Annotated Ed.

FIDELER SOCIAL STUDIES

Families
Family life: sharing, caring, and working together
A Chartbook of discussion pictures

Families Around the World
How families live in communities around the world.

Our Needs
The needs of people in families and in communities

Our Earth
Our Earth, its geography, its people and communities.

Great Americans and Great Ideas
Biographies of thirteen great Americans.
The great ideas that built our nation.

The United States
The people, geography, and history of the United States. The Northeast, The South, Midwest and Great Plains, The West, Pictorial Story of Our Country. Depth Studies.

American Neighbors
The people, geography, and history of Canada, Mexico, Caribbean Lands, and South America. Depth Studies.

World Cultures
The people, geography, and history of ten world regions. British Isles, Germany, France, Soviet Union, China, Japan, India, Southeast Asia, Africa, South America. Depth Studies.

Inquiring About Freedom
United States history. Depth Studies of the "freedom" concepts that built our nation.

Jerry E. Jennings

Jerry E. Jennings is an author and editor of textbooks. A graduate of Michigan State University, he continued his education at Columbia University. Through extensive travel and study, he has gained a comprehensive knowledge of our country and its people. Mr. Jennings has a deep interest in young people and a desire to share with them important concepts of American life and culture in terms they can readily understand.

Marion H. Smith

Marion H. Smith is a writer and editor of textbooks. She is a graduate of Michigan State University, and has also studied at the University of Michigan. Mrs. Smith has traveled widely throughout the United States and has done extensive research in the social sciences. As a parent and an educator, she is keenly interested in helping students meet their essential learning needs.

Walter Havighurst

Walter Havighurst is known as an authority on American history and geography and has won wide acclaim as a gifted author. He is now professor emeritus in the Department of English at Miami University, Oxford, Ohio. Professor Havighurst writes from a background of years of travel and study. Among his books are *The Upper Mississippi* in the Rivers of America Series, *The Long Ships Passing,* and *Land of Promise.*

Contributors to The United States

BENJAMIN CHINITZ
 Deputy Assistant Secretary
  for Economic Development
 U.S. Department of Commerce
 Washington, D.C.

JOHN FRASER HART
 Professor of Geography
 University of Minnesota
 Minneapolis, Minnesota

J. R. T. HUGHES
 Professor of Economics
 Northwestern University
 Evanston, Illinois

JOHN F. LOUNSBURY
 Chairman of Department
  of Geography
 Arizona State University
 Tempe, Arizona

VINCENT M. MALMSTRÖM
 Professor of Geography
 Dartmouth University
 Hanover, New Hampshire

ASHLEY MONTAGU
 Anthropologist
 Princeton, New Jersey

WALTER T. K. NUGENT
 Professor of History
 Indiana University
 Bloomington, Indiana

G. ETZEL PEARCY
 Chairman, Department
  of Geography
 California State College
 Los Angeles, California

JACOB L. SUSSKIND
 Professor of Social Science
  and Education
 Pennsylvania State University
  Capital Campus
 Middletown, Pennsylvania

WILLIAM H. WAKE
 Professor of Geography
 Fresno State College
 Bakersfield, California

LEE ABBOTT
SILENCE M. ANDREWS
CHERYL BALAVITCH
BETTY-JO BUELL
LYNNE A. DEUR
MARGARET S. DeWITT
MARY A. DOWNEY
EVELYN M. DOWNING
RAYMOND E. FIDELER
SUSAN R. GROOVER
MARGARET F. HERTEL
MARY MITUS
CAROL S. PRESCOTT
BEV J. ROCHE
MARY JANE SACK
VIRGINIA A. SKALSKY
BARBARA M. SMITH
JUDY A. TAYLOR
ALICE VAIL
JOANNA VAN ZOEST
AUDREY WITHAM
LISA WRIGHT

THE UNITED STATES

Jennings, Smith, Havighurst

The Northeast

The South

Midwest and Great Plains

The West

Pictorial Story of Our Country

COPYRIGHT 1979, THE FIDELER COMPANY

All rights reserved in the U.S.A. and foreign countries. This book or parts thereof must not be reproduced in any form without permission. Printed in the U.S.A. by offset lithography.

LIBRARY OF CONGRESS CATALOG CARD NUMBER: 78-62083
ISBN: 0-88296-477-1

THE FIDELER COMPANY   GRAND RAPIDS, MICHIGAN • TORONTO, CANADA

Contents

The Northeast

Part 1 Land and Climate

1 A Global View.............. 4
2 Land...................... 12
3 Climate................... 26

Part 2 People

4 People.................... 40
5 Cities.................... 48
6 Citizenship and Government..... 60
7 The Arts.................. 72

Part 3 Earning a Living

8 Farming................... 80
9 Natural Resources and Energy.... 90
10 Industry................. 114

Index........................ 129
Acknowledgments.............. 132

The South

Part 1 Land and Climate

1 A Global View.............. 4
2 Land...................... 10
3 Climate................... 24

Part 2 People

4 People.................... 40
5 Cities.................... 48
6 Citizenship and Government..... 58
7 The Arts.................. 74

Part 3 Earning a Living

8 Farming................... 84
9 Natural Resources and Energy.... 98
10 Industry................. 116

Index........................ 129
Acknowledgments.............. 132

Midwest and Great Plains

Part 1 Land and Climate
1 A Global View   4
2 Land 12
3 Climate 30

Part 2 People
4 People 48
5 Cities 56
6 Citizenship and Government 64
7 The Arts 76

Part 3 Earning a Living
8 Farming 82
9 Natural Resources and Energy 96
10 Industry 114
Index 129
Acknowledgments 132

The West

Part 1 Land and Climate
1 A Global View   4
2 Land 12
3 Climate 26

Part 2 People
4 People 42
5 Cities 52
6 Citizenship and Government 62
7 The Arts 74

Part 3 Earning a Living
8 Farming 80
9 Natural Resources and Energy 92
10 Industry 112
Alaska and Hawaii 124
Index 129
Acknowledgments 132

Pictorial Story of Our Country
Our Country   2
1 People Build Communities in America   4
2 American Communities Form a Nation 20
3 The Nation Grows 30
4 The Union Is Saved 41
5 Our Country Becomes a World Leader 46
6 Years of Amazing Change 56
Index 65
Acknowledgments 66

Thinking Aids
Skills Manual
  Thinking   1
  Solving Problems   2
  Learning Social Studies Skills   3
    How To Find Information   4
    Evaluating Information   5
    Making Reports   7
    Holding a Group Discussion   9
    Working With Others   9
    Building Your Vocabulary 10
  Learning Map Skills 10
Needs of People 17
Great Ideas That Built Our Nation 19
Word List (Glossary) 35
Acknowledgments 48

v

Maps, Charts, and Special Features

The Northeast

PART 1 Land and Climate

The Solar System, 4-5
A Global View, 6
The United States, 7
The United States, 8-9
The Northeast, 13
Land Regions, 14
The Seasons of the Year, 30-31
Average Length of Growing Season, 32
Average Yearly Rainfall, 34
Average January and July Temperatures, 36

PART 2 People

United States Population Distribution, 41
Main Cities of the Northeast, 50
Eight Metropolitan Areas, 51
New York City, 55
Washington, D.C., 59
Our Federal Government, 62
Seven Important Beliefs Shared
   by People in a Democracy, 65
Responsibilities of Citizens, 66
Seven Social Problems, 67

PART 3 Earning a Living

Major Types of Farming
   in the United States, 83
Poultry and Poultry Products,
   and Dairy Products, 85
Coalfields of the United States, 93
Oil, Natural Gas, Iron Ore, and
   Limestone, 94
Natural Forest Regions, 99
Leading Fishing States
   of the Northeast, 100
Where We Get Our Energy, 102
How Electricity Is Produced, 107
Energy Used and Value of Goods
   per Person, 108
A Steel Plant, 116
Waterways, 121
Main Industrial Areas, 122

The South

PART 1 Land and Climate

The United States, 6
Main Groups of States, 7
The United States, 8-9
Land Regions, 13
Exploring Waterways, 17
Average Yearly Rainfall, 30
Average January and July Temperatures, 32
Thunderstorms, 34
Hurricanes, 35

PART 2 People

United States Population Distribution, 43
Six Metropolitan Areas, 53
Cities of the South, 54
Seven Important Beliefs Shared
   by People in a Democracy, 61
Responsibilities of Citizens, 65
Seven Social Problems, 68

PART 3 Earning a Living

Fruits and Nuts, and Vegetables, 86
Exploring the Growing Season,
   and Cotton Harvested, 88
Soybean Production, Soybeans Harvested, 91
Major Types of Farming
   in the United States, 92
Dairy Products, Sheep and Lambs, and
   Poultry and Poultry Products, 95
Cattle and Calves, and Hogs and Pigs, 96
Coalfields of the United States, 103
Iron and Steel, 104
Oil, Natural Gas, Iron Ore, Limestone, 105
Timber Harvested, and Distribution of
   Forestland, 109
Leading Fishing States of the South, 110
Tennessee Valley Authority, 112-115
Main Industrial Areas, 121

Midwest and Great Plains

PART 1 Land and Climate

Our Solar System, 5

vi

Main Planets, 5
The United States, 7
The United States, 8-9
Main Groups of States, 10
Our Trip, 14
Land Regions, 14-15
The Story of Glaciers, 18-19
Mississippi River System, 20
Average Yearly Rainfall, 34
Average January and July Temperatures, 39
Tornadoes, 41
Average Length of Growing Season, 42

PART 2 People

United States Population Distribution, 50
Six Metropolitan Areas, 57
Cities, 59
Our State Governments, 67
Responsibilities of Citizens, 68
Seven Important Beliefs Shared by People in a Democracy, 71
Seven Social Problems, 73

PART 3 Earning a Living

Major Types of Farming in the United States, 87
Dairy Products, Hogs and Pigs, Corn, and Soybeans, 89
Wheat, Sheep and Lambs, Cattle and Calves, and Cotton, 94
A Visit to a Coal Mine, 99
Coalfields of the United States, 99
Oil, Natural Gas, Iron Ore, Limestone, 102
Water Resources, 105
Natural Forest Regions, 108
Great Lakes-St. Lawrence Waterway, 120
Main Industrial Areas, 122

The West

PART 1 Land and Climate

Our Earth, 5
The United States, 7
The United States, 8-9
Main Groups of States, 10

Land Regions, 24
Average Yearly Rainfall, 27
Average January and July Temperatures, 30
The Seasons of the Year, 34-35
Average Length of Growing Season, 38

PART 2 People

United States Population Distribution, 46
Six Metropolitan Areas, 53
Cities of the West, 61
Seven Important Beliefs That Build Strong Communities, 64
Responsibilities of Citizens in a Strong Community, 68
Seven Social Problems, 70

PART 3 Earning a Living

Major Types of Farming in the United States, 82
Fruits and Nuts, Vegetables, Sugar Beets, and Wheat, 86
Cattle and Calves, and Sheep and Lambs, 87
Water Resources, 94
Copper, Lead, Uranium, and Oil, 96
Where We Get Our Energy, 97
Lumber Production, and National Forests in the West, 107
Leading Fishing States in the West, 108
Main Industrial Areas of the West, 115
Alaska, 125

Pictorial Story of Our Country

Routes of Indian Settlers, 5
Routes of Explorers and Traders, 7
Routes of Spanish Explorers, 10
Dutch and Swedish Settlements, 13
Thirteen British Colonies, 17
Before and After the French and Indian War, 21
How Our Country Grew, 34
The United States and Mexico in 1821, 35
Routes to the West, 36
A Divided Country, 43
Our Changing Nation, 57
The United States, 60-61

New York, the largest city in the United States, is located in the Northeast. The photograph at right shows skyscrapers on the southern end of Manhattan Island, which is part of New York City. Brooklyn, another section of New York, lies in the foreground. It is separated from Manhattan by the East River. Crossing the East River are Brooklyn Bridge (left) and Manhattan Bridge (right). The state of New Jersey lies beyond the Hudson River, in the background of the picture. (For additional information see Chapter 5 of "The Northeast" and the New York City map in that chapter.)

THE NORTHEAST

New York City. Skyscrapers on the southern end of Manhattan Island.

Part 1

Land and Climate

One group of states in our country is known as the Northeast. Do you know exactly where the Northeast is located? What do you know about the land and climate of the states in the Northeast? Do you know the answers to the following questions?

- How many states are in the Northeast? What are their names?
- Parts of three of our country's main land regions lie in the Northeast. What are these regions? (See map on page 14.)
- The growing season differs from one place to another in the Northeast. (See map on page 32.) What facts help to explain why this is so?

As you read the chapters in Part 1, you will discover answers to these and many other questions. The pictures and maps provide additional information that will be helpful.

Use Fideler Discovery Cards 1-36 for additional activities.

Skiers in the Green Mountains. Winters are cold and snowy in many parts of the Northeast. What facts help explain why this is so?

† Use these questions to start students thinking about the universe and our solar system.

1 A Global View

Explore the Universe

† 1. What is a star? About how many stars do you think there are in the universe?
2. What is a galaxy? What is the solar system?
3. What is the name of the galaxy in which the solar system is located?
4. What are two differences between a star and a planet?
5. What main planets does the solar system include?

The universe

Scattered through the vast, nearly empty space of the universe are billions of stars. These are huge, whirling balls of burning gases. Some of them are many times larger than our sun, which is also a star. But when we look at the stars in the night sky they appear to be much smaller than the sun. This is because they are such a long distance away.

There are so many stars in space that no one could ever count them all. The stars are divided into huge groups called galaxies. Our sun is in a galaxy called the Milky Way. It contains about 100 billion stars. Scientists believe there are billions of galaxies in the universe.

Our solar system

Not all of the lights that we can see in the night sky are stars. A few are balls of fairly solid material, like our earth. These are called planets. They do not give off any light of their own, as the stars do. Instead, they reflect the light of the sun.

The earth on which we live is one of nine main planets that travel around the sun. These planets differ greatly in size. Some planets are much larger than

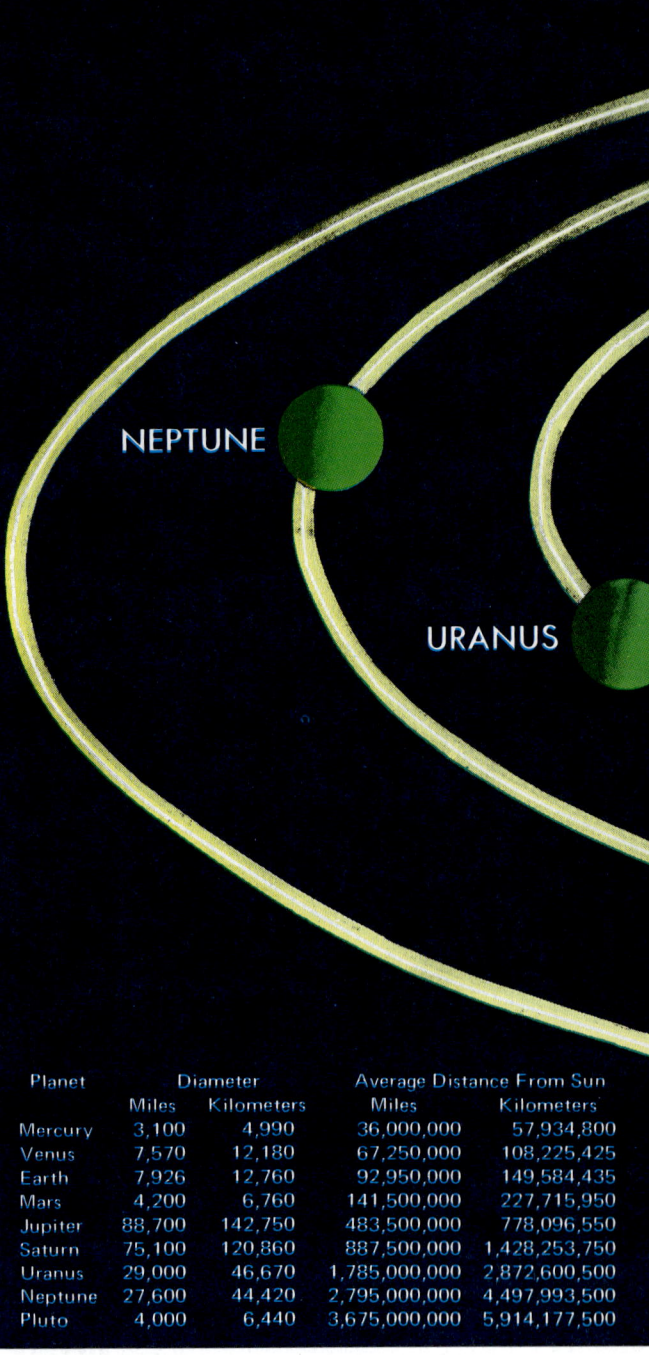

Planet	Diameter		Average Distance From Sun	
	Miles	Kilometers	Miles	Kilometers
Mercury	3,100	4,990	36,000,000	57,934,800
Venus	7,570	12,180	67,250,000	108,225,425
Earth	7,926	12,760	92,950,000	149,584,435
Mars	4,200	6,760	141,500,000	227,715,950
Jupiter	88,700	142,750	483,500,000	778,096,550
Saturn	75,100	120,860	887,500,000	1,428,253,750
Uranus	29,000	46,670	1,785,000,000	2,872,600,500
Neptune	27,600	44,420	2,795,000,000	4,497,993,500
Pluto	4,000	6,440	3,675,000,000	5,914,177,500

the earth, and some are smaller. The planets also differ in their distance from the sun. Several of the planets have one or more moons. There are also many smaller planets, called asteroids. Together, our sun and its family of planets and smaller bodies are called the solar system. (See the chart above.)

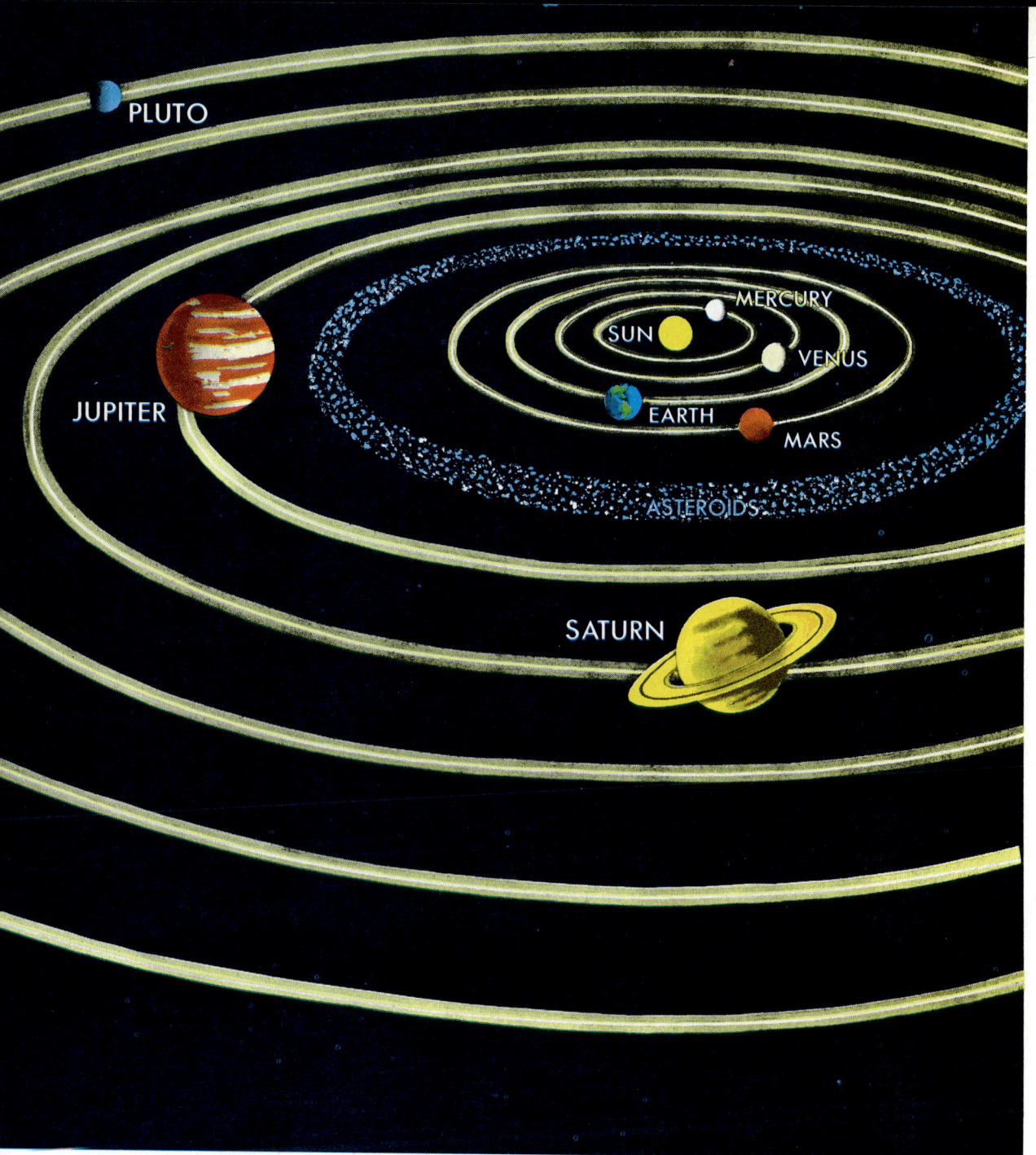

The solar system includes nine main planets. It also includes thousands of small planets, called asteroids. Which two planets are our nearest neighbors? Which planet is farthest from the sun?

The earth

The surface of our own planet, the earth, is made up partly of water and partly of land. The largest bodies of water are called oceans. They cover about three fourths of the earth's surface. The largest bodies of land are called continents.

North America

The land area of the earth is divided into about 162 independent countries. There are also a number of territories that are not independent. Some countries, such as the United States and Canada, are very large. Others are very small. On maps, boundary lines may be

Use a globe or world map to show the area covered by continents as compared to the area covered by oceans.

A global view. This picture of a globe shows the continents of North America and South America. These continents are bordered by two large bodies of water, the Atlantic and Pacific oceans. The dotted line in eastern North America outlines the group of states that make up the Northeast.

drawn to show where different countries are located. These lines are imaginary, however. If you were to fly over the earth in a spacecraft, you would not see any boundary lines. You would not be able to tell where one country ends and another begins.

Most of our country, the United States, is located on the continent of North America. The map on the opposite page shows that the countries of Canada and Mexico are our closest neighbors on this continent.

The United States

Our country is made up of fifty states. Two of these, Alaska and Hawaii, are separated from the others.

† Ask a student to look up the word "conterminous" in the Glossary or dictionary and read the definition aloud. Call attention to the conterminous states on the map on this page.

Alaska, like most of our country, is on the North American continent. Hawaii, however, is an island state in the Pacific Ocean. The part of our country that is made up of the other forty-eight states is called the conterminous* United States. (See map below.)

The Northeast

The Northeast is a group of twelve states in the northeastern part of the conterminous United States. It also includes a small area called the District of Columbia, which is the home of our national government.

The states of the Northeast may be divided into two groups, New England and the Middle Atlantic states. New England is made up of Maine, New Hampshire, Vermont, Massachusetts, Connecticut, and Rhode Island. The Middle Atlantic states are New York, Pennsylvania, New Jersey, Delaware, Maryland, and West Virginia.

An important region

Although the Northeast covers less than one tenth of the area of the United States, it has about one fourth of our country's population. More than 56 million people make their homes in the Northeast. New York, the largest city in the United States, lies in this region. Several other great cities are also in the Northeast. Among them is our nation's capital city, Washington, D.C.

*See Glossary

The United States

This map shows the location of the fifty states that make up our country. Two of these, Alaska and Hawaii, are separated from the others. Alaska is in the far northern part of North America. Hawaii is an island state in the Pacific Ocean. The other forty-eight states form the part of our country known as the conterminous* United States.

† Ask a student to read aloud (from the map on pages 8-9) the names of the states that make up the Northeast. Note the location of each of these states on the map.

† The Northeast was one of the first parts of our country to be settled by people from Europe. There were busy cities here when most of America was still a wilderness. Many great events in our nation's history took place in the Northeast. Over the years, the Northeast continued to grow in population and wealth.

Today the Northeast is a great manufacturing and trading region. There are thousands of factories here, producing many different goods. The Northeast provides other regions of our country with items they need. In return, it buys many things that other regions have to sell.

There are other reasons, too, why the Northeast is an important part of the United States. Many large companies have their main offices here. In the Northeast there are also some of our

Discuss some of the major industries of the Northeast.

country's largest banks. Many of the television programs watched by people throughout the United States are broadcast from studios in the Northeast. Here, too, are companies that publish most of our country's books and magazines. The cities of the Northeast are noted for their fine museums, libraries, theaters, and concert halls. Some of our country's best-known colleges and universities are in the Northeast. This region is also the home of the United Nations.*

In the following chapters of this book, you will learn about the land and the climate of the Northeast. You will also learn about the people of this region and the ways in which they earn their living. In addition, you will come to understand some of the problems and opportunities facing the people of the Northeast today.

Cooperation
See Great Ideas

Penn Center, in downtown Philadelphia. In this busy center, there are hotels, business offices, department stores, restaurants, and theaters. Philadelphia is one of several large cities in the Northeast. Do you think the great idea of cooperation is important to people who live in large cities? Why? Why not? What are some of the ways people who live in large cities cooperate with one another? Do you think people who live in smaller cities and towns must also cooperate with one another? Give reasons for your answers.

† Refer to the map on pages 8-9 and to the Skills Manual. Have students answer these questions.

Learn To Read Maps
Maps will help you gain much information during your study of the Northeast. To use maps well, there are certain things you must know. Study "Learning Map Skills" in the Skills Manual. Then answer the following questions.
1. What is the "scale" of a map?
2. What does a map legend, or key, show?
3. What do the terms longitude and latitude mean?
4. What do the terms parallel and meridian mean?
5. What is a topographic map?

The Northeast 11

Boothbay Harbor, on the coast of Maine. Hundreds of bays and inlets indent the lowlands along the Atlantic coast of New England. Some of them are natural harbors. In what ways have harbors and other physical features helped to determine where the cities in the Northeast grew up?

2 Land

A Problem To Solve

Mountains and rolling hills make up much of the Northeast. Very little of this part of our country is low and level. How do the land features of the Northeast affect the lives of the people? In forming hypotheses* to solve this problem, you will need to think about how the land features of the Northeast affect the following:

a. where the cities grew up
b. industry
c. farming

Information in Chapters 5, 8, and 10 will also be helpful in solving this problem.

See Skills Manual, "Thinking and Solving Problems"

If you were to take a trip through the Northeast, you would notice that the land is very different from place to place. In some areas there are forest-covered mountains. In others there are plateaus and rolling hills. Only a small part of the Northeast is low and level. The lowlands are very important, however, since many of the people in the Northeast live here. To find out more about the Northeast we will take a trip by helicopter over this important part of our country.

*See Glossary

† Have students find the highlands and the lowlands of the Northeast by using the maps on pages 8-9, 13, and 14.

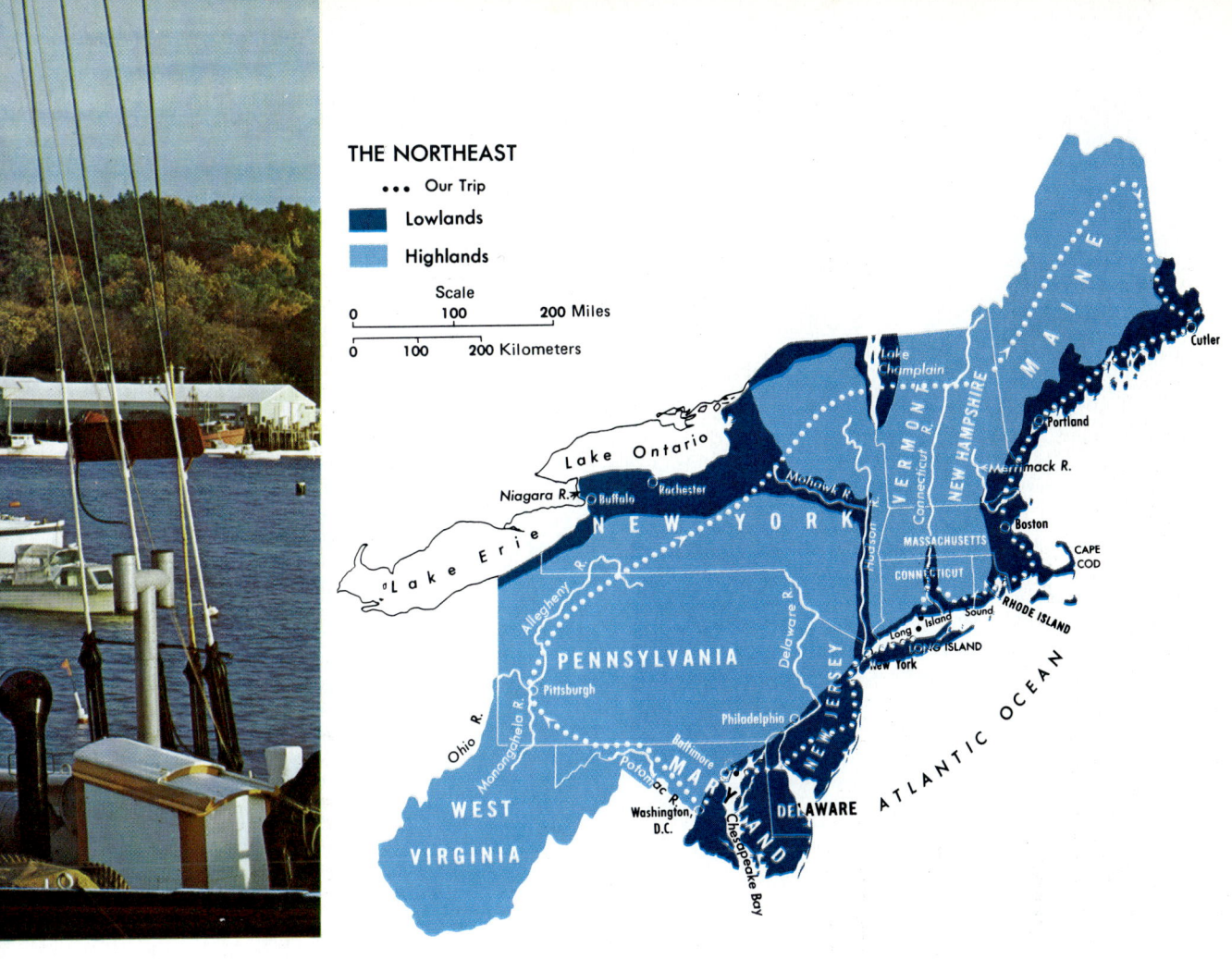

The Lowlands

Our trip will first take us over lowlands along the Atlantic coast of the Northeast. We will also learn about the Northeast's other lowland areas. Some of these lowlands lie along rivers that cut far inland through highland areas. Others lie along Lake Ontario, Lake Erie, and Lake Champlain.

Lowlands of New England

The sun is rising as we board our helicopter at Cutler, a small fishing village in eastern Maine. (See map above.) As our helicopter rises high in the air, we see the blue green waters of the Atlantic Ocean.

Our trip will take us southward. We will fly over the coastal lowlands of Maine, New Hampshire, Massachusetts, Rhode Island, and Connecticut. Most of the people in New England live on these coastal lowlands.

The coast of Maine

As we fly southwest along the coast of Maine, we notice hundreds of little bays and inlets. In sheltered inlets, we can see small fishing villages. Some

Refer to the picture on these pages. Ask: What can you discover about the way some people live in Maine? What does this picture tell you about how some people earn their living there?

LAND REGIONS

- COASTAL PLAIN
- APPALACHIAN HIGHLANDS
  1. The Piedmont Plateau
  2. Blue Ridge
  3. Appalachian Ridges and Valleys
  4. Appalachian Plateau
  5. New England Lowlands
  6. New England Highlands
  7. Adirondack Mountains
  8. St. Lawrence Valley
- INTERIOR PLAINS
- INTERIOR HIGHLANDS
  9. Ozark Plateau
  10. Arkansas Valley
  11. Ouachita Mountains
- SUPERIOR UPLAND
- The Northeast

fishers wave to us from their boats that are heading out to sea. Our guide tells us that these people earn their living by catching lobster.

Looking inland from the coast, we notice that large forests of evergreen trees cover much of the land. From time to time we see neat white farmhouses surrounded by green pastures and fields of crops. As we fly farther along the coast, we see more towns and villages. Soon a large seaport comes into view. This is Portland. Although it is the largest city in Maine, fewer than sixty thousand people live here.

Massachusetts

Now we are flying over northeastern Massachusetts. Below us is the winding Merrimack River. Along its banks are the manufacturing cities of Lowell, Lawrence, and Haverhill. Our guide tells us that the Merrimack helped these cities grow. In the 1800's, waterpower was used to run factory machinery. Textile* mills and other factories were built near falls in the river. Today, waterpower is used by hydroelectric* plants along the banks of the Merrimack to produce electricity for factories and homes.

† Waterpower is one of our important resources. You may assign a class activity using Fideler Discovery Card 90. (Make a diagram that shows how waterpower is transformed into hydroelectricity. See page 107 of THE NORTHEAST.)

Farther south, we come to the city of Boston, the capital of Massachusetts. Along the harbor of the city we see docks and warehouses. In the water below us, we notice ocean liners, freighters, and fishing vessels. Inland from the harbor, the city seems to stretch out as far as we can see. Our guide tells us that this is not just one city, but about seventy-five separate cities and towns. Boston and its neighboring communities are so close together that they appear to be one great city. Together they are called Greater Boston. About three million people live here.

Flying southeast from Boston, we see Cape Cod, a peninsula that reaches far out into the Atlantic Ocean. (See map on page 13.) Many visitors come to Cape Cod each year to spend their summer vacations.

Rhode Island

Our helicopter turns westward toward the tiny state of Rhode Island. Soon we pass over Narragansett Bay. This narrow inlet almost divides the state into two parts. Rhode Island is the smallest state in our country.

Connecticut

West of Rhode Island, we see the sandy beaches and gently rolling hills of Connecticut's coastal lowland. We turn northwest and fly to the central

Hartford, the capital of Connecticut, is located along the banks of the Connecticut River. The valley of this river contains some of the most fertile farmland in the entire Northeast.

part of the state. Soon we are over the Connecticut River. This is the longest river in New England. It begins far to the north, in the mountains of New Hampshire.

The valley of the Connecticut River has some of the best farmland in the Northeast. Farmers here grow fruits, vegetables, and tobacco.* They also raise poultry and dairy cattle.

Middle Atlantic Lowlands

Now we turn southward and fly back to the coast of Connecticut. Our guide tells us that we will next visit the Middle Atlantic lowlands. These important lowlands stretch along the Atlantic coast between Connecticut and Virginia. They are part of a vast region called the Coastal Plain. The land here is level or gently rolling, and the soil is generally sandy. Only a small part of the Northeast lies in the Coastal Plain. (See map on page 14.)

†

New York

Ahead of us is Long Island Sound. This is an arm of the Atlantic Ocean. (See map on page 13.) After crossing the sound, we fly westward over Long Island. This island is in New York State. Our guide tells us that part of the great city of New York is on the western end of Long Island. In a short while, our helicopter lands at New York's busy La Guardia Airport to get more fuel.

Soon we are ready to go on with our flight. As our helicopter rises, we have a beautiful view of New York City. Tall buildings reach high into the sky. In the harbor are huge ocean liners, tugboats, freighters, and ferryboats. More ships load and unload cargo at New

York than at any other seaport in the United States.

New Jersey

As we fly southward over the lowlands of New Jersey, we notice long, sandy beaches along the coast. People are swimming in the ocean below us. We also see many large hotels along the beach. New Jersey is famous for its seashore resorts.

When our helicopter turns inland over New Jersey, we begin to see fields

† Call attention to this area (Coastal Plain) on the map on page 14.

A ship in New York Harbor. New York is our country's greatest trading city. More ships load and unload cargo here than at any other seaport in the United States. New York City lies on the Atlantic coast at the mouth of the Hudson River. In which lowland region is New York located?

of green beans, tomatoes, and other vegetables. Vegetables raised here are shipped to nearby cities, where they are sold to supermarkets and restaurants. Raising vegetables for sale is called truck farming. This type of farming is usually very profitable in the Northeast. There are millions of people in the cities of this region to buy and eat the vegetables raised here.

In the distance we can see the buildings of several cities. Our guide tells us that these are the cities of Trenton and Camden in New Jersey and Philadelphia in Pennsylvania. All of these cities are along the Delaware River.

Delaware and Maryland

Soon we leave New Jersey and cross Delaware Bay. Now we are flying over

Refer to the picture on these pages. Ask: What can you discover about New York City from this picture? (Seaport, harbor, skyscrapers.) In what ways is water transportation important to the people of New York? Explain.

a large peninsula that stretches far southward into the Atlantic Ocean. Most of Delaware and part of Maryland are located on this peninsula. The land here is very low and level. We see few large towns, but there are a great number of farms. Many are truck farms, and there are also poultry farms. Farmers in Delaware and Maryland raise millions of chickens each year to ship to the great cities of the Northeast.

Chesapeake Bay

Now we are flying over Chesapeake Bay. (See map on page 13.) The water below us is crowded with fishing boats and ocean freighters. To our right, we see tall buildings and the smoke from many factories. Our guide tells us that this is the great port city of Baltimore, Maryland. We are approaching our nation's capital, Washington, D.C., where we will spend the night before continuing our trip.

Other Lowlands

In our trip along the Atlantic coast, we could not see all the lowland areas of the Northeast. There are some important lowlands that lie far inland.

The Erie-Ontario Lowland

† The Erie-Ontario Lowland is a broad fertile plain in the western part of New York and the northwestern part of Pennsylvania. This lowland lies along Lake Ontario and Lake Erie. (See map on page 13.)

If you could visit this part of the Northeast, you would see people working in vineyards and orchards and on dairy farms. In large cities like Buffalo and Rochester, you would see many factories and mills.

One of the most interesting sights in the Erie-Ontario Lowland is beautiful Niagara Falls. These falls are located on the Niagara River, which forms part of the border between the United States and Canada. The Niagara River flows northward from Lake Erie to Lake Ontario. About halfway between these two lakes, the river plunges over a steep cliff, forming Niagara Falls. Each year, thousands of tourists come to see these famous falls. Waterpower from the falls is used to produce electricity for factories and homes in both the United States and Canada.

† Call attention to this area on the map on page 13.

† **Niagara Falls**, on the border between the United States and Canada. These falls are an important natural resource to people who live in the nearby area. Can you explain why this is so?

Hudson-Mohawk Lowland

East of the plain along Lake Erie and Lake Ontario is another important lowland area. Here, the valleys of the Hudson and Mohawk rivers form a natural pathway through the highlands of New York. Large boats carry goods up the Hudson River from New York City as far north as Albany. From a point near here the goods are transported westward on the New York State Barge Canal, which extends through the Mohawk Valley and the Erie-Ontario Lowland to Buffalo, on Lake Erie. Good roads and railroads in the Hudson-Mohawk Lowland also help to make this part of the Northeast an important trade route.

St. Lawrence Valley

In northern New York and Vermont is another lowland area, which extends along the St. Lawrence River and Lake Champlain. This is the St. Lawrence Valley. (See map on page 14.) Most of the land in this section is flat or gently rolling. Dairy farms here supply milk to people in New York and other large cities. Fruit growing is also important in this area.

† Have a student read the caption to this picture aloud. In what ways is Niagara Falls an important natural resource to the people who live nearby?

† Use the maps on pages 13 and 14 to show the Appalachian Highlands. You may assign a class activity using Fideler Discovery Cards 10-16, or Fideler Discovery Sheets, Volume 1, pages 5-8.

The Highlands

More than three fourths of the Northeast lies in a vast region called the Appalachian Highlands. (See map on page 14.) These highlands extend for more than 1,600 miles (2,574 km.)† from central Alabama northeastward into Canada. In this region are mountain ranges, high ridges, and deep valleys. Plateaus and hilly land also make up a large part of the Appalachian Highlands. During the remainder of our trip, we will be flying over these highlands.

Piedmont Plateau

Our helicopter rises over Washington, D.C., and we follow the winding Potomac River northwestward. The land below is gently rolling. We are flying over a plateau that slopes gradually upward from the Coastal Plain to the mountainous land that lies to the west. This part of the Appalachian Highlands is called the Piedmont Plateau. (See map on page 14.) The word piedmont means "foot of the mountain."

Fall Line

Many fast-flowing rivers cross the Piedmont on their way to the Atlantic Ocean. As these rivers drop from the plateau onto the Coastal Plain, they form swift rapids and waterfalls. For this reason, the dividing line between the Piedmont and the Coastal Plain is called the Fall Line.

Some of the Northeast's largest cities lie along the Fall Line. In the early days of our country, settlers traveling upstream by boat were stopped at the Fall Line by the falls and rapids. Here they had to unload their goods, and many of them settled nearby. Water-

† km. means kilometer

power from the falls was used to run machines in small mills and factories. Gradually, many of the settlements along the Fall Line grew into important cities.

Blue Ridge

Soon we leave the Piedmont Plateau and fly over a broad, forest-covered ridge. This is part of the Blue Ridge, a chain of mountain ranges that extends from Pennsylvania southwestward into Georgia. It is called the Blue Ridge because its slopes often look blue from a distance.

Refer to the picture below. What can you discover about the way people live in the Appalachian Plateau? How do some people earn their living here?

Appalachian Ridges and Valleys

Beyond the Blue Ridge, we come to a broad valley. We learn that this is the easternmost part of the Appalachian Ridges and Valleys section of the Appalachian Highlands. The valley below us is part of a long chain of valleys, called the Great Valley. On the valley floor, we see herds of dairy cattle grazing in green meadows.

Northwestward from the Great Valley, we cross a series of heavily wooded ridges separated by narrow valleys. Occasionally we fly over a small town, but we have not seen a large city since leaving Washington. One reason why this area has not been heavily settled is lack of transportation. It has been difficult to build roads and railroads through this mountainous area.

Appalachian Plateau

Our guide tells us that we have crossed into southern Pennsylvania and are now flying over the Appalachian

The **Appalachian Plateau** section of the Northeast is an area of rugged hills and low mountains. Long ago, the surface of this plateau was smooth and unbroken. What caused changes in the land?

Plateau. In the Northeast, this section of the Appalachian Highlands extends over large areas of Pennsylvania, New York, and West Virginia. (See map on page 14.)

† The land below us is hilly and rugged. Usually we think of a plateau as an area of high, flat land. We learn that at one time the surface of the Appalachian Plateau was smooth and unbroken. Through the centuries, however, rivers and streams have cut thousands of valleys into the plateau, leaving rugged hills and mountains. We see few farms in this area, but in some of the valleys below us there are small mining communities. The hills of the Appalachian Plateau contain large deposits of bituminous* coal. West Virginia and Pennsylvania rank among the leading coal-producing states in the nation.

Ahead of us we see the tall buildings of a large city. This is Pittsburgh, one of the greatest steelmaking cities in the world. It is situated at the point where the Allegheny and Monongahela rivers meet to form the Ohio River. (See map on page 13.) Tall furnaces of steel mills rise near the riverbanks. Towboats are pushing barges loaded with coal and other raw materials needed to make steel. Nearby raw materials and cheap transportation have helped Pittsburgh become a great manufacturing city.

Adirondack Mountains

†† From Pittsburgh, our trip takes us far northeastward to the Adirondack Mountains of New York. (Compare maps on pages 13 and 14.) These are the oldest mountains in the Appalachian Highlands.

As we fly over the Adirondacks, we notice that the mountain peaks are not very high or rugged. Through countless centuries, the forces of nature have worn down the slopes and rounded the peaks of these mountains. Many thousands of years ago, the land here was covered with huge masses of ice called glaciers.* As the glaciers moved slowly

† Look up the word "bituminous" in the Glossary. Read and discuss the definition.
†† Point out the Adirondack Mountains on the map on page 14.

A river in the Adirondack Mountains. The Adirondacks lie in the northern part of New York State. They are the oldest mountains in the Appalachian Highlands region. Every year many people visit the Adirondacks to hunt and fish, and enjoy the beautiful scenery.

over the land, they smoothed the mountain peaks, carved out hollows, and deposited stones and gravel.

In the forested valleys below us, hundreds of lakes glisten like jewels. Our guide points out hotels and hunting lodges along many of the lakes. The beautiful scenery and the wildlife of the Adirondacks attract thousands of tourists each year.

Highlands of New England

To the east of the Adirondack Mountains are the highlands of New England.

† Why is this a popular vacation area? Read the caption to this picture and discuss the picture.

These highlands, like the Adirondacks, are very old. They, too, were covered by glaciers thousands of years ago. As the glaciers moved down the mountains and valleys, they scraped away the soil in many places. When the glaciers melted, they left large amounts of stones and gravel behind. As a result, much of the soil in New England is thin and stony. It is difficult to raise crops in this area.

Green Mountains

We begin our trip over the highlands of New England by flying eastward across Lake Champlain. Soon we are over the gently rounded Green Mountains of Vermont. The Green Moun-

† **A village in the Green Mountains of Vermont.** These mountains are popular with vacationers both in summer and in winter. Why do you suppose they are called the Green Mountains?

† Class activity: Ask each student to do a report using one of the three trips listed below. All research can be done from the text, maps, and pictures in THE NORTHEAST.

tains owe their name to the forests of evergreen trees that cover their slopes. We notice there are many resort hotels here, as in the Adirondacks. Tourists come to the cool mountains during the summer months to escape the heat of the cities. Many vacationers also come during the winter to ski and enjoy other sports.

White Mountains

Now we are flying over the White Mountains of New Hampshire. These mountains seem to rise higher than any others we have seen on our trip. Our guide tells us that one of these peaks, Mt. Washington, rises to nearly 6,300 feet (1,920 m.)† above sea level. This is the highest point in the Northeast.

Soon we cross the border between New Hampshire and Maine and fly northeastward. As far as we can see there are forested mountains and hills. Forests cover more than four fifths of the land in Maine. Very seldom do we see any farmland or a town.

Northeastern Maine

When our helicopter reaches northeastern Maine, we see many farms below us. Our guide tells us that this is Aroostook County. It has the only large area of fertile land in Maine. This county is famous for its fine potatoes.

Now our trip is almost over. Our flight over the Northeast has helped us to understand how land features affect the ways in which people live and work.

† m. means meter

Imagine You Are a Geographer †
Imagine you are a geographer who has been asked to write a magazine article about a trip through the Northeast. Choose one of the following trips, or plan your own.
1. an automobile trip from New York City to the Adirondack Mountains
2. a boat trip on the New York State Barge Canal from Lake Champlain to Lake Erie
3. a helicopter trip from Philadelphia to Pittsburgh, Pennsylvania

You will need to do research about land and water features along your route. Illustrate your article with a map showing the route and the names of places to visit.

† Use "A Problem To Solve" to start students thinking about climate in the Northeast.

3 Climate

† **A Problem To Solve**

In the Northeast, temperatures differ considerably from place to place. Why is this true? In order to solve this problem, you will need to find out what the climate is like in different parts of the Northeast. Then you will need to make a number of "educated guesses," or hypotheses, that you think explain these differences. In forming your hypotheses, you may find it helpful to consider each of the following questions.
a. How are temperatures in different places affected by distance from the equator?
b. How does altitude affect temperature?
c. How are temperatures in different places affected by distance from large bodies of water?

See Skills Manual, "Thinking and Solving Problems"

In the Northeast, each season brings great changes in the weather. Summer days in most parts of this region are often hot and damp. Winter days are usually cold. In some places, snow covers the ground for weeks at a time. During the spring and autumn months, the weather is not often very hot or very cold.

The weather in the Northeast differs not only from season to season but also from place to place. In the northern part of this region, temperatures are usually different from those in the southern part. The weather in the highlands is not the same as that in the lowlands. There are also differences between the weather along the seacoast and the weather farther inland.

To learn more about the climate of the Northeast, let us imagine that we are spending a year in this part of our country. We will begin our visit in the winter.

Winter

A visit to the White Mountains

We are visiting a ski resort in the White Mountains of New Hampshire. The temperature on this January afternoon is 20° F. (-7° C.).† The mountains and the valleys are covered with a blanket of fresh, white snow. In many places, strong winds have piled the snow into deep drifts. We notice that a pond nearby is covered with ice. All around us, skiers dressed in bright winter clothing are gliding down the snowy mountains.

† F. means Fahrenheit scale
C. means Celsius scale

Winter in New York City. In parts of the Northeast, heavy snowfall sometimes makes it hard for people to travel from place to place. They must wait while snowplows clear the streets and highways. What are some other ways in which snowfall affects the lives of people in the Northeast?

Shortly after four o'clock, the sun sets behind a mountain peak to the west. Here in New Hampshire, January days are short. The time between sunrise and sunset is less than ten hours long. As the sky grows darker, the evening air becomes very cold. Tonight the temperature will probably go down to 0° F. (-18° C.)

Why winters are cold and snowy

One reason winters are so cold in the Northeast is that this region lies in the northern part of the United States. The weather in the northern part of our country is generally cooler than the weather in the southern part. (See the feature on pages 30 and 31.)

There is also another reason why the Northeast has such cold winters. During the winter months, the winds that pass over this region are often from the northwest. These winds, which come from northern Canada, are very cold and dry. They help to bring bitterly cold weather to the Northeast.

Not all of the winds that blow across the Northeast during the winter come

† Ask someone to call or write to the local weather bureau to find out what the average annual snowfall is in your area.

from Canada. Often a large amount of warm, moist air moves northward from the Gulf of Mexico. When this air meets the cold air from the north, it rises and becomes cooler. As it becomes cooler, it drops some of its moisture in the form of snow. This helps to explain why many areas in the Northeast receive heavy snowfall.

How winter affects the people

There are many ways in which cold, snowy winters affect the lives of people in the Northeast. The houses in this region are well built to keep out the cold. They are usually heated by furnaces. People in the Northeast need to wear warm clothing in the winter. Although a snowy land is a beautiful sight, snowstorms can cause much trouble. After a storm, people must shovel the snow off their walks and driveways. Cities must use snowplows to clear the streets. Cars often become stuck in snowdrifts, and icy roads make driving dangerous. Buses and trains sometimes cannot run on time because of heavy snow. Airport runways are sometimes blocked by drifts or covered with ice so that planes cannot take off or land.

Winters in the highlands

Winters are cold and snowy in most of the highlands of the Northeast. Temperatures often stay below freezing for weeks at a time, and snowstorms are frequent. In some of the mountains of the Northeast, more than 144 inches (366 cm.)† may fall during the winter. Many people go to the mountains in winter to enjoy skiing and other winter sports.

† cm. means centimeter

Winters in the lowlands

In the lowlands along the Atlantic coast, winter weather is not as cold as it is in the highlands. Large bodies of water lose their heat more slowly than land does. For this reason, the Atlantic Ocean is warmer during the winter than the land nearby. Breezes from the ocean bring mild weather to the lowlands along the coast. In the lowlands of Maryland and Delaware, winters are so mild that snow does not often stay on the ground for more than a day or two at a time.

Can anyone identify the building in this picture? (The Jefferson Memorial, built on the Tidal Basin near the Potomac River in honor of Thomas Jefferson, our third president.)

On the plain along Lake Erie and Lake Ontario, winters are a little milder than they are in the highlands. Winds from the north and west are warmed as they blow across the Great Lakes. They help to keep very cold weather from coming to the eastern and southern shores of the lakes. As these winds pass over the lakes, they take up much moisture. Some of this moisture later returns to the earth in the form of snow. Buffalo and other cities in western New York often receive large amounts of snow in the winter.

Spring

It is April, and we are visiting the city of Washington, D.C. (See map on page 13.) The air is warm, and a soft breeze is blowing. The cherry trees are in bloom. The gardens and parks that we see as we tour the city are fresh and green.

In the countryside around Washington, we see farmers plowing their fields. They are turning over the soil so it will be ready for spring planting. The weather should be warm enough from

In Washington, D.C., cherry trees blossom in April. Here, as in some other lowland areas of the Northeast, spring comes early. How does an early spring help farmers in these areas?

THE SEASONS

The year is divided into four natural periods, or seasons. We call them summer, autumn, winter, and spring. Each season is marked by changes in the length of day and night and by changes in temperature.

The seasons are caused by the tilt of the earth's axis and the revolution of the earth around the sun. It takes one year for the earth to revolve around the sun. On this trip, the earth remains tilted at the same angle to the path along which it travels. The chart below shows how this causes the Northern Hemisphere to be tilted toward the sun on June 21 and away from the sun on December 22. On March 21 and September 22, the Northern Hemisphere is tilted neither toward the sun nor away from it.

The chart on the left shows that on June 21 the sun shines directly on the Tropic of Cancer.* This is the northernmost point ever reached by the sun's direct rays. In the Northern Hemisphere, June 21 is the first day of summer and the longest day of the year.

The chart on the right shows that on December 22 the sun shines directly on the Tropic of Capricorn.* This is the southernmost point ever reached by the sun's direct

SUMMER IN THE NORTHERN HEMISPHERE

The chart above shows how the earth is lighted by the sun at noon on June 21, the first day of summer in the Northern Hemisphere.

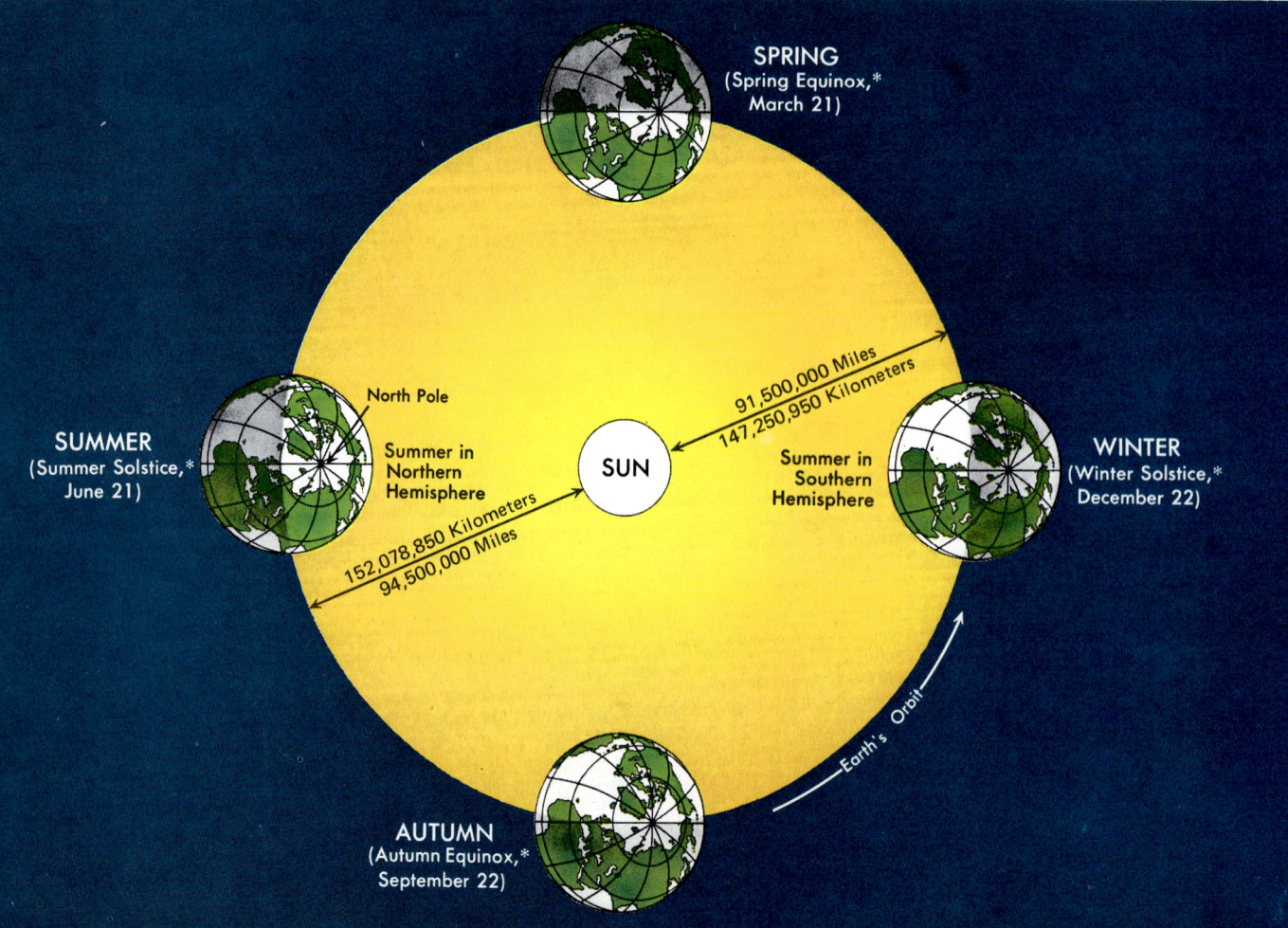

OF THE YEAR

rays. In the Northern Hemisphere, December 22 is the first day of winter and the shortest day of the year.

When one hemisphere is tilted toward the sun, the other is tilted away from the sun. For this reason, the seasons in the Southern Hemisphere are just the opposite of those in the Northern Hemisphere. Summer in the Southern Hemisphere begins on December 22, and winter begins on June 21.

Temperatures are affected by the slant of the sun's rays as they strike the surface of the earth. Study the chart below, and the picture of Washington, D.C., to help you understand why this is true.

Near the equator, the sun is almost directly overhead throughout the year. For this reason, the weather near the equator is always hot, except in the mountains. In areas farther away from the equator, the sun's rays are more slanted. Therefore, the weather is usually cooler.

The southern part of the United States is nearer the equator than the northern part. This helps to explain why the weather is generally warmer in the southern part of our country than it is in the northern part.

*See Glossary

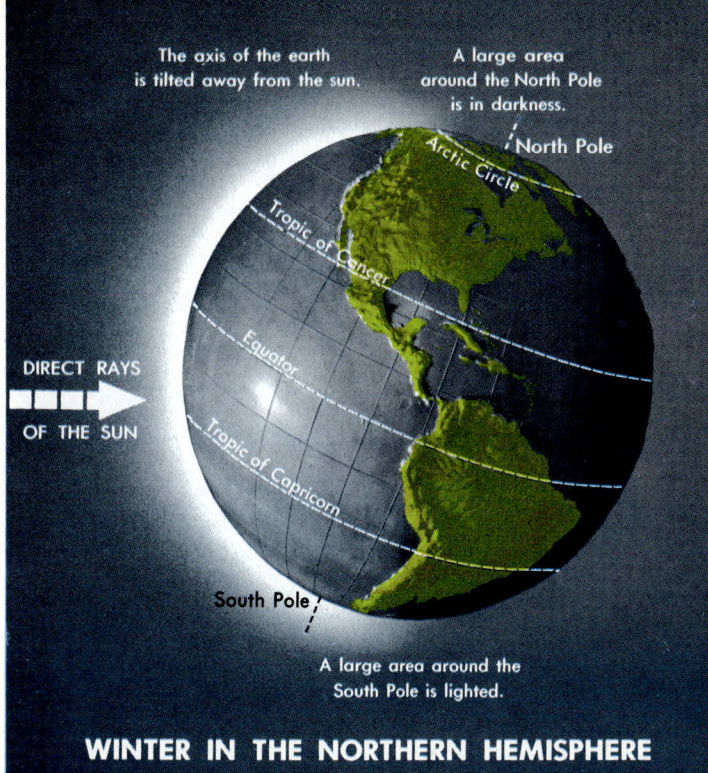

WINTER IN THE NORTHERN HEMISPHERE

The chart above shows how the earth is lighted by the sun at noon on December 22, the first day of winter in the Northern Hemisphere.

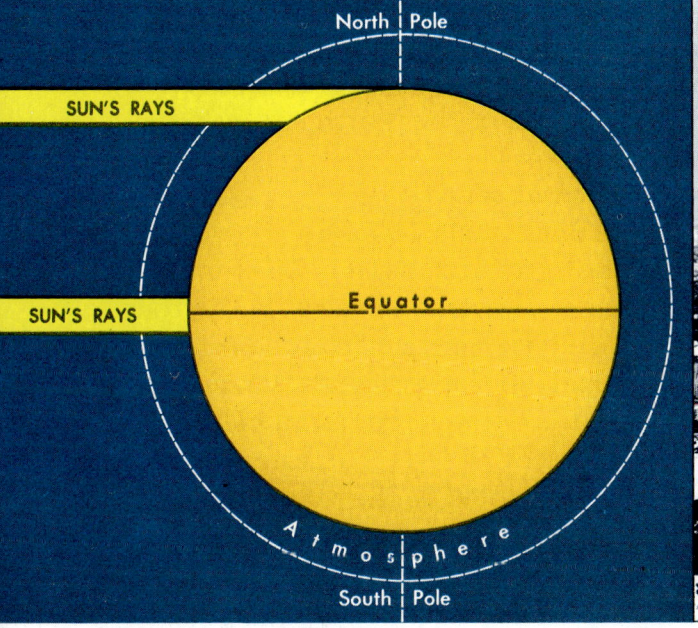

The chart above shows that when the sun's rays strike the earth at a slant, they must travel through more atmosphere, or air, than when they strike it directly. This affects temperatures because the air soaks up heat from the sun's rays. The more air the rays must pass through, the less heat they hold to warm the earth. This is one reason why temperatures are higher if the sun is directly overhead than they are if the sun is low in the sky.

This picture also helps to explain how changes in temperature are caused by the different angles at which the sun's rays strike the earth. During the summer, the noon sun is high in the sky. The rays of the sun are concentrated into small areas. For this reason, they give large amounts of heat. During the winter, the noon sun is lower in the sky. The slanting rays of the sun are spread over much wider areas, so they give less heat.

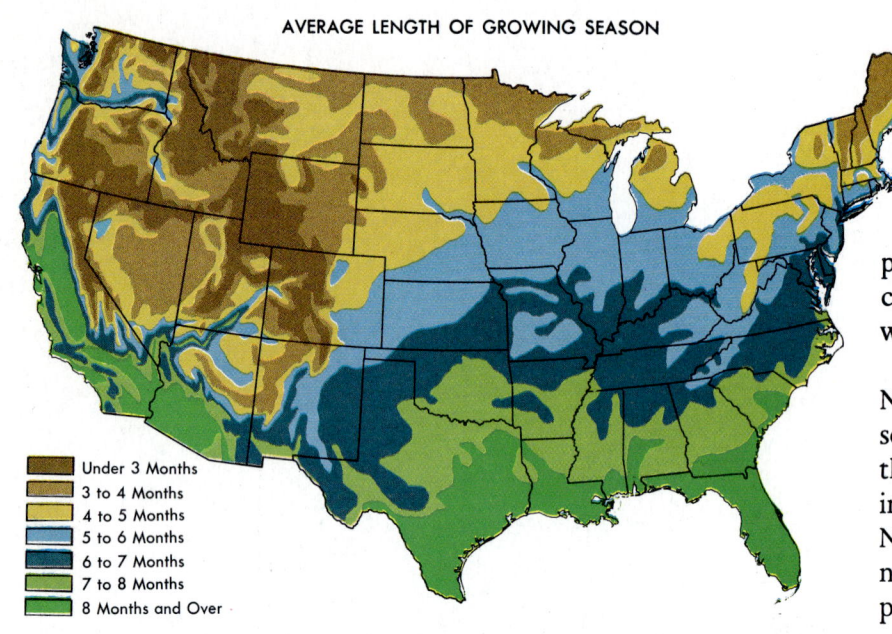

AVERAGE LENGTH OF GROWING SEASON

- Under 3 Months
- 3 to 4 Months
- 4 to 5 Months
- 5 to 6 Months
- 6 to 7 Months
- 7 to 8 Months
- 8 Months and Over

The growing season is the period of time during which crops can be grown outdoors without being killed by frost.

The growing season in the Northeast lasts from three to seven months. It is shortest in the Adirondack Mountains and in the highlands of northern New England. It is longest near the coast in the southern part of the Northeast.

now on so that tender young plants will not be killed by frost.

What is the growing season?

In this part of the Northeast, the last hard frost comes in early April. The first hard frost of autumn usually comes some time in October. Therefore, crops can be grown outdoors for six months of the year without danger of being killed by frost. This frost-free period is known as the growing season.

The growing season along the Atlantic coast

The map above shows the length of the growing season in different parts of the Northeast. You can see that the growing season is quite long in the lowlands along the Atlantic coast. In some places, farmers can grow crops outdoors for nearly seven months.

The long growing season along the Atlantic coast is helpful to farmers. There are many truck farms on Long Island, and in New Jersey, Delaware, and Maryland. Vegetables are grown on these farms and sold to people in the large cities of the Northeast. Because the farmers can plant their crops early in the spring, they can get their vegetables to market sooner than farmers in other parts of the Northeast.

The growing season in the Erie-Ontario Lowland

The growing season in the Erie-Ontario Lowland is also fairly long. The climate here is very good for growing fruit. In the spring, the Great Lakes do not become warm as quickly as the land nearby. Winds from the north and west are cooled as they blow across the lakes. The cool winds keep fruit trees and grapevines from budding while there is danger of frost. In the fall, the Great Lakes are warmer than the land. Warm winds from the lakes help to protect ripening fruit from early frosts. Large amounts of apples, peaches, grapes, and other fruit are grown in the Erie-Ontario Lowland.

† How does the growing season help determine the type of crops farmers can grow?

The growing season in the highlands

At the same time that flowers are blooming in the lowlands, snow still covers many hills and mountains in the Northeast. The growing season in the highlands is generally shorter than the growing season in the lowlands.

† The growing season is quite short in the Adirondack Mountains and the highlands of northern New England. In some places, farmers cannot plant their crops until late May. The first killing frost may come in September. Therefore, farmers here cannot raise crops that need a long growing season. They must grow crops such as hay and potatoes, which do not take long to ripen.

Summer

We are strolling along Fifth Avenue in New York City on a hot day in July. The sun is shining brightly, and the temperature is 90° F. (32° C.). Because the air is very humid,* we feel even warmer than we would if it were dry. We wish that we could drive to one of the beaches on Long Island for a cooling swim in the Atlantic Ocean.

In the middle of the afternoon, large, dark clouds called thunderheads appear in the west. The air is very still. Suddenly we hear a loud crash of thunder, and rain begins to fall in large drops. We stand in a doorway to get out of

*See Glossary

A hot summer day in New York City. Water from a fire hydrant helps these children cool off on a hot summer day. Why are summers hot and humid in most parts of the Northeast?

† Why do we consider rain a natural resource? (It's a gift of nature.) Why is rain important to farmers?

the rain. Within an hour, the storm is over. Now the air feels cooler.

Why summers are hot and humid

There are many hot, humid days like this in most parts of the Northeast in the summer. The feature on pages 30 and 31 helps to explain why. During the summer months, the northern part of the earth is tilted toward the sun. Therefore, lands in the Northern Hemisphere receive large amounts of warm sunshine.

There is also another reason why summers are so warm in the Northeast. During the summer, many of the winds that blow across this region come from the Gulf of Mexico. (See map on page 7.) These winds are very warm and moist. They bring hot, humid weather to many parts of the Northeast.

The winds from the Gulf of Mexico also bring frequent rains to the Northeast during the summer. As the moist air passes over the hot land, it rises and cools quickly, losing some of its moisture in the form of rain. There is often thunder and lightning with this kind of rainfall.

Summers in large cities

Hot, humid weather can be very unpleasant for people in large cities, where the buildings and pavements reflect the sun's heat. Sometimes a "heat wave" may last for weeks. It is hard to work when the weather is hot and humid. It is hard to sleep. On hot days, city dwellers go to parks or sit on porches and balconies. On weekends, many people go to the seacoast or to the mountains to escape the heat.

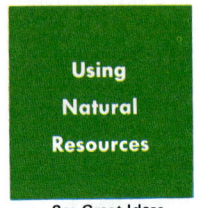
Using Natural Resources
See Great Ideas

The map below shows average annual rainfall in different parts of the United States. The term "rainfall" includes the amount of water that falls as rain, snow, and sleet. Rainfall is an important natural resource in the Northeast, as it is in other parts of our country. Almost all parts of the Northeast receive enough rainfall for growing most kinds of crops. What other natural resources do people need for growing crops? †

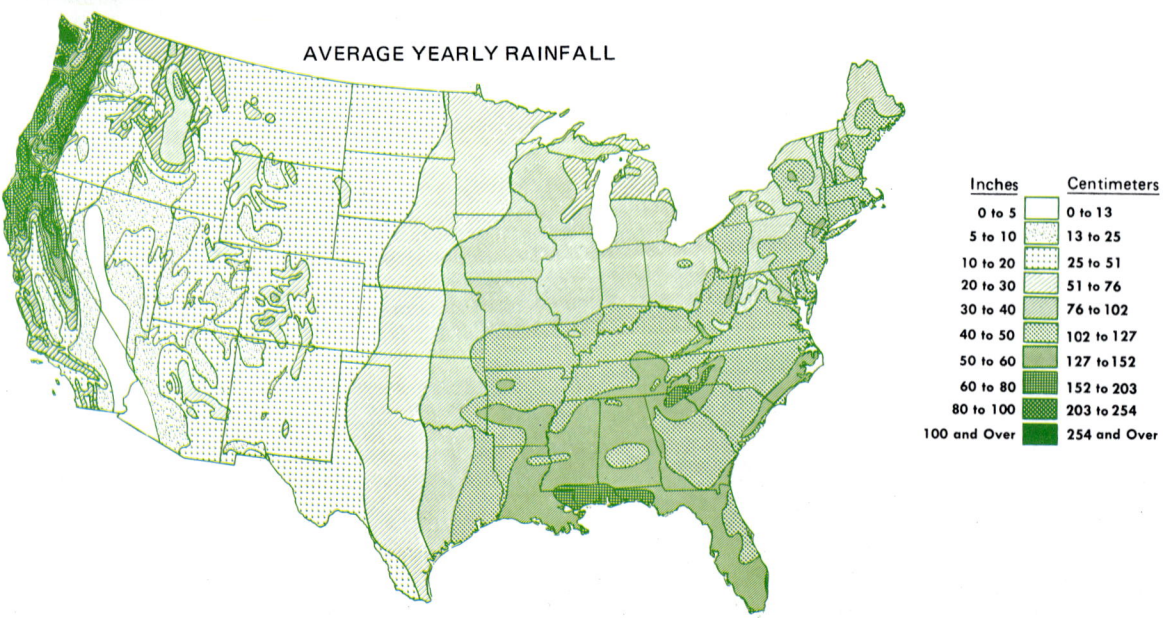

AVERAGE YEARLY RAINFALL

Inches	Centimeters
0 to 5	0 to 13
5 to 10	13 to 25
10 to 20	25 to 51
20 to 30	51 to 76
30 to 40	76 to 102
40 to 50	102 to 127
50 to 60	127 to 152
60 to 80	152 to 203
80 to 100	203 to 254
100 and Over	254 and Over

A beach on the Atlantic coast of Delaware. In the summer, some city people go to the seacoast to escape the hot, humid weather. Other people visit mountainous areas where it is cooler than it is in the lowlands. What facts help explain why it is cooler in the mountains?

Summers in the highlands

From New York City we take a trip to the Adirondack Mountains. We find that the summer weather here is cooler and more pleasant than it is in the lowlands. Summers are also pleasant in other mountainous areas in the Northeast. Many people come to these areas during the summer to enjoy the cool mountain air.

Mountainous parts of the Northeast † are generally cooler than nearby lowlands because they are so much higher above the level of the sea. The higher you go above sea level, the cooler the air becomes. As you may have learned in your science class, the earth gives off heat that it has received from the sun. At low elevations, much of this heat is taken up by the moisture and

† How is summer weather in the highlands generally different from summer weather in the lowlands?

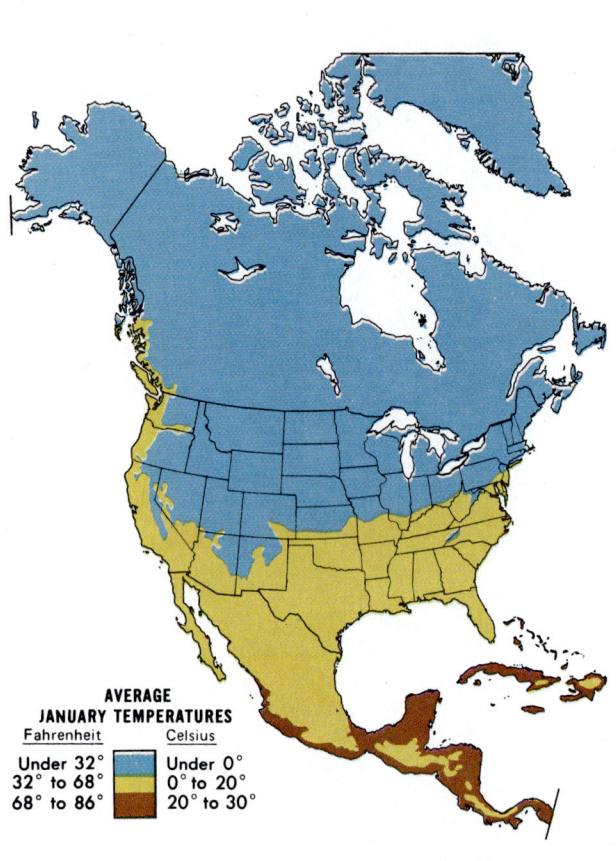

AVERAGE JANUARY TEMPERATURES

Fahrenheit	Celsius
Under 32°	Under 0°
32° to 68°	0° to 20°
68° to 86°	20° to 30°

AVERAGE JULY TEMPERATURES

Fahrenheit	Celsius
Under 32°	Under 0°
32° to 68°	0° to 20°
68° to 86°	20° to 30°
86° and Over	30° and Over

dust in the air. At high elevations, however, the air is much cleaner and drier. Therefore, it cannot take up as much heat. As a result, the temperature is usually cooler at high elevations.

Summers along the Atlantic coast

Another place where summers are mild is the Atlantic coast of New England. Cool breezes from the ocean keep the temperature from becoming very hot. This is one reason why many people spend their vacations on Cape Cod or along the coast of Maine.

Autumn

Now it is October, and we are hiking through the Berkshire Hills in western Massachusetts. We are wearing light

Call attention to the average temperature maps above. Refer to the map keys. Ask: What is the average July temperature where we live? What is our average temperature in January?

Autumn in the highlands of Vermont. In the Northeast, autumn is a season of many colors. It brings cool, pleasant weather and shorter days to this part of our country.

jackets, because the temperature here is about 50° F. (10° C.). The air here is so cool and fresh that it makes us feel very healthy. Wherever we go in the Northeast during the autumn, we are likely to find cool, pleasant weather.

The oaks, maples, and birches that cover the hills around us are clothed in red and gold. Although the sky above is blue and without clouds, the air seems smoky. Farmers are busy harvesting the last of their crops. Tomorrow morning, the ground will probably have a white coating of frost.

† The days are growing shorter. Each day the sun is a little lower in the sky. Winter will soon be here.

Explore the Climate of the Northeast
1. What facts help to explain why many areas in the Northeast receive heavy snowfall?
2. How does the long growing season along the Atlantic coast help farmers here?
3. Why is the climate along Lake Ontario and Lake Erie good for growing fruit?

Climate Where You Live ††
What is the climate like where you live? How does it affect your everyday life? Think carefully about these two questions. Then, draw or paint several pictures that show how the weather affects your life during each season of the year. You may wish to write labels for your pictures. Share the pictures with your class.

† Why do the days grow shorter in autumn in the Northeast? Refer to pages 30 and 31.
†† Have your students do the activity explained above.

Part 2

People

† Use these questions to start students thinking about people in the Northeast.

The people of the Northeast are very much like people in other parts of our country. They share the same basic human needs and the same important beliefs about how our country should be governed. As you learn about the people of this region, you may wish to discover answers to the following questions:

†
- Who lives in the Northeast?
- Why is the Northeast thickly populated?
- What are some of the ways in which the people of the Northeast meet their basic needs? (See "Needs of People" at the back of this book. Part 3 also has information that will help you answer this question.)
- What is the "super city?"
- What are some of the rights that people of the Northeast share as citizens of our country?
- What are some of the responsibilities the people of this region have as citizens of our country?

Use Fideler Discovery Cards 57-82, or Fideler Discovery Sheets, Volume 1, pages 25-36 for additional activities.

People at a street fair in New York City. People of many different national* origins, races, and religions live in the great cities of the Northeast.

*See Glossary

† Refer to the text on these pages and to the map on the opposite page to answer the question in the caption below.

4 People

Population of the Northeast

The Northeast is the most thickly populated part of our country. More than 56 million people live in the Northeast. This is about one fourth of the entire population of the United States. However, the Northeast covers less than one tenth of the total land area of our country.

Where do the people live?

About four fifths of the people who make their homes in the Northeast live in large cities or other thickly populated areas. Others live on farms or in small towns and villages.

Most of the Northeast's towns and cities have grown up in the lowland areas along the Atlantic Ocean and the Great Lakes, or in river valleys. Many early colonists settled near the fine natural harbors along the coast. Others settled along rivers, which provided good water transportation routes. As people moved westward, they settled mainly on plains or in river valleys. In

† **Shoppers at a sidewalk market in New York City.** Millions of people live and work in the Northeast. This region is the most thickly populated part of our country. What are some of the reasons why so many people have made their homes in the Northeast?

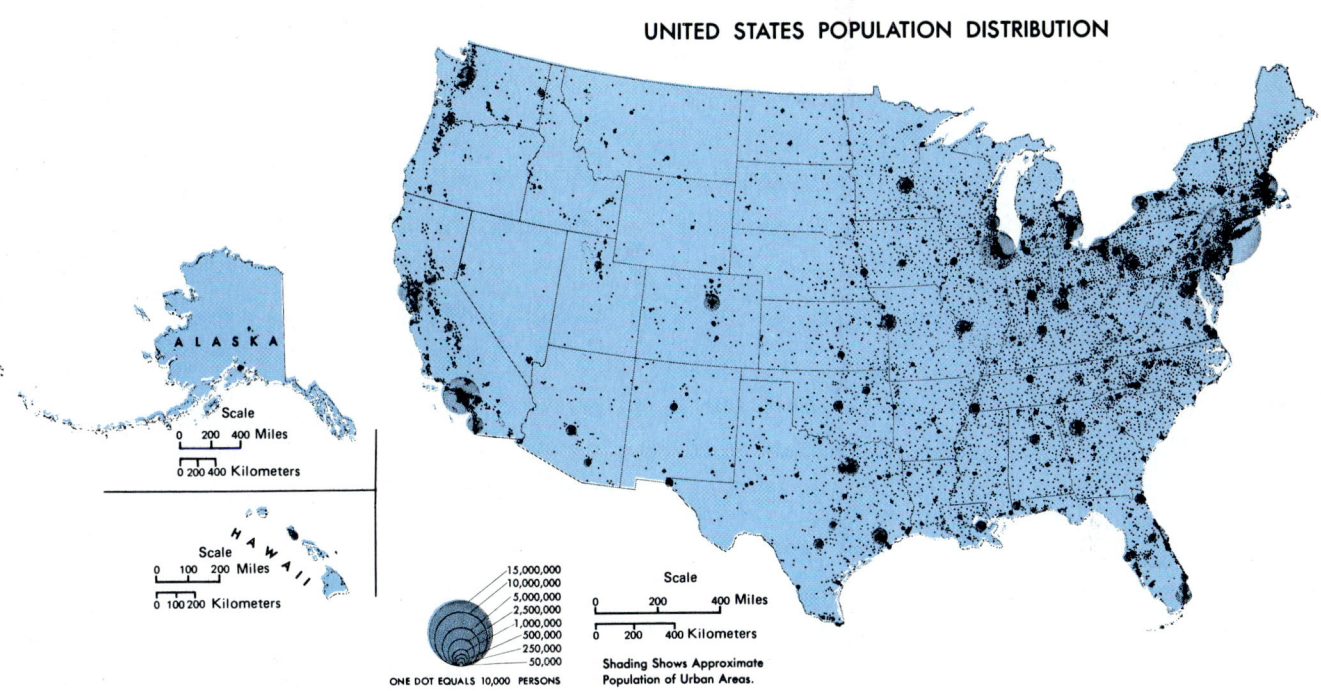

UNITED STATES POPULATION DISTRIBUTION

these areas, they generally found the land and climate well suited to farming. Also, it was easier to build roads and railroads through plains and valleys than through the highlands. Few people settled in the mountainous parts of the Northeast, such as the Adirondacks in New York or the highlands of Maine. Today, these areas are still thinly populated. (Compare map on page 14 with map above.)

Three main areas with many people

The most thickly populated part of the Northeast begins in southern New Hampshire and extends south along the Atlantic coast. This area is known as Megalopolis, or the "super city." (See Chapter 5.) Megalopolis includes the great Atlantic port cities of Boston, New York, Philadelphia, and Baltimore, as well as Washington, D.C. It also includes the many smaller cities, towns, and suburban communities between these larger cities.

Another thickly populated part of the Northeast is in western Pennsylvania, along the Ohio River and its branches. Large supplies of coal have helped this to become one of our country's leading industrial areas. More steel is made here than in any other part of the Northeast. Pittsburgh is the largest city in western Pennsylvania, and one of the oldest.

Still another thickly populated area extends from east to west across central New York. It lies along the route of the Erie Canal. This area includes the cities of Albany, Utica, Syracuse, Rochester, and Buffalo.

People from many lands

† Most people in the Northeast are American-born citizens, just as most people are in other regions of the United States. In our country, however, almost all American-born citizens are descended from immigrants who have come here during the last four hundred years. Indians, Eskimos, and Hawaiians are the only exceptions. In the Northeast, by far the largest number of American-born citizens are of European descent. Their ancestors came to America from many different countries in Europe. The blacks in the Northeast are descended from people who lived in Africa.

Immigration in early times

People from several different European countries came to America during colonial times. Most of the colonists in the Northeast came from England. Others came from Scotland and Ireland. There were Dutch settlers in New York and New Jersey, Germans in Pennsylvania, and Swedes in Delaware. French Huguenots* also settled in the Northeast, mainly in New York. In addition to the settlers who came from Europe, there were also many black people who were brought from Africa to work as slaves.

The years 1820 to 1900

After the Revolutionary War* few settlers came to the United States.

About 1820, however, immigration to America began to increase rapidly. By this time, the United States was a successful democracy. It was a land of freedom and opportunity. Many Americans were moving from the east into the vast lands that had been opened up for settlement in the west. This left a shortage of workers in the factories that were growing up in the Northeast.

At this same time, many people in Europe were becoming unhappy and restless. One reason for this was that thousands of workers could not find

*See Glossary

42   The Northeast   † Does anyone have parents or grandparents who came to America from other countries? Does anyone have parents or grandparents who are Native Americans?

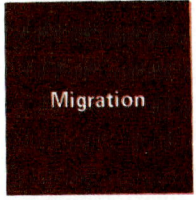

A Problem To Solve

The picture at left shows immigrants arriving in the Northeast. Ever since the United States became a nation, people from many different lands have come to the Northeast to live. Why have so many immigrants made their homes in the Northeast? In forming hypotheses* to solve this problem, you may wish to think about each of the following questions.

a. What facts about religious and political freedom in the United States help to solve this problem?
b. What facts about job opportunities in the Northeast help solve it?
c. How has the location of the Northeast affected the number of immigrants who have come to this region?

See Skills Manual, "Thinking and Solving Problems"

jobs. Everywhere in Europe, the population was getting larger. There was no new land for farming, and the cities could not provide jobs for all the people who needed work. In addition, many Europeans were dissatisfied with the governments under which they lived. Democracy and religious freedom were unknown in most of the countries in Europe. Also, crop failures made it difficult for some people in Europe to obtain enough food.

Between 1840 and 1860, more than one and one-half million people left their homes in Ireland and came to America. Many left Ireland because crop failures were causing great hardship and suffering.

A steady stream of German immigrants came to America during the second half of the nineteenth century. Many of these people came because they were unhappy with their government at home. Crop failures also caused people from Germany to come to the United States. Some of these Germans had saved enough money to buy farmland. They generally moved farther

† Discuss "A Problem To Solve." Do we still have immigration into the United States?

† The Statue of Liberty was a gift to the people of America from the people of France.

west, where more land was available. Many settled in the towns and cities of the Northeast, however.

In addition to the large number of immigrants from Ireland and Germany, people came to America from many other parts of the world. They came from England as they always had. They also came from Sweden, Norway, Finland, and the Netherlands. After the Civil War, many French Canadians also came to the United States. Most of them settled in New England.

Altogether, about twenty million immigrants came to America between 1820 and 1900. Most of these people entered our country through the great port cities of the Northeast. Large numbers of these immigrants found jobs in the cities where they landed. Some moved on to other parts of the Northeast or to other regions of our country.

The twentieth century

During the first ten years of the twentieth century, almost nine million immigrants came to the United States. By that time immigration from the countries of northern and western Europe was decreasing. More people were coming from southern and eastern Europe. Each year, thousands of Italians, Poles, Greeks, Russians, Jews, and

Refer to the caption below. You may use the questions for a class discussion.

Freedom
See Great Ideas

The Statue of Liberty, in † New York Harbor, reminds people of freedom. Millions of people have come to America from other lands in search of freedom. What different kinds of freedom were these people looking for? What kinds of freedom do people enjoy in the United States?

Puerto Ricans taking part in a parade in New York City. Many Spanish-speaking people of Puerto Rican descent make their homes in the cities of the Northeast.

Czechs came to America. Most of these immigrants became industrial workers in the great cities of the Northeast and the Midwest. Some found jobs in the coal mines of West Virginia and western Pennsylvania.

Other newcomers

Although immigration from Europe declined after 1910, the great industrial cities of the Northeast continued to grow. Many farm workers left rural areas to take factory jobs in the cities. Among these people were large numbers of blacks from the South. In the past, most of them had made their living by farming small plots of land, or by working at other jobs that paid them very little money. They came to New York and other cities of the Northeast hoping to find work in industry.

In the late 1930's, Spanish-speaking † Americans from the island of Puerto Rico* began to move into the cities of the Northeast. At that time, many of the people in Puerto Rico were very poor. Large numbers of Puerto Ricans came to the Northeast to look for better-paying jobs. Today there are more than 800,000 people of Puerto Rican descent living in New York City.

† Have a student look up "Puerto Rico" in the Glossary and read the definition aloud. Have another student locate Puerto Rico on the classroom globe or map.

The Northeast today

As you have seen, people have been moving to the Northeast for hundreds of years. Today, people of many different races and national origins live here. About nine tenths of the people are white. Nearly all of the others are black. Most of the rest are of Asian descent. They are mainly Chinese, Japanese, or Filipino.* A small number of Native Americans (Indians) also live in the Northeast.

Christianity is the leading religion in the Northeast, just as it is in other parts of our country. Roman Catholics make up the largest single religious group.

Education

See Great Ideas

A drugstore owner in the Northeast. This picture shows a successful pharmacist at work in his drugstore. He earns his living partly by preparing medicines for customers according to their doctors' instructions. How do you suppose this man learned the skills needed to prepare medicines? Do you think this man could be successful in his job without the great idea of education? Give reasons for your answer.

The Eastern Orthodox* churches also have many members. Some of the main Protestant groups in the Northeast are the Methodists, the Presbyterians, and the Baptists.

Another large religious group in the Northeast is made up of Jews. There are hundreds of Jewish congregations in this region, especially in New York and other large cities. In addition, people of other faiths such as Islam* and Buddhism* live in the Northeast.

Americans all

Life in the Northeast, as in all of America, is more interesting because of the many races, religions, and nationalities that are represented among the people. Each group, in its own way, has had an influence on the American way of life.

People of almost every different group in the Northeast have made important contributions to American life. For example, Andrew Carnegie, an immigrant from Scotland, helped to develop America's steel industry. Gian-Carlo Menotti, who came to the Northeast from Italy, is a world-famous composer of music. Senator Edward Brooke and Representative Shirley Chisholm are black Americans. The German-born scientist Albert Einstein was a Jew. John F. Kennedy, whose great-grandparents came from Ireland, was our first Roman Catholic president.

The people of the Northeast, through their labor, their skills, and their talents, have all helped to make the United States the strong country it is today. Whatever their race, religion, or national origin, the people of the Northeast have one very important thing in common. They are all Americans.

The famous scientist Albert Einstein was a German-born Jew who lived in New Jersey. People of almost every group in the Northeast have made important contributions to America.

Famous People †

People of many different races and nationalities have influenced life in our country. Eight of these people are listed below. Make a chart for your classroom that shows the national origin of each person and how he or she has influenced American life. As you do your research, you may find other names to add to your chart.

John James Audubon   Lin Yutang
Marian Anderson   Maria Tallchief
Arturo Toscanini   Knute Rockne
Wernher von Braun   Igor Stravinsky

For help in finding information, see "Learning Social Studies Skills" in the Skills Manual.

† Ask your students to prepare a report on any one of the people listed above. Or, you may assign your students to give a class report using Fideler Discovery Card 59. (Give a report about the people who live in the area you are studying.)

Boston, Massachusetts, is part of a long chain of cities, towns, and suburbs. This chain extends along the Atlantic coast of our country from southern New Hampshire into northern Virginia. This densely populated part of the Northeast is known as Megalopolis, or the "super city."

5 Cities

† **A Problem To Solve**

<u>Why have so many great cities grown up in the Northeast?</u> In forming your hypotheses,* think about the following:
1. location of early settlements in this region
2. location of industry
3. transportation routes
4. immigration to our country

This chapter, as well as other chapters in this book, contain much useful information for solving this problem.

See Skills Manual, "Thinking and Solving Problems"

A region of great cities

If you were to go by train from Washington, D.C., to Boston, Massachusetts, you would travel through an almost unbroken line of cities, towns, and suburbs.* You would see open countryside and farmland from time to time. But, you would sometimes find it difficult to tell where one city ends and another begins.

*See Glossary

48 The Northeast   † Have your students solve this problem to start them thinking about cities in the Northeast. Use Fideler Discovery Card 68 for an additional activity.

Pittsburgh is the only one of these areas that is not located in New York State. More than two million people live in or near Pittsburgh, Pennsylvania. The Buffalo metropolitan area has a population of more than one million. Other large metropolitan areas in western or central New York are Rochester and Syracuse. Also, Albany and its neighboring cities of Schenectady and Troy make up a large metropolitan area.

The Northeast has not always been a region of great cities. Three hundred years ago, very few people lived here. Only along the coast and in some of the river valleys were there small towns and settlements. Today, about four out of every five people in this region live in or near cities or towns. Let us learn how the Northeast became a region of great cities.

How Cities Grew

Cities do not grow up in a certain place by accident. There are always reasons for their growth. To understand why the Northeast has become a region of great cities, we need to know about the history of some of these cities.

Early settlements along the coast

Many of the Europeans who came to the Northeast in early colonial days settled along bays and inlets on the Atlantic coast. Some of these settlers turned to the sea for their living. They became shipbuilders, sailors, and fishers. Many of the early settlements along the coast became seaports. Some ships sailed from these ports to the nearby fishing grounds in the Atlantic Ocean. Others made long trips to trade with other parts of the world. This

The entire area along the Atlantic coast from southern New Hampshire into northern Virginia appears to be a single huge city. For this reason, this area has been called Megalopolis, or the "super city." (See map on page 50.) Several of the largest metropolitan* areas in the Northeast form part of the super city. In addition to these great metropolitan areas, there are many smaller urban* areas in the super city.

There are also large metropolitan areas in other parts of the Northeast.

The Northeast 49

Have students use the map below to find out how many large cities (250,000 population or more) are included in Megalopolis.

trade helped the seacoast towns to grow. Even before the Revolutionary War,* seaports such as New York, Boston, and Philadelphia had become important cities.

Early settlements in the river valleys

Some early settlements were made in the river valleys of the Northeast. Since there were no roads through the forests, the early settlers usually traveled by river. They found some places along the rivers favorable for starting settlements. Other settlements started as fur-trading posts. One of these is Albany, New York, on the west bank of the Hudson River. Pittsburgh, in western Pennsylvania, also started as a fur-trading post.

Early industrial cities

Many of the first settlements in the Northeast became important manufacturing cities. Textile* mills and other

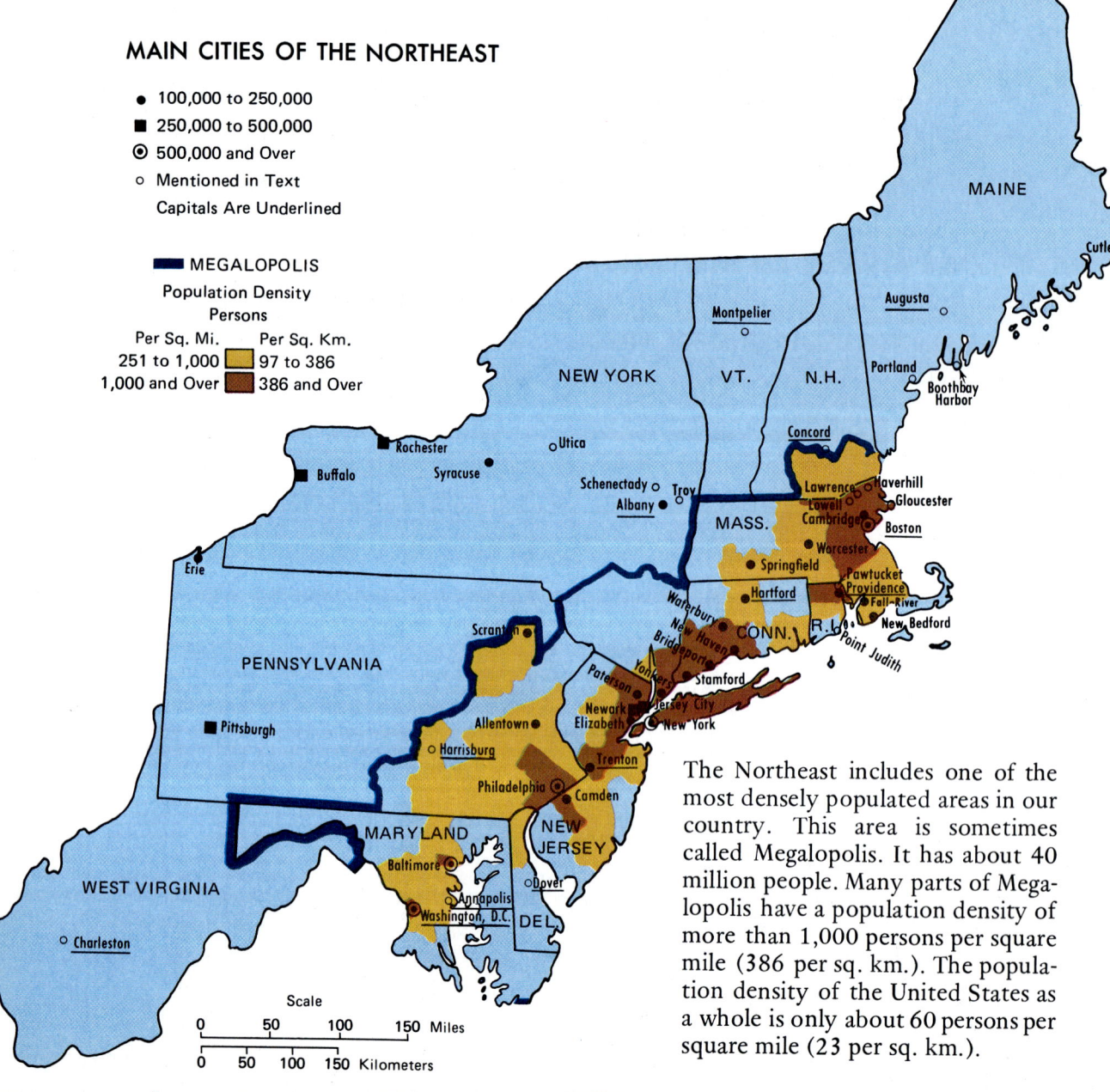

The Northeast includes one of the most densely populated areas in our country. This area is sometimes called Megalopolis. It has about 40 million people. Many parts of Megalopolis have a population density of more than 1,000 persons per square mile (386 per sq. km.). The population density of the United States as a whole is only about 60 persons per square mile (23 per sq. km.).

† Have someone look up "Erie Canal" in the Glossary and read the definition aloud.

factories were built in this region in the early 1800's. Many of these factories were started in port cities. Here, there were store owners and ship owners who had money to help build factories. Also, most of the people lived near the coast. The large population here provided workers for factories and customers for manufactured goods.

Some industrial cities grew up around factories located near waterfalls. The force of falling water was used to run machines in certain types of factories, such as gristmills* and textile mills. Among the New England cities that grew up near waterfalls were Lowell, in Massachusetts, and Pawtucket, in Rhode Island.

Good transportation routes

Good transportation routes helped some cities in the Northeast grow. From the Atlantic coast, several river valleys lead through the Appalachian Mountains. The most important of these is the Hudson-Mohawk Lowland in New York State. Others are in Pennsylvania and Maryland. In the 1800's, roads, canals, and railroads were built through these lowland areas. These transportation routes led westward from three of the region's largest cities —New York, Philadelphia, and Baltimore.

Many people from the Northeast moved westward along these routes. They began to farm, and settlements grew up in the lands beyond the mountains. A lively trade began between the manufacturing cities near the coast and the inland farming settlements. This trade helped the coastal cities to grow. It also helped settlements along the transportation routes to grow rapidly. For example, the small settlements of Buffalo, Rochester, and Syracuse became important cities after the Erie Canal* was finished in 1825.

Newcomers help the cities grow

About the middle of the 1800's, the cities of the Northeast began to grow very rapidly. Between 1840 and 1870, Philadelphia and Boston more than tripled in population. New York grew even more rapidly. By 1900, it was the world's second largest city. Only London, England, was larger.

There were several reasons for this rapid growth of the cities. One reason was the great increase in the number of immigrants coming to the United States. (See pages 43-44.) Many of these immigrants settled in the cities of the Northeast, where they could find jobs.

EIGHT METROPOLITAN AREAS

Metropolitan Area	Population of Entire Area	Population of Central City
New York City	9,526,800	7,509,300
Philadelphia	4,822,400	1,804,100
Boston	2,890,000	621,300
Washington, D.C.	3,035,900	713,900
Nassau-Suffolk	2,675,300	
Pittsburgh	2,306,300	448,900
Baltimore	2,152,400	826,400
Newark	1,988,300	352,600

The eight largest metropolitan* areas in the Northeast are listed above. Their populations are given in the middle column. For seven of these areas, the population of the central city is also given. The counties of Nassau and Suffolk are on Long Island, near New York City. They form a separate metropolitan area, even though this area has no central city.

*See Glossary

The Northeast 51

† What are some reasons why people moved from cities to the suburbs? (More room for children to play, more land for building, movement of industry to suburban areas.)

During the last half of the 1800's, many people from farming areas in the Northeast also moved to the cities. New kinds of farm machinery and better ways of farming had come into use. As a result, farmers were producing larger harvests than ever before. Since fewer farmers were needed to supply our country with food, many people decided to leave their farms. They moved to cities to work in the rapidly growing businesses and industries. After 1900, the cities grew still more in population. (See pages 44-45.)

Great Cities Today

People are still coming to the great cities of the Northeast. However, most of the central cities have smaller populations today than they did fifteen years ago. This is because many people have left the crowded cities and moved to the suburbs. Unlike the central cities, most of the metropolitan areas are still growing in population.

From cities to suburbs

† Many people have moved to the suburbs because the central cities have become so crowded. In the suburbs, the streets are not usually so busy with traffic. Also, there is more open land where people can build houses. People can have larger lawns and more room for their children to play.

Many people have also moved to the suburbs to be near the places where they work. As the cities became more and more crowded, they had less open land where large factories could be built. Many new factories were then built in less crowded areas, outside the cities. The suburbs grew as people moved from the cities to be near the factories where they worked.

New York City

A visit to New York

We are flying northward along the coast of New Jersey. Soon we see the tall buildings of a great city. This is New York. Below us, we see a wide harbor. Miles of docks line the water-

52   The Northeast

> Refer to the picture below. Call attention to the tall buildings (skyscrapers). Ask: What can you discover about living in New York City from this picture?

front. In the harbor we see many different kinds of ships. Most of the city is located on islands. As far as we can see, the land is covered with tall buildings, factories, and homes.

New York is located in the southeastern part of New York State, at the mouth of the Hudson River. Across the Hudson from New York City is the state of New Jersey. Here are several densely populated cities. They are part of the New York metropolitan area.

Our country's largest city

New York, with a population of about seven and one-half million, is the largest city in the United States. In addition to the people who live in the central city, millions of others live in cities and suburbs close to New York.

New York City is in the southeastern part of New York State, at the mouth of the Hudson River. It is the largest city in our country. About how many people live in the New York metropolitan area?

Apartment buildings in New York City. People who live in this city share the same needs that all other people do. Do you think it is easier for people in a large city like New York to meet their needs than it is for people who live on farms? Explain.

Meeting Needs

See Needs of People

About nine and one-half million people live in the New York metropolitan area.

An important gateway for trade

New York is our country's leading seaport. Each year, thousands of ships enter and leave New York Harbor. These ships carry many different kinds of raw materials and manufactured goods. Much of the freight entering New York is shipped to other cities throughout the country. Goods produced in the Northeast and other regions of the nation are shipped to all parts of the world through the port of New York. In addition, most of the freight that is shipped by air between the United States and other countries passes through New York's John F. Kennedy International Airport. †

More wholesale* and retail* trade is carried on in New York than in any other city in our nation. Wholesale companies in this city sell goods to people throughout the United States and in many other parts of the world. Hundreds of thousands of New Yorkers earn their living from wholesale trade. Retail stores in New York also employ large numbers of people. These stores sell food, clothing, furniture, and hundreds of other goods needed by people in the city. New York has some of the country's largest department stores. Along Fifth Avenue in Manhattan* are many fine clothing stores and other shops. People from hundreds of miles away come to shop in stores in New York City.

Our country's banking capital

Some of our nation's largest banks and insurance companies are located in New York City. They provide money

† How do seaports, like New York City, help people in other parts of the country meet their needs?

New York City is made up of five sections called boroughs. These are Manhattan, Brooklyn, Queens, the Bronx, and Staten Island. (See map at right.) A visitor to New York can see the Statue of Liberty in New York Bay. Nearby is Ellis Island, where millions of immigrants first landed in our country. Central Park, in Manhattan, is also a popular place to visit. North of Central Park is Harlem, one of the best-known black communities in the United States. Many New Yorkers go to the beaches on Coney Island during the summer.

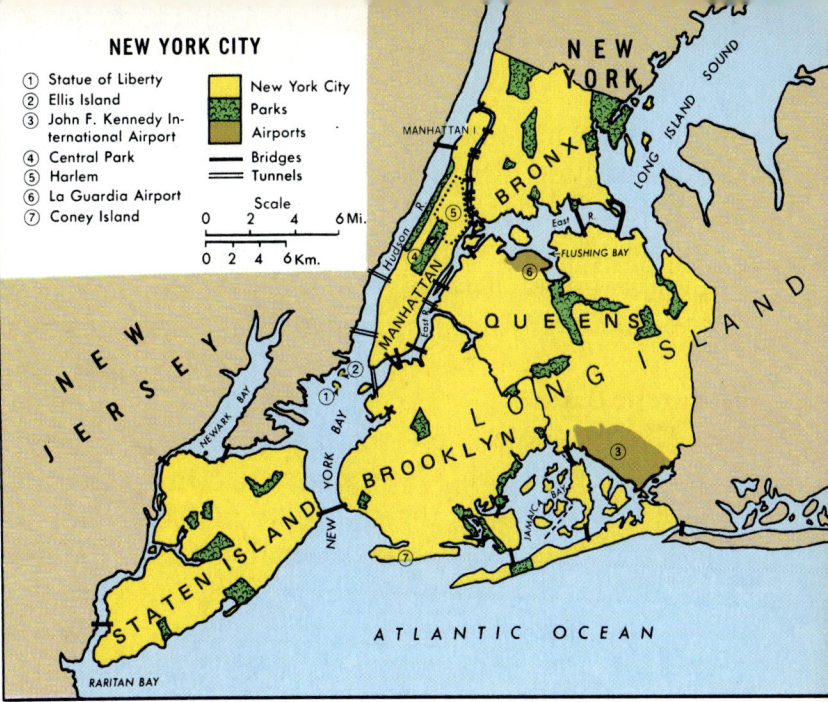

for businesses throughout the United States as well as in many countries around the world. Many of the banks and insurance companies are located on or near Wall Street in Manhattan.

A leading industrial city

Most people who visit New York do not think of it as a great manufacturing city. They see few tall smokestacks or huge factories, like those in other industrial cities. Yet New York earns more money from manufacturing than any other American city except Chicago. Because of the high cost of land in this city, manufacturers here specialize in industries that do not need a large amount of factory space. Among New York's most important industries are printing and publishing and the manufacture of clothing.

Boston

The largest city in the northern part of Megalopolis is Boston. (See map on page 50.) Boston is located on the Atlantic coast where the Charles River empties into Massachusetts Bay. Many fine harbors along the bay help make Boston an important port city.

Boston is the capital of Massachusetts, and the state's largest city. About three million people live in the Boston metropolitan area.

Industry

There are more than 5,000 factories in the Boston metropolitan area. They produce machinery, medical instruments, and many other products. Printing and publishing are also important.

Education and the arts

Since colonial times, Boston has been a leading center of education. Our country's oldest public school, the Boston Latin School, was started here by settlers in 1635. Today, more than forty colleges and universities are in the Boston area. One of these is Harvard, the oldest college in the United States. Harvard is in the city of Cambridge, across the Charles River from Boston. It was founded in 1636 and has become one of our country's leading universities.

The Northeast 55

† What do Boston, Philadelphia, and Baltimore have in common? (All are port cities and large manufacturing centers.)

Boston has many fine museums and concert halls. Many people enjoy looking at paintings and other works of art in the Museum of Fine Arts. Other people enjoy listening to concerts by the Boston Symphony Orchestra.

Historic Boston

Many people come to Boston every year to walk the Freedom Trail. This trail is a walkway through part of the city. It guides visitors to many old buildings where important events in our country's history took place. They see the Old State House,* which was built in 1713. They also see Paul Revere's House and the place where Benjamin Franklin was born.

Philadelphia

Philadelphia was founded in 1682. It grew from a small settlement to become the largest city in the state of Pennsylvania. Philadelphia is now the fourth largest city in the United States. About five million people live in the Philadelphia metropolitan area.

An important inland port

Although Philadelphia is about 100 miles (161 km.)† from the Atlantic Ocean, it is one of our country's most important ports. It is in the southeastern part of the state. (See map on page 50.) Philadelphia lies along the Delaware River, which flows to the Atlantic Ocean. Dock workers at the port of Philadelphia load and unload more than 5,000 ships every year.

Industry

Philadelphia is the third largest clothing and manufacturing city in our country. Oil refining and shipbuilding are two other major industries in the Philadelphia area. Some of Philadelphia's plants process* farm products that are raised nearby. Other industries produce chemicals and machinery.

An historic city

If you were to visit Philadelphia, you might be reminded of many events in our country's history. Thousands of tourists visit the city each day to see Independence Hall, where the Declaration of Independence and the Constitution were signed. The Liberty Bell, a well-loved symbol of American freedom, can be seen in Independence Hall.

Baltimore

Baltimore is Maryland's largest city. More than two million people live in the Baltimore metropolitan area. Parts of this city have not changed for a hundred years. There are old streets that are lined with narrow, brick buildings, called row houses. In other parts of Baltimore are skyscrapers and modern apartment buildings.

A major seaport

Baltimore lies along a wide harbor where the Patapsco River empties into Chesapeake Bay. (See map on page 13.) This fine harbor and miles of docks help make Baltimore one of the leading port cities in our country. Ships from other parts of the United States and around the world carry goods to and from this port city every day.

Industry

Baltimore's leading industry is the metals industry. The Bethlehem Steel plant near this city is one of the largest steel producers in the world. Copper is

† km. means kilometer

also produced in the Baltimore area. Other main industries here produce chemicals and electronic* equipment.

Pittsburgh

Pittsburgh is one of the few major cities in the Northeast that are not part of Megalopolis. (See map on page 50.) It is located in the southwestern part of Pennsylvania. Pittsburgh is the second largest city in the state. More than two million people live in the Pittsburgh metropolitan area.

The Golden Triangle

Downtown Pittsburgh is beautiful and modern. This area, located between the Allegheny and Monongahela rivers, is called the Golden Triangle. New skyscrapers and large, green parks have taken the place of some of the old buildings that used to be here.

Industry

Pittsburgh is one of the great iron and steel centers of the world. At night, flames from the huge steelmaking furnaces are seen for many miles. Large amounts of coal from nearby mines are used in making the iron and steel.

Pittsburgh also ranks high in the production of bottles and window glass. The Pittsburgh area's 2,500 manufacturing plants also make chemicals, metal products, and machinery. Food processing is another leading industry.

Pittsburgh is the second largest city in Pennsylvania. It began in the 1700's as a trading post. This city is at the point where the Allegheny and Monongahela rivers join to form the Ohio River.

Washington, D.C.

Washington, D.C., is our country's capital. It is also one of our most beautiful cities. It lies in the eastern part of our country, between Maryland and Virginia. (See map on the opposite page.) Washington is the only city or town in our country that is not part of a state. It covers the entire area of the District of Columbia. This area is a piece of land set apart as the home of our federal government. More than three million people live in the Washington metropolitan area. This area spreads into Maryland and Virginia.

Earning a living

More than one fourth of the people in the Washington metropolitan area have government jobs. Many others earn their living by working in hotels and restaurants. They serve the millions of people who visit Washington every year. Stores and shops also provide many jobs.

The White House, in Washington, D.C. Washington is our country's capital. The president of our country lives and works in the White House. Thousands of Americans visit the White House each year.

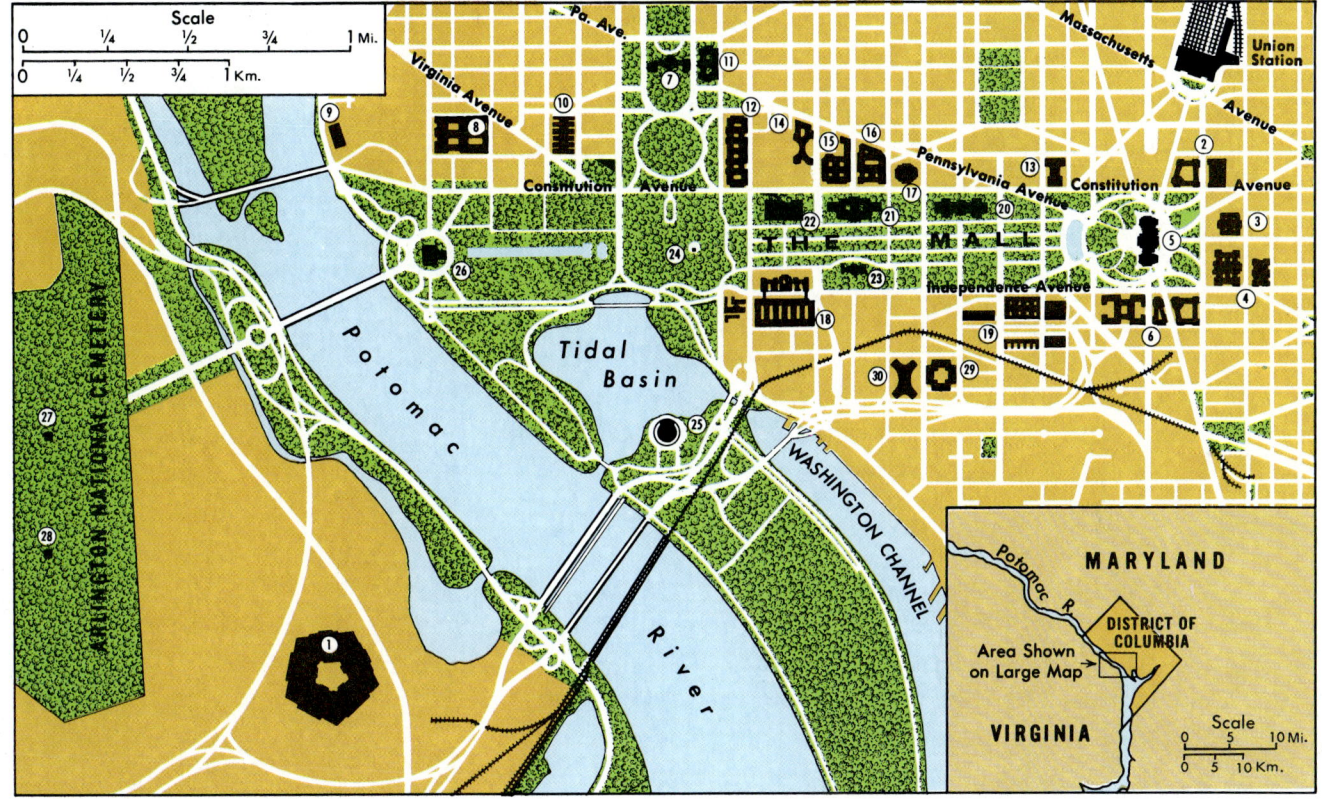

PLACES OF INTEREST

1. The Pentagon
2. Senate Office Buildings
3. Supreme Court
4. Library of Congress
5. Capitol
6. House of Representatives Office Buildings
7. White House
8. Department of State
9. John F. Kennedy Center for the Performing Arts
10. Department of the Interior
11. Department of the Treasury
12. Department of Commerce
13. Department of Labor
14. United States Postal Service
15. Internal Revenue Service
16. Department of Justice
17. National Archives
18. Department of Agriculture
19. Department of Health, Education, and Welfare
20. National Gallery of Art
21. National Museum of Natural History
22. National Museum of History and Technology
23. Smithsonian Building (Administration Offices)
24. Washington Monument
25. Jefferson Memorial
26. Lincoln Memorial
27. Grave of President Kennedy
28. Tomb of the Unknowns
29. Department of Transportation
30. Department of Housing and Urban Development

Early history

In 1783 Congress decided that our country needed a permanent capital. In 1790 they finally agreed that it should be built along the Potomac River. President George Washington chose the place along the river where the city was to be built. He also hired a French engineer to draw up plans for the city. The federal government moved from Philadelphia to Washington, D.C., in 1800.

A Visit to New York City

New York City is an interesting place to visit. Do research in other sources about one or more of the following:
1. the arts of New York City
2. the United Nations
3. the Statue of Liberty
4. the Empire State Building

Take careful notes as you do your research. Then imagine you have visited New York City and prepare a report about one or more of the above subjects. Share the report with your class.

† Have your students do research on one of the four subjects listed above. Or, you may assign a student activity using Fideler Discovery Sheets, Volume 1, page 32.

6 Citizenship and Government

Our National Government

In Chapter 5, you discovered that our nation's capital city is in the Northeast. This city is Washington, D.C. The main offices of our national government are located here. Let's take a trip to Washington to find out how the government works.

How our government began
In Washington, we hire a guide to show us around the city. Our guide tells us there are certain things we ought to know before we begin our tour.

She reminds us that our country was founded more than two hundred years ago. At that time, there were thirteen colonies along the Atlantic coast of North America. (See pages 17-18 in "Pictorial Story of Our Country.") These thirteen colonies belonged to the country of Great Britain.

People in the colonies wanted more freedom than the British government would give them. In 1775 a war broke out between the colonies and Great Britain. This became known as the Revolutionary War. It lasted for eight years. When it ended, the colonists had won their freedom from British rule. They formed a new nation called the United States of America.

The government of the new nation was very weak. It could make laws. But it had no way to make sure these laws were carried out. Many Americans felt a stronger government was needed. In 1787, some of our country's leaders met in the city of Philadelphia. They drew up a new plan of government. This was the United States Constitution.

Our government today
The Constitution is the most important set of laws in the United States. It tells how our government is supposed to be run. All other laws that are passed in our country must agree with the Constitution.

Rules and Government

See Great Ideas

President Jimmy Carter speaking to the United States Congress. Congress makes the laws for our country. What two groups make up the Congress? How are the members of each of these two groups chosen? Would you like to be a member of Congress some day? Give reasons for your answer.

60 The Northeast — Make students aware of the members of Congress who represent our area.

Under the Constitution, the United States has a federal form of government. This means that power is divided between the national government in Washington and the governments of the fifty states. (See pages 6-7.) The federal government can do certain things that the states cannot do. For example, it can issue money. It can also carry on wars against other countries. The states can do certain things that the federal government is not supposed to do. One of these is running the schools.

In the United States, all citizens of voting age can take part in running the government. They do this by electing men and women to make and carry out the laws. A country with this kind of government is known as a democracy.

Congress

Now we are ready to begin our tour. Our first stop is the Capitol. (See picture on Table of Contents pages.) The United States Congress meets here. Congress is a group of men and women who are elected by the people. They make laws for our nation.

Our guide says that Congress is made up of two groups. These are the Senate and the House of Representatives. The Senate has one hundred members—two

Refer to the picture above. Ask if any students have visited our nation's capitol. Have them tell about their experiences.

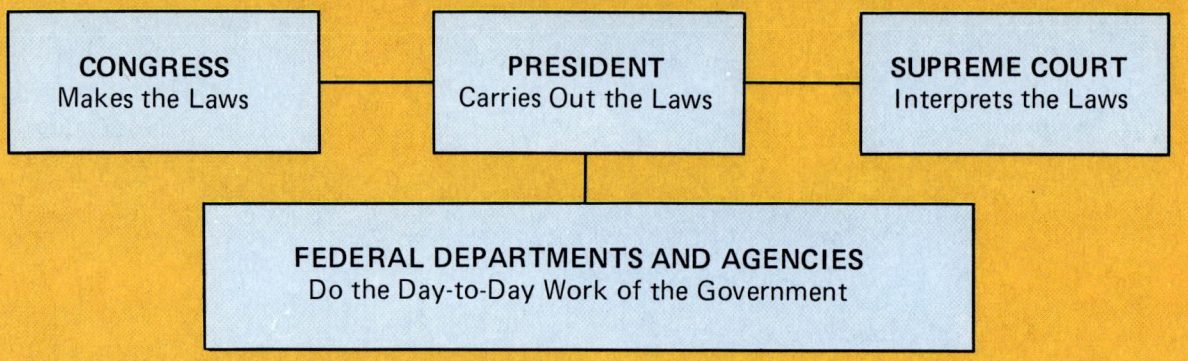

from each state in our country. These people are elected for terms of six years. The House of Representatives has 435 members. They are elected for two-year terms. Each state chooses a certain number of representatives according to its population. For example, California—the state with the most people—has forty-three representatives. Wyoming—the state with the fewest people—has only one representative.

Now we enter the Capitol and go into a large room where the Senate is meeting. From our seats in the balcony, we can watch the senators at work. One senator is making a speech. The others are sitting at their desks. They are listening to the speaker or talking quietly among themselves.

Our guide tells us that the speaker is trying to talk the other senators into voting for a bill.* Before a bill can become a law, it must be approved by both the Senate and the House of Representatives. All decisions are made by majority* vote.

The president and vice-president

Leaving the Capitol, we drive along a wide, busy street called Pennsylvania Avenue. (See map on page 59.) Soon we come to a large, beautiful house with lawns and gardens around it. This is the White House. The president of the United States lives and works here.

Our guide says the president is in charge of carrying out the laws Congress has made. A president is elected every four years by the citizens of our country. At the same time, the voters also choose a vice-president. If the president dies, the vice-president becomes the president.

Our guide tells us about the president's duties. For instance, the president is in charge of our dealings with other countries. The president is also the commander of our army, navy, and air force. The president suggests laws for Congress to vote on. Another of the president's duties is taking part in ceremonies, such as welcoming foreign leaders.

Federal departments and agencies

After we leave the White House, we drive past several office buildings. Our guide tells us that these are the offices of some of the people who work for the federal government.

Our guide explains that there are many people who help the president carry out the nation's laws. In fact, nearly three million people work for the federal government. Some of these people live in Washington. A much

*See Glossary

† In what ways do you think the members of the Cabinet help the president? (Advise on policies, provide information for decisions, carry out policies.)

larger number live in cities all over the country.

The people who work for the federal government are grouped into a number of departments and agencies. Each has a different job to do. For example:

... The Department of State handles our dealings with other countries.

... The Department of Defense helps protect our country from being attacked by our enemies.

... The Department of Justice makes sure people obey federal laws.

... The Department of the Interior helps to protect our natural resources.

... The United States Postal Service delivers our mail.

The people in charge of all the main departments in the government are chosen by the president. Together they make up a group called the Cabinet. Members of the Cabinet meet with the president about once a week to talk about important problems.

The Supreme Court

The last stop on our tour is the Supreme Court Building. (See map on page 59.) The United States Supreme Court is the most important law court in our country. It is made up of nine judges called justices, who are chosen by the president. The justices serve on the court until they die or resign.

A Cabinet meeting. The people in charge of the main departments in our federal government are chosen by the president. Together they make up a group called the Cabinet. Members of the Cabinet meet with the president about once a week to talk about important problems.

† Class activity: Hold a class election to demonstrate the voting process. Require "candidates" for office to give campaign speeches explaining their qualifications for class office.

The main job of the Supreme Court is to decide whether the people who make and carry out our laws are following the Constitution. Important cases are brought to the Supreme Court from other law courts in the United States. When the Supreme Court makes a decision, all other courts in our country must follow that decision.

Our tour of Washington is over now. But our guide has one more thing to say. She tells us that in a democracy like the United States, the government is not able to do its job well without the help of all of the citizens. "If you want to have a good government," she says, "you must be a good citizen and be willing to do your part."

Your Job as a Citizen

† When you are eighteen years old, you will be able to vote. Then you can help choose the men and women who run our government. To vote wisely, you need to learn as much as you can about how our government works. You also need to learn about some of the ideas that make our democracy possible.

A worker in a factory where television tubes are made. People in a democracy share seven important beliefs. For example, they believe that citizens have responsibilities as well as rights. One of these responsibilities is doing useful work. What are some other responsibilities of citizens?

SEVEN IMPORTANT BELIEFS SHARED BY PEOPLE IN A DEMOCRACY

1. Every person is important.

Most Americans believe that every person is important. It does not matter if you are young or old, a man or a woman. You are just as important as every other person. You are important whether your skin is black, white, or some other color. You are important no matter what religion you follow or what country your grandparents came from.

2. People have the right to govern themselves.

Americans believe the citizens of a country have the right to govern themselves. We think every person should be able to have some part in running our government.

3. Decisions should be made by majority* vote.

In the United States, all citizens have a chance to help choose the people who run the government. They do this by voting in elections. The candidate* with the most votes is elected. This is known as majority vote. Most Americans believe the fairest way for people to govern themselves is by majority vote.

4. All citizens should have a chance to get a good education.

Education is very important in a democracy. To have good government, citizens must be able to vote wisely for the people who make and carry out the laws. Most Americans believe that all young people should have a chance for a good education.

5. Laws should be the same for all citizens.

Most Americans believe all citizens should be treated the same by their government. Everyone should be required to obey the same laws. People should never gain or lose any rights because of such things as the color of their skin, or how much money they have.

6. All people have certain rights that no one can take away from them.

Most Americans believe that every person has a number of important rights and freedoms. Among these are freedom of speech and freedom of religion. Also every person has the right to a fair trial in a court of law. We believe that these rights cannot be taken away from any person, even by a majority vote. In a democracy, the government is expected to protect the rights of all citizens.

7. Citizens have responsibilities as well as rights.

For a democracy to work, all citizens must be willing to do their part. In other words, citizens have responsibilities as well as rights. Among these responsibilities are obeying the laws of the community, taking part in the government, and doing useful work.

*See Glossary

Seven important beliefs

The feature above tells about seven important beliefs shared by people in a democracy. These beliefs touch our lives every day—at home, at school, at church, and at work. Wherever we go, we find people who are either following or not following these beliefs in their daily lives.

Study these seven beliefs carefully, and decide whether they are important to you. Do you understand all seven beliefs? Do you agree with them? Are there any that you do not agree with?

You may wish to assign a student activity using Fideler Discovery Card 54. (Do research to make discoveries about three types of government.)

RESPONSIBILITIES OF CITIZENS

Obeying the laws

Good citizens obey the laws of their community, state, and country. Even if they think a law is unfair, they will not disobey it. Instead, they will work in a peaceful way to get the law changed.

Treating other people with respect

Good citizens treat other people the same way they would like to be treated. They try to be friendly and polite to everyone. This is because they truly believe that every person is important.

Getting a good education

In the United States, most people have an opportunity for an education. Young people are responsible for making good use of this opportunity. By learning as much as they can, they are preparing to become useful citizens when they grow up.

Doing useful work

Most Americans feel they are responsible for doing useful work. When they become adults they do not expect other people to take care of them. Instead, they expect to work hard and do their job well.

Taking part in the government

In the United States, it is important for every citizen to take part in the government. People who are over eighteen can do this by voting in all elections. Also they can work for candidates* they think would do a good job. Young people have a responsibility to learn as much as they can about their government. This will help prepare them to make wise decisions when they are older.

Cooperating with other people

Many jobs in a community cannot be done well by persons working alone. Instead, there must be cooperation among many people. Citizens of a community have a responsibility to work together. In this way, they can make their community a better place to live.

*See Glossary

Discuss the relationship between freedom and responsible citizenship.

If so, which ones? Give reasons for your answer.

Why the seven beliefs are important

Most Americans are loyal to the seven beliefs. They know that if people did not follow these beliefs, it would not be possible to have a democracy like ours.

Suppose people did not think it was important for everyone to have an education. They might not be willing to pay taxes to support free public schools. If people wanted to go to school, they would have to pay a fee. Many families would not have enough money to send their children to school. As a result, many young people would grow up without learning how to read and write. When it came time to vote, they would not have enough knowledge to make wise decisions.

Here is another example. Imagine what might happen if Americans did not believe citizens have responsibilities as well as rights. Every person would feel free to do just as he or she pleased. Some people would break the laws or cheat others whenever they wanted. Soon, no one would be able to trust anyone else. People would be too busy protecting their own lives and property. They would not have time to do any useful work.

Becoming a responsible citizen

You are already a citizen, even though you cannot vote until you are eighteen. As a citizen, you enjoy a number of rights and freedoms. In return for these rights and freedoms, you have certain responsibilities. Some of these are shown in the feature at left.

† Do you think it is always a person's fault if he or she does not have a job and cannot meet the basic needs? Explain your answer.

Problems Facing Our Nation

One of the main duties of each citizen is to think carefully about the problems that face our country. Today there are several important problems that keep many Americans from meeting their basic needs. (See "Needs of People" at the back of this book.) These are known as social problems.

The feature below shows seven social problems facing our country. Let's look more closely at two of these.

The Need for More Jobs

† The greatest problem many Americans face is that of earning a living. Some people work at jobs that pay them very little money. Others cannot find jobs at all. Today, about six out of every one hundred workers in the United States do not have jobs. Let's look at some of the reasons why.

Recessions*

Sometimes the United States goes through a time of business troubles known as a recession. When this happens, many stores and factories are not able to make a profit.* Some of them have to lay off many workers. Others may go out of business. As a result, there are not enough jobs for all the people who need them.

Depressed* areas

In some parts of our country, there is always a shortage of jobs. These are

---

SEVEN SOCIAL PROBLEMS

In our country, a number of serious problems prevent people from meeting their needs. These are called social problems. The government and the people of our country have been working hard to solve these problems. As we make progress toward this goal, more Americans will have happier and more successful lives. Our country's social problems include:

1. **The need for more jobs.** At the present time, about six out of every hundred workers in the United States are unable to find jobs.
2. **The high cost of living.** In recent years, the high cost of goods and services has kept many people from meeting their needs. This continuing rise in prices is called inflation.
3. **The need for better education.** Many people in our country are not getting a good education. They are not gaining the knowledge they need for good citizenship.
4. **Illness and handicaps.** Americans are among the healthiest people in the world. However, millions of people in our country suffer from serious illnesses and handicaps.
5. **Lack of freedom for certain groups.** In the past, some groups of people in our country did not have the same freedoms as other people. Today, our laws give every person the right to fair treatment and equal opportunity. Even so, some Americans still do not have all the rights and freedoms promised by our laws.
6. **Crime.** Over the years, there has been a great increase in the number of major crimes in our country. In many areas, people live in fear for their lives.
7. **Unsuccessful communities.** In many parts of the United States there are unsuccessful communities. Many of the people in these communities are not doing useful work. They are not getting the education they need to get jobs or to be good citizens. The crime rate in these communities is very high.

The Northeast

known as depressed areas. There are several reasons why areas become depressed. In some places, poor farming methods or strip* mining has ruined good farmland. Sometimes mines have been closed because all the valuable minerals have been removed. In other cases, businesses have moved from a community because the owners could no longer make a profit there. Factories have sometimes closed down because people stopped buying the goods they were making.

Discrimination*

Even in communities where there are plenty of jobs, many people cannot find work. Sometimes this is because they are thought to be too old for certain jobs. Other times, it is because they belong to a group of people who are not treated the same as other Americans. For example, women, blacks, or Mexican-Americans are sometimes refused jobs that others might get easily. This kind of unfair treatment is called discrimination.

The control panel of a steelmaking furnace. Many jobs in our country today are done by machines like the one in this picture. These machines need only a few skilled workers to run them. The use of machines that need few people to run them is called automation. Automation has created many new jobs for skilled workers. But fewer jobs are now open to unskilled workers.

† In what ways does the federal government help people who cannot find jobs?

Lack of education

There is another important reason why many Americans do not have jobs today. They do not have the education or the skills needed for the jobs they can find.

In the past, many jobs were open to people who did not have much education. Today, most of these jobs are done by machines. The use of machines that need few people to run them is called automation. Automation has created many new jobs for engineers* and other specially trained people. Many skilled workers are needed to build the new machines and keep them running. But fewer jobs are now open to unskilled workers.

† Helping people without jobs

Today, a number of things are being done to help people who cannot find jobs. Our government is studying ways to help business grow and to prevent recessions. Sometimes the government lends money to companies that are in trouble. To provide more jobs, a state or a city will sometimes give help to business people who want to build a new factory there.

The federal government has passed laws against job discrimination. So have many of our states. These laws say that anyone who hires workers must treat them all the same. An employer cannot refuse to hire or promote a person because that person belongs to a certain group. For example, an employer cannot discriminate against women or blacks. These laws are helping many people who used to find it hard to get well-paying jobs.

Many companies and community groups have started programs to help people find work. They have also set up job-training centers. There, people can learn the skills they need to hold good jobs in factories or offices. A number of businesses have classes for workers who are losing their jobs because of automation. In these classes, workers learn new skills that they can use both now and in the future.

Our federal government also helps provide job training. For example, it runs a program called the Job Corps. Young men and women who do not have jobs can stay a few months at special Job Corps centers. There they learn valuable skills. They are also given a chance to earn money.

The High Cost of Living

There is another reason why many people find it hard to meet their needs. They have to pay higher prices than they used to for the things they buy. The problem of rising prices is known as inflation. For example, in 1966 a loaf of bread cost about fifteen cents. Today it costs almost three times that much.

The causes of inflation

Prices go up for a number of different reasons. Sometimes there are many people who want to buy a certain product, but there is only a small amount available. Some people are then willing to pay higher prices to make sure they get this product. For example, in 1973 †† there was not enough gasoline in the United States for everyone who wanted to buy it. (See pages 102-103.) This helped cause the price of gasoline to go up very rapidly.

Sometimes a business company will raise the price it charges for a certain

†† Discuss the relationships between "supply and demand" and the price of gasoline.

Buying groceries. The problem of rising prices makes it difficult for many people to meet their needs. They have to pay higher prices than they used to for groceries and other things they buy.

product. It does this to make more money. If there are many different companies that make the same product, each company will be slow to raise its prices. Otherwise, it may lose customers to companies whose prices are lower. But in many industries, a few companies make nearly all of a certain product. If one company raises its prices, the others often do the same.

† Labor* unions may also bring about a rise in prices. If a union feels that its members are not being paid enough money, it can call a strike.* In this way, it can sometimes force a company to pay more money to its workers. When this happens, the company may have to raise its prices to stay in business.

Our government also helps cause inflation. Each year, the federal government spends many billions of dollars. Some of this money is used to defend our country against possible enemies. Much is spent for new schools, better health care, and other services.

Usually, the federal government spends more money each year than it receives in taxes. When this happens, the government simply issues more money. Then people have more money in their pockets to buy the things they need and want. But there are not

† Hold a class discussion on labor union strikes. Do you think strikes are always a good thing? Why? Why not?

enough goods and services for all the people who want to buy them. As a result, prices go up.

How inflation affects our lives

Inflation hurts nearly everyone in our country. However, some people are hurt worse than others. These are people whose incomes* have not been rising as fast as prices. Some of these people work at jobs that pay little more than they did ten years ago. Others are older people who are living on money they saved when they were younger. Although their income stays about the same, they have to pay more money for the things they buy. As a result, they cannot buy as many things as they could before.

Inflation also hurts business companies. They must pay higher wages to keep their workers happy. Also, they must pay more money for the goods they use. If they charge higher prices for their products to meet these costs, they may lose some of their customers. It is hard for some companies to stay in business during times of inflation.

The fight against inflation

Today, government leaders and other people in the United States are studying ways to stop inflation. Some people believe the government should pass laws to control wages and prices. Then workers could not get raises without the government's permission. Also, companies would need the government's permission to raise prices.

Wages and prices have been controlled by the government at certain times in the past. But many Americans are against wage and price controls. They believe people should be free to decide on wages and prices without being told what to do by the government.

Some people think inflation cannot be stopped as long as our government spends more money than it receives. These people say the government should either spend less money or raise taxes, or both. If the government cut down on its spending, it would not have to issue so much new money. People would then have less money to spend for goods and services. The same thing would happen if taxes were raised. In either case, prices would go up more slowly than they did before.

There is still much that people need to learn about inflation. Only as we gain more facts will we be able to make much progress toward solving this important problem.

A Citizenship Project

† You may assign this activity to students. Hold a class discussion on some of the news stories.

Many of the problems that we face today have come about because people were not living by the seven important beliefs of a democracy. To understand this more clearly, you may want to carry out the following project.

When you go home tonight, read your daily newspaper. Or listen to a news report on radio or television. Take notes about some of the news stories of the day. Bring your notes to class, and be prepared to answer the following questions about each story:

- How does this news story relate to the seven beliefs that make democracy possible?
- Are the people in the news story being loyal to the seven beliefs? Or are they acting against these beliefs? Explain your answer.
- Are the actions of these people making life better or worse for other citizens of our country? Give facts to support your answer.

The Northeast

† Assign "A Problem To Solve" to start students thinking about the arts of the Northeast. Use Fideler Discovery Cards 75-82 for additional activities.

7 The Arts

A Problem To Solve
How do the arts of the Northeast help us to understand our country's history? In forming hypotheses* to solve this problem, you will need to consider the works of art created since colonial times by each of the following:

a. writers of the Northeast
b. painters of the Northeast
c. composers of the Northeast

As you try to solve this problem, you may wish to do research in this book as well as in other books.

See Skills Manual, "Thinking and Solving Problems"

In New York City's Guggenheim Museum, visitors can view paintings by many of the artists of our own time. The Northeast offers opportunities for people to enjoy many different kinds of art. Cities throughout the region have fine museums, art galleries, theaters, and concert halls.

The arts help tell America's story

The arts are much more than collections of paintings, books, and music for people to enjoy. The arts also tell us about a country's way of life and about people's thoughts, feelings, and goals. Learning about America's arts and artists can bring us to a richer understanding of our country and its history.

Many of America's greatest artists have lived in the Northeast. In the early years of our country, almost all of our large cities were in this region. Painters, writers, and musicians came to study and to work in some of these early cities, such as New York and Boston.

The Arts in Early America

During the early years of our country's history, most people had little time for the arts. When they were not hard at work, the early settlers spent a great deal of time in church. Most writing was about religion, and hymns were almost the only kind of music. A number of artists were able to earn their living by painting people's pictures, however. John Singleton Copley is considered the best American painter of these early times.

During the Revolutionary War,* American writers became less interested in writing about religion and more interested in writing about our country and its leaders. Thomas Paine, for example, wrote articles to encourage the American people in their fight for independence. One of his writings is called *Common Sense*.

The interest that Americans felt in their history and their leaders was also shown in paintings. Gilbert Stuart and Charles Willson Peale were two of the many artists who painted pictures of George Washington and other great Americans. John Trumbull painted some of the great events in American history. Among his paintings are *The Battle of Bunker's Hill* and *The Declaration of Independence*.

The Arts in the 1800's

Painting

Three of the leading American painters of the 1800's were George Inness, James McNeill Whistler, and Mary Cassatt. Inness painted peaceful, dreamy pictures of the countryside. Whistler's paintings were known for their unusual use of color. Cassatt was best known for her paintings of mothers and children. Although Whistler was a native of

*See Glossary

The Northeast 73

A nineteenth-century painting called *The Lackawanna Valley*, by George Inness. What feelings do you suppose the artist was trying to express in this painting? How does the picture make you feel?

New England and Cassatt was born near Pittsburgh, both artists spent much of their lives in Europe.

Two other leading artists were Thomas Eakins and Winslow Homer. Eakins painted pictures of hospital scenes and sporting events. Homer, one of our country's best-known artists, painted pictures that showed the might and power of the sea.

Music

The well-known songwriter Stephen Foster lived in the Northeast, but he wrote mostly about the South. His songs include "Old Folks at Home" and "Oh! Susanna."

Edward MacDowell was one of America's greatest composers of the 1800's. He was born in New York City. MacDowell wrote piano and orchestra

Have students compare the picture on this page with the picture on pages 72-73. Do you think George Inness' painting would look out of place with the paintings in the Guggenheim Museum? Explain your answer.

music. Two of his works are *Indian Suite* and *New England Idyls*.

Writers of fiction*

Washington Irving lived in New York State during the early 1800's. He wrote several well-liked books about American life. One of these was a group of stories called *The Sketch Book*. This book includes "The Legend of Sleepy Hollow" and "Rip Van Winkle." James Fenimore Cooper was also a great writer of the early 1800's. Cooper wrote several novels* about life on the frontier.*

Nathaniel Hawthorne, who wrote during the mid-1800's, was one of New England's best-known writers. He wrote several novels, including *The House of Seven Gables*, and also many short stories. Herman Melville wrote a number of books. His *Moby Dick* is one of the greatest American novels. Edgar Allan Poe wrote both short stories and poetry. Some of his stories, such as "The Fall of the House of Usher," are spooky and scary. Another author of the mid-1800's was Louisa May Alcott. She wrote *Little Women* and other stories about young people.

Stephen Crane and Henry James also lived in the Northeast. In *The Red Badge of Courage*, Crane described the fear and the courage of soldiers in the Civil War. James wrote many novels about Americans in Europe, describing the lives of wealthy people.

Poets

Several of America's best-loved poets of the 1800's lived in the Northeast. William Cullen Bryant was important both as a poet and a newspaper writer. Perhaps you have read his poem "To a Waterfowl." John Greenleaf Whittier wrote "Snow-Bound" and many other well-known poems. You might know some of Henry Wadsworth Longfellow's poems. These include "The Village Blacksmith" and "Paul Revere's Ride."

Emily Dickinson and Walt Whitman wrote poetry that was very different from that of other American poets. Dickinson wrote hundreds of poems that describe her own feelings about life and death. In many poems she used words in unusual ways. Whitman's poems show his love of America and democracy. His poetry was very different because he wrote in a freer style than earlier poets. He did not always follow the usual rules of writing.

Writers of nonfiction*

Several of America's leading writers of nonfiction during the 1800's lived in the Northeast. George Bancroft and Francis Parkman wrote important books about our country's history. Ralph Waldo Emerson and Henry David Thoreau were thinkers who believed that all people are good and should follow their own best feelings. Emerson's essay* "Self-Reliance" and Thoreau's book *Walden* are among our country's best-known writings.

The Arts in the 1900's
Literature

Eugene O'Neill is one of America's greatest playwrights. Many of his plays, such as *The Emperor Jones* and *Long Day's Journey Into Night*, show people living unhappy and hopeless lives.

One of the best-known American poets of the 1900's is Robert Frost.

† Assign students to prepare reports on one or more of these books. They may be found in your school library. Students may present oral reports to the class.

Have students bring in several short poems by Robert Frost and Marianne Moore. Then discuss why they are considered important poets.

Although Frost was born in San Francisco, he spent much of his life in New England. His poetry shows both the beautiful and the unhappy sides of life.

Many other poets of the 1900's have made their homes in the Northeast. Among these writers are Marianne Moore, Wallace Stevens, Amy Lowell, William Carlos Williams, and E.E. Cummings. In their poems, they often used unusual groups of words to tell their own ideas about life and art. Edwin Arlington Robinson wrote clever poems about people who are mixed-up and lonely. Well-known black poets who have lived and worked in New York City are Langston Hughes, Countee Cullen, and Claude McKay.

Other important writers of the Northeast, such as John O'Hara and John Marquand, wrote novels and short stories that tell about America's changing values. Conrad Richter and Kenneth Roberts wrote interesting stories about the history of the Northeast. In novels such as *Go Tell It on the Mountain*, James Baldwin has described the hopes and problems of

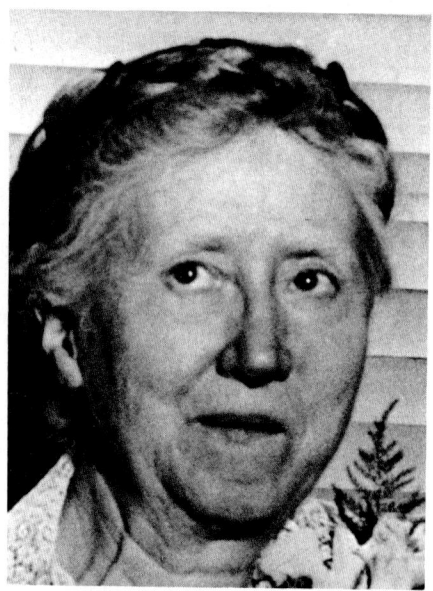
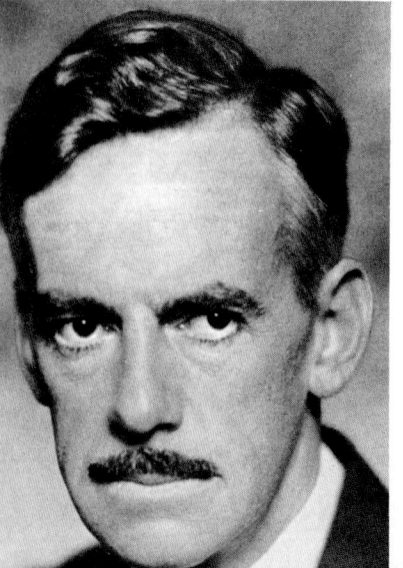
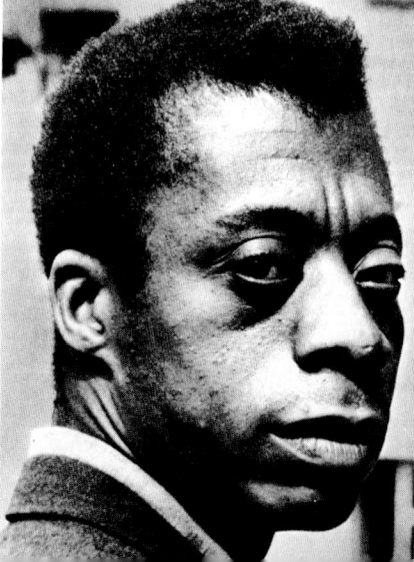

Language

See Great Ideas

Four of the many important writers of the 1900's who made their homes in the Northeast are shown in these pictures. Robert Frost (upper left) and Marianne Moore (upper right) are two of America's best-known poets. The plays of Eugene O'Neill (lower left) are famous all over the world. James Baldwin (lower right) is noted for his powerful novels about black Americans. Writers use words to tell about their ideas and feelings. What are some other ways in which people express their ideas and feelings?

Beverly Sills is a world-famous opera singer who was born in New York City and has performed in many operas there. What other well-known artists have lived and worked in the Northeast?

black people living in large cities. Bernard Malamud has written about the lives of Jewish Americans.

Painting

Important painters of the Northeast during the 1900's are John Marin, Anna Mary ("Grandma") Moses, and Andrew Wyeth. Marin painted many pictures of the Maine seacoast and New York City. "Grandma" Moses, who began painting at the age of seventy-six, painted many simple, colorful scenes of country life. Wyeth also painted pictures of country life in Pennsylvania and Maine.

Music

One of America's greatest composers of the 1900's is Charles Ives. He was a New York businessman who wrote music in his spare time. Other important composers from the Northeast are Aaron Copland and George Gershwin. Copland's works include the music for three ballets, *Appalachian Spring*, *Billy the Kid*, and *Rodeo*. Gershwin wrote the musical play *Porgy and Bess*.

Express Your Opinion

Read one of the following poems in class:

"Annabel Lee," by Poe
"I Never Saw a Moor," by Dickinson
"Richard Cory," by Robinson
"The Runaway," by Frost

Discuss the following questions.

1. How did the poem make you feel?
2. Did you like the poem? Why? Why not?

† Assign the activity described above, or Fideler Discovery Card 78 (Use Your Creativity), or Fideler Discovery Sheets, Volume 1, page 35.

Part 3

Earning a Living

† Read this aloud to start students thinking about how people earn a living.

† In the Northeast, as in other parts of our country, people earn their living in many different ways. The Northeast is one of the most important manufacturing regions of our country. This region is also good for farming, and it has many valuable natural* resources. Below is a list of just a few ways people in the Northeast earn their living.
- mining coal
- tree farming
- fishing for lobsters
- raising vegetables
- raising dairy cattle
- working in an office in a steel plant
- working in a clothing factory
- working in a department store

As you do research in Part 3, make a list of additional ways in which people in the Northeast earn their living. You may wish to compare your list with the lists made by the other members of your class.

A nuclear* power plant in Pennsylvania. About 3% of the energy we use in the United States is nuclear energy. It produces electricity that is used by many people working in business and industry.

Planting celery on a truck farm in Pennsylvania. Truck farming is an important way of earning a living in the Northeast. What are some of the other types of farming in this region?

8 Farming

A Problem To Solve

Farmers in the Northeast earn more money from milk than from any other product. <u>Why is dairying the most important type of farming in this part of our country?</u> In forming hypotheses,* you will need to consider the following:

a. climate of the Northeast
b. land features of this part of our country
c. markets for dairy products

See Skills Manual, "Thinking and Solving Problems"

A New Jersey truck farm

It is a hot summer afternoon. As we drive across the level countryside of southern New Jersey, we see many green fields of crops. A sign along the road tells us that there is a vegetable stand at the farm ahead.

We stop at the stand and pick out some nice, ripe, red tomatoes. As we

*See Glossary

Use Fideler Discovery Cards 93-102, and Fideler Discovery Sheets, Volume 1, pages 41-44 for activities about farming.

are paying for the tomatoes, the woman who owns this farm comes over to talk with us. We ask her whether she grows any crops besides tomatoes. The farmer says that she also raises green beans, peppers, and cauliflower. She explains that raising vegetables for sale is known as truck farming.

We learn that this farm is very small compared with many farms in the United States. It covers only 50 acres (20 ha.).† But the farmer knows how to earn a good living from this small piece of land. First, she grows crops that sell for high prices. Second, she makes sure that each acre of land produces as much as possible.

The farmer tells us that vegetables are a profitable crop. She explains that her farm is only 40 miles (64 km.)† from Philadelphia and 100 miles (161 km.) from New York City. In both of these cities, there are many people who will pay a good price for fresh vegetables. The farmer never sees most of these people because she sells her crops mainly to large grocery stores. Trucks can deliver the farmer's vegetables to stores in New York on the same day they are picked.

To produce good crops, the farmer must give them a great deal of care. In the spring, she and her son and daughter plow and fertilize the land. Then they set out the young vegetable plants. As the plants grow, they are weeded. They are also sprayed with chemicals that kill harmful insects. If the weather is dry, the plants must be irrigated.* At harvesttime, the farmer has to hire more workers to pick the vegetables before they spoil.

As we tell the farmer good-bye, she smiles and says she wishes all her sales were this easy. She tells us that in order to be a truck farmer she also needs to understand business. She must have enough money to buy fertilizer and insect spray. At times, she must buy a new piece of farm machinery. To make a profit, she needs to sell her crops at the highest possible prices.

Other kinds of farms

Not all farms in the Northeast are like the one we have just visited. Some of them are much larger. There are farms that raise fruit or other crops. Many farms raise only livestock, such as cattle or poultry. In spite of these differences, many northeastern farms have certain things in common. You will learn what some of

† ha. means hectare
† km. means kilometer

Refer to the picture below. What can you discover about truck farming from this picture? Are machines (tools) important in farming today? these things are as you read more about farming in the Northeast.

Efficient farming methods

Although less land in the Northeast is being used for farming today than in the past, this region produces more farm products than ever before. Northeastern farmers are able to get large yields because they use their land very efficiently. They try to choose the best kinds of plants and livestock. They use large amounts of fertilizer, and chemicals are used to kill weeds and insects. When the weather is dry, the farmers irrigate their fields.

Farmers in the Northeast have machines to help them do much of this work. For example, milking machines are used on most dairy farms. Many kinds of vegetables can be planted and harvested by machine. But people are still needed to run the machines. They are also needed to do work that machines cannot yet do, such as harvesting peaches and other fruits that are easily damaged.

Long growing season

Another reason why some farmers in the Northeast are able to harvest more crops is that they live in areas where the growing season is long. (See map on page 32.) In some places along the Atlantic coast, the frost-free period is long enough for growing two crops on the same land in a single year. A truck farmer in Delaware may plant green

Using Tools

See Great Ideas

A truck farmer in Delaware harvesting lima beans with modern machinery. Today, there are fewer farmers in the Northeast than there were in the past. Yet they produce larger amounts of crops than ever before. One reason for this is that farmers now use many farm machines. What are some of these machines? How do these machines help each farmer to produce more crops? How has this change in farming affected the lives of nearly everyone in the United States?

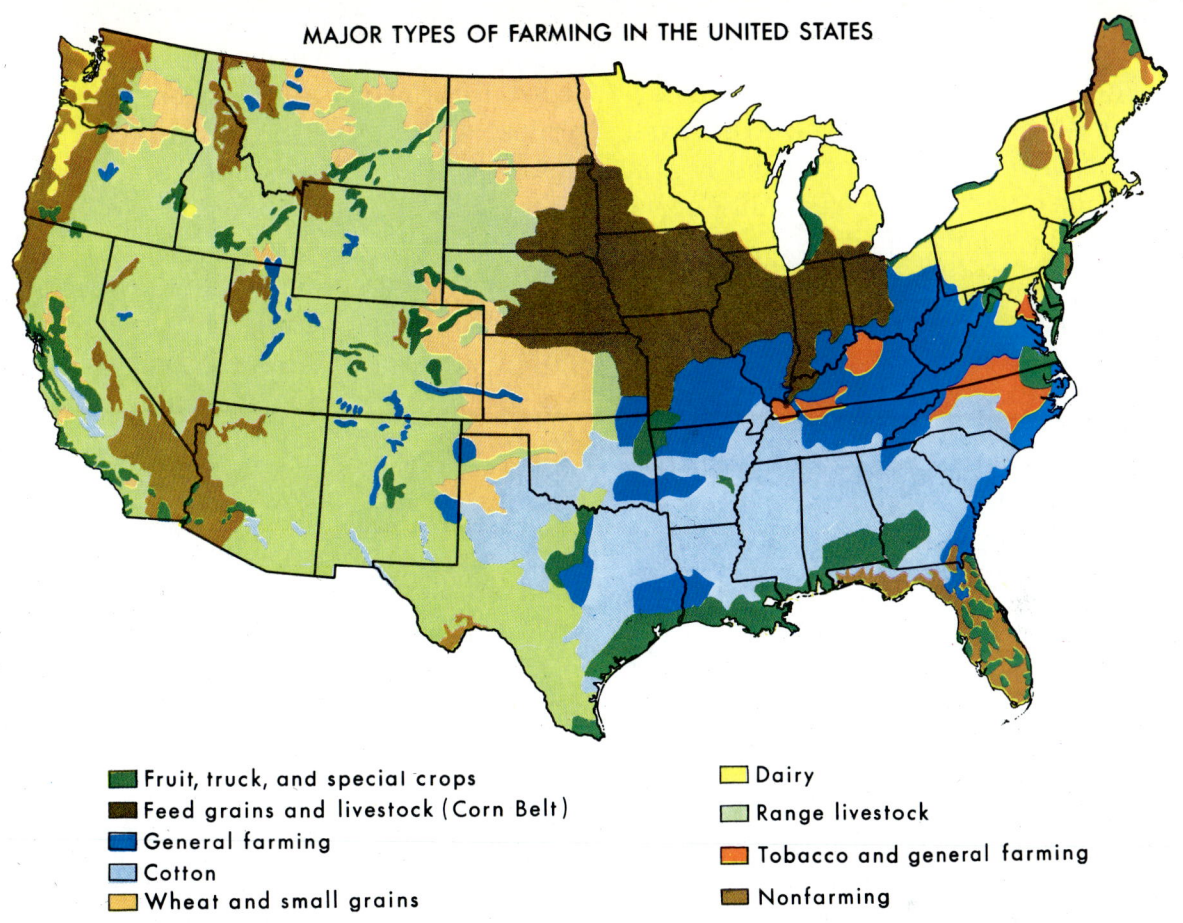

MAJOR TYPES OF FARMING IN THE UNITED STATES

- Fruit, truck, and special crops
- Feed grains and livestock (Corn Belt)
- General farming
- Cotton
- Wheat and small grains
- Dairy
- Range livestock
- Tobacco and general farming
- Nonfarming

beans as soon as the soil warms up in the spring. By the end of June, the beans will be ready to pick. After they have been harvested, the land will be plowed again and fertilized. Then the farmer will plant some other vegetable that will ripen before the first frost of autumn.

The use of labor, machinery, and efficient methods to produce a large harvest in a small area is called intensive farming. Much of the farming done in the Northeast is intensive.

Markets for farm products

Farmers in the Northeast have been helped by their location in the most heavily populated part of our country. Millions of people live in the great cities of the Northeast. Each day these people buy huge quantities of food such as milk, eggs, vegetables, and fruit. All of these products must be sold and used quickly before they spoil. Therefore, farms that are close to cities have an advantage over farms that are located farther away. It is no surprise that there are many dairy and poultry farms, orchards, and truck farms in the Northeast. Farmers here use trucks and trains to rush their products to customers in the cities.

Livestock

Dairy cattle

Raising cows for milk is the most important type of farming in the Northeast. Farmers here earn more money from milk than from any other product. Dairy farms can be found in nearly all parts of this region. (See map on page 85.)

Call attention to the map and legend above. Looking at the map, what are the main types of farming in the Northeast?

The Northeast

Refer to the picture below. What can you discover about modern dairy farming from this picture?

There are several reasons why dairying is so important in the Northeast. People in the large cities of this region use huge quantities of fresh milk every day. Milk spoils quickly. Even with fast, refrigerated trucks and trains, fresh milk is usually not shipped farther than 200 miles (322 km.). Because of this, most dairy farms are near cities or towns.

The land and climate of the Northeast also help to explain why there are so many dairy farms here. Land that is too rough for growing crops can often be used as pasture for dairy cows. Grasses used for hay and grazing grow well where summers are too short and cool for raising most other kinds of crops. Cows give more milk if the weather is not too hot. In the Northeast, there is usually enough rainfall to provide drinking water for cattle.

Most dairy farms in the Northeast are rather small. A typical farm covers about 100 acres (40 ha.). Dairy farmers use most of their land for pasture, or for growing hay and other feed crops. Also, some farmers feed their cattle grain from the Midwest.* In this way, they do not need to own as much land as they would if they grew their own feed crops.

Dairy farming requires skill and care. On most farms, there may be as many

Milking time on a modern dairy farm in the Northeast. Dairy farms can be found in nearly all parts of the Northeast. Farmers here earn more money from milk than from any other farm product.

as forty cows. These cows must be milked twice a day all through the year. Milking machines and other equipment must be kept very clean. The cows must be given just the right amounts of certain feeds if they are to produce large amounts of good milk.

Farmers sell most of their milk to dairies. Here it is pasteurized* and put into bottles or cartons. Most of this milk is sold to grocery stores or is delivered to people's homes. Dairies also use some of the milk to make butter, cheese, or other products.

Poultry

Poultry and eggs are second in value among the farm products of the Northeast. Like dairy cows, poultry can be raised in areas where the land is too poor for growing most crops. Also, farmers can raise a lot of poultry on only a few acres of land. There is a huge market for eggs and fresh poultry in the large cities of the Northeast. Broiler chickens are among the main types of poultry raised in this region of our country.

Many farmers in the Northeast raise chickens for their eggs. Pennsylvania and New York are the main egg-producing states in this region. There are also many chicken farms in the southern part of New England. Each day, these farms supply many thousands of eggs to customers in nearby cities.

Other kinds of poultry are also raised in the Northeast. Farms on Long Island produce about half of the ducks raised in the United States. Large numbers of turkeys are raised in Pennsylvania and West Virginia.

People who specialize in other kinds of farming sometimes raise a few chick-

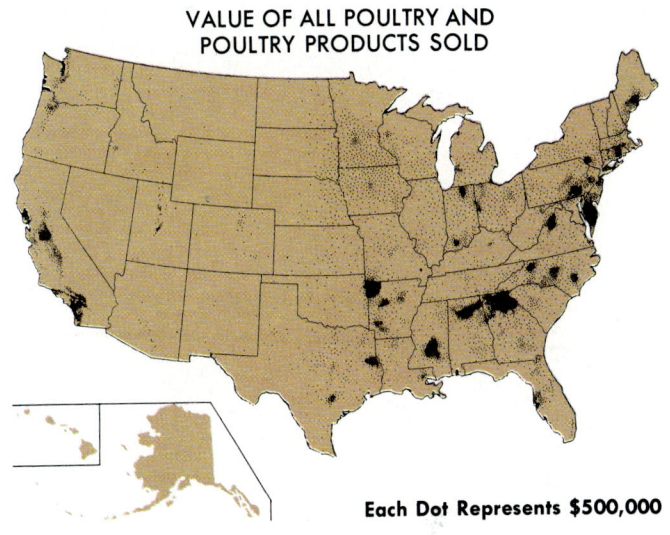

VALUE OF ALL POULTRY AND POULTRY PRODUCTS SOLD

Each Dot Represents $500,000

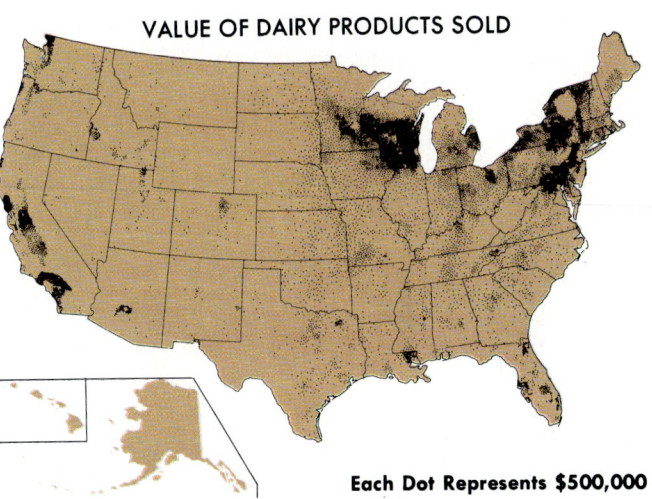

VALUE OF DAIRY PRODUCTS SOLD

Each Dot Represents $500,000

ens. However, most poultry farming in the Northeast today is a full-time business. Some farmers care for many thousands of birds. To do this, farmers must have a great deal of knowledge and skill. They must select the kinds of birds that will provide the most meat or eggs at the lowest cost. They must spend much money to build poultry houses and to equip them with automatic feeders and other modern machinery. The farmers must make sure that their birds receive the right amounts of food and water. They must protect the birds from disease by giving

† You might point out that today's farmers have to know many different things to be successful. (Farmers must understand business, machinery, and how to sell.)

A turkey farm in the Northeast. Poultry and eggs are second in value among the farm products of the Northeast. In addition to turkeys, what other kinds of poultry are raised in this region?

them "shots" and keeping their houses clean. It is also important for farmers to know how to sell their poultry and eggs at a good price so that they can make a profit.

Beef cattle

The raising of cattle for beef is less important in the Northeast than the raising of dairy cattle. However, many herds of beef cattle graze on hillside pastures in West Virginia. Much of the land in this state is too rough for growing crops, but it can be used for pasture.

The cattle raised in West Virginia are usually thin, because they feed mainly on grass. They must be fed corn and other grains to fatten them before they can be sold for meat. Although it is difficult to grow corn and other grains on the rough land of West Virginia, these crops grow well on the fertile, rolling Piedmont Plateau. Each fall, large numbers of beef cattle are shipped by train or truck from West Virginia to farms on the Piedmont in Maryland and southeastern Pennsylvania. There they are kept in feedlots* and fed a rich diet of hay and grain. When they are fat enough, they are shipped to meat-packing plants in New York and other cities of the Northeast.

† Why are beef cattle from West Virginia shipped to farms on the Piedmont Plateau each fall? (To fatten them with hay and grain.)

Vegetables

In the Northeast, there are thousands of truck farms like the one we visited at the start of this chapter. Many truck farms are located on Long Island, on the Delmarva Peninsula,* and in southern New Jersey. All three of these areas are in the Coastal Plain region of our country.

The land and climate of the Coastal Plain help explain why truck farming is so important here. Most of the land is level enough for growing crops. The loose, sandy soil is easy to cultivate, even though it must be fertilized heavily to produce good harvests. This kind of soil is very well suited to growing root crops, such as carrots and beets. The Coastal Plain has a long growing season. Also, the sandy soil warms up quickly in the spring. As a result, farmers here can plant their crops earlier than farmers in other parts of the Northeast. They can harvest their vegetables and send them to market earlier in the season. In this way, they are likely to get a better price.

Many different kinds of vegetables are raised on the Coastal Plain. Among the most important are tomatoes, potatoes, beans, peas, and cucumbers. A large part of the vegetable crop is sold fresh in nearby cities. The rest is sent to canning or freezing plants.

Not all truck farms are as small as the one we visited. Some of them cover thousands of acres. These large farms may grow only one vegetable, or they may raise many crops. Some of them are owned by food companies. The large farms use many kinds of machinery for planting, cultivating,* and harvesting their crops.

The Coastal Plain is not the only truck-farming area in the Northeast. Large crops of cabbages, beans, and other vegetables are grown on the Lake Ontario plain in New York State. Northern Maine is one of the best potato-farming areas in the United States.

Fruits

In some parts of the Northeast, fruit growing is an important kind of farming. There are many orchards on the Erie-Ontario Lowland in western New York and Pennsylvania. The climate here is very good for growing fruit. Among the kinds of fruit grown here are apples, peaches, pears, and cherries. In western New York, grapes are also grown. These are used mainly for grape juice and wine.

Apples are grown in every state of the Northeast. They can be raised in places where the climate is too cold for other kinds of fruit. In fact, they grow best where summers are not extremely hot. Some of our country's best apple-growing areas are in the Appalachian Ridges and Valleys section in Pennsylvania, Maryland, and West Virginia. In the springtime, many hillsides and mountain slopes here are covered with white rows of blossoming apple trees.

Among the other fruit crops grown in the Northeast are blueberries and cranberries. Large amounts of blueberries are grown in New Jersey. They are also grown along the eastern coast of Maine. In these places, the soil is well suited for growing this crop. Massachusetts is our country's leading producer of cranberries. Large amounts of this crop are grown in the southeastern part of the state.

Discuss how farm machinery has affected the number of farm jobs.

Refer to the picture below. How is the method of farming shown here different from the method shown on pages 80-81? Explain.

Other Crops

In addition to vegetables and fruits, many other crops are produced in the Northeast. Among these are wheat, corn, oats, hay, and tobacco.* In some parts of the Northeast, several different crops are grown on the same farm. This kind of farming is called mixed farming.

Farming in Lancaster County

To learn more about mixed farming, we will visit Lancaster County in southeastern Pennsylvania. This part of Pennsylvania is one of our country's most fertile farming areas. The soil is rich, and the land is gently rolling. Rainfall is plentiful, and the growing season is long enough for many kinds of crops.

It is a bright morning in June as we drive through the countryside of Lancaster County. Here we see golden fields of wheat and green rows of corn and tobacco plants. There are neat farmhouses and sturdy barns. The people who own these farms are mainly of German descent. Many are members of a religious group known as the Amish. They are noted for their hard work and their love of farming.

The main crops grown in Lancaster County are wheat, potatoes, corn, hay,

Farming in Lancaster County, Pennsylvania. This county lies in one of the most fertile farming areas in the United States. Farmers here grow several different kinds of crops. In Lancaster County, members of certain religious groups, such as the Amish, still use horses instead of tractors.

and tobacco. To help keep the soil fertile, farmers practice crop* rotation. Many farmers in Lancaster County raise beef cattle. In the fall, after their crops are harvested, they buy lean cattle from West Virginia and other states. They feed the cattle corn and other grains that they have grown on their own farms. When the cattle are fat enough, the farmers sell them for meat.

Grain crops

As you have learned, much of the Northeast is not well suited to growing corn, wheat, and other grains. However, these crops are important in some areas. Wheat is raised on the lowland that borders Lake Erie and Lake Ontario. It is also raised on the Piedmont Plateau. Some of it is used in making flour, and some is fed to livestock. In many parts of the Northeast, dairy farmers raise corn for silage.* Other grain crops grown in the Northeast include barley, oats, and rye.

Nurseries and greenhouses

Near the large cities of the Northeast, there are many nurseries and greenhouses. Nurseries are places where trees, shrubs, and flowering plants are grown for sale. People buy these plants for their lawns and gardens. Flowers, vegetables, and other plants are raised in greenhouses the year around. Many of the orchids, carnations, and gardenias sold in the United States come from greenhouses in southeastern Pennsylvania. This is also the chief mushroom-growing area in the United States.

Explore Truck Farming in the Northeast
Imagine that you are a truck farmer in the Northeast and have been asked to write a story about your farm for a leading farm magazine. Before writing your story, you will need to do research. Take careful notes and then make an outline before you begin to write. Some of the things your readers will be interested in are:
1. where your truck farm is located
2. why this is a good location
3. what crops you grow
4. how your farm products are sent to market and who buys them
5. what kinds of work you do on the farm

This chapter provides much useful information for this project. For help in finding additional information, see "Learning Social Studies Skills" in the Skills Manual.

The Northeast

† Use "A Problem To Solve" to start students thinking about natural resources in the Northeast.

9 Natural Resources and Energy

† **A Problem To Solve**
How have the natural resources of the Northeast affected the development of manufacturing in this region? To solve this problem, you will first need to know what natural resources are found in the Northeast. Then you will need to make hypotheses* that explain how these resources have affected:
a. the location of industries in the Northeast
b. the types of manufacturing that have developed here

See Skills Manual, "Thinking and Solving Problems"

Natural Resources

If you take a trip on the Ohio River, you will see many towboats pushing long barges upstream. Some barges are loaded with coal. Others are filled with crushed limestone. Both the coal and the limestone will be used by steel mills in or near the city of Pittsburgh.

Coal, limestone, and other minerals are valuable gifts from nature. These gifts are called natural resources. The people of the Northeast have used their natural resources to develop many important industries.

In addition to minerals, there are many other valuable natural resources in the Northeast. Forests cover more than half of the land. Each year, millions of pounds of fish are caught in the waters along the coast of this region. Rivers and lakes generally supply the Northeast with enough water for its great cities and industries. Fertile soil, sunny days, and rainfall are also valuable natural resources. (See Chapters 2 and 3.) They help farmers provide much of the food needed by the people who live in this part of our country.

Water Resources

Water is a valuable resource

The people in the Northeast, like people everywhere, use water in many ways. In their homes, they need water for drinking, cooking, and other uses. On warm summer days they enjoy sports such as swimming and boating. Farmers in the Northeast need water in order to raise crops and livestock.

*See Glossary

Using Natural Resources

See Great Ideas

Robert Moses Power Dam at Niagara Falls, in New York State. Water is one of the most valuable natural resources of the Northeast. People in this region, like people everywhere, need water for drinking, bathing, and many other uses. Large amounts of water are also used on farms and in factories. The force of running water is also an important source of energy. Do research in this chapter to discover how waterpower is used to produce electricity.

Water is also important to the industries of the Northeast. It is used in the manufacture of most products. For example, as much as 65,000 gallons of water are used to make one ton of steel. Water is also a source of some of the electric energy in the Northeast. (See feature on page 107.)

Using water wisely

The rivers and lakes of the Northeast supply most of the water needed by the people who live here. However, many rivers and lakes that could be used to supply water have become polluted* with wastes from factories and homes. For example, factories often dump harmful wastes into nearby rivers and lakes.

Most people in the Northeast understand that water is a valuable resource and that it must be used wisely. Like people in other parts of our country, they are trying to reduce pollution in their rivers and lakes. Industries in the Northeast must follow new laws that limit the amount and kinds of wastes that can be dumped into the water. If the pollution of lakes and rivers can be controlled, the Northeast will become a healthier as well as a more beautiful place in which to live.

Mineral Resources

There are only a few important mineral deposits in the Northeast. Many of the minerals needed by industries in this region are brought in from other

Mining coal in Pennsylvania. Coal is one of our country's most valuable mineral resources. Do research in this book and other sources to find some of the different ways we use coal.

parts of the United States. Some are brought in from other countries.

Coal in the Northeast

Coal is the most important mineral resource of the Northeast. Deposits of high-grade soft coal, called bituminous coal, are found in the Appalachian Plateau. Deposits of anthracite, or hard coal, are found in eastern Pennsylvania. Industries in the Northeast use much of the region's coal. Some coal is transported to Lake Erie for shipment to steel plants in the Midwest.

More bituminous coal than anthracite is mined in the Northeast. Anthracite was once used widely for heating homes. Today, oil or natural gas is used in most homes and there is little demand for anthracite. However, bituminous coal is used for many purposes. For example, it is needed in the manufacture of steel, chemicals, and many other products.

A coal mine in West Virginia

We are visiting a coal mine in the northern part of West Virginia. The main tunnel of the mine leads into the side of a large hill. This kind of mine is called a drift* mine.

The workers in the mine are running machines. One of the machines tears pieces of coal from a wall of the tunnel. The pieces fall onto a conveyor* belt. This belt carries the coal to a "shuttle car," which looks like a long, open trailer.

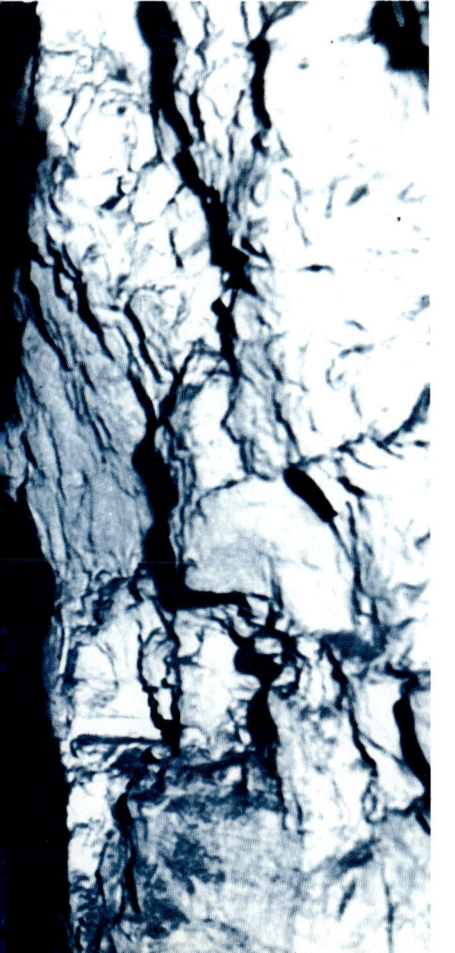

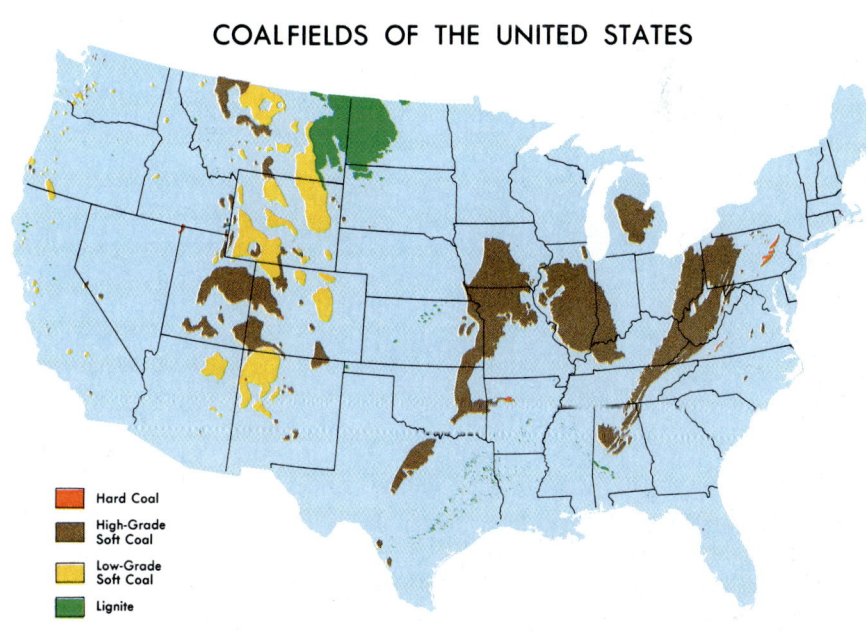

COALFIELDS OF THE UNITED STATES

- Hard Coal
- High-Grade Soft Coal
- Low-Grade Soft Coal
- Lignite

The map above shows the main coal deposits in the conterminous* United States. Deposits of high-grade soft coal are found in West Virginia and western Pennsylvania. They are part of a huge coalfield in the Appalachian Plateau. Hard coal is found in eastern Pennsylvania. West Virginia and Pennsylvania are two of the most important coal-producing states in our country.

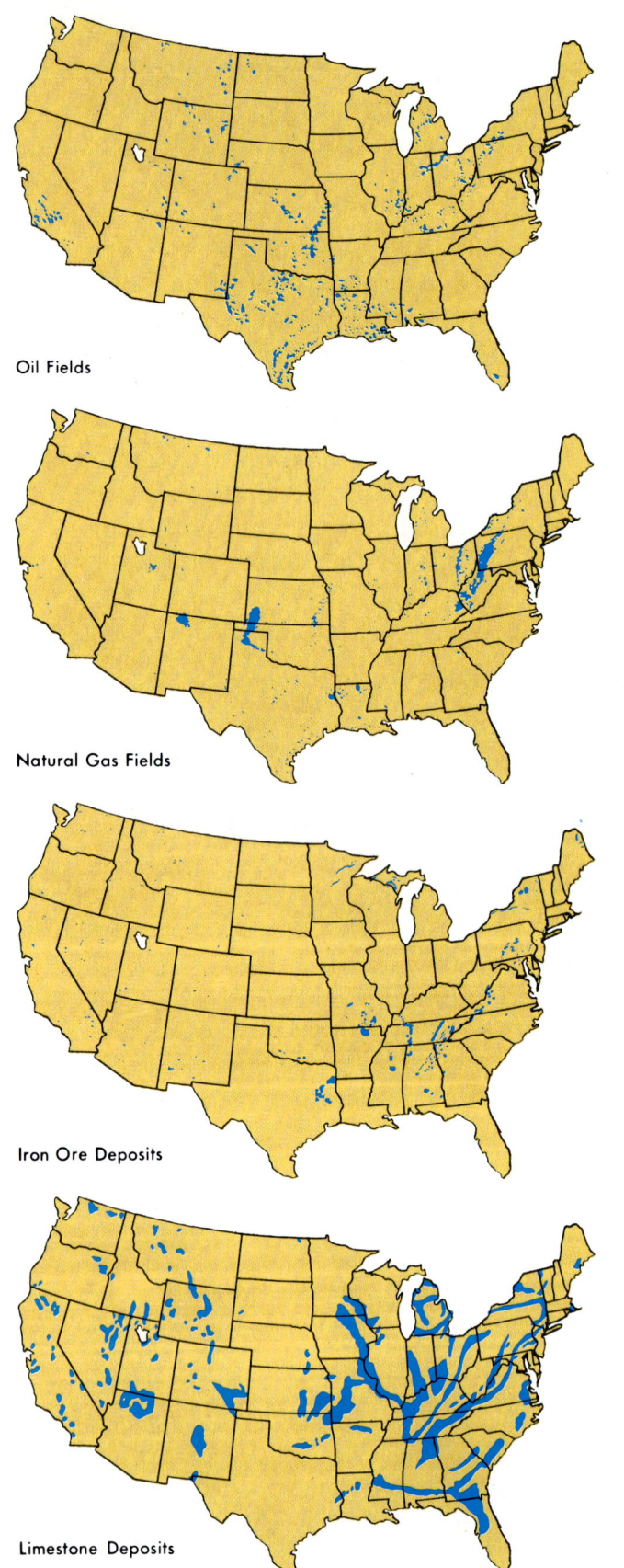

Oil Fields

Natural Gas Fields

Iron Ore Deposits

Limestone Deposits

When the car is loaded, it is driven to a large building near the front of the mine. Here, machines wash and sort the pieces of coal by size. Then the coal is taken by train to a river, a few miles away. There it is put on barges and taken down the river to large steel mills in the Pittsburgh area.

Changes in coal mining

Early in the 1900's, hundreds of thousands of people worked in the coal mines of West Virginia. These people worked long hours for very little pay. Their job was hard and dangerous. Sometimes gases or coal dust would collect in the mines and cause an explosion, or the ceiling of a mine would cave in. When such accidents happened, many miners lost their lives.

As time passed, coal-mining companies found it more and more difficult to make any money. Many Americans had begun to use oil or natural gas, instead of coal, to heat houses and other buildings. Oil also replaced coal as the main fuel for railroad engines. Since there were fewer customers for coal, some of the mines were shut down and thousands of people lost their jobs. Meanwhile, new machines had been invented to do much of the work once done by miners using picks and shovels. As more machinery was used, fewer miners were needed.

The unemployed miners had a hard time finding other work in the coal-mining areas. Many of them left home to find jobs in other parts of our

These maps show deposits of four valuable minerals in the conterminous United States. It is important to remember that these maps show both developed and undeveloped deposits.

Call attention to the mineral deposit maps. Ask: Do these maps show any valuable mineral deposits where we live?

† In what ways would our way of life change if we ran out of petroleum and natural gas? What kinds of things would we have to do without if this happened?

country. Those who stayed behind often lived in poverty. They received just enough money from the government for their most important needs.

† Today there are signs of growing prosperity in the coal-mining areas. Our country faces a shortage of oil and natural gas to meet its needs for energy. (See pages 102-113.) These fuels can be imported from other countries, but only at a high price. Since the United States has huge deposits of coal, there is growing interest in this mineral as a source of energy. New mines are being opened, and more workers are being hired. Also the miners now earn higher wages and enjoy safer working conditions than they did before.

Petroleum and natural gas

There are deposits of petroleum, or oil, and natural gas in several states of the Northeast. America's first oil well was drilled in northwestern Pennsylvania in 1859. Ways of pumping and refining crude* oil were also developed here. Until 1895, the Northeast produced more oil than any other part of the United States.

†† Today, other parts of our country are far ahead of the Northeast in petroleum production. However, the oil found in the Northeast is valuable because of its high quality. It is used to make gasoline, kerosene,* and other products.

West Virginia leads the Northeast in the production of natural gas. This resource has many uses. Some of it is carried by pipes to homes where it is used for heating and cooking. Chemicals made from natural gas are used in manufacturing many products, such as medicines and plastics.

Metal ores

There are only a few deposits of metal ores in the Northeast. The main deposits of iron ore in this region are found in the Adirondack Mountains of New York. Zinc ore is mined in New York, New Jersey, Maine, and Pennsylvania. New York is one of our country's leading producers of zinc. This metal is combined with copper to make brass, and it is also used as a coating to prevent rust.

Other minerals

There are large deposits of limestone in several states of the Northeast. This nonmetallic* mineral has many important uses. In the Northeast, large amounts of limestone are used to make steel. This mineral is also used in making cement. Pennsylvania and New York, which have large deposits of limestone, are among our nation's leading producers of cement. Blocks of limestone are used in the construction of buildings.

Several other nonmetallic minerals are also produced in the Northeast. Sand and gravel, which are found in every state of this region, are used mainly as construction materials. Some high-quality sand is used in the manufacture of glass. Vermont produces large quantities of granite and marble. These are used in the construction of buildings. Several states of the Northeast also produce slate.*

Among the other minerals produced in the Northeast are salt and clay. New York produces large amounts of salt. Various types of clay are found throughout the region. These are used in making pottery, china, tile, bricks, and many other products.

†† Have a student look up the word "kerosene" in the Glossary and read the definition aloud.

Forest Resources

Although the Northeast is our country's most densely populated region, more than half of the land is forested. Large forests are found in nearly every part of this region.

Many different kinds of trees grow in the Northeast. Softwoods, such as spruce and fir, grow mainly in the north. Hardwoods, such as oak, birch, and maple, are found throughout this region. (See map on page 99.) To learn more about the trees in the Northeast, let us visit a tree farm.

A tree farm in Maine

It is a cool fall day, and we are visiting a tree farm in northern Maine. Many acres of the farm are green with fir

Using Tools

See Great Ideas

Harvesting timber. Forests are an important resource in the Northeast. Large amounts of timber are harvested here every year. Loggers use big power saws to cut down the trees. They also use other tools to lift the heavy logs and to move them from the forests to mills and factories. What tools do you see in this picture? Do you think it would be possible to harvest so much timber without the use of tools like these? Why do you think this? Do you think it would be possible to make forest products such as lumber and newsprint without the use of tools? Give reasons for your answer.

trees. There is also a large grove of brightly colored beech and maple trees. The farmer tells us that the beeches and maples were growing here when he bought the land. However, he planted and raised the fir trees, just as other farmers raise crops such as wheat or oats.

The farmer says that he began raising trees nearly twenty-five years ago. The first fir trees that he planted have just been sold. They will be made into wood pulp.* Through the years, he has sold many of his beech and maple trees to a nearby lumber company.

We ask the farmer if tree farming takes much time and work. He tells us that after the trees are planted, they must be protected against fire and other enemies. Sometimes the trees must be sprayed to prevent damage from insects or disease. The farmer also says he spends long hours pruning* and cutting the trees. However, he does have enough time to raise some livestock to sell.

As it is getting late, we thank the farmer and leave for home.

Forest products

When European settlers first came to the Northeast, they discovered that the vast forests in this region were a valuable resource. They cut down trees and used the lumber to build homes, schools, churches, and ships. Much lumber was exported to other countries.

Today, many products are made from wood. One of the most important forest products of the Northeast is wood pulp. It is used to make newsprint, cardboard boxes, and other paper products. Some of the wood from the Northeast is cut into lumber, which is used to make furniture and to build homes and other buildings.

† Do you know what the pages of this book are made from? (Wood pulp.)

The Northeast 97

Maple syrup and maple sugar are also forest products of the Northeast. In late winter, when days become warmer but nights are still cold, the sap begins to flow in sugar maple trees. This sap is collected and made into maple syrup and maple sugar. New York and Vermont lead all of our states in the manufacture of these two products.

Other uses of forests

In addition to providing the raw materials for many products, forests are valuable in other ways. The roots of trees help hold the soil in place, preventing erosion.* Forests also give shelter and food for wildlife.

Forests help in saving water. During a heavy rainfall in open country, water often flows away quickly in ditches and streams. Where there are trees, however, rain must fall through leaves and branches. Therefore, a heavy rainfall reaches the ground more slowly in a forest than it does in open country. This gives the ground time to soak up the water. In addition, snow melts slowly in a forest and is soaked up by

Collecting maple sap in New York. The forests of the Northeast provide raw materials that are used in making a variety of products. In what other ways are forests valuable to the people of the Northeast?

the soil. Much of the rain and melted snow that collects in the ground beneath the forest drains slowly into rivers and lakes, helping to give them a steady supply of water.

Forests are also important to the tourist industry of the Northeast. They provide beautiful scenery for the people of this region and for visitors from other parts of our country. People can hike, camp, or hunt in the Northeast's many state and national forests.

Conserving the forests

In the past, the forests of the Northeast were not used wisely. Trees were cut until much of the land was barren. Soil once protected by trees was carried away by wind and water. Some forests were destroyed by fire. No efforts were made to replace the trees that were lost.

Today, people in the Northeast are trying to conserve forest resources. When forests are cut, new trees are usually planted. Sometimes several large healthy trees, called "seed trees," are left standing. These trees drop their seeds, and new trees begin to grow where others were cut. Better ways of controlling insects and disease are being discovered. Also, much land that is not good for growing food crops is now used for raising trees. For these reasons, forests will be an important natural resource in the Northeast for many years.

Fishing Grounds

The Atlantic coast of the Northeast † is an important fishing area. There are several reasons why this is so. One of the world's best fishing grounds lies in the coastal waters that extend northward from Massachusetts. There are also many fish in Chesapeake Bay and other inlets along the Atlantic coast. In addition, the Northeast has fine natural harbors where fishing boats can anchor.

Fishing in the Middle Atlantic states

Fishing is important in several Middle Atlantic states. Boats sailing from ports in New York State bring back large catches of fish from Long Island Sound. Off the Atlantic coast of New York and New Jersey is one of the most important clam-producing areas

Natural Forest Regions
- River bottom hardwoods and cypress
- Longleaf — loblolly — slash pine
- Mangrove or subtropical forest
- Oak — hickory
- Oak — pine
- Oak — chestnut — yellow poplar
- Spruce — fir with some hardwoods
- Birch — beech — maple — hemlock
- White, red, and jack pine

† Why is the Atlantic coast of the Northeast an important fishing area?

in the United States. Each year, Maryland fishers bring in thousands of tons of oysters. They also harvest other shellfish from Chesapeake Bay.

Large amounts of menhaden* are caught in the coastal waters of the Middle Atlantic states. The oil from menhaden is used in making soap and paint. Menhaden are also ground up and used as fertilizer.

Fishing in New England

Fishing is an important occupation along the Atlantic coast of New England. Massachusetts leads all the states of the Northeast in the value of fish caught. (See graph below.) New Bedford, Gloucester, and Boston are the leading fishing ports in this state. Other important fishing ports are Point Judith, Rhode Island, and Portland, Maine. Some of the fish that are brought to ports in New England are sold fresh in the cities of the Northeast. Others are frozen or canned and sold throughout our country.

Many different kinds of fish are caught off the coast of New England. Whiting, ocean perch, haddock, cod, and menhaden are brought to the ports at Boston and Gloucester. Flounder and scallops are important types of fish brought into the port of New Bedford. Thousands of tons of lobsters and clams are also caught off the coast of New England.

A visit to Gloucester Harbor

We are visiting the busy harbor of Gloucester, Massachusetts. Several fishing boats are entering or leaving the harbor. Others are docked here. Many of the boats

This graph shows the value in dollars of the 1974 fish catch in six northeastern states. Massachusetts leads the Northeast in the value of fish caught, and ranks sixth among all states. Ships from this state bring in huge catches of haddock, ocean perch, and other fish. Each year, Maine fishers catch thousands of tons of lobsters. Maryland fishers take large quantities of oysters from Chesapeake Bay.

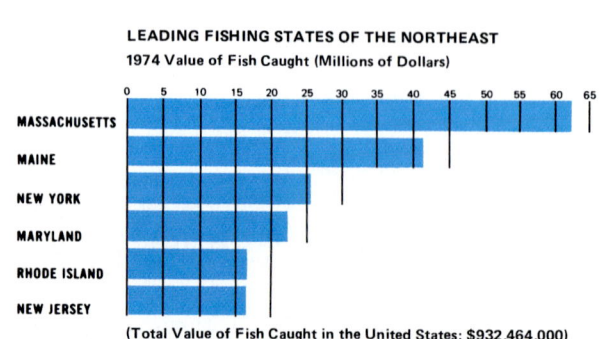

LEADING FISHING STATES OF THE NORTHEAST
1974 Value of Fish Caught (Millions of Dollars)

(Total Value of Fish Caught in the United States: $932,464,000)

Maine lobster fishers. The Atlantic coast of the Northeast is an important fishing area. Massachusetts and Maine are the region's leading fishing states. What kinds of fish do Northeast fishers catch?

that we see are trawlers. Some of these boats are as long as one hundred feet and are powered by diesel* engines.

A fisher working on the deck of his trawler invites us to come aboard. He shows us a huge net called an otter trawl. This net is towed along the bottom of the ocean with long cables. Two boards, called otter boards, keep the mouth of the net open so that fish can swim in. When the net is full, it is pulled into the boat with a machine called a winch.

The fisher tells us that he and his crew travel northward toward Newfoundland to fish for haddock, cod, and ocean perch. As soon as the fish are caught, they are refrigerated. This keeps them fresh until the ship arrives in port.

Energy

The Gasoline Shortage

In 1973, something happened that surprised many people in the United States. There was a shortage of gasoline. Gas stations could no longer get all the gas they needed from the companies that had always supplied them. Some stations had to close down because they did not have any gas to sell. Others stayed open for only a few hours each day. Sometimes drivers had to wait in line for hours to buy gas for their cars.

This was a new experience for most Americans. In the past, there had always been plenty of gasoline. What caused the gasoline shortage?

Where our gasoline comes from

As you discovered earlier, gasoline is made from petroleum, or oil. This dark-colored liquid is found in layers of rock far beneath the ground. To get oil, people drill wells deep into the earth. Then they pump the oil to the surface. The oil is sent to factories called refineries. There it is made into gasoline, fuel oil, and other kinds of fuel. Much of the fuel oil is burned to make electricity. Oil is the most important source of energy in the United States today. (See chart at right.)

A growing need for oil

In the past, the United States produced most of the oil it needed. There were thousands of oil wells in Texas, California, and other parts of our country. As time passed, many of these wells ran out of oil. New deposits of oil were discovered from time to time. However, these were not large enough to take care of all of our country's needs. This was because Americans were using larger amounts of gasoline and other fuels.

Oil from the Arab* nations

To get the oil it needed, the United States began buying oil from other countries. Some of these countries were Saudi Arabia, Iraq, and other Arab

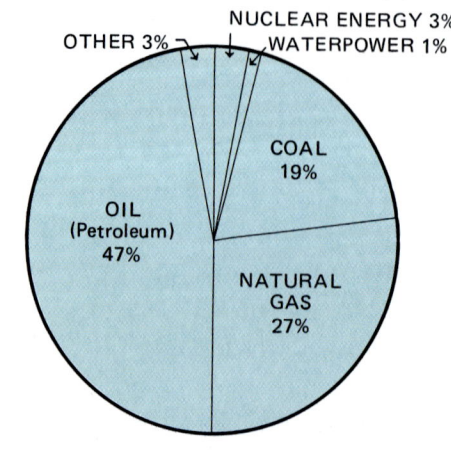

WHERE WE GET OUR ENERGY

Traffic in New York City. The many cars, trucks, and buses in our country use huge amounts of gasoline. This fuel is made from petroleum, or oil. Where does our country get the oil it needs?

nations. These nations have the largest deposits of oil in the world.

In 1973, some of the Arab nations were at war with the neighboring country of Israel. They were angry because the United States seemed to be taking Israel's side in this war. In the fall of 1973, the Arab nations stopped selling oil to the United States. This caused problems for the American refineries. They could not get enough oil to make gasoline for all the people who wanted it.

An unsolved problem

The gasoline shortage lasted for several months. Then the Arab nations began selling oil to the United States again. Americans could again buy all the gasoline they wanted. But they had to pay a much higher price than they had paid before.

Have students answer the question in the caption below.

The gasoline shortage was over for the time being. But the United States still faces a serious problem. The world's supply of oil is growing smaller each day. Scientists say that most of the known oil deposits will be used up within the next forty years. Before this happens, the United States and other countries will have to find new ways of producing the energy they need. Otherwise, people's lives will be much less comfortable than today.

What Is Energy?

Why is energy so important to people? To answer this question, we need to know what energy is.

Energy is power that can be used to do work. For example, we use energy in the form of heat to cook our meals.

The port of New Orleans in the 1880's. Long ago, people knew only a few ways of getting the energy they needed. They depended mostly on their own muscles or the muscles of animals to do work. Later, they found out how to use other sources of energy. What sources of energy does this picture illustrate?

We also use energy to keep our houses warm. We use other kinds of energy to run cars, boats, trains, and airplanes. Energy is needed to build houses and other buildings. It is needed to plant and harvest the farm crops so we have food. Electric energy is needed to light our homes. It is also needed to run the machines that make all the different kinds of goods we use. We could not live at all without using some form of energy.

Changes in the Use of Energy

Muscle power

Long ago, people knew only a few ways of getting the energy they needed. For thousands of years, they depended largely on their own muscles to do work. They lifted, carried, pushed, and pulled heavy objects. They hunted wild animals with simple weapons. These weapons were made from stone, wood, and bones. People built fires out of wood to keep warm and to cook their food.

Thousands of years ago, people began using animals to help them do work. They rode on the backs of horses and camels. They used donkeys or oxen to pull their plows and wagons. Sometimes they hitched these animals to simple machines. These machines ground grain or did other jobs.

Wind and water

As time passed, two new sources of energy were discovered. These were wind and water. People began to build sailboats. These boats depended on the wind to move them from place to place. Later, windmills were invented. They were used for such tasks as grinding grain and pumping water out of the ground. People also built gristmills* along the banks of rivers. The flowing water turned a large wooden wheel. This provided energy to run machinery for grinding grain.

The steam engine

During the 1700's, the steam engine was developed in Great Britain. A

The Northeast 105

steam engine works in this way: Coal or some other fuel is burned to heat water in a large tank. The water turns to steam and expands. This means it takes up more space. The power of the expanding steam can be used to run machinery. The steam engine was soon being used to run many kinds of factory machines. It was also used to run ships and trains.

The gasoline engine

In the 1800's, another new source of energy was discovered. Scientists found that oil could be used to make kerosene, gasoline, and other kinds of fuel. Soon many people were using kerosene for lighting their houses and cooking food. Then inventors in Europe developed a new kind of engine that ran on gasoline. This engine was lighter than the steam engine. Also, it took up less space. By the end of the 1800's, it was being used to run the world's first automobiles.

Electricity

For years, scientists had been studying the strange force known as electricity. Then inventors developed machines that could produce electric power. They also found ways to use electricity in homes and factories. One of these people was an American named Thomas Edison. In 1879 he invented an electric light bulb that was cheap and easy to make. Later, Edison built our country's first electric power plant. The electricity produced here was used to light nearby houses, stores, and offices. As the years passed, people began using electricity to run many different kinds of machines.

Meeting Our Energy Needs Today

In the United States today, people get energy from several different sources. The most important of these are named on the chart on page 102. They are oil, natural gas, and coal. These three provide about 93 percent of the energy we use. They are called fossil* fuels. They were formed from the remains of plants and animals that lived on the earth millions of years ago.

Fossil fuels

Nearly one half of all the energy we use in the United States today comes from oil. As you have seen, oil is made into gasoline and other kinds of fuel. Some of these are used to run cars, boats, trains, and airplanes. Petroleum is also made into fuel oil. Fuel oil is used mostly to heat houses and to produce electricity.

Natural gas is the second most important source of energy in our country today. Millions of Americans burn natural gas to heat their houses. Many of them also use gas for cooking food and heating water. Factories use natural gas as a fuel in making hundreds of different things.

Coal provides about one fifth of our country's energy needs. It is used mostly as a fuel in power plants that produce electricity. But some coal is also used to heat schools and other buildings.

Waterpower

Another source of energy used in the United States today is waterpower. Dams and power plants have been built on many rushing rivers in our country.

† Have students refer to the chart on page 102 when discussing our energy needs.

How Electricity Is Produced

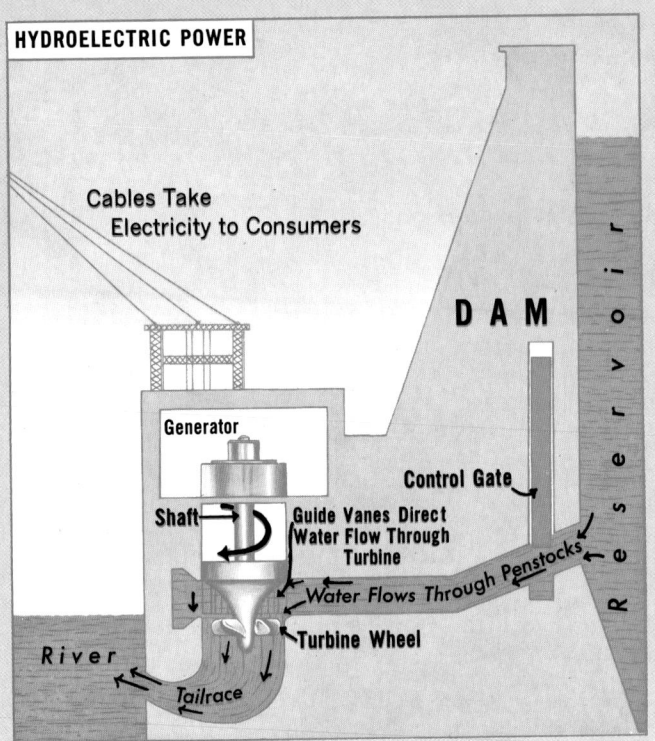

Most electricity is produced in power plants by large machines called generators.* These generators are usually driven by turbines.* There are two main kinds of turbines. One kind is powered by steam. The other is powered by falling water.

Steam-powered turbines are used in producing almost nine tenths of the electricity generated in the Northeast. To make steam for the turbines, water is heated in large boilers. In the Northeast, coal is the fuel most commonly used to heat the water. Oil or natural gas is used in some places. However, a few plants use nuclear energy.

About one tenth of the Northeast's electricity is produced by generators driven by water turbines. Electric power produced in this way is called hydroelectricity.

The chart on this page shows how waterpower is changed into electrical energy. A dam has been built across a river to hold back the water. This creates a large reservoir.* Turbines are placed at the bottom of the dam. When the control gate is opened, water rushes downward through pipes and turns the turbines. Shafts leading from the turbines turn the generators, which produce electricity.

The power of the moving water is used to run machines that produce large amounts of electricity.

Nuclear energy

During the last few years, people in the United States have begun to use a new source of energy. This is the energy stored in tiny bits of matter called atoms.* When atoms are split or combined in certain ways, huge amounts of energy are given off. This is known as nuclear energy. Today there are a number of nuclear power plants in our
† country. Here, the energy stored in atoms is used to produce electricity for homes and factories.

Energy and Our Way of Life

Today, most Americans have a better way of life than even the richest people enjoyed in earlier times. This is because we have so many different ways of getting the energy we need. We can produce many more goods and services than people could when they used their muscles for energy.

There is a close connection between people's standard* of living and the amount of energy they use. To see an example of this, look at the chart on page 108. This chart shows that the average person in the United States uses almost twenty times as much energy as the average person in China. At the same time, the average American produces more than twenty-five times as many goods and services each year as the average Chinese.

This helps to explain why the standard of living in our country is one of the highest in the world. We use large amounts of energy to help us meet our needs.

† Discuss other ways nuclear energy is used. (Nuclear submarines, nuclear weapons.) What do you think is the best way to use this energy? Explain.

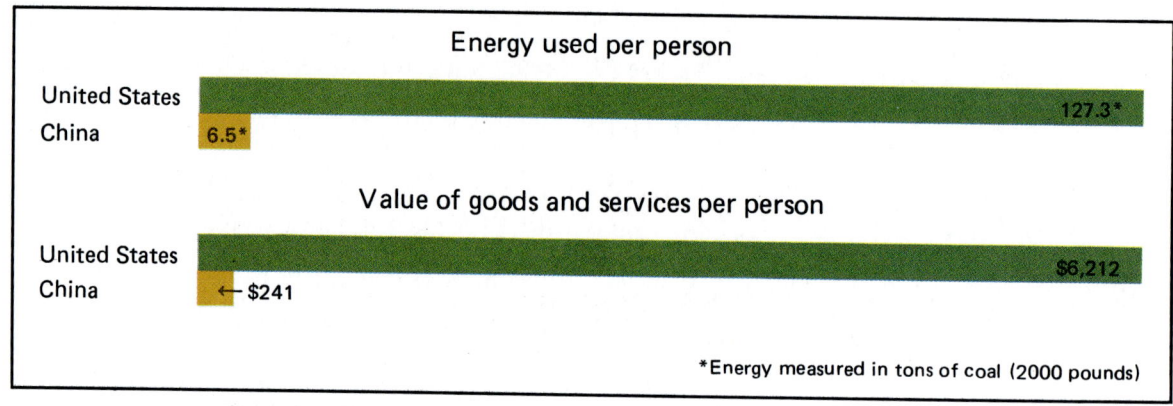

Many Americans wonder how long we will be able to enjoy our present way of life. They point out that we are rapidly using up the natural resources that supply most of our energy.

The Energy Problem

As you have discovered, about 93 percent of the energy we use each year comes from the fossil fuels. These are oil, natural gas, and coal. It is becoming harder to find new deposits of oil. Our country is also starting to run out of natural gas. Scientists say that the natural gas we now have will only last for another twenty or thirty years.

As energy fuels become harder to find, they also become more costly. Today, Americans are paying much higher prices for gasoline than they did in the past. They are also paying more for fuel oil and natural gas to heat their houses. This is because much of our electricity is produced by burning fuel oil or natural gas.

Dark houses and empty factories

Unless we can find new ways to meet our need for energy, we will likely face a number of serious problems. For example, factories might have to shut down because they could not get fuel oil or natural gas for heating. Also, they could not get electricity to run their machines. If this happened, thousands of people might be left without jobs. Also, many Americans might have to stop using their cars because gasoline prices were too high. And, there might not be gasoline to buy.

A shortage of fuel might cause power companies to cut off electricity to some of their customers for hours or days at a time. If this happened, lights would go out. People would not be able to use any electrical appliances such as stoves and refrigerators. Blackouts* have already taken place in New York and other cities.

Solving the Energy Problem

What can be done to make sure that our country has enough energy to meet its needs? Let us explore some of the different answers to this question.

Finding more oil and natural gas

Today, people who work for oil companies are trying hard to find new deposits of oil and natural gas. They are going to far-off places to search for them. And they are using new tools that make it easier to find these deposits that lie deep in the earth.

The Alaskan pipeline. A few years ago, a huge deposit of oil was found along the coast of northern Alaska. Oil from this deposit is now being shipped to refineries in other parts of our country.

† Underground coal mining is very dangerous. Many miners have been trapped in cave-ins. Also, miners who work for long periods in the coal mines often get a disease called "black lung."

In some cases, their search has been successful. A huge deposit of oil was discovered a few years ago along the coast of northern Alaska. Oil from this deposit is now being shipped to refineries in other parts of the United States. Scientists believe that other large oil deposits lie under the Atlantic Ocean, near our country's eastern coast. The ocean is not deep there. It would be possible to get the oil.

These new deposits can help to meet our needs for a short time. But they will not solve the energy problem. Sooner or later, we will have to use something other than oil and natural gas.

Coal

The only fossil fuel that we have plenty of today is coal. Some experts believe that there is enough coal in the United States to meet all of our energy needs for the next four hundred years or more. But the use of coal as a fuel leads to certain problems.

First is the problem of removing the coal from the earth. There are two † main ways of mining coal. One is to dig tunnels deep under the ground. This is costly. It is often dangerous. The other way is to dig giant holes in the earth with power shovels. This is safer and less costly than underground mining. However, it causes great damage to the land.

Coal has other disadvantages too. In general, it gives off large amounts of smoke when it burns. For this reason, it is a major cause of air pollution. Also, coal cannot be used now to run cars or trucks.

To use coal as our chief energy fuel, these problems must be solved. Scientists are looking for a way to change coal into a new form. They hope to make a kind of fuel that will burn without causing air pollution.

Waterpower

The power of rushing water can be used to make electricity. Waterpower does not cause air pollution, as the burning of fuel does. Also, we won't run out of waterpower as long as rivers flow. But waterpower cannot be used without building large dams and power plants. These are costly. Also, they can be built only in certain places. Water must flow down from a higher level to a lower level. For these reasons, waterpower will never supply more than a small part of our energy needs.

Wind power

For thousands of years, people have been using the wind as a source of energy. The wind is free. It can never be used up. Also, wind power does not cause any pollution. Today, some people are using windmills to produce electricity for farms. But this works only in places where the wind blows strongly for hours at a time.

Solar energy

Every day great amounts of energy come to our earth as sunlight. This is known as solar energy. It does not cause pollution. And it will never run out. If all the solar energy that reaches the earth could be used, it would take care of all of our energy needs for millions of years.

Certain devices are needed to collect the sunlight and change it into heat and electricity. These cost a great deal. They take up a large amount of space.

Using Natural Resources

See Great Ideas

A solar house. Panels on the roof of this house collect sunlight, or solar energy. This energy is used to provide the house with heat and hot water. Do you think solar energy is an important natural resource? What are some good things about using sunlight as a source of energy? What are some of the drawbacks of this kind of energy?

Also, solar energy cannot be collected at night or when dark clouds hide the sun.

However, many Americans today are interested in making use of solar energy. Thousands of people now use sunlight to heat houses and other buildings. Solar energy is also being used to heat water for homes and business places.

Nuclear energy

As you have discovered, nuclear energy can be used in making electricity. A few years ago, many people believed that nuclear energy would soon be our main source of energy. They thought it would take the place of oil, natural gas, and coal. So far this has not happened.

To understand why, you need to know that there are two main ways of producing nuclear energy. One is by splitting atoms into smaller parts. This is called fission.* The other way is by combining atoms into larger ones. This is known as fusion.*

At the present time, only fission is being used to produce nuclear energy. Fission has a number of disadvantages. First, fission power plants are costly to build. Second, it is difficult to keep them working properly. Also, a mineral called uranium* is needed as a fuel in these plants. Uranium is costly, and new deposits are becoming hard to find.

Many people believe that fission power plants are unsafe. They are afraid that an accident might kill or

Inside a nuclear power plant. Here, nuclear energy is made into electricity. What mineral is used as a fuel in nuclear power plants?

hurt thousands of people. Also, fission makes large amounts of harmful waste matter. These wastes can cause illness or death to people unless they are stored carefully.

Scientists are now working on these problems. They are also trying to find a cheap, practical way of using fusion to produce nuclear energy. This will be much safer than fission. Also it will not leave harmful waste matter. With fusion, water can be used as a fuel instead of uranium. As a result, our supply of fuel would never run out.

Using Energy More Wisely

Someday, we may have all the energy we need. Perhaps we will find ways to produce nuclear energy cheaply and safely. Or we may find practical ways of using solar energy. Until then, we cannot take a chance on running out of oil and other energy fuels. We must be more careful in using the energy we have.

In the past, the United States has always had enough energy. Americans have been more wasteful of energy than people in most other countries.

There are many things that Americans can do to make better use of their energy. For instance, engineers can develop new machines that will run on less electricity. Builders can construct buildings that do not need so much fuel to keep them heated.

How we can do our part

All of us can help to save energy in a number of different ways. For example, we can buy smaller cars. We can drive them more slowly. In this way, we can go farther on every gallon of gasoline. We can also save energy by riding buses or trains instead of driving our own cars. We can make sure that our houses are well insulated to save heat during the winter. We can turn down our furnaces in the wintertime. We can use less air conditioning in the summertime. We can turn out all electric lights that are not being used. And we can save energy in the ways we use stoves and other appliances.

All citizens of the United States must work together to help solve the energy problem. Our way of life in the future will depend on the steps we take to save energy today.

Energy and You

All of us can help to save energy in a number of different ways. For example, we can turn off the TV set when no one is watching it. We can ride a bike instead of asking someone to take us in a car. Prepare to discuss the following questions with the other members of your class.

1. What things do you and your family use that need energy?
2. What are some of the ways you can help to save energy?

To prepare for your discussion, list the things you and your family use that need energy in order to work. Your list might include appliances, such as a refrigerator and a stove. It might also include means of transportation and sports or recreational equipment. Think about the energy each of these things uses. What are some things you and your family could do to save some of this energy?

The Northeast

10 Industry

A Tour Through a Steel Plant

We are driving along a highway in Pennsylvania, about 30 miles (48 km.)† northeast of Philadelphia. In the distance, we see a row of smokestacks and the towers of three giant blast* furnaces. These are part of one of the largest steel plants in the Northeast. To learn how steel is made, we will take a tour of this plant. (See page 116.)

This plant is owned by a large steel company. Before the tour starts, our guide tells us about the plant we are visiting. He says that the plant belongs to the United States Steel Corporation. This is a huge company. It has factories and offices in many parts of our country. Only a company with large amounts of capital* could build a plant like this one. This plant cost about 400 million dollars.

Our guide tells us this company began over seventy years ago. It was started by a group of people in the Northeast and the Midwest.* Several small steel companies were joined to form one larger company. Shares of stock* were bought by the people who started the company. More shares were sold to other people who wanted to invest* their money. These investments helped the company to grow larger and brought profits* to the people who owned stock. Today, about 250,000 people own stock in the United States Steel Corporation. Much of the money needed to start new plants comes from profits. The company may also borrow money from banks or offer more shares of stock for sale.

Thousands of workers

Many workers are needed to make steel. We learn that about 9,000 people work in this plant. Some

† km. means kilometer
*See Glossary

Inside a steel plant. Hot, melted iron is being poured into a furnace. There it will be made into steel. The making of steel is one of the leading industries in the Northeast. What are some important products that are made from this metal?

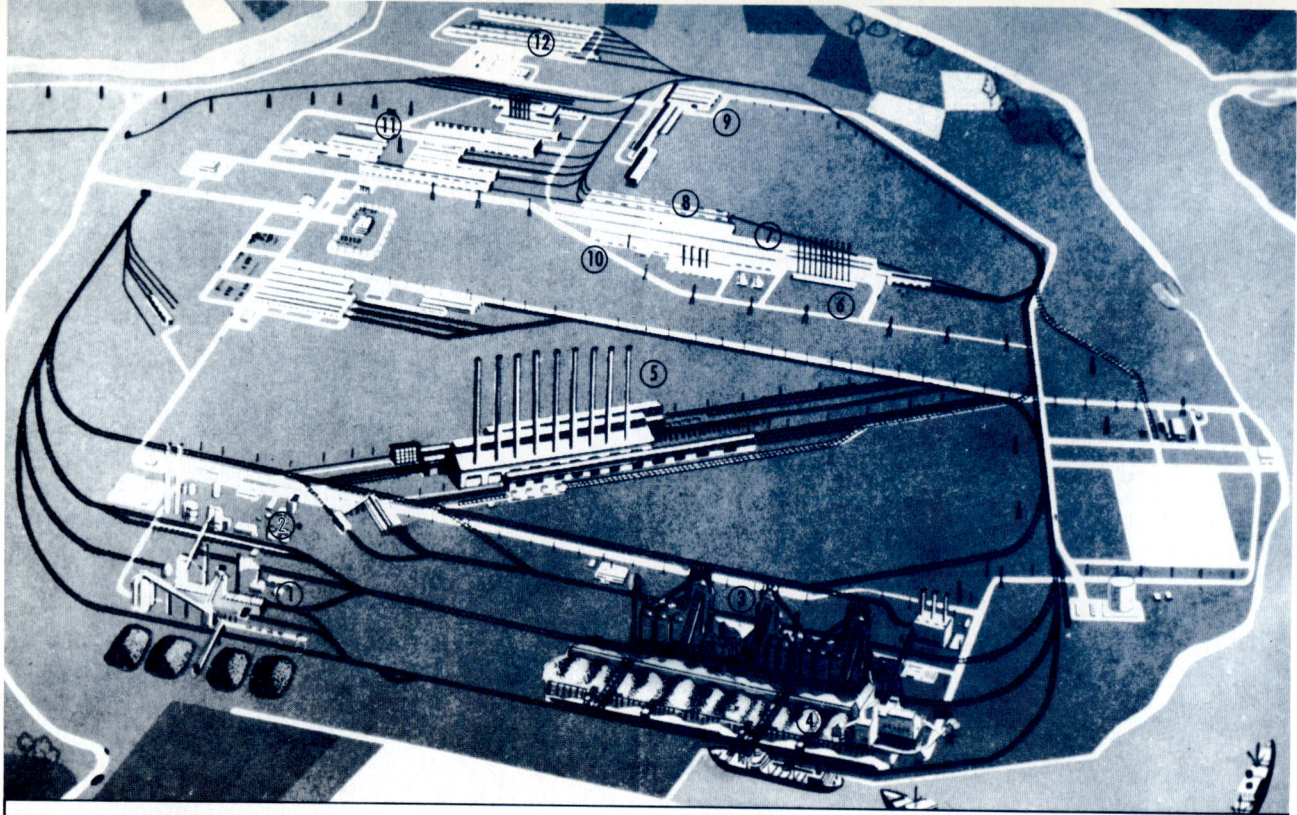

1. Coke Ovens
2. Coal-Chemicals Plant
3. Blast Furnaces
4. Docks and Ore Storage Yard
5. Open-Hearth Building
6. Soaking Pits
7. Slab—Bloom Mill
8. Billet Mill
9. Bar Mill
10. Hot-Strip Mill
11. Sheet and Tin Finishing Mill
12. Pipe Mill

A Steel Plant

Our tour of the steel plant pictured above will show us how three important raw* materials are used in making steel. These raw materials are iron ore, coal, and limestone.

We begin our tour at the coke ovens (1). Here, coal is unloaded from trains and heated in airtight ovens. The heat drives gases from the coal, leaving a hard, gray substance called coke. This is a fuel that burns with a hot flame. Coke is needed in the making of iron and steel. The gases given off when the coal is heated are piped to the coal-chemicals plant (2), where they are made into valuable chemicals.* A conveyor* belt more than a mile long carries the coke from the ovens to the blast* furnaces (3).

Now we visit the docks along the Delaware River (4). Here we watch a ship unloading reddish brown iron ore. Large amounts of iron ore, coke, and limestone are fed into the three giant blast furnaces nearby. Powerful machines then blow a blast of very hot air into each furnace. This air makes the coke burn with a very high heat that melts the iron ore. The limestone mixes with waste materials in the ore to form slag,* which rises to the top. Melted iron containing carbon and other substances settles at the bottom of the furnace. The iron is now ready to be made into steel.

Our next stop is the open-hearth building (5), where steel is made. Here we watch iron ore, limestone, and steel scrap* being loaded into a huge open-hearth furnace. These materials are heated until they melt. Then melted iron is brought from the blast furnace and added to the mixture. Small amounts of special metals may also be added. The mixture is cooked for several hours to burn out some of the carbon and other unwanted materials from the iron. Finally, melted steel is drained from the furnace and poured into molds.* As the steel cools, it hardens into huge blocks called ingots. The molds are removed and the ingots are taken to the soaking pits (6). Here they are reheated until they are an even temperature throughout.

The steel now goes to the mills (7-12). At the mills it will be formed into different shapes that can be used in making steel products. Some of the steel is rolled into thin sheets or strips. Some is formed into other shapes. In one of the mills, sheets and strips of steel are used in making tinplate.* Steel pipes and tubes are made in another mill.

*See Glossary

† You may assign student activities using Fideler Discovery Card 111, or Fideler Discovery Sheets, Volume 1, pages 45-48.

of these workers run the machines. Others are managers or office workers. Most of them live in towns or cities within 20 miles (32 km.) of the plant.

Raw* materials for steelmaking

We ask where this steel plant gets the iron ore and other raw materials it needs. Our guide says large amounts of iron ore are imported* from other countries. The cheapest way to bring iron ore a long way is by water. Our guide explains that the plant is on the Delaware River. This river empties into Delaware Bay, an arm of the Atlantic Ocean. Ships bringing iron ore from other countries can travel up the river to the plant.

This steel plant is also in a good place for getting the other raw materials it needs. Coal is brought by train from mines in western Pennsylvania and West Virginia. Trucks bring limestone from central Pennsylvania.

Electricity runs the machinery

As we tour the plant, we see that many kinds of machinery are needed for making steel. These machines are run by electric* power. Our guide says the plant has its own powerhouse. There, gas from the blast furnaces and coke* ovens is burned to heat water. The water turns to steam. The steam is used to run generators* that produce electricity for the steel plant. About half of the electricity this plant needs comes from the powerhouse. The rest is bought from a company that supplies power to homes, stores, and factories.

The Delaware River supplies water

Large amounts of water are needed in making steel. Our guide says this plant uses about 250 million gallons of Delaware River water each day. After the water has been used, it is treated to purify* it. Then it is returned to the river.

Many customers

A factory cannot do business without customers to buy its products. In other words, every factory must have a market. This steel plant is in a very good place. It lies between the two largest cities in the Northeast, New York and Philadelphia. There are many factories in this area. Some of them use large amounts of steel in making their products. For example, automobile plants use sheets of steel in making cars. Other plants use steel in making tools. Steel is also used in making electrical appliances such as washing machines.

After the steel has been made, it must be delivered to the people who buy it. This steel plant is near several very good highways and railroad lines. Most of the steel made here is shipped to customers by train or truck.

A Great Manufacturing Region

The plant we just visited is only one of many factories in the Northeast. There are more than 100,000 factories here. They make many kinds of products, from nails and buttons to airplanes and ocean liners. The total value of goods made each year in the Northeast is more than 100 billion dollars. No other part of our country except the Midwest has so much industry.

What industries need

Our tour of the steel plant showed us a factory needs many things. First, capital is needed to start the factory

The Northeast 117

† What do you think might happen if people did not invest money in new industry? Explain.

and to keep it going. Skilled people are needed to run machines and work in the factory offices. People are also needed to manage these offices. The factory needs raw materials. It must also have power to run its machinery. Trucks, trains, and other kinds of transportation are needed to bring raw materials to the factory. They are also needed to ship goods to customers. Finally, every factory must have a market for its goods.

The Northeast has most of the things factories need. Some things it does not have. But these can easily be gotten from other regions of the United States or other countries. Let us learn more about why the Northeast has so much industry.

Early history

The history of the Northeast helps explain why it has so much industry today. The first factories in our country were started in the Northeast. Therefore, the people here have long known how to manufacture goods. Also people in other regions are used to buying goods from factories in the Northeast.

All through its history, the Northeast has been the home of skillful people. Some of these people developed new products or new ways of making things. Inventions such as the telephone and the electric light were first tried out in the Northeast. They led to the growth of several new industries in this region.

The capital industries need

† The Northeast has long been the home of people who are willing to invest money in new industries. Today it still has the capital industries need. In this region are many banks that lend money to businesses that want to build new factories. Here, too, are large stock exchanges, where people can buy and sell shares in many different companies.

Many workers

The Northeast has many industrial workers, for more than 56 million people live here. Many of these people have the skills needed to run complicated* machinery. Others make beautiful things by hand. New England is noted for its skillful craft workers. The

A worker in a factory in Buffalo. What are some of the things that factories need besides workers? Which of these things does the Northeast have? Which of these does the Northeast lack?

Northeast also has many office workers and managers.

To make good products, workers and managers must be well trained. There are many fine schools in the Northeast that train people for jobs in industry.

Raw materials

The Northeast has a number of raw materials that factories need. The most important of these is coal. Other minerals here include limestone, natural gas, and salt. There are large forests that supply wood for certain industries. Raw materials also come from farms and fishing grounds in the Northeast.

At the same time, the Northeast does not have many raw materials it needs. For example, it does not produce nearly enough oil for its refineries.* It also has little iron ore, bauxite, and other metal ores. Many farm products cannot be raised in the Northeast as the land and climate are not suitable.

Being without these raw materials has not kept industry from growing in the Northeast, however. Industries can get raw materials from other parts of the United States or from other countries. Also, the Northeast has made good use of its resources. New England, for instance, has few mineral resources. But it has many skilled workers. Therefore, many factories in New England make products that need skilled workers but few raw materials. Among these products are clocks, machine tools, and electronic* products.

Well supplied with power

Nearly all machines in northeastern factories are run by electric power. Most of this power comes from steam plants. But some power comes from

A chemist for a large oil company in the Northeast. The Northeast does not have large deposits of petroleum, or crude oil. But there are many oil refineries in this region. Much of the oil used in these refineries is shipped here from other parts of the United States or from other countries. Where are some of the Northeast's oil refineries located?

Ports and waterways have helped the Northeast become an important manufacturing region. A number of cities along the Atlantic coast have fine deep-water harbors. Ships from all over the world bring goods of many kinds to these harbors. Ships also carry goods from these harbors to many faraway ports.

Inland waterways are also important in the Northeast. One of these is the Great Lakes–St. Lawrence Waterway.* It connects lake ports in the Northeast, the Midwest, and Canada. It also connects these ports with the Atlantic Ocean. The Ohio River connects the Northeast with parts of the South and the Midwest.

hydroelectric* plants. (See page 107.) Coal from Pennsylvania and West Virginia is used in many steam power plants. There are hydroelectric plants along several rivers in the Northeast.

Industry got an early start in New England. This was partly because of the many small streams here to provide waterpower. In time, New England's factories needed more power than these streams could give. Today, most factories here use electricity made in steam power plants. Coal for these plants is brought by train and ship from Pennsylvania and West Virginia.

Good transportation

The Northeast is served by many good roads, railroads, and airways. The main waterways are also good transportation routes. (See map below.) Because this region is on the Atlantic Ocean, raw materials can be shipped here from all parts of the world. Factories in the Northeast can send their products by ship to other countries.

A huge market

A business person choosing a place for a new factory might decide to build it in the Northeast. For one reason,

Refer to the map and caption above. Discuss the importance of these waterways to industry in the Northeast.

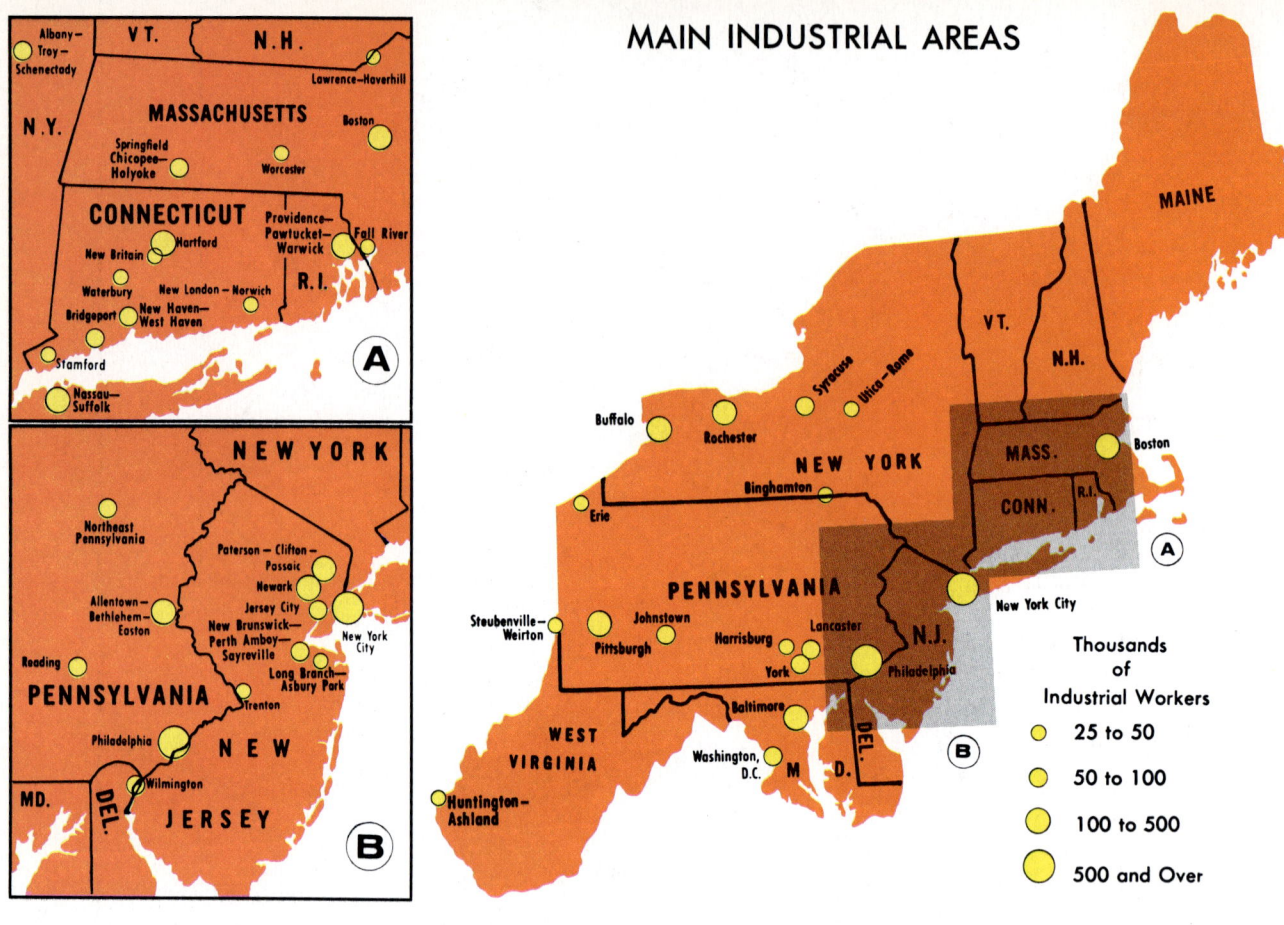

MAIN INDUSTRIAL AREAS

the millions of people here buy many manufactured products. Also, many factories in the Northeast use goods other factories make. This large market helps explain why there is so much industry in the Northeast today.

Main industrial areas

All parts of the Northeast do not have factories. There are few industries in some parts, such as the Adirondack Mountains and northern New England. Other parts have many industries.

The three maps above show the main industrial areas of the Northeast. You can see that many of these areas are along the Atlantic coast, from New Hampshire to Washington, D.C. This is a densely populated area, with many large cities. (See map on page 50.)

Another great manufacturing belt crosses the central part of New York State. It goes from Albany to Buffalo. This area lies along one of the main transportation routes through the Appalachian Highlands. Cities that have grown up here are served by roads, railroads, and the New York State Barge Canal. (See map on page 121.)

There are also many factories in western Pennsylvania and West Virginia. This area is rich in coal, natural gas, and other minerals used in industry.

Products of Industry

Iron and steel

The manufacture of iron and steel is one of the Northeast's most important industries. There are more than three hundred steel plants here. Plants in

Call attention to the map above. Refer to the legend. Which states have the most industrial workers? Which states have the least?

Pennsylvania alone make nearly one fourth of our country's steel.

The greatest steelmaking area in the Northeast is around Pittsburgh. Steel plants here can get coal and limestone from large deposits nearby. Iron ore is brought from mines near Lake Superior. Factories in the cities of the Northeast and Midwest buy much of Pittsburgh's steel. The Pittsburgh area is well served by railroads, waterways, and other means of transportation.

Not all of the steel plants in the Northeast are in the Pittsburgh area. There are some plants in eastern Pennsylvania. Also, there are large plants near Buffalo and Baltimore. There are no large steel plants in New England, however. This area does not have enough coal and iron ore for making steel. Factories here must buy most of their steel from plants in other parts of the Northeast.

Machinery

Factories in the Northeast use steel and other metals to make thousands of useful things. More people work in the manufacture of machinery than in any other industry in the Northeast. Electrical machinery such as motors and generators are important products of this region. Air conditioners, washing machines, and other household appliances are also made here.

Many factories in the Northeast make parts for electronic products such as radios and television sets. There

Workers in a television factory. Many of the manufacturing plants in the Northeast make parts for electronic* products. Among these products are radios, television sets, and computers.

† Ask: What would happen to the refineries and chemical plants if there were no more oil available? Explain. What would happen to the people who worked in the refineries and plants?

are also factories that make different kinds of telephone equipment.

Many other kinds of machinery are also made in the Northeast. Among these are typewriters and other kinds of office equipment. An important industry in New England is the manufacture of machine tools. These are machines that cut, grind, and shape metal. Other types of factory machinery are also made in the Northeast. For example, textile* machinery is made in New England. Printing machinery is made in the New York City area.

Transportation equipment

Some of the metal produced in the Northeast is used in making transportation equipment. Factories in Connecticut, Maryland, and other states make airplanes or airplane parts. There are automobile plants in New Jersey and Delaware. Factories in Pennsylvania, New York, and New Jersey make railroad cars. Shipbuilding has been carried on in the Northeast since colonial days. Today there are large shipyards near Boston, New York, Philadelphia, and Baltimore. They build all kinds of ships, from tugboats to huge naval and passenger ships. Nuclear* submarines and helicopters are made in Connecticut.

Other metal products

Factories in the Northeast make many other products from metal. Steel sections used in building bridges are made in Pennsylvania. Many northeastern factories make nails, locks, and other hardware. Connecticut is noted for products made from copper and brass. Here, too, are factories that make ball and roller bearings* for industry.

Petroleum products

In the Northeast, there are many refineries that make gasoline, fuel oil, and other products from petroleum. Although these plants do not use many workers, the goods they make are very important. There are several huge refineries along the Atlantic coast, near Philadelphia and other cities. They use petroleum shipped in from other states and other countries. There are some small refineries near oil fields in western Pennsylvania and New York.

Chemicals* and chemical products

The chemical industry is another important manufacturing industry in the Northeast. Many plants here make basic chemicals, such as ammonia, sulfuric acid, and chlorine. Basic chemicals are used in making many different products. These include plastics, synthetic* fibers, soap, medicines, paint, and fertilizer.

Chemical plants in the Northeast are usually built near sources of raw materials or power. Many of these plants are around New York City or along the Delaware River. Some of these chemical plants use products from nearby oil refineries to make chemical products. In West Virginia there are plants that use coal, natural gas, and other minerals found nearby. Some chemical plants that need large amounts of electricity are around Buffalo. They get hydroelectric power from Niagara Falls. Some chemical plants in the Northeast also use raw materials that come from other countries. †

Textiles, clothing, and shoes

In 1920, textile manufacturing was the most important industry in New

A Connecticut factory that makes products out of brass. Brass is a metal made of copper and zinc. It is used to make hardware, such as screws. Some musical instruments are also made of brass.

England. Then, in the 1920's and 1930's, many New England textile plants had to close. They could not make textiles as cheaply as mills in the South. Even today, however, textile manufacturing is important in New England and other parts of the Northeast. Some textile mills spin natural or synthetic fibers into yarn. Others use yarn to make cloth. There are also factories that use textiles to make such things as sheets, blankets, tablecloths, and clothing.

Much of the clothing worn by people in the United States is made in the Northeast. New York City is the center

Refer to the picture below. Have a student read the caption. Use the questions for a class discussion.

of our country's clothing industry. Factories here make dresses, slacks, shirts, coats, and many other kinds of clothes. Clothing is also made in Philadelphia and other cities.

Making shoes is another important industry in the Northeast. Boston and New York are among the leading shoe-manufacturing cities in our country. There are also many shoe factories in the smaller cities and towns of New England. Many animal skins used in making shoe leather come by ship from Argentina and other countries.

Food

Food processing* is also a leading industry in the Northeast. The farms and fishing grounds of the Northeast provide many raw materials for this industry. There are canneries and freezing plants in New Jersey, Maryland, and other states. They process fruits and vegetables from nearby farms. Cattle raised on West Virginia and Pennsylvania farms are processed in meat-packing plants. Other factories process chickens raised on nearby farms or seafood caught by northeastern fishers.

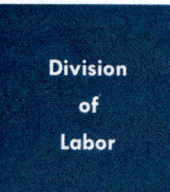

Division of Labor

See Great Ideas

Inspecting shirts in a New Jersey factory. Much of the clothing worn by people in the United States is made in the Northeast. Some factories spin wool, cotton, or synthetic fibers into yarn. Other factories weave the yarn into cloth. Still other factories use cloth to make dresses, shirts, and many other kinds of clothing. Do you think it helps to meet people's need for clothing by dividing work in this way? Explain your answer. What do you think would happen if each person in our country tried to make all of his or her own clothing?

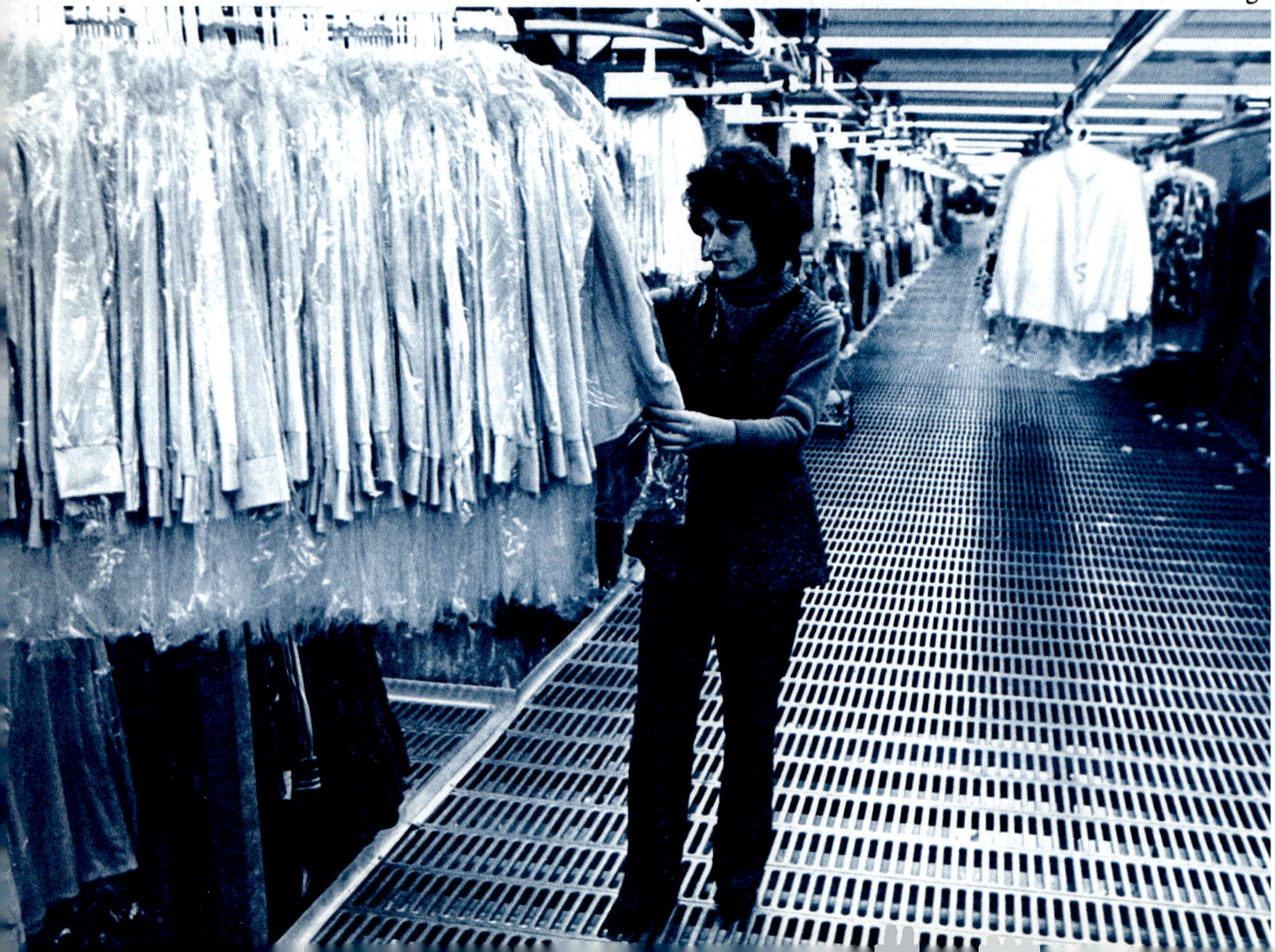

Dairy farms in the Northeast send milk to creameries, cheese factories, and ice cream plants.

Some of the factories in the Northeast use farm products from outside this region. There are large sugar refineries in New York, Baltimore, and other seaports. They process raw* sugar that comes by ship from the West Indies. The city of Buffalo is noted for its breakfast-food plants and flour mills. These plants use grain that is shipped on the Great Lakes from farming areas in the Midwest and Great Plains.* Bakeries in many northeastern cities use flour from Buffalo in making bread, cakes, and other products.

An Important Trading Region

Trade is another important way of earning a living in the Northeast. More people here are employed in trade than in any other kind of work except manufacturing. Some people have jobs in the importing and exporting* businesses. Others work in department stores or small shops.

Trade with other countries

† Much of the trade between the United States and other countries is carried on by businesses in the Northeast. Many goods made in other parts of the world come by ship to ports in the Northeast. Many goods are also exported from this region to other parts of the world.

Trade with other regions

The Northeast also carries on much trade with other parts of the United States. For example, fresh fruits and vegetables grown in California and Florida are shipped to the Northeast.

† Use Fideler Discovery Cards 118 and 120.

A ship docked in New York Harbor. The Northeast has some of our country's largest seaports. They help make this part of our country an important trading region.

See Great Ideas

A drugstore in the Northeast. There are many stores in the Northeast that sell goods directly to people. This is called retail trade. Most people get nearly all the goods they need through retail trade. What do people give in exchange for the things they buy? What are some of the things you and your family buy through retail trade? Would you be able to obtain these things without the great idea of exchange? Give reasons for your answer.

This region, in turn, ships many goods to other parts of our country.

Retail* trade

The Northeast has many stores that sell goods directly to the people who use them. Most of this kind of trade is in the Northeast's large cities. Besides large department stores, these cities have many smaller stores that sell unusual things. People come from hundreds of miles away to shop in the great cities of the Northeast. Here they find many goods they cannot buy in their own cities or towns.

A Problem To Solve

The Northeast is one of the most important industrial regions of the United States and also of the world. Why is this true? In forming hypotheses* to solve this problem, you need to know how the growth of industry in the Northeast has been affected by:

a. its location
b. its history
c. the raw materials available here
d. the markets for manufactured goods
e. transportation routes
f. the sources of power available
g. the skills of the people

Information in other chapters of this book will be helpful in solving this problem.

See Skills Manual, "Thinking and Solving Problems"

Use Fideler Discovery Card 115 (Discover How Exchange Helps People) and Fideler Discovery Sheets, Volume 1, pages 49-52 for additional activities.

Index

Explanation of abbreviations used in this Index: p — picture   m — map

Adirondack Mountains, 22-23, 33, 35, 41, 95, 122; p 22-23; m 14
Albany, New York, 42, 49, 50, 122; m 50
Alcott, Louisa May, 75
Allegheny River, 22; p 57; m 13
Amish, 88; p 88-89
Appalachian Highlands, 20-25, 122; p 20-25; m 14
Appalachian Plateau, 21-22, 93; p 20-21; m 14
Appalachian Ridges and Valleys, 21; m 14
arts, 56, 72-77
  in colonial times, 73
  literature, 75-77; p 76
  music, 74-75, 77; p 77
  painting, 73-74, 77; p 72-74
Atlantic Ocean, 13, 15, 16, 28, 117; p 35; m 121
Baldwin, James, 76-77; p 76
Baltimore, Maryland, 18, 41, 51, 56-57, 124, 127; m 13, 50; chart 51
Bancroft, George, 75
Berkshire Hills, 36-37
Blue Ridge, 20; m 14
Boothbay Harbor, Maine, p 12-13
Boston, Massachusetts, 15, 41, 51, 55-56, 73, 100, 124, 126; p 48-49; m 13, 50; chart 51
Boston Latin School, 55
Brooke, Senator Edward, 47
Bryant, William Cullen, 75
Buddhism, 47
Buffalo, New York, 18, 42, 49, 122, 123, 124; m 13, 50

Cabinet, 63; p 63
Cape Cod, Massachusetts, 15; m 13
Capitol, see Washington, D.C.
Carnegie (kär nā′gē), Andrew, 47
Cassatt, Mary, 73
Charles River, 55
Chesapeake Bay, 18, 56, 99, 100; m 13
Chisholm, Shirley, 47
Christianity, 46-47
cities, 48-59; p 10-11, 48-49, 52-54, 57, 58; m 50, 55; chart 51. See also Megalopolis and names of cities
citizenship, 61, 64-66; p 64
climate, 26-37; p 2-3, 26-29, 33, 35-37; m 30-32, 34, 36
  autumn, 26, 36-37; p 36-37
  growing season, 32-33; m 32
  rainfall, 34; m 34
  snowfall, 26, 28, 29; p 26-27
  spring, 26, 29, 32-33; p 28-29
  summer, 26, 33-36; p 33, 35
  temperature, 26-27, 32, 33, 34, 36-37; m 36
  winter, 26-29; p 2-3, 26-27
Coastal Plain, 16, 87; m 14
Congress, 61-62; p 60-61; chart 62
Connecticut, 15-16; p 125; m 13, 50
  cities, p 15; m 50
  farming, 16
  farm products, 16
  industry, 124; p 125; m 122
  land, 15-16; p 15; m 8-9, 13
  rivers, p 15
Connecticut River, 16; p 15; m 13
conservation, 92, 98-99, 113
Constitution, 60-61, 64
continents, 5
Cooper, James Fenimore, 75
cooperation, see great ideas
Copland, Aaron, 77
Copley, John Singleton, 73
Crane, Stephen, 75
Cullen, Countee, 76
Cummings, E.E., 76
Cutler, Maine, 13; m 13

Declaration of Independence, 56
Delaware, m 13, 50
  climate, 28; p 35
  farming, 18, 32, 82-83; p 82
  farm products, 18, 124
  industry, m 122
  land, 17-18; m 8-9, 13
  people, 42
Delaware Bay, 17, 117
Delaware River, 17, 56, 117, 124; m 13, 121
Delmarva Peninsula, 87
democracy, 42, 43, 61
  beliefs in, 65-66
  citizenship in, 64-66
  education in, 65, 66
  responsibilities in, 65, 66
  rights in, 65
  voting in, 61, 64, 65, 66
Dickinson, Emily, 75
discrimination, see social problems
District of Columbia, see Washington, D.C.

Eakins, Thomas, 74
earning a living, see farming, industry, natural resources, and trade
Edison, Thomas, 106
education, 55, 65, 66, 67, 69, 120. See also great ideas
Einstein, Albert, 47; p 47
electricity, see energy, electric
Emerson, Ralph Waldo, 75
energy, 102-113; p 102-105, 109, 111, 112; charts 102, 108
  from coal, 108, 110
  electric, 92, 106-107, 108, 110-111, 113, 117, 120-121
  from gasoline, 102-104, 106, 108, 113; p 102-103
  from natural gas, 108
  nuclear, 107, 111-113; p 78-79, 112
  from oil, 94, 95, 102-104, 106, 108-110; p 109
  problems, 94-95, 102-104, 108, 110-111, 113
  solar, 110-111; p 111
  from steam, 105-106, 117, 120
  from wind and water, 105-107, 110, 117
  See also hydroelectricity and waterpower
equator, 31; m 30, 31
Erie Canal, 42
Erie-Ontario Lowland, 18, 32

Fall Line, 20
farming, 16, 18, 80-89, 96-97, 126-127; p 80-82, 84, 86, 88-89; m 83, 85
  intensive, 83
  mixed, 88-89
  truck, 32, 80-81, 87; p 80-82; m 83
farming methods, 68, 80-81, 82-86, 87, 88-89; p 80-82, 88-89
farmland, 68, 84, 85, 87-89; p 80-82, 88-89
farm products,
  barley, 89
  beef cattle, 81, 86, 89, 126
  corn, 88-89; m 83
  dairy, 16, 18, 19, 21, 83-85, 127; p 84; m 83, 85
  fruit, 16, 19, 32, 81, 82, 87, 126
  hay, 33, 88
  marketing, 81, 83-84, 86, 87, 89
  mushrooms, 89
  oats, 88, 89

PRONUNCIATION KEY: hat, āge, cāre, fär; let, ēqual, tėrm; it, īce; hot, ōpen, ôrder; oil, out; cup, pùt, rüle, ūse; child; long; thin; ᴛHen; zh, measure; ə represents a in about, e in taken, i in pencil, o in lemon, u in circus.

poultry and eggs, 16, 18, 81, 85-86, 126; *p* 86; *m* 85
rye, 89
tobacco, 16, 88-89
vegetables, 16-17, 25, 32-33, 80-81, 87, 126; *p* 80-81
wheat, 88-89; *m* 83
federal government, *see* government, national
fisheries, 13-14, 99-101, 126; *p* 100-101; *graph* 100
forest products, 97-98; *p* 98
forests, 90, 96-99, 120; *p* 96-97; *m* 99
Foster, Stephen, 74
Franklin, Benjamin, 56
freedom, *see* great ideas
Freedom Trail, 56
Frost, Robert, 75-76; *p* 76

Gershwin, George, 77
glaciers (glā'shərz), 22-24
global view, 4-11; *p* 10-11; *m* 6-9; *chart* 4-5
Gloucester, Massachusetts, 100-101; *m* 50
Golden Triangle, 57; *p* 57
government, 60-71; *p* 60-61, 63, 64, 68, 70; *chart* 62
   courts, 63-64
   departments and agencies, 62-63; *chart* 62
   history, 60
   laws, 60, 61, 62, 63, 64, 65; *chart* 62
   national government, 7, 60-64; *p* 60-61, 63; *chart* 62
   president, 62; *p* 60-61; *chart* 62
   problems of, 67-71; *p* 68, 70
   state government, 61
   vice-president, 62
great ideas,
   cooperation, *p* 10-11
   division of labor, *p* 126
   education, *p* 46
   exchange, *p* 128
   freedom, *p* 44
   language, *p* 76
   rules and government, *p* 60-61
   using natural resources, *p* 90-91, 111; *m* 34
Great Lakes, *m* 121
Great Lakes-St. Lawrence Waterway, *m* 121
Great Valley, 21
Green Mountains, 24-25; *p* 2-3, 24-25
Guggenheim Museum, *p* 72-73

Hartford, Connecticut, *p* 15; *m* 50
Harvard University, 55
Haverhill, Massachusetts, 14; *m* 50

Hawthorne, Nathaniel, 75
history, 40-41, 42-45, 60; *p* 104-105
Homer, Winslow, 74
House of Representatives, *see* Congress
Hudson-Mohawk Lowland, 19, 51
Hudson River, 19; *p* 52-53; *m* 13
Hughes, Langston, 76
hydroelectricity, 14, 106-107, 120-121, 124; *p* 90-91; *chart* 107. *See also* **waterpower**

immigrants, 42-45, 51; *p* 42-43
immigration, *see* immigrants
Independence Hall, 56
industry, 99-101, 114-128; *p* 68, 114-116, 118-120, 123, 125, 126; *m* 122
   aircraft, 124
   areas, 122; *m* 122
   automotive, 124
   capital for, 114, 117-118
   chemicals, 56, 57, 124
   clothing, 54, 55, 56, 124-126; *p* 126
   development of, 114, 118, 124-125
   electronic, 57, 120; *p* 64, 123
   fishing, 99-101; *p* 100-101; *graph* 100
   food-processing, 56, 57, 126-127
   glass, 57
   iron and steel, 56, 57, 114-117, 122-123; *p* 68, 114-116
   machinery, 55, 123-124
   metals, 56-57, 124; *p* 125
   mining, 92-95; *p* 92
   oil refining, 56, 124; *p* 120
   pollution problems, 92
   printing and publishing, 55, 124
   raw materials for, 117, 120, 121, 124
   shipbuilding, 56, 124
   textile, 50-51, 124-125; *p* 126
   tourist, 99
   transportation equipment, 124
inflation, *see* social problems
Inness, George, 73; *p* 74
Irving, Washington, 75
Islam, 47
Ives, Charles, 77

Jews, 47
John F. Kennedy International Airport, 54; *m* 55

Kennedy, John F., 47

labor unions, 70
La Guardia (lə gwär'dē ə) Airport, 16; *m* 55

Lake Champlain, 19; *m* 13
Lake Erie, 29, 93; *m* 13, 121
Lake Ontario, 29; *m* 13, 121
Lake Superior, 123; *m* 121
Lancaster County, Pennsylvania, 88-89; *p* 88-89
land, 12-25; *p* 2-3, 12-13, 15-25; *m* 13, 14
   highlands, 20-25; *p* 20-25; *m* 13, 14
   lowlands, 12, 13-19, 28-29; *p* 12-13, 15-19; *m* 13, 14
Lawrence, Massachusetts, 14; *m* 50
Liberty Bell, 56
Longfellow, Henry Wadsworth, 75
Long Island, 16, 32,33, 85, 87; *m* 13, 55
Long Island Sound, 16, 99; *m* 13
Lowell, Amy, 76
Lowell, Massachusetts, 14, 51; *m* 50

MacDowell, Edward, 74
McKay, Claude, 76
Maine, 13-14; *p* 12-13, 100-101; *m* 13, 50
   cities, 13, 14; *m* 50
   farming, 25, 87
   fisheries, 13-14, 100; *p* 100-101; *graph* 100
   forests, 96-97
   land, 13-14, 25; *p* 12-13; *m* 8-9
   minerals, 95
   people, 41
Malamud, Bernard, 77
Marin, John, 77
Marquand, John, 76
Maryland, 18, 58; *m* 13, 50
   cities, 18, 41; *m* 50; *chart* 51
   climate, 28
   farming, 32, 86,87
   fisheries, 100; *graph* 100
   industry, 124, 126; *m* 122
   land, 17-18; *m* 8-9, 13
   people, 41
Massachusetts, 14-15; *m* 13, 50
   cities, 14-15, 41; *p* 48-49; *m* 50; *chart* 51
   climate, 36-37
   farming, 87
   fisheries, 99, 100-101; *graph* 100
   industry, 14; *m* 122
   land, 14-15; *m* 8-9, 13
   people, 41
Massachusetts Bay, 55
Megalopolis (meg'ə lop'ə lis), 41, 49, 55; *m* 50
Melville, Herman, 75
Menotti, Gian-Carlo, 47
Merrimack River, 14; *m* 13
Middle Atlantic Lowlands, 16-18
Middle Atlantic states, 7

migration, p 42-43
Milky Way, 4
minerals, 92-95
  bauxite, 120
  clay, 95
  coal, 22, 41, 57, 90, 93-95, 106, 108, 110, 117, 121, 122, 123, 124; p 92-93; m 93
  copper, 95, 124
  granite, 95
  iron ore, 95, 117, 120, 123; m 94
  limestone, 90, 95, 117, 120, 123; m 94
  marble, 95
  natural gas, 94, 95, 106, 108, 120, 122, 124; m 94
  oil, 95, 106, 108, 120, 124; p 109; m 94
  salt, 95, 120
  sand and gravel, 95
  uranium, 111, 113
  zinc, 95
mining, 68. See also minerals
Mohawk River, 19; m 13
Monongahela River, 22; p 57; m 13
Moore, Marianne, 76; p 76
Moses, Anna Mary ("Grandma"), 77
mountains, see land, highlands
Mount Washington, 25

Narragansett Bay, 15
Nassau-Suffolk, Long Island, chart 51
natural resources, 90-113. See also fisheries, forests, minerals, and water
needs of people 67; p 54
New Bedford, Massachusetts, 100; m 50
New England, 7, 13-16, 44, 118, 120, 124-125; p 12-13
New Hampshire, 122; m 13, 50
  climate, 26-27
  land, 25; m 8-9, 13
  people, 41
New Jersey, m 13, 50
  cities, 17; m 50; chart 51
  farming, 17, 32, 80-81, 87
  farm products, 17
  fisheries, 99-100; graph 100
  industry, 124, 126; m 122
  land, 16-17; m 8-9, 13
  minerals, 95
  people, 42
New York City, 7, 16, 19, 41, 52-55, 73, 74, 76, 108, 117, 124; p 1, 16-17, 44, 52-54, 72-73, 102-103, 127; m 13, 50, 55
  banking, 54-55
  climate, 33-34; p 26-27, 33
  harbor, 52-53, 54; p 16-17, 127
  industry, 54-55, 124, 125-126
  people, 53-54; p 38-41, 45, 77
  trade, 54
  transportation, 54
New York State, 16, 18-19, 122; p 22-23; m 13, 50
  cities, 16, 18, 29, 33, 41, 42, 45, 47, 49, 52-55; p 26-27, 33, 52-54, 102-103; m 50; chart 51
  climate, 29
  farming, 85, 87
  fisheries, 99-100; graph 100
  forests, 98; p 98
  industry, 124; m 122
  land, 16, 18-19; m 8-9, 13
  minerals, 95
  people, 41, 42, 45, 47
  rivers, 19
New York State Barge Canal, 19, 122; m 121
Niagara Falls, 18, 124; p 18-19, 90-91
Niagara River, 18; m 13, 121
North America, 5-6; m 6

oceans, 5
O'Hara, John, 76
Ohio River, 41, 90; p 57; m 13, 121
Old State House, 56
O'Neill, Eugene, 75; p 76

Paine, Thomas, 73
Parkman, Francis, 75
Patapsco River, 56
Pawtucket, Rhode Island, 51; m 50
Peale, Charles Willson, 73
Pennsylvania, 122, 123; m 13, 50
  cities, 22, 41; p 10-11, 57; m 50; chart 51
  farming, 85, 86, 87, 88-89; p 80-81, 88-89
  industry, 22, 41, 114, 116, 117, 123, 124, 126; m 122
  land, 20-22; m 8-9, 13
  minerals, 22, 41, 93, 95, 121; p 92-93
  people, 41, 42, 45
people, 40-47. See also social problems
petroleum, see minerals, oil
Philadelphia, Pennsylvania, 41, 51, 56, 60, 124; p 10-11; m 50; chart 51
Piedmont Plateau, 20, 86, 89; m 14
Pittsburgh, Pennsylvania, 22, 41, 49, 50, 57, 123; p 57; m 13, 50; chart 51
planets, 4; chart 4-5
Poe, Edgar Allan, 75
Point Judith, Rhode Island, 100; m 50
pollution, 92
population, 7, 40-42, 122
  density, m 50
  distribution, 40-42; m 41
Portland, Maine, 14, 100; m 13, 50
ports, 14, 15, 16, 18, 41, 44, 49-51, 53-57, 127; p 16-17, 104-105, 127; m 121
Potomac River, 59; m 59
president, see government
Protestants, 47

recessions, 67
recreation, 16, 23, 25, 99; p 2-3, 22-23, 35
religion, 46-47, 73
Revolutionary War, 60, 73
Rhode Island, 15; m 13, 50
  fisheries, 100; graph 100
  industry, m 122
  land, 15; m 8-9, 13
Richter, Conrad, 76
rivers, m 121. See also names of rivers
Roberts, Kenneth, 76
Robinson, Edwin Arlington, 76
Rochester, New York, 42, 49; m 50
Roman Catholics, 46
rules and government, see great ideas

St. Lawrence Seaway, m 121
St. Lawrence Valley, 19; m 14
seasons of the year, 30-31; m 30-31
Senate, see Congress
shipbuilding, 124
Sills, Beverly, p 77
skiing, p 2-3
social problems, 67-71
  crime, 67
  depressed areas, 67-68
  discrimination, 68, 69
  illness and handicaps, 67
  inflation, 67, 69-71
  jobs, 67, 68-69
  lack of education, 67, 69
  recessions, 67
  unemployment, 67, 68, 69
  unsuccessful communities, 67
solar system, 4; chart 4-5
sports, p 2-3. See also recreation

PRONUNCIATION KEY: hat, āge, cāre, fär; let, ēqual, tėrm; it, īce; hot, ōpen, ôrder; oil, out; cup, put, rüle, ūse; child; long; thin; ᴛHen; zh, measure; ə represents a in about, e in taken, i in pencil, o in lemon, u in circus.

standard of living, 107
Statue of Liberty, *p* 44
Stevens, Wallace, 76
stocks, 114, 118
Stuart, Gilbert, 73
Supreme Court, *see* United States Supreme Court
Syracuse, New York, 42, 49; *m* 50

textiles, 14. *See also* industry
Thoreau, Henry David, 75
trade, 19, 49-51, 54, 127-128; *p* 70, 127, 128
transportation, 19, 22, 40, 51, 54, 121, 122, 123
  problems, 21, 28
  waterways, 19, 42; *m* 121
Tropic of Cancer, 30; *m* 30, 31
Tropic of Capricorn, 30; *m* 30, 31
Trumbull, John, 73

United Nations, 11
United States, 6-7; *m* 7-9

conterminous, 7; *m* 7
See also government
United States Supreme Court, 63-64; *chart* 62
universe, 4
Utica, New York, 42; *m* 50

Vermont, *m* 13, 50
  climate, *p* 36-37
  forests, 98
  land, 19, 24-25; *p* 24-25; *m* 8-9, 13
  minerals, 95
vice-president, *see* government

Wall Street, 55
Washington, D.C., 7, 41, 58-59, 122; *p* 31; *m* 13, 59
  Capitol, 61-62; *m* 59
  climate, 29; *p* 28-29
  history, 59
  land, 18, 20; *m* 8-9, 13
  Pennsylvania Avenue, 62; *m* 59
  people, 41

White House, 62; *p* 58; *m* 59
Washington, George, 59, 73
water, 90-92, 105; *p* 90-91
  pollution, 92
  See also waterpower
waterpower, 14, 18, 20, 121; *p* 90-91; *chart* 107. *See also* hydroelectricity
waterways, *see* transportation
West Virginia, *m* 13, 50
  farming, 85, 86, 87, 89
  industry, 124, 126; *m* 122
  land, 22; *m* 8-9, 13
  minerals, 22, 93-95, 117, 121
  people, 45
Whistler, James McNeill, 73
White House, *see* Washington, D.C.
White Mountains, 25, 26-27
Whitman, Walt, 75
Whittier, John Greenleaf, 75
Williams, William Carlos, 76
Wyeth, Andrew, 77
Wyoming, 62

Acknowledgments

Grateful acknowledgment is made to the following for permission to use the illustrations found in this book:

A. Devaney, Inc.: Pages 92-93
Alpha Photo Associates, Inc.: Pages 28-29; page 112 by J. Zimmerman
Bethlehem Steel: Pages 114-115
Black Star: Pages 60-61 by Dennis Brack
Cyr Color Photo Agency: Page 98
De Wys, Inc.: Pages 46, 70, and 126
Frederic Lewis: Page 33 by Alon Reininger
Freelance Photographers Guild: Pages 36-37 and 102-103; pages 40-41 by Ward Allan Howe; page 58 by Werner Stoy
Gene Ahrens: Pages 12-13 and 22-23
Glass Image: Pages 38-39 by J. Glab
Grant Heilman: Pages 78-79, 80-81, 82, 84, and 86
Grumman Energy Systems: Page 111
H. Armstrong Roberts: Pages 44, 64, 68, 88-89, 96-97, and 123
Hartford Chamber of Commerce: Page 15
Historical Pictures Service: Pages 42-43
James H. Pickerell: Page 77
Joan Kramer and Associates: Pages 26-27
Killington Ski Resort: Pages 2-3
Knox College Library: Pages 104-105

New York State Department of Commerce: Pages 18-19
Pennsylvania Bureau of Travel Development: Page 57
Philadelphia Convention and Visitors Bureau: Pages 10-11
Photo Researchers, Inc.: Pages 72-73; page 128 by Van Bucher
Photo Trends: Pages 24-25
Rapho Guillumette Pictures: Page 127 by Jan Lukas
Sanford Associates: Pages 100-101
Shostal Associates, Inc.: Pages 16-17, 20-21, 45, 48-49, 52-53, 54, 90-91, and 118-119
Sohio: Page 109
Texaco: Page 120 by J. Motiekaitis
The Bettmann Archive: Page 47
The National Gallery of Art, Washington, D.C.: Page 74, painting by George Inness
The White House: Page 63
United States Industrials Chemical Co.: Page 125
Wide World Photos: Page 76 (all)
Williams: Page 35
Zentrale Farbbild Agentur: Page 1 by Kurt Goebel

Grateful acknowledgment is made to Scott, Foresman and Company for the pronunciation system used in this book, which is taken from the Thorndike-Barnhart Dictionary Series. Grateful acknowledgment is made to the following for permission to use cartographic data in this book: Creative Arts: Pages 30 and 31; Base maps courtesy of the Nystrom Raised Relief Map Company, Chicago 60618: Page 14; Rand McNally & Company: Pages 6 and 8-9; United States Department of Commerce: Bureau of the Census: Pages 41 and 85.

THE SOUTH

Miami, Florida. Miami is in the southern part of Florida, on the Atlantic coast.

† Use these questions to start students thinking about the land and climate of the South.

Part 1
Land and Climate

In the southern part of our country is a large area known as the South. Imagine that you are taking a trip to learn what this part of our country is like. You would see low plains near the blue waters of the Atlantic Ocean and the Gulf of Mexico. In other parts of the South you would see rolling plateaus and rich farmlands. You would also see beautiful forest-covered mountains and deep, green valleys.

During your trip, you would discover many differences in climate in this large area of our country. For example, in winter, you might go skiing in the higher mountains of Virginia. A few days later, you might go swimming in the waters off the coast of Florida.

As you read about the South, try to find answers to the following questions:

†
- How many states are there in the South? What are their names?
- What are the four main land regions of the South?
- How does the climate differ from one part of the South to another?

Use Fideler Discovery Cards 10-36.

In the Blue Ridge section of North Carolina. This mountainous part of the South is in the Appalachian Highlands region of our country. What is the climate like in the Blue Ridge?

2 The South

The Milky Way is a great galaxy of stars in the shape of a pinwheel. Our solar system is located in one arm of the pinwheel. What kinds of heavenly bodies make up our solar system?

1 A Global View

The Milky Way

When you look at the sky on a clear night, you see hundreds of stars shining against the deep blackness of space. These stars are part of a huge star system, or galaxy, called the Milky Way.

The Milky Way is one of billions of separate galaxies scattered through the vast, nearly empty space of the universe. Each of these galaxies is made up of billions of stars and other heavenly bodies.

Call attention to the picture and caption above. Have a student answer the question. Then use Fideler Discovery Sheets, Volume 1, pages 1-4 to guide students in making discoveries about our planet.

A spiral galaxy

As the painting at left shows, the Milky Way has a spiral shape like that of a pinwheel. In one arm of the pinwheel is our own star, the sun, together with the earth and the other heavenly bodies that make up our solar system.

† Our sun

Our sun, like the other stars in the universe, is a huge, whirling ball of burning gases. The other parts of our solar system are balls of fairly solid material that revolve around the sun. These include nine main planets. Some of the main planets, such as our earth, have one or more moons. Our solar system also has thousands of small planets, called asteroids, that circle the sun between Mars and Jupiter.

The nine main planets are different in size and in distance from the sun. The time it takes for each of them to go around the sun is also different. Our earth makes this trip around the sun once each year. Our moon circles the earth about once each month.

An envelope of air

Pictures of the sunlit earth taken from far out in space show that the curving surface of our planet is partly hidden by a layer of white clouds. These clouds are part of the atmosphere, which is the precious envelope of air around our planet. Without this envelope of air, people could not live on the earth. The atmosphere provides the oxygen* we breathe. It protects us by night from the bitter cold of outer space. It also protects us by day from the burning rays of the sun. If there were no atmosphere to hold moisture, there would be no rain on the earth. Plants could not live, and without plants there could be no animal life. Plants provide food for human beings and other animals. They also put back into the air the oxygen we use up. Thus, the atmosphere is our planet's greatest treasure.

The earth's surface

Pictures of the earth taken from far out in space also show the shining blue waters of the earth's great oceans and seas. These waters cover about three fourths of the earth's surface. The largest areas of land on the earth are called continents. The earth's six continents, together with its many islands, make up about one fourth of the surface of our planet.

If we were to fly over the continents, we would not see any boundary lines. We could not tell where one country ends and another begins. On maps, boundary lines are drawn to show where different countries are located. Sometimes, a boundary may follow a physical feature such as a river or a mountain range. Boundaries are made by agreements, or treaties, among the different countries. As new agreements are made, boundaries change. Sometimes the changes are very great, but often they are small.

North America

The continent of North America is where most of our country, the United States, is located. The map on page 6 shows us the boundary lines between the different countries of North America. We can see that our closest neighbors are Canada and Mexico.

*See Glossary

† Use Fideler Discovery Card 6 (Explore the Sun).

† Refer students to the map on page 9. Have them identify and locate the states of the South.

There are fifty states in the United States. Two of these, Alaska and Hawaii, are separated from all the others. Alaska, like most of our country, is on the continent of North America. Hawaii, however, is an island state in the Pacific Ocean. (See map below.) The part of our country that is made up of the other forty-eight states is called the conterminous* United States.

† **The South**

The states in the conterminous United States may be divided into groups. One of these is the South, which is made up of eleven states in the southeastern part of our country. These states are Alabama, Arkansas, Florida, Georgia, Kentucky, Louisiana, Mississippi, North Carolina, South Carolina, Tennessee, and Virginia. The South is bordered on the east by the Atlantic Ocean, and on the south by the Gulf of Mexico.

Great changes in the South

At the beginning of the 1900's, the South was not as well off as most other parts of the United States. More than half of the people earned their living

The United States

This map shows the location of the fifty states that make up our country. Two of these, Alaska and Hawaii, are separated from the others. Alaska is in the far northern part of North America. Hawaii is an island state in the Pacific Ocean. The other forty-eight states form the part of our country known as the conterminous* United States.

6 The South

The states in the conterminous United States may be divided into five main groups. These are the Northeast, the South, the Midwest, the Great Plains states, and the West. Sometimes the Midwest and the Great Plains states are combined into one group, known as the Midwest and Great Plains. Compare the map at right with the large map on pages 8-9. Then list the states in each of the five main groups.

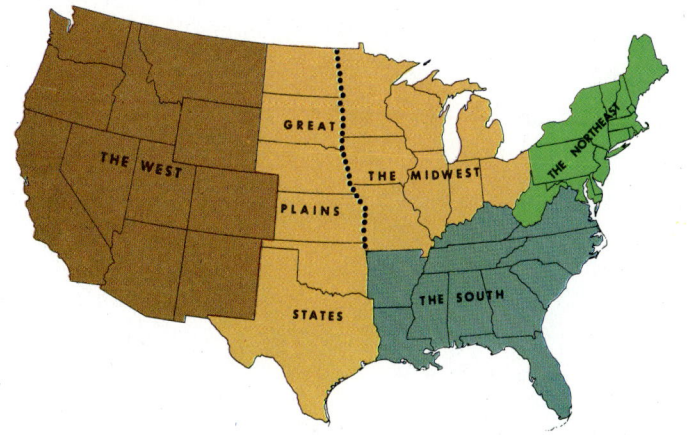

by farming. There were few factories. Most manufactured goods came from northern states, where there was more industry. Nearly all of the South's main crop, cotton, was shipped to other parts of the country to be made into cloth.

Today, improved ways of farming and new industries have brought the South a better way of life. Many different products come from its farms and factories. Crops such as soybeans and peanuts are grown, as well as cotton and tobacco.* Furniture, paper, textiles,* and many other goods are made in the South and sold throughout the country. In exchange, the South buys things that other states sell. In the chapters that follow, you will learn more about the South. You will also learn many things about the people who make their homes in this important part of our country.

Modern office buildings near the city of Atlanta, Georgia. Since 1900, business and industry have been growing rapidly in the South.

Using Natural Resources

See Great Ideas

Nature has given the South many valuable resources. Among these are sunshine, rich soil, and plenty of rainfall.
1. How did colonists in the South use these resources during the early days of our country?
2. What are some of the ways in which the people of the South use these resources today?

Chapters 3 and 8, as well as this chapter, will help you discover answers to these questions.

† Use this problem to start students thinking about the land features of the South.

2 Land

A Problem To Solve †
The South has many different kinds of land features. How do these features affect the people who live in the South? The following questions suggest hypotheses* you may need to make to solve this problem.
1. How do the land features of the South affect the way people earn a living?
2. How do the land features help to determine where people live?

The chapters in Part 3 of this book, as well as this chapter, will help you solve this problem.

See Skills Manual, "Thinking and Solving Problems"

If you were to fly over the South in an airplane, you would see that all parts of it are not alike. You would notice that some areas are low and almost level. In other parts of the South, you would see plateaus and rolling hills. The South also has forest-covered mountains and deep valleys.

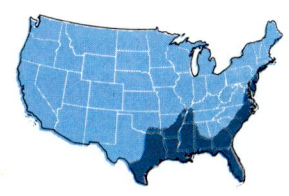

The Coastal Plain

The picture above shows farmers harvesting rice on the Coastal Plain in Arkansas. More than half of the South lies in the huge Coastal Plain region, which borders the Atlantic Ocean and the Gulf of Mexico. (See map at right.) Much of the Coastal Plain is low and level. In other parts of the South, there are rolling plateaus, wooded mountains, and deep valleys.

More than half of the South lies in a large region of the United States called the Coastal Plain. The map on page 13 shows us that this region stretches along most of the Atlantic coast of our country. In the north, the Coastal Plain

*See Glossary

The South 11

† Refer to the map on the opposite page. Have students identify the states of the South which lie in the Coastal Plain.

† is narrow. Farther south, it becomes wider. It spreads out westward along the Gulf of Mexico. The map also shows us that part or all of every state in the South lies in the Coastal Plain.

Near the sea

The Coastal Plain is low and flat near the sea. Sandy beaches stretch for miles along parts of the coast. Many very low areas are covered with water much of the time. Some of these areas are freshwater swamps. Others are covered with salt water. Where the land is not so wet, there are huge forests of pine trees. In some places, there are fields of vegetables, rice, sugarcane, or other crops.

Jacksonville, Florida, is on the Coastal Plain of the South. The St. Johns River flows through the city. Many broad, winding rivers flow across the Coastal Plain. They empty into the Atlantic Ocean or the Gulf of Mexico. Most of the South's large port cities are in the Coastal Plain region.

LAND REGIONS
- COASTAL PLAIN
- APPALACHIAN HIGHLANDS
  1. The Piedmont Plateau
  2. Blue Ridge
  3. Appalachian Ridges and Valleys
  4. Appalachian Plateau
  5. New England Lowlands
  6. New England Highlands
  7. Adirondack Mountains
  8. St. Lawrence Valley
- INTERIOR PLAINS
- INTERIOR HIGHLANDS
  9. Ozark Plateau
  10. Arkansas Valley
  11. Ouachita Mountains
- SUPERIOR UPLAND
- The South

Farther inland

Farther inland, the Coastal Plain rises higher above sea* level and becomes gently rolling. The light, sandy soil of this area is good for growing such crops as corn, tobacco,* and peanuts.

Along the rivers

Many broad, muddy rivers wind across the Coastal Plain on their way to the Atlantic Ocean or the Gulf of Mexico. They carry soil that rainwater has washed away from the land farther upstream. Time after time, these rivers have overflowed their banks and left some of this soil on the flooded land. For this reason, much of the land along the rivers is covered with a deep layer of rich, dark soil. Cotton and other crops grow well on these rich lowlands.

Some of the largest cities in the South have grown up near the mouths of rivers or along bays on the seacoast. Here there are fine harbors where ships from many parts of the world can come to load and unload their freight.

The South 13

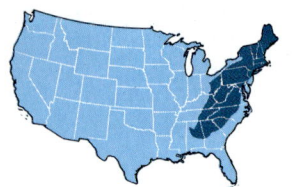

The Appalachian Highlands

The Appalachian Highlands region of our country stretches from central Georgia and Alabama northeast to Canada. (Compare maps on pages 9 and 13.) In this region are mountains, plateaus, and valleys. The land here is higher and more rugged than the land in the Coastal Plain region. In the South, the Appalachian Highlands region is divided into four sections.† These are the Piedmont Plateau, the Blue Ridge, the Appalachian Ridges and Valleys, and the Appalachian Plateau.

The Piedmont Plateau

Most of the Piedmont Plateau section of the Appalachian Highlands lies in the South. The name of this broad, rolling plateau means "foot of the mountain." The Piedmont rises gently upward from east to west. In some places, the Piedmont is more than 125 miles (200 km.)† wide. (See map on page 13.)

An important farming region

The Piedmont Plateau has some of the South's best farmland. Fields of cotton, soybeans, and other crops cover much of the land. In order to have good harvests, however, Piedmont farmers must use up-to-date ways of farming. They must use contour plowing and add fertilizer to the soil. (See page 93.)

In earlier times, many farmers in the South did not know how to keep the land fertile* so that it would grow large crops. In some parts of the Piedmont Plateau, the topsoil has been worn

† km. means kilometer

† Locate these four sections of the Appalachian Highlands region on the map on page 13.

This picture shows hikers in the Appalachian Highlands. In the South, the Appalachian Highlands region is divided into four sections. These are the Piedmont Plateau, the Blue Ridge, the Appalachian Ridges and Valleys, and the Appalachian Plateau. The South's highest mountains are in the Blue Ridge. Some of the peaks rise more than 6,000 feet (1,829 m.)†above sea level.

†m. means meter

Use this picture to make discoveries about the Appalachian Highlands. In which of the four parts of the Appalachian Highlands do you think this picture was taken? (Appalachian Ridges and Valleys.)

† Why did cities grow up along the Fall Line? List five or more cities that grew up along the Fall Line. Use the map on page 17.

out or washed away. In areas where this has happened, the land can no longer be used for growing crops. Forests, orchards, and pastures now cover many of these areas.

The Fall Line

Many swift rivers cross the Piedmont as they flow toward the Atlantic Ocean or the Gulf of Mexico. Rapids and waterfalls are formed as these rivers drop from the plateau onto the Coastal Plain. For this reason, the border between the Piedmont Plateau and Coastal Plain is called the Fall Line. The map on page 17 shows this line. By comparing this map with the map on page 9, you can see that the Fall Line stretches all the way from New Jersey to central Alabama.

The drawing below shows that the land of the Coastal Plain rises gently upward from the ocean to the Piedmont Plateau. In most places along the Fall Line, there is not much difference in elevation between the Piedmont and the Coastal Plain. In places where rivers flow from the plateau to the plain, the elevation drops sharply. The drawing also helps to explain how rapids and waterfalls were formed at these places. Under the surface soil of the Piedmont is hard rock. However, the Coastal Plain is made up of soft sand and clay. Rivers flowing to the sea carry away much more soil from the plain than from the plateau. Through the years, these rivers have carved valleys in the plain, almost down to sea level. Near the ocean, where the land is low, the valleys are not very deep. Farther inland, however, where the land slopes upward, the valleys are deeper. As the rivers drop from the rocky Piedmont into these valleys, they form rapids and waterfalls.

Cities grow along the Fall Line

During the early days of our country, settlers went upstream from the coast by boat. They were stopped by the falls and rapids at the Fall Line. Here the settlers had to unload their goods. Many of them settled nearby. Later, people in settlements along the Fall Line found that they could use the power of the falling water to run machines in mills and factories. Some of the early settlements that started on rivers along the Fall Line have grown into important cities. (See map on page 17.)

†

Today there are many electric* power plants along the Fall Line and on the Piedmont Plateau. They produce electricity for homes and factories. More factories are found here than in any other part of the South.

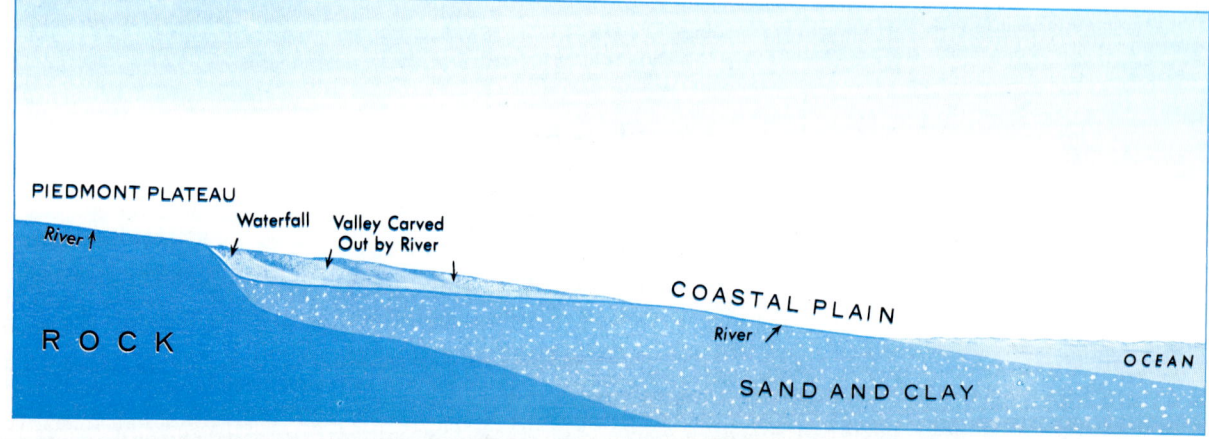

Exploring Waterways

A network of water highways connects the South with other parts of our country and the world. Boats and barges carry freight along the Atlantic and Gulf coasts by way of the Intracoastal Waterway. Freight is also shipped up and down the Ohio, the Mississippi, and other rivers. By using rivers and canals, boats can travel between the Gulf of Mexico and the Great Lakes. The South has several important seaports, such as New Orleans and Norfolk. Memphis and Louisville are leading river ports.

Refer students to the map and key above. Have them list the main rivers that flow from the Fall Line to the ocean.

† Refer students to the map on page 17. Have them locate the cities of Chattanooga and Knoxville, Tennessee on the map.

The Blue Ridge

From northern Georgia into southern Pennsylvania, ranges of forest-covered mountains overlook the Piedmont Plateau. Because its wooded slopes often appear blue from a distance, this chain of mountain ranges is called the Blue Ridge. These mountains are millions of years old. Through the years, wind and water have rounded the tops of the mountains and smoothed their sides.

The map on page 13 shows that the southern part of the Blue Ridge Mountains is wider than the northern part. On the Tennessee-North Carolina border, the Blue Ridge is about 70 miles (113 km.) wide. Here are the Great Smoky Mountains, the Black Mountains, and several other mountain ranges. Mount Mitchell, in the Black Mountains, is the highest peak in the South. It rises to 6,684 feet (2,037 m.) above sea level.

Thick forests cover the mountains

Most mountain sides in the Blue Ridge are too steep for farming. They are covered with thick forests of oak, walnut, and other hardwood* trees. However, many small farms lie in the valleys between the mountains.

When our country was being settled, people moving west into Kentucky and Tennessee found it hard to cross the Blue Ridge. These mountains still make transportation difficult here. It is hard to build roads and railroads through this rugged area.

The Appalachian Ridges and Valleys

West of the Blue Ridge is an area of many ridges and valleys. This section is called the Appalachian Ridges and Valleys. It is shown on the map on page 13. The most important part of this section is a long chain of river valleys known as the Great Valley. In the South, most of the land in the Great Valley is flat or gently rolling, and the soil is very rich. A patchwork* of farms, meadows, and orchards covers the countryside. Flowing through different parts of the Great Valley are several large rivers, such as the Shenandoah, the Tennessee, and the Coosa.

Cities and towns

There are many cities and towns in the Great Valley. Among the largest are Chattanooga and Knoxville, both in Tennessee. Important highways and railroads run along the valley floor. Electric power is produced by dams and power plants that have been built on rivers in the valley. Factories in Chattanooga and other cities use much of this power in making chemicals,* textiles,* and many other products.

West of the Great Valley are long, parallel ridges. The steep sides of these ridges are blanketed with forests. Between the ridges are narrow valleys that are used for farming.

The Appalachian Plateau

A large highland area lies west of the Appalachian Ridges and Valleys. This is the Appalachian Plateau. (See map on page 13.) Most of this section of the South is called the Cumberland Plateau.

The Appalachian Plateau slopes downward from east to west. If you were to look down at the plateau from an airplane flying high above it, the surface of the land would appear

†† Have students locate the Appalachian Plateau on the map on page 13.

The **Great Valley** is part of the Appalachian Ridges and Valleys section of the Appalachian Highlands. Much of the land in the Great Valley is flat or gently rolling. Several large rivers flow through this part of the South. Douglas Dam, shown above, is on a branch of the Tennessee River.

smooth. If you were to fly lower, however, you could see the thousands of valleys that have been cut into the plateau. Long ago, the surface of the plateau was smooth. As time passed, however, rushing streams and rivers carved out narrow, steep-sided valleys.

A poor farming area

In most of the Appalachian Plateau section of the South, the land is not good for farming. Forests of oak, hickory, and other hardwoods cover some of the more rugged areas. There are small fields of corn and tobacco in the narrow valleys. However, much soil has been washed away by rain or worn out by careless farming. The land no longer produces good crops. For this reason, many farmers in this section of the South are very poor.

Few towns or factories

If you were to take a trip through the Appalachian Plateau, you would not see many large towns. There are few factories. This area has rich coal deposits, but most of the coal mined here is sent by rail to other parts of our country. There are few highways, for the deep valleys make it hard to build good roads.

Change and Continuity

The picture above shows a farm in the Bluegrass of Kentucky. Farming has been important in the South since the days when the first settlers arrived. Today, the land in many parts of this region still looks much as it did long ago. For example, much of the Bluegrass is still covered with rich pastureland where horses and cattle may graze. What are some of the ways in which people have changed the land in other areas of the South? Information in Chapters 5, 8, 9, and 10 will help you answer this question.

Have students read the caption above, and do research in this book to answer the question.

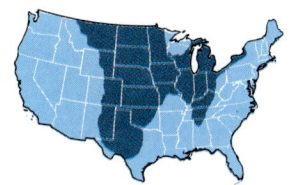

The Interior Plains

West of the Appalachian Plateau is an area of hilly land that extends southward across Kentucky and Tennessee and into northern Alabama. This area of the South is lower than the Appalachian Plateau, but it is not as low as the Coastal Plain. It is part of a huge region in the central part of our country known as the Interior Plains. (See map on page 13.)

Two important lowlands

There are two important lowlands within the Interior Plains region of the South. These are the Bluegrass in northern Kentucky and the Nashville Basin in Tennessee. In these areas, much of the land is flat or gently rolling, and the soil is very good for growing crops. In the summer, green fields of tobacco cover much of the Bluegrass. There are also many large pastures where cattle and horses graze on the rich bluegrass* that gives this area its name. In the Nashville Basin are many dairy and tobacco farms.

Hills and valleys

The rest of the Interior Plains region in the South is hillier than the Bluegrass and the Nashville Basin. Also, the soil is not as rich. Much of the land is wooded, but there are fields of corn and tobacco in the valleys and on many of the hillsides.

The South

The Interior Highlands

The northwestern part of Arkansas is in a region of our country called the Interior Highlands. This region stretches from the Mississippi and Missouri rivers southwest into eastern Oklahoma. The mountains and plateaus in this region are not as high as those in the Appalachian Highlands.

The Ozark Plateau

The northern part of the Interior Highlands is known as the Ozark Plateau. (See map on page 13.) In Arkansas, farm fields and forests cover the broad, rolling hills of this area. There are also orchards of peach and apple trees. Along the southern edge of the Ozark Plateau are steep ridges separated by deep river valleys. These ridges are called the Boston Mountains.

The Ouachita Mountains

In the southern part of the Interior Highlands region are the Ouachita Mountains. They reach from east to west across part of Arkansas and into Oklahoma. (See map on page 13.) The highest peaks in the Ouachita range are only about 2,800 feet (853 m.) above sea level. Most of the mountain sides are covered with thick forests of hardwood trees. Lumbering is important in this area.

The Arkansas Valley

Between the Ozark Plateau and the Ouachita Mountains is a narrow lowland called the Arkansas Valley. (See map on page 13.) Here the land is gently rolling, and the soil is good for growing crops. In the Arkansas Valley are many fields of cotton, strawberries, and other crops.

Fishing on the White River, in the Interior Highlands. The three main areas of the Interior Highlands extend through part of the South. What are the names of these areas and where are they?

Share New Understandings

Imagine that you have a pen pal in another country and that you want to tell your friend about the main land regions of the South. Do research in this book to discover the most important land and water features of each of the South's regions. Then write your pen pal a letter. Describe what you might see if you were to take a trip through these regions. Be sure to use words that will create pictures in your friend's mind.

† Have students do research to answer these questions.

3 Climate

Develop Important Understandings
Use the following questions to guide your research about the climate of the South.

†
1. What is the difference between "weather" and "climate"? (See the Glossary.)
2. What is the main reason why winters are mild in the South?
3. Why are winters milder along the coasts of the South than they are farther inland?
4. How does a long growing season help farmers in the South?
5. Which parts of the South have the longest growing season? (See top map on page 88.)
6. Why are summers cooler in the Blue Ridge than in other parts of the South?

Imagine that we are visiting the city of Miami Beach, Florida, on the first day of February. We notice that the air is warm and the sun is bright. The people we meet are dressed in light summer clothing. In a park nearby, we see colorful flowers in bloom. Because there are palm trees growing in the park, we know that the weather here is never very cold.

We stop at a drugstore to buy a newspaper. On the front page, we read that a storm is sweeping across the northern part of the United States. Snow has been falling for three days. The temperature is below 0° F. (-18° C.).† We are glad to be here in Miami Beach, enjoying the warm sunshine.

Mild winters
In order to learn more about the climate of the South, turn to the map on the left-hand side of page 32. This map shows average temperatures in North America during the month of January. Notice that in most of the northern part of the United States, the average temperature in January is below 32° F.

† F. means Fahrenheit scale
C. means Celsius scale

24 The South

Truckloads of oranges in a Florida orchard. In some parts of Florida, winters are so mild that oranges and other warm-weather crops can be grown. What is the climate like in other parts of the South?

† ($0°$ C.). You will realize that winters are cold there when you remember that this is the temperature at which water freezes. In nearly all of the South, however, the average temperature in January is above freezing. The only places in the South that receive much snow are high in the mountains.

The main reason why winters are mild in the South is that the southern part of our country is nearer the equator than the northern part.

† How does this compare with the average January temperature where we live? Refer students to the left-hand map and key on page 32.

Winters in the South are milder along the coasts than they are farther inland. This is because large bodies of water lose their heat more slowly than the land. Warm winds from the Gulf of Mexico and the Atlantic Ocean help to delay the coming of frost to the coastal areas.

Warm summers

Except in the mountains, summers in the South are long and warm. Crops can be grown without danger of frost for a longer time in the South than farther north. This frost-free period is called the growing season. As you can see by the map on page 88, most of the South has a growing season of more than two hundred days. In southern Florida, crops can be grown outdoors all year round.

A long growing season helps farmers. In the South, crops can be planted and harvested earlier than they can in northern states. These crops can be sold in parts of the country where winters are long and cold. Also, farmers in some parts of the South can grow such crops as cotton and oranges. These crops cannot be grown in the northern part of the United States.

Heavy rainfall

People sometimes talk about "the sunny South." However, the South receives more rainfall than any other main group of states. The map on page 30 shows that most parts of the South receive more than 40 inches (102 cm.)† of rainfall each year.

Warm winds from the Gulf of Mexico bring most of the South's rainfall. These winds blow northward from the sea toward the land. They contain

moisture that has evaporated* from the surface of the Gulf. As these winds blow over the land, they drop their moisture as rain. Along the Atlantic coast, some rain is brought by winds that blow in from the ocean.

You have learned that the climate in most parts of the South is much the same. Winters are mild, summers are warm, and rainfall is heavy. However, there are some differences in climate from place to place. For example, the climate of southern Florida is not like

† cm. means centimeter

*See Glossary

† How does this compare with the annual rainfall in our area? Refer students to the map and key on page 30.

A sandy beach on Jekyll Island, Georgia. Jekyll Island is part of a chain of islands that lies in the Coastal Plain region of the South. These islands, called the Sea Islands, stretch along the Atlantic coast of South Carolina, Georgia, and the northern part of Florida. What kinds of weather might you find here during the summer months? What kinds during the winter months?

the climate in the Blue Ridge of Virginia. The rest of this chapter describes the climate in different parts of the South.

Coastal Plain

If you could visit the Coastal Plain region of the South, you might discover many facts about the climate. Let's imagine that you are going to stay with friends in Montgomery, Alabama, for a whole year. (See map on page 9.) The climate in most parts of the Coastal Plain is much like the climate in this city.

Summer

In the summer, the weather in Montgomery is warm and humid. It is like this nearly everywhere on the Coastal

You may use the caption below for a class discussion about physical needs.

Plain. During your stay, the weather is sometimes hot. The temperature does not often rise as high as it does in some other parts of our country. The deserts and plains of the West are hotter, but the air is dry. Here on the Coastal Plain the air is moist. You feel warmer and more uncomfortable than you would if the air were dry.

During the summer, the weather in the parts of the South near the coasts is likely to be a little cooler than it is inland. Large bodies of water like the Atlantic Ocean and the Gulf of Mexico become warm more slowly in summer than the land does. Cool sea breezes bring pleasant weather to coastal areas of the South.

Thunderstorms

It is an afternoon in July. All day long, the weather in Montgomery has been so hot and damp that you have been uncomfortable. Now large, black clouds fill the sky. Thunder rolls, lightning flashes, and rain pours down. When the thunderstorm finally ends, the air seems cooler and fresher.

During the summer, Montgomery has many thunderstorms. (See page 34.) Some parts of the Coastal Plain of the South receive more than seventy thunderstorms each year.

Thunderstorms bring heavy rains. Sometimes they bring as much as 10 inches (25 cm.) of rain within twenty-four hours. Heavy summer rains are good for growing crops, but they wash much soil into rivers and streams.

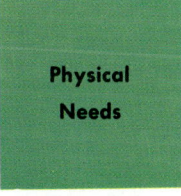

Physical Needs

See Needs of People

The picture at left shows a family camping at a state park in Louisiana, in the Coastal Plain region of the South. Do you think that the members of this family have the same physical needs that you do? Do they need food? Exercise? Fresh air? Protection from heat and cold? How does this picture suggest ways in which the members of the family meet their physical needs?

Hurricanes

During the summer and early fall, hurricanes sometimes strike the Coastal Plain. Hurricanes are terrible storms that begin in the tropics, over large bodies of water. The hurricanes that strike the United States begin over the Atlantic Ocean or the Caribbean Sea. (See page 35.) During a hurricane, rainfall is heavy and winds blow at 75 miles (121 km.)† an hour or more. Hurricanes can uproot trees and smash houses. The high waves that come with hurricanes often sink boats and cause great damage along low-lying coasts. Sometimes many people are killed.

Winter

During your year in Montgomery, the weather never becomes very cold. Winters are short and mild in the Coastal Plain region of the South. Snow does not fall very often in this area. When it does, it is likely to melt quickly. Winters are mildest near the coasts.

In the southern half of Florida, several years may pass without a heavy frost. Farmers here can grow oranges and other fruits that need a year-round growing season.

† km. means kilometer

As this map shows, the average yearly rainfall varies from place to place in the United States. Throughout the South, rainfall is plentiful.

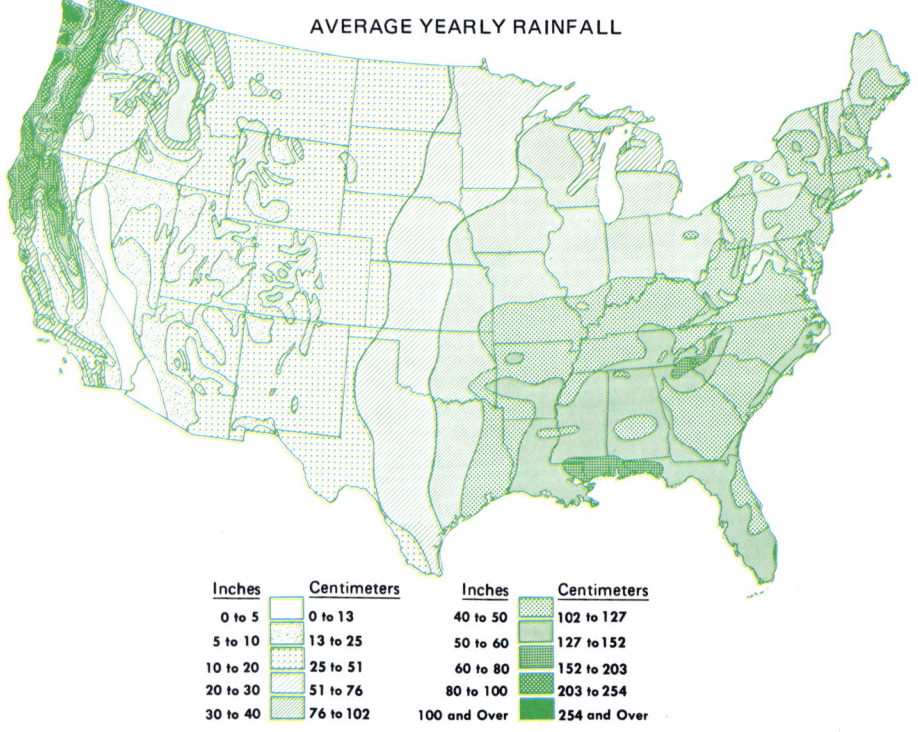

Hurricanes sometimes strike the Coastal Plain region of the South. They uproot trees and smash buildings. Near the sea, high waves may also cause great damage. Where do hurricanes form?

Have students study the temperature maps and keys below. What is the average temperature in Florida in January? In July?

They can also grow vegetables in the winter to sell to people in the northern part of our country. During the winter, millions of people come to Florida to enjoy the mild, sunny climate.

Even in Florida, however, the temperature may drop below freezing during the winter. Freezing temperatures are caused by cold air from the north, which sometimes brings a few days of cold weather. A heavy frost may cause great damage to crops.

Appalachian Highlands

In the Appalachian Highlands region, climate changes with elevation. The higher you go above sea level, the cooler the air becomes. The earth gives off heat that it has received from the sun. At low elevations, much of this heat is soaked up by the moisture and dust in the air. At high elevations, however, the air is much cleaner and drier. Therefore, it cannot soak up as much heat. For this reason, the temperature is likely to be cooler at high elevations than it is at low elevations.

Summer

In the Piedmont Plateau section of the Appalachian Highlands, the climate is much like that of the Coastal Plain. Summers here are warm and humid. The growing season on the Piedmont lasts from about 180 days in Virginia to 240 days in Georgia.

Continued on page 36

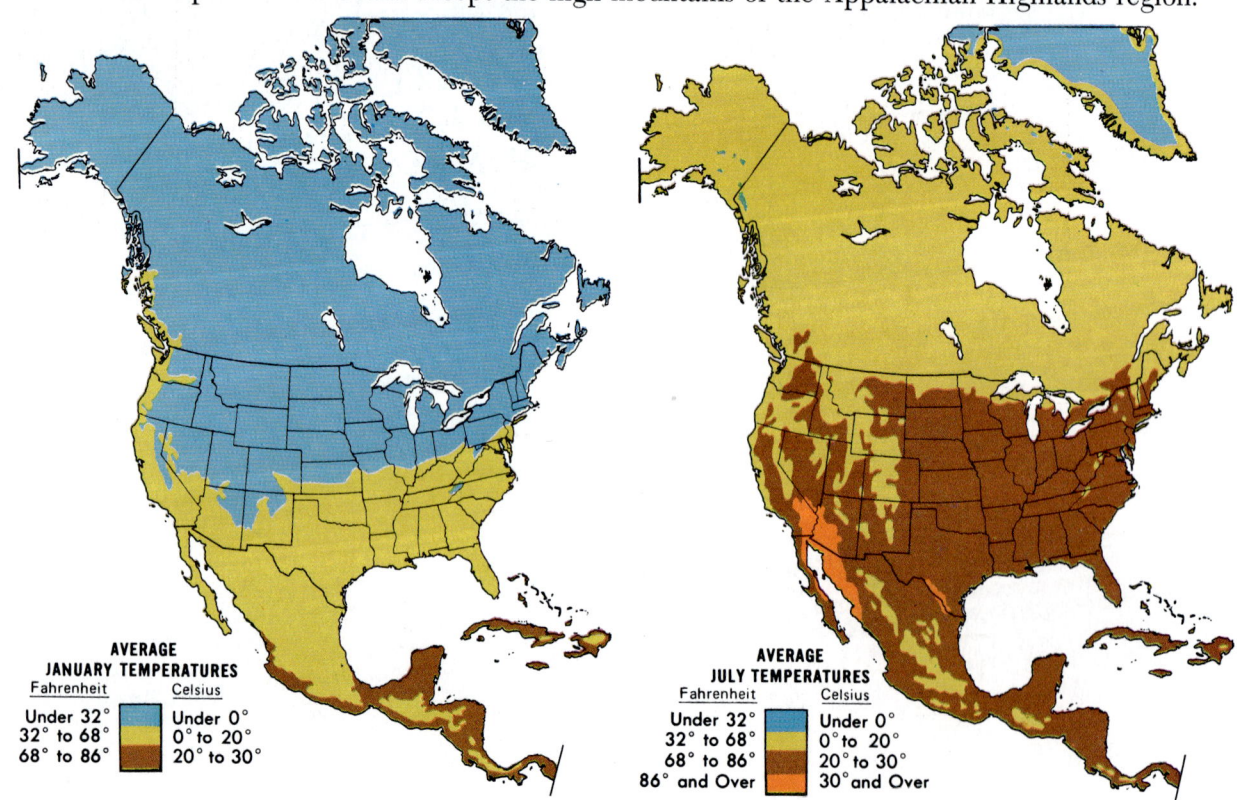

Average temperatures in North America during January and July. Winters are mild and summers are warm in all parts of the South except the high mountains of the Appalachian Highlands region.

32 The South

Fontana Lake in the Blue Ridge, in North Carolina. Many people visit the high mountains of the Blue Ridge during the summer months. At that time of year, the weather is cool and pleasant.

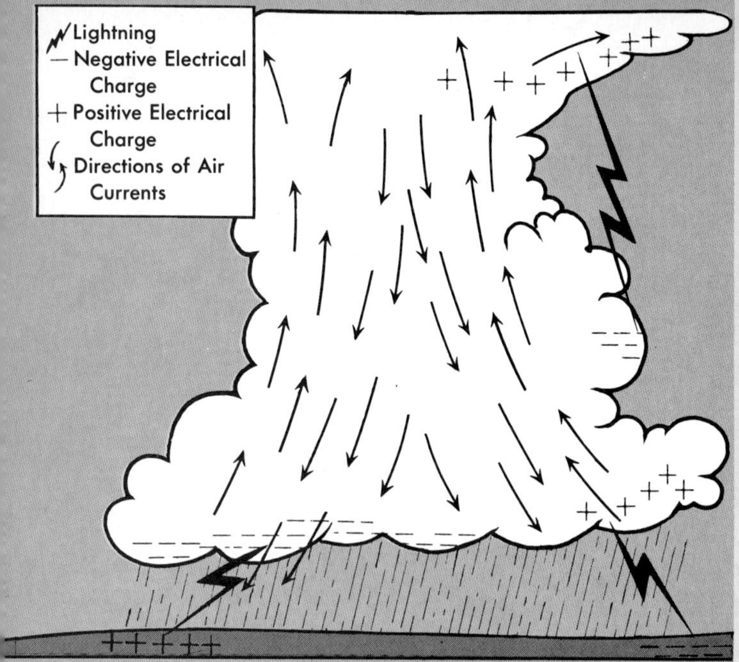

Legend:
- Lightning
- Negative Electrical Charge
- + Positive Electrical Charge
- Directions of Air Currents

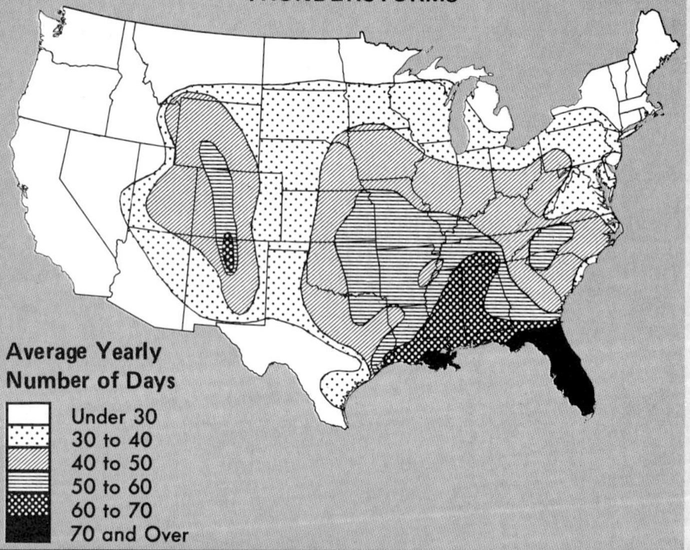

THUNDERSTORMS

Average Yearly Number of Days
- Under 30
- 30 to 40
- 40 to 50
- 50 to 60
- 60 to 70
- 70 and Over

Thunderstorms

A thunderstorm is a heavy shower of rain that comes with strong winds, thunder, lightning, and sometimes hail. Thunderstorms most often happen over the warm land in or near the tropics.* Few such storms take place beyond 60 degrees north or south latitude.*

Almost all rain is formed by the rising and cooling of moist air. As the air cools, moisture forms into tiny droplets of water. If there are enough droplets, they form a rain cloud. Then the droplets join together to become raindrops, and rain begins to fall.

A thunderstorm may come up when a warm land surface heats moist air very rapidly. This heating causes strong currents of rising air. When rain clouds form, the rising air currents sweep them upward. They rise several miles above the earth's surface. Falling raindrops are broken up into fine particles by the rising air. These particles develop electrical charges, some negative (-) and some positive (+). Particles with the same charge collect in different parts of a cloud. Or, they form new raindrops that fall to earth. When the difference in charge becomes great enough, electricity may be given off between parts of one cloud, between two clouds, or between a cloud and the ground. This electricity, or flash of lightning, heats the air through which it passes. The heated air expands so rapidly that it makes the sound waves we call thunder. It takes about five seconds for a sound wave to travel a mile. A person can tell how far away a storm is by counting the seconds between a flash of lightning and the thunder that follows.

*See Glossary

Hurricanes

A hurricane is the most damaging storm in the world. It is made up of very, very strong winds that circle around a quiet center, called the eye. The eye is generally about fifteen miles in diameter, but the whole storm may be as much as five hundred miles across. Such a storm is not called a true hurricane unless the winds near the center blow at a speed of seventy-five miles an hour or more. The hurricane itself, however, travels rather slowly. It moves at only about fifteen or twenty miles an hour.

Hurricanes form in the tropics, over large bodies of warm water. They are formed most often in summer and fall. North of the equator,* hurricanes move northwestward until they reach about 25 or 30 degrees north latitude. Then they may change direction and move northeastward. South of the equator, hurricanes move first southwestward and then southeastward. The map below shows where hurricanes are most often formed, and the directions they generally follow.

Usually, several hurricanes form each year over the Atlantic Ocean. Some of these storms remain over the sea. Others blow across the islands of the West Indies or the coast of North America. The strong, roaring winds of a hurricane often cause great damage to houses and other buildings. Sometimes many people are killed. The huge ocean waves and heavy rains that come with hurricanes may also cause damage. Fortunately, hurricanes do not very often reach far inland. This is because their winds are slowed down when they blow over the land.

*See Glossary

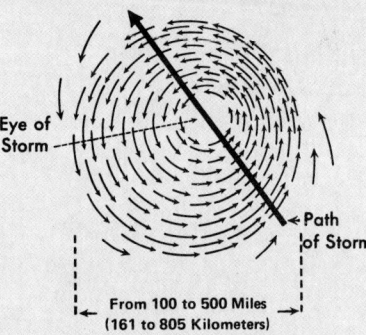

ROTATION OF WINDS IN A HURRICANE

Eye of Storm
Path of Storm
From 100 to 500 Miles
(161 to 805 Kilometers)

A hurricane is made up of very strong winds that circle around a quiet center called the eye. (See above.) In the Northern Hemisphere, the winds of hurricanes and other circular storms blow in a counterclockwise direction. (See chart at left.) In the Southern Hemisphere, they blow in a clockwise direction. In some parts of the world, hurricanes are called typhoons.

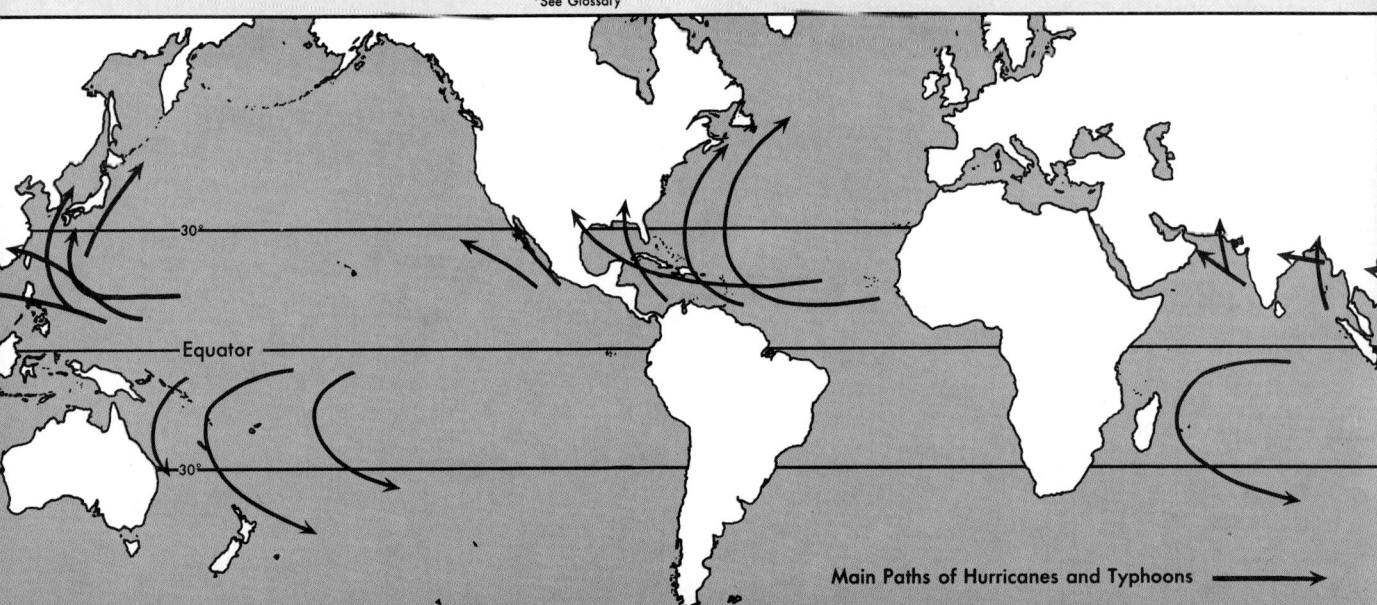

Main Paths of Hurricanes and Typhoons →

Winter in the Appalachian Highlands of Virginia. The high mountains are the only places in the South that receive much snow. Winters are generally less severe at lower elevations.

In the higher parts of the Appalachian Highlands, summers are cooler and more pleasant than they are on the Piedmont Plateau. The coolest summer weather in the Appalachian Highlands is found in the high mountains of the Blue Ridge. Many people spend their summers in these mountains.

Winter

Winters in the Appalachian Highlands are colder in the high mountains than they are at lower elevations. The first frost comes earlier in the fall. Often, a white blanket of snow covers the high peaks. As soon as the danger of frost is over in the spring, crops such as corn may be planted on the mountain sides. The growing season in the mountains is only about 160 days long.

Rainfall

Most parts of the Appalachian Highlands region receive more than 40 inches (102 cm.) of rainfall each year. Rainfall is heaviest in the Blue Ridge. Here, the mountain sides are covered with thick, green forests. The heavy rainfall helps the trees to grow. Also, because it is cooler in the mountains, water does not evaporate quickly from the soil. Trees grow well where the ground holds plenty of water for their roots.

All year round, the Blue Ridge receives large amounts of moisture. Warm moist air blows in from the Atlantic Ocean and the Gulf of Mexico. When the air reaches the mountains, it is forced to rise. The higher it rises, the cooler it becomes. Some of the moisture falls as rain or snow.

Interior Plains

Summers are warm in the Interior Plains region of the South. However, the growing season here is generally shorter than it is in the Coastal Plain. This is mainly because the Interior Plains region lies farther north than most parts of the Coastal Plain. Also, the warm sea winds that delay the coming of frosts to the coasts do not reach this far inland.

Farmers in the Interior Plains grow crops such as corn. Many horses, cattle, and other livestock are also raised here. Cotton, which needs a growing season of about two hundred days, is grown in Alabama and in some parts of Tennessee.

Because it is farther north, the Interior Plains region has longer and somewhat cooler winters than the Coastal Plain. During the winter months, the parts of Kentucky and Tennessee that lie in the Interior Plains usually receive about 10 inches (25 cm.) of snow.

Interior Highlands

The climate in the Interior Highlands region of the South is a little cooler and less humid than it is in the Coastal Plain nearby. This is because the Interior Highlands region is higher above sea level than the Coastal Plain. Summer days are hot, but nights are cool. Winters are short and mild, with very little snow. The snow that does fall does not remain on the ground very long.

A Problem To Solve

Some parts of the Coastal Plain of the South receive more than seventy thunderstorms each year. Why do so many of these storms take place here? The following questions suggest hypotheses* you will need to think about.
1. How do the high temperatures in these parts of the Coastal Plain affect the forming of thunderstorms?
2. How does warm moist air from the Gulf of Mexico and the Atlantic Ocean affect the forming of thunderstorms?

See Skills Manual, "Thinking and Solving Problems"

Summer in the Ozark Plateau of Arkansas. The Ozark Plateau is part of the Interior Highlands region of the South. What is the climate like in this region? Would you like to visit the Ozark Plateau? Explain.

† Use these questions to start students thinking about the people of the South.

Part 2
People

The people of the South have the same basic human needs as people everywhere. They also share several important beliefs with other people in our country. As you do research in Part 2, see if you can discover answers to the following questions:

†
- Who settled in the South during colonial times? Who lives in the South today?
- What are the six largest metropolitan* areas in the South? Where are they located? Which southern city would you most like to visit? Give reasons for your answer.
- What is democracy? What seven beliefs do people in a democracy share? Do you think that all of these beliefs are important? Explain.
- Who are some well-known southern artists?

*See Glossary

Use Fideler Discovery Cards 57-82.

People enjoying a parade in New Orleans. About 47 million people make their homes in the South. Many of these people live in or near large cities, such as New Orleans.

4 People

A fast-growing region

In the South, just as in most other parts of our country, population has been growing rapidly. Today, about 47 million people live in the eleven states that make up the South. This is more than one fifth of the population of the whole United States.

Some states of the South have been growing more rapidly in population than others. Florida, for example, is one of the fastest-growing states in our country. Its population has grown by nearly two million people in less than ten years.

The map on page 43 shows the distribution of people in the United States. Each tiny dot on the map stands for ten thousand people. If you compare this map with the one on page 54,

New buildings in a growing area near Atlanta, Georgia. Population in the South has been growing rapidly in the past few years. More than one fifth of the people in our country now live in the South.

A southerner of European descent. Many people in the South are descended from early settlers who came to America from the British Isles. Other settlers have come from France and Spain.

you will notice that the population of the South is distributed quite evenly. There are no large areas where few people live, as there are in the West. There are only a few large areas that are very thickly populated.

For hundreds of years, people have been coming to the South from many parts of the world. Today, people of all races and many different national* origins make their homes in the South.

People of European descent

Many southerners are descended from early settlers who came to America from the British Isles. In much of

*See Glossary

The South 41

the South, the people still bear the English, Scotch, or Irish names of their ancestors* who came here two or three hundred years ago.

The English brought their language and ways of living to the colonies. Among the southern cities founded and named by the English are Charleston, South Carolina, and Richmond, Virginia. Many beautiful Georgian-style* houses built in the South by the English colonists are still standing.

† There are also people of French descent in the South. Most of them live in southern Louisiana. Some are descendants of families that came to Louisiana from France early in the 1700's. Others are descended from Acadians who settled here a little later. The Acadians were people of French descent who lived in a part of Canada called Nova Scotia. They were driven out of Nova Scotia by the British during and after the French and Indian War.*

People from other parts of Europe also settled in the South. In Louisiana there are descendants of Spanish families who settled here long ago. On Florida's Gulf coast there are people of

† Some of your students may have visited Louisiana. Have them tell about any of their experiences with French-speaking people who live there.

Greek descent. In Kentucky, many people of German descent live in towns along the Ohio River.

People of African descent

More than ten million black people live in the South today. Nearly all of them are descended from people who

Refer to this picture and caption. Use the caption for a class discussion on the arts. Use Fideler Discovery Card 75 as an additional activity.

A southern mansion. This beautiful house was built by English colonists who came to the South in the 1700's. It is built in a style of architecture called Georgian.* The English built many beautiful houses in this style. Architecture is the art of designing houses and other buildings. Why do you suppose architecture is thought of as an art? What are some other arts? (See Chapter 7.) Do you think the arts are important in your life? Explain.

UNITED STATES POPULATION DISTRIBUTION

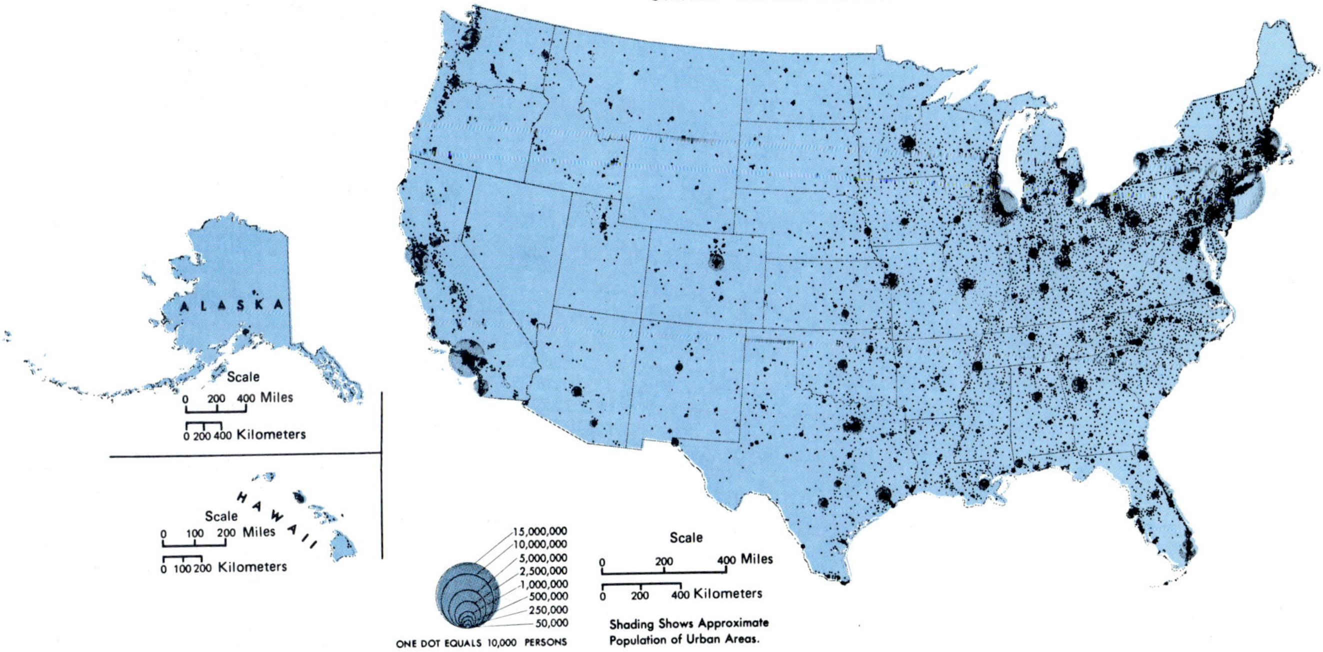

The South 43

were brought here from Africa during the 1600's and 1700's.

Many people of African descent have helped to shape our country's history. During the Revolutionary War,* thousands of black soldiers fought bravely against the British. Nearly 200,000 blacks served with the Union armies during the Civil War.* President Lincoln believed these troops were a great help in winning the war.

Black people have enriched life in America in many different ways. For example, blacks have played an important part in the growth of certain kinds of American music, such as jazz, rock, and "soul" music. Some of our country's leading writers, teachers, and government leaders have been black people. Other blacks have been well known in sports, science, and show business.

People of Asian descent

Some of the people in the South are descended from people who came from China, Japan, and other countries in Asia. Florida and Virginia are the states with the most people of Asian descent.

People of Latin-American descent

Since 1900, many people have come to the South from Spanish-speaking countries in Latin America. The largest number of these are from the island country of Cuba. In 1959 Fidel Castro came to power in Cuba and began to set up a new form of government. Large numbers of Cubans moved to the United States because they did not want to live under this new government. Many of them settled in or near Miami, Florida. Today, more than

44 The South

Freedom

See Great Ideas

The picture below shows a southern family enjoying a backyard cookout. Do you think the members of this family have very much freedom to live as they please? What makes you think this? Are there any people in our country today who do not have as much freedom as other Americans? If so, who are they? What do you think might be done to help these people gain more freedom?

The South 45

250,000 people in Florida are of Cuban descent. People have also come to the South from the island of Puerto Rico. Still other people in the South are of Mexican descent.

American Indians

More than 75,000 Indians, or Native Americans, live in the southern states. Most of them are in North Carolina. This state has a Cherokee Indian reservation, which is located at the edge of Great Smoky Mountains National Park. There are some Choctaw Indians in Mississippi and Seminole Indians in Florida. Most of the Indians in the South no longer live on reservations. Their way of life is much like that of other people who make their homes in the South.

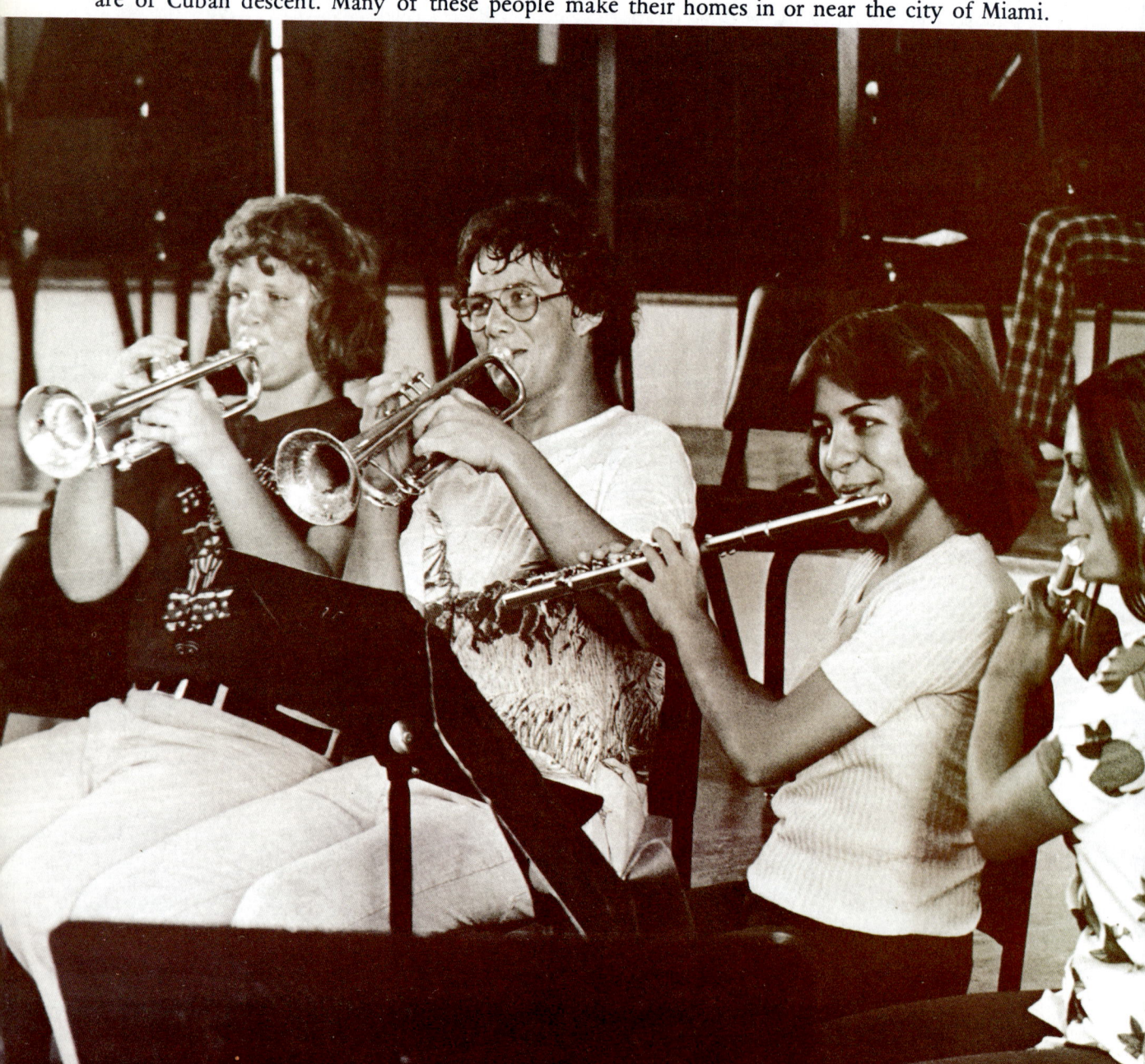

Young people of Cuban descent in Florida. More than 250,000 people who live in Florida today are of Cuban descent. Many of these people make their homes in or near the city of Miami.

Seminole Indians in Florida. More than 75,000 Indians live in the southern states. Most of these people enjoy a way of life that is very much like that of other people who live in the South. Some Indians, however, live in much the same way as their ancestors did long ago. What does the picture above tell you about the way in which this Indian family lives? In what ways is this family like your family? In what ways is it different?

Many religions

The people of the South worship God in many different ways. A Protestant group called the Baptists is the largest single religious group. Some of the other main Protestant groups are the Methodists, the Presbyterians, and the Episcopalians. Many southerners are members of the Roman Catholic Church. Some people of the Jewish faith also live in the South.

Explore Population †

1. About how many people live in the South?
2. Which state of the South is one of the fastest-growing states in our country?
3. Compare maps on pages 43 and 54. Which cities are in densely populated areas?
4. Over the years, people from many different countries have made their homes in the South. Name several of the countries from which these people have come.

† Have students answer these questions.

5 Cities

Metropolitan* areas in the South have been growing rapidly in population in recent years. In the early 1900's, the cities of the South were much smaller than they are today. Most people in this region lived on farms or in small towns. As time passed, more and more people moved from farming areas into the cities. People from other parts of the United States also came to the cities in the South. Today, about six out of every ten people in the South live in metropolitan areas.

Atlanta

The largest city in Georgia is the capital city, Atlanta. It is an inland city. (See map on page 54.) Atlanta is located on the rolling land of the Piedmont Plateau. The Atlanta metropolitan area has grown rapidly during the last few years. It is still growing. Today it is the largest metropolitan area in the South.

Atlanta began as a railroad terminus.* It soon became an important transportation city. During the Civil War,* Union troops under General Sherman set fire to Atlanta. The city was almost destroyed. After it was rebuilt, Atlanta became the state capital. Today, Atlanta is a modern city with many fine parks and schools. It is sometimes called the "Dogwood City" because of the beautiful dogwood trees that line many of its streets.

A trade center

Atlanta has become an important trading and business city. Railroads and highways stretch out from Atlanta like the spokes of a wheel. A number of airlines also serve the city. Many products manufactured in the South are shipped to northern markets by way of Atlanta. This city is also a market for farm products such as cotton and cattle. Because it is a major trading and business center, Atlanta has many banks and other business offices.

Thousands of people in Atlanta earn their living in government work or in manufacturing. Atlanta has many state government offices. It also has many federal government offices. Factories in the Atlanta area make over three thousand different products. Among these are clothing, furniture, soft drinks, and paper. Many workers have jobs in a huge airplane factory nearby.

*See Glossary

Atlanta is the state capital and largest city in Georgia. More than 1,800,000 people live in the Atlanta metropolitan* area. Atlanta, in northwestern Georgia, lies on the Piedmont Plateau.

The city of Miami is located on Biscayne Bay in Florida. Each year, millions of people spend their vacations here. The most important industry in the city of Miami is the resort business.

Miami

The city of Miami is in the southern part of Florida. It lies along the Atlantic coast. (See map on page 54.) To the east of downtown Miami are the bright blue waters of Biscayne Bay. This bay is an arm of the Atlantic Ocean. It is dotted with many kinds of fishing boats and sailboats. The eastern shore of the bay is made up of long, narrow islands just off the coast. Beyond these islands is the open ocean.

A large metropolitan area

Miami and its neighboring communities have grown close together. It is impossible to tell where Miami ends and other cities begin. There are more than twenty-five cities and towns in

the Miami metropolitan area. Among these are Miami Shores, North Miami, Hialeah, and Coral Gables. The island city of Miami Beach is also part of the Miami metropolitan area. It is one of the best-known resorts in the world. Here, tall hotels and apartment buildings line the Atlantic shore. The population of the Miami area has † grown rapidly. Today this metropolitan area is the second largest in the South. (See chart on page 53.)

Many visitors every year

Miami's most important industry is the resort business. Each year, millions of visitors come to the city. Many of the people who live in Miami work in hotels and restaurants. Others work for transportation companies such as railroads and airlines. Miami is also a manufacturing, trading, and shipping city. Furniture, clothing, and chemicals* are among the products made in Miami's factories. Vegetables and fruit grown in rich farming areas nearby are sent to packing plants in Miami. Foods and manufactured goods produced in Miami are shipped to many other parts of our country.

New Orleans

The South's chief port city is New Orleans. (See map on page 17.) New Orleans is the largest city in Louisiana. New Orleans is located on a bend in the Mississippi River. It is not far from the Gulf of Mexico. The oldest part of the city lies along the north bank of the river. Much of the newer part of New Orleans spreads along the shores of a body of salt water called Lake Pontchartrain.

A French settlement

New Orleans was founded in 1718 by French settlers. The following year, the little settlement was badly damaged by floodwaters from the Mississippi River. In order to protect their land from floods, the settlers built levees* along the banks

† Refer to the map on page 54. How does the population of Miami compare with that of New Orleans? With Orlando? With Atlanta?

of the river. More and more settlers soon came to New Orleans. The town spread into nearby areas. Swamps were drained, and more levees were built.

The South's chief port

The location of New Orleans near the mouth of the Mississippi River has helped it become a leading port city. Among our country's ports, New Orleans is second only to New York in the amount of freight handled. The docks of the port of New Orleans stretch for miles along both sides of the river. Oceangoing ships carry passengers and freight between New Orleans and other ports all over the world. Boats also travel between New Orleans and port cities on the Mississippi River and its branches.

During the 1900's, industry has grown rapidly in New Orleans. Minerals found nearby, such as petroleum, natural gas, sulfur, and salt, are processed in the city's refineries* and chemical plants. Some of the natural gas is used to make the electricity needed by factories. Many of the crops from Louisiana's farms, such as sugarcane, cotton, and rice, are sent to factories in New Orleans for processing. Many kinds of manufactured goods, as well as minerals and farm products, are shipped from New Orleans to other states and to countries around the world.

An interesting place to visit

Each year, millions of visitors come to New Orleans. Many people come to

The French Quarter of New Orleans. This is the oldest part of New Orleans. The city was settled by the French early in the 1700's.

† Have students look up the word "peninsula" in the Glossary.

the city to see the French Quarter. (See picture at left.) This is the oldest part of New Orleans, settled by the French in the early 1700's. Here, there are narrow streets, small shops, and old buildings trimmed with lacy, iron grillwork. Other people come to New Orleans for Mardi Gras. This well-known festival lasts for about two weeks just before Lent.*

Tampa Bay Area

About halfway up the Florida peninsula,* a large arm of the Gulf of Mexico cuts into the west coast. This is Tampa Bay. Along the shores of the bay are several cities, the largest of which are Tampa and St. Petersburg.

Tampa

The largest city on Florida's west coast is Tampa. (See map on page 54.)

SIX METROPOLITAN AREAS		
Metropolitan Area	Population of Entire Area	Population of Central City (or Cities)
Atlanta	1,802,700	445,300
Miami	1,466,800	371,700
Tampa-St. Petersburg	1,370,400	293,300 237,000
New Orleans	1,109,700	575,200
Louisville	884,200	331,900
Memphis	874,800	666,300

The six largest metropolitan* areas in the South are listed above. Their populations are given in the middle column. For each of these areas, the population of the central city or cities is also given.

*See Glossary

Cities of the South

It has a fine harbor at the northeast end of Tampa Bay. Tampa is Florida's most important trading, manufacturing, and port city on the Gulf coast. Ships bring products such as oil and sugar to Tampa. They come from other American ports and from other countries. The city's leading export is phosphate* rock. This rock comes from mines nearby. Lumber, canned fruit, and other items produced in the Tampa area are also exported.

The tourist business is one of Tampa's most important industries. Many thousands of people come here. They enjoy such sports as fishing, sailing, and golfing.

St. Petersburg

The second largest city in the Tampa Bay area is St. Petersburg. It is on the peninsula that separates the Tampa Bay area from the Gulf of Mexico. (See map above.)

St. Petersburg is mainly a resort city. Because the sun shines here almost every day of the year, it is sometimes called the "Sunshine City." Visitors come here to swim, fish, sail, or just to enjoy the sunshine.

Louisville

The largest city in Kentucky is Louisville. (See map on opposite page.) It is on the Ohio River, which forms the state's northern and western borders. The Louisville metropolitan area includes some towns on the other side of the Ohio River, in Indiana.

An important river port

Louisville is one of our country's leading river ports. At one time, ships sailing on the Ohio River had to stop at Louisville because of falls in the river. Goods were unloaded, carried around the falls, and reloaded onto ships on the other side. Since 1830, when a canal was opened at Louisville, ships have been able to go around the falls.

Louisville is one of the South's most important business and manufacturing cities. Factories in Louisville make furniture, electrical appliances, and other products. The largest baseball-bat factory in the United States is located here.

Each year, Louisville draws large numbers of visitors. Many people come here to watch the Kentucky Derby. This well-known horse race is held in May at Churchill Downs racetrack.

About 30 miles (48 km.)† south of Louisville is Fort Knox. Here the United States government keeps much of our country's gold.

† km. means kilometer

Louisville is the largest city in Kentucky. Nearly 900,000 people live in the Louisville metropolitan area. The city is located on the Ohio River and is one of our country's important river ports.

Memphis

Memphis is another great river port of the South. (See map on page 54.) This city is in the southwest corner of Tennessee, on the Mississippi River. Memphis was founded in 1819. The city soon became a busy river port. Steamboats stopped at its docks to load cotton and other goods. Today, Memphis is one of the largest cities on the Mississippi River.

Memphis is an up-to-date city, with many new office buildings, factories, and homes. It also has many fine old houses that were built by wealthy planters before the Civil War.

A leading inland port

Memphis is one of our country's leading inland ports. If you were to take a sight-seeing trip on the Mississippi River, you would see miles of docks along the waterfront. You would notice workers loading barges with lumber, cotton, and other products of the area. These goods are shipped to many parts of the world. On the river, tugboats move slowly along, pushing strings of barges. Many of these barges are heading downstream toward New Orleans, where their freight will be loaded aboard oceangoing ships. Others are heading for ports upstream.

A major trading city

Memphis is the main trading and business city for western Tennessee and parts of neighboring states. It is one of the world's largest markets for cotton and hardwood* lumber. Memphis is also a market for cattle, grain, and other products of farms in the area. Many drug companies, grocery dealers, and other businesses have branch offices in Memphis.

Manufacturing is also important in Memphis. Many people work in plants where cottonseed, rice, and other farm products are processed. This city is one of the leading meat-packing centers in the South. Other important products made in Memphis are paper, chemicals, and farm machinery.

Memphis is the largest city in the state of Tennessee. Its location on the Mississippi River has helped Memphis become one of our country's major inland ports.

Discover New Cities

Choose a city in the South where you would like to spend your summer vacation. What are some of the interesting places you would like to visit? Use information from this book and other books to describe these places. Use pictures to illustrate* your report.

Using Maps To Find Information

Compare the map on page 54 with the map on page 17. Study these maps to find more information about the cities of the South. Using these two maps, try to answer the following questions:

1. Which eleven cities in the South have a population of 250,000 or more?
2. Eight of these eleven large cities are port cities. Which ones are they?
3. Which of these eight large port cities are located on rivers?
4. Which of these eight large port cities are located on the Intracoastal Waterway?

Do you think that rules, or laws, are important? Can you think of ways in which they are important in your life?

6 Citizenship and Government

Citizenship in a Democracy

Why all communities need laws

We live in communities where most of the people work together to make life pleasant for each other. Imagine what it would be like if this were not true. Suppose the people around us refused to follow any rules. It would not be possible to play games, because there can be no games without rules. People could not work together very well. They would not be able to trust each other, either. We would never feel completely safe. We probably would not be very happy.

All groups of people in the world have certain rules, or laws, to live by. Laws help people to live happy, useful lives and to meet their basic needs. (See "Needs of People" at the back of this book.) In communities where the laws are fair and the people obey them, life is safer and more pleasant for everybody.

Why all communities need government

Laws do not just "happen." In every community, there must be someone to make the laws and to see that the laws are carried out. In other words, all communities need government.

Not all governments are the same, however. In some communities, one person alone has the power to make the laws. This person also sees that they are carried out. The rest of the people do not have any share in making the laws. But they have to obey them anyway. In other communities, a small number of people have the power to make and carry out the laws all by themselves.

There are also communities where all of the people have a share in making and carrying out the laws. These communities are called democracies.

Rules and Government

See Great Ideas

Crossing the street safely. The "safety" in the left of this picture is helping younger students cross the street safely. All people in the world have certain rules, or laws, to live by. What rules do you think the "safety" is following? What rules are the younger students following? What might happen if they did not follow these rules? What are some of the rules you follow in school? What are some of the rules you follow at home? Write a story telling what it might be like if everyone at home or at school refused to follow these rules. Share your story with your teacher and with the other members of your class.

The Florida House of Representatives. The members of this group are elected by the people of Florida. They help make laws for the state. In our country, people have the right to govern themselves.

Making the laws in a democracy

In a very small community, such as a family or a village, all of the people can meet in one place and make their own laws. They can also work together to see that the laws are carried out.

People in larger communities cannot govern themselves in the same way. Imagine what it would be like if everyone in New York City or the state of Florida met together to make laws. There would be too many people to get any real work done. It would take a very long time to make any laws. People would not have time to work at other jobs.

SEVEN IMPORTANT BELIEFS SHARED BY PEOPLE IN A DEMOCRACY

1. Every person is important.
2. People have the right to govern themselves.
3. Decisions should be made by majority* vote.
4. All citizens should have a chance to get a good education.
5. Laws should be the same for all citizens of a country.
6. All people have certain rights that no one can take away from them.
7. Citizens have responsibilities as well as rights.

*See Glossary

A way has been worked out for the members of large communities to govern themselves. The people of the community choose men and women to run the government for them. These men and women make the laws and see that they are carried out. In the United States, for example, we choose members of a group called Congress. This group makes laws for our nation. We also choose a president and vice-president. They see that the laws are carried out. Because it has this kind of government, the United States is called a democracy.

Seven important beliefs shared by people in a democracy

Many people in the world today believe that democracy gives us the best way of making laws and carrying them out wisely. But democracy will not work unless the citizens of a country agree on seven important ideas, or beliefs. These ideas are listed in the box above. Let us examine each of these ideas more closely to see why it is important to people in a democracy.

1. Every person is important.

Most Americans believe that every person is important. It does not matter whether you are tall or short, blue-eyed or brown-eyed, young or old, a man or a woman. You are as important as

The South 61

every other person. You are important whether you are rich or poor, or whether your skin is black, white, or some other color. You are important no matter what religion you follow or what country your grandparents may have come from.

There are several reasons for believing that every person is important. In the first place, we know that all people have almost exactly the same needs. (See "Needs of People.") Second, most Americans follow religions which teach that all people are equal under God. Third, we know that problems cannot be solved unless each person thinks about them and does something about them.

Loyalty

See Great Ideas

Voting in an election. In democracies like the United States, citizens have a chance to help choose the people who run the government. They do this when they vote in elections. By voting, people show their loyalty to certain beliefs. What seven important beliefs do people in a democracy share? Besides voting, what are some additional ways in which people show their loyalty to these beliefs?

† Why is it important to treat others the way you want to be treated? Explain.

† When we really believe that every person is important, we are more likely to treat other people the way we would like to be treated. We are also more careful not to harm other people in order to meet our own needs. For example, if you forgot to bring your lunch to school, you would not take someone else's lunch for yourself.

2. **People have the right to govern themselves.**

Most Americans believe that the citizens of a country have the right to govern themselves. We think every person should be able to have some part—no matter how small—in running the government under which we live.

3. **Decisions should be made by majority vote.**

In democracies like the United States, all citizens have a chance to help choose the people who run the government. They do this by voting in elections. For example, an election is held once every four years to choose a new president of the United States.

In most elections, there are several different people who are running for the same job in government. The person who receives the most votes is elected. This is known as majority vote. Most Americans believe that the fairest way for people to govern themselves is by majority vote.

In some elections, the citizens not only vote for people to run the government but they also help to decide important questions. For instance, the people of a community may have a chance to vote on whether they wish to pay more taxes in order to build a new school.

In every election, there are winners and losers. But even though people are on the losing side, their opinions are still important. In a democracy, people who do not agree with the majority are free to express their ideas and offer suggestions. Perhaps they can persuade other people to agree with their point of view. Then, in the next election, they may have a majority on their side.

4. **All citizens should have a chance to get a good education.**

In every community on earth, young people must learn many things to meet

The South 63

An auto-mechanics class. Most Americans believe that all people should have an opportunity to get a good education. In this class, students learn skills that will help them get a good job. Students also need to develop thinking skills that will help them live successfully in today's world.

their needs successfully. The older people help them learn these things. Helping people learn is known as education.

Education is very important in a democracy like the United States. In order to have good government, citizens must be able to vote wisely. They must choose people to make and carry out the laws. This means that citizens must be able to understand the things they read about in the newspapers and hear on radio and television. They must also be able to think clearly about the
† problems that face their nation. They cannot do any of these things successfully unless they have had a good education.

Most Americans believe that <u>all</u> young people—even those from the poorest families—should have an opportunity to get a good education. At the same time, young people have a duty to make the best possible use of this opportunity. Only in this way can they become useful citizens.

5. **Laws should be the same for all citizens of a country.**

Most Americans believe that all the citizens of a country should be treated in the same way by their government. Everyone should be required to obey the same laws. Each person's vote should count exactly the same as every

† In what other ways is education important to you? Explain.

other person's. People should never gain or lose any rights just because of such things as their religion, the color of their skin, or the amount of money they have.

6. All people have certain rights that no one can take away from them.

Most people who live in democracies believe that every person has a number of important rights. For example, in the United States we believe that:

. . . People have the right to express their ideas on any subject.

. . . People have the right to worship God in any way they choose, or not at all.

. . . People have the right to choose the kind of work they want to do. They also have the right to change jobs whenever they like.

. . . A person who is accused of a crime has the right to a fair trial.

We also believe that these rights cannot be taken away from any person, even by a majority vote. In a democracy, the government is expected to protect the rights of all citizens.

7. Citizens have responsibilities as well as rights.

As you have discovered, people in a democracy enjoy many important rights and freedoms. But these rights and freedoms do not just come to us without any effort. They have to be earned.

For a democracy to be successful, all citizens must be willing to do their part. In other words, citizens have <u>responsibilities</u> as well as rights. Most Americans would agree that the responsibilities of a citizen include those that are shown at right.

Have students read "Responsibilities of Citizens" and discuss them as a class.

RESPONSIBILITIES OF CITIZENS

Obeying the laws

Good citizens obey the laws of their community, state, and country. Even if they think a law is unfair, they will not disobey it. Instead, they will work in a peaceful way to get the law changed.

Treating other people with respect

Good citizens treat other people the same way they would like to be treated. They try to be friendly and polite to everyone. This is because they truly believe that every person is important.

Getting a good education

In the United States, most people have an opportunity for an education. Young people are responsible for making good use of this opportunity. By learning as much as they can, they are preparing to become useful citizens when they grow up.

Doing useful work

Most Americans feel they are responsible for doing useful work. When they become adults they do not expect other people to take care of them. Instead, they expect to work hard and do their job well.

Taking part in the government

In the United States, it is important for every citizen to take part in the government. People who are over eighteen can do this by voting in all elections. Also they can work for candidates* they think would do a good job. Young people have a responsibility to learn as much as they can about their government. This will help prepare them to make wise decisions when they are older.

Cooperating with other people

Many jobs in a community cannot be done well by persons working alone. Instead, there must be cooperation among many people. Citizens of a community have a responsibility to work together. In this way, they can make their community a better place to live.

*See Glossary

† Have you thought about how you might want to earn your living when you are older? How important is education to your goal? Explain.

Problems of Democracy

In the United States today, there are certain problems that keep many people from meeting all of their basic needs. These are known as social problems. The box on page 68 lists seven important social problems that people in our country are trying to solve. Let's look more closely at two of these problems.

The Need for Better Education

Today, most people in our country need a better education than they would have needed in earlier times. Most jobs today can only be done by people who have learned certain skills. Education is important for other reasons as well. A good education helps people develop their abilities and reach important goals in life. †

Children in school. Most people in our country today have a chance to get a good education. What are some of the things you can do as a student to make the most of this opportunity to learn?

Opportunities for education

In the United States today, most people have a chance to get a good education. There are many fine schools in all parts of our country. Most of these are public schools. The money needed to run the public schools comes from taxes that people pay to the government. Public grade schools and high schools are free to all students. Nearly every young person in our country can attend school for twelve or thirteen years without paying any money.

There are also many private grade schools and high schools in the United States. These are usually run by churches or other groups. The private schools are not supported with tax money as the public schools are. Instead, they are supported with money that comes from churches or other groups. Also, the parents usually pay fees for sending their children to these schools.

Today, millions of Americans continue their education beyond high school. Many of them attend colleges or universities. Others go to special kinds of schools. These might be business schools or schools of nursing. There they can learn the skills they need to hold certain jobs.

Many adults who work at full-time jobs are now getting more education. They are doing this to learn new skills or to have more satisfying lives. Some attend classes where they work. Others go to special classes during their spare time.

Problems of education

In spite of these opportunities, there are still many Americans who do not receive the education they need to lead happy, useful lives. Let's look at some of the reasons for this.

Some communities in our nation do not have enough tax money. They cannot pay for the kind of schools they need. In these communities, the school buildings may be old and run-down because there is no money to build new ones. Or the schools may be overcrowded with students. Sometimes there are not as many teachers in a school as there should be. Also, some schools do not have the books or equipment they need to help all their students learn.

Even if young people attend good schools, they do not always learn as much as they should. This may be partly because they are not prepared to do schoolwork. In many families, the parents must work long hours in order to earn a living. They do not have time to teach their children the things they must know in order to do well in school. Some children come from homes where there are few toys, books, or writing materials. These children often do not know as many words as other children do. It is not surprising that they make less progress in school, even though they may be just as smart as other children. They need special help in order to make full use of their abilities.

Many young people fail to do well in school because they do not understand why education is important to them. Some of these students do not receive the help they need to succeed in school. As a result, they dislike schoolwork. Or they may be bored with schoolwork, and feel that it is a waste of time. They do not study hard enough to get a good education. Sometimes they make trouble for their

Have students read "Seven Social Problems" and then discuss them as a class.

teachers and the other students. When this happens, the whole class may make less progress than it should.

In most states today, children are required by law to attend school until they are at least sixteen years old. But some young people drop out of school soon after reaching this age. They leave school before they have learned the skills they need to earn a good living. On the other hand, many students who would like to go on to college after finishing high school do not have the money to do so.

Helping people get a good education

Today, people in the United States are trying in many ways to provide students better opportunities for getting an education. For example, our national and state governments have been giving large amounts of money to local communities. Some of this money is being used to build new schools and to hire more teachers. Some of it is used to buy new books and equipment.

As you have seen, many children make slow progress in school. This is because their experiences at home have not prepared them for doing schoolwork. It has been found that these children can often be helped by sending them to nursery school. They attend when they are three or four years old. At nursery school they can be taught the things that most other children learn at home.

Many communities have begun programs planned to give children a "head start." In nursery schools or special classes, very young children are prepared for kindergarten or first grade. Our national government is helping to pay for these programs.

SEVEN SOCIAL PROBLEMS

In our country, a number of serious problems prevent people from meeting their needs. These are called social problems. The government and the people of our country have been working hard to solve these problems. As we make progress toward this goal, more Americans will have happier and more successful lives. Our country's social problems include:

1. **The need for more jobs.** At the present time, about six out of every hundred workers in the United States are unable to find jobs.
2. **The high cost of living.** In recent years, the high cost of goods and services has kept many people from meeting their needs. This continuing rise in prices is called inflation.
3. **The need for better education.** Many people in our country are not getting a good education. They are not gaining the knowledge they need for good citizenship.
4. **Illness and handicaps.** Americans are among the healthiest people in the world. However, millions of people in our country suffer from serious illnesses and handicaps.
5. **Lack of freedom for certain groups.** In the past, some groups of people in our country did not have the same freedoms as other people. Today, our laws give every person the right to fair treatment and equal opportunity. Even so, some Americans still do not have all the rights and freedoms promised by our laws.
6. **Crime.** Over the years, there has been a great increase in the number of major crimes in our country. In many areas, people live in fear for their lives.
7. **Unsuccessful communities.** In many parts of the United States there are unsuccessful communities. Many of the people in these communities are not doing useful work. They are not getting the education they need to get jobs or to be good citizens. The crime rate in these communities is very high.

Children in a nursery school. Many communities have started programs that help prepare very young children for kindergarten or first grade. In nursery schools or special classes, these young people learn many things they have not had a chance to learn in their own homes.

Older children are also being helped to get a good education. For instance, many communities have programs to help students who have trouble keeping up with their schoolwork. These programs are often run by churches, clubs, or other community groups. In some communities, there are classes for young people who have dropped out of high school.

Today, young people are being encouraged to stay in school until they get all the education they need. Our government carries on a program to explain why a good education helps people succeed in later life. Many communities have set up special schools or classes for students who plan to get jobs as soon as they finish high school. There students can learn valuable job skills such as typing, carpentry, and auto repairing.

Today, many young people from poor families have a chance to go on to college after they finish high school. Each year, thousands of students receive gifts of money to help pay for a college education. These gifts are called scholarships. Some of the money for these scholarships comes from clubs or churches. Some money comes from business companies or labor unions. Some is provided by our government. The government also has a program to help students who need jobs while they are in college.

The South 69

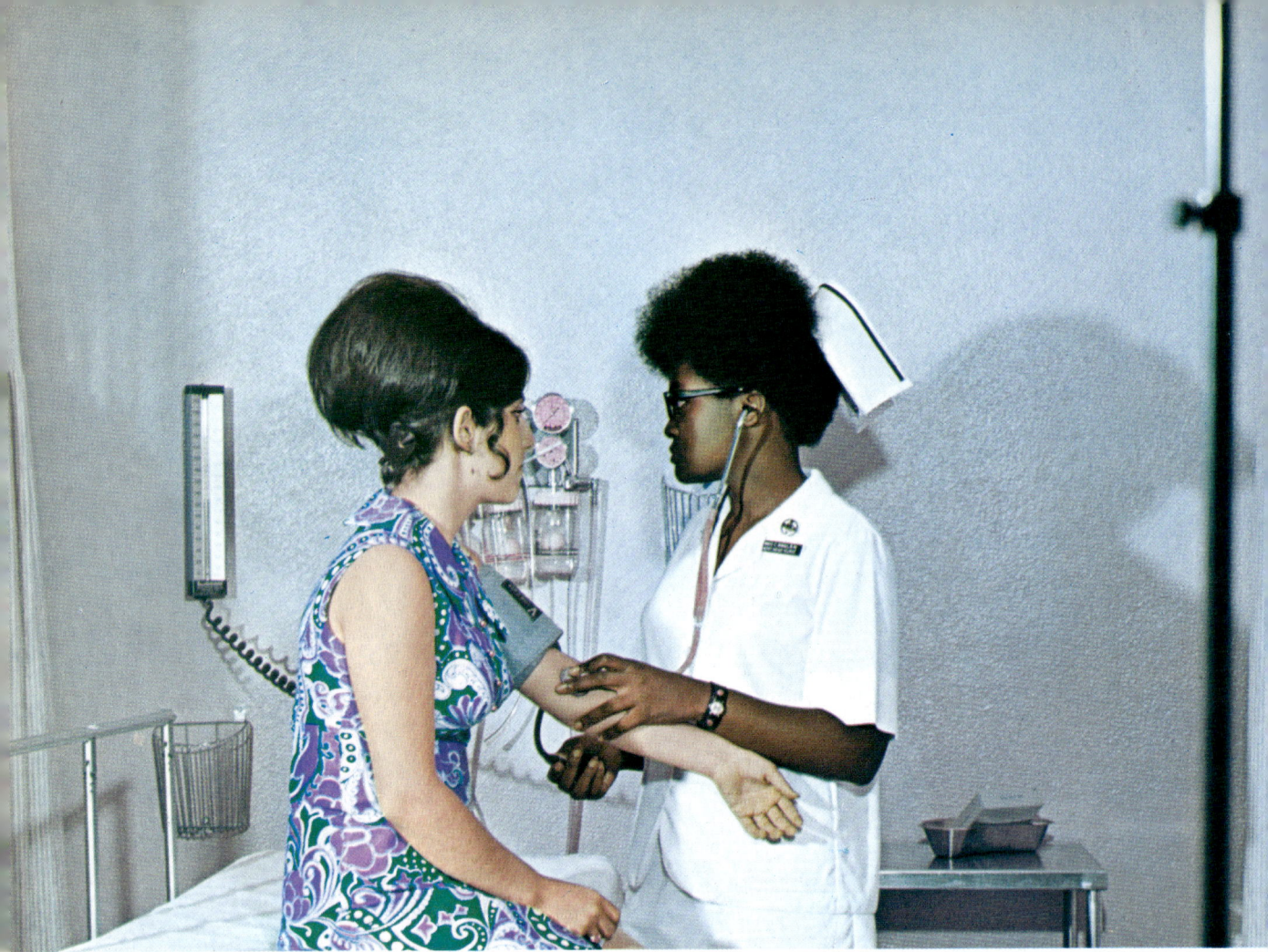

In a modern hospital. Americans enjoy better health than people in most other countries of the world. Yet sickness is a serious problem for many people in our country. What are some of the things being done to provide better health care for all the people who need it?

Illness and Handicaps

Americans enjoy better health than people in most other countries of the world. Yet sickness is a serious problem for many of our citizens. Millions of people suffer from long-lasting illnesses such as cancer* and heart disease. Others have some kind of weakness in their bodies. This weakness makes it harder for them to lead a normal life. For example, there are many people who are blind, deaf, or crippled. Weaknesses such as these are known as handicaps.

Illness and handicaps keep large numbers of Americans from meeting all of their basic needs. Some of these people are children who cannot go to regular schools. Others are older people who can work only part of the time or not at all.

Helping people to have better health

In the last one hundred years, scientists and doctors have found many ways of helping people who are ill. Many serious diseases can now be entirely cured with the use of modern medicines. People who have certain diseases that cannot be cured are given medicines that allow them to lead fairly normal lives.

Our country has also made great progress in keeping people from becoming ill. For example, few Americans now suffer from rickets.* This disease can be avoided by eating foods that are rich in vitamin D. People can now get "shots" and other medicines that protect them from being harmed by disease germs. As a result, diseases such as polio* have almost been wiped out. In the past, people often became sick from eating food or drinking water that contained germs. This seldom happens today. People are more careful about keeping food and water clean.

Americans are not only more healthy than they used to be but they are also living longer. In 1900, a ten-year-old child could expect to live to about fifty years of age. Today, a ten-year-old child can expect to reach the age of seventy-one.

Much is now being done to make life easier for people who have handicaps. For instance, a person who cannot walk can move around in an electric wheelchair. A person who has lost an arm or a leg can sometimes get a new arm or leg made out of plastic and metal. Many people who are partly deaf can use hearing aids to help them hear better. People who have very poor eyesight can be fitted with special eyeglasses.

† The high cost of medical care

Even though these gains are important ones, not all of our country's health problems have been solved. For example, the cost of medical care has been rising rapidly. If there is a serious illness, a family may have to spend thousands of dollars for doctors' fees and medical care.

This problem is especially serious for families who do not have much money. Sometimes the members of these families do not have good health because they do not eat enough of the right foods. Also, they sometimes live in places that are not clean. When these people become sick, they may not be able to pay for good medical care. Also, they may not know where they can go for help.

Sickness also causes many problems for older people. As you have seen, people are living longer today than they did in the past. For this reason, more people suffer from illnesses that come with old age. Sickness keeps many older people from working at steady jobs. To meet their needs, they must depend on money they saved during the years when they were working. This is seldom enough money to pay for expensive medical care.

Health care for the poor and elderly

Today, a number of things are being done to provide better health care for all the people who need it. "Shots" and other kinds of medicine are sometimes provided free or at a very low cost to all citizens. In many communities, there are places where people who do not have much money can get free medical care.

Many families in the United States have insurance* to help them pay the costs of a serious illness. Sometimes workers pay for this insurance out of the money they earn. In other cases, the insurance is paid for by business companies. Our national government

† Can you think of reasons why medical care is so expensive? Explain your reasons.

Providing better health care. The scientist in the picture at left is using an electron* microscope to do medical research. In the past one hundred years, scientists and doctors have found many ways of curing people who are ill. Modern machines also help provide better health care. In the picture at right, a medical worker is using an X-ray* machine to help find out what is wrong with a patient.

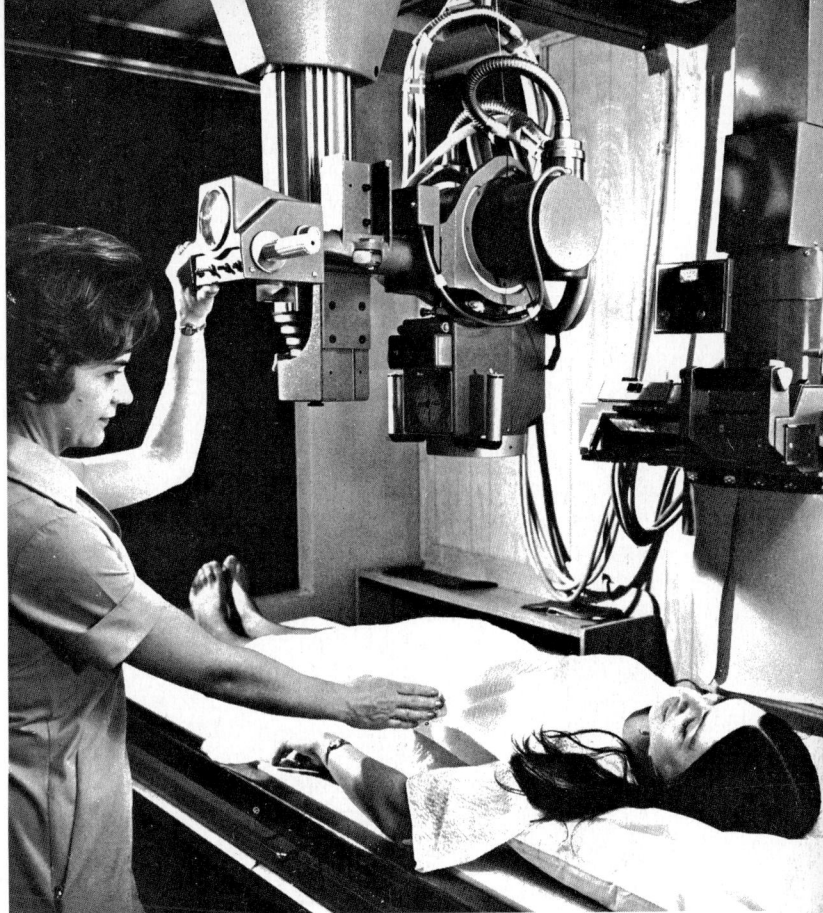

has set up programs called Medicare and Medicaid. These programs help poor and elderly people pay for medical care. There are still many medical costs that are not covered by any insurance.

Other health problems

Other health problems also face our nation today. In many small towns and farming communities, there are not enough doctors to care for all the people who are sick. This is also true in poorer neighborhoods of large cities. Some communities do not have modern hospitals. Also, scientists who have been seeking cures for diseases such as cancer are finding it hard to raise the money they need for their work. There is still much to be done before all Americans receive the kind of health care they need.

Make a Poster †
This chapter tells about seven important beliefs shared by people in a democracy. Do research about these beliefs. Then choose one of them. Make a poster showing how this belief is important in your life. Draw or paint pictures for your poster. Or, you may wish to cut pictures out of old magazines or newspapers.

Thinking Together ††
In our country today, most people have a chance to get a good education. With the other members of your class, discuss the following question. Why is it important for people in a democracy to get a good education? In preparing for your discussion, do research in this chapter. Think about the ways in which education affects the following:
1. voting wisely
2. getting a good job
3. meeting other basic needs

† Have individual students make posters.
†† Hold a class discussion.

† Have students solve this problem to start them thinking about the arts of the South.

7 The Arts

† **A Problem To Solve**
How do the arts of the South help us understand the people of this region? In forming hypotheses* to solve this problem, you will need to think about the following:
1. southern painting and architecture*
2. literature of the South
3. music of the South
4. southern crafts
To help solve this problem, you will need to do research in other sources.

See Skills Manual, "Thinking and Solving Problems"

Many of our country's great writers, painters, architects, and musicians have lived in the South. Through their works artists let us know their thoughts and feelings. As you learn about the different works of southern artists, you will gain a better understanding of this area's history. You will also discover some of the values important to the people of the South.

Architecture
In the South you can see many fine examples of architecture. During the early days of our country, southern planters built beautiful Georgian-style* homes, which were very much like a style of architecture used in England.

After the Revolutionary War,* Greek and Roman styles of architecture became well-liked in the United States. Our third president, Thomas Jefferson, borrowed ideas from the Roman style in designing his own home, Monticello. (See picture at right.) Jefferson also designed the Capitol at Richmond and several buildings for the University of Virginia.

*See Glossary

Monticello, Thomas Jefferson's home, is an example of architecture in the South. Jefferson used ideas from the Roman style of architecture in designing this house.

74 The South

Daniel Boone Coming Through the Cumberland Gap is one of George Caleb Bingham's best-known paintings. Bingham, who grew up in Virginia, became famous for his paintings of early American life.

Wealthy cotton planters in Mississippi, Alabama, and Georgia built homes in a style known as Greek Revival. These homes are known for their large white columns and two-story porches. The porches protected the rooms from sun and allowed space for outdoor living. Many such homes can still be seen in Natchez, Mississippi, on the banks of the Mississippi River. In parts of Louisiana, houses with beautiful wrought-iron balconies and gates show the influence of the early French settlers.

Painting

Many American painters have made their homes in the South. Perhaps the best known is George Caleb Bingham, who was born in Virginia. He was one of our country's leading painters of the 1800's and is well known for his paintings of subjects from American history. One of his most famous pictures is titled *Daniel Boone Coming Through the Cumberland Gap*. In his later years, Bingham lived in Missouri and painted many pictures showing life in the Midwest.

How do paintings, such as the one above, help us to learn about historical events? Discuss how historical events are recorded today.

Frank Duveneck was a Kentucky-born artist who spent much of his life in Europe. Duveneck's style of painting influenced many other American artists. He used broad, flat strokes to show scenes from everyday life. Duveneck was also a sculptor* and an etcher.*

Literature

In the early days of our country, some of the major writers in the South were also government leaders. Thomas Jefferson wrote the Declaration of Independence and many papers on government and science. James Madison, who also lived in Virginia, was one of the authors of *The Federalist*. This was a series of papers about the United States Constitution.

By the end of the 1800's, several southern writers of fiction* had become widely known. Joel Chandler Harris wrote some delightful animal tales known as the "Uncle Remus" stories. His characters such as Brer Rabbit, Brer Fox, and Tar Baby are still popular today.

Many of America's important writers of novels* in the 1900's were born in the South. William Faulkner used his home state of Mississippi as the setting for many novels, such as *The Sound and the Fury* and *Light in August*. In 1949 he was given the Nobel Prize* for literature. Faulkner and several other southern writers have received Pulitzer* prizes for their novels. Among these are Margaret Mitchell, for *Gone With the Wind*, and Harper Lee, for *To Kill a Mockingbird*.

Another important southern writer was Thomas Wolfe. He wrote several long novels that describe the beautiful countryside in North Carolina, where he was born. His best-known work, *Look Homeward, Angel*, is based on his own life.

Many novelists born in the South have written about the problems faced by farm families and small-town southerners. One of these was Carson McCullers. In her most famous novel, *The Member of the Wedding*, she wrote about a small-town girl and the pains of growing up. Erskine Caldwell, Eudora Welty, and Du Bose Heyward also wrote about life in the South.

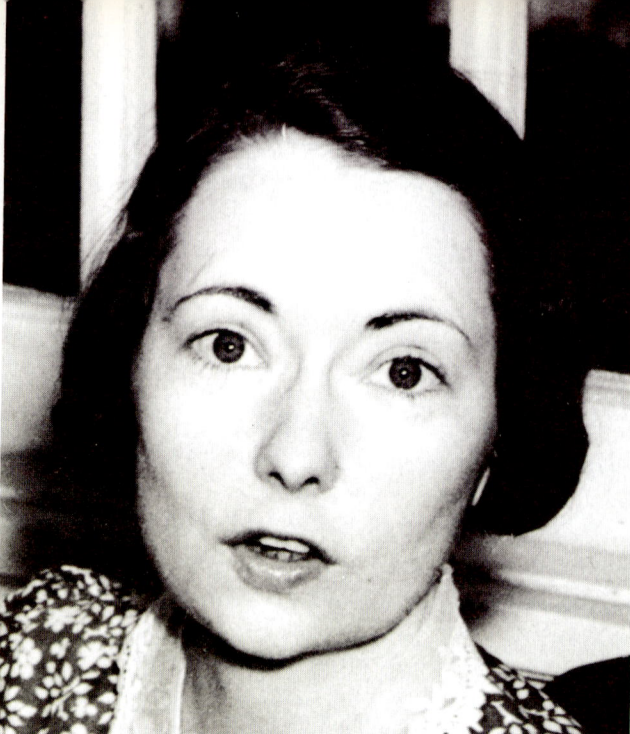
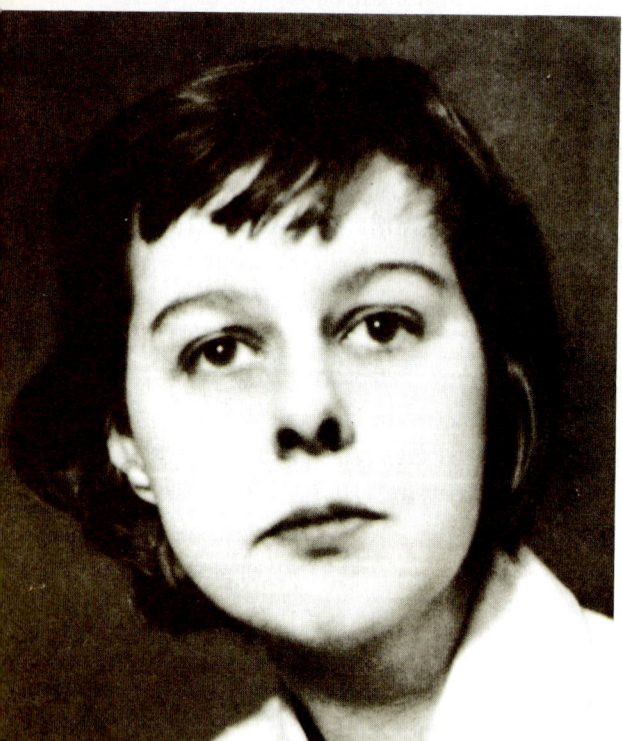

Language

See Great Ideas

Four of the most important novelists of the 1900's who made their homes in the South are shown in these pictures. They are: Thomas Wolfe (upper left), Margaret Mitchell (upper right), Carson McCullers (lower left), and William Faulkner (lower right). All four of these people wrote about life in the South. Why do you think they used southern people and places in their novels? Do you think they could have written important books about the South if they had not lived there? Give reasons for your answers.

Refer to the pictures and caption above. You may wish to use the caption for a class discussion about sharing ideas with language.

† Have you ever listened to jazz? Describe your feelings about this kind of music.

Another novelist was Richard Wright, one of America's first major black writers. Other southern-born writers include Frank Yerby and Truman Capote.

The South has also been the home of many fine poets and playwrights. Important poets born in the South include Sidney Lanier, John Gould Fletcher, John Crowe Ransom, and Robert Penn Warren. Warren has received Pulitzer prizes for both poetry and fiction. Tennessee Williams, one of our leading playwrights, has twice received the Pulitzer Prize. Many of his plays are about people in the South.

Music

Much of our country's popular music had its beginnings in the South. In fact, New Orleans is often called the "cradle of jazz," although no one knows exactly where or when jazz began. Around 1890-1910 young musicians in New Orleans and other parts of the South created a new form of music. This new music was a mixture of Negro spirituals, marching tunes, and other kinds of music. It became known as jazz. The jazz artist Louis Armstrong was born in New Orleans and started his career in that city. He became

Louis Armstrong was one of the best-known jazz artists in the world. Jazz is a form of music created by young southern musicians sometime around the beginning of the 1900's.

† Use this activity, and hold a class discussion about two types of music that began in the South.

known all over the world. W. C. Handy was a jazz composer who was born in Alabama but spent part of his life in New Orleans. He is best known for his "St. Louis Blues."

The Negro spirituals that influenced early jazz musicians were often sung by field hands as they worked in the cotton fields of the South. "Swing Low, Sweet Chariot" is one of these spirituals.

Many well-known folk songs have come from the mountains and valleys of the South. The lovely song "Down in the Valley," once heard only in the mountains of Kentucky, is now known all over the United States.

The style of popular music known as "country and western" comes mainly from the South. For many years, the "Grand Ole Opry" show, which features country-and-western music, has been broadcast from Nashville, Tennessee. Most of the country-and-western recordings made in the United States are also produced in this city. Many leading singers and composers live in Nashville.

Crafts

Early settlers in the Appalachian Highlands of the South made nearly everything they needed by hand. They skillfully made clothing, dishes, furniture, and other goods for their homes. Even after stores began to sell machine-made goods, many mountain people still made things by hand. They took pride in tanning their own leather, dyeing their own wool, spinning their own cloth, and making their own dishes. In recent years, community

Chet Atkins is one of our country's most popular country-and-western artists. Like jazz, this type of music had its beginnings in the South. Perhaps you would like to play a country-and-western record and a jazz record. Then, as a class, discuss the following questions. †
1. Do you think country-and-western and jazz are both "arts"? Why do you think this?
2. Which of these kinds of music do you like better? Why?

A **North Carolina woman weaving cloth** on a handloom. Skilled workers throughout the South create beautiful handicrafts such as bedspreads, pottery, and furniture.

leaders have encouraged mountain people to make and sell their handicrafts. This helps increase the income of the mountain people. It also helps make sure that knowledge of these arts will not be lost. All over the South, people show their love for art by making beautiful and useful things.

In North Carolina, for instance, workers make rocking chairs and tables by hand, out of hickory or walnut wood. Others carve beautiful stringed instruments called dulcimers from maple or cherry. In the western part of the state, potters shape clay into lovely teapots, candlesticks, bowls, and other things. Many mountain people raise their own sheep. They clip off the wool, spin it, and dye it with bark. Then they weave beautiful woolen bedspreads. Many people are willing to pay good prices for these handmade spreads. Other craft workers make patchwork* quilts or cornhusk dolls.

Discover Arts and Crafts in Your Area †
As a class, do research to discover what kinds of arts and crafts are carried on in your community. Then make a bulletin-board display with newspaper and magazine clippings about artists and craft workers in your community. Perhaps an artist or craft worker would be willing to talk to your class about his or her work.

† Use this as a class activity.

Part 3

Earning a Living

The people of the South, like people in other parts of our country, earn their living in many different ways. Some southerners are farmers. Others work in mines. Some people in the South earn their living by fishing. Many southerners work in factories and offices. In which areas or states of the South would you find people who earn their living in the following ways:
- drilling for oil
- mining iron ore
- mining coal
- raising oranges
- raising peanuts
- raising soybeans
- working in a textile* mill
- working in a furniture factory
- working in a steel mill

Part 3 has information that will help you answer this question.

*See Glossary

Canning shrimp in Biloxi, Mississippi. The processing of food products is an important industry in the South. What are some other important industries here? Where do industries in the South get the raw materials they need?

Use Fideler Discovery Cards 93-102, or Fideler Discovery Sheets, Volume 1, pages 41-44 for activities about farming.

8 Farming

A region good for farming

Most parts of the South have been given the valuable gifts of nature needed for farming. This part of our country has rich soil and plenty of rainfall. The South also receives many months of warm sunshine. Therefore, it has a long growing season. The growing season is the length of time when crops can be grown outdoors. Most of the South has a growing season of 200 days or more. (See map on page 88.)

The long growing season helps southern farmers in two important ways. It allows them to grow crops that cannot be grown in many other parts of our country. Some of these crops are cotton, oranges, rice, and sugarcane. The long growing season also makes it possible for some southern farmers to grow two crops on the same land in a single year.

In some parts of Florida, the weather is warm all year round. During the winter months, farmers here can grow fruits and vegetables. Large amounts of tomatoes, lettuce, and other fresh vegetables are shipped to northern cities. Strawberries, melons, and other fresh fruits are also shipped to northern markets.

Growing Crops

A visit to an orange grove

To learn more about farming in the South, let's visit an orange grove in Florida. As we drive along a highway in central Florida, we see row after row of trees. The rows stretch as far as we can see. The green trees are dotted with many oranges. When we drive into the grove, we see workers on ladders. They are picking the fruit.

Refer to the picture on these pages. What can you discover about farming in the South? List your discoveries.

Workers picking oranges in Florida. The South has a long growing season. This allows southern farmers to grow crops that cannot be grown in many other parts of our country. One of these crops is oranges.

We watch as the oranges are loaded into large trucks. The owner of the orange grove tells us that more oranges are grown in Florida than in any other state in our country. Some of the oranges are sold in stores throughout our country. Many others are made into orange juice.

Florida also leads our country in growing grapefruit. In fact, this state produces more than three fourths of the citrus* fruit grown in our country.

*See Glossary

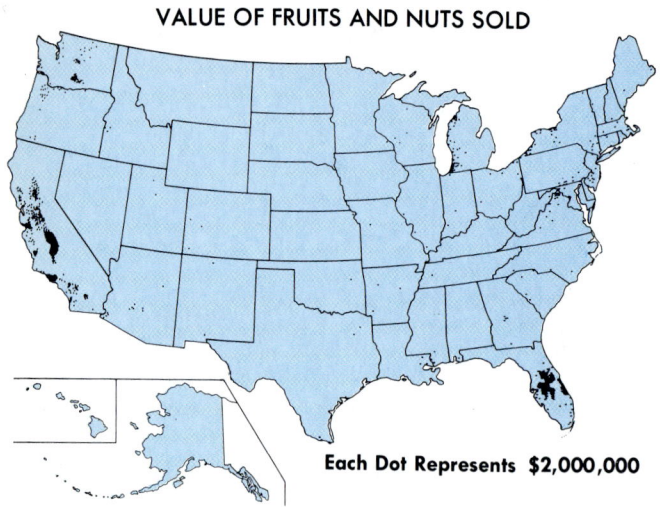

VALUE OF FRUITS AND NUTS SOLD

Each Dot Represents $2,000,000

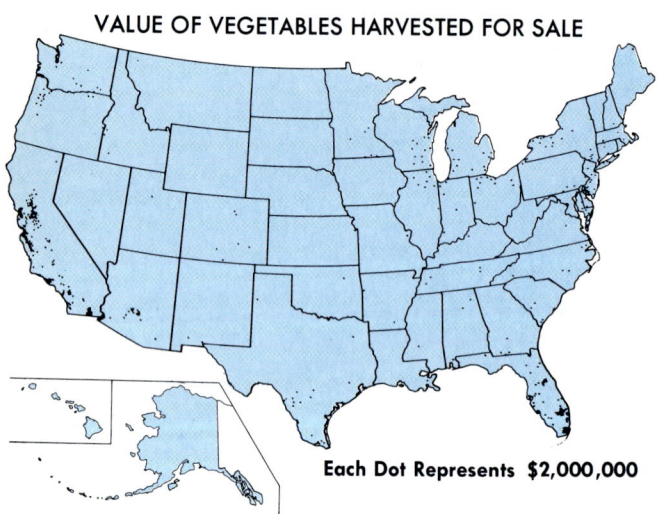

VALUE OF VEGETABLES HARVESTED FOR SALE

Each Dot Represents $2,000,000

grow well in the light, sandy soil of the Coastal Plain. Celery, beans, tomatoes, cabbages, and peppers are grown on truck* farms. Most of these farms are along the Atlantic and Gulf coasts.

Other fruits

Many other kinds of fruits are grown in the South. Apples are grown on the western part of the Piedmont Plateau* in Virginia. Apples are also grown in parts of the Great Valley.* (See page 18.) In South Carolina, Georgia, and other states there are huge orchards of peach trees. Strawberries, pears, plums, and watermelons are also grown in the South.

Vegetables

Farmers grow vegetables in many parts of the South. Sweet potatoes

Refer to the picture and caption below. Use the question to start a class discussion about exchange.

Exchange
See Great Ideas

Harvesting strawberries in Florida. In some parts of the South, the weather is warm all year round. During the winter months, farmers here can grow fruits and vegetables for northern markets. For example, the strawberries shown here will be shipped to New York City and other large cities in the north. Would it be possible for people in the north to have fresh fruits and vegetables during the winter months without the great idea of exchange? Give reasons for your answer.

Refer to the maps and caption below. Have students compare with map on pages 8-9. Could cotton be grown in Maine? In South Carolina? Why? Why not?

Cotton

The southern states grow about one third of our country's cotton. Most of it is raised in an area known as the cotton belt. A very important part of this belt lies along the Mississippi River. It extends from northern Louisiana to northern Tennessee. The land in this part of the South is level and very rich. The rainfall is not too heavy. The growing season is long enough for raising cotton. It lasts 200 days or more. (See below.) Mississippi and Arkansas lead the southern states in the growing of cotton.

Let's visit a cotton farm near the Mississippi River. It is September. The cotton is ready to be harvested. Rows of plants stretch as far as the eye can see. The plants are covered with snowy-white cotton bolls. Huge cotton-picking machines rumble slowly through the fields. We watch as they strip the cotton bolls from the plants. The bolls are taken to buildings where machines called gins separate the seeds from the cotton fibers. Then the fibers are pressed into giant bales.* The bales are taken to a nearby railroad to be shipped to textile mills.

Exploring the Growing Season

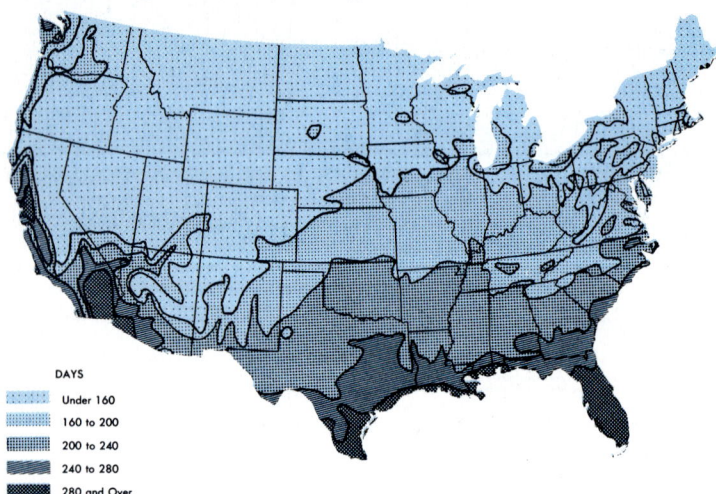

Cotton Harvested

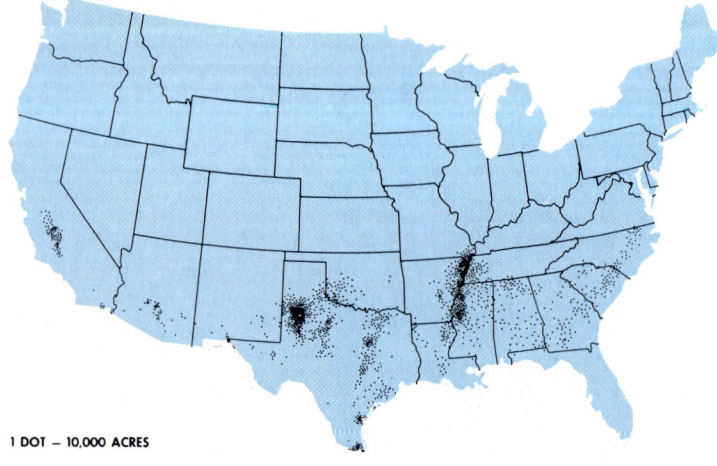

1 DOT = 10,000 ACRES

The growing season is the period of time when crops can be grown outdoors without danger of being killed by frost. Most of the South has a growing season of 200 days or more.

Some crops can be raised only in areas where the growing season is fairly long. One of these crops is cotton, which needs at least 200 days in a row without frost. If you will compare the two maps on this page, you will see that the cotton-growing areas of the South have a frost-free period of 200 days or more. Other crops raised in the South that need a long growing season are oranges, rice, and sugarcane. The South also produces many crops that do not require such a long growing season.

Emptying a cotton harvester. About one third of our country's cotton is raised in the South. Most of it is grown in an area called the cotton belt. Where is the cotton belt located? What are some of the reasons why this part of our country is very good for raising cotton?

Soybeans

Southern farmers earn more money from soybeans than from any other crop. Soybeans are used in making many food products. Among the foods made from soybean oil are oleo and cooking oils. Soybean flour is used to make breads, soups, and many other foods. Soybeans can also be made into food that looks and tastes like beef, pork, and other kinds of meat. Soybean meal is a good food for livestock.

Think as a Social Scientist*
The picture at left shows a farmer cultivating* a field of soybeans. Use this picture to think as a social scientist would. Look at the picture carefully. What does it tell you about farming in the South? As you answer this question, think of what the picture tells you about each of the following:
1. the kind of soil here
2. the weather
3. the kinds of tools this farmer uses
4. earning a living in the South
5. crops raised in the South

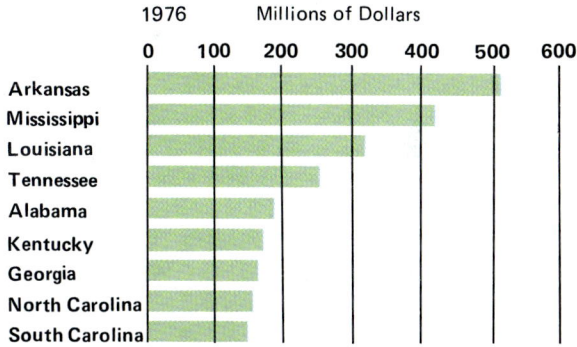

SOYBEAN PRODUCTION IN THE SOUTH

(Total Value of Soybeans Produced in the United States: About 8 Billion Dollars)

SOYBEANS HARVESTED FOR ALL PURPOSES

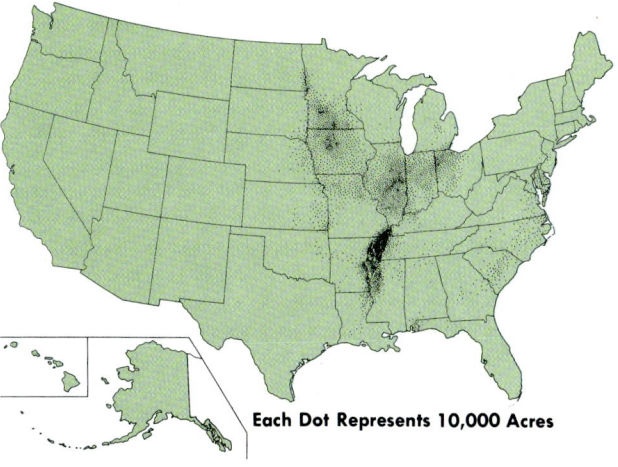

Each Dot Represents 10,000 Acres

Soybeans are grown in many parts of the South. However, the main area for growing this crop is the rich soil of the Mississippi Valley. Arkansas and Mississippi raise more soybeans than any other states in the South.

The South

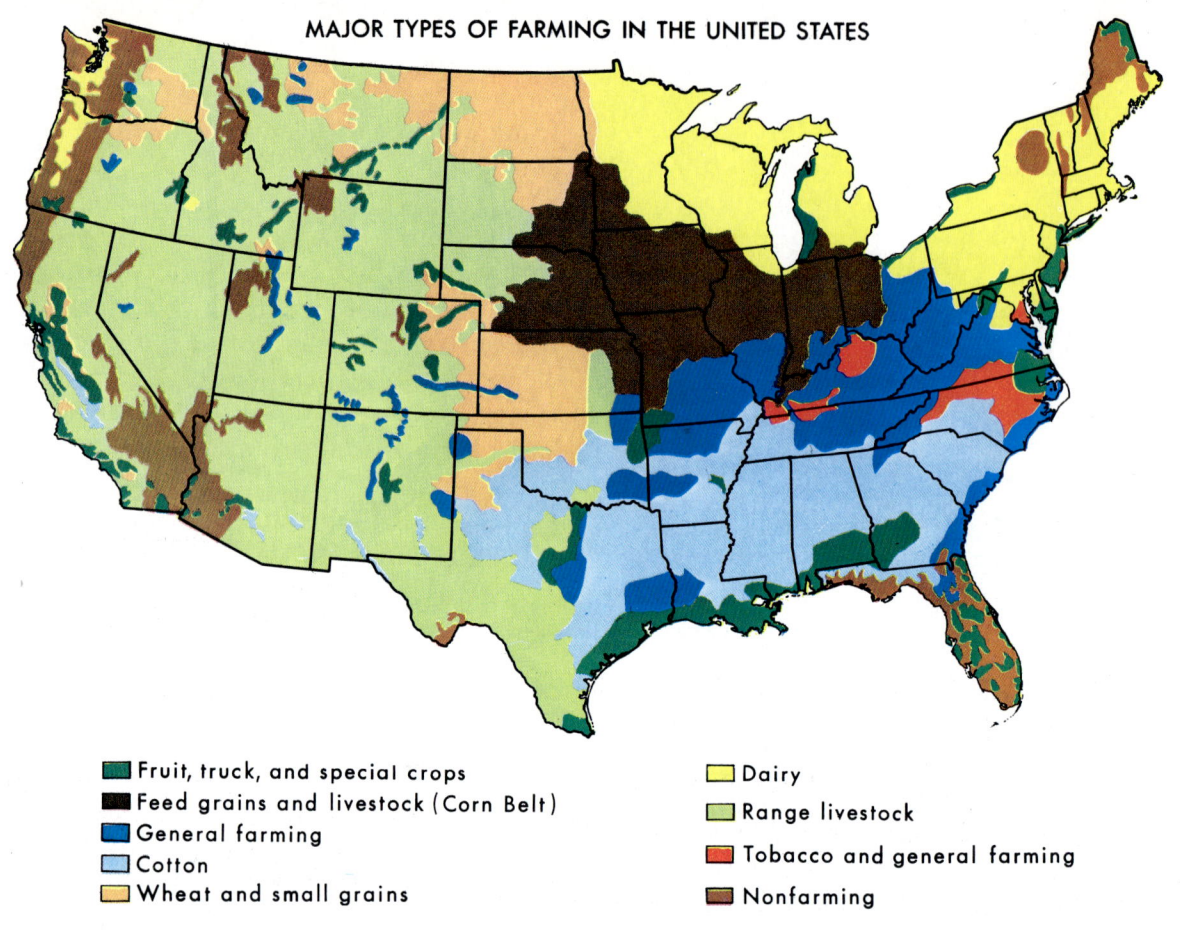

MAJOR TYPES OF FARMING IN THE UNITED STATES

- Fruit, truck, and special crops
- Feed grains and livestock (Corn Belt)
- General farming
- Cotton
- Wheat and small grains
- Dairy
- Range livestock
- Tobacco and general farming
- Nonfarming

Using Natural Resources

See Great Ideas

The map above shows the major types of farming in the United States. What major types of farming are there in the South? Southern farmers, like those in the other parts of our country, use several different natural resources. What are they? How is each of these resources used in growing crops? In raising livestock? Do you think it is important for farmers to be careful in their use of natural resources? Explain.

Grain crops

Many farmers in the South raise grain crops. Rice is grown in parts of Arkansas and Louisiana. In these places, the soil is very moist. The land is also low and easily flooded. Rice fields must be covered with several inches of water for the young plants to grow well.

Corn is raised in every southern state. It is used in making many different kinds of foods, such as corn bread and breakfast cereals. Corn is also important as a feed for animals.

Other farm crops

Peanuts grow well in the sandy soil and warm climate of the Coastal Plain. Georgia raises more peanuts than any other state in our country. Large quantities are also grown in Alabama, North Carolina, and Virginia. Peanut oil, peanut butter, and many other foods are made from this crop.

About nine tenths of our country's tobacco* is grown in the South. North Carolina and Kentucky are the leading tobacco-growing states.

Some parts of the South are very good for growing other crops. Sugarcane is raised in the Florida Everglades and in parts of southern Louisiana. There the soil is very rich and moist. Orchards of tung trees can be found near the Gulf coast. This tree grows very well in the warm and rainy climate there. Tung nuts contain a quick-drying oil that is used in making paints and other products. There are many large orchards of pecan trees on the Coastal Plain of the South. More pecan nuts are grown in Georgia than in any other state.

Making Good Use of the Land

Farming in the South today is very different than it was years ago. Farmers have learned that they must take good care of their land if they want to grow large amounts of crops.

† Some of the old ways of farming were not good for the land. Years ago, farmers used to plow their rows straight up and down on the hillsides. When it rained, the rainwater would wash away large amounts of the rich topsoil. Today, farmers plow rows that curve around the hillsides. This is known as contour plowing. The cuts made into the land by the plow catch rainwater. When it rains, the rainwater cannot rush down the hillside and wash the soil away.

Southern farmers use other modern ways of farming. They use chemical fertilizers to help keep their soil rich. These fertilizers put back into the soil some of the plant foods their crops use up. Chemicals are also used to kill weeds and harmful insects.

Peanuts grow under the ground. At harvesttime, the plants are plowed up. They are left in the fields to dry in the sun. Later, machines are used to remove the peanuts from the dried plants. More peanuts are raised in Georgia than in any other state in our country.

† What do you think happens when the soil is washed away? Explain. Review and discuss erosion.

Using Tools

See Great Ideas

The picture above shows early settlers harvesting grain. The man in the bottom part of the picture is cutting grain with a tool called a sickle. What tool is the man in the top part of the picture holding? How do you think he will use this tool? Compare this picture with the picture at right. The picture at right shows farming in the South today. What tool is the farmer in this picture using? What are some of the ways in which the use of new machines helps farmers make good use of their land?

Refer to these pictures and caption. Have students answer the questions.

New machines have also changed southern farming. Machines such as tractors and cotton pickers are doing work that people used to have to do themselves. A cotton picker can harvest cotton fifty times faster than a person can harvest it by hand.

Livestock

Poultry and eggs

Poultry and eggs rank first in value among the farm products of the South. This region has many farms where chickens are raised for their eggs and for meat. Georgia, Arkansas, Alabama, and North Carolina lead our country in raising broiler chickens. Georgia produces more eggs than any state except California. Turkeys are also raised in the South. Many turkey farms are in North Carolina and Arkansas.

INTERNATIONAL

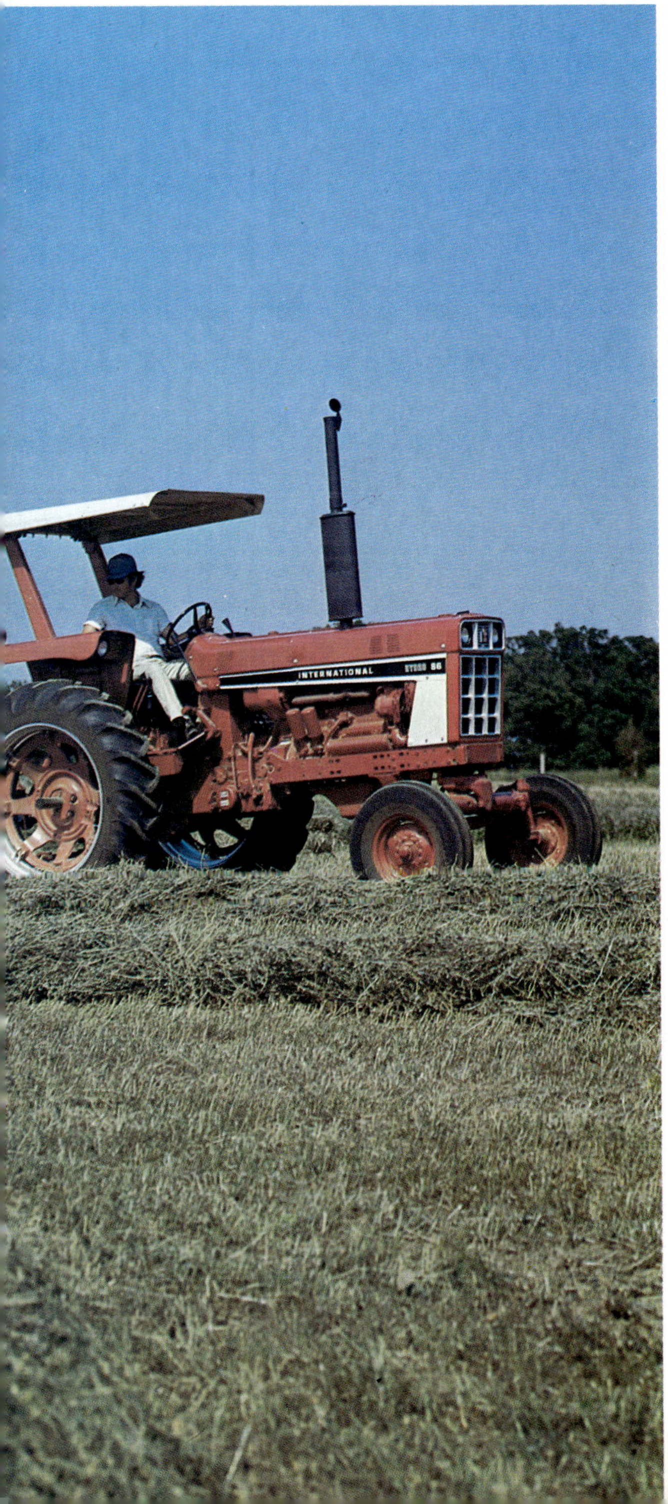

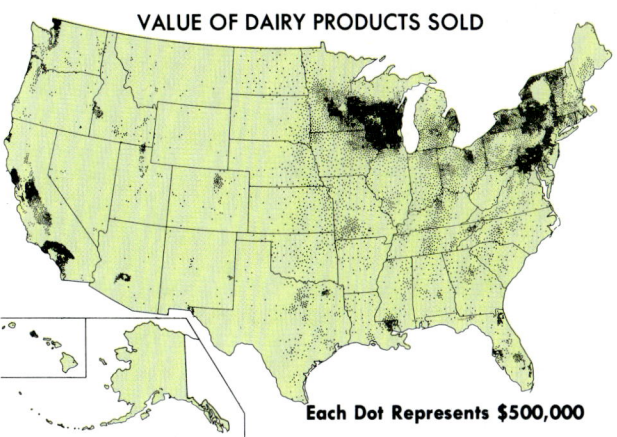

VALUE OF DAIRY PRODUCTS SOLD
Each Dot Represents $500,000

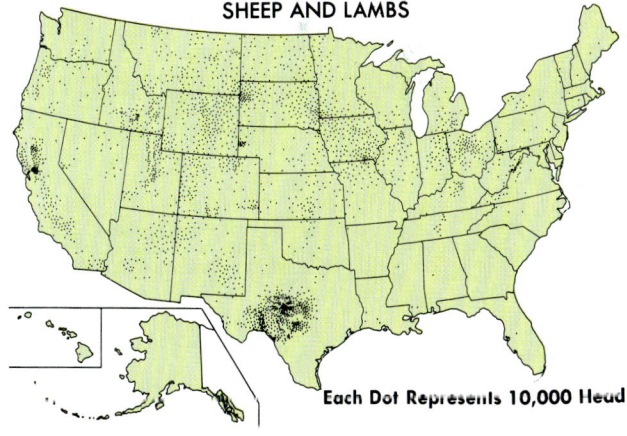

SHEEP AND LAMBS
Each Dot Represents 10,000 Head

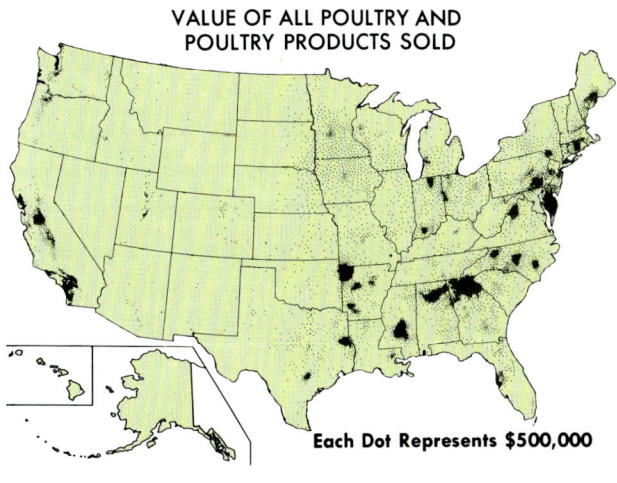

VALUE OF ALL POULTRY AND POULTRY PRODUCTS SOLD
Each Dot Represents $500,000

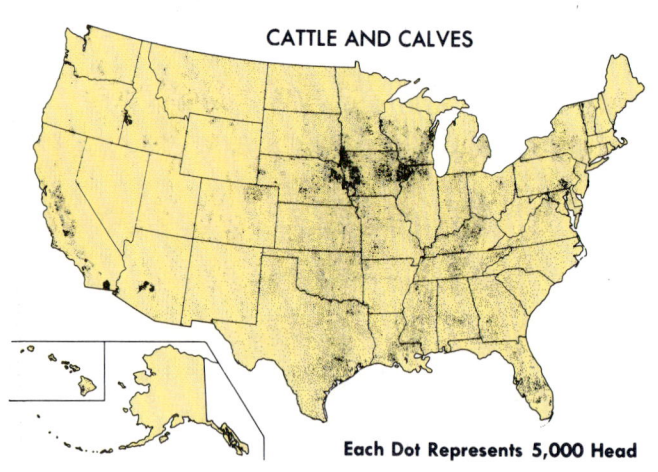

CATTLE AND CALVES

Each Dot Represents 5,000 Head

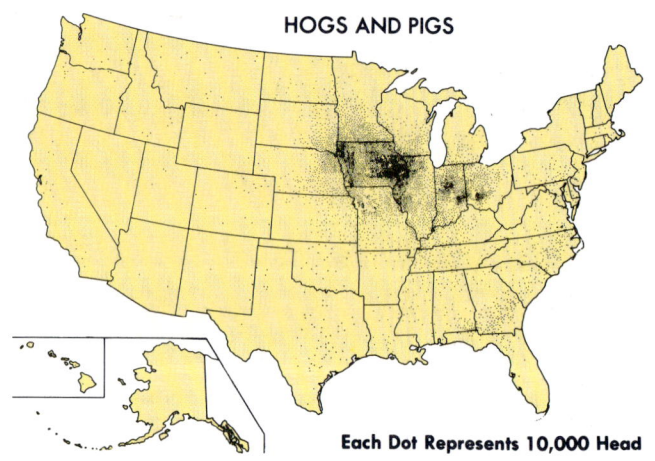

HOGS AND PIGS

Each Dot Represents 10,000 Head

Cattle

The raising of cattle is another important kind of farming in the South. Large herds of beef cattle graze on rich green pastures in Kentucky. They are also raised in Alabama, Tennessee, and other states. Some of these cattle are later sent to feedlots. There they are fed corn and other grains to fatten them for market.

Large numbers of dairy cows are also raised in the South. Kentucky, Florida, Tennessee, and Virginia lead the South in the value of dairy products sold. Many dairy farms are near large cities. † They supply fresh milk to city people.

Other livestock

Southern farmers also raise several other kinds of livestock. Hogs are raised in all parts of the South. The leading hog-producing states are North Carolina and Georgia. Sheep farming is important in Virginia and Kentucky. Valuable horses are raised on large farms in the Bluegrass area of Kentucky. They are also raised in the Nashville Basin of Tennessee.

96 The South

† Why do you think many dairy farms are located near large cities? (Due to spoilage, fresh dairy products cannot be shipped long distances.)

Cattle on a feedlot in Florida. The raising of beef cattle and dairy cows is an important kind of farming in the South. What other kinds of livestock are raised in this part of our country?

Think With a Picture

The picture on these two pages was taken in Florida. Use this picture to think as a social scientist. What does this picture tell you about raising cattle in the South? As you answer this question, think of what the picture tells you about the following:
1. the land
2. the weather
3. kinds of cattle raised here
4. how the cattle are fed
5. earning a living in the South

You may wish to look at other pictures in this chapter to see what they tell you about farming in the South.

Make a Crop Map

Do research in this chapter to find out what main crops are raised in the South. Also find out where in the South these crops are grown. Then do the following:
1. Using the map on page 54, trace an outline map of the South.
2. Choose a symbol for each crop you want to show on your map.
3. Draw the symbol for each crop in the right places on the map. The symbols should show where in the South each crop is grown.
4. Include a key with your map. (The key tells the meaning of the symbols.)

You may wish to assign these as special student activities.

Use Fideler Discovery Cards 83-92, or Fideler Discovery Sheets, Volume 1, pages 37-40 for activities about natural resources.

9 Natural Resources and Energy

The South has many natural resources that people can use to meet their needs. In this part of our country are rich deposits of oil, coal, iron ore,* and other minerals.* There are also large forests. Great numbers of fish live in the waters of the Atlantic Ocean and the Gulf of Mexico. In some parts of the South, there are fast-flowing rivers. These can be used to make electricity.

Energy Fuels

Among the most important minerals found in the South are oil (or petroleum), natural gas, and coal. All of these minerals can be burned to produce energy* for homes and factories. For this reason, they are called energy fuels.

Oil and natural gas

There are huge deposits of oil and natural gas in the South. Oil is an important resource in Louisiana, Florida, Mississippi, Arkansas, and Alabama. Most states in the South have deposits of natural gas. Louisiana produces more oil and natural gas than any other state in our country except Texas.

Oil is usually found deep under the ground. Most scientists believe that oil was formed millions of years ago. This was long before people lived on the earth. Much of the earth that is now dry land was then covered by shallow seas. Billions of tiny plants and animals lived in the water. As they died, they sank to the bottom. Over millions of years, rivers carried sand and soil into the sea. The dead plants and animals were covered by these materials. As time passed, the sand and soil turned into rock. The weight of the rock helped change the remains of the dead plants and animals into oil.

*See Glossary

Drilling for oil in the Gulf of Mexico. The South has huge deposits of oil. Some of these lie beneath the Gulf of Mexico. From large platforms, like the one in the picture at left, oil wells are drilled deep into the ocean floor. The platform holds the drilling machinery. It also has rooms where the workers eat and sleep.

† To get oil, people drill wells deep into the earth. The drilling machinery is held up by tall towers called derricks. These are usually made of steel. The oil is pumped to the surface. It is then sent through large pipes to factories called refineries. There it is changed into many useful products. One of these products is the gasoline we use in our cars. Another is the fuel burned in jet airplanes.

Some of the South's deposits of oil lie beneath the Gulf of Mexico. In many places along the coast of Louisiana, oil derricks rise high above the waters of the Gulf. Some of the derricks are on floating platforms that can be moved from place to place. Others are attached to the floor of the Gulf. Although many oil wells are near the shore, others are as far as 80 miles (129 km.)† from land.

Natural gas is usually found in the same places as oil. But sometimes it is found alone. Large pipes carry natural gas produced in the South to cities and towns in the eastern part of our country. Natural gas is used in many homes for heating, cooking, and other purposes. It is also used as a fuel in factories.

Oil and natural gas can be used in making many valuable chemicals.* These are called petrochemicals. Among the different products made from petrochemicals are medicines, plastics, and fertilizer.

Coal

The South has large deposits of high-grade soft coal. (See page 103.) Most of these deposits are in the Appalachian Highlands. They are part of a huge

† km. means kilometer

† Perhaps some of your students have seen or visited an oil well or refinery. Have them tell about their experiences.

Using Natural Resources

See Great Ideas

Workers drilling for oil. The South has valuable energy fuels and many other mineral resources. Do research about them in this chapter. Then make a mineral resources chart. In the first column of your chart, list the energy fuels and other mineral resources of the South. In the second column, list the states in the South in which each resource is found. In the third column, list some of the ways in which each resource is used.

Refer to the picture and caption. Have students do the activity described in the caption.

Use Fideler Discovery Cards 123-131, or Fideler Discovery Sheets, Volume 1, pages 53-56 for activities about ecology.

Ecology

Strip-mining coal in Kentucky. Much of the South's coal is mined in this way. Huge power shovels like the one below are used. They remove layers of soil and rock that lie on top of the coal deposits. When the coal is uncovered, it can be broken up and removed. Many people feel strip-mining is harmful to the ecology of the area. What is the meaning of the term "ecology"? Why is strip-mining thought to be so harmful? To answer these questions, you may wish to read about ecology in the Glossary and do further research.

Coalfields of the United States

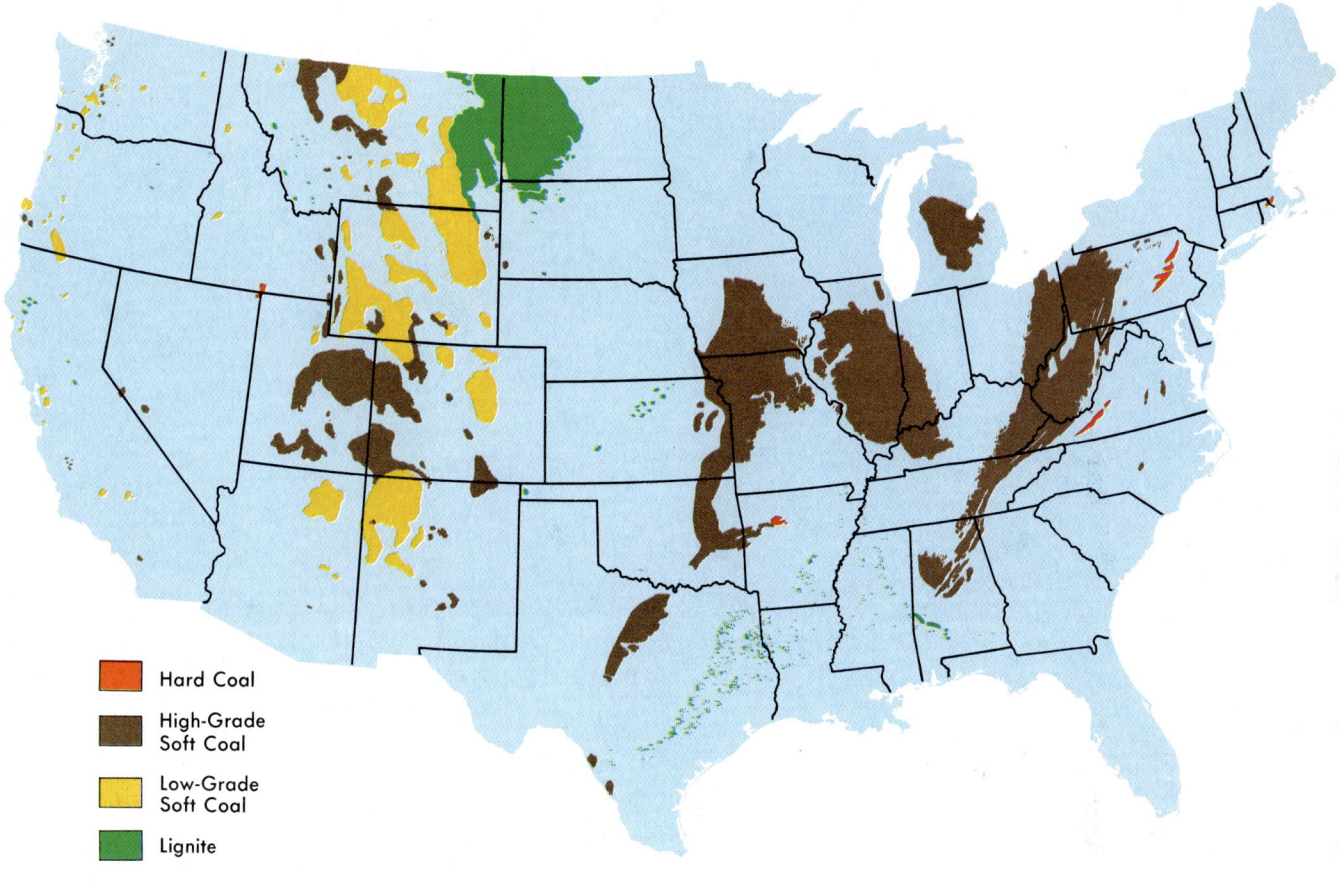

coalfield that stretches from northwestern Pennsylvania into Alabama. More than one third of the coal mined in the United States comes from Kentucky, Virginia, Alabama, and Tennessee. Kentucky produces more coal than any other state in our country.

Coal produced in the South is used in many ways. Much of it is burned as fuel in homes and factories. Iron and steel plants in Alabama and Tennessee use large amounts of coal from nearby mines. Much of the coal used by these plants is made into a fuel called coke.* Certain chemicals are obtained from gases that are given off when coke is made. These chemicals are used in making paint and other useful products.

Trains carry coal from southern mines to seaports on the Atlantic coast such as Norfolk, Virginia, and Charleston, South Carolina. (See map on page 17.) From these cities, coal is shipped to other seaports in the United States, Canada, and western Europe. Coal is also taken by train to Toledo, Ohio, and other ports on Lake Erie. There, the coal is loaded onto large boats that carry it to other cities on the Great Lakes.*

Operating a loading machine in an iron mine. Iron ore is one of many valuable minerals found in the South. The most important deposits are near Birmingham, Alabama.

Coalfields
Iron Ore Deposits
▲ Limestone Quarries

IRON AND STEEL

Three main minerals are needed for making iron and steel. They are iron ore, coal, and limestone. As the map at left shows, these three minerals are found near Birmingham, Alabama. This is one of the few places in the world where deposits of all three minerals are found close together. Trucks and trains carry these minerals to steel plants in the Birmingham area.

Making iron

Large amounts of iron ore, coke,* and limestone are placed in a giant blast furnace. Then a blast of very hot air is blown into the furnace. The air makes the coke burn with a great heat. This melts the iron ore. The limestone mixes with waste matter in the ore to form slag. The slag rises to the top of the furnace. Melted iron containing carbon* collects at the bottom.

Making steel

Some of the carbon and other unwanted matter must be removed from the melted iron to make steel. This may be done in different ways. But most of the steel made in the United States is produced by a method called the basic oxygen* process. In this process, oxygen is blown into a special furnace through a tube. It is blown at very high speed. The oxygen helps burn out unwanted matter in the melted metal. This produces steel.

*See Glossary

Other Minerals

Besides the energy fuels, many other kinds of valuable minerals are found in the South. Some of these are ores that can be used to make metals such as iron and aluminum. Other minerals produced in the South include salt, sulfur, and clay, as well as several different kinds of rock.

Iron ore

There are rich deposits of iron ore in the Appalachian Highlands. The most important deposits in the South are in Alabama, near the city of Birmingham. Alabama is one of our country's leading producers of iron ore. It is the only state in the South that mines very much of this mineral. Two important metals—iron and steel—are made from iron ore at huge plants in or near Birmingham. The feature at left gives more facts about Alabama's iron and steel industry.

Bauxite

Another valuable resource in the South is bauxite. This is an ore used in making aluminum. All of the bauxite mined in our country comes from the South, mainly from Arkansas. The bauxite is dug from huge open pits. Then it is sent to factories to be made into aluminum. More aluminum is used in the United States than any other kind of metal except iron and steel.

† The large amounts of bauxite mined in the South are not nearly enough to meet our country's need for aluminum. Most of the aluminum produced in the United States is made from bauxite mined in other countries.

Four important mineral resources of the South are iron ore, limestone, oil, and natural gas.

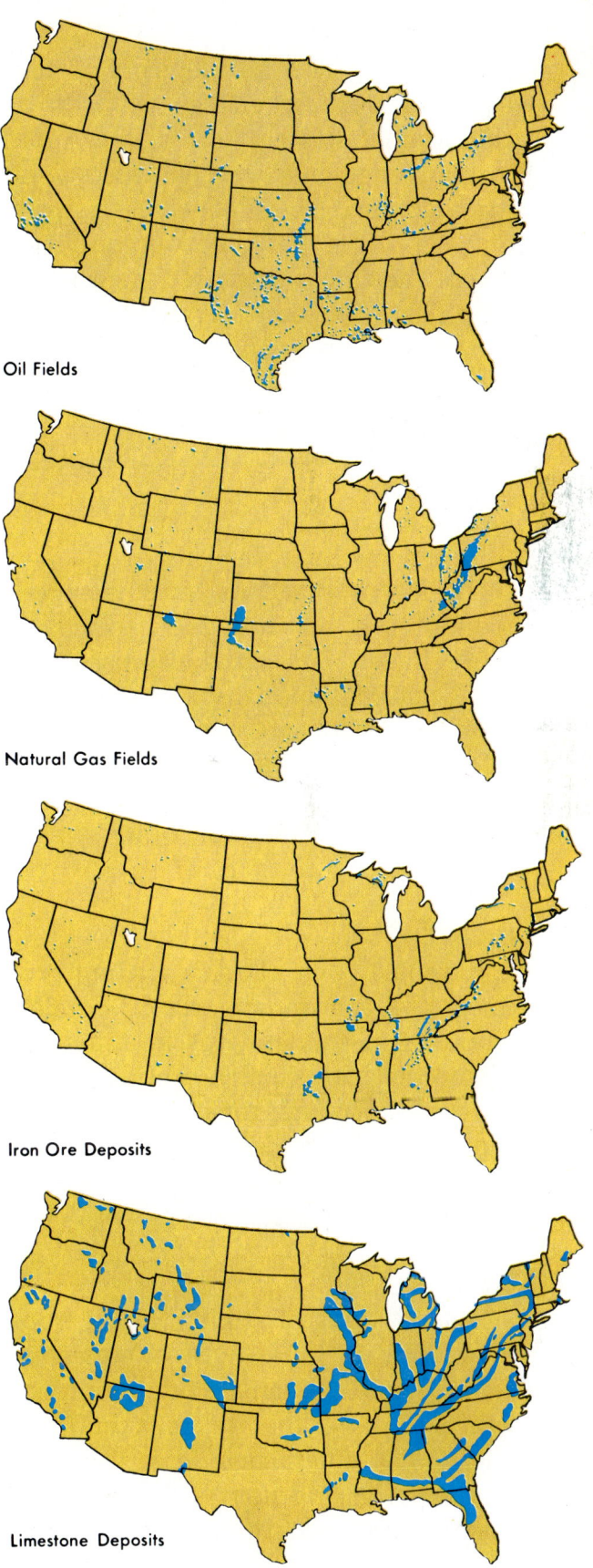

Oil Fields

Natural Gas Fields

Iron Ore Deposits

Limestone Deposits

† Is it wise to be dependent on other countries for important resources? Explain.

Zinc and pyrites

The South also has deposits of zinc ore and pyrites.* Large deposits of these minerals are found in the Appalachian Highlands in Tennessee. Zinc ore is shipped from Tennessee to smelters* in other parts of our country. There the zinc is separated from waste materials in the ore. At factories near the mines, copper and sulfuric acid are made from pyrites. Sulfuric acid is used in making many chemicals and chemical products.

Salt and sulfur

There are huge deposits of salt and sulfur in Louisiana. As you know, people put salt on their food to give it more flavor. But salt is also used as a raw* material by many industries. For instance, chemical companies use salt in making hundreds of different products. Much of the sulfur mined in Louisiana is combined with other chemicals to make sulfuric acid.

Phosphate rock

Florida is our nation's leading producer of phosphate rock. Smaller amounts of this mineral are mined in Tennessee and North Carolina. Much of the phosphate rock is made into fertilizer. This is done by heating the rock or by treating it with a chemical such as sulfuric acid.

Stone

Several kinds of stone are dug from quarries* in the South. Tennessee, Georgia, and Alabama produce marble, which is used mainly as a building stone. The finest marble is used for monuments* and statues. Georgia produces more granite than any other state in our country. Granite is often used to build bridges and large buildings because it is very strong. In several states of the South there are limestone quarries. Limestone is a good building stone because it can be cut easily and does not split. It is also used in making cement, and in producing iron and steel. (See feature on page 104.)

Several kinds of clay are found in the South. Georgia and South Carolina are leading producers of kaolin,* which

Mining zinc ore in Tennessee. Large amounts of zinc ore are mined in Tennessee. Zinc is important in industry. It is used to coat metals, such as steel. The zinc coating prevents the steel from rusting.

is also called china clay. Most of the kaolin is used in making paper or as a filler for rubber products. Some kaolin is used to make fine china and pottery. Clays used in making bricks are found in every state of the South.

Forest Resources

More than half of the land in the South is covered with forests. (See map on page 109.) As you know, the South has a warm climate, a long growing season, and plenty of rainfall. Trees grow rapidly here. Huge forests of pine trees grow on much of the Coastal Plain. They also grow on the mountain ranges in the Appalachian Highlands. Hardwoods such as oak, hickory, gum, and walnut are found mostly in highland areas of the South. Many farmers in this part of our country raise pine trees on tree farms.

Logging in the South. Nearly one half of all the wood produced in our country comes from forests of the South. Much of the wood is sawed into lumber. What are some other forest products of the South?

A visit to a logging camp

To learn how the forests of the South are used, let's watch a logging crew at work. The loggers have driven to work from their homes a few miles away. Sometimes they live in a logging camp in the forest. This is only when they are working far from home in areas that are hard to reach by car.

Before the loggers begin work, a forester marks the trees that will be cut. Only large trees or diseased trees are marked. The healthy young trees will not be cut. Now we watch the loggers at work. The whine of their saws and the crash of the falling trees are so loud that we can hardly hear each other talk. The fallen trees will be cut into logs and sent to sawmills. There they will be sawed into lumber.

Products from southern forests

Nearly one half of all the timber harvested in the United States comes from forests in the South. Georgia, Alabama, Mississippi, Louisiana, and North Carolina are among the leading states in our country in timber harvested.

Much of the wood that comes from southern forests is sawed into lumber. Pine trees are the main source of lumber. However, oak, cypress, and other trees are also used. Part of the lumber is used to build houses and other buildings. The rest is used in making furniture and other wood products.

Several other products come from the forests of the South. Valuable oils are obtained from pine trees. These oils are made into turpentine and rosin. Turpentine is used mainly as a paint thinner. Rosin is used in making paint, paper, soap, and many other products. Some of the wood from southern forests is made into wood pulp, which is used in making paper. There are many pulp and paper mills located in the South.

TIMBER HARVESTED IN THE SOUTH 1970 — Millions of Cubic Feet

(Amount of Timber Harvested in the United States: About 12 Billion Cubic Feet)

DISTRIBUTION OF FORESTLAND

Each Dot Represents 25,000 Acres

The graph above shows the estimated amounts of timber harvested in 1970 by the states of the South. Nearly one half of all the timber harvested in our country comes from the South.

This map shows the distribution of forests in the southern part of our country. Notice that every state in the South has many areas that are covered with forests. More than one half the land in the South is wooded.

† Use Fideler Discovery Card 91 for an activity about forest resources.

Fish Resources

Each year, fishing boats bring hundreds of millions of pounds of fish to ports in the South. Most of these fish come from the Atlantic Ocean or the Gulf of Mexico. Louisiana, Florida, and Virginia lead the South in the amount of money they receive from fishing. (See graph below.)

Many different kinds of fish are caught in the South. Among these are red snapper, mullet, and groupers. All of these are used for food. Large numbers of menhaden are also caught. They are made into fertilizer, fish oil, and meal.

Shellfish such as shrimp, oysters, and crabs are taken in great numbers from the waters off the coasts of the South. Most of the shellfish are canned or frozen. Then they are shipped to different parts of the country. Shrimp bring more money to people in the South than any other kind of fish.

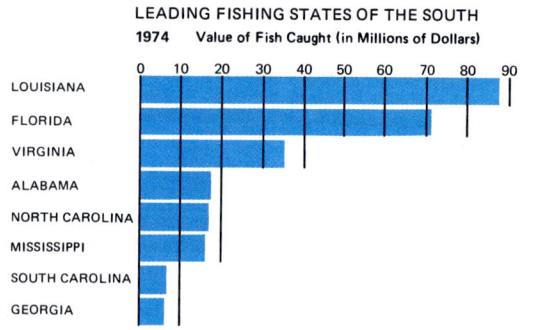

This graph shows the value in dollars of the fish catch in eight states of the South. Some of these fish are red snapper, mullet, and groupers. Others are shellfish, such as shrimp, oysters, and crabs.

Waterpower

The South has many rivers that can be used to produce electricity. Most of these rivers begin in the Appalachian Highlands. They flow into the Atlantic Ocean or the Gulf of Mexico.

Electricity that comes from waterpower is called hydroelectricity. Let's find out how it is produced. First, a dam is built on a river to hold the water back. The water forms a large lake behind the dam. Then water from the lake is allowed to flow downward through large pipes, which are usually inside the dam. In a powerhouse at the

Refer to the picture on these pages. Do you think you would like to become a commercial fisher? Why? Why not?

Fishing for shrimp in Florida. Shrimp bring more money to people in the South than any other kind of fish. Louisiana and Florida lead this part of our country in the amount of money earned from fishing.

foot of the dam, the rushing water turns engines called turbines. The turbines run machines called generators, which produce electricity.

The Tennessee Valley Authority

Many hydroelectric power plants have been built on the Tennessee River and its branches. A government agency called The Tennessee Valley Authority runs most of these power plants. You can learn more about TVA on pages 112-115.

Dams and powerhouses have been built on a number of other rivers in the South. But only a small part of the electricity produced in this region comes from hydroelectric power plants. Most of the South's electricity is produced in steam power plants. These burn coal, oil, or natural gas.

Thinking With Pictures †
Use the pictures in this chapter to think and work as a social scientist.* Study these pictures and record your findings.
1. What do you see in each picture that relates to natural resources?
2. What is being done with each resource?
3. What else have you discovered from these pictures?

† Have students do this activity.
Use Fideler Discovery Sheets, Volume 1, page 39 for additional activities.

TVA's Wilson Dam and chemical plants. The Wilson Dam is on the Tennessee River in northern Alabama. In what ways has the TVA helped to protect and develop the resources of the Tennessee Valley?

Tennessee Valley Authority

The Tennessee Valley Authority (TVA) was created by the federal government in 1933. Its goal was to protect and develop the resources of the Tennessee Valley. This great valley stretches through parts of seven states. (See map on pages 114-115.)

When our country was first being settled, much of the Tennessee Valley was covered with forests. The tree roots helped to hold the soil in place. They also helped to stop rainwater from draining quickly away. As people settled in the valley, great changes took place. Most of the forests were cut down to use as lumber or to clear the land for farming. Few trees were left on the valley's steep sides. Rainwater began to carry much of the topsoil away. Crops could no longer be grown on much of the land. It became difficult for many farmers to earn a living. There were few other jobs in the Tennessee Valley because the valley did not have many factories.

Rainwater also drained more quickly into the rivers. This caused the rivers to rise and overflow their banks. Sometimes these floods caused millions of dollars' worth of damage.

TVA went to work to improve things for the people who lived in the valley. It was given control of Wilson Dam in Alabama and two nearby chemical* plants. These plants had been built by the government during World War I. Then TVA began building other dams and power plants. These helped to protect against floods and they produced electric power. They also helped improve the rivers so that ships could use them more safely. Factories were built in the Tennessee Valley because they could get electric power at a low price.

TVA has helped develop the resources of the Tennessee Valley in other ways also. It has developed new fertilizers at its chemical plants near Wilson Dam. It has also planted trees on steep hillsides. These steps have helped to conserve* soil, water, and forests.

*See Glossary

Refer to the picture on these pages. What can you discover about the Tennessee Valley? List your discoveries.

Pickwick Landing Dam. This TVA dam is on the Tennessee River in the western part of Tennessee. The TVA has built several dams in the Tennessee Valley. These dams help control floods. They also produce electric power.

Read a TVA map. The green area of this map is the Tennessee River Valley. It stretches through parts of seven southern states. The map also shows the dams of the Tennessee Valley Authority. The key box shows that some of the dams on this map were built by the Aluminum Company of America. Others were built by the Corps of Engineers. The key box can also be used to help find the area where electric power is provided by the TVA.

Refer to the map and caption above. Have students list the rivers in the Tennessee Valley.

Refer to the picture and caption below. Use the questions in a class discussion about division of labor in your community.

10 Industry

Division of Labor

See Great Ideas

The workers shown below are making lighting fixtures in a factory in North Carolina. Look at the other pictures in this chapter to discover some additional kinds of work people do in the South. Dividing up the work among different people is called division of labor. What are some of the kinds of jobs that people have in your community? Does your community have much division of labor? Explain.

† How important to factories are raw materials? How important are workers? Explain.

Imagine that you are taking a trip on horseback from Boston, Massachusetts, to Savannah, Georgia, in the year 1830. In the northeastern part of the country, the cities and towns are close together. As you ride through the cities, you notice clouds of gray smoke pouring from the chimneys of many factories. Farther south, in Virginia and the Carolinas, you see large fields of cotton and tobacco.* You ride for many miles between cities, and in the cities you see very few factories.

A slow beginning

In 1830, and for many years afterward, the South was mainly a farming region. Southern planters were earning a lot of money from cotton and tobacco. They were not interested in manufacturing. Most of the other people in the South had little money to use for building factories. The cotton grown in the South was sold to textile* mills in Europe or the northern part of the United States. From these same areas, the South bought manufactured goods.

During the Civil War,* factories were set up in the South to make weapons, uniforms, and other things for the Confederate army. By the end of the war, however, many of these factories had been destroyed.

A good place for industry

Toward the end of the 1800's, many business people found that there were good reasons for building factories in the South. The southern states were † rich in raw materials such as cotton, tobacco, iron ore, coal, and timber. Rivers on the Piedmont Plateau could provide waterpower. Many workers could be found for factory jobs, and taxes were low.

Soon many factories were built in the South. Among these were sawmills, textile mills, and chemical* plants. Iron and steel mills were built in Birmingham, Alabama. During World War I* and World War II,* factories were built to produce war materials.

A textile mill in North Carolina. The manufacture of textiles is one of the most important industries in the South. Most of our country's cotton cloth is made in this region. What facts help explain why this is so? What are some of the other products made from cotton?

Industry grows

The growth of industry helped many people in the South. Men and women who went to work in southern factories earned money they needed. They were able to buy more goods than before. As sales grew, stores hired more clerks and bought more goods from factories. New plants were built to produce more goods. These factories bought more of the farm products and other raw materials produced by southern workers.

Today, industry is still growing in the southern states. Some state and local governments help businesses to build factories in the South. They help businesses find land and buildings. Favorable tax laws have also been passed. Today, nearly four times as many people work in manufacturing in the South as work in farming. In the years ahead, many more industries will make use of the rich resources of the South.

Textiles and clothing

Textile manufacturing is one of the most important industries in the South today. More people here work in the manufacture of textiles and clothing than in any other industry.

Most of our nation's cotton cloth is made in textile mills built along the Fall Line and on the Piedmont Plateau in the South. Large amounts of electric power for running machinery are produced in this area. Although much of the cotton used by the mills is grown nearby, some of it comes from states to the west.

Let's visit two textile mills in North Carolina. At the first mill, we see machines that spin cotton fibers into thread. This thread, which is called yarn, is woven into cloth by giant power looms at the second mill. Instead of cotton, some mills use rayon, nylon, or other synthetic* fibers.

Some southern factories manufacture clothing from textiles made in the South. In the past thirty years, many clothing factories have been built in the South, mainly in Georgia and North Carolina. These factories make dresses, shirts, overalls, stockings, and many other kinds of clothing.

Do you think the great change from farm work to factory work has been good for the people who live in the South? Why? Why not?

Other cotton products

Cotton grown in the South provides raw materials for several industries in addition to the textile industry. When cottonseeds are separated from the cotton lint* by machines called gins, some tiny fibers stick to the seeds. These fibers are used in making such products as camera film and phonograph records. Oil is squeezed from the cottonseeds and used to make food products such as margarine, cooking oil, and salad dressing. After the oil has been removed from the seeds, the material that is left is made into fertilizer and cattle feed.

Food products

The manufacture of food products is an important industry all through the South. Oil for cooking is made from corn, peanuts, and soybeans, as well as from cottonseeds. In many places, fruits and vegetables are processed in

A meat-processing and freezing plant in Alabama. The workers shown below are cutting and packaging pork. Food processing is an important industry in all parts of the South. What are some of the other foods that are processed in this part of our country?

canning factories and freezing plants. Large amounts of oranges and grapefruits are processed in Florida. Meatpacking plants can be found in Memphis and other large cities. In Louisiana, sugarcane is processed to make the snowy-white sugar that you sprinkle on your breakfast cereal.

Tobacco products

The South produces most of the pipe tobacco and cigarettes used in our country. The factories are near tobacco-farming areas, mainly in North Carolina, Virginia, and Kentucky.

Petroleum products

One of the South's important industries is the processing of petroleum. In refineries,* petroleum is made into gasoline, fuel oil, and other products. Louisiana leads the southern states in the manufacture of petroleum products.

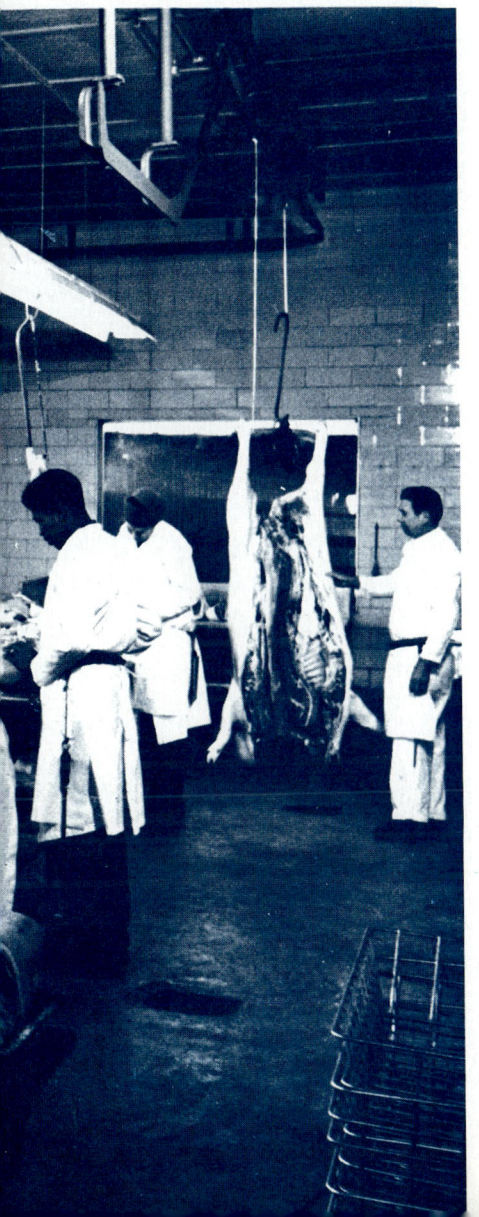

Main Industrial Areas

The map above shows the areas of the South that have the largest number of industrial workers. Use this map, the map on page 17, and information in Chapter 5 to help you answer the following questions.

1. Which of the South's main industrial areas include important seaports or river ports?
2. What are some of the main industries in Atlanta? Miami? New Orleans? Louisville? Memphis?
3. Which southern state has no large industrial area?

A laboratory worker in a chemical plant in Florida. The South has many plants where chemical products are made. What are some of the chemical products manufactured in this part of our country?

Chemical products

The South produces large amounts of chemicals and chemical products. It is rich in raw materials used by the chemical industry. Among these are coal, sulfur, salt, and phosphate* rock. Petroleum and natural gas provide raw materials for chemical plants. The chemicals made in these plants are called petrochemicals.

Other factories use petrochemicals in the manufacture of chemical products such as synthetic rubber and certain plastics. Some of these factories, which need large amounts of fresh water, are near the Mississippi River. The river provides the water, and also serves as a transportation route.

Chemical plants in the South produce large amounts of fertilizer. Plants in Florida and other states make fertilizer out of phosphate rock. In several states, chemical plants make nitrogen fertilizers from ammonia.* Many of the newer ways of making fertilizer were first tried at TVA's fertilizer-testing plant near Muscle Shoals, in northern Alabama.

Factories in the South also make many other chemical products. Plants in Tennessee and North Carolina produce chemicals from which different plastics and other synthetic materials are made. Among the many synthetic fibers manufactured in the South are rayon, nylon, orlon, and dacron. Much of the sulfur mined in Louisiana is made into sulfuric acid. Large amounts of sulfuric acid are made in Tennessee from pyrites. (See page 106.) Sulfuric acid is used in making products such as paper, glass, steel, paint, fertilizer, and camera film.

Forest products

There are huge pine and hardwood* forests in many parts of the South. Timber cut from these forests has helped the southern states become leaders in the manufacture of paper, lumber, and many other wood products.

To learn about the paper industry in the South, let's visit a mill near a pine forest in southern Alabama. Here we see wood chips and chemicals being cooked together to make wood pulp. The pulp from this plant will be made

The South 123

† Have you ever seen newsprint? Where? (Have students look up "newsprint" in the Glossary to answer these questions.)

† into the heavy brown paper used in grocery bags. Factories in the South also make newsprint* and other kinds of paper.

Building materials are produced by many factories in the South. At some plants, there are machines that glue together thin sheets of wood to form plywood. At other plants, wood fibers are pressed together to make a building material called fiberboard. Sawmills all through the South produce large amounts of lumber.

The South has a large furniture industry. North Carolina is the leading furniture producer in this region. In fact,

A paper mill in Georgia. The South has a large forest-products industry. Huge forests of pine and hardwood trees provide raw materials for making paper, furniture, and other wood products.

more household furniture is made in North Carolina than in any other state in our country. Many of North Carolina's furniture factories are in the city of High Point. These factories use lumber from sawmills in the area. The sawmills produce this lumber from hardwood logs cut in the great forests of the Appalachian Highlands.

A furniture factory in North Carolina. More household furniture is made in North Carolina than in any other state in our country.

Metal products

The South has large amounts of the three main raw materials needed to make iron and steel. Limestone is found in many parts of the South, and there are large deposits of coal and iron ore in the Appalachian Highlands. However, the only area where large amounts

The South 125

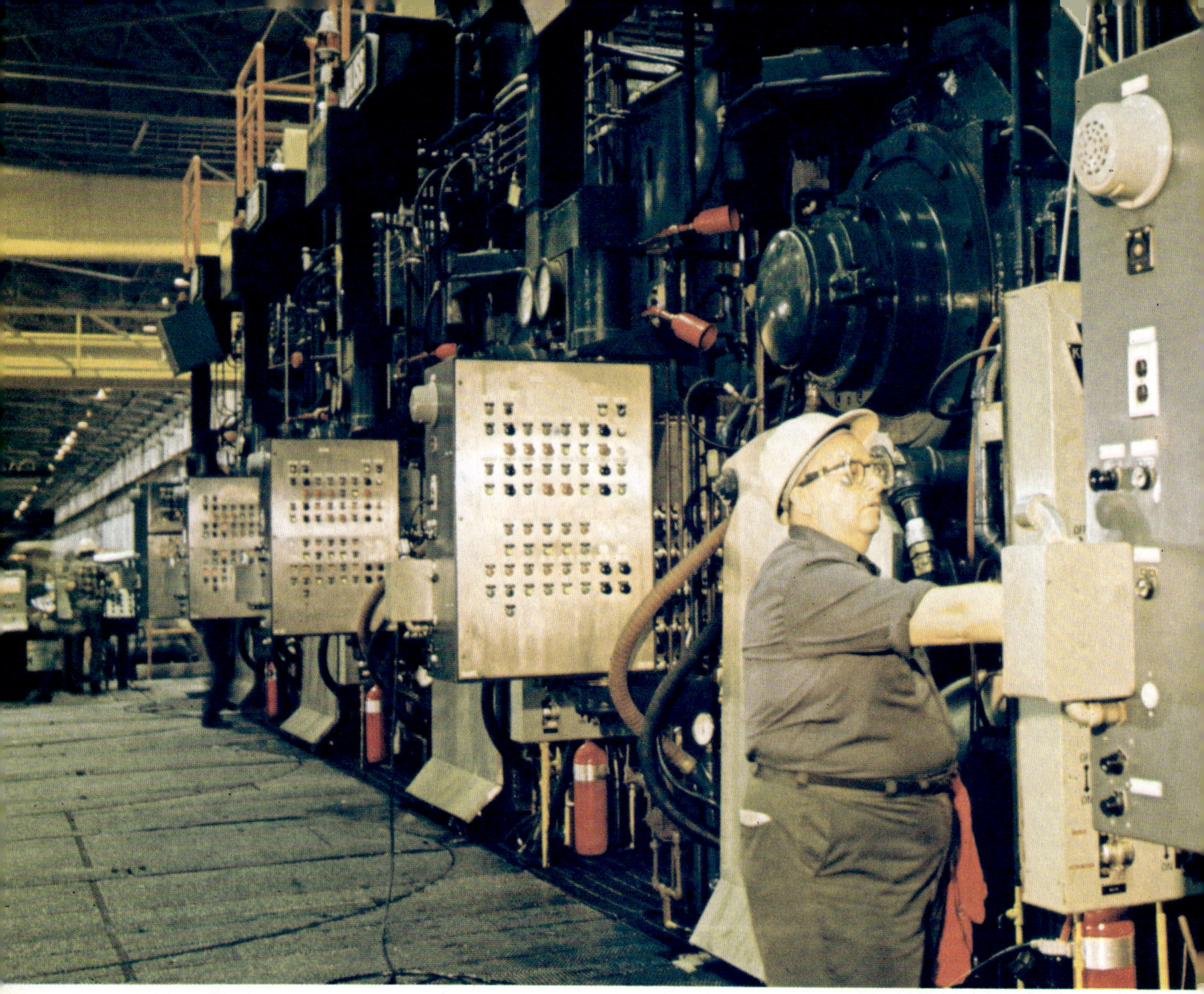

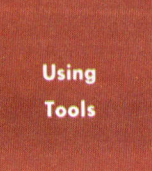

Using Tools

An aluminum mill. The workers in this picture are using machines to roll aluminum into thin sheets. Machines are some of the most important tools we have. As you can see by the pictures in this chapter, many different kinds of machines are used in industry. What are some of the machines used in obtaining raw materials such as metal ores and timber? What are some machines used in farming? What machines do you use at home? What machines do you use in school?

See Great Ideas

of all three are found close together is near Birmingham, Alabama. Plants in this area help to make Alabama the leading producer of iron and steel in the South.

Aluminum is another important metal produced in the South. It is made from an ore called bauxite.* The bauxite is first made into alumina, which contains both aluminum and oxygen.* To produce aluminum, the oxygen must be removed from the alumina. Great amounts of electric power are needed to do this.

In Louisiana, there are several plants that make alumina out of bauxite imported from the West Indies and South America. A large plant in southern

Refer to the picture and caption above. Use the questions in a class discussion about using tools.

Alabama also makes alumina from imported bauxite. Other alumina plants are located in Arkansas near bauxite mines. (See page 105.)

Several states in the South have factories where alumina is made into aluminum. Some of the alumina comes from alumina plants in the South and some is imported. Aluminum factories in northern Alabama and eastern Tennessee are near dams and power stations that provide the large amounts of electricity needed by these factories. Aluminum factories in Louisiana use electricity produced mainly at power plants that burn natural gas.

Transportation equipment

The manufacture of transportation equipment is a major industry in the South. The largest shipyard in the United States is in Newport News, Virginia. Many large naval ships, passenger liners, and freighters have been built here. There are other large shipyards along the Atlantic and Gulf coasts. The South also has several airplane factories and a number of plants where automobiles are made.

Other products

Nearly every kind of industry can be found in the South today. Among the many household appliances made here are stoves, refrigerators, and sewing machines. The South also produces farm equipment, air conditioners, and many other kinds of machinery. There are factories that make many kinds of electrical and electronic* equipment such as that used to guide our spacecraft. Huge plants in Kentucky, Tennessee, and South Carolina supply materials used to produce nuclear* energy.

Many of the South's new industries are not like the older ones such as those that manufacture textiles. They do not depend so much on having raw materials nearby. Their most important "resources" are the skills and ideas of southern workers.

Why are the skills and ideas of workers important resources? Explain.

Researchers at a space flight center in Alabama. These women are making tests in a laboratory that is just like one being built for a new space station. They are doing some of the same tests that researchers will do in the space station laboratory far above the earth's surface.

† Gain Important Understandings
1. What kinds of transportation equipment are made in the South?
2. What state is the South's leading producer of iron and steel?
3. What other important metal is produced in the South?
4. What industry provides the most jobs for southern workers?
5. In which southern state is sugar produced?
6. Which southern state produces more household furniture than any other state in our country?
7. In which two southern states would you find many clothing factories?

Paper in Your Life ††

An important forest-products industry in the South is the making of paper. How important is paper in your life? To answer this question, you may do the following:
1. List some of the ways in which you and your family use paper and things made of paper, such as cups and envelopes.
2. From old newspapers and magazines, cut out pictures that show the uses you have listed. Arrange the pictures in a display to share with your class.
3. You and the other members of your class may wish to discuss what your lives might be like without paper and things made of paper.

† Have students write their answers to these questions.
†† Have students work alone or in groups to prepare for a discussion.

Index

Explanation of abbreviations used in this Index:
p — picture   *m* — map

Alabama, 14, 16, 21, 27, 29, 30, 37, 76, 92, 95, 96, 99, 103, 104, 105, 106, 109, 113, 123, 126; *p* 112-113, 120-121, 128; *m* 9, 54, 104, 121
alumina (ə lü′mə nə), 126-127
aluminum, 105, 126, 127; *p* 126-127
Appalachian (ap′ə lā′chən) Highlands, 14-16, 18-19, 80, 100, 105, 106, 107, 125; *p* 2-3, 14-15, 19; *m* 13, 14
climate, 32, 36-37
forests in, 18, 19; *p* 14-15
Appalachian Plateau, 18-19; *m* 13
Appalachian Ridges and Valleys, 18; *p* 19; *m* 13
architecture, *see* arts
Arkansas, 22, 91, 92, 95, 99, 105, 127; *p* 10-11, 37; *m* 9, 54, 121
Arkansas Valley, 22; *m* 13
Armstrong, Louis, 79-80; *p* 79
arts, 74-81; *p* 74-81
architecture, 74-76; *p* 42-43, 74-75
crafts, 80-81; *p* 81
literature, 77-79; *p* 78
music, 44, 79-80; *p* 79, 80
painting, 76-77; *p* 76-77
Atkins, Chet, *p* 80
Atlanta, Georgia, 48; *p* 7, 48-49; *m* 54, 121; *chart* 53

bauxite (bôk′sīt), *see* minerals
Biloxi, Mississippi, *p* 82-83
Bingham, George Caleb, 76; *p* 76-77
Birmingham, Alabama, 105, 117, 126; *m* 54, 104, 121
Biscayne Bay, 50; *p* 50-51
Black Mountains, 18
bluegrass, 21; *p* 20-21
Blue Ridge, 18, 27, 36-37; *p* 2-3, 33; *m* 13

Charleston, South Carolina, 42, 103; *m* 17, 54
Charlotte, North Carolina, *m* 54, 121
Chattanooga, Tennessee, 18; *m* 17, 54, 121

chemicals, *see* industry
Cherokee Indians, *see* people, American Indians
Chesapeake (ches′ ə pēk) Bay, *m* 17, 54
Choctaw Indians, *see* people, American Indians
cities, 13, 18, 48-57; *p* 12, 38-40, 48-53, 55, 56; *m* 17, 54, 121; *chart* 53
development of, 16, 48, 51-52, 55, 57
metropolitan areas, 48, 51, 55; *chart* 53
See also names of cities *and* ports
citizenship, 58-73
responsibilities of, 65
citizenship and government, 58-73; *p* 58-64, 66, 69, 70, 72, 73
Civil War, *see* history
climate, 2, 24-37, 107; *p* 24-31, 33, 34, 36, 37; *m* 30, 32, 34, 35
Appalachian Highlands, 32, 36-37; *p* 33, 36
Coastal Plain, 27-32; *p* 24-31
hurricanes, 30, 35; *p* 30-31; *m* 35; *chart* 35
Interior Highlands, 37; *p* 37
Interior Plains, 37
rainfall, 26-27, 29, 30, 34, 35, 36, 107; *m* 30
summer, 26, 27, 29, 30, 32, 36, 37; *p* 33, 37; *m* 32
temperature, 24-25, 29, 32; *m* 32
thunderstorms, 29, 34; *chart* 34
winter, 24-26, 30, 32, 36, 37; *p* 36
coal, *see* minerals
Coastal Plain, 11-13, 16, 27-32, 107; *p* 10-12, 24-31; *m* 11, 13
coke, *see* minerals, coal
Congress, 61
contour plowing, 93
Coosa River, 18; *m* 17
Coral Gables, Florida, 51; *m* 54
cotton, *see* farm products
cotton products, *see* industry
crafts, *see* arts
crops, *see* farm products

Cubans, *see* people, of Latin-American descent
culture, *p* 47
Cumberland Plateau, 18

Declaration of Independence, 77
democracy,
beliefs in, 61-65; *p* 62-64
citizenship in, 58-65
education in, 63-64, 66-69; *p* 64, 66, 69
making laws, 60-61; *p* 60-61
problems of, 66-73
responsibilities in, 65
rights in, 65
voting in, 63; *p* 62-63
Douglas Dam, *p* 19
Duveneck, Frank, 77

ecology, *p* 102
education, 63-64, 66-69; *p* 64, 66, 69
electrical equipment, *see* industry
electricity, 16, 52, 110-111, 127
electric power, 18, 113, 119, 127; *m* 114-115
energy fuels, *see* natural resources and energy

Fall Line, 16, 119; *m* 16, 17
farming, 6-7, 18, 22, 51, 84-97, 107, 113; *p* 20-21, 84-87, 89, 91, 93-97; *m* 86, 88, 91, 92, 95, 96
growing season, 84, 88; *m* 88
in the Appalachian Highlands, 14, 16, 19
in the Interior Plains, 21, 37
on the Coastal Plain, 12, 13, 26, 30, 32; *p* 10-11, 24-25
orchards, 22, 86
farming methods, 14, 93-94; *p* 10-11, 89, 94-95
farmland, 18, 19, 21, 22
farm products,
corn, 13, 19, 21, 37, 92, 120
cotton, 7, 13, 14, 22, 26, 37, 48, 52, 57, 84, 88, 117, 119, 120; *p* 89; *m* 88, 92
cotton seed, 57
dairy, 21, 96; *m* 92, 95

PRONUNCIATION KEY: hat, āge, cāre, fär; let, ēqual, tėrm; it, īce; hot, ōpen, ôrder; oil, out; cup, pùt, rüle, ūse; child; long; thin; ᴛHen; zh, measure; ə represents a in about, e in taken, i in pencil, o in lemon, u in circus.

The South 129

fruit, 22, 26, 30, 51, 54, 84-85, 86, 120-121; *p* 24-25, 84-87; *m* 86, 92
grain, 57; *m* 92
livestock, 21, 37, 48, 57, 95-96; *p* 96-97; *m* 92, 95, 96
nuts, 93; *m* 86
peanuts, 7, 13, 92, 120; *p* 93
poultry and eggs, 95; *m* 95
rice, 12, 52, 57, 84, 92; *p* 10-11
soybeans, 7, 14, 90-91, 120; *p* 90-91; *m* 91; *graph* 91
sugarcane, 12, 52, 84, 93, 121
tobacco, 7, 13, 19, 21, 92, 117
vegetables, 12, 32, 51, 84, 86, 120-121; *m* 86
Faulkner, William, 77; *p* 78
fish, *see* natural resources and energy
Florida, 24, 26-27, 30, 32, 40, 44, 46, 50-51, 53-54, 84-85, 93, 96, 99, 123; *p* 1, 12, 24-25, 46, 47, 50-51, 60-61, 84-87, 96-97, 110-111, 122-123; *m* 9, 54, 121
Florida House of Representatives, *p* 60-61
food processing, *see* industry
forest products, *see* industry
forests, *see* natural resources and energy
French Quarter, 53; *p* 52-53
fruit, *see* farm products
furniture, *see* industry

galaxy, 4-5; *p* 4
Georgia, 14, 32, 48-49, 76, 86, 92, 93, 95, 96, 106, 119; *p* 7, 26-27, 40, 48-49, 124-125; *m* 9, 54, 121
global view, 4-9; *p* 4, 7; *m* 6-9
government, 58-73; *p* 58-63
great ideas,
 division of labor, *p* 116-117
 exchange, *p* 86-87
 freedom, *p* 44-45
 language, *p* 78
 loyalty, *p* 62-63
 rules and government, *p* 58-59
 using natural resources, *p* 10-11, 100-101; *m* 92
 using tools, *p* 94-95, 126-127
Great Valley, 18, 86; *p* 19
growing season, 26, 30, 32, 37, 84, 88, 107; *m* 88
Gulf of Mexico, 6, 51, 53, 100, 110; *p* 98-99; *m* 6, 54, 121

Handy, W. C., 80
Harris, Joel Chandler, 77
health, 70-73; *p* 70, 72, 73

Hialeah, Florida, 51; *m* 54
High Point, North Carolina, 125
history, 6-7
 Civil War, 44, 48, 57, 117
 French and Indian War, 42
 Revolutionary War, 44, 74
 World War I, 113, 117
 World War II, 117
hurricanes, *see* climate
hydroelectricity (hī′ drō i lek ′tris′- ə tē), *see* natural resources and energy, waterpower

Indians, *see* people, American Indians
industrial areas, *m* 121
industry, 7, 48, 51, 52, 54, 55, 57, 116-128; *p* 116-128; *m* 121
 appliance, 127
 chemical, 18, 51, 52, 57, 100, 103, 106, 113, 117, 123; *p* 122-123
 clothing, 48, 51, 119
 cotton products, 120
 development of, 117, 119
 electrical equipment, 55, 127; *p* 116-117
 electronic equipment, 127
 food processing, 51, 52, 90, 120-121; *p* 82-83, 120-121
 forest products, 109, 123-125; *p* 124-125
 furniture, 7, 48, 51, 55, 124-125; *p* 125
 iron and steel, 104, 105, 117, 125-126
 lumber, 22, 54, 57
 meat-packing, 57; *p* 120-121
 metal, 104, 105
 metal products, 125-127; *p* 126-127
 petroleum products, 121
 pulp and paper, 7, 48, 57, 109, 123-124; *p* 124-125
 space, 127; *p* 128
 textiles, 7, 18, 117, 119, 120; *p* 118-119
 tobacco products, 121
 tourist, 51, 52-53, 54, 55
 transportation, 48, 51
 transportation equipment, 48, 127
Interior Highlands, 22, 37; *p* 22-23; *m* 13, 22
Interior Plains, 21, 37; *p* 20-21; *m* 13, 21
Intracoastal Waterway, *m* 17
iron ore, *see* minerals

Jacksonville, Florida, *p* 12; *m* 17, 54, 121

Jefferson, Thomas, 74, 77; *p* 74-75
Jekyll Island, Georgia, *p* 26-27

Kentucky, 18, 21, 37, 43, 55, 92, 96, 103, 121, 127; *p* 20-21, 55, 102; *m* 9, 54, 121
Kentucky Derby, 55
Knoxville, Tennessee, 18; *m* 17, 54, 121

land, 2-3, 10-23; *p* 2-3, 10-12, 14-15, 19, 20-23; *m* 11, 13, 14, 16, 17, 21, 22. *See also* Appalachian Highlands, Coastal Plain, Interior Highlands, *and* Interior Plains
Lee, Harper, 77
limestone, *see* minerals
Lincoln, Abraham, 44
literature, *see* arts
livestock, *see* farm products
logging, 109; *p* 108
Louisiana, 42, 51-53, 76, 92, 93, 99, 100, 106, 110, 121, 126-127; *p* 28-29, 38-39, 52-53; *m* 9, 54, 121
Louisville (lü′ i vil), Kentucky, 55; *p* 55; *m* 17, 54, 121; *chart* 53

Madison, James, 77
majority vote, 63, 65
manufacturing, *see* industry
Mardi Gras (mär′ dē grä), 53
McCullers, Carson, 77; *p* 78
Medicaid, 73
Medicare, 73
Memphis (mem′fis), Tennessee, 56-57; *p* 56; *m* 17, 54, 121; *chart* 53
metal products, *see* industry
metropolitan area, 48, 50-51, 55; *p* 48-51, 55; *chart* 53
Mexicans, *see* people, of Latin-American descent
Miami, Florida, 50-51; *p* 1, 50-51; *m* 17, 54, 121; *chart* 53
Miami Beach, Florida, 24, 51; *m* 54
Milky Way, 4-5; *p* 4
minerals, 99-107; *p* 98-102, 104, 106-107; *m* 103-105
 bauxite, 105, 126-127
 clay, 106-107
 coal, 19, 100, 103, 111, 117, 123, 125; *p* 102; *m* 103, 104
 granite, 106
 iron ore, 104, 105, 117, 125; *p* 104; *m* 104
 limestone, 104, 106, 125; *m* 104, 105
 marble, 106
 natural gas, 52, 99-100, 111, 123; *m* 105

oil, 52, 99-100, 111, 121, 123; *p* 98-101; *m* 105
phosphate rock, 54, 106, 123
pyrites, 106
salt, 52, 106, 123
stone, 106
sulfur, 52, 106, 123
zinc, 106; *p* 106-107
Mississippi, 46, 76, 91, 99, 109; *p* 82-83; *m* 9, 54, 121
Mississippi River, 22, 51-52, 57, 123; *m* 17
Mitchell, Margaret, 77; *p* 78
Montgomery, Alabama, 27, 29, 30; *m* 54
Monticello (mon′tə sel′ō), *p* 74-75
Mount Mitchell, 18
music, *see* arts

Nashville Basin, 21
Nashville, Tennessee, 80; *m* 17, 54, 121
Native Americans, *see* people, American Indians
natural gas, *see* minerals
natural resources and energy, 98-115; *p* 98-102, 104, 106-108, 110-114; *m* 103-105, 109, 114-115; *graphs* 109, 110
 energy fuels, 99-103; *p* 98-102; *m* 103, 105
 fish, 110; *p* 110-111; *graph* 110
 forests, 12, 18, 19, 22, 107-109; *p* 14-15, 108; *m* 109
 waterpower, 16, 110-111, 117; *p* 19, 112-114; *m* 114-115
 See also minerals *and* great ideas
New Orleans (ôr′ lē ənz), Louisiana, 51-53, 79; *p* 38-39, 52-53; *m* 17, 54, 121; *chart* 53
Newport News, Virginia, 127; *m* 54
Nobel Prize, 77
Norfolk, Virginia, 103; *m* 17, 54
North America, 5, 6; *m* 6
North Carolina, 18, 46, 81, 92, 95, 96, 106, 109, 121, 123, 124-125; *p* 2-3, 33, 116-119, 125; *m* 9, 54, 121
North Miami, Florida, 51; *m* 54
nuclear energy, 127

Ohio River, 43, 55; *m* 17
oil, *see* minerals
Ouachita (wäsh′ə tô) Mountains, 22; *m* 13
Ozark Plateau, 22; *p* 37; *m* 13

painting, *see* arts
paper, *see* industry, pulp and paper
people, 38-47; *p* 38-47
 American Indians, 46; *p* 47
 ancestry, 41-44, 46
 blacks, 43-44; *p* 44-45
 colonial times, 41-42
 Cubans, 44, 46; *p* 46
 national origin, 41-44, 46
 needs of, 29; *p* 28-29
 of African descent, 43-44
 of Asian descent, 44
 of European descent, 41-43; *p* 41
 of Latin-American descent, 44, 46
 population, 40-41, 43-44, 46, 48; *m* 43; *chart* 53
 religion, 47
petroleum, *see* minerals, oil
petroleum products, *see* industry
Pickwick Landing Dam, *p* 114; *m* 114-115
Piedmont (pēd′mont) Plateau, 14, 16, 32, 86, 117, 119; *p* 48-49; *m* 13
population, *see* people
ports, 50-57, 103; *p* 12, 50-53, 55, 56; *m* 17
Puerto Ricans, *see* people, of Latin-American descent
Pulitzer (pu̇′lit sər) Prize, 77, 79

rainfall, *see* climate
recreation, 53, 54; *p* 14-15, 22-23, 26-29, 33, 38-39, 44-45
religion, *see* people
Revolutionary War, *see* history
Richmond, Virginia, 42, 74; *m* 17, 54, 121
rivers, 13, 16, 18, 19; *p* 12, 19, 22-23, 55, 57; *m* 17

St. Petersburg, Florida, 54; *m* 17, 54; *chart* 53

schools, *see* education
Seminole Indians, *p* 47. *See also* people, American Indians
Shenandoah (shen′ən dō′ə) River, 18; *m* 17
Sherman, General, 48
social problems, 68. *See also* democracy, problems of
South Carolina, 42, 86, 103, 106, 127; *m* 9, 54, 121
strip-mining, *p* 102

Tampa, Florida, 53-54; *m* 17, 54, 121; *chart* 53
Tampa Bay, 53-54
temperature, *see* climate
Tennessee, 18, 21, 37, 57, 96, 103, 106, 123, 127; *p* 56, 106-107, 114; *m* 9, 54, 121
Tennessee River, 18; *p* 19, 114; *m* 17
Tennessee Valley Authority, 111-115; *p* 112-114; *m* 114-115
textiles, *see* industry
thunderstorms, *see* climate
timber, 109; *p* 108; *graph* 109
trade, 48, 51, 54, 57
transportation, 18, 48, 123
transportation equipment, *see* industry

United States, 5-6; *m* 6-9
United States Constitution, 77

Virginia, 27, 32, 42, 86, 92, 96, 103, 117, 121, 127; *p* 36; *m* 9, 54, 121

Warren, Robert Penn, 79
waterpower, *see* natural resources and energy
waterways, *m* 17
White River, *p* 22-23
Williams, Tennessee, 79
Wilson Dam, 113; *p* 112-113; *m* 114-115
Wolfe, Thomas, 77; *p* 78
World War I, *see* history
World War II, *see* history
Wright, Richard, 79

PRONUNCIATION KEY: hat, āge, cãre, fär; let, ēqual, tėrm; it, īce; hot, ōpen, ôrder; oil, out; cup, pu̇t, rüle, ūse; child; long; thin; ᴛHen; zh, measure; ə represents a in about, e in taken, i in pencil, o in lemon, u in circus.

Acknowledgments

Grateful acknowledgment is made to the following for permission to use the illustrations found in this book:

A. Devaney, Inc.: Pages 7, 40, and 60-61; pages 74-75 by David W. Carson
Alpha Photo Associates, Inc.: Pages 84-85
American Automobile Association: Pages 58-59
American Museum of Natural History: Page 4
Arkansas Department of Parks and Tourism: Page 37
Bob Hahn: Pages 106-107
Colfield's Studio: Page 78 (lower right)
Cyr Color Photo Agency: Pages 90-91
David Redfern Photography: Page 79
De Wys, Inc.: Page 70
Edward L. DuPuy: Page 81
Florida Department of Commerce: Pages 86-87 and 110-111
Florida Development Commission: Pages 122-123
Freelance Photographers Guild, Inc.: Pages 73 and 120-121; pages 2-3 by A. C. Shelton; pages 20-21 by Lehrt; page 41 by A. Felix
Globe Photos: Pages 1 and 50-51 by Eamon Kennedy
Grant Heilman: Pages 10-11, 22-23, and 93; pages 28-29 by Alan Pitcairn
H. Armstrong Roberts: Pages 12, 14-15, and 44-45
Harold M. Lambert Studios, Inc.: Pages 30-31 and 62-63
Harrison Forman: Page 36
International Harvester: Pages 89 and 94-95
Library of Congress: Pages 42-43
Louisville Chamber of Commerce: Page 55
Memphis Chamber of Commerce: Page 56
Minute Maid Company: Pages 24-25
Mobil Oil Corporation: Pages 100-101

NASA: Page 128
National Coal Association: Page 102
Paul Meyer: Page 64
Photo Researchers, Inc.: Pages 52-53; pages 38-39 by Glaubach; page 66 by Gerry Souter
RCA Records: Page 80
Reynolds Metals Company: Pages 126-127
Richard Marsh: Page 46
Shostal Associates, Inc.: Pages 26-27, 82-83, 96-97, 108, 116-117, 118-119, and 124-125
State of Florida Development Commission—Florida News Bureau: Page 47 by Ozzie Sweet
Taurus: Pages 48-49 by Russell Thompson
Tennessee Valley Authority: Pages 19, 33, 112-113, and 114 (left)
The Fideler Company: Page 94 (upper left) by Janet Johnson
Tom Stack: Pages 98-99 by Ron Church
Travel and Promotion Division, Department of Construction and Development—Raleigh, North Carolina: Page 125 (upper right)
United Methodist Community House—Grand Rapids, Michigan: Page 69
United States Department of Commerce, Weather Bureau: Page 34 by Klein
United States Department of Health, Education, and Welfare: Page 72 by Robert Pumphrey
Washington University Gallery of Art—St. Louis, Mo.: Pages 76-77, painting by Bronson
Wide World Photos: Page 78 (upper left, upper right, and lower left)
Woodward Iron Company: Page 104

Grateful acknowledgment is made to Scott, Foresman and Company for the pronunciation system used in this book, which is taken from the Thorndike-Barnhart Dictionary Series.

Grateful acknowledgment is made to the following for permission to use cartographic data in this book: Nystrom Raised Relief Map Company, Chicago 60618: Page 13; Rand McNally & Company: Pages 8 and 9; United States Department of Agriculture, Forest Service: Page 109; United States Department of Commerce, Bureau of the Census: Pages 43, 86, 91, 95, and 96.

MIDWEST AND GREAT PLAINS

Chicago, Illinois. This city stretches for many miles along the southwestern shore of Lake Michigan.

Part 1

Land and Climate

Use these activities to start students thinking about the land and climate of the Midwest and Great Plains.

Most of the Midwest and Great Plains is flat or gently rolling. However, the land in this part of our country differs in some ways from one area to another. The climate also differs from place to place. Choose one of the cities listed below and do research about the land and climate of the area in which it is located.

- Akron, Ohio
- Indianapolis, Indiana
- Duluth, Minnesota
- Bismarck, North Dakota
- Houston, Texas

Now, imagine that you moved to this city a year ago. Write a letter to a friend telling how the land and climate there have made a difference in your way of life.

The map on pages 8-9 will help you find the cities listed above. To find information in other sources, use the suggestions in the Skills Manual. You may find useful information in Chapters 2, 3, and 5.

Rolling hills in Wisconsin. The fourteen states that make up the Midwest and Great Plains lie in the central part of North America. Most of the land in this part of the United States is flat or gently rolling.

Have students write a definition of each of the following: (a) Solar system (b) Our sun (c) Our earth. As a group decide which definitions are best.

1 A Global View

Our Solar System Is in the Milky Way

Our own star

It is a sunny, summer afternoon. The sun is a bright ball of light in the sky. This ball of light is so bright that we cannot look at it directly. We can hardly believe that our sun is a star just like the stars that look so small on a clear night. But our sun is a star. Like other stars in the universe, our sun is a huge ball of burning gases. The sun is the center of our solar* system, and it is much closer to us than any other star.

The sun and all of the other stars we can see are part of a huge star system, or galaxy, called the Milky Way. The Milky Way is one of billions of separate galaxies scattered through the nearly empty space of the universe. Each one of these separate galaxies is made up of billions of stars and other heavenly bodies.

*See Glossary

Our sun is a star just like the stars we see in the sky on a clear night. To us, our sun is the most important star of all. Without it, there could be no life on our planet. It gives off heat and light that all people, plants, and animals need in order to live.

Our solar system includes nine main planets. It also includes many small planets, called asteroids. These asteroids circle the sun between Mars and Jupiter. Some of the main planets, including our earth, have one or more moons. Which main planet is the largest? Which is the smallest?

Exploring Our Solar System

The solar system

The earth is one of the solar system's nine main planets. (See chart at right.) These are balls of fairly solid material that revolve around the sun. The solar system also includes thousands of small planets, called asteroids. Some of the main planets, including the earth, have one or more moons.

Our neighbors in the solar system

In recent years, we have begun to explore some of our neighbors in the solar system. The Soviet Union and

Main Planets

Planet	Diameter		Average Distance From Sun	
	Miles	Kilometers	Miles	Kilometers
Mercury	3,100	4,990	36,000,000	57,934,800
Venus	7,570	12,180	67,250,000	108,225,425
Earth	7,926	12,760	92,950,000	149,584,435
Mars	4,200	6,760	141,500,000	227,715,950
Jupiter	88,700	142,750	483,500,000	778,096,550
Saturn	75,100	120,860	887,500,000	1,428,253,750
Uranus	29,000	46,670	1,785,000,000	2,872,600,500
Neptune	27,600	44,420	2,795,000,000	4,497,993,500
Pluto	4,000	6,440	3,675,000,000	5,914,177,500

† What would you see if you looked down at North America from a distance of 500 miles? Describe.

the United States have sent several unmanned spacecraft to find out more about Mars and Venus. On July 20, 1969, United States astronauts Neil A. Armstrong and Edwin E. Aldrin, Jr., became the first people to set foot on the moon. These men and other Apollo astronauts have set up experiments on the moon's surface to gather facts for scientists on earth. The astronauts have also brought back rocks from the moon. Information gained from these space explorations is helping scientists learn more about our solar system.

Observing Our Earth

The earth from space

We have also learned much about our own planet by looking at the earth from space. Astronauts have taken many pictures of the earth from high above its surface. For example, the picture below was taken from the spacecraft Gemini 11. In this picture and others taken by astronauts, the surface of the earth is partly hidden by clouds. These clouds are part of the atmosphere, the envelope of air that is all around our earth. The atmosphere is our planet's greatest treasure. It provides the air we breathe. It holds the moisture that brings life-giving rain to the earth. The atmosphere also protects us by night from the bitter cold of outer space, and by day from the burning rays of the sun.

† The earth as seen from the spacecraft Gemini 11. This picture was taken from more than 500 miles (805 kilometers) above the earth's surface. The white patches in the picture are clouds.

The United States

This map shows the location of the fifty states that make up our country. Two of these, Alaska and Hawaii, are separated from the others. Alaska is in the far northern part of North America. Hawaii is an island state in the Pacific Ocean. The other forty-eight states form the part of our country known as the conterminous* United States.

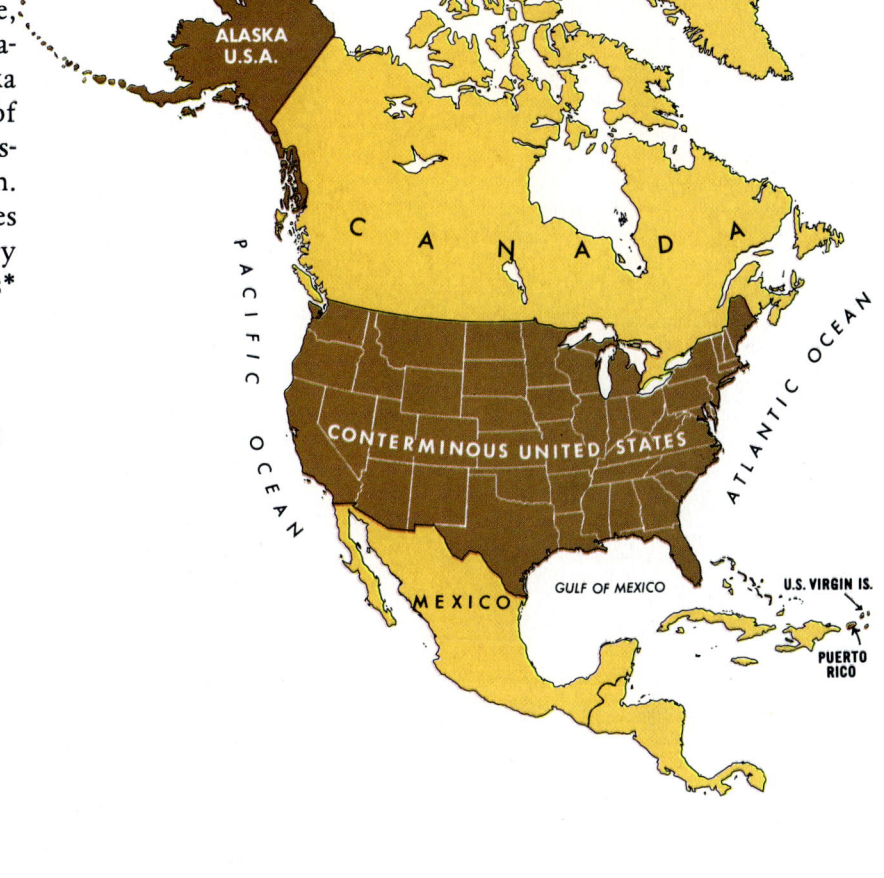

The earth's surface

As astronauts ride in their spacecraft above the earth's surface, they often catch sight of the shining blue waters of our planet's great oceans. These waters make up about three fourths of the earth's surface. The largest areas of land on the earth are called continents. Our earth's six continents, together with many islands, make up about one fourth of the surface of our planet.

The continent of North America

If we were to fly over North America, we would not see any boundary lines. We could not tell where one country ends and another begins. On maps, boundary lines are drawn to show different countries. If we look at the map of North America above, we can see that most of the United States is located on this continent. The countries of Canada and Mexico, our closest neighbors, are also on this continent.

Have students look up the word "conterminous" in the Glossary. Refer to the conterminous United States on the map above. Are Hawaii and Alaska part of the conterminous United States?

Midwest and Great Plains

Exploring Our Country

Our country is made up of fifty states. Two of these, Alaska and Hawaii, are separated from the others. The part of our country that is made up of the remaining forty-eight states is called the conterminous* United States. (See the map on page 7.)

In addition to the fifty states, our country also includes a small area called the District of Columbia. This is the home of our national government.

Over the years, the United States has gained control of various areas. One of these is the island of Puerto Rico, in the West Indies.* Today, Puerto Rico governs itself with the help of the United States. Another American possession in the West Indies is an island group called the Virgin Islands of the United States. Several islands and island groups in the Pacific Ocean also belong to us. At the present time, the United States also controls the Panama Canal Zone.

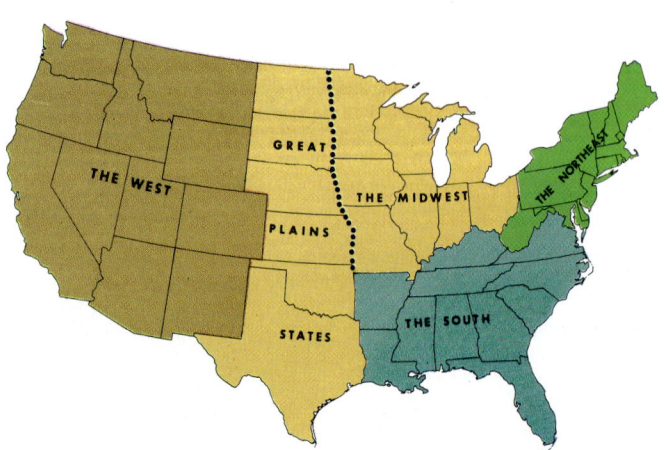

The states in the conterminous United States may be divided into five main groups. These are the Northeast, the South, the Midwest, the Great Plains states, and the West. Sometimes the Midwest and the Great Plains states are combined into one group, known as the Midwest and Great Plains.

† Have students read the caption. What main group of states do we live in?

† **Detroit** is located on the busy Detroit River in southeastern Michigan. It is the largest city in the state and the sixth largest in the nation. What other large cities are located in the Midwest and Great Plains?

The Midwest and Great Plains

An important part of the United States

A group of states known as the Midwest and Great Plains lies in the central part of our country. (See map on opposite page.) At the time our country was founded, this area was nothing but forests and grasslands. Small groups of Indians roamed the land, hunting buffalo and other wild animals.

Today, about 73 million people live in the Midwest and Great Plains. Much of our country's best farmland is found here. Many of our leading industrial cities, such as Chicago and Detroit, are also in this area. A network of highways, railroads, airways, and waterways connects the Midwest and Great Plains with other parts of our country and the world.

In the chapters that follow, you will learn about the land and the climate of the Midwest and Great Plains. You will also learn about the people here and how they live.

† What can you discover about Detroit from this picture? List your discoveries.

Growing corn on rich farmland in the Midwest and Great Plains. Most of the Midwest and Great Plains lies in one main land region of our country. This region is called the Interior Plains. The Interior Plains may be divided into two parts. What are these two parts called?

2 Land

† **A Problem To Solve**
How do the land features of the Midwest and Great Plains affect the people who live there? In order to solve this problem you will need to make hypotheses* about how the land and water features of this part of our country affect:

a. where the people live
b. how the people earn their living
c. transportation

Chapters 4, 8, and 10 contain additional information that will be useful in solving this problem.

See Skills Manual, "Thinking and Solving Problems"
*See Glossary

† Use "A Problem To Solve" to start students thinking about the land of the Midwest and Great Plains. Have all students participate.

Four important facts about the Midwest and Great Plains

1. The Midwest and Great Plains is made up of fourteen states that lie in the central part of North America. †

2. Most of the land in the Midwest and Great Plains is flat or gently rolling.

3. Only a few parts of the Midwest and Great Plains rise very high above sea* level.

4. Four of the five Great Lakes border or lie in the Midwest. These are among the largest lakes in the world.

Land regions of the Midwest and Great Plains

The map on pages 14-15 shows the different land regions in the United States. When you study this map, you will see that most of the Midwest and Great Plains lies in one region of our country. This region is called the Interior Plains.

The map shows that the Interior Plains may be divided into two parts. One part is called the Central Lowland. Here most of the land is low and flat or gently rolling. To the west of the Central Lowland are the Great Plains. These plains are generally flat, but they are higher above sea level than the Central Lowland. The states of North Dakota, South Dakota, Nebraska, Kansas, Oklahoma, and Texas lie partly in the Great Plains. This is why they are called the Great Plains states.

Some parts of the Midwest and Great Plains lie in another great lowland region. This is the Coastal Plain. It extends most of the way along the Atlantic coast of our country. It also forms a wide band along the Gulf of Mexico.

As you study the map on pages 14-15, you will see only four small highland areas in the Midwest and Great Plains. One of these is

† Refer students to the map on pages 8-9. Have them list the fourteen states that make up the Midwest and Great Plains.

part of the Appalachian Highlands. Another is part of the Interior Highlands. The third is part of the Superior Upland, and the fourth is in the Plateau Country.

To learn more about the land features of the Midwest and Great Plains, we will take a trip by helicopter over this part of our country. The route that we will follow is shown on the small map at the bottom of this page.

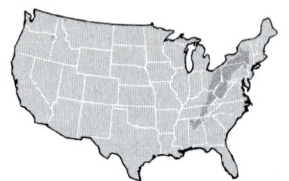

The Appalachian Plateau

We board our helicopter in the city of Youngstown, Ohio. As we take our seats, our guide tells us that Youngstown is in the Appalachian Plateau. This is part of a much larger land region known as the Appalachian Highlands. (See map at right.) The Appalachian Highlands region extends from Alabama northeastward into Canada.

Our helicopter is rising now. Soon we are high enough to see for many miles in every direction. We notice that most of the land around Youngstown is hilly or gently rolling. In some places, herds of cows are grazing on grassy hillsides. In much of this area the land is too hilly or the soil is too thin and stony for growing crops. But under the ground there are large deposits of coal and limestone. These valuable minerals are used by many industries. We learn from our guide that there are several important manufacturing cities besides Youngstown in this section of the Midwest.

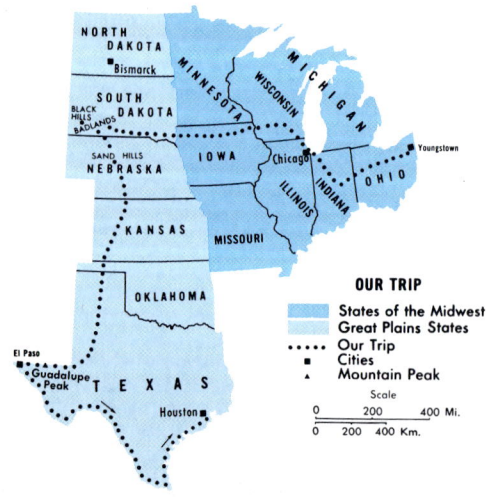

Refer to the small map on this page. Have students trace the helicopter route from Youngstown to Houston. Have them list the major cities on the trip.

14 Midwest and Great Plains

LAND REGIONS

 **PACIFIC MOUNTAINS AND VALLEYS**
  1 San Diego Ranges
  2 Los Angeles Ranges
  3 California Coast Ranges
  4 Klamath Mountains
  5 Oregon Coast Range
  6 Olympic Mountains
  7 Puget-Willamette Lowland
  8 Central Valley
  9 Cascade Range
 10 Sierra Nevada

THE PLATEAU COUNTRY
 11 Basin and Range Country

 12 Colorado Plateau
 13 Columbia Plateau

THE ROCKY MOUNTAINS

INTERIOR PLAINS
 14 Great Plains
 15 Central Lowland

SUPERIOR UPLAND

INTERIOR HIGHLANDS
 16 Ozark Plateau
 17 Arkansas Valley
 18 Ouachita Mountains

APPALACHIAN HIGHLANDS
 19 The Piedmont Plateau
 20 Blue Ridge
 21 Appalachian Ridges and Valleys
 22 Appalachian Plateau
 23 New England Lowlands
 24 New England Highlands
 25 Adirondack Mountains
 26 St. Lawrence Valley

COASTAL PLAIN

 Midwest and Great Plains

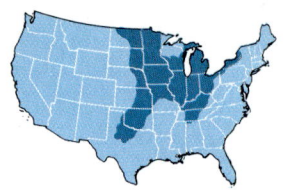

The Central Lowland

Now our helicopter heads westward from Youngstown. As we fly across Ohio, the land gradually becomes flatter. Our guide tells us that we are now in the Central Lowland. (See map on pages 14-15.) This large section covers more than three fourths of the Midwest. It also extends westward into the Great Plains states.

Large farms and busy cities

We learn that the Central Lowland contains some of the best farmland in the United States. Here are many fields

Refer to the picture below. Have students read the caption and answer the question.

Using Tools

See Great Ideas

Harvesting corn. The corn belt is a huge area of fertile farmland that stretches through the heart of the Midwest and Great Plains. Why do farmers find it easy to use tractors and other machines to work the land here?

of corn, hay, and other crops. Farmers in the Central Lowland raise large numbers of cattle and hogs.

Our guide tells us that several large cities are located in the Central Lowland. Among these are Cleveland, Detroit, Chicago, Minneapolis, St. Louis, and Oklahoma City.

As we look down from our helicopter, we notice that the land is crossed by many highways and railroad tracks. Because the Central Lowland is mostly level, it has been easy to build roads and railroads here. Good transportation routes have helped farming and industry to grow in the Midwest.

The corn belt

The land that we now see below us looks somewhat like a checkerboard. It is marked off in neat squares of green and tan. These squares are fields of corn, oats, and other crops. Our guide tells us we are flying over the corn belt. This is a huge area of fertile farmland that stretches through the heart of the Midwest and Great Plains. (See map on page 87.)

We learn that more food is produced in the corn belt than in any other area of the same size in the world. There are several reasons for this. First, most parts of the corn belt have rich, dark soil. Summers here are warm, and there is plenty of rainfall. These conditions are just right for growing corn. Soybeans and many other crops also grow well here. Because most parts of the corn belt are level, farmers find it easy to use tractors and other machines to work their land.

We ask our guide to tell us what is done with all the corn grown in the corn belt. She says that most of this corn is not the kind we eat as a vegetable. Instead, it is a type of corn that is fed to cattle and hogs to fatten them for market. For this reason, people often say that corn grown in the corn belt "travels to market on four legs." A small part of the corn grown here is used in making breakfast cereal, corn syrup, and other products.

The Great Lakes

When we reach the central part of Indiana, our helicopter turns toward the northwest. Soon we see

Midwest and Great Plains

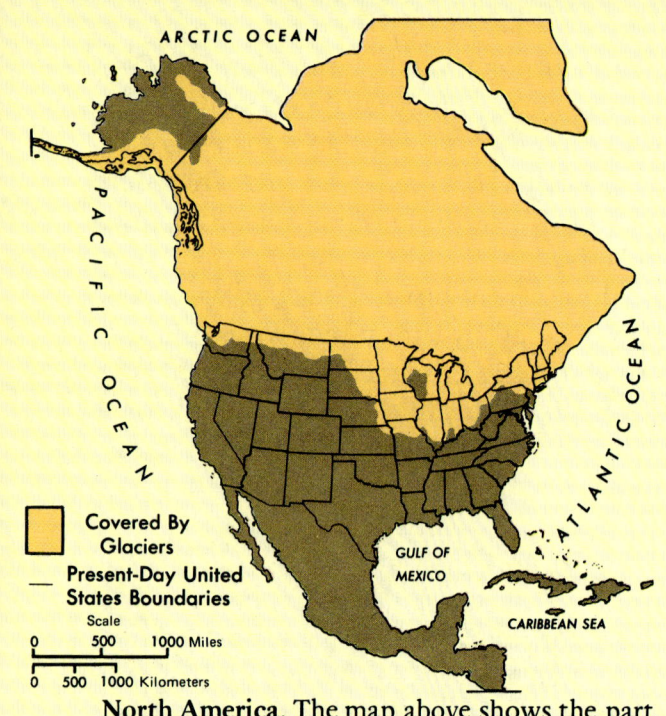

North America. The map above shows the part of North America that was covered by glaciers at one time or another during the Great Ice Age.

The Story of Glaciers

The Great Ice Age. About one million years ago, the climate of the earth was colder than it is today. Great quantities of snow fell in and near Arctic regions of the world. In some places more snow fell in winter than melted in summer. The snow piled higher and higher each year, and the bottom layers gradually turned to ice. Finally, the enormous weight of the snow on top caused the ice below to spread out in all directions. A mass of moving ice formed in this way is called a glacier.

As the centuries passed, glaciers spread over large areas in Europe, Asia, and North America. In some places, they were almost two miles thick. As glaciers moved across the land, they carried away soil and rocks, scooped out deep hollows, and rounded off mountaintops.

Gradually, the climate of the earth became warmer. The glaciers began to melt. As they melted, they left behind the soil and rocks

before us a great expanse of bright-blue water. Our guide tells us that this is Lake Michigan, one of the five Great Lakes. The others are Lake Superior, Lake Huron, Lake Erie, and Lake Ontario. (See map on pages 8-9.)

We ask our guide how the Great Lakes were formed. She tells us that many thousands of years ago, great sheets of ice called glaciers formed in northern Canada. (See feature above.) As the glaciers moved southward, they dug out large hollows in the earth. Later, the climate became warmer and the glaciers slowly melted. Water from the melting ice filled the hollows dug by the glaciers, forming the Great Lakes.

An important waterway

As we fly over the southern end of Lake Michigan, we see several large boats in the water below us. Some of these boats are carrying iron ore.* Others are loaded with grain or coal. We also see boats that are carrying automobiles and other manufactured products. Our guide says that Lake Michigan is part of the Great Lakes-St. Lawrence Waterway. (See map on page 120.) By using this waterway, large ships can travel more than 2,000 miles (3,218 km.)† inland from the Atlantic Ocean.

We learn that the Great Lakes are important for reasons other than transportation. For one thing, they provide large amounts of fresh water to homes and factories in nearby cities. Thousands of people spend their vacations along the Great Lakes. Here they can enjoy swimming, boating, and other water sports. Fish caught in the Great Lakes are sold in many parts of our

† km. means kilometer

they had carried. Water from the melting ice filled some of the hollows they had made. In this way, many lakes and ponds were formed.

Three more times during the Great Ice Age the earth's climate cooled and then became warmer again. Each time, glaciers spread over large areas of the earth's surface and then melted. The last of these ice sheets retreated only about 18,000 years ago.

How glaciers affected the Midwest and Great Plains. During the Great Ice Age, glaciers spread over much of the Midwest and Great Plains. (Compare the map on the opposite page with the map on page 10.) They scooped out thousands of hollows in the earth. Later, water from the melting glaciers filled many of these hollows, forming the Great Lakes and thousands of smaller lakes. The melting glaciers also left a thick layer of sand, clay, and finely ground rock over large areas of land. In many parts of the Midwest and Great Plains these materials helped to form very fertile soil.

country. Also, the Great Lakes have an important effect on the climate of the lands along their shores. You can learn more about this in Chapter 3.

† **Chicago**

Along the shore of Lake Michigan, we see what appears to be a single great city spreading out for many miles across the plains. We are coming near Chicago, Illinois. (See trip map on page 14.) More people live in Chicago than any other city in the United States except New York. Chicago and its neighboring communities have grown so close together that we cannot tell one city from another. About seven million people make their homes in the Chicago metropolitan* area.

As our helicopter flies closer, we can see different kinds of buildings. We see houses, stores, schools, and churches. We also see the smokestacks of steel mills and other factories. In the distance are tall hotels and office buildings. Railroad tracks and broad highways form a crisscross pattern like the threads in a spider's web.

The dairy belt

Our helicopter heads northwestward from Chicago, and we are soon flying over the state of Wisconsin. Below us we see rolling hills that are covered with green pastures. Large herds of cows are grazing on the hillsides. Our guide tells us that these cows are raised for their milk.

We are now in the dairy belt of the Midwest. This area covers most of Wisconsin, Michigan, and Minnesota. (See map on page 87.) The land here is generally more hilly and less fertile than in the corn belt. In many parts of the dairy belt, summers are too cool and the growing season is too short for corn to ripen fully. But this kind of climate is very good for raising grass, which can be used to feed dairy cattle. There are many fine dairy farms in this area.

Crossing the Mississippi River

Our helicopter turns westward now. Before long, we are crossing the broad, winding Mississippi River. Trace the route of this river on the map on page 20. You will see that it begins in the northern part of Minnesota and flows southward into the Gulf of Mexico.

Most of the other large rivers in the Midwest and Great Plains flow into the Mississippi. A river that empties into a larger river is called a tributary. The largest tributaries of the Mississippi are the Ohio River and the Missouri River.

† Refer to the map on pages 8-9. Have students locate Chicago on this map.

MISSISSIPPI RIVER SYSTEM

The Mississippi River, together with its tributaries, drains a vast area in the central part of our country. This area includes most of the Midwest and Great Plains. The Mississippi begins in northern Minnesota and flows southward into the Gulf of Mexico. The Ohio and the Missouri rivers are the Mississippi's chief tributaries.

Together, the Mississippi and its tributaries form the Mississippi River system. This is one of the largest river systems in the world.

The Mississippi River in early times

Our guide tells us that the Mississippi River and its tributaries played an important part in the history of the United States. In the early days of our country, there were few roads and no railroads. Rivers and other waterways were important for transportation.

Pioneer families on their way to make new homes on the frontier journeyed by flatboat down the Ohio and other rivers. These people often settled near the rivers, which they used to send their goods to market. Flatboats loaded

Pushing barges up the Mississippi River. The Mississippi River system is one of the largest river systems in the world. What two rivers are the Mississippi's main branches, or tributaries?

† How did the Mississippi River help cities like Minneapolis, St. Louis, and Kansas City grow?

with furs, lumber, and farm products were floated down the Mississippi River to the port of New Orleans. From New Orleans, these goods were sent by ship to many cities in the eastern part of the United States and to cities in Europe.

As time passed, the flatboats were replaced by steamboats. These were much faster than flatboats, and they could go upstream as well as downstream. By the middle of the 1800's, there were hundreds of steamboats carrying passengers and goods up and down the Mississippi.

† Many port towns grew up along the Mississippi and its tributaries. Some of these towns have become important cities. Among them are Minneapolis, St. Paul, St. Louis, Kansas City, and Cincinnati.

The Mississippi River today

Today, few people travel by boat on the Mississippi River. But the river is still an important transportation route. Large amounts of grain, oil, and other bulky products are carried by barges on the Mississippi. These products can be carried more cheaply by boat than by train or truck.

Our guide says that the rivers in the Mississippi River system can be harmful as well as helpful to the people living nearby. In the spring, melting snow or heavy rains sometimes cause a river to overflow its banks. The rising water may destroy millions of dollars' worth of property. Sometimes many people are drowned.

Dams have been built on the Mississippi River and some of its tributaries to control the flow of water and prevent floods. You can learn more about these dams on pages 106 and 107.

An important farming state

Now we have crossed the Mississippi River and are flying westward across the state of Iowa. Nearly all of Iowa lies in the corn belt. Our guide says that most of the corn grown in this state is fed to livestock. Iowa produces more hogs than any other state. It is also a leading producer of beef cattle.

As we continue our trip, our guide tells us about two highland regions that lie partly in the Midwest and Great Plains. We are not going to visit these regions, but we can see them on the map on page 15. They are the Interior Highlands and the Superior Upland.

The Interior Highlands

A region of hills and low mountains

The Interior Highlands region extends from the southern tip of Illinois to the eastern part of Oklahoma. The Ozark Plateau forms the northern part of this region. In the Ozark Plateau, there are many steep-sided hills covered with thick forests. A number of small farms are scattered through this section, but most of the land is too rugged for growing crops.

The scenery in much of the Ozark Plateau is very beautiful. Rushing streams flow between wooded hills. In some places there are clear blue lakes. Each summer, thousands of people come to the Ozark Plateau to spend their vacations.

The map on pages 14-15 shows that there are two other parts of the Interior Highlands. South of the Ozark Plateau is the fertile valley of the Arkansas River. Still farther south are the Ouachita Mountains. These mountains are low but quite rugged. Most of their slopes are covered with thick forests of pine, oak, and other trees. Lumbering is an important way of earning a living in this area.

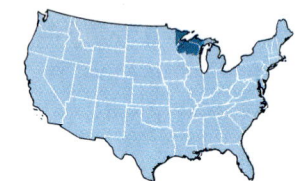

The Superior Upland

A hilly and wooded region

To the north of us is the Superior Upland. Parts of Minnesota, Wisconsin, and Michigan lie in this region. Here there are rolling hills and low mountains with gentle slopes.

Along Lake Superior, in Michigan's Upper Peninsula. The western half of this part of Michigan lies in the Superior Upland. Parts of two other states also lie in this region. Which two states are they?

† Why are there few factories in this area? (Dense forests, small population.)

Much of the land in the Superior Upland is covered with dense forests. In only a few places are there towns or farms. Our guide says that most of the soil in the Superior Upland is too poor for farming. In addition, summers are too cool for growing many kinds of crops. Not many factories have been built in this region. But there are sawmills and paper mills that use wood from nearby forests.

Iron mines and tourists

Our guide tells us that there are many large iron mines in the Superior Upland. About four fifths of all the iron ore mined in the United States each year comes from this region. To learn more about iron mining in the Superior Upland, see pages 100-103.

Although the Superior Upland is thinly populated, it attracts large numbers of tourists each year. In this region are wooded hills, swift-flowing rivers, and thousands of sparkling lakes.

The Great Plains

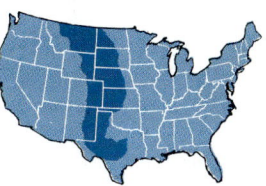

A flat, treeless land

After leaving Iowa, we fly westward across the state of South Dakota. Soon we notice the broad, muddy Missouri River below us. We are now flying over the Great Plains. This part of our country forms a wide band extending from Canada to Mexico. (See map on pages 14-15.) The eastern edge of the Great Plains is less than 2,000 feet (610 m.)† above sea level. From there the land slopes gently upward toward the west until it reaches the Rocky Mountains. Near the western edge of the Great Plains, some places are more than one mile (1.6 km.) above sea level.

Most of the land in the Great Plains appears to be nearly as flat as a tabletop. But in some places, steep-sided hills called buttes* rise like skyscrapers above the plains. Rivers flowing eastward across the plains have carved deep valleys in the level surface of the land.

During our trip over the Great Plains we will not see many forests. One reason why there are few forests in the

† m. means meter

Great Plains is the lack of rainfall here. Much of this area receives less than 20 inches (51 cm.)† of rainfall a year. (Compare maps on pages 10 and 34.)

Cattle country

Now we are flying over the western part of South Dakota. Here much of the land is too dry for growing crops. We travel for many miles without seeing any towns or cultivated fields. The plains below us are covered with short, brown grass on which herds of cattle are grazing. Our guide tells us that cattle ranches on the Great Plains are usually very large. The reason for this is that many acres of grassland are needed to provide enough food for a herd of cattle. Now and then we fly over a lonely ranch house with a tall windmill used to pump water for livestock.

The Badlands of South Dakota

As we continue westward, we fly over the Badlands of South Dakota. Our guide tells us that millions of years ago this area was a high, level plain. Rainfall was usually very light here. But once in a while there were heavy rainstorms that washed deep gullies in the dry, bare earth. As time passed, rainwater carried away still more soil and rock, forming many jagged peaks. When we fly over the Badlands, we see that they are strangely beautiful. The layers of rock in these peaks are tinted every color of the rainbow.

We learn that the Badlands were given their name many years ago by the Indians. Today the name "badlands" is used for any area that looks like this. There are badlands in North Dakota, Nebraska, and other states.

The Black Hills

Near the western border of South Dakota, we see a group of mountains rising from the plains. From a distance, these mountains appear black. But as we come closer, we can see that they are covered with forests of dark green pine trees. These are the Black Hills. Some of the peaks here rise more than 7,000 feet (2,134 m.) above sea level. Between the mountains are rushing streams and sparkling lakes.

We ask our guide how the Black Hills were formed. She says that millions of years ago, movements deep within the earth raised the surface of the land to form a huge dome about 50 miles (80 km.) across. As time passed, rainwater wore away parts of the dome to form a number of rugged peaks. The wearing away of rock and soil by water, wind, and other natural forces is called erosion.

Our guide tells us more about the Black Hills. She says they contain rich deposits of gold and other minerals. The forests on their slopes provide much wood for lumber. In the summer, thousands of people come to the Black Hills to enjoy the beautiful mountain scenery.

The Sand Hills of Nebraska

From the Black Hills, our helicopter flies southeastward. Before long we see below us rolling hills covered with a thick carpet of light green grass. These are the Sand Hills of Nebraska. They are made up of sand that was piled here thousands of years ago by strong winds blowing across the Great Plains. It is almost impossible to grow crops in the sandy soil of this area. But the grassy

† cm. means centimeter

The **Badlands** in the southwestern part of South Dakota. The Badlands are one of several different kinds of land features found in the Great Plains region. What other kinds of land features make up the Great Plains? Which part of this region would you most like to visit? Why?

hillsides provide excellent pasture for cattle.

Our nation's "breadbasket"

Soon after crossing the wide, muddy Platte River, we reach the state of Kansas. We notice that the land below us is marked off into long, narrow strips. Some of the strips are bright gold in color, and others are dark brown. Our guide tells us that the golden strips are fields of wheat that is ripe and ready to harvest. The brown strips are patches of earth on which no crops are being grown. To save water in this land of little rainfall, farmers grow crops on only part of their land at one time. (See page 85.)

Our guide tells us that more wheat is grown on the Great Plains than in any other part of our country. The soil here is fertile, and the dry, sunny climate is well suited to growing wheat. Most of the land is level enough to be

Refer to the picture above. What do you think it would be like to live in the Badlands?

Camping in Big Bend National Park. This park is in the Basin and Range Country, which extends across southwestern Texas. In this area are many rugged mountain ranges separated by basins.

worked with large machines. The state of Kansas produces so much wheat that it is sometimes known as the "breadbasket" of the United States.

From our helicopter, we see machines that look like giant bugs moving slowly over the fields. These are combines. They cut the wheat and separate the grain from the stalks. The grain is loaded into trucks. Then it is carried to tall buildings called elevators, which are located near railroads. The grain is stored in the elevators until it can be loaded onto trains that will carry it to flour mills in the cities. As we keep on flying over Kansas, we see many grain elevators rising like watchtowers over the plains.

Refer to the picture above. What can you discover from this picture about some of the land features of southwestern Texas?

From Kansas we fly southward across Oklahoma and into Texas. (See map on page 14.) We continue to see many large wheat fields, but we also see cattle ranches. Under the ground are rich deposits of oil and natural gas.

Cotton fields and cattle ranches

As we continue southward, we notice that some of the land below us is covered with neat squares of bright green. Our guide tells us that these are cotton fields. She says that Texas produces more cotton than any other state. Because rainfall is light on the Great Plains, farmers here must bring water from wells and streams to put on their crops. This is called irrigation. Many irrigation ditches have been dug to carry water to the thirsty cotton plants.

Now we leave the cotton fields behind and fly over dry plains where few crops are grown. Here most of the land is covered with clumps of brown grass or low, thorny bushes. We see a cloud of dust formed by a large herd of cattle moving across the plains. The cattle are being guided by a group of cowhands* on horseback. Our guide tells us that Texas is our country's leading producer of beef cattle.

The Basin and Range Country

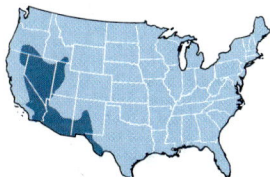

Our helicopter is turning westward now, and we leave the dry plains behind. Soon we are flying over ranges of rugged mountains that are separated by wide, level basins.* Our guide tells us that we are now in the Basin and Range Country. This is part of a great land region called the Plateau Country, which covers much of the western United States. (See map on pages 14-15.)

From our helicopter, the land below us looks dusty gray or tan. Most of the land in the Basin and Range Country is so dry that it can be used only for grazing. The basins are dotted with mesquite* and other plants that can live without much water. Now we are flying over Guadalupe Peak, which rises more than 8,700 feet (2,652 m.) above sea level. This is the highest point in the Midwest and Great Plains.

The Coastal Plain

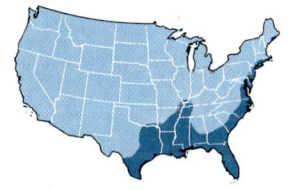

When we reach the city of El Paso, Texas, our helicopter turns toward the southeast. Our guide tells us that we will follow a river called the Rio Grande all the way to the Gulf of Mexico. After we have been traveling for a while, we enter the huge region of our country known as the Coastal Plain. (See map on pages 14-15.) Near the Gulf of Mexico, the Coastal Plain is very low and flat. Farther inland, it is a little higher and more rolling. But only a very few places in the Coastal Plain are more than 1,000 feet (305 m.) above sea level.

Farms, forests, and oil fields

† Our guide tells us that the Coastal Plain is a very important part of Texas. In this region are large areas of nearly level land with soil that is good for growing peanuts, cotton, and many other crops. Under the surface of the Coastal Plain are huge deposits of oil and natural gas. Texas produces larger amounts of these minerals than any other state. In some parts of the Coastal Plain are large forests that supply wood for making paper, lumber, and other products.

As we come near the Gulf of Mexico, we begin to see many large orchards of orange and grapefruit trees. We also notice many fields of tomatoes, lettuce, and other vegetables. Our guide tells us that the soil in the lower Rio Grande Valley is very fertile. Winters here are so mild that crops can be grown the year around. But the fields and orchards must be irrigated, because there is not enough rainfall here.

Flying along the Gulf coast

When we reach the Gulf of Mexico, our helicopter turns northward and flies along the seacoast. We notice that most of the land near the coast is low and marshy. Rice, a crop that needs much water, is grown in some areas. Along the coast are many large bays. Now and then we fly over a harbor crowded with fishing boats and cargo ships. A few miles off the coast are long, narrow islands made up largely of sand. Here are fine beaches where people come to swim and to enjoy the sunshine.

Now we see a city that stretches for many miles across the Texas plains. This is Houston. Although it is nearly 50 miles (80 km.) from the coast, it is connected to the Gulf of Mexico by a channel that is deep enough for large ocean ships. Houston is a leading seaport and a great manufacturing city. It has a larger population* than any other city in the Great Plains states.

Our helicopter is preparing to land at the Houston airport now. During our trip, we have seen the main land features of the Midwest and Great Plains. We have also seen some of the ways in which land features affect the lives of people in this part of our country.

† Is oil important in your life? Is natural gas important in your life? Is gold? Which resources are most important to you? Why?

Corpus Christi, Texas, lies in the Coastal Plain, along the Gulf of Mexico. Our country's Coastal Plain extends across much of eastern and southern Texas. Most of the land here is very low and flat. In what ways is the Coastal Plain region an important part of Texas?

† **Explore a Great River System**
The Mississippi River and its tributaries form one of the largest river systems in the world. Do research about this great river system. Then, with a group of your classmates, draw pictures to make a wall mural. Show ways in which people have used the Mississippi River and its tributaries over the past three hundred years. Books such as *Life on the Mississippi* by Mark Twain and *The Upper Mississippi* by Walter Havighurst will provide helpful information. You might also like to make a map of the Mississippi River and its tributaries. On your map, show the states through which these rivers flow and the states they border. Print the names of these states on your map. You may also wish to show the names and locations of important port cities along these rivers.

† You may wish to assign this activity to your students. You might also have students read the books and make special class reports about them.

† Use this problem to start students thinking about climate in the Midwest and Great Plains.

3 Climate

† **A Problem To Solve**
How does the climate of the Midwest and Great Plains affect the people who live here?
In forming hypotheses* to solve this problem, you will need to think about ways in which climate affects each of the following:
1. the clothing people wear
2. the kinds of homes people live in
3. transportation
4. sports and recreation
This chapter contains much of the information you will need in order to solve this problem.
See Skills Manual, "Thinking and Solving Problems"

Summer in Iowa

It is a sunny afternoon in July, and we are standing in an Iowa cornfield. The temperature is 101° F. (38° C.).† Not a breeze is stirring. The hot, moist air seems to shimmer above the green rows of corn. The farmer, who has been working in his field, stops to talk with us. He is wearing a hat to shade his head from the glaring sun. The farmer says that rain is expected tonight, but it will probably not cool the air very much. Here in Iowa, summer nights are usually warm and humid.

We remark that the weather makes us feel hot. The farmer agrees, but he adds, "I like it just the same. This is wonderful weather for raising corn. On a still summer night, you can actually hear the corn growing." The farmer tells us that hot, humid weather has helped to make Iowa one of our country's leading corn-producing states.

Iowa in winter

Six months later, we visit the farm once more. We can hardly believe that we are in the same place. The weather is bitterly cold. Now, the temperature is only 3° F. (-16° C.). The sky is dark and cloudy. Snow is blowing across the bare fields. It is piling into drifts against barns and fences. People are being warned to stay at home. The drifting snow may soon block all roads. Cold, snowy weather like this is common in Iowa during the winter months.

† F. means Fahrenheit scale
C. means Celsius scale
*See Glossary

30 Midwest and Great Plains

For additional activities, use Fideler Discovery Card 29 (Climate and You), and Fideler Discovery Sheets, Volume 1, page 16.

An Iowa cornfield in the summer. The weather is usually hot and humid in Iowa during the summer. Even the nights are usually warm. What is the weather like in Iowa during the winter months?

A Continental Climate

Temperatures change greatly

On our visits to the farm in Iowa, we found two kinds of weather. It was very warm in July and very cold in January. In most other parts of the Midwest and Great Plains, there are also large differences in temperatures between summer and winter.

This part of our country, like the rest of the conterminous* United States, is far north of the equator. The weather in lands near the equator is hot all year long, except in the mountains. In lands that are far away from the equator, however, there are great differences between temperatures in

Refer to the picture above. Use the caption in a class discussion about weather in Iowa.

Call attention to the picture below. What can you tell from this picture about the way some people earn their living in the Midwest?

the summertime and temperatures in the wintertime.

You might think that all places that are the same distance from the equator would have the same kind of climate. This is not true, however. In Seattle, Washington, the average temperature in July is about 66° F. (19° C.), and the average temperature in January is about 42° F. (6° C.). Bismarck, North Dakota, lies at about the same latitude* as Seattle. But Bismarck's average July temperature is nearly 72° F. (22° C.), and its average January temperature is only 10° F. (-12° C.). In most parts of the Midwest and Great Plains, summers are warmer and winters are colder than they are in other areas at the same latitude.

Distance from the ocean

The map on pages 8-9 will help you understand why there is such a great difference between summer and win-

Summer in the Midwest. In most parts of the Midwest and Great Plains, there are great differences in temperatures between summer and winter. Summers are generally very warm and winters are very cold. What do we call this kind of climate? Why do you think it is called this?

ter weather in most parts of the Midwest and Great Plains. When you study the map, you will see that most parts of the Midwest and Great Plains lie far from any ocean. Large bodies of water, such as the oceans, gain or lose heat more slowly than the land does. Therefore, the water is warmer than the land in winter. It is cooler than the land in summer. Winds blowing from the oceans bring mild weather to lands along the coasts. Only a small part of the land in the Midwest and Great Plains is cooled in summer or warmed in winter by ocean breezes. Because of this, changes in temperature are greater in most of the Midwest and Great Plains than they are along our coasts. The kind of climate that is found in most of the Midwest and Great Plains is known as a continental climate.

Winds and Rainfall

Winds affect temperature

The winds that sweep across the Midwest and Great Plains help to cause changeable weather here. Like other parts of our country, the Midwest and Great Plains lies in a belt of westerly winds. These winds sweep across the United States from west to east. However, they are joined by winds blowing from other directions.

In the wintertime, the winds that pass over the Midwest and Great Plains are often from the north. These winds come from northern Canada. They are cold and dry. The weather they bring is bitterly cold.

The warm winds that sweep across the Midwest and Great Plains in the summertime come mainly from the south. Some of these winds contain large amounts of moisture that has evaporated from the Gulf of Mexico. These moist winds bring hot, humid weather to the areas over which they move.

In the Midwest and Great Plains, the weather often changes rapidly from day to day. There are no high mountains in this part of our country. For this reason, winds from the north and the south can move swiftly over the land, bringing sudden changes in temperature.

Refer to the Average Yearly Rainfall map below. Have students use this map and the map key to find out the average annual rainfall where we live.

Cyclonic rainfall

The winds that pass over the Midwest and Great Plains not only cause changes in temperature, they also bring rain. Much of this rain occurs when a mass of warm, damp air from the south meets a mass of cold, dry air from Canada. Since the warm air is lighter than the cold air, it rises. As it rises, it becomes cooler. Some of the moisture in the air condenses and falls to earth as rain or snow. The kind of rainfall that comes from the meeting of a warm air mass and a cold air mass is known as cyclonic rainfall.

Convectional rainfall

On hot summer days, rainfall may be caused in a different way. As warm, moist air from the Gulf of Mexico moves northward over the land, it is heated still more. This hot, damp air rises very rapidly. As it rises, it becomes cool. Some of the moisture in the air condenses, bringing heavy summer rains. The kind of rainfall that is formed in this way is called convectional rainfall. It is often accompanied by thunder and lightning.

The Midwest receives plenty of rain

In the Midwest, rainfall is usually plentiful the year around. This part of our country lies in the path of the moist winds that move northward from the Gulf of Mexico. Rainfall is heaviest in the part of the Midwest that lies nearest to the Gulf. Some places here receive about 50 inches (127 cm.)† of rainfall a year. (See map below.) Less rain falls in the northern part of the Midwest. In some of the northern areas, the average yearly rainfall is less than 30 inches (76 cm.).

Rainfall has helped determine the kinds of plants that grow in the Midwest. Before this part of our country was settled, thick, green forests cov-

† cm. means centimeter

The map below shows the average yearly rainfall in different parts of the conterminous United States. Rainfall is plentiful in the Midwest and along the eastern edge of the Great Plains states. Much of the rain that falls here is brought by moist winds from the Gulf of Mexico. These winds seldom reach the western part of the Great Plains states. Also, this part of the Great Plains states lies in the rain* shadow of the Rocky Mountains. As a result, the climate here is dry.

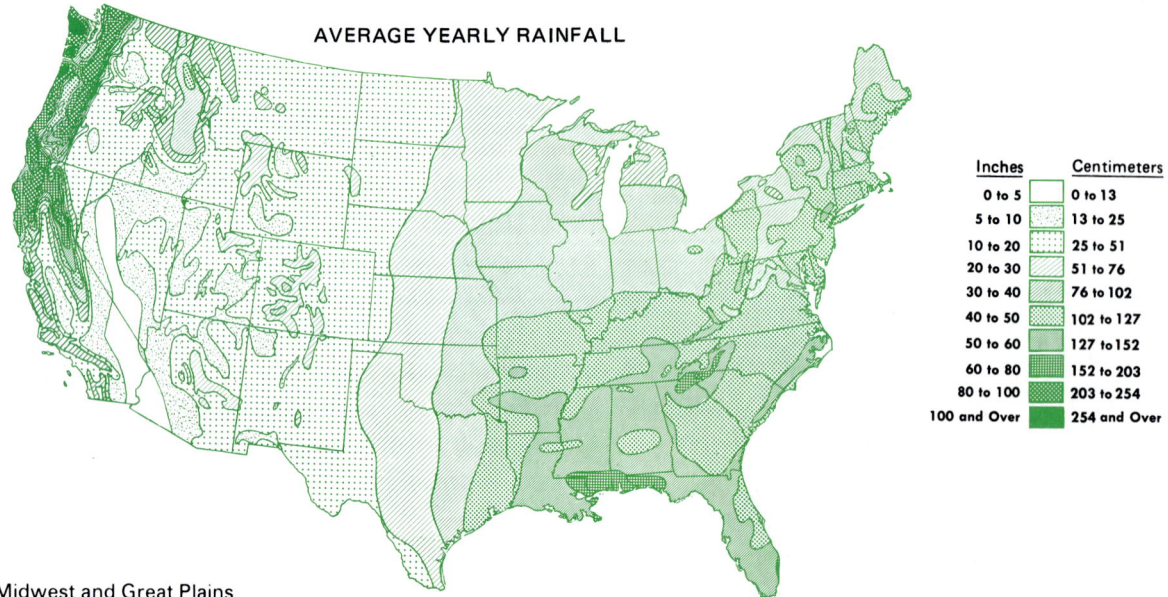

ered most of the land. Tall grasses grew in many areas that were not forested. Trees and tall grasses can grow only where there is plenty of rainfall.

In all parts of the Midwest, there is enough rainfall for farming. Most crops grow well on 30 inches (76 cm.) of rainfall a year. Even less rainfall is needed in places where summers are not too warm. Less water is lost from the soil in cool weather than in hot weather. Long periods of dry weather, known as droughts, do not happen very often in the Midwest. When they do, they seldom last long enough to cause much damage. The plentiful rain has helped farmers to produce large harvests.

Because rainfall is plentiful in the Midwest, people here usually have enough water for all their needs. There are many lakes and rivers in this part of our country, as well as a large supply of groundwater.* Most communities have the water they need for homes and industries. Pages 104-108 provide more information about the Midwest's water resources.

Rainfall in the Great Plains states

If you compare the map on the opposite page with the map on page 10, you will see that there are great differences in rainfall within the Great Plains states. Rainfall is heaviest along the eastern border of these states, especially in Texas and Oklahoma. Some places here receive about 50 inches (127 cm.) of rainfall a year. As you go westward across the Great Plains states, the amount of rainfall grows less. In the western part of these states, the average rainfall is less than 20 inches (51 cm.) a year. Most kinds of crops do not grow well with so little rain.

Fishing in the Midwest. There are many lakes and rivers in this part of our country. Most parts of the Midwest have plenty of water.

† Have a student look up the word "groundwater" in the Glossary and read the definition aloud.

Physical Needs

See Needs of People

Winter in Michigan. Winters are cold and snowy in the northern part of the Midwest and Great Plains. The skiers in this picture are enjoying a winter day in Michigan. Skiing helps these people meet their physical needs for fresh air and exercise. How do you suppose these people meet those physical needs during the summer months? In what ways do you meet these needs during the winter? In what ways do you meet them during the summer?

There is also too little rainfall for trees to grow.

There are two reasons why the rainfall is so light in the western part of the Great Plains states. First, the western part of these states does not lie in the path of moist air moving northward from the Gulf of Mexico. Usually this air drifts toward the Atlantic Ocean.

The other reason why this area receives so little rainfall is that it lies in the rain* shadow of the Rocky Mountains. All through the year, moist winds from the Pacific Ocean blow toward the western coast of the United States. When these winds reach the mountains in the western part of our country, they rise. As they rise, they become cooler and lose most of their moisture as rain or snow. By the time these winds have finally crossed the Rocky Mountains, they are very dry. As they move down the eastern slopes of the mountains, the winds become warmer. Instead of giving off water, they take up water from the land. This helps explain why the climate in the western part of the Great Plains states is so dry.

In this area, rainfall is also very uncertain. The amount changes greatly from year to year. In some years, there is enough rain for growing good crops of wheat. In other years, so little rain falls that crops wither and die. Sometimes, droughts last for a long time. This makes life very hard for the farmers.

The Changing Seasons

This chapter has explained why there are great differences in temperature between summer and winter in the Midwest and Great Plains. It has also shown why rainfall differs from place to place in this part of our country. To learn more about the climate of the Midwest and Great Plains, let us see what the weather is like during each of the four seasons of the year.

Winter

Winters are cold in the north

The top map on page 39 shows the average temperatures in North America during January. You will see that the average January temperature in the northern part of the Midwest and Great Plains is below freezing. Winters are especially cold in the far northern states, such as North Dakota and Minnesota. These states lie in the path of icy winds from Canada. In these states, the temperature often drops far below zero.

In the northern part of the Midwest and Great Plains, snow may blanket the ground for months at a time. Snowfall is especially heavy along the eastern and southern shores of the Great Lakes. As cold winds from the north and west blow across the lakes, they become warmer and take up much moisture. In winter, they drop this moisture over the cold land in the form of snow. Along the southern shore of Lake Superior, over eight feet of snow may fall each winter.

Snowfall is lighter in the Great Plains states, because the climate is drier. Sometimes, however, the strong winds that blow here pick up snow and send it whirling through the air. A snowstorm like this is called a blizzard. † People or animals who are caught outdoors in a blizzard may lose their way in the blinding snow. They may even freeze to death if they cannot find shelter.

† Perhaps some of your students have been in a blizzard. You may wish to have them tell about their experiences.

The Mackinac Bridge in wintertime. This huge bridge crosses the Straits of Mackinac between Lake Michigan and Lake Huron. (See map on pages 8-9.) It connects two large peninsulas that make up the state of Michigan. In the northern part of the Midwest and Great Plains, winters are long and cold. How does the cold winter weather affect shipping on the Great Lakes?

The people who live in the northern part of the Midwest and Great Plains have learned to prepare for cold winter weather. Their homes and other buildings are heated with furnaces that burn gas, oil, or coal. Houses in this area are built to keep out the cold. When people go outdoors in the wintertime, they wear heavy clothing to keep themselves warm.

Cold, snowy weather sometimes slows down travel in the northern part of the Midwest and Great Plains. Cars often become stuck in snowdrifts. Icy roads make driving dangerous. Buses and trains may be delayed by a heavy snowfall. Snowplows are used to clear the streets and highways so that traffic can move. For about three or four months each winter, ice covers parts

What can you discover about winter on the Great Lakes from this picture? (Cold, thick ice, no ships.)

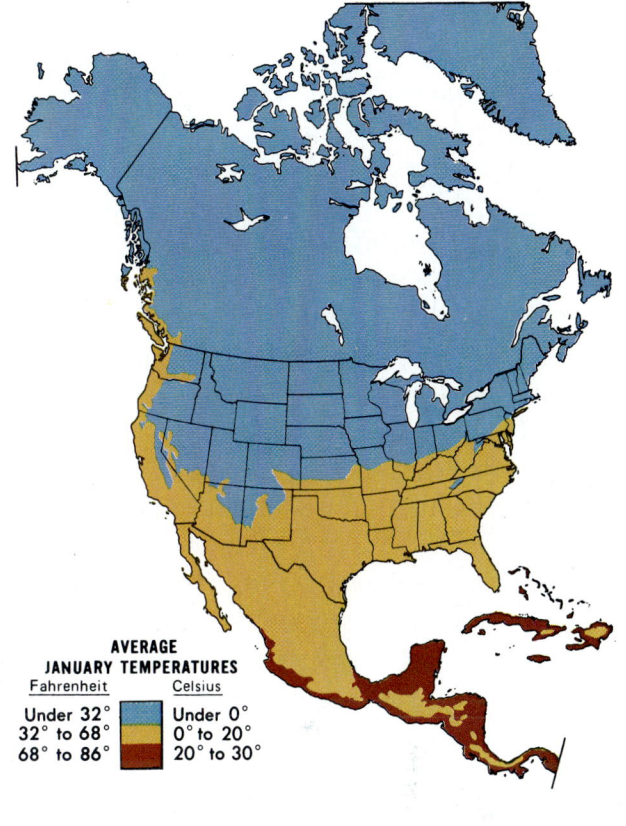

AVERAGE
JANUARY TEMPERATURES
Fahrenheit   Celsius
Under 32°   Under 0°
32° to 68°   0° to 20°
68° to 86°   20° to 30°

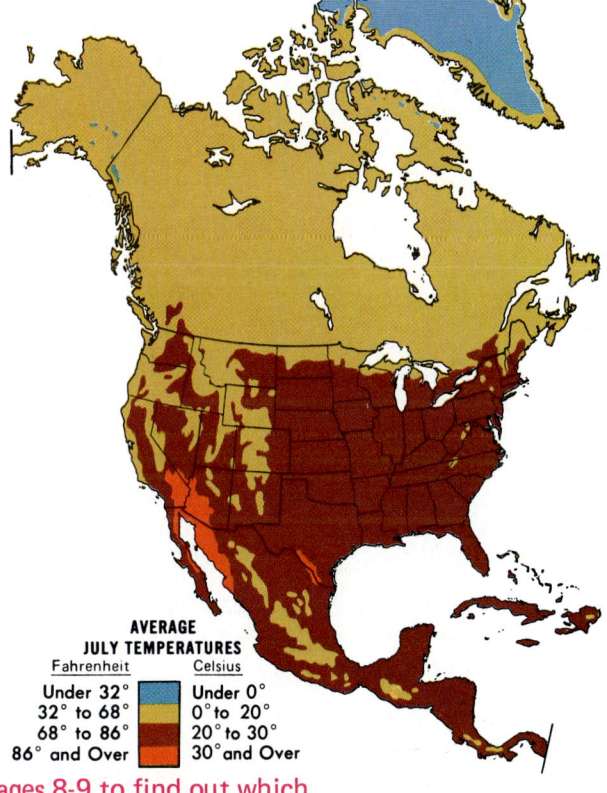

AVERAGE
JULY TEMPERATURES
Fahrenheit   Celsius
Under 32°   Under 0°
32° to 68°   0° to 20°
68° to 86°   20° to 30°
86° and Over   30° and Over

of the Great Lakes. Ships cannot travel unless special boats called icebreakers clear a path through the ice for them.

Farmers in the northern part of the Midwest and Great Plains do not work in their fields during the winter. The ground is frozen and covered with snow. The farmers must care for their livestock, however. They have to provide warm barns and plenty of food for their animals during the wintertime. Many people in this area look

Have students use these maps and the map on pages 8-9 to find out which states in the Midwest and Great Plains have the greatest temperature changes from January to July.

Midwest and Great Plains

forward to the winter months. They enjoy skiing, ice-skating, and other winter sports. There are many ski resorts in Michigan, Wisconsin, and Minnesota.

Winters are milder in the south

If you were to travel southward through the Midwest and Great Plains during the winter, you would find that the weather becomes warmer. Winters are mild in the southern part of the Midwest and Great Plains.

Winters are very mild along the Gulf coast of Texas. As you learned earlier, large bodies of water such as the Gulf of Mexico are warmer than the land in winter. Warm winds from the Gulf bring mild weather to the land along the coast. In Houston, Texas, the average January temperature is 55° F. (12° C.).

Sometimes during the winter, cold winds from the north sweep southward all the way across Texas. Temperatures may fall below freezing, but it rarely snows in the southern part of the state. When snow does fall, it seldom stays on the ground more than a few days at a time.

People who live where winters are very mild can work and play comfortably outdoors all year long. They do not have to wear heavy clothing or heat their houses for many months. During the winter, they can sometimes enjoy swimming, boating, and other outdoor sports. In the lower Rio Grande Valley of Texas, farmers grow fruits and vegetables during the winter months. They sell them to people in the cold northern part of our country. Some of these crops, such as oranges and grapefruit, cannot be grown in areas where winters are colder.

Spring

In the Midwest and Great Plains, spring weather is usually very changeable. One day the weather may be so sunny and pleasant that people can go outdoors without coats. The next day, the temperature may drop below freezing, and snow may fall. These sudden changes in the weather are caused by cold winds from the north and warm winds from the south.

Spring is a stormy time of year in the Midwest and Great Plains. The clashing of cold and warm air often results in windstorms and heavy rainfall. Terrible storms known as tornadoes sometimes develop in spring or early summer. (See feature on opposite page.) More tornadoes strike the Midwest and Great Plains than any other part of our country.

Growing seasons

During the springtime, farmers in the Midwest and Great Plains are busy plowing the land to prepare for planting. Before crops can be planted, farmers must be sure that the danger of hard frost is past. The period of time when crops can be grown outdoors without being killed by frost is known as the growing season.

The map on page 42 shows the average length of the growing season in different parts of the United States. You can see that the length of the growing season varies greatly in the Midwest and Great Plains.

Some areas in the northern part of the Midwest and Great Plains have a growing season that is less than four months long. Farmers in areas like these must grow crops such as potatoes,

Continued on page 42

† What do you think it would be like to be caught in a tornado?
†† Refer to the map. What region has the greatest number of tornadoes?

The black funnel cloud of a tornado moves slowly across the plains of Kansas.

† Tornadoes

We are visiting a small town in the eastern part of Kansas. It is a warm afternoon in early May. The air is very still. Far away, we can hear the low rumble of thunder. Large, black storm clouds are gathering in the western sky. The people we are visiting have turned on a radio to hear the latest weather report. They know that this kind of weather sometimes produces strong windstorms called tornadoes.

Suddenly we hear the loud sound of a warning siren. We rush to the window and look out. In the distance, we can see a black, twisting cloud shaped somewhat like a funnel. It reaches all the way down to the ground. (See picture above.) This is the funnel cloud of a tornado.

As the tornado moves toward the town, we hurry to the basement. We will be safer there if the house should blow off its foundation. It is raining very hard now, and lightning flashes across the sky. When the tornado strikes the town, the noise is like the roaring of a hundred freight trains. Buildings in the path of the tornado suddenly explode. Trees are ripped from the ground. Cars are tossed into the air like toys. Soon the tornado has passed, leaving a path of wreckage about a hundred yards (91 m.)† wide. It will take many months to repair the damage that the tornado caused in less than a minute.

A tornado is one of nature's most terrible storms. It is made up of very strong winds that whirl rapidly in a circle. Scientists believe that the whirling winds in a tornado may sometimes blow at speeds of more than three hundred miles an hour. The storm itself, however, travels forward rather slowly.

The exact way in which tornadoes are formed is not yet known. They seem to occur when a mass of warm, moist air and a mass of cold, dry air come together in a certain way. In the Midwest and Great Plains, this usually happens in spring or early summer when cold air from Canada meets warm air from the Gulf of Mexico.

There are more tornadoes in the Midwest and Great Plains than anywhere else in the world. Each year they destroy millions of dollars' worth of property. Sometimes many people are killed. In recent years, however, scientists have found better methods of predicting tornadoes and of warning people when one of these storms is coming. These warnings have surely helped to save many lives.

† m. means meter

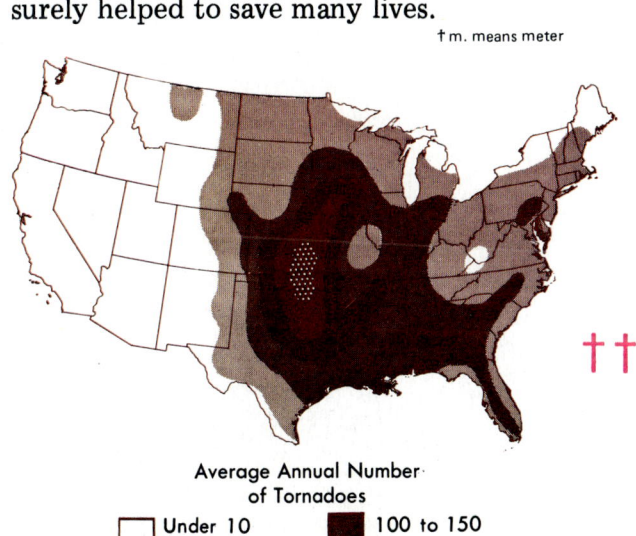

††

Average Annual Number of Tornadoes

- Under 10
- 10 to 50
- 50 to 100
- 100 to 150
- 150 to 200
- 200 and Over

AVERAGE LENGTH OF GROWING SEASON

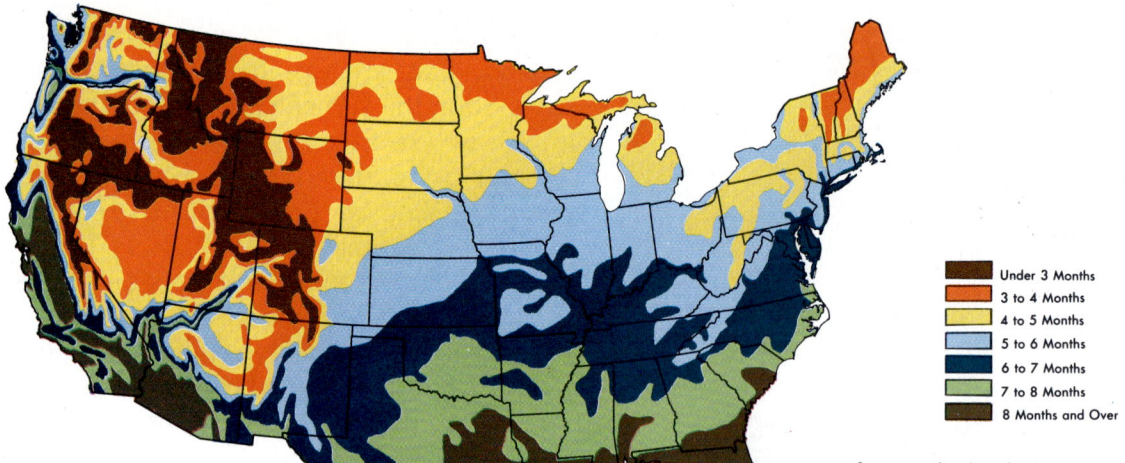

- Under 3 Months
- 3 to 4 Months
- 4 to 5 Months
- 5 to 6 Months
- 6 to 7 Months
- 7 to 8 Months
- 8 Months and Over

The period of time when crops can be grown outdoors without danger of being killed by frost is known as the growing season.

hay, and barley. These are crops that do not take a very long time to ripen.

In much of the Midwest and Great Plains, the growing season is between four and seven months long. (See map above.) Here the period without frost is long enough for growing corn, soybeans, and many other crops. The fertile farming area known as the corn belt lies entirely within this part of the Midwest and Great Plains.

The map above also shows that in parts of Texas and Oklahoma the growing season is more than seven months long. A long growing season is helpful to the farmers here. They can grow cotton and other crops that need many months to ripen. They are also able to plant their crops earlier in the year than farmers in the northern part of our country. As a result, they can harvest their crops and send them to market earlier. In this way, they are likely to get a better price.

The effect of the Great Lakes

The growing season in parts of the Midwest is affected by the Great Lakes. Like other large bodies of water, these lakes gain and lose heat more slowly than the land. In the spring, winds from the north and west are cooled as they blow across the lakes. The cool winds help keep fruit trees from budding until the danger of frost is past. In the fall, the Great Lakes

How long is the average growing season in southern Texas? In northern Illinois? Use the map on pages 8-9 to identify states.

Refer to the picture below. Read the caption aloud. Use the question for a class discussion.

are warmer than the land. Warm winds from the lakes help to protect the fruit from the danger of early frost. This climate is very good for growing fruit. There are many large orchards and vineyards along the eastern shore of Lake Michigan and the southern shore of Lake Erie.

Summer

Summers are warm or hot throughout the Midwest and Great Plains, except for a small area along the northern border of our country. During July and August, daytime temperatures in the Midwest and Great Plains often rise above 80° F. (27° C.). Winds from the north sometimes bring cooler weather, but this does not usually last long.

In the Midwest, summers are not only warm but humid. The warm air that drifts northward from the Gulf of Mexico during the summertime is very moist. Moisture in the air makes people

A grapefruit grove in the Rio Grande Valley of Texas. The growing season is more than seven months long in some parts of Texas and Oklahoma. In what ways is a long growing season helpful to farmers?

feel even warmer and more uncomfortable than they would if the air were dry. Many people do not like warm, humid weather. However, it is excellent for growing many kinds of crops. Rainfall is plentiful in the Midwest during the summer months.

In the Great Plains states, summers are often warmer than they are in the Midwest. In North Dakota, for example, daytime temperatures sometimes rise above 100° F. (38° C.). However, people usually do not mind the heat so much because the air is drier. In the western part of the Great Plains states, droughts may occur during the summer months. Hot, dry winds from the southwestern part of our country often blow across the plains. These winds can cause the crops to wither.

Summers are milder in the north

In the northernmost part of the Midwest and Great Plains, summers are

Summer in the northern part of the Midwest. Summers are cooler in the northern part of the Midwest and Great Plains than they are in the south. Compare the lower map on page 39 with the map on pages 8-9 to discover which four states in this region have areas in which the summers are mild.

milder than they are farther south. (See the bottom map on page 39.) Summer weather is especially pleasant near the Great Lakes. In the summer, these lakes are cooler than the land nearby. Breezes from the Great Lakes help to keep the weather along the shores from becoming very hot. During the summer months, millions of people come to northern Minnesota, Wisconsin, and Michigan. Here they enjoy the cooler weather and beautiful scenery.

Autumn

Autumn is a favorite time of year for many people in the Midwest and Great Plains. During this season, masses of cool, dry air from Canada often drift southward over the United States. They bring cool, refreshing weather and clear, blue skies. The leaves of oaks, maples, and other hardwood trees turn bright shades of gold, orange, and red.

Autumn is harvesttime in the Midwest and Great Plains. Corn and many other kinds of crops are ripe and ready to be picked. Tender crops, such as tomatoes, cucumbers, and certain kinds of fruit, must be harvested before the first hard frost of autumn.

Late in autumn, people in the northern part of the Midwest and Great Plains often enjoy a period of fine weather known as "Indian summer." Before long, however, the sky turns gray and a cold wind blows down from the north. Autumn is almost over, and winter is on its way.

Making Discoveries

Violent storms sometimes strike parts of the Midwest and Great Plains. Do research about one of the following types of storms:

tornado   blizzard

Share your findings with your classmates in an oral report. Look in magazines and newspapers to find pictures and articles to illustrate your report. The following questions will guide your research.

1. What weather conditions cause this kind of storm?
2. Where in the Midwest and Great Plains is this kind of storm most likely to strike?
3. How does this storm affect life and property when it strikes?
4. How do people protect themselves during this kind of storm?

Part 2

People

† Use these questions to start students thinking about the people of the Midwest and Great Plains.

About 73 million people live in the Midwest and Great Plains today. What do the people in this part of our country have in common with people in other parts of our country? Part 2 will help you discover answers to this question. You may also wish to answer the questions listed below.

- Who lives in the Midwest and Great †
  Plains today?
- What are the four largest cities in this part of our country? Why do you think so many people have chosen to live in these cities?
- What are some of the responsibilities that citizens have to the communities in which they live? What are some things you can do as a good citizen of your community?
- What can you do to help solve the problems of prejudice* and discrimination* in our country?
- What have you discovered about the arts in the Midwest and Great Plains?

*See Glossary

People in the Midwest and Great Plains. More than one third of all the people in the United States now live in this part of our country. Who first settled in the Midwest and Great Plains?

Midwest and Great Plains 47

4 People

About 73 million people live in the Midwest and Great Plains today. They make up more than one third of our country's population. Study the map on page 50. You will see that the population is not spread evenly throughout the Midwest and Great Plains. There are some places where very few people live. Other areas are crowded with people. To learn more about the population of the Midwest and Great Plains, we will make two trips.

A visit to the Midwest

We drive along the shore of Lake Michigan. We are going from Chicago, Illinois, to Milwaukee, Wisconsin. (See map on page 59.) During our 90 mile (145 km.)† journey, we do not see very much open countryside. In fact, we are inside a city or town almost all the time. In some of the cities that we visit, we see large apartment buildings where many families live. We also pass through large suburbs* with thousands of homes. Any crowded area like the one we are driving through is said to be densely populated.

A visit to the Great Plains

On our next trip, we cross the Great Plains in western Nebraska. Our highway passes through broad grasslands. Few people live here. Sometimes we drive for miles without seeing a single farmhouse. At last we reach a crossroads with a gasoline station. There are two or three houses nearby. A worker at the gas station tells us that the nearest town of any size is 40 miles (64 km.) away. Any area like this one, which has very few people, is said to be thinly populated.

Population in the Midwest

More than 52 million people live in the Midwest. Except for the Northeast, this is the most densely populated part of our country.

There are many ways for people to meet their basic needs in the Midwest. This is the main reason why it is so densely populated. The Midwest

† km. means kilometer
*See Glossary

Students and teachers at a university in Houston, Texas. People of many different national* origins, races, and religions live in the Midwest and Great Plains. What are some of the different groups these people belong to?

Cooperation

See Great Ideas

The students shown in the picture above want to get a good education. Do you think it would be possible for them to do this if they did not cooperate with their teachers? Do you think the teachers cooperate with their students? With one another? What might be some of the ways in which the students cooperate with one another? What are some of the ways in which the students and teachers in your school use the great idea of cooperation?

Use these questions in a class discussion.

Midwest and Great Plains

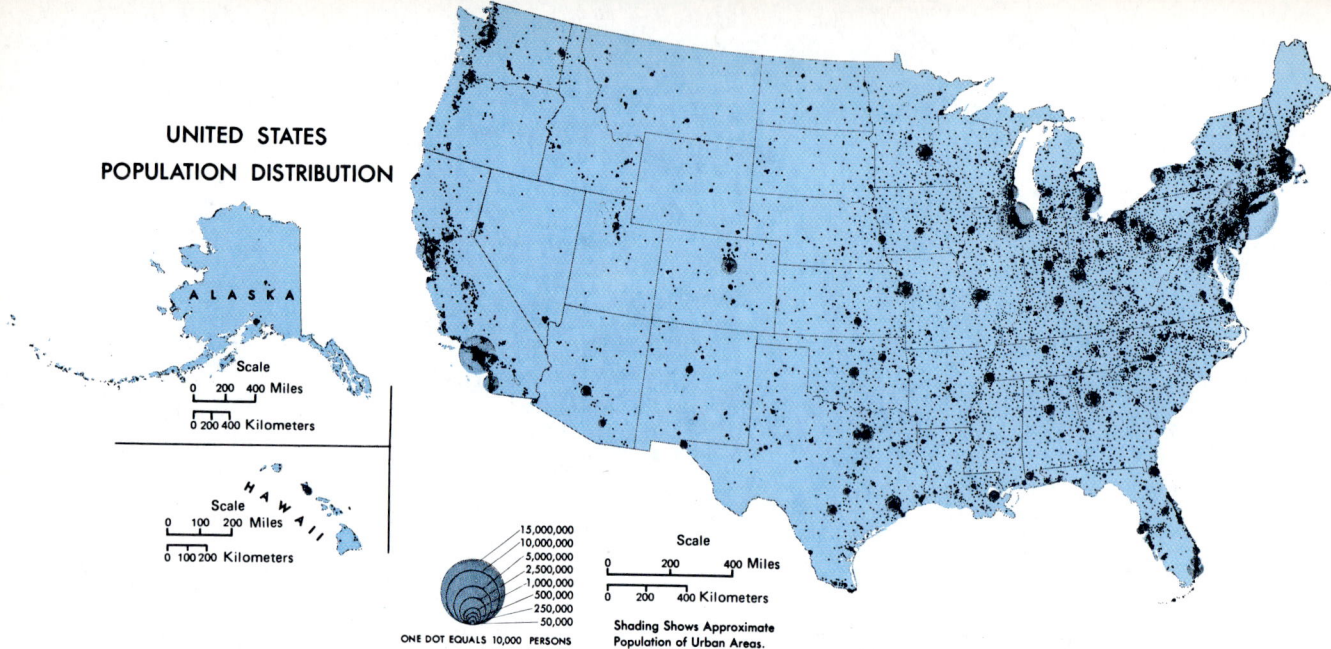

is an important manufacturing, farming, and trading region. Many workers are needed in factories, stores, and offices. Most people in the Midwest are able to earn the money they need.

Some of the most thinly populated areas in the Midwest are in northern Michigan, Wisconsin, and Minnesota. Winters here are very cold. The growing season is too short for many kinds of crops. Also, much of the soil is thin and sandy. Only a small part of the land is used for farming. Most of the rest is covered with forests. There is little manufacturing in these areas. Therefore, there are fewer jobs here than in most other parts of the Midwest.

Population of the Great Plains states

The Great Plains states cover a larger area than the Midwest. However, they have only about one-third as many people. Almost 21 million people live in the Great Plains states. About six out of ten of these people live in Texas.

There are fewer ways for people to meet their basic needs in the Great Plains states. This is the main reason why this area is more thinly populated than the Midwest. The Great Plains states have less industry than the Midwest. (See Chapter 10.) Huge cattle ranches and wheat farms cover much of the land. Few people are needed to work on the wheat farms. With modern machinery, one person can farm many acres. A few workers can take care of thousands of cattle on a large ranch. It is not surprising that there are not many jobs in many parts of the Great Plains states.

The populations of some Great Plains states have been growing rapidly during the past few years. For example, the number of people living in Texas has more than doubled since 1930. Texas has several large manufacturing cities. Factories, stores, and offices provide jobs for many people. Other Texans work on farms or in oil fields. The United States government has been carrying on space projects in Texas. These projects use thousands of workers. Some people have moved to Texas because they enjoy the mild, sunny climate along the Gulf coast.

† Do you think there were more jobs on farms and cattle ranches before modern machines were used? Explain.

Who Lives in the Midwest and Great Plains?

People of many national* origins, races, and religions live in the Midwest and Great Plains. Many people in this part of our country are the descendants of Europeans who came to the United States hundreds of years ago. Others are of Latin American descent or of African descent. Some American Indians also make their homes in the Midwest and Great Plains.

People of European Descent

People from many different countries in Europe have been coming to live in the Midwest and Great Plains since the late 1700's.

The British Isles

The pioneers who settled the Midwest in the late 1700's and early 1800's were mostly of British descent. They were English, Scotch, or Irish. All during the 1800's, people came to America from Ireland and other parts of the British Isles. Some of these immigrants* settled in the Midwest and Great Plains. They brought the English language with them. They also brought many

At a Dutch festival in Holland, Michigan. Many people who live in the Midwest and Great Plains are the descendants of people who came from Europe many years ago. What are some of the countries these people came from?

ideas and customs that have become part of our way of life.

Germany

During the last half of the 1800's, many immigrants came to the Midwest and Great Plains from Germany. Some of them became farmers. Others settled in the cities. There they worked in factories, stores, or offices. Today, you can still notice the German influence in such cities as Milwaukee, St. Louis, and Cincinnati.

Other northern Europeans

People from other countries in northern Europe also came to the Midwest and Great Plains during the last half of the 1800's. Dutch immigrants settled in Michigan, Iowa, and other states. Many other people came from the Scandinavian countries of Norway, Sweden, and Denmark. They settled mainly in Wisconsin, Minnesota, and the Dakotas. Many of them became farmers. Some helped to harvest timber in the northern forests. Others earned their living by fishing on the Great Lakes.

Eastern and southern Europe

After 1890, millions of people came to America from eastern and southern Europe. Many of these people came from Poland, Italy, and Hungary. Some came from Greece. Others came from Russia. Some of these people were Jews. By the time they arrived, most of the good farmland in the Midwest had been taken. Some of these newcomers went farther west to farm on the Great Plains. Many more settled in Chicago and other cities. Some of them worked in steel mills. Many worked in factories. They helped make the Midwest a great manufacturing region. Other immigrants became doctors, lawyers, or teachers. The descendants of many of these people still live in the cities of the Midwest today.

People of African Descent

About one tenth of the people in the Midwest and Great Plains are of African descent. During World War I* and World War II,* factories in the Midwest

Education

See Great Ideas

The man in the picture above works in a laboratory. Many black people in the Midwest and Great Plains have good jobs in business and industry. Do you think it would be possible for them to get these jobs without a good education? Explain.

needed many workers. Hundreds of thousands of black people moved from the South to the Midwest. They hoped to get good jobs in industry. Many blacks are still moving from the South to the Midwest today.

A better way of life

Most of the black people who moved to the Midwest came in search of a better way of life. Today, many black people in the Midwest and Great Plains have good jobs in stores, offices, and factories. Some blacks are managers or own their own businesses. Others are government leaders, teachers, doctors, or lawyers. However, there are not enough jobs in our country. Some people are not able to find work.

Most black people live in cities

There are many black people in all the large cities of the Midwest. More than one million black people live in Chicago. About two out of every five people in Detroit are of African descent. More than one and one-half million black Americans live in Texas. Most of these people live in Dallas, Houston, and the state's other large cities. Texas is the only Great Plains state with a large black population.

† Do you think the government was right in forcing Indians to move onto reservations? Why? Why not?

People of Latin American Descent

Many Spanish-speaking people live in the Midwest and Great Plains. Most of these people live in Texas, Illinois, and Michigan.

Mexican-Americans

About two million people of Mexican descent live in the Midwest and Great Plains. Most of these people live in Texas. Some are descendants of people who lived here when Texas was part of Mexico. (See page 35 of "Pictorial Story of Our Country.") Many have come from Mexico since that time. Some work on farms or orchards. Others work in businesses or factories. Spanish is still spoken by many Mexican-Americans today.

Other Spanish-speaking peoples

Other people of Latin American descent live in the Midwest and Great Plains. Some of these people came from Puerto Rico. Others came from Cuba. Most of these Spanish-speaking people make their homes in Illinois.

People of Asian Descent

The descendants of people from several Asian countries also live in the Midwest and Great Plains. Some people moved to this part of our country from Japan, China, and Korea. Others came from the Philippines to settle in this region.

American Indians

There are about 178,000 Native Americans in the Great Plains states. Another 89,000 live in the Midwest. Some are descended from the Indians who lived on the prairies* and in the forests here long ago. Others are descended from the Cherokee and Choctaw Indians, who moved here from the eastern part of our country during the 1800's.

When our country was being settled, † the United States government forced most Indians to move onto reservations.* These reservations were generally in areas where few white people cared to live. Much of the land in these areas was not good for farming. Today many Indians still live on reservations. Most of them earn their living by grow-

A Mexican-American. About two million Mexican-Americans live in the Midwest and Great Plains. What other groups of people live here?

American Indians in South Dakota. Several thousand American Indians live in the Midwest and Great Plains. Some of them are descended from the Indians who lived in this part of our country long ago.

ing crops or raising livestock. Some Indians, however, have moved to cities to get jobs in business and industry.

Many Religious Faiths

In the Midwest and Great Plains, as in other parts of our country, people of different religious beliefs live side by side in friendship. Some are members of the Roman Catholic Church. Others belong to different Protestant groups. In a number of cities, there are Eastern Orthodox* churches. Thousands of people in the Midwest and Great Plains are Jews.

Explore Population

Imagine you have taken a trip through parts of the Midwest and Great Plains. You began your trip in Milwaukee, Wisconsin, and went to Chicago, Illinois. Then from Chicago you went to Sioux City, Iowa. Write a letter to a friend and tell what you saw. In your letter, you should tell about the following:
1. a densely populated area
2. a thinly populated area
3. some of the different people you saw

This chapter provides information that will help you tell about your trip and the people along the way. "Learning Social Studies Skills" in the Skills Manual will help you write a good letter.

† You may wish to have all students participate in this activity.

Midwest and Great Plains 55

5 Cities

Use the questions on page 63, "Make Discoveries About Cities," to start students thinking about cities in the Midwest and Great Plains.

Many large cities

About seven out of every ten people in the Midwest and Great Plains live in cities or large towns. The map on page 59 shows where the main cities in this part of our country are located.

Just as in other parts of our country, cities have grown up in the Midwest and Great Plains because they help to meet human needs. If you compare the map on page 59 with the one on page 122, you can see that many of the cities are centers of large industrial areas. During the past one hundred years, well-paying jobs in factories brought millions of people to cities in the Midwest and Great Plains. Other people have come to the cities to work in stores and offices.

As the map on page 59 shows, some parts of the Midwest and Great Plains have no large cities. In these thinly populated areas, most of the people earn their living by farming.

The following pages tell about four of the largest cities in the Midwest and Great Plains. As you read, try to find out why each city grew up where it did, and why so many people chose to live there.

Chicago grew up on the site of an early fur-trading post. What facts about land, transportation, natural resources, industry, and history help explain why Chicago eventually became such a large city?

56 Midwest and Great Plains

Chicago

The largest city in the Midwest and Great Plains is Chicago, Illinois. It is larger than any other city in the United States except New York.

The city of Chicago stretches for about thirty miles along the southwest shore of Lake Michigan. (See map on page 59.) North of Chicago, a group of smaller cities and towns reaches to the Wisconsin border. West of the city, the land is dotted with towns and factories. To the southeast, a huge industrial area extends into northwest Indiana. Altogether, a little more than seven million people live in the Chicago metropolitan* area.

History

The first settler in the Chicago area was a black fur trader named Jean Baptiste Point du Sable. In 1779 he built a trading post near the mouth of the Chicago River. This lay on the main

*See Glossary

SIX METROPOLITAN AREAS		
Metropolitan Area	Population of Entire Area	Population of Central City (or Cities)
Chicago	7,006,400	3,109,000
Detroit	4,389,900	1,304,000
Dallas-Fort Worth	2,585,300	831,000 364,000
Houston	2,392,100	1,402,000
St. Louis	2,386,300	520,000
Minneapolis-St. Paul	2,033,400	364,000 273,000

The six largest metropolitan* areas in the Midwest and Great Plains are listed above. Their populations are given in the middle column. For each of these areas, the population of the central city or cities is also given.

*See Glossary

route between the Great Lakes and the Mississippi River. Explorers and fur traders had used this route for many years. They paddled their canoes from Lake Michigan up the Chicago River and traveled a few miles overland to a branch of the Illinois River. Then they paddled down the Illinois River into the Mississippi.

In 1803 a group of American soldiers † built a fort near the site of Du Sable's trading post. A small settlement grew up around the fort. For many years Chicago grew slowly. Then, in the 1850's, railroads were built connecting settlements in the Midwest with cities in the east. Many new settlers came to the Midwest. They shipped their grain, livestock, and other farm products to Chicago. Many factories were started in this city to produce the things the growing population of the Midwest needed. Thousands of people came from eastern cities and from Europe to live and work in Chicago. By 1890, the tiny settlement along the Chicago River had become one of the great cities of the world.

A transportation center

Today Chicago is the most important transportation center in the nation. A great web of highways and railroads leads into this city. More travelers pass through O'Hare International Airport than any other airport in the world. Water transportation is also important. Millions of tons of oil, coal, and other products are carried on the Illinois Waterway, which now connects Lake Michigan with the Mississippi River. Ships from all parts of the world come to Chicago by way of the Great Lakes-St. Lawrence Waterway.

See Great Ideas

Shoppers on State Street, in downtown Chicago. There are many fine department stores in the Chicago area, and thousands of people shop here each day. In addition to retail trade, what other kinds of exchange are carried on in Chicago? How did exchange help Chicago to become one of the largest cities in the United States? Do research in this book and in other sources to find answers to these questions.

† Refer students to the picture of Chicago on pages 56-57. In what main ways is Chicago different today than it was in the 1700's?

† Why do you think so many people in the Midwest and Great Plains live in or near the main cities shown on this map?

Trade and industry

Factories in the Chicago area produce almost eighteen billion dollars' worth of goods each year. There are large iron and steel plants in Chicago and in neighboring cities in Indiana. Much of the iron and steel produced here is used in making many kinds of machinery. Huge factories in the Chicago area produce kitchen stoves, television sets, radios, and other electrical equipment. Chicago is also a big producer of clothing and food products. Some other important industries in the Chicago area are printing and publishing, oil refining, and chemicals.

More trade is carried on in Chicago than in any other city of the United States except New York. A number of large department stores and mail-order companies are located in this city. Owners and managers of stores and factories send buyers to Chicago to see products at huge trade shows.

The arts

If you visited Chicago, you would find many things to do. You could go to several different plays. You could also hear concerts by the Chicago Symphony Orchestra and other musical groups. Each day, thousands of people visit the city's great museums, such as the Art Institute, the Field Museum of Natural History, and the huge Museum of Science and Industry.

Houston

The largest city in the Great Plains states is Houston, Texas. (See map below.) It is located in the southeastern part of the state, about fifty miles

This map shows the locations of the main cities of the Midwest and Great Plains. It includes all cities with a population of 100,000 or more. It also shows all state capitals, including those with a population of less than 100,000. More than half of the people in the Midwest and Great Plains live in or near the cities shown on this map.

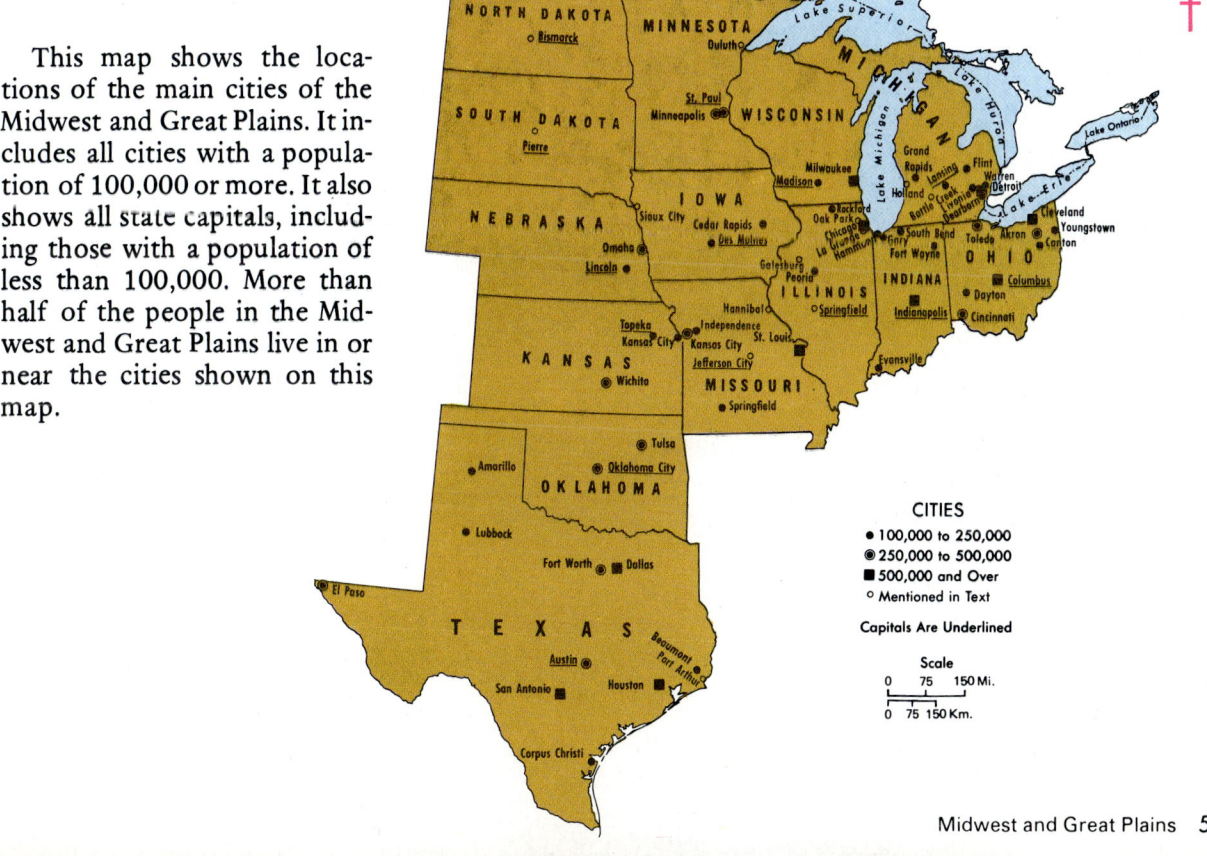

Midwest and Great Plains 59

† How has oil helped Houston grow?

from the Gulf of Mexico. The Houston Ship Channel connects the city with the Gulf.

History

Houston was founded in 1836. It was named for General Sam Houston, who led the people of Texas in their revolt against Mexican rule. Rich deposits of oil were discovered in southeast Texas in about 1900. Houston became an important oil-refining center. The ship channel was deepened and the port was improved to allow more ships to dock at the city. Since then, Houston's population has grown rapidly. Today almost two and one-half million people live in the metropolitan area that surrounds Houston.

A leading port city

Houston is our country's third leading port city. Only New York and New Orleans are larger. Ships from all over the world load and unload goods along the Houston Ship Channel. Many of the city's factories are located along this waterway.

Houston is the largest city in the Great Plains states. It is located in southeastern Texas, about fifty miles from the Gulf of Mexico. What facts help to explain why Houston became such a great city?

† In what ways has the automobile industry helped Detroit grow? List your discoveries.

Industry

Houston is the central city of one of our country's major industrial areas. (See map on page 122.) There are several chemical plants and oil refineries in the Houston area. Several other industries are also important here. Many people work in factories that make metal products. Others work in plants that prepare rice, meats, and other foods for sale.

In the Houston metropolitan area is the huge Manned Spacecraft Center of the National Aeronautics and Space Administration (NASA). Here, NASA trains astronauts and controls space flights. In addition, spacecraft are planned at this center.

Detroit

Detroit is the largest city in Michigan. (See map on page 59.) It is the sixth largest in the nation. About four and one-half million people live in the Detroit metropolitan area.

History

Detroit is located on the busy Detroit River. This is part of a waterway that connects Lake Erie with Lake Huron. (See map on page 120.) In 1701 French settlers built a fort on the Detroit River. Here they traded with the Indians for furs. Later the fort and the settlement that grew up around it were taken over by Great Britain and then by the United States.

Industry

After the Civil War, manufacturing grew rapidly in Detroit. Among the city's products were bicycles and carriages. In the early 1900's, people such as Henry Ford and Ransom E. Olds began to make automobiles. The † first small factories grew into huge automobile plants. They brought thousands of people to work in Detroit.

Today, America's three largest automobile manufacturers have their main offices in the Detroit area. Detroit leads the world in the production of automobiles and trucks. Detroit also has many factories that make automobile parts. Here, too, automobiles are planned and tested.

Many other products are also made in the Detroit area. Steel plants here

Midwest and Great Plains 61

produce much of the metal needed by the automobile industry. Some of the other kinds of goods made in the Detroit area are machine tools, hardware, chemicals, and rubber products.

A changing city

In recent years, Detroit has been changing rapidly. A large, modern civic center has been built on Detroit's waterfront. Many slums have been replaced with new housing. Several broad highways connect Detroit with different parts of the fast-growing urban area that has spread out from the city.

St. Louis

St. Louis, Missouri, is on the west bank of the Mississippi River, a few miles south of the place where the muddy waters of the Missouri River flow into the Mississippi. It is the central city of a huge metropolitan area that spreads across the Mississippi into Illinois. Almost two and one-half million people live in this area. St. Louis is an important manufacturing city and one of our country's leading river ports.

History

St. Louis began in 1764 as a French fur-trading post. During the 1800's, it was the main gateway to the west. Many explorers and settlers set out from St. Louis on their way to the west. They carried food and other supplies they had bought here.

Industry

Today, many different products are made in St. Louis. The production of airplanes and automobiles are two of the most important industries. Foods such as fruits, vegetables, and meats

are also canned in the St. Louis area. Animal hides are made into leather for shoes and other products.

Gateway Arch

Near the riverfront of this modern city stands a reminder of the past. The Gateway Arch recalls the time when St. Louis was the gateway to the west. The arch stands 630 feet high. From its top you can see the city stretching along the Mississippi River.

† **Gateway Arch, in St. Louis, Missouri.** This arch is a part of the Jefferson National Expansion Memorial. It stands on the bank of the Mississippi River in downtown St. Louis. It was built to remind people of the time when this city was the gateway to the western part of our country.

Make Discoveries About Cities

1. Which city in the Midwest and Great Plains is the most important transportation center in the United States?
2. Which city is the largest city in the Great Plains states?
3. Name two important cities in the Midwest and Great Plains that were founded by the French.
4. Which city in the Midwest is famous for the manufacture of automobiles?
5. Which states in the Midwest and Great Plains have cities with populations of 500,000 or more? Name these cities.
6. Two cities in the Midwest and Great Plains have populations of 500,000 or more and are also the capitals of their states. Which cities are these?
7. Two states in the Great Plains have no cities with populations of 100,000 or more. Name these states. Why do you think these states have no large cities?

† Why was this arch built?

Read a picture. What does this picture of the Indiana House of Representatives show you about the government of Indiana?

6 Citizenship and Government

Our State Governments

Our country, the United States, is made up of fifty states. There is a government for the nation as a whole. But each state also has its own government. These state governments are not all just the same. There are a number of differences between them. Still, they are alike in certain important ways. For instance, every state has a group of people who make the laws.

The capital of Indiana

To learn how state governments work, let's visit the capital of a single state in the Midwest. We will go to Indianapolis, Indiana. The main offices of Indiana's government are in this city.

We start our visit to Indianapolis by going to the state capitol.* This is a huge stone building with a gold-colored dome. It is near the center of the city.

The state constitution

At the capitol, we meet a woman who will be our guide. She tells us that Indiana became a state in 1816. At that time, the people of Indiana approved a plan of government for the state. This plan was called a constitution. It told how Indiana's government was supposed to be run.

In 1851 the people of Indiana approved a new constitution. This plan of government is still being used today. However, a number of changes have been made in the constitution since 1851. These are called amendments.

Our guide tells us that every state in our country has a constitution. These constitutions are very different from each other in many ways. But all are alike in one way. They all tell how the state government should be run.

The state legislature

Our guide says that the laws of Indiana are made by the legislature. This is a group of men and women elected by the people of the state. In many ways the legislature is like

*See Glossary

The Indiana state legislature. Every state in our country has a legislature. This is a group of men and women elected by the people of the state. The legislature makes the laws for the state. Do research in other sources to discover what some of your state's laws are. Do you think it is important for people to obey these laws? Explain.

Rules and Government

See Great Ideas

† In what ways is the governor of a state like the president of the United States?

the United States Congress.* Every state in our country has a legislature, but it is sometimes known by another name. In Indiana, for example, the legislature is called the General Assembly.

The General Assembly is made up of two parts, or houses. One of these is the Senate. It has fifty members, who are elected to serve four-year terms. The other is the House of Representatives. It has one hundred members, who are elected for two-year terms. The General Assembly decides on new laws by voting on bills* suggested by its members. A bill cannot become a law until it has been approved by both of the houses. All of the decisions are made by majority* vote.

Otis R. Bowen, the governor of Indiana. Every state in our country has a governor. The governor makes sure that the laws made by the state legislature are carried out.

We learn that other state legislatures are much like Indiana's. In every state except Nebraska, the legislature is made up of two houses. Nebraska has a one-house legislature.

The governor and other state officers

While we are in the capitol, we visit the office of Indiana's governor. Our guide says that this person is like the president of the United States in many ways. The governor is in charge of carrying out the laws that the legislature has made. Also, the governor suggests new laws for the legislature to pass.

A governor is elected every four years by the people of Indiana. At the same time, they elect a lieutenant governor. If the governor dies or cannot perform the duties, the lieutenant governor takes the governor's place. Several other state officers are also elected every four years. Among these are the state treasurer and secretary of state.

The governor has thousands of people to help do the work of government. These people are grouped into many departments. Each department has a special job to do. For instance, the Department of Public Instruction is in charge of running the schools.

Every state has a governor. However, state governments are different from one another in a number of ways. For instance, not all governors serve four-year terms. In some states, they are elected for two years. In many states, officers such as the treasurer are not elected by the people. Instead, they are chosen by the governor.

The state supreme court

From the governor's office, we go to another large room in the capitol. Our

†† In our school library or public library find information about the Supreme Court of our state.

Our State Governments

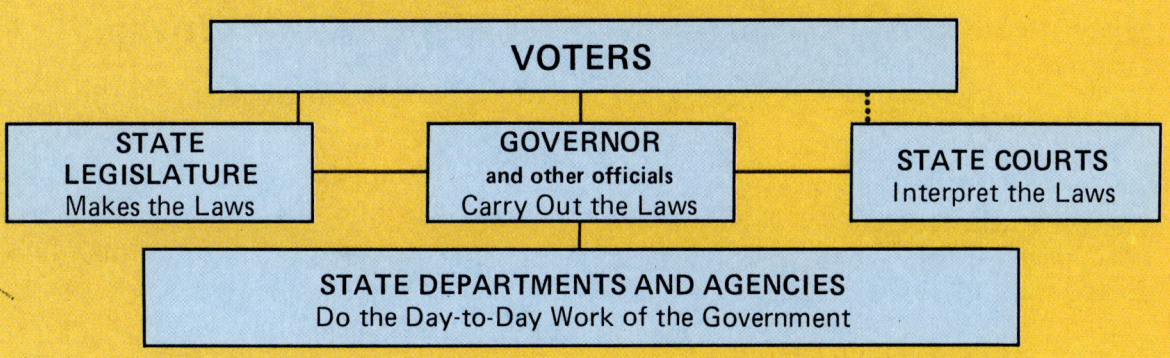

guide says that this is where the Indiana Supreme Court meets.

Like other states, Indiana has many different law courts. The highest of these is the Indiana Supreme Court. To see how this court works, imagine that a man is arrested for a crime. This man feels that he has been treated unfairly in a lower court. He can ask the Indiana Supreme Court to hear his case. When the supreme court makes a decision, all other courts in the state must follow that decision. There is only one court higher than the state supreme court. That is the United States Supreme Court.*

Indiana's Supreme Court is made up of five judges, called justices. Each judge is chosen by the governor to serve for two years. At the end of that time, an election is held. The voters decide whether the judge should be allowed to serve for ten more years.

Other states also have supreme courts. These courts are sometimes called by other names. And they are different in other ways. In some states, the judges are elected by the people. In other states, they are chosen by the governor or the legislature. In some states, the judges serve until they die or resign. In other states, they serve for only a few years at a time.

Local governments

Now we walk to a large, modern building near the center of Indianapolis. This is the city-county building. The offices of the Indianapolis city government are located here.

Our guide tells us about local governments in Indiana. She says that the state is divided into ninety-two counties. Each county is divided into smaller parts called townships. Both the counties and the townships have their own governments. Each city and town in Indiana has a government also.

Indianapolis is different from any other city in Indiana. At one time, it was part of Marion County. The city and the county each had its own government. But Indianapolis has grown so large that it now covers the same area as the county. Both the city and the county have the same government. This is known as Unigov.

We learn that other states have local governments also. But these are not all alike. For example, some states do not have townships. In some states, county governments are quite powerful. In others, they have very little power.

Our visit to Indianapolis is over now. During our trip, we have learned many things about state governments and how they work.

Midwest and Great Plains 67

RESPONSIBILITIES OF CITIZENS

Obeying the laws

Good citizens obey the laws of their community, state, and country. Even if they think a law is unfair, they will not disobey it. Instead, they will work in a peaceful way to get the law changed.

Treating other people with respect

Good citizens treat other people the same way they would like to be treated. They try to be friendly and polite to everyone. This is because they truly believe that every person is important.

Getting a good education

In the United States, most people have an opportunity for an education. Young people are responsible for making good use of this opportunity. By learning as much as they can, they are preparing to become useful citizens when they grow up.

Doing useful work

Most Americans feel they are responsible for doing useful work. When they become adults they do not expect other people to take care of them. Instead, they expect to work hard and do their job well.

Taking part in the government

In the United States, it is important for every citizen to take part in the government. People who are over eighteen can do this by voting in all elections. Also they can work for candidates* they think would do a good job. Young people have a responsibility to learn as much as they can about their government. This will help prepare them to make wise decisions when they are older.

Cooperating with other people

Many jobs in a community cannot be done well by persons working alone. Instead, there must be cooperation among many people. Citizens of a community have a responsibility to work together. In this way, they can make their community a better place to live.

*See Glossary

Being a Good Citizen of a State

As an American citizen, you probably live in one of the fifty states that make up our country. Or you may live in the District of Columbia,* where our nation's capital is located.

A citizen's rights

Citizens of a state have the same rights that they do as citizens of the United States. For example, they are free to worship God in any way they please, or not at all. They are free to express their ideas on any subject. Citizens are free to live anywhere they please. They are free to work at jobs they have chosen themselves. If a person is arrested for a crime, he or she has a right to a fair trial.

A citizen's responsibilities

Most of the good things that people have in life do not come to them free. These things must be paid for in some way. This is true of the rights and freedoms that we enjoy in the United States. To protect these rights and freedoms, we must be willing to do our part as citizens. In other words, we have certain <u>responsibilities</u> to our community, our state, and our nation.

Some of the main responsibilities of citizens are described in the feature at left. Study each item on the list carefully. Then decide for yourself how you feel about it. Do you agree that this is an important responsibility of citizens? Give reasons for each answer. Can you think of any other items that should be added to the list? If so, what are they?

† List and describe the responsibilities of a citizen that you feel you should meet.

† What kinds of problems occur when people do not meet their responsibilities as citizens?

When citizens do their part

You probably live in a community where most citizens meet their responsibilities. For example, most people obey the laws of their community, state, and nation. They try to treat other people as <u>they</u> would like to be treated. They try to get as much education as they can. They earn their living by doing some kind of useful work.

When citizens fail to do their part

In every community, there are some people who do not meet their responsibilities as citizens. For example, there are people who break the laws. Some people do not treat others with respect. In fact, they often do things that cause harm to other people. Many people do not do any kind of useful work. Yet they expect other people to help them meet their needs.

† People who fail to do their part as citizens can cause great harm to a community. Sometimes they can even destroy it. Many of the problems that our country faces today have come about because some people are not meeting their responsibilities.

To understand why this is so, think about an example from real life. Suppose that a person makes a living by stealing cars. This person is disobeying the laws of the community. He is not treating other people the way he would like to be treated. Instead, he is causing them harm. By breaking the law, he is taking away other people's rights.

The person who steals cars is also hurting the community. When people are the victims of crime, they often become angry and afraid. They stop trusting their neighbors. As a result, they are less likely to work with other people to do things that help the community. If crimes take place often, people no longer feel proud of their community. As soon as they have a chance, they move away. They go to places where they think life will be safer and more pleasant.

The car thief is hurting not only other people but also himself. Sooner or later, he will probably be caught and sent to prison. Then he will lose some of his own rights and freedoms.

People who break the law have little respect for themselves. Usually there is no one they can really trust. Such people will never feel very safe or happy.

A decision you must make

Even though you are not old enough to vote, you are already a citizen. In the years to come, you will need to make an important decision. You will have to decide whether you are going to meet your responsibilities as a citizen. Are you going to help build a stronger community, state, and nation? Or are you going to make them weaker? The choice is up to you.

A Problem Facing Our Nation

As you have seen, many problems arise when citizens do not meet their responsibilities. Let's explore one important problem facing our country today. This problem is caused by people who do not treat others as they would like to be treated.

Lack of freedom for certain groups

Freedom is one of the great ideas that built our nation. (See "Great Ideas" in the Table of Contents.) Our country is often called "the land of the free." There are some people, however, who have not always enjoyed as much freedom as other Americans. Many of them belong to groups that are different in some way from the majority of people. Their skin color may be different. They may speak a different language than the majority. Or they may follow a different religion. Such groups are called minority groups.

Minority groups that have not always had their full share of rights and freedoms include:

... blacks.
... American Indians.
... Latinos (people from Spanish-speaking countries such as Mexico).
... people from Asian countries such as China and Japan.
... Roman Catholics.*
... Jews.*

Not all people who lack freedom belong to minority groups. There are more women than men in our country. Yet women have not always had the same rights and freedoms as men.

The meaning of prejudice

Why have so many Americans found it hard to get equal rights? Mostly because other people have feelings of prejudice toward them.

† Prejudice means having a feeling about someone without knowing the facts. People who have prejudices do not judge other people by their actions. Instead, they judge them simply by the fact that they belong to a certain group. For instance, some people may believe that women are not as smart or as brave as men. Such a belief is not based on facts.

People who have prejudices may not mean to hurt other people. They may not even realize that they have any prejudices. Often they have learned these feelings from friends or relatives. They have never asked themselves whether these feelings are true. People who have prejudices may not realize that people in other groups have the same needs as they do. (See "Needs of People" in the Table of Contents.) They may not understand that these people, too, have a right to meet their needs.

The meaning of discrimination

Sometimes people who have prejudices do things that keep other people from enjoying all their rights. This is known as discrimination.

In the past, many kinds of discrimination could be found in the United States. Here are some examples.

The right to vote

The United States, as you know, is a democracy.* Yet in earlier times, many Americans were not allowed to take part in our country's government. Until the 1900's, most states did not allow women to vote. Several states kept black people from voting until the 1960's. In some places, Indians also lacked the right to vote.

Legal* rights

In the past, women and members of minority groups often did not have the same legal rights as other Americans. For instance, women were not allowed to serve on juries.* And they could not appear as witnesses in a court of law. When a woman married, she lost the right to own property. All of her property belonged to her husband. In some states, blacks could not serve on juries. A black or an Indian who was

† Have you ever felt prejudiced against someone? Explain.

SEVEN IMPORTANT BELIEFS SHARED BY PEOPLE IN A DEMOCRACY

1. **Every person is important.**

   Most Americans believe that every person is important. It does not matter if you are young or old, a man or a woman. You are just as important as every other person. You are important whether your skin is black, white, or some other color. You are important no matter what religion you follow or what country your grandparents came from.

2. **People have the right to govern themselves.**

   Americans believe the citizens of a country have the right to govern themselves. We think every person should be able to have some part in running our government.

3. **Decisions should be made by majority* vote.**

   In the United States, all citizens have a chance to help choose the people who run the government. They do this by voting in elections. The candidate* with the most votes is elected. This is known as majority vote. Most Americans believe the fairest way for people to govern themselves is by majority vote.

4. **All citizens should have a chance to get a good education.**

   Education is very important in a democracy. To have good government, citizens must be able to vote wisely for the people who make and carry out the laws. Most Americans believe that all young people should have a chance for a good education.

5. **Laws should be the same for all citizens.**

   Most Americans believe all citizens should be treated the same by their government. Everyone should be required to obey the same laws. People should never gain or lose any rights because of such things as the color of their skin, or how much money they have.

6. **All people have certain rights that no one can take away from them.**

   Most Americans believe that every person has a number of important rights and freedoms. Among these are freedom of speech and freedom of religion. Also every person has the right to a fair trial in a court of law. We believe that these rights cannot be taken away from any person, even by a majority vote. In a democracy, the government is expected to protect the rights of all citizens.

7. **Citizens have responsibilities as well as rights.**

   For a democracy to work, all citizens must be willing to do their part. In other words, citizens have responsibilities as well as rights. Among these responsibilities are obeying the laws of the community, taking part in the government, and doing useful work.

   *See Glossary

---

arrested for a crime sometimes found it hard to get a fair trial.

Asian-Americans also lacked some of their legal rights. During World War II, our country was at war with Japan. Most Japanese-Americans were loyal citizens. Yet thousands of these people were taken from their homes without a trial. They were sent to camps far away. There they had to stay until the war was over.

Employment

Because of discrimination, many Americans have found it hard to earn a good living. In the past, most kinds

How would you feel if someone discriminated against you? What would you do about it?

of jobs were not open to women. There was also job discrimination against minority groups. Many employers would not hire blacks, Indians, Latinos, or Asian-Americans. Or they would hire them only for jobs that were hard or unpleasant. Often these jobs paid them very little money.

Housing

In the past, members of minority groups often had trouble getting good housing. Many people would not sell houses or rent apartments to them. When minority families moved into certain neighborhoods, people sometimes made trouble for them.

Education

During the early days of our country, it was hard for women to get a good education. Few girls went to high school, and colleges would not admit women students. Even in the 1900's, colleges sometimes tried to keep women from studying certain subjects, such as medicine and engineering.

Members of some minority groups also had few chances for an education. After the Civil War,* most states in the South passed segregation* laws. These laws kept black children from attending the same schools as white children. Often the schools that were built for blacks were not as good as those for

Workers in an engineering* office. Until a few years ago, job discrimination was a serious problem in our country. Today, a growing number of jobs are being filled by people who belong to minority groups.

Lead a class discussion about "Seven Social Problems."

whites. In the West, Indians and Asian-Americans sometimes had to attend separate schools. Some colleges in our country would not admit Jews. Some would accept only a small number of Jewish students.

Use of public facilities

In the past, other kinds of segregation were also allowed in our country. Some states had laws that kept black people from using the same parks, playgrounds, and beaches as white people. Blacks also had to sit apart from whites in trains and buses. Some communities discriminated against Indians, Latinos, and Asian-Americans. For instance, Latinos were sometimes kept from using the same parks and playgrounds as other citizens. All over the country, there were restaurants that would not serve blacks or Asian-Americans. Many hotels would not admit Jews as guests.

Gaining more rights for women

The fight to end discrimination in our country began in the 1800's. Some women began to demand the same rights as men. They wrote books and made speeches to call attention to their views. As time passed, they accomplished some of their goals. Most states passed laws that gave women the same legal rights as men. In 1920 the people of our country approved the Nineteenth Amendment to the Constitution. This amendment gave women the right to vote in all elections.

The civil rights movement

During the first half of the 1900's, members of minority groups still did not have equal rights. But a great change began to take place in the

SEVEN SOCIAL PROBLEMS

In our country, a number of serious problems prevent people from meeting their needs. These are called social problems. The government and the people of our country have been working hard to solve these problems. As we make progress toward this goal, more Americans will have happier and more successful lives. Our country's social problems include:

1. **The need for more jobs.** At the present time, about six out of every hundred workers in the United States are unable to find jobs.
2. **The high cost of living.** In recent years, the high cost of goods and services has kept many people from meeting their needs. This continuing rise in prices is called inflation.
3. **The need for better education.** Many people in our country are not getting a good education. They are not gaining the knowledge they need for good citizenship.
4. **Illness and handicaps.** Americans are among the healthiest people in the world. However, millions of people in our country suffer from serious illnesses and handicaps.
5. **Lack of freedom for certain groups.** In the past, some groups of people in our country did not have the same freedoms as other people. Today, our laws give every person the right to fair treatment and equal opportunity. Even so, some Americans still do not have all the rights and freedoms promised by our laws.
6. **Crime.** Over the years, there has been a great increase in the number of major crimes in our country. In many areas, people live in fear for their lives.
7. **Unsuccessful communities.** In many parts of the United States there are unsuccessful communities. Many of the people in these communities are not doing useful work. They are not getting the education they need to get jobs or to be good citizens. The crime rate in these communities is very high.

Freedom

See Great Ideas

The woman in this picture is training for work as a machinist. During the past few years, women have been seeking greater freedom to choose the kind of work they wish to do. Do you think women should have this kind of freedom? Should men and women receive the same amount of money for the same kind of work? Do you think women and members of certain minority groups in our country are ever discriminated against? Give reasons for your answers.

1950's. Black people in our country began to demand the same rights as other citizens. Other minority groups, such as Indians and Latinos, also began to demand equal rights. This was the start of the civil* rights movement. You can read more about the civil rights movement on page 62 of "Pictorial Story of Our Country."

A change in people's feelings

The civil rights movement helped bring about important changes in people's feelings. Many Americans have begun to lose their prejudice toward members of minority groups. Today, most Americans try to live by the seven important beliefs of democracy shown on page 71. For example, they believe that the law should be the same for all citizens of a country.

Supreme Court decisions

The United States Supreme Court has helped to end discrimination in our country. In 1954, it said that segregation in public schools is against the Constitution. In spite of this, many communities still provided separate schools for blacks. Then, in 1969, the Supreme Court ordered all schools to end segregation at once. The Court has also made other decisions that have helped minority groups to gain equal rights.

Laws against discrimination

In the last fifteen years, many laws have been passed to end discrimination. One of these is a federal* law known as the Civil Rights Act. It says that employers must not discriminate against women or members of minority groups. This law has also helped to end segregation in places such as schools, parks, hotels, and restaurants. Another federal law is called the Voting Rights Act. It forbids state and local governments to do certain things that would keep members of minority groups from voting. Still another federal law has helped to end discrimination in housing. Many state governments have also passed laws to do away with different kinds of discrimination.

Civil rights in America today

Today, women and members of minority groups enjoy more rights and freedoms than ever before. But there is still much to be done before all Americans have equal rights. For example, some companies still refuse to hire women for certain jobs. Black people still have trouble buying or renting homes in certain areas.

All Americans must work together to solve the problem of discrimination. They must treat other people as they would like to be treated themselves. And they must live by the seven important beliefs that make our democracy possible.

Exploring Citizenship †

Try to think of different situations in which people <u>are</u> or <u>are not</u> doing their part as citizens.

Make a list with two columns. In the first column, give examples of citizens who are meeting their responsibilities. In the second column, give examples of citizens who are not meeting their responsibilities. Use newspapers, magazines, radio, and television to get the facts you need. For each example on your list, do the dollowing:

1. Give the facts about the situation. Also, tell where you got these facts.
2. Tell how you feel about this situation. Are the people helping their community, or are they hurting it? Explain.
3. If people are not meeting their responsibilities, tell what you think should be done about it. How can we get more people to do their part as citizens?

When you have finished your research, share your findings with other people in your class. Find out how they feel about the examples you have described. You may also want to present your findings in a written report.

† Use "Exploring Citizenship" as a culminating activity for this unit.

7 The Arts

Literature

Writers of the 1800's

In the 1800's, the Midwest and Great Plains produced one of America's greatest writers. This was Samuel Clemens, who wrote under the name of Mark Twain. Clemens grew up in Hannibal, Missouri, a town on the Mississippi River. He wrote of his boyhood experiences in some of his best-loved books, such as *The Adventures of Tom Sawyer* and *Life on the Mississippi*.

Several other writers of the Midwest and Great Plains became famous during the late 1800's. One of these was Hamlin Garland, who was born in Wisconsin and grew up in Iowa and South Dakota. Garland wrote many novels and short stories. He is best known, however, for his autobiography *A Son of the Middle Border*.

Indiana's James Whitcomb Riley was a well-loved poet of this period. You may have read some of his poems, such as "Little Orphant Annie." Eugene Field was another midwestern poet. He wrote "Wynken, Blynken, and Nod" and many other poems for young people.

See Great Ideas

Mark Twain was a great American writer of the 1800's. Perhaps you have read *The Adventures of Tom Sawyer* or *The Prince and the Pauper*. In his works, Twain expressed his ideas about people and the ways in which they live. Could he have shared his ideas without the use of language? Explain your answer. Do you think it is important for people to write books? To read books? Why? Why not?

† Use your school library to do research about Mark Twain or another person mentioned in this chapter.

† Have a student read aloud part of one of these poems. What does it tell you about the author?

† **Poets of the 1900's**

The Midwest has produced many important poets during the twentieth century. These include Vachel Lindsay and Carl Sandburg. Lindsay used new and interesting verse rhythms in poems such as "The Congo." Some of his poems, such as "Abraham Lincoln Walks at Midnight" and "Bryan, Bryan, Bryan, Bryan" were about famous people of the Midwest. Carl Sandburg's works include *Chicago Poems* and *The People, Yes*. He has also written a fine book about the life of Abraham Lincoln.

Some of the more recent poets who were born in the Midwest include Marianne Moore, Archibald MacLeish, Mark Van Doren, and Richard Eberhart.

Poets of the Great Plains states include Edgar Lee Masters, who was born in Kansas. His most famous book is *Spoon River Anthology*. The poems in this book tell about the lives of the people buried in the cemetery of a midwestern village. Gwendolyn Brooks was also born in Kansas. Two of her books of poems are *Annie Allen* and *A Street in Bronzeville*.

Novelists of the 1900's

During the 1900's, the Midwest has produced dozens of fine writers. Many of these men and women have written

The famous poet Carl Sandburg (below left) was born in Galesburg, Illinois. Gwendolyn Brooks (below right), another well-known poet of the 1900's, was born in Topeka, Kansas. Both of these poets spent much of their lives in Chicago. They wrote many poems about how hard life can be in a big city.

novels and short stories about the people and history of this part of our country.

Booth Tarkington and Edna Ferber wrote many enjoyable novels that are popular with young people as well as grown-ups. Tarkington's books include *Penrod, Seventeen,* and *The Gentleman from Indiana.* Some of Ferber's novels, such as *So Big,* are about people in the Midwest. *Cimarron* tells about people who settled the Great Plains states.

Several of our country's greatest novelists of the 1900's were born in the Midwest. These include Sherwood Anderson, Theodore Dreiser, Sinclair Lewis, and James T. Farrell. In their books, these writers told about people who faced some of the hard problems of life in modern America. Anderson's best-known books include *Poor White* and *Winesburg, Ohio.* Among Dreiser's novels are *An American Tragedy* and *Sister Carrie.* Many of Lewis's novels became best sellers. One of these is *Main Street,* which is about life in a small town in Minnesota. Farrell's most famous work is *Studs Lonigan,* a series of novels about a young man growing up in Chicago.

F. Scott Fitzgerald and Ernest Hemingway were also born in the Midwest but later moved to other areas. Fitzgerald was born in St. Paul, Minnesota. One of his most important novels is *The Great Gatsby.* Hemingway grew up in Oak Park, Illinois, and began his career in Kansas City. He wrote *A Farewell to Arms* and many other novels and short stories.

Many fine writers of the present century have lived in the Great Plains states. Willa Cather, who grew up in Nebraska, wrote a number of novels and short stories about the settlement of the western prairies. Among these are *O Pioneers!* and *My Ántonia.* O.E. Rölvaag was a Norwegian immigrant who lived in South Dakota. His greatest work, *Giants in the Earth,* describes the lives of Norwegian settlers in South Dakota. Katherine Anne Porter, who was born in Texas, is known for her fine short stories and also for her novel *Ship of Fools.*

Other Arts
Painters and sculptors

During the 1800's, George Caleb Bingham painted many scenes showing life in the Midwest. Among his paintings are *Fur Traders Descending the Missouri* and *The Jolly Flatboatmen.*

Three more recent artists of the Midwest and Great Plains also became famous for their paintings of everyday life in this part of our country. The paintings of Iowa's Grant Wood include *American Gothic,* which is shown on the opposite page. Thomas Hart Benton, who lived in Missouri, created many murals* and other paintings showing life in the Midwest. John Steuart Curry's paintings show farm life on the plains of Kansas.

Other artists who lived and worked in the Midwest and Great Plains include the sculptors Lorado Taft and Carl Milles. In some of the cities of the Midwest are beautiful fountains and statues created by these men.

Architects

Some of our country's greatest architects worked in the Midwest and Great Plains. Louis H. Sullivan designed many of Chicago's early skyscrapers. Houses and other buildings designed by Frank

† Grant Wood's *American Gothic*. Wood was one of a group of twentieth-century artists who painted scenes of everyday life in the Midwest and Great Plains. Do you think paintings such as *American Gothic* can help us understand the people of this area? Give reasons for your answer.

Lloyd Wright are found in many different parts of the Midwest and Great Plains. Eliel Saarinen and his son Eero Saarinen came to America from Finland in 1923. Each designed many buildings. Eero Saarinen made the design for the huge steel arch that is part of the Jefferson National Expansion Memorial in downtown St. Louis. (See picture on pages 62-63.)

† Call attention to the picture above and discuss the question.

Part 3

Earning a Living

The Midwest and Great Plains is an important farming region. It also has large amounts of useful minerals. It has valuable forests and fisheries. In addition, the Midwest and Great Plains has many factories. Because of this, people in this part of our country earn their living in many different ways. In which areas or states would you find people who earn their living in the following ways:
- drilling for oil
- mining iron ore
- harvesting evergreen trees
- fishing for shrimp
- raising dairy cattle
- raising wheat
- raising fruit
- assembling automobiles
- working in a flour mill
- working in a chemical plant

Part 3 has information that will help you answer this question.

Workers in a luggage factory in Detroit. The Midwest and Great Plains is an important industrial region of the United States. It is also our country's leading agricultural region.

† Use this problem to start students thinking about farming in the Midwest and Great Plains.

8 Farming

† **A Problem To Solve**

The Midwest and Great Plains is one of the greatest farming areas in the world. Why has farming become so important in this part of our country? To solve this problem, you will need to make several hypotheses.* In forming your hypotheses, you will want to consider facts about each of the following:

a. the soil and land features of the Midwest and Great Plains
b. the climate here
c. the farming methods used in this part of our country

Chapters 2 and 3 provide additional information that will be helpful in solving this problem. You may also wish to do research in other sources.

See Skills Manual, "Thinking and Solving Problems"

The Midwest and Great Plains is the most important farming area in the United States. Each year, farmers here earn about half of the money that comes from farming in our country. Eight of our ten leading farming states are located in the Midwest and Great Plains. Farms in this part of our country provide us with many of the foods we eat. Two major crops are wheat and corn. More than half of our country's beef cattle and most of its hogs are raised here. Some of our clothing is made from cotton or wool produced in the Midwest and Great Plains. Hundreds of other products also come

*See Glossary

Harvesting corn in Indiana. Most of our country's corn is grown in the corn belt. This is a fertile farming area in the Midwest and Great Plains. Nearly half of all the corn in the world is grown here.

† Why is farming so successful in the Midwest and Great Plains? Students should use the pictures, maps, and text to answer this question.

from the huge farmlands in this part of our country.

† There are several reasons why farming is so important in the Midwest and Great Plains. Nowhere else in the world are there such large areas of fertile soil. Most of the land in the Midwest and Great Plains is level enough to be farmed with modern machinery. The long, warm summers in most of this area are very good for growing crops. Rainfall is plentiful in the Midwest. Although many parts of the Great Plains states receive little rainfall, farmers here can earn a good living if they use the soil and water wisely.

Saving nature's riches

Nature gave farmers in the Midwest and Great Plains huge areas of fertile land. In the past, however, many farmers did not use this valuable land wisely. Some farmers planted the same crop, such as corn, on the same land year after year. This removed large amounts of plant foods from the soil. As a result, the soil became less fertile.

Sometimes poor ways of farming caused soil erosion.* Before the Midwest and Great Plains was settled, most of the land was covered with grass or trees. The roots of these plants held the soil in place. They kept it from being washed away by rainwater or carried away by the wind. When the land was cleared and used for growing crops, the soil was no longer protected. In some places, rainwater washed away much of the fertile topsoil and cut deep gullies in the surface of the earth. In other places, strong winds picked up large amounts of topsoil and carried it away. After the fertile topsoil had been removed, the land could no longer be used for growing crops.

Farmers have learned that if they wish to produce large crops, they must take good care of their land. In other words, they must practice conservation. In the Midwest and Great Plains, just as in other parts of our country, farmers keep their soil fertile and help prevent erosion in several different ways.

Many farmers no longer grow the same crop on the same land year after year. Instead, they grow different crops on the same land in different years. This is called crop rotation. For example, one year a farmer may plant a crop such as corn, which removes large amounts of plant foods from the soil. The next year or two, the farmer may raise a rotation crop such as soybeans,

Midwest and Great Plains 83

Soybeans are grown in the Midwest and Great Plains. Illinois ranks first and Iowa second in growing soybeans. Indiana and Ohio also grow large amounts of soybeans.

clover, or alfalfa. These crops need smaller amounts of some plant foods than corn does. Sometimes the farmer may plow a rotation crop into the soil to help restore fertility. By the third or fourth year, the land is ready for growing corn again.

Many farmers today use chemical fertilizers to help keep their soil fertile. These fertilizers replace some of the plant foods that corn and other crops take out of the soil.

Farmers use various methods to stop soil from being carried away by water or wind. To conserve soil on sloping land, they often plow rows that curve around the hillsides instead of up-and-down rows. This is known as contour plowing. The rows made by the plow catch the rainwater so that it cannot rush down the hillside and wash the fertile topsoil away.

Dry farming

In parts of the Great Plains states where rainfall is light, farmers must conserve water as well as soil. They have worked out certain ways of growing crops without irrigation. This kind of farming is known as "dry farming."

† What information do the picture below and the map on page 87 provide about the dairy belt? Prepare a list of discoveries you make.

Farmers who use dry farming methods leave part of their land idle, or fallow, each year. Rain that falls on the fallow land is stored in the soil. When crops are grown on this land the following year, they can use the stored-up moisture. Therefore, they will not need so much rainfall.

When land is left fallow, the strong winds that sweep across the plains may blow much soil away. To prevent this, many wheat farmers plant their wheat in long, narrow rows between strips of fallow land. The stalks of wheat slow down the wind so that it does not sweep across the bare soil with its full force. Many farmers also plant rows of trees along the edges of their fields. These are known as "windbreaks." They, too, break the force of the wind and help to keep the soil from being blown away.

Main Farming Areas

In order to make a good profit, farmers raise the crops and animals best suited to the land and climate where they live. Within the Midwest and Great Plains there are several large areas where the land and climate favor a certain kind of farming. The map on page 87 shows these main farming areas. It is important to remember, however, that many other crops and animals are raised in addition to the main ones listed for each area.

The dairy belt †

In the dairy belt, raising cows for milk is the main type of farming. This

Dairying is important in some parts of the Midwest and Great Plains. Many farmers raise Holstein cows, like the ones pictured below. Holstein cows produce more milk than any other cows.

belt includes most parts of Wisconsin, Minnesota, and Michigan. Several facts help explain why dairying is so important in these areas. Summers here are cooler than they are in other parts of the Midwest, and rain is plentiful. This kind of climate is very good for growing grass, which can be cut for hay or used for grazing. Also, cows give more milk if the weather is not too hot in the summer. In many parts of the dairy belt, the land is too hilly or the soil too poor for growing most crops. These areas can be used as grazing land for dairy cattle.

A number of large cities in the Midwest lie in or near the dairy belt. (Compare the map on the opposite page with the map on page 59.) Because fresh milk spoils quickly, it is seldom shipped far away. For this reason, dairy farms are usually located as close as possible to customers. The cities of the Midwest provide a huge market for dairy products.

Wisconsin produces more milk than any other state in our country. If you were to travel through this state in the summer, you would see many herds of dairy cattle grazing in rolling green pastures. You would also see well-kept barns and other farm buildings.

Most farms in the dairy belt are not very large. The grass here is thick and nourishing, so large areas of grazing land are not needed. Many dairy farmers raise alfalfa, clover, or timothy for hay. Corn is also grown on many farms. In places where the growing season is too short for corn to ripen fully, the corn is harvested before it is ripe and chopped into silage.*

Farmers who live near cities usually sell their milk to dairies. These plants pasteurize* the milk and put it into bottles or cartons for sale to customers. Farmers who do not live close to cities sell their milk to nearby plants that make such products as butter, cheese, and ice cream. If they are properly stored, these products keep for a long time without spoiling. Therefore, they can be shipped long distances. Nearly half of the cheese made in the United States comes from Wisconsin. Minnesota produces more butter than any other state. Large quantities of ice cream are made in Michigan.

The corn belt †

The corn belt covers a part of every state in the Midwest and Great Plains except Texas and Oklahoma. It is the most fertile farming area of its size in the world. The rich, dark soil and warm, humid summers here are well suited for growing corn.

Each year, farms in the corn belt produce about four fifths of our country's corn. This is nearly half of all the corn grown in the world. Illinois and Iowa are our nation's leading corn-producing states.

The corn belt could also be called the "meat belt." Most of the corn grown here is used by farmers to fatten millions of hogs and cattle. When these animals are fat enough, they are sold to stockyards in Nebraska, Illinois, and other states. Nearly half of the money earned by farmers in the corn belt comes from the sale of livestock and livestock products. Iowa and Illinois lead all the states in money earned from the sale of hogs. Iowa ranks second to Texas in earnings from beef cattle.

Corn is not only used as feed for livestock, but it is also an important raw

† Make a map showing the corn belt. Students should use the map on page 87 to identify the corn belt and the map on pages 8-9 for naming the states.

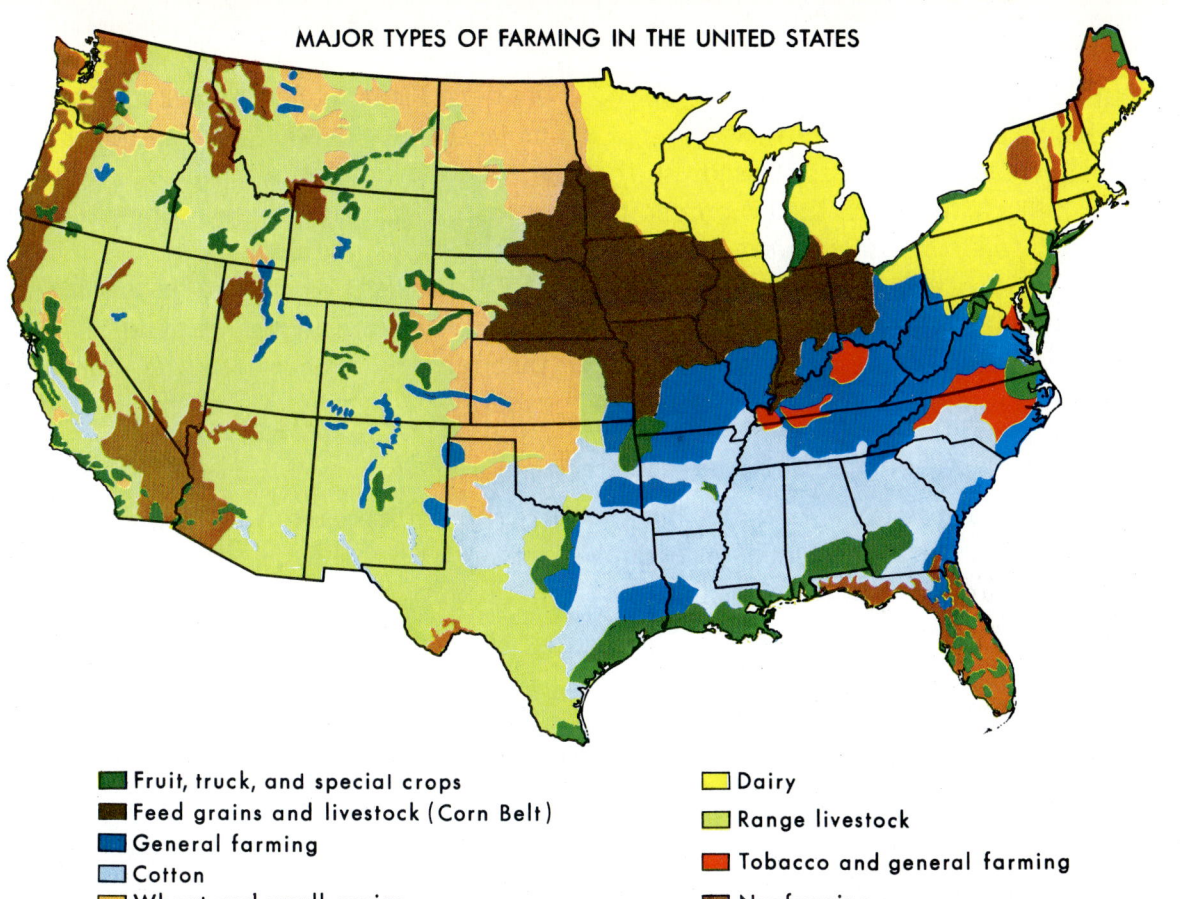

MAJOR TYPES OF FARMING IN THE UNITED STATES

- Fruit, truck, and special crops
- Feed grains and livestock (Corn Belt)
- General farming
- Cotton
- Wheat and small grains
- Dairy
- Range livestock
- Tobacco and general farming
- Nonfarming

Using Natural Resources

See Great Ideas

The map above shows the major types of farming in the conterminous United States. Within the Midwest and Great Plains are several large areas, such as the corn belt, where a certain kind of farming is important.

1. Why are certain kinds of crops and livestock produced in some areas and not in others? Do you suppose the answer to this question has anything to do with the natural resources in the area? Among the natural resources used by farmers are sunshine, water, and soil. Do all areas receive the same amount of sunshine and rainfall? Do all areas have the same kind of soil? How do differences in the supply of these natural resources affect the raising of crops and livestock?

2. Sometimes, through hard work and careful planning, people can overcome problems in the supply of natural resources. Pages 106-108 provide information about the dams that have been built on rivers in the Great Plains states. How do these dams help people in the Great Plains states to make better use of their resources?

material for industry. Factories use it in making cornstarch, cooking oil, breakfast cereal, and other items that you can probably find in your kitchen. Corn is also used in manufacturing hundreds of different products, including soap, glue, and paper.

In recent years, soybeans have become an imporant cash* crop in the corn belt. The soybean plant has many uses. Farmers feed the vines to animals. They also plow the vines back into the soil to replace plant foods taken from it by other crops. Manufacturers make both meal and oil from the beans. Soybean meal is a good feed for livestock, and the oil is used in making margarine, linoleum, and many other products.

† Use this map and the questions to make additional discoveries about farming in the Midwest and Great Plains, and in other parts of our country.

Refer to the picture below. What can you discover about wheat farming from this picture and from the maps on pages 87 and 94? List your discoveries.

Our country's leading producers of soybeans are Illinois and Iowa.

Other crops are also raised in the corn belt. After corn, the two most important feed crops are oats and hay. These are often planted as rotation crops on land where corn is grown. Soybeans or wheat sometimes take the place of oats or hay as rotation crops.

Wheat farming

It is a warm sunny morning in late June. We are visiting a wheat farm that covers nearly 500 acres (202 ha.)† in western Kansas. The owner has invited us to see how wheat is harvested. From the cab of the truck, we look out on golden fields of wheat separated by brown strips of fallow land.

To the right of the truck, a machine called a combine is moving slowly through the wheat. As the combine moves, it cuts and threshes* all the wheat in its path. Then the grain is fed through a spout into the back of the truck. Before long, the farmer tells us that we have a full load of wheat. We take the wheat to a nearby railroad

† ha. means hectare

Harvest season in South Dakota. Huge combines are used to cut and thresh wheat. The Great Plains states produce more wheat than any other part of our country.

station, where it is put into a huge building called a grain elevator. The wheat will be kept in this building until a train comes to carry it to Kansas City, where it will be made into flour.

More wheat is produced in the Great Plains states than in any other part of our country. In much of this area, the land and climate are better suited to growing wheat than any other crop. There are large areas of fertile soil. Rainfall in many parts of the Great Plains states is too light for growing such crops as corn and soybeans, but there is usually enough rain for wheat. Because so much of the land here is level, farmers can use modern farm machines to plant and harvest their wheat.

Winter wheat

There are two main wheat-growing areas in the Great Plains states. The most important is the winter wheat belt. This belt extends across central and western Kansas and Oklahoma and into Texas. Here, farmers plant their wheat in late summer or early fall. The young plants grow about six inches before winter comes, and then do not grow again until spring. By early summer, the grain is ripe and ready to harvest. More than three fourths of all the wheat grown in our country is winter wheat. Kansas produces more wheat than any other state.

Sometimes, in the winter wheat belt, rainfall may be especially light for months or even years at a time. A severe drought* can ruin the wheat crop and cost farmers large sums of money. To protect themselves against such a loss, many farmers raise other crops as well as wheat. For example, some farmers in the winter wheat belt also raise

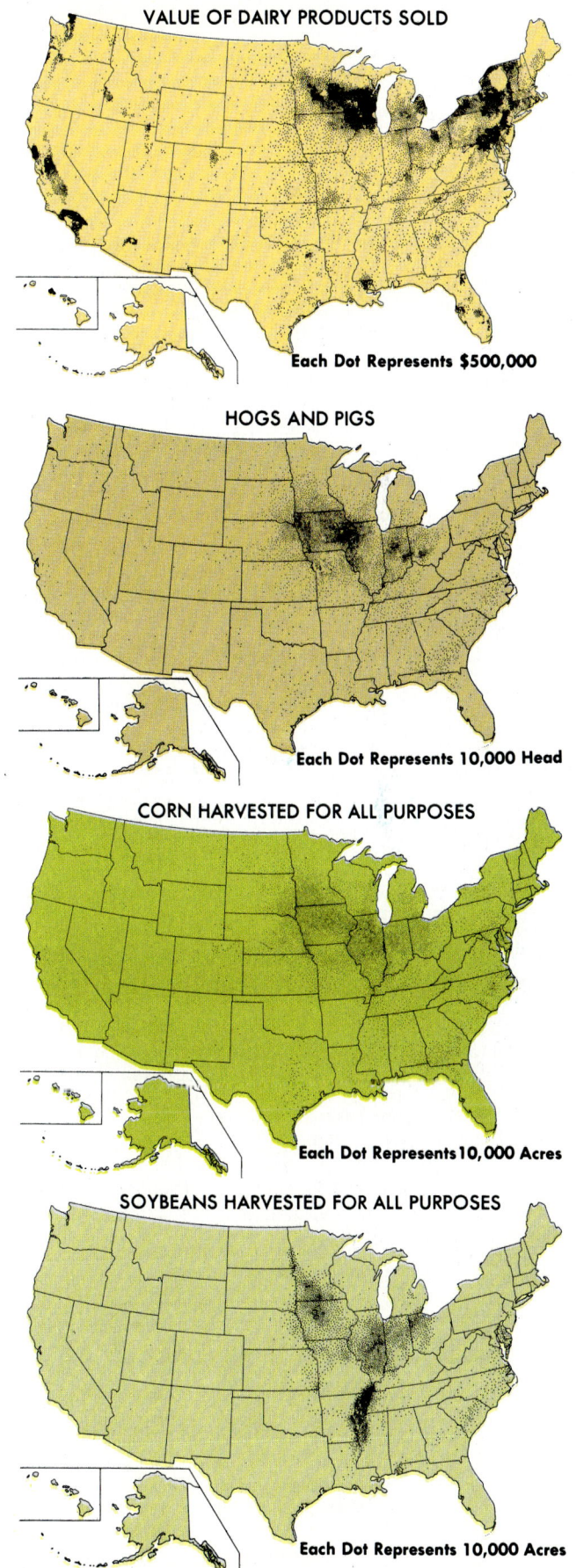

A feedlot in Kansas. More than half of our country's beef cattle are raised in the Midwest and Great Plains. Which three states in this region rank high in earnings from beef cattle?

sorghum. This crop grows well even in places where the weather is very dry. Large amounts of sorghum are used for fattening cattle in feedlots in the Great Plains states. Often, beef cattle are also raised on wheat farms.

Spring wheat

North of the winter wheat belt is another large wheat-growing area. Here, winters are too cold for young wheat plants to live. Farmers in this area plant their wheat in the spring. For this reason, the area is called the spring wheat belt. Spring wheat is ready to harvest in late summer or early fall. North Dakota is our country's leading producer of spring wheat.

† Rangelands

Some parts of the Great Plains states are too dry or too rough for growing crops. Here much of the land is covered with short grass. At one time, great herds of buffalo fed on these grasslands, which are called ranges. Today the rangelands are used for grazing beef cattle and other livestock.

In the rangelands, livestock are usually raised on large farms called ranches. These vary in size from two or three thousand acres to more than one-half million acres. Ranches must be large because as many as fifty acres of grassland may be needed to feed each animal. In some places, cattle drink from streams or water holes. Where these are scarce, wells are an important source of drinking water for cattle. On many ranches, tall windmills pump this water from deep underground.

Two of the Great Plains states rank high in earnings from beef cattle. These are Texas, which ranks first, and Nebraska, which ranks third. Some of the cattle raised on grasslands in these states are shipped directly to stockyards in cities such as Omaha, Nebraska, and Kansas City, Missouri. However, cattle fed only on grass may be too thin to slaughter for meat. Many grass-fed cattle are sold to farmers in the corn belt. These cattle are put into feedlots, where they are fattened on corn and other grains. After they have been fattened, trucks or trains carry them to the stockyards.

Ranchers in the drier parts of the Great Plains states also raise many thousands of sheep and Angora goats. These animals do not need as much grass and water as cattle do. Sometimes, cattle, sheep, and goats are raised on the same ranch. Cattle are given the best land, and the goats and sheep graze on the rest. Angora goats are valued for their long, silky hair. It is used to make mohair.* Most of the sheep that graze on the Great Plains are raised for their wool. Those raised for meat are sent to feedlots for fattening.

The cotton belt

Every fall, many fields in Texas turn almost snow-white. These are fields of cotton. During the long, warm summer, the seedpods, or bolls, on the cotton plants have been ripening. When they are fully ripe, they burst open, showing the white, fluffy cotton fibers. Cotton-picking machines move slowly along the rows, stripping the ripe bolls from the plants. The cotton is taken to large buildings in nearby towns. There, gins* separate the fibers from the sticky cotton seeds. Then machines press the cotton into tightly packed bundles, called bales. The baled cotton is

---

† Use the picture on page 90 and the map on page 87 to make additional discoveries about cattle raising on the rangelands of our country.

shipped to textile mills, where it is spun into yarn for making cloth.

Texas produces nearly one third of all the cotton grown in our nation. This crop is raised in many parts of the state. However, the state's most important cotton-growing area is in western Texas, near New Mexico. (Compare the map on pages 8-9 with the bottom map on page 94.) This is one of the

Harvesting cotton. Texas produces nearly one third of all the cotton grown in the United States. The most important cotton-growing area in Texas is in the western part of the state. What facts help to explain why western Texas is one of the best cotton-growing areas in our country?

† Use this picture and the maps on pages 87 and 94 to answer the question: Where is most cotton produced in our country today, and how is it harvested?

best cotton-growing areas in the United States.

Western Texas has become a major cotton-growing area only within the last sixty years. Before 1900, nearly all of our country's cotton was grown in an area extending from South Carolina and Georgia westward into eastern Texas.

In the early 1900's, many cotton farmers faced a number of problems. In some areas, the land had been used so many years for growing cotton that it was no longer very fertile. Poor ways of farming had caused soil erosion in some places. Also, an insect known as the boll weevil had begun to destroy cotton crops all the way from Texas to the Atlantic coast.

Cotton farms in western Texas

Gradually, many new cotton farms were started in areas west of the old cotton belt. One of these areas was western Texas. Here, there were large stretches of level, fertile land. The growing season was long enough for cotton. Although rainfall was fairly light in this area, there was generally enough for growing cotton. Also, farmers could irrigate their fields with water from nearby wells. Even more important, the boll weevil was not a problem to farmers in western Texas. Here, the weather was too dry and the winters were too cold for this insect to live.

Cotton-harvesting machines were developed in the 1930's and 1940's. They gave farmers in western Texas another advantage over farmers in other cotton-growing areas. With the new machines, farmers could harvest their cotton much faster and better than they could by hand. However, in states east of Texas, much of the land where cotton was grown was too hilly for using these machines. Also, the machines were expensive to buy and operate. Many farms in the old cotton belt were small,

Midwest and Great Plains

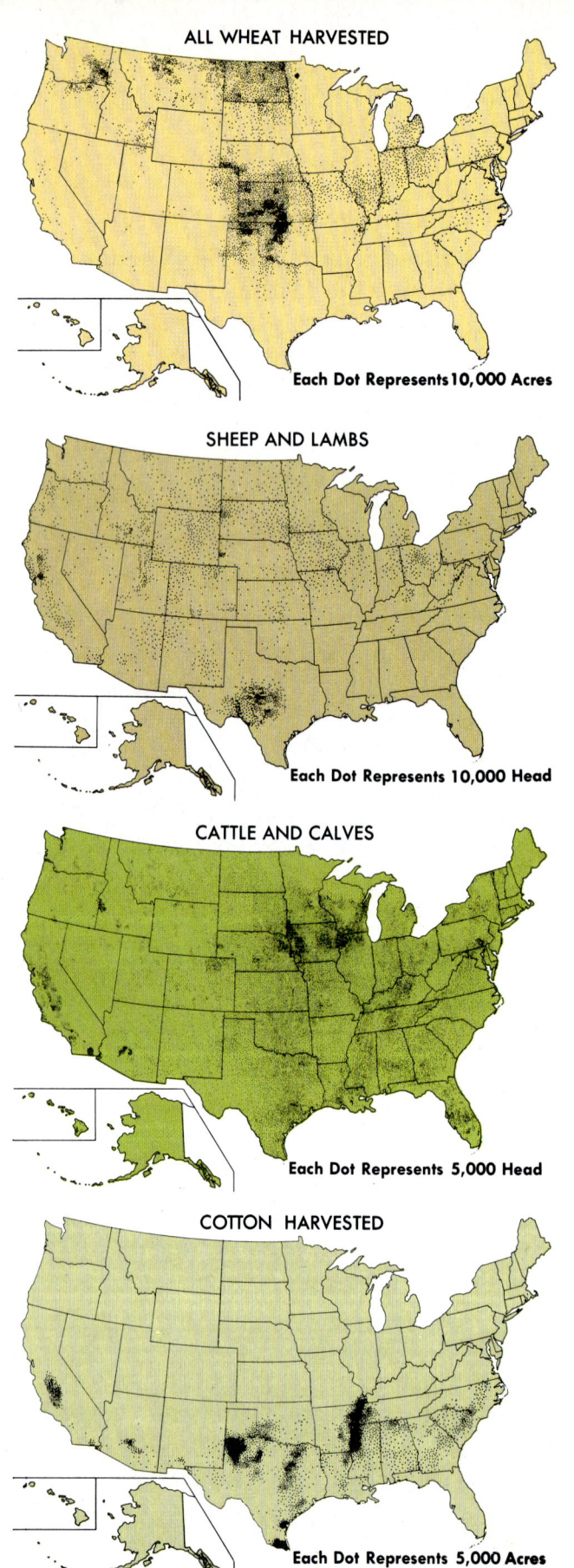

and it was not profitable for farmers to buy such expensive machines.

Although Texas is by far the most important cotton-growing state in the Midwest and Great Plains, cotton is also produced in Missouri and Oklahoma. (See lower map on this page.) Missouri's cotton-growing area is located in the southeastern tip of the state, in the Coastal Plain. Oklahoma's cotton is grown mainly in the southwestern part of the state.

Orchards and truck farms

In a few parts of the Midwest and Great Plains, farmers grow large amounts of fruits and vegetables. Along the eastern shore of Lake Michigan and the southern shore of Lake Erie, the climate is well suited to growing fruit. (See pages 42-43.) For example, Michigan is one of the nation's leading fruit-growing states. Farmers here grow such fruits as apples, cherries, peaches, and blueberries.

In the lower Rio Grande Valley of Texas, there are many groves of grapefruit and orange trees. Citrus fruits such as these cannot be grown where winters are cold. Winters in the lower Rio Grande Valley are usually mild and sunny. Sometimes, however, cold winds from the north sweep across the valley, killing thousands of fruit trees. Rainfall is light here, so the fruit trees must be irrigated with water from the Rio Grande.

Many different kinds of vegetables are grown on irrigated truck* farms in the lower Rio Grande Valley. During the winter months, large crops of carrots, cabbages, and other vegetables are shipped from here to colder parts of our country.

Tomatoes and other kinds of vegetables are grown in the lower Rio Grande Valley. During the winter, vegetables such as tomatoes, carrots, and cabbages are shipped from here to colder parts of our country.

During the summer months, vegetables are raised in many parts of the Midwest and Great Plains. Farmers in each area grow the kinds of vegetables that are best suited to the soil and climate of that area. For example, potatoes can be raised where the growing season is too short and cool for many other kinds of crops.

Use Your Reasoning Ability †

Choose a state in the Midwest and Great Plains that you, as a farmer, would find well suited to raising each of the following:

spring wheat	cotton
beef cattle	dairy cows
corn	winter wheat

Give reasons for each choice.

† Use this project as a culminating activity. It will help students develop their thinking skills.

Use Fideler Discovery Cards 83-92.

9 Natural Resources and Energy

Nature has given many valuable gifts to the people of the Midwest and Great Plains. Among these gifts are rich soil, plentiful rainfall, and warm sunshine. Chapter 8 tells how these resources have helped make the Midwest and Great Plains an important farming area.

This part of our country has other natural resources as well. There are huge deposits of useful minerals here. There are also valuable forests and fishing grounds. Rivers and lakes here provide large amounts of fresh water for cities, farms, and factories.

Mineral Resources

Many kinds of valuable minerals have been found in the Midwest and Great Plains. Each year, this region produces* minerals that are worth more than twenty billion dollars. Some of these minerals are used to produce electricity and other forms of energy. Other minerals are used by factories in making hundreds of different products.

Energy Fuels

The most valuable minerals produced in the Midwest and Great Plains are oil, natural gas, and coal. These are known as energy* fuels, because they can be burned to produce energy. We need energy to run our cars, to heat our houses, and to cook our meals. Energy is also needed to run all the different machines we use in our homes and factories.

*See Glossary

† Use the questions in this caption for a class discussion.

Oil and natural gas

There are huge deposits of oil and natural gas in the Great Plains states. (See maps on page 102.) These deposits provide almost half the oil and natural gas produced in our country. No other part of the United States has such large supplies of these important minerals.

Most deposits of oil are located far beneath the earth's surface. To get oil, people drill wells deep into the earth. Sometimes the oil flows to the surface by itself. At other times, it has to be pumped to the surface. The oil is sent to factories called refineries. There it is used to make gasoline and other products.

Natural gas is found wherever there is oil. But it is also found in some places in the earth where there is no oil. After the natural gas is taken from the earth, it is sent through large pipes to homes and factories. There it is burned as a fuel.

Texas produces more oil and natural gas than any other state in our country. Large amounts of oil have been produced in Texas since 1901. That

Using Natural Resources

See Great Ideas

The picture at left shows an † oil well in Oklahoma. Oil, or petroleum,* is an important natural resource of the Midwest and Great Plains. What are some of the products made from petroleum? In what ways would your life be different if there were no more of these products? In recent years, people have realized that the use of petroleum products can lead to harmful air pollution. What can be done to stop this pollution? Do research to find answers to this question.

Midwest and Great Plains 97

Strip-mining coal in southern Illinois. There are huge deposits of coal in the Midwest and Great Plains. Most of the coal mined in this part of our country is used as fuel for producing electricity.

was when the state's first large oil field was discovered. Today, Texas has about 160,000 producing oil wells. Some of these are off the coast of Texas. Here, oil is pumped from deposits that lie deep in the earth beneath the Gulf of Mexico. Several other Great Plains states also produce large amounts of oil and natural gas. These are Oklahoma, Kansas, and North Dakota.

The Midwest is not nearly as rich in oil and natural gas as the Great Plains states. But there are valuable deposits of these minerals in some areas. Illinois, Michigan, Ohio, and Indiana produce most of the oil in the Midwest. Ohio and Michigan are the leading producers of natural gas.

Coal

Huge deposits of coal are found in the Midwest. (See map on opposite page.) Illinois, Ohio, and Indiana rank among the ten leading producers of coal in our country.

A Visit to a Coal Mine

To learn how coal is mined in the Midwest, let's visit a strip mine in southern Illinois. (See picture at left.) This mine looks like a huge ditch several blocks long. The land that has not been stripped of coal is shown at the left. The land that has already been stripped of coal is at the right.

The largest machine in the ditch is called an excavator. It is taking soil from the surface of the land at the left and dumping it at the right. After the soil has been removed, the rock that lies under it will be blasted with explosives.* This loosens the rock so that it, too, can be removed.

A giant power shovel is picking up rock that has already been loosened. It is dumping the rock along the other side of the ditch. In this way, it is uncovering the coal that lies under the rock. A smaller power shovel is digging the coal from the bottom of the ditch and loading it onto a truck. The truck will carry the coal to a nearby factory. There the coal will be cleaned and sorted into different sizes. Then it will be loaded onto railroad cars and barges. These will carry the coal to the people who will use it.

About half of the coal produced in the United States today comes from strip-mines. The rest comes from underground mines. Strip-mining causes great harm to the land. But many mining companies try to restore land that has been strip mined. Sometimes the land is smoothed and planted with grass. Then it can be used for grazing. Much of the strip-mined land in Illinois and Indiana has been made into lakes and parks.

*See Glossary

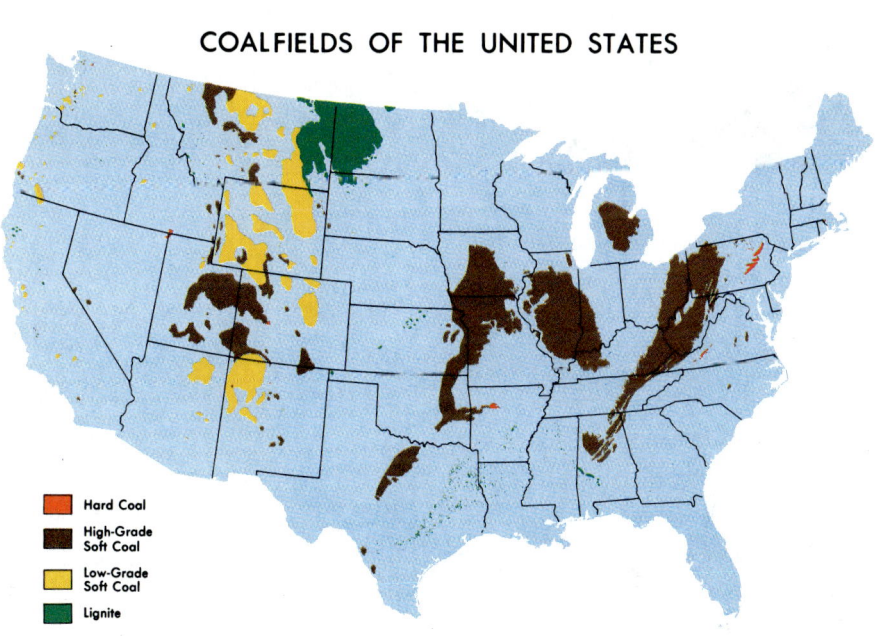

COALFIELDS OF THE UNITED STATES

- Hard Coal
- High-Grade Soft Coal
- Low-Grade Soft Coal
- Lignite

Nearly all the coal mined in the Midwest is high-grade soft coal. This is also known as bituminous* coal. It has several important uses. Some of it is burned to heat houses, factories, and other buildings. Some is used as a fuel in making cement. But most of the coal mined in the Midwest is used for producing electricity. At power plants, the coal is burned to heat water. The water turns to steam, which runs powerful engines called turbines. The turbines run machines called generators. These machines produce electricity. Most of the electricity used in the Midwest comes from power plants that burn coal.

Very little bituminous coal is mined in the Great Plains states. However, North Dakota has our country's largest deposits of lignite.* Lignite is used in the same ways as bituminous coal. However, it is much less valuable. It contains large amounts of water. When it is burned, it does not give off as much heat as bituminous coal.

Metals

Several different kinds of metal ores* are found in the Midwest and Great Plains. By far the most important of these is iron ore. It is used in making iron and steel.

Iron mining in Minnesota

About two thirds of all the iron ore produced in our country comes from Minnesota. Thousands of people in Minnesota earn their living by working in iron mines.

The largest iron ore deposits in the state of Minnesota are found in the Mesabi Range. This is a line of low hills that extends for more than 100 miles

(161 km.)† through northeastern Minnesota. Ore is also mined from two smaller ranges in the northern part of the state.

Most of the iron ore that comes from the Mesabi Range is dug from open-pit mines. (See picture above.) An open-pit iron mine may be as much as a mile across and five hundred feet deep. At the bottom, workers run huge power

† km. means kilometer

Refer to the picture and text on these pages. Discuss the process used to mine iron ore.

Rouchleau Mine in the Mesabi Range. Each year, millions of tons of iron ore are dug from mines in the Mesabi Range. Minnesota produces about two thirds of the iron ore produced in our country.

shovels that scoop up tons of iron ore. Trucks or conveyor* belts carry the ore out of the mine.

The iron ore is taken by train to Duluth and other ports on Lake Superior. (See map on page 120.) There it is dumped into huge ore boats. These boats carry it to Chicago, Detroit, and other cities around the Great Lakes.

The history of the Mesabi Range

Iron ore was first discovered in Minnesota in the 1850's. By the end of the 1800's, several companies were mining ore from the Mesabi Range. This ore was very rich in iron. Until the 1950's, the Mesabi Range continued to produce great amounts of high-grade ore. But as time passed, much of the richest

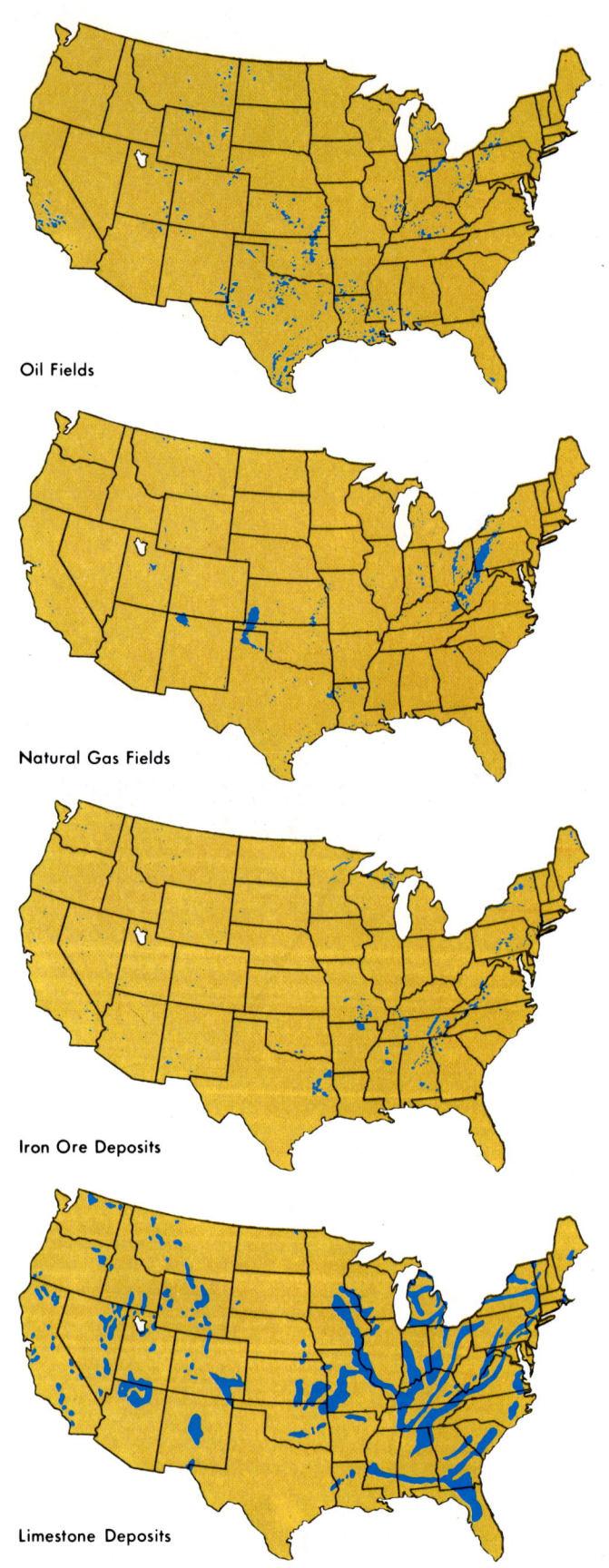

Oil Fields

Natural Gas Fields

Iron Ore Deposits

Limestone Deposits

ore was used up. Some mines were forced to close.

There was still one hope for Minnesota's iron-mining industry. In the Mesabi Range were huge deposits of taconite. This is a hard rock that is only about one-fourth iron. Because it contains so little iron, taconite cannot be used in making iron and steel. But a way might be found to change taconite into a richer ore. Then the Mesabi Range could keep on producing large amounts of iron.

After years of trying, scientists found a way to change taconite into a highgrade ore. The taconite is crushed and ground into a fine powder. Magnets are used to separate bits of iron from waste materials in the powder. Then these bits are formed into small, round pellets and baked. The pellets are very rich in iron. They can be used to make iron and steel.

Since the 1950's, many taconite mines have been opened in the Mesabi Range. Also, a number of mills have been built to make pellets of taconite. Each year, millions of tons of pellets are made in northern Minnesota. They are shipped to steel plants all around the Great Lakes. Someday, the taconite will be used up also. But by then, there may be ways of using ore from the Mesabi Range that is even less rich.

Iron mining in other states

The Mesabi Range is part of a large iron-mining area near Lake Superior. This area extends into northern Wisconsin and the Upper Peninsula* of Michigan. At one time, Michigan produced more iron ore than Minnesota. Today it still ranks second among our states in iron mining. In Michigan, too,

† **What information do this picture and caption give you about the process of gold mining?**

there are mills that make pellets from low-grade ore.

Iron ore has been mined in Missouri for many years. Today this state ranks fourth in the nation in iron mining. Most of the iron ore deposits are on the Ozark Plateau, in the southeastern part of the state.

Copper, lead, and gold

The Midwest and Great Plains has deposits of several other valuable minerals. For example, Michigan is an important producer of copper. Almost all of this copper is found in the Upper Peninsula, near Lake Superior. Most of it is so pure that it needs very little smelting* to remove waste materials. Copper is used in making electrical wire, water pipes, and other products.

Missouri ranks first among all our states in producing lead ore. Lead is a soft, heavy metal. It is used in making car batteries, bullets, and many other products. Chemicals* that contain lead may be used to make rubber, printing inks, and gasoline.

South Dakota is our country's chief producer of gold. In the Black Hills is a huge mine called the Homestake Mine. It produces more gold each year than any other mine in the United States.

† **Drilling blast holes in the Homestake Gold Mine,** in South Dakota. This huge mine is located in the rugged Black Hills. It has helped South Dakota to become our country's leading producer of gold.

Other Minerals

Limestone

In the Midwest and Great Plains, there are large deposits of limestone. (See map on page 102.) This kind of rock varies in color from white to dark gray or brown. It is taken from huge open pits called quarries.

Limestone is the main raw material used in making cement. It is ground up with a smaller amount of shale* or clay. This mixture is heated in a large oven until it forms lumps called clinkers. The clinkers are cooled and ground into powder. This powder is cement. Texas, Michigan, and Missouri are important cement-producing states.

Limestone is also needed for making iron and steel. For this purpose, it must be very pure. Michigan produces large amounts of limestone for the iron and steel industry.

Some limestone can be cut into large blocks. These blocks are then used to build the outside walls of buildings. Indiana leads the nation in producing this kind of limestone.

Crushed limestone is widely used in building roads and railroads. It is produced in many parts of the Midwest and Great Plains.

Salt

Almost half of the salt produced in our country comes from Texas, Ohio, and Michigan. Some of this salt is dug from mines deep in the earth. The rest is obtained by drilling wells. Fresh water is pumped down the wells to the salt deposits below. The salt dissolves in the water and rises to the surface.

Most of the salt produced in the Midwest and Great Plains is used in making chemicals. Salt is also used as a seasoning for food.

Sulfur

Texas produces about one third of our country's sulfur. Large amounts of this mineral are found along the Gulf coast. To get sulfur, people usually drill wells into the earth. Then they pump hot water down into the sulfur. The hot water melts this mineral. Air is then pumped into the well. This pushes the mixture of sulfur and water to the surface.

Large amounts of sulfur are used in making chemicals. One of the most important is sulfuric* acid. It is used by factories in making hundreds of products. Among these are fertilizers* and synthetic* fibers.

Water Resources

The Midwest

Water is an important natural resource in the Midwest. There is enough rainfall for growing crops. Farmers here seldom need to irrigate* their fields.

Much of the rain that falls in the Midwest flows into rivers and streams. The Mississippi River and its branches make up the largest river system in our country. (See page 20.) Rivers in the Midwest provide large amounts of water for cities and factories along their banks.

Some of the Midwest's rainwater flows into lakes. Four of the five Great Lakes are in this part of our country. (See map on pages 8-9.) Cities and factories near these lakes have plenty of fresh water. Many smaller lakes also supply water to people in the Midwest.

Water Resources

As this map shows, there are a number of major dams in the Great Plains states. These dams were built to control floods or to store water for irrigation. The water stored in reservoirs* behind the dams may also be used for recreation or for the production of hydroelectric* power.

The map also shows that there are many thousands of acres of irrigated farmland in the northwestern part of Texas. Here, water for irrigating crops is brought from nearby wells. Other large areas of irrigated farmland lie near the Platte River in Nebraska and along the Rio Grande in southern Texas.

*See Glossary

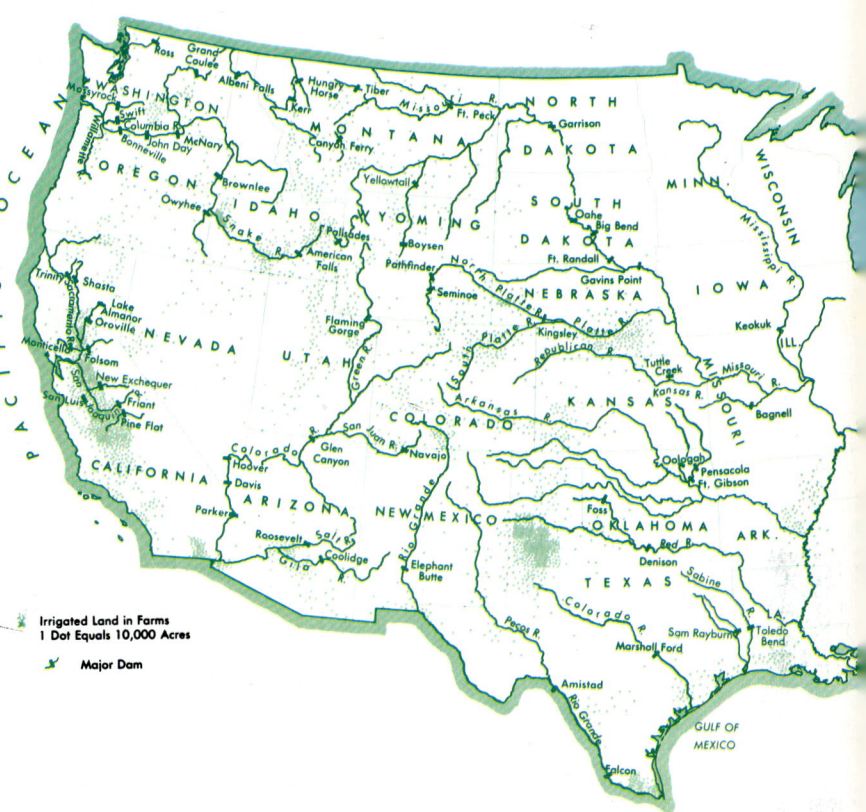

Part of the rain that falls in the Midwest soaks into the ground. It sinks down into layers of rock and soil beneath the surface. These layers are full of tiny holes and cracks. As a result, they can hold large amounts of water. The water stored in rock and soil beneath the ground is called groundwater. It can be obtained by drilling wells. Many towns and farms in the Midwest use wells to get the water they need.

Taking care of water resources

People in the Midwest have not always used their water resources wisely. Sometimes, waste materials from factories and homes have been dumped in rivers and lakes. This has caused water pollution.* Water that is polluted may contain germs or harmful chemicals. It may also have an unpleasant smell. Polluted water cannot be used for drinking, bathing, or other purposes.

A few years ago, Lake Erie was called a "dying lake." Cities and factories had been dumping all kinds of waste materials into the lake. It became so polluted that fish could not live in it. This fine lake could not be used for swimming.

Many people felt something should be done about pollution in Lake Erie. Our government began working with community groups and businesses to clean up the lake. Today, Lake Erie is much cleaner than it used to be. People are once again fishing and swimming in the lake.

In the future, people in the Midwest must take better care of their water resources. Cities and factories must not dump waste materials into rivers and lakes. Each citizen must learn that

† Use this problem to start students thinking about the need for water in the western part of the Great Plains states.

water is a valuable resource. Only then can people in the Midwest have enough pure, fresh water to meet their needs.

The Great Plains States

Where water is plentiful

In the eastern part of the Great Plains states, people usually have enough water. Rainfall is heavy enough for growing crops without irrigation. (See map on page 34.) Rivers and lakes provide water for many cities and factories.

Where water is scarce

In the western part of the Great Plains states, people sometimes have trouble getting water. The average rainfall here is less than twenty inches a year. Also, there are very few lakes and only a few large rivers in this area. Most of the rivers flow down from the Rocky Mountains, which lie farther west. There, rainfall is heavier.

The lack of water affects people in many ways. To grow crops, farmers must irrigate their fields or use dry* farming. The dry climate has kept some companies from building factories here. This is because many factories use large amounts of water. When rainfall is very light, people must be careful not to waste any water. Sometimes they are not allowed to wash their cars or water their lawns.

Dams

People in dry areas of the Great Plains states have worked hard to get water. Dams have been built on the Missouri and other rivers that flow across the plains. (See map on page 105.) These dams hold back the river water to form large reservoirs.*

Some of the water stored in reservoirs is used for irrigation. It flows

† **A Problem To Solve**
The western part of the Great Plains states has very little water. The average rainfall is less than 20 inches (51 cm.)† a year. Also, there are very few lakes and rivers here. How does the lack of water affect the western part of the Great Plains states? In forming hypotheses* to solve this problem, think about how the lack of water affects:
1. the number of people who live in the western part of the Great Plains states
2. the kinds of farming carried on here
3. the amount of industry in this area

See Skills Manual, "Thinking and Solving Problems"

† cm. means centimeter

Use the picture and caption below in a discussion about irrigation.

through pipes, canals, and ditches to farms where it is needed. There are about twelve million acres of irrigated land in the Great Plains states.

Dams and reservoirs are also useful for other reasons. They help control the amount of water in the Missouri and other rivers. In the past, these rivers would often rise above their banks. They would flood the land nearby, causing great damage. Today, the dams help to prevent floods. When the rivers are high, some of the water is stored behind the dams. This keeps it from flooding the land. When the rivers are low, some of the water in the reservoirs is let out. Reservoirs are also used for swimming, boating, and other water sports.

Power plants have been built near some of the dams in the Great Plains states. Water from the reservoirs flows through large pipes inside the dams. The rushing water is used to run generators that produce electricity. Hydroelectric* power is important in some parts of the Great Plains states. But most of the electricity used in this

Irrigating a Nebraska farm. Water is scarce in the western part of the Great Plains states. Many farmers must irrigate their land. Where do farmers here get the water they need for irrigation?

Have students use this map to identify the forest types found in our state.

area comes from steam power plants. These plants burn coal, oil, or natural gas as fuel.

Wells

People in the Great Plains states also get water from wells. Each winter, large amounts of snow fall on the Rocky Mountains. As the snow melts, some of it sinks into layers of rock under the ground. These layers extend all the way from the mountains to the Great Plains. People get water from these rock layers by drilling wells. Then they pump the water to the surface. There are thousands of wells in the Great Plains states. They supply pure water to many towns and farms here.

Forest Resources

Great forests of long ago

When settlers first came to the Midwest, they found huge forests here. The map below shows some of the main kinds of trees in these forests. In the north were pines, hemlocks, and other evergreen trees. Farther south were forests of hardwoods, such as oak, maple, and hickory. Even on bright summer days, these forests were cool and dark.

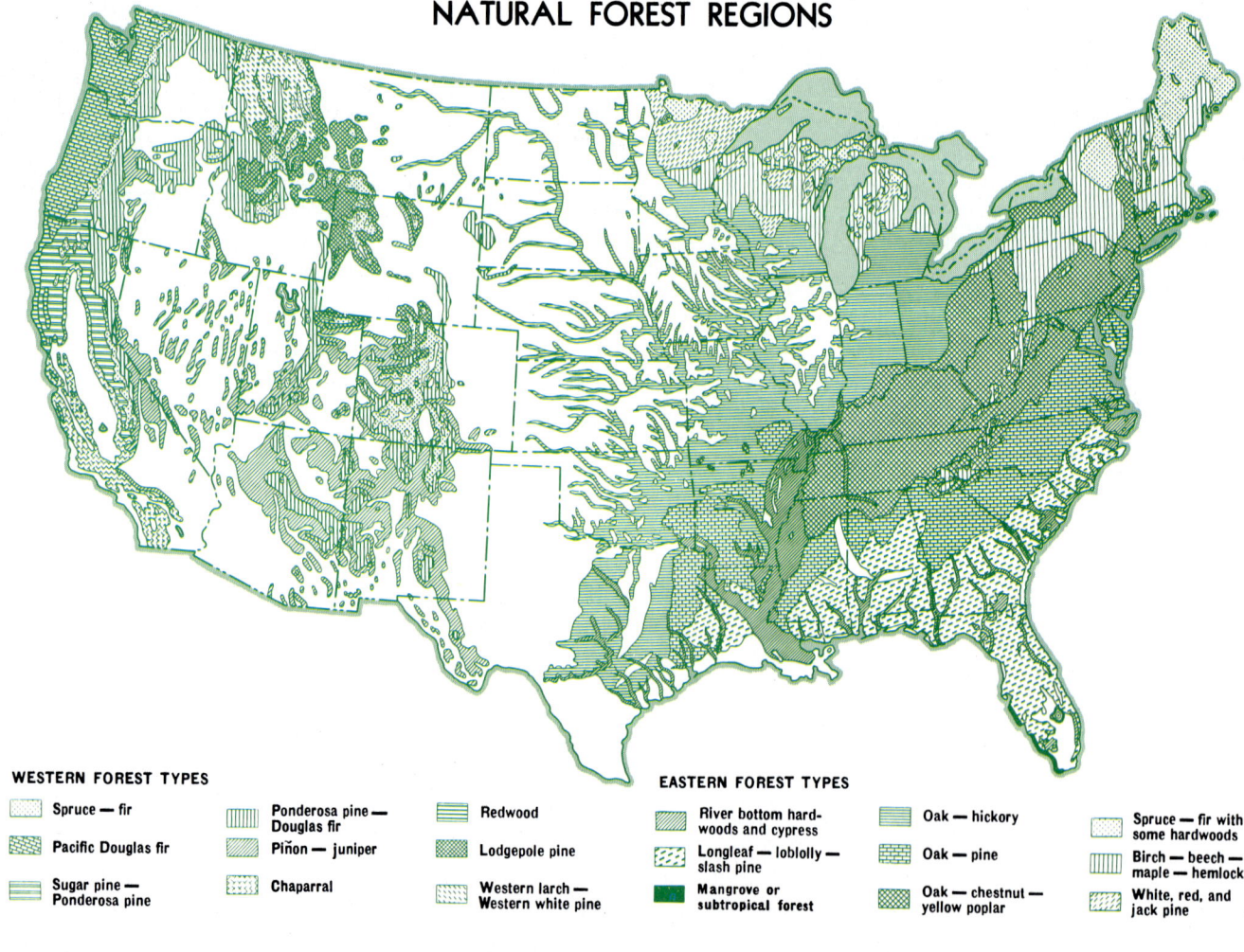

NATURAL FOREST REGIONS

WESTERN FOREST TYPES
- Spruce — fir
- Pacific Douglas fir
- Sugar pine — Ponderosa pine
- Ponderosa pine — Douglas fir
- Piñon — juniper
- Chaparral
- Redwood
- Lodgepole pine
- Western larch — Western white pine

EASTERN FOREST TYPES
- River bottom hardwoods and cypress
- Longleaf — loblolly — slash pine
- Mangrove or subtropical forest
- Oak — hickory
- Oak — pine
- Oak — chestnut — yellow poplar
- Spruce — fir with some hardwoods
- Birch — beech — maple — hemlock
- White, red, and jack pine

Early loggers in Michigan. Most of the great forests in the Midwest were cut down during the 1800's. What are some of the many uses people made of the lumber that came from these forests?

A thick roof of leaves shut out most of the sunlight.

The climate of the Midwest helps explain why forests were so large here. Trees need about twenty inches of rainfall a year. They cannot stand long stretches of dry weather. Trees also need about fourteen straight weeks without heavy frosts each year. In the Midwest, there is plenty of rainfall all year long. Also, the growing season is long enough for trees.

In some parts of the Midwest, the settlers found grasslands instead of forests. These treeless areas were called prairies. They covered large parts of Illinois, Iowa, and western Minnesota. (See map on opposite page.) No one knows for sure why these areas were not forested. They have the same climate as other parts of the Midwest.

Cutting down the forests

Most of the great forests in the Midwest were cut down during the 1800's. The early settlers removed thousands of trees. They did this to clear the land so they could grow crops. Later,

Using Tools

See Great Ideas

Logging in Michigan today. What kind of tool do you see in the picture at right? Compare this picture with the picture on page 109. What kinds of tools do you think loggers used in the 1800's? How do you think they were different from the tools used today? In what ways do you think today's tools make logging easier?

logging companies began cutting down pine forests in northern Michigan, Wisconsin, and Minnesota. At that time, cities in the Midwest were growing rapidly. Large amounts of lumber were needed for building houses. Lumber was also needed for making such things as furniture, wagons, and railroad ties. Logs from the northern forests were floated down rivers to sawmills. There they were cut into lumber. The lumber was shipped by boat to Chicago and other cities.

Forests of the Midwest today

Today, forests cover about one third of the land in the Midwest. Most of the trees in these forests are "second growth." They have grown up in place of trees that were cut down years ago. These trees are usually smaller than the ones that grew here before.

Most forests in the Midwest today are in places that are not good for farming. There are large forests of evergreen trees in northern Michigan, Wisconsin, and Minnesota. Here the soil is poor. Also, the growing season is too short for most crops. Forests cover much of the hilly land in the Ozarks of southern Missouri. Most of the trees here are oaks and other hardwoods. Forests like these also grow on the Appalachian Plateau* of eastern Ohio.

Forests of Texas and Oklahoma

The largest forests in the Great Plains states are in eastern Texas and Oklahoma. (See map on page 108.) Here summers are very warm. The growing season is long, and there is plenty of rainfall. Trees can grow rapidly here. In some places, there are large forests of oaks and other hardwoods. In other

places, huge pine forests stretch for many miles.

Grasslands of the Great Plains states

In the 1800's, American settlers came to the Great Plains states. They found much of the land covered with grass instead of trees. This was mainly because rainfall is so light here. In pioneer days, most trees grew along river banks. There were also forests in the Black Hills of South Dakota. Rainfall was heavier there than on the plains nearby.

The farmers who settled on the grassland often planted trees near their houses. The trees protected them from the strong winds that swept across the plains. In recent years, many farmers have planted rows of trees around their fields. This helps prevent wind erosion.*

Products of the forests

Wood from the forests of the Midwest and Great Plains is used in making many different products. The most important are wood pulp and lumber.

Wood pulp is a soft, damp material made up of tiny wood fibers.* It is used in making paper, cardboard, and other products. Many trees in the second-growth forests of the Midwest are too

† Make a list of the useful products made of wood from the forests of the Midwest and Great Plains.

small to be cut into lumber. But they are fine for making wood pulp. Logs of pine, hemlock, and other evergreens are taken to nearby pulp mills. At the mills, the logs are cut into small chips. These are cooked with chemicals to make pulp. There are many pulp and paper mills in Wisconsin and neighboring states. The making of pulp and paper is also an important industry in eastern Texas.

Lumber is another forest product of the Midwest and Great Plains. Each year, thousands of hardwood trees are cut down in Missouri, Ohio, and other states. The logs go to nearby sawmills, where they are cut into lumber. The wood of oak, maple, and other hardwoods is strong and beautiful. Much of it is used in making furniture. Some is used to build houses and other buildings. There are many sawmills in eastern Texas and Oklahoma. They produce lumber from pine logs cut in nearby forests.

Several other products come from the forests of the Midwest and Great Plains. Logs of certain sizes are used as telephone poles or fence posts. A building material called fiberboard is made from wood chips. Sap is taken from pine trees in Texas. It is used in making turpentine* and rosin.* Many farmers in the Midwest earn money by raising Christmas trees.

Other ways that forests are used

Forests not only supply us with many products, but they are useful in other ways. For example, the roots of trees help hold the soil in place. This helps prevent erosion by wind and rainwater. People come to the woods for camping, hiking, hunting, and other outdoor sports. Also, forests provide food and shelter for wild animals.

Fishing Grounds

Fishing is not a major way of earning a living in the Midwest and Great Plains. Most of the states in this region are far from any ocean. Texas is the only state that has a seacoast. It leads the Midwest and Great Plains in the value of fish caught.

Fishing in the Gulf of Mexico

There are several fishing ports along the Gulf coast of Texas. Each year, fishing boats bring millions of pounds of fish to these ports. Most of the fish are shrimp or menhaden.* Large numbers of shrimp are packaged and frozen in factories along the coast. Then they are sent by train or truck to stores all over our country. Menhaden are usually made into oil, fertilizer, and livestock feed. Menhaden oil is used in making soap, paint, and other products.

Fishing in lakes and rivers

Hundreds of people make their living by fishing in Michigan and other states along the Great Lakes. These people catch yellow perch, lake trout, and chubs. Whitefish, salmon, and other fish are also caught. Some of the fish are smoked or frozen. Others are sold fresh in grocery stores and fish markets. People who fish on the Great Lakes also catch large numbers of alewives.* These are used mostly for pet food and oil.

Many fish are caught in large rivers, such as the Mississippi and the Illinois. Among these fish are catfish and carp. They are mostly sold fresh in nearby towns and cities.

Unloading shrimp in Texas. This is the only state in the Midwest and Great Plains that has a seacoast. Texas has several fishing ports along its Gulf coast. Large amounts of shrimp are caught here.

Make a Minerals Chart

The Midwest and Great Plains has many valuable minerals. Do research about them in this chapter. Then make a chart of these minerals. Your chart should have three columns. In the first column, name the minerals found in the Midwest and Great Plains. In the second column, tell where the mineral is mined. In the third column, tell some of the ways in which this mineral is used. Share your chart with your class.

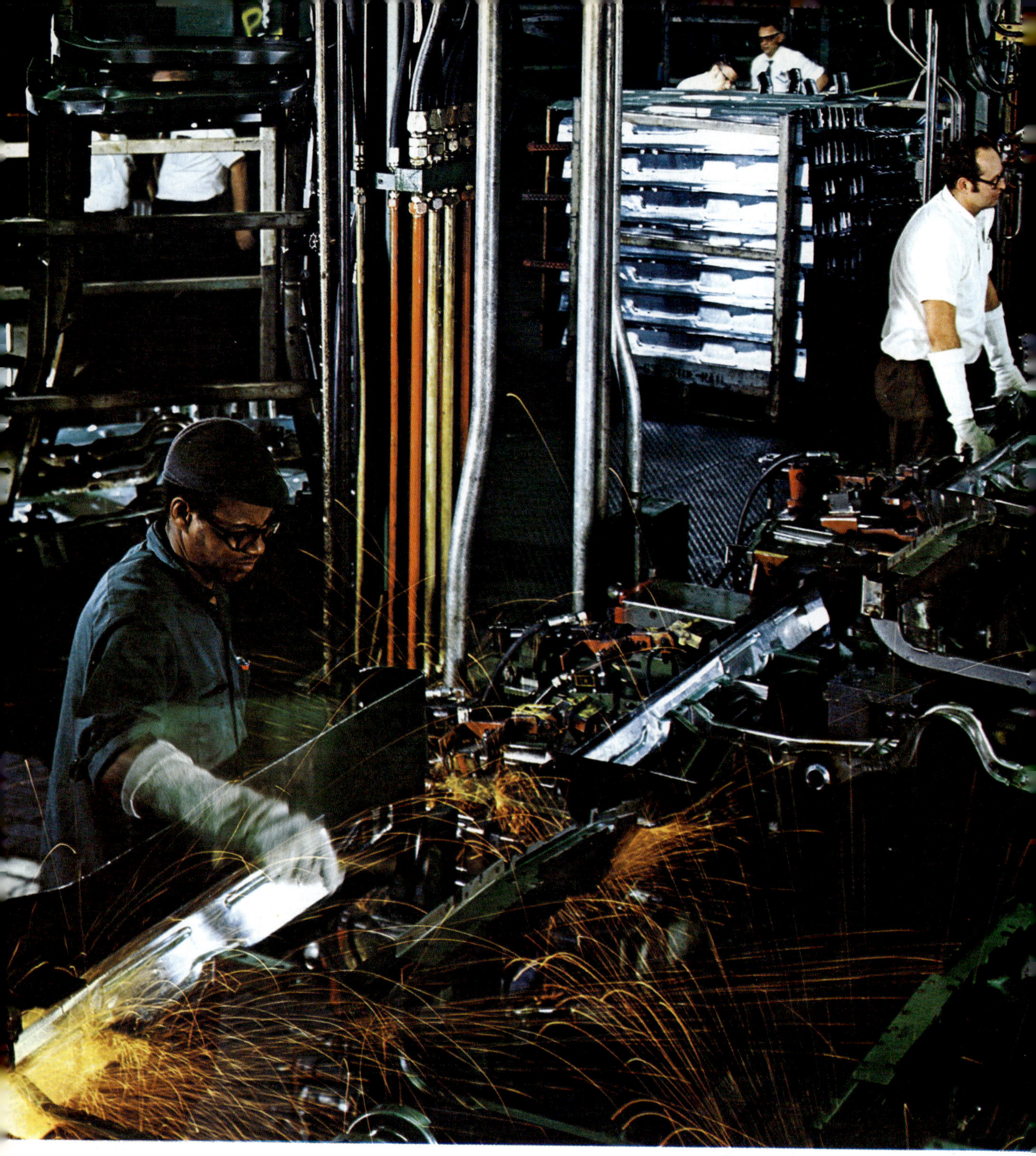

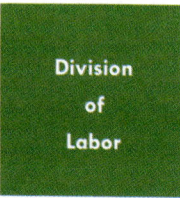

Division
of
Labor

See Great Ideas

Making automobile parts in a factory in Detroit. The parts these people are helping to make will be sent on to another kind of factory called an assembly plant. Here, other workers will put the parts together to make automobiles. To do this, they work on an assembly line. What is an assembly line? Do you think assembly lines make it easier to manufacture automobiles? Explain. Do you think it would be possible to have an assembly line without division of labor? Why? Why not?

Use this caption and picture in a class discussion.

† Use "A Problem To Solve" to start students thinking about industry in the Midwest and Great Plains.

10 Industry

A Problem To Solve †

The Great Plains states have much less industry than the Midwest. Why is this so? In order to solve this problem, you will need to make hypotheses* about how each of the following has affected the growth of industry in these two parts of our country:

a. transportation
b. location of raw materials
c. location of markets
d. number of skilled workers
e. water supplies

See Skills Manual, "Thinking and Solving Problems"

A Visit to a Manufacturing Plant

In southeastern Michigan is one of the greatest manufacturing plants in the United States. It is made up of dozens of buildings. It spreads out over as much land as a small town might use. If you were to fly over this plant in a helicopter, you could look down at large factories with tall smokestacks. You could see blast* furnaces as tall as ten-story buildings. You would see raw materials being unloaded from large boats at the company's docks. Also, you would notice the many miles of roads and railroad tracks connecting the different parts of this plant.

The River Rouge plant

All of these buildings, docks, and roads are part of the huge River Rouge plant of the Ford Motor Company at Dearborn, Michigan. To learn about this plant, we will go on a guided tour. Our tour begins at the company's main office building. This building is about two miles from the plant. Here we board a bus and are welcomed by our guide.

Our guide tells us the Ford Motor Company is a very large manufacturing company. It has plants and offices in many parts of the world. It was founded in the early 1900's by Henry Ford, a pioneer of the automobile industry. Ford made his first automobiles in a small workshop. Then, a group of business people lent Ford the money he needed to build a factory.

*See Glossary

Take a picture-trip through the Ford plant. Have students locate in the picture and caption each of the parts of the plant that are numbered.

Mass production

Henry Ford was the first person to produce an automobile that large numbers of people could afford to buy. In order to do this, Ford used a new way of manufacturing called mass production. Thousands of each automobile part were made in his factory. The automobile frames were placed on a moving belt called a conveyor belt. The belt carried the frames along, past a row of workers. As each frame came along, a worker on the "assembly line" added a different part, such as a wheel or a nut and bolt. By using this method, Ford lowered the cost of making each car. The price charged to customers was also lowered. At the Rouge plant, we will learn more about the mass production of automobiles.

Ideas and skills

During our bus ride, our guide tells us that the ideas and skills of many thousands of workers are needed to mass-produce automobiles. In another part of Dearborn, more than twelve thousand workers plan the kind of car that they think people will buy and that will bring the company a profit.* They spend many months designing the car and the ways in which the car will be produced. When these designs are finished, test models of the car are manufactured. These models are given a series of rugged tests. Finally, the car is ready to be mass-produced.

Thousands of workers

The Rouge plant itself needs thousands of workers to perform hundreds of different jobs. Some people work in the company's steel mill. Others work in the foundry,* in the glass factory, or at the company's docks. There are also factories where engines, frames, and other automobile parts are made. Workers at the Rouge plant also have jobs such as running locomotives and cranes.

The Rouge plant also needs managers to direct the many activities that take

The Ford Motor Company's River Rouge plant is in Dearborn, Michigan. It has dozens of buildings spread out over many, many acres.

116 Midwest and Great Plains

place here. Without good management, it would be impossible to run a plant as large as this one. The managers must run each part of the plant carefully so that the company can make a profit. People who have invested* money in the company want a good profit on their investment.

Raw materials

Our bus has now entered the plant grounds. The first stop on our tour is the company's docks. From early spring to late fall, boats arrive here carrying huge loads of iron ore,* coal, and limestone. These raw materials are piled high in bins near the three blast

This picture shows many parts of the plant: (1) coal, iron ore, and limestone storage bins, (2) blast furnaces, (3) coke* ovens, (4) powerhouse, (5) steelmaking plant, (6) warehouse, (7) ore boats, (8) boat slip, (9) and (10) steel-shaping plants.

† Do you think cooperation is important in an automobile assembly plant? Explain.

furnaces of the company's steel mill. Iron ore, coal, and limestone are the three main raw materials needed for making iron and steel. About half of the iron and steel needed by the Ford Motor Company is made here.

The assembly plant

Our next stop is the assembly plant. Here workers put together more than fifteen thousand parts to make one shiny new automobile. Our guide explains that there are several assembly lines in this plant. The frame of the automobile is carried by the moving conveyor belt along the main assembly line. Certain parts of the car, such as the body, move along other assembly lines to the main line, where they are added to the frame.

Checking the car

At many places along the assembly line, we notice workers checking the car. They must make sure that it is well made. After the car has been completely assembled, other workers give it a final test. Then it is driven from the assembly plant. Less than a minute later, another new car follows this one off the assembly line. These cars will be shipped by truck or train to an automobile showroom somewhere in our country.

Many assembly plants

Our guide tells us that not all Ford cars are assembled here at the Rouge plant. The Ford Motor Company, like other major automobile manufacturers, has assembly plants in many parts of the United States and in some other countries as well. Automobile parts are shipped to these plants to be assembled. It is much cheaper to ship automobile parts than to ship fully assembled automobiles.

As we leave the plant, our guide tells us that the kind of production we have seen at the Rouge plant is not limited to the automobile industry. We could see many examples of mass production in manufacturing plants throughout our country.

Industry in the Midwest

Automobiles are only one of many thousands of products manufactured in this part of our country. Each year, factories in the Midwest turn out more than 118 billion dollars' worth of steel, machinery, food products, and other goods. This is more than one third the value of all goods manufactured in the United States.

A good transportation system

The Midwest is a great manufacturing region because it has nearly all the things industry needs. One of the most important things the Midwest has is its good transportation system. By comparing the map on pages 8-9 with the map on page 122, you can see that most of the Midwest's main industrial areas are on or near important inland waterways.

The Midwest is served by the greatest inland waterway in the world. This is the Great Lakes–St. Lawrence Waterway. It is made up of the five Great Lakes, the St. Lawrence River, and several smaller connecting waterways. (See map on page 120.)

Ships traveling on the Great Lakes carry many kinds of raw materials and manufactured products. Although water transportation is slower than other

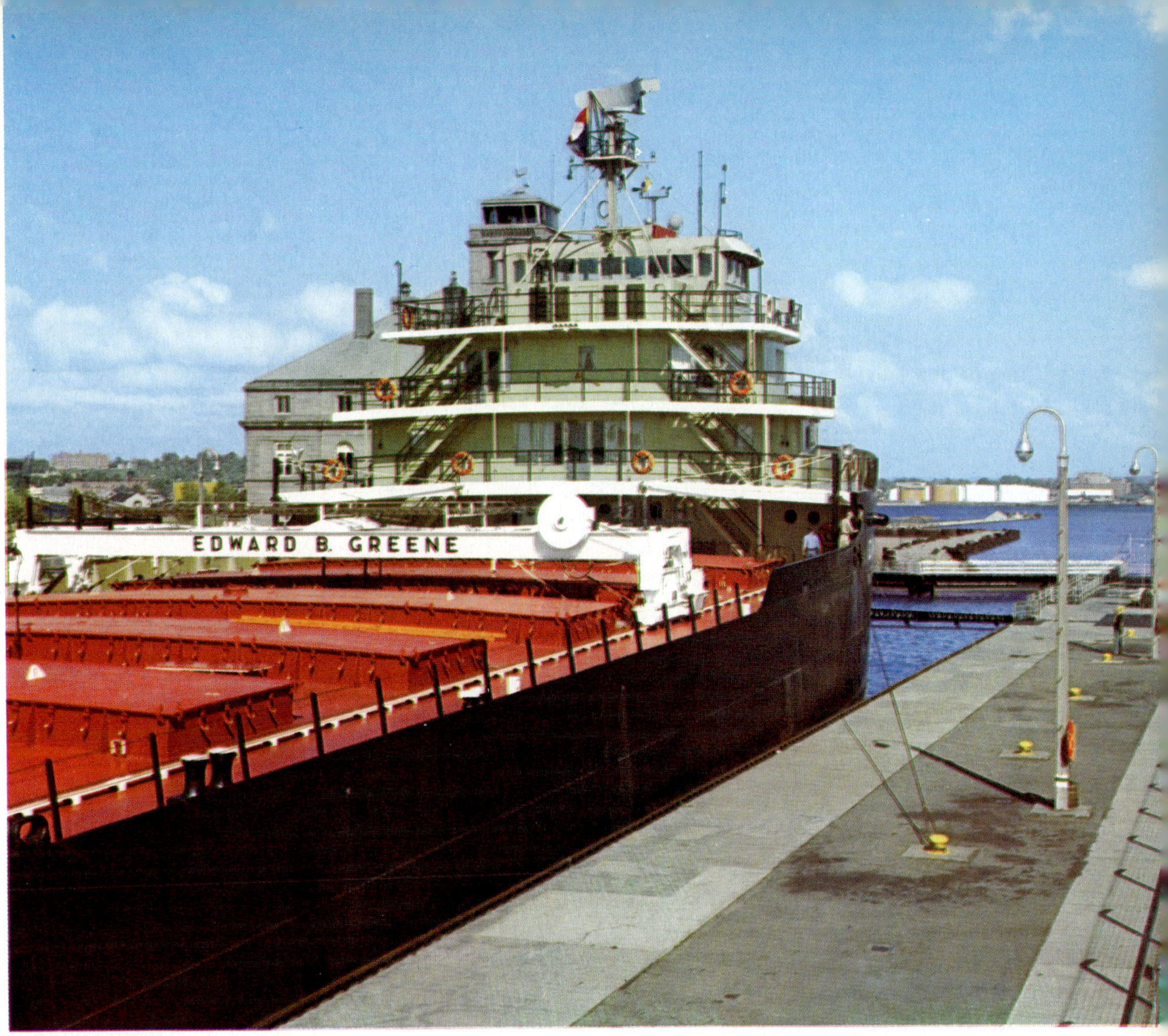

Exchange

See Great Ideas

The Soo Canals make it possible for ships to travel between Lake Huron and Lake Superior. (See map on page 120.) These canals are part of the Great Lakes-St. Lawrence Waterway. This great waterway helps people in the Midwest exchange many products with people in other parts of our country and the world. Why is trade carried on between people in different communities? Do you think trade helps people have a better way of life? Explain.

means of transportation, it is generally cheaper. Therefore, ships are often used to carry heavy loads that do not need to be moved in a hurry. Many boats carry wheat, iron ore, and other raw materials to mills and factories. Other ships carry products, such as automobiles and steel, between lake ports. Most shipping on the Great Lakes must stop during the winter, however. Ice blocks many harbors from about December to April.

If you were to visit the large ports along the Great Lakes, you would see ships from many different countries. The Great Lakes-St. Lawrence Waterway makes it possible for large, ocean-going ships to sail from the Atlantic Ocean through the Great Lakes to the western end of Lake Superior.

Use the caption in a class discussion about exchange. You may also assign Fideler Discovery Card 120 for an additional activity.

The Great Lakes–St. Lawrence Waterway is made up of the five Great Lakes, the St. Lawrence River, and several smaller connecting waterways. Ships can sail all the way from the Atlantic Ocean to the western end of Lake Superior. This is about 2,300 miles (3,701 kilometers).

The Ohio and Mississippi rivers are also important transportation routes. Barges move up and down these rivers carrying loads of coal, grain, sand, oil, or other raw materials. Waterways connect the Mississippi River with the Great Lakes. At Chicago, goods can be moved directly from riverboats to lake freighters and oceangoing ships. A waterway system connects the Mississippi River with ports along the Arkansas and Verdigris rivers in Oklahoma.

Other needs of industry

Factories need raw materials, water, and power to make goods. The Midwest has large amounts of iron ore, coal, and other important raw materials for factories. The farms and forests here also provide valuable raw materials. Many industries need huge amounts of water. Rivers, lakes, and underground water supplies in the Midwest have plenty of water for factories. Industries also need electric power to run machinery. Coal mined in the Midwest is used as fuel for plants that produce electricity.

More than 52 million people live in the Midwest. Many of these people have skills and ideas needed by industry. The people of the Midwest also

† Why is manufacturing much less important in the Great Plains states than in the Midwest? List the reasons.

make up a huge market for manufactured goods. Every day, they buy food, clothing, and hundreds of other items made here. Midwestern factories also sell large amounts of goods such as machinery to other factories.

Industry in the Great Plains States

† Manufacturing is much less important in the Great Plains states than in the Midwest. Factories here make only about twenty-three billion dollars' worth of goods every year. As the map on page 122 shows, there are about four times as many main industrial areas in the Midwest as there are in the Great Plains states.

Several things have held back the growth of industry in the Great Plains states. First, most parts of this region are not served by major waterways. Goods such as coal and steel have to be shipped by train or truck. It costs more to ship goods by these means of transportation than by boat. Second, the Great Plains states do not have some of the mineral resources needed for modern industry, especially iron ore and high-grade coal. Iron ore, for example, is needed to make steel. This metal is the main raw material used by factories that make machinery and hundreds of other products. Many parts of the Great Plains states also do not have enough water for industry. Finally, fewer people live here than in the Midwest. Therefore, there are not as many workers here.

Industry in Texas

Although there is little industry in most parts of the Great Plains states, Texas is one of our nation's ten leading manufacturing states. It is the only Great Plains state with ports that can handle oceangoing ships. This state is on the Gulf of Mexico, an arm of the Atlantic Ocean. Ships carry large amounts of goods to and from ports at Houston, Corpus Christi, Port Arthur, and other Texas cities. Among the goods shipped from ports in Texas are petroleum products, chemicals, cotton, and sulfur. Goods shipped into Texas include bauxite, iron ore, and other raw materials for Texas industries. Houston's port is one of the busiest in the United States. (See page 60.)

Texas is also served by the Gulf Intracoastal Waterway. This waterway extends along the coast from Texas to Florida. Boats using this waterway can move goods between Gulf coast ports without going into the open sea. In some places, the waterway is protected by offshore islands. In others, it lies inland. Many barges carry freight on this waterway from ports in Texas to New Orleans. From there, barges can go northward on the Mississippi River and connecting waterways to Chicago, St. Paul, and other ports in the Midwest.

In addition, Texas has many rich deposits of minerals that can be used by industry. In eastern Texas, where most of the state's industries are located, there is also enough water for manufacturing. Texas also has a large population. About six tenths of the people in the Great Plains states live here. There are plenty of workers for factories and large markets for manufactured goods.

Products of Industry

Iron and steel

The manufacture of iron and steel is one of the leading industries in

Refer to the map and map key below. Have students list the cities with 25,000-50,000 workers, and also the cities with 500,000 or more workers.

the Midwest and Great Plains. Much of the steel made in the United States comes from the Midwest. Ohio, Indiana, Michigan, and Illinois rank just after Pennsylvania as our country's most important iron- and steel-producing states.

Most of the steel produced in the Midwest comes from five main industrial areas. These are Youngstown, Cleveland, Detroit, Gary-Hammond-East Chicago, and Chicago. (See map below.) The main raw materials needed to make iron and steel can easily be shipped to these areas. Freighters carry iron ore from iron-mining areas near Lake Superior to ports along the southern shores of Lake Michigan and Lake Erie. Trains carry the ore to steel plants that lie inland. Limestone from the Midwest and coking* coal from the Appalachian Plateau are also carried to steel plants by water and by rail.

Much of the steel made in the Midwest is sold to nearby factories. The steel is used in making machinery, automobiles, and other products. These factories can obtain the steel they need without having to pay high transportation costs.

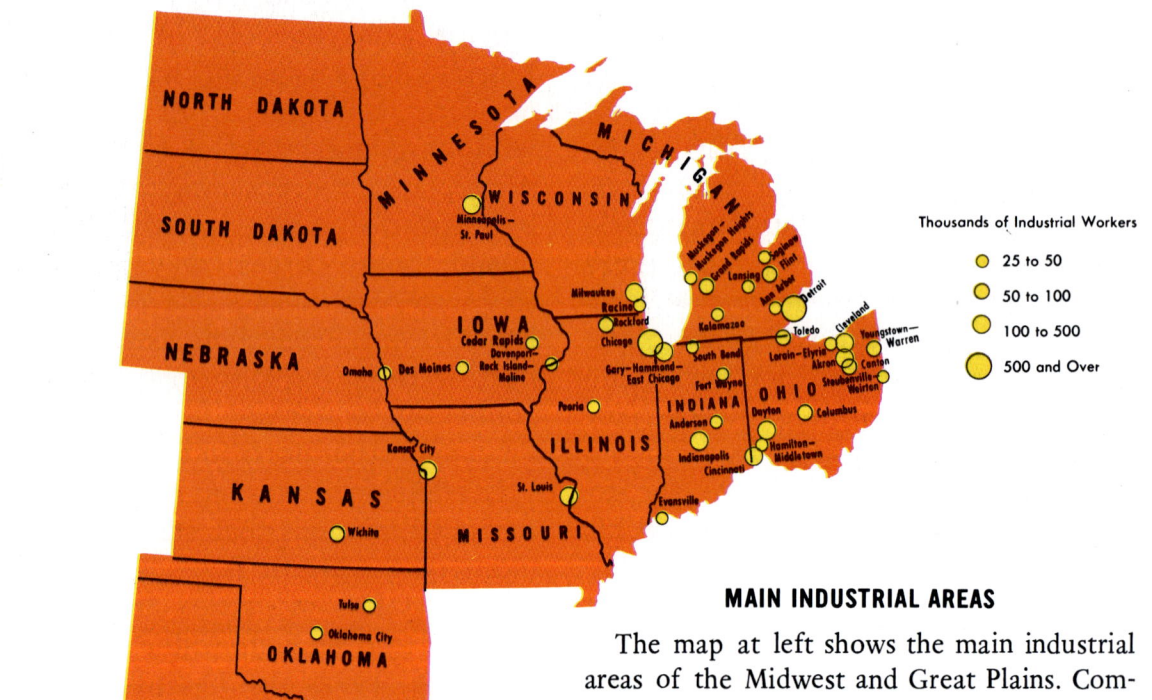

MAIN INDUSTRIAL AREAS

The map at left shows the main industrial areas of the Midwest and Great Plains. Compare this map with the map on page 50. You will notice that all of these industrial areas are densely populated. In these areas are large numbers of workers for factories and customers to buy manufactured goods.

Most of the main industrial areas in the Midwest and Great Plains are located in the states of Ohio, Illinois, Michigan, Texas, and Indiana. All of these states offer many advantages for industry. They are among the ten leading manufacturing states in our country.

A steel mill in the Midwest. Making iron and steel is one of the leading industries in the Midwest and Great Plains. Ohio, Indiana, Michigan, and Illinois rank just after Pennsylvania as our country's most important iron- and steel-producing states.

Machinery

Another leading industry in the Midwest and Great Plains is the manufacture of machinery. Each year factories here produce more than half of the total value of machinery made in our country.

Hundreds of factories in the Midwest and Great Plains make industrial or construction machinery. Plants in Ohio, Michigan, and other midwestern states make nearly two thirds of the nation's machine tools. These machines cut, grind, and shape metal to make parts needed in the manufacture of other machines. Factories in this part of our country also manufacture such industrial machinery as refrigeration equipment and printing presses. The Chicago industrial area is a leading producer of construction equipment, such as bulldozers and concrete mixers. Texas and Oklahoma, which are important oil-producing states, have plants that make oil-field equipment.

Factories in Illinois, Iowa, Wisconsin, and Michigan make much of our nation's farm machinery. Farmers in the Midwest and Great Plains need machines for planting, cultivating,* and harvesting crops.

Plants in the Midwest and Great Plains also produce several other kinds of machinery. Many people here work in factories that manufacture appliances, such as refrigerators and air conditioners. Electronic* equipment, such as computers* and television sets, is made in Chicago, Dallas, and other cities.

Transportation equipment

The manufacture of transportation equipment is another main industry in the Midwest and Great Plains. More transportation equipment is made here than in any other part of our country. This industry includes the production of airplanes and railroad equipment, as well as cars, trucks, and buses.

Michigan ranks first in our country in the production of cars and other motor vehicles. The world's three leading automobile manufacturers—General Motors, Ford, and Chrysler—have their main offices in the Detroit area. They have large factories in Michigan.

A meat-packing plant in the Midwest. Farms and ranches in the Midwest and Great Plains provide raw materials for industry. Plants here prepare meat, grain, and other farm products for sale.

Several other industries supply automobile manufacturers with products they need. Plants in Toledo, Ohio, supply auto makers in nearby Michigan with glass for car windows. Most of the tires used by the automobile industry come from factories in Akron, Ohio.

Plants in the Midwest and Great Plains also make railroad equipment and airplanes. Locomotives are manufactured in La Grange, Illinois. More than half of the small airplanes made in this country come from Wichita, Kansas. In Texas, there are plants that make helicopters, large airplanes, and spacecraft.

Food products

Farms in the Midwest and Great Plains produce raw materials for industry here. Food-processing plants prepare meat, grain, and other farm products for sale to customers.

An important kind of food processing in this part of our country is meat-packing. More meat is processed in Omaha, Nebraska, than in any other city in the United States. There are also large meat-packing plants in many other cities in the Midwest and Great Plains. Farmers like to sell their livestock to meat-packing plants that are fairly close to their farms. Livestock may lose too much valuable weight if they are shipped to markets far away.

In many cities of the Midwest and Great Plains, there are mills and factories that make food products from grain. Trains and trucks bring grain from our country's wheatlands to flour mills in Kansas City, Missouri. Flour milling is an important industry in this city. Large plants at Battle Creek, Michigan, make much of our country's breakfast cereal from wheat, corn, and other grains.

In the dairy belt of the Midwest, there are many plants that process milk to make cheese and butter. More cheese is produced in Wisconsin than in any other state. Minnesota, Wisconsin, and Iowa are our country's leading butter producers.

An oil refinery in Oklahoma. The Midwest and Great Plains has many refineries that make gasoline and other products from petroleum. Texas produces more petroleum products than any other state.

† What facts make it possible for Texas to produce more petroleum products than any other state?

Petroleum products

The Midwest and Great Plains has many refineries that make gasoline, fuel oil, and other products from petroleum. A large number of these refineries are on the Gulf coast of Texas. Here they can get the petroleum they need from nearby oil wells. Texas produces more petroleum products than any other state. Ocean tankers and pipelines carry large amounts of these products to other parts of our country.

Chemicals and chemical products

Texas, Illinois, Ohio, and Indiana are among our country's leading producers of chemicals and chemical products. Many plants in these states make basic* chemicals, such as hydrochloric* acid and ammonia. Basic chemicals are used in the making of hundreds of different products, from soaps to drugs.

Texas ranks second only to New Jersey in the manufacture of chemicals and chemical products. The chemical plants of Texas are located near the state's oil refineries. These refineries are mainly along the Gulf coast. Chemical plants in this part of Texas use large quantities of raw materials from nearby refineries to make petrochemicals.*

Oil refining is also an important industry in Oklahoma Kansas, and Indiana. Do research in other sources to discover more about the many different products that are made from petroleum.

Using Tools

See Great Ideas

The people in this picture work in a plant that makes truck parts. The worker at right is using a machine called a lift truck. This lift truck will pick up and move a large roll of aluminum. Do you think it would be possible to make trucks, cars, and other kinds of transportation equipment without the use of machines? Why do you think this? What are some other industries in the Midwest and Great Plains that use machines and other tools?

† **Choose a Place To Build**

Imagine that you are a business person who would like to build a manufacturing plant in the Midwest and Great Plains. Choose one of the following plants and decide the best location for it.

An automobile plant   A steel mill
A farm machinery plant   An oil refinery

In choosing the place to build your plant, you will have to think about:
1. the location of raw materials
2. the supply of workers
3. transportation routes

† Use "Choose a Place To Build" as a culminating activity for this unit.

Index

Explanation of abbreviations used in this Index: *p* — picture   *m* — map

Akron, Ohio, 125; *m* 59
Aldrin, Edwin E., Jr., 6
American Indians, *see* people
Anderson, Sherwood, 78
Appalachian (ap′ ə lā′ chən) Highlands, *see* land
Appalachian Plateau, *see* land
Arkansas River, 22; *m* 8-9, 105
Armstrong, Neil A., 6
arts, 59, 76-79; *p* 76, 77, 79
   architects, 78-79
   literature, 76-78; *p* 76, 77
   painters and sculptors, 78; *p* 79
astronauts, 6

Badlands, 24; *p* 25; *m* 14
Basin and Range Country, *see* land
Battle Creek, Michigan, 126; *m* 59
Black Hills, 24, 103, 111; *m* 14
Bowen, Otis R., *p* 66

cement, 104
Central Lowland, *see* land
Chicago, Illinois, 17, 19, 48, 52, 53, 57-59, 122, 124; *p* 56-58; *m* 59, 120; *chart* 57
Chicago River, 57-58
Cincinnati, Ohio, 52; *m* 59
cities, 14, 17, 19, 27, 28, 40, 48, 52, 53, 56-63, 64-67, 76, 115-118, 121, 122, 124, 125, 126; *p* 10-11, 28-29, 51, 56-58, 60-63; *m* 59, 120; *chart* 57
   population, 56, 57, 60, 61, 62; *m* 59; *chart* 57
   citizenship and government, 64-75; *p* 64-66, 72, 74; *chart* 67
   citizenship, 68-69
   civil rights movement, 73-75
   democracy, 71
   local government, 67
   minority groups, 70-75; *p* 72
   social problems, 69-75
   state government, 64-67; *chart* 67
Clemens, Samuel, 76; *p* 76
Cleveland, Ohio, 17, 122; *m* 59, 120

climate, 30-45, 50, 106; *p* 30-33, 35, 36, 38-39, 41-45; *m* 34, 41, 42
   blizzard, 37
   continental, 31-37
   droughts, 35, 37, 44
   growing season, 40, 42-43; *m* 42
   rainfall, 34-35, 37, 44, 106; *m* 34
   rain shadow, 37
   seasons of the year, 37-45
   snowfall, 37, 38, 40
   temperature, 31-33, 37, 40, 43-44; *m* 39
   tornadoes, 40, 41; *p* 41; *m* 41
   winds, 33, 34
coal, *see* minerals
Coastal Plain, *see* land
conservation, 83
copper, *see* minerals
corn, *see* farm products
Corpus Christi, Texas, 121; *p* 28-29; *m* 59
cotton, *see* farm products

Dallas, Texas, 53, 124; *m* 59; *chart* 57
dams, *see* water resources
Dearborn, Michigan, 115-118; *m* 59
Detroit, Michigan, 17, 61-62, 122, 124; *p* 10-11; *m* 59, 120; *chart* 57
Detroit River, 61; *m* 120
discrimination, 70-75

East Chicago, Indiana, 122
electricity, 100, 107-108
El Paso, Texas, 27; *m* 14, 59
energy fuels, 96-98, 100; *p* 96-99
   use of, 96, 100
erosion, 24

farming, 25-26, 27, 28, 50, 82-95, 104, 106-107; *p* 12-13, 16-17, 82-85, 88, 90, 92-93, 95, 106-107; *m* 87, 89, 94, 105
   corn belt, 17, 21, 86-88; *p* 16-17, 30-31, 82-83; *m* 87
   cotton belt, 91-94; *p* 92-93
   dairy belt, 19, 85-86
   growing season, 40, 42-43; *m* 42
   methods, 83-85, 93-94, 104, 106-107; *p* 106-107
   wheat belts, 89, 91
farm products, 17, 19, 21, 24-27, 28, 30, 40, 42-43, 45, 82, 84-95; *p* 12-13, 16-17, 30-31, 42-43, 82-85, 88, 90, 92-93, 95; *m* 87, 89, 94
   Angora goats, 91
   barley, 42
   cattle, 17, 21, 24, 25, 27, 82, 86, 91; *p* 90; *m* 94
   corn, 17, 21, 30, 42, 82, 86-88; *p* 12-13, 16-17, 30-31, 82-83; *m* 87, 89
   cotton, 27, 42, 82, 91-94; *p* 92-93; *m* 87, 94
   dairy products, 19, 85-86; *p* 85; *m* 87, 89
   fruit, 28, 40, 42-43, 45, 94; *p* 42-43; *m* 87
   hay, 17, 42
   hogs, 17, 21, 82; *m* 89
   rice, 28
   sheep, 91; *m* 94
   soybeans, 17, 42, 87-88; *p* 84; *m* 89
   tobacco, *m* 87
   value of, 82
   vegetables, 28, 40, 45, 94-95; *p* 95
   wheat, 25-26, 82, 88-89, 91; *p* 88; *m* 87, 94
   wool, 82
fisheries, 112-113; *p* 113
Ford, Henry, 61, 115-116
Ford Motor Company, 115-118, 124; *p* 116-117
forest products, 28, 111-112
forests, 34-35, 108-112; *p* 109-111; *m* 108
   logging, 109-110; *p* 110-111
Fort Worth, Texas, *m* 59; *chart* 57

Pronunciation Key: hat, āge, cāre, fär; let, ēqual, tėrm; it, īce; hot, ōpen, ôrder; oil, out; cup, pút, rüle, ūse; child; long; thin; ᴛʜen; zh, measure; ə represents a in about, e in taken, i in pencil, o in lemon, u in circus.

glaciers, 18-19; *m* 18
global view, 4-11; *p* 4, 6, 10-11; *m* 7-10; *chart* 5
government, *see* citizenship and government
great ideas,
  cooperation, *p* 48-49
  division of labor, *p* 114-115
  education, *p* 52-53
  exchange, *p* 58, 119
  freedom, *p* 74
  language, *p* 76
  rules and government, *p* 64-65
  using natural resources, *p* 96-97; *m* 87
  using tools, *p* 16-17, 110-111, 128
Great Lakes, 17-19, 37, 39, 42-43, 45, 104, 112, 118-119; *p* 38-39; *m* 8-9, 14-15, 59
Great Lakes–St. Lawrence Waterway, 18, 58, 118-119; *p* 119; *m* 120
Great Plains, *see* land
growing season, *see* climate
Guadalupe (gwäd′əl üp′) Peak, 27; *m* 14
Gulf Intracoastal Waterway, 121
Gulf of Mexico, 28, 40, 112; *p* 28-29; *m* 7, 105

Hammond, Indiana, 122; *m* 59
Hannibal, Missouri, 76; *m* 59
Holland, Michigan, *p* 51; *m* 59
Houston, Texas, 28, 40, 53, 59-61, 121; *p* 48-49, 60-61; *m* 59; *chart* 57
Houston Ship Channel, 60

Illinois, 19, 48, 54, 57-59, 86, 88, 109, 122, 124, 125, 127; *p* 56-58, 98-99; *m* 8-9, 59, 120, 122; *chart* 57
  cities, 57-59; *p* 56-58; *m* 59
  farming, 86, 88
  industry, 122, 124, 125, 127; *m* 122
  land, 109; *m* 8-9
  minerals, 98; *p* 98-99
  people, 54
Illinois River, 58, 112
Illinois Waterway, 58
Indiana, 17, 64-67, 98, 122, 127; *p* 64-66, 82-83; *m* 8-9, 59, 120, 122

  cities, 64-67; *m* 59, 120
  government of, 64-67; *p* 64-66
  industry, 122, 127; *m* 122
  land, 17; *m* 8-9
  minerals, 98
Indianapolis, Indiana, 64-67; *m* 59
industrial areas, *m* 122
industry, 50, 52-53, 114-128; *p* 114-117, 119, 123-128; *m* 120, 122
  chemical, 127
  fishing, 112; *p* 113
  food-processing, 125-126; *p* 124-125
  iron and steel, 121-122; *p* 123
  logging, 109-110; *p* 109-111
  machinery, 124
  petroleum products, 127; *p* 126-127
  raw materials for, 86-87, 117-118, 120, 121, 122
  transportation equipment, 61-62, 115-118, 124-125; *p* 114-117, 128
Interior Highlands, *see* land
Interior Plains, *see* land
Iowa, 21, 30-31, 86, 88, 109, 124, 126; *p* 30-31; *m* 8-9, 59, 122
  climate, 30-31
  farming, 21, 86, 88
  farm products, 21, 30, 88; *p* 30-31
  industry, 124, 126
  land, 21, 109; *m* 8-9
iron ore, *see* minerals
irrigation, 27, 28, 93, 94, 106-107; *p* 106-107; *m* 105

Kansas, 13, 25-26, 41, 88-89, 98, 125, 126; *p* 41, 90; *m* 8-9, 59, 122
  climate, 41; *p* 41
  farming, 88-89; *p* 90
  industry, 125; *m* 122
  land, 13, 25-26; *m* 8-9
  minerals, 98
Kansas City, Missouri, 126; *m* 59

LaGrange, Illinois, 125; *m* 59
Lake Erie, 43, 61, 94, 105; *m* 59, 120
Lake Huron, 61; *m* 59, 120
Lake Michigan, 18, 43, 57, 58, 94; *m* 59, 120
Lake Ontario, *m* 59, 120

Lake Superior, 37, 119; *p* 22-23; *m* 59, 120
land, 12-29, 109; *p* 12-13, 16-17, 20, 22-23, 25, 26, 28-29; *m* 14-15, 18, 20
  Appalachian Highlands, 14; *m* 14-15
  Appalachian Plateau, 14; *m* 14-15
  Arkansas Valley, 22; *m* 14-15
  Basin and Range Country, 27; *p* 26; *m* 14-15
  Central Lowland, 13, 16-21; *m* 14-15
  Coastal Plain, 13, 27-28; *p* 28-29; *m* 14-15
  glaciers, 18-19; *m* 18
  Great Plains, 13, 23-27; *p* 25; *m* 14-15
  Interior Highlands, 14, 21-22; *m* 14-15
  Interior Plains, 13; *m* 14-15
  Ouachita (wash′ə tô′) Mountains, 22; *m* 14-15
  Ozark Plateau, 21; *m* 14-15
  Plateau Country, 14; *m* 14-15
  Rio Grande Valley, 28
  Superior Upland, 14, 22-23; *p* 22-23; *m* 14-15
Latin Americans, *see* people

Mesabi (mə säb′ bē) Range, 100-102; *p* 100-101
metropolitan areas, 57, 60-62; *chart* 57
Michigan, 22-23, 45, 50, 52, 54, 61-62, 86, 94, 98, 102, 103, 104, 110, 115-118, 122, 124, 126; *p* 10-11, 22-23, 36, 38-39, 51, 109-111, 114-117; *m* 8-9, 59, 120, 122
  climate, 45; *p* 36, 38-39
  farming, 86, 94
  forests, 110; *p* 109-111
  industry, 115-118, 122, 124, 126; *p* 114-117; *m* 122
  land, 22-23; *m* 8-9
  minerals, 98, 102, 103, 104
  people, 52, 54
Milwaukee, Wisconsin, 48, 52; *m* 59, 120
minerals, 14, 23, 24, 28, 60, 96-104; *p* 96-101, 103; *m* 99, 102

coal, 14, 98-100; *p* 98-99; *m* 99
copper, 103
gold, 24, 103; *p* 103
iron ore, 23, 100-103; *p* 100-101; *m* 102
lead, 103
limestone, 14, 104; *m* 102
natural gas, 28, 97-98; *m* 102
oil, 28, 60, 96-98; *p* 96-97; *m* 102
salt, 104
sulfur, 104
taconite, 102
uses of, 96, 100, 103, 104
mining, *see* minerals
Minneapolis, Minnesota, 17; *m* 59; *chart* 57
Minnesota, 22, 37, 45, 50, 52, 86, 100-102, 109, 110, 126; *p* 100-101; *m* 8-9, 59, 122
climate, 37, 45
farming, 86
forests, 110
industry, 126; *m* 122
land, 22, 109; *m* 8-9
minerals, 100-102; *p* 100-101
people, 52
Mississippi River, 19-21, 29, 58, 62, 76, 104, 112, 120, 121; *p* 20; *m* 8-9, 20, 105
Missouri, 62, 76, 91, 94, 103, 104, 110, 112, 126; *m* 8-9, 122
farming, 91, 94
forests, 110, 112
industry, 126; *m* 122
minerals, 103, 104
Missouri River, 19, 23, 62, 106, 107; *m* 8-9, 20, 105

natural resources and energy, 96-113; *p* 96-101, 103, 106-107, 109-111, 113; *m* 99, 102, 105, 108
Nebraska, 13, 24-25, 48, 66, 91, 126; *p* 106-107; *m* 8-9, 59, 122
farming, 91; *p* 106-107
government, 66
industry, 126; *m* 122
land, 13, 24-25; *m* 8-9

North Dakota, 13, 32, 37, 44, 52, 91, 98, 100; *m* 8-9, 59, 122
climate, 32, 37, 44
farming, 91
land, 13; *m* 8-9
minerals, 98, 100
people, 52

O'Hare International Airport, 58
Ohio, 14, 16, 52, 98, 112, 122, 124, 125, 127; *m* 8-9, 59, 122
forests, 112
industry, 122, 124, 125, 127; *m* 122
land, 14, 16; *m* 8-9
minerals, 14, 98, 104
Ohio River, 19, 120; *m* 20
oil, *see* minerals
Oklahoma, 13, 17, 21, 35, 42, 98, 110, 124; *p* 96-97, 126-127; *m* 8-9, 59, 122
climate, 35, 42
forests, 110
industry, 124; *p* 126-127; *m* 122
land, 13, 21; *m* 8-9
minerals, 98; *p* 96-97
Oklahoma City, Oklahoma, 17; *m* 59
Olds, Ransom E., 61
Omaha, Nebraska, 126; *m* 59
Ouachita (wäsh′ə tô) Mountains, *see* land
Ozark Plateau, *see* land

people, 46-55, 70-75; *p* 46-49, 51-55; *m* 50
American Indians, 54-55; *p* 55
Asian-Americans, 54
blacks, 52-53; *p* 52-53
of European descent, 51-52; *p* 51
immigrants, 51-52
Latin Americans, 54; *p* 54
minority groups, 70-75
petroleum, *see* minerals, oil
Plateau Country, *see* land
Platte River, 25; *m* 8-9, 105
population, 48, 50, 53, 54, 56, 57, 60, 61, 62; *m* 50; *chart* 57
Port Arthur, Texas, 121; *m* 59

ports, 21, 28, 60, 62, 119, 120, 121, 122; *p* 60-63, 119; *m* 120

religion, 55
Rio Grande, 27; *m* 8-9, 105
Rio Grande Valley, 28, 94

St. Lawrence River, 118; *m* 120
St. Louis, Missouri, 17, 52, 62; *p* 62-63; *m* 59; *chart* 57
St. Paul, Minnesota, *m* 59; *chart* 57
Sand Hills, 24-25; *m* 14
seasons of the year, *see* climate
Soo Canals, *p* 119; *m* 120
South Dakota, 13, 23-24, 52, 103, 111; *p* 25, 55, 88, 103; *m* 8-9, 59, 122
Badlands, 24; *p* 25; *m* 14
Black Hills, 24, 103, 111; *m* 14
farming, *p* 88
forests, 111
land, 13, 23-24; *m* 8-9
minerals, 103; *p* 103
people, 52; *p* 55
soybeans, *see* farm products
Superior Upland, *see* land

temperature, *see* climate
Texas, 13, 27, 28, 35, 40, 42, 50, 53, 54, 59-61, 86, 89, 91-94, 97-98, 104, 110-111, 112, 121, 124, 125, 127; *p* 26, 28-29, 42-43, 48-49, 113; *m* 8-9, 59, 122
climate, 35, 40, 42, 50; *p* 42-43
farming, 86, 89, 91-94
farm products, 28, 40; *p* 42-43, 92-93, 95
fisheries, 112; *p* 113
forests, 110-111
history, 60
industry, 50, 112, 121, 124, 125, 127; *m* 122
land, 13, 27; *p* 26; *m* 8-9
minerals, 28, 97-98, 104
people, 53, 54
population, 50, 53
Toledo, Ohio, 125; *m* 59
tornadoes, 41; *p* 41; *m* 41

PRONUNCIATION KEY: hat, āge, cāre, fär; let, ēqual, tėrm; it, īce; hot, ōpen, ôrder; oil, out; cup, pu̇t, rüle, ūse; child; long; thin; ᴛʜen; zh, measure; ə represents a in about, e in taken, i in pencil, o in lemon, u in circus.

transportation, 17, 18, 20-21, 38-39, 58, 60, 61, 118-120, 121; *p* 119; *m* 120
Twain, Mark, *see* Clemens, Samuel

water resources, 104-108; *p* 106-107; *m* 105
    dams, 21, 106, 107; *m* 105
    hydroelectric power, 107

wells, 108
waterways, 18, 20-21, 58, 60, 61, 118-120, 121; *p* 20, 119; *m* 120
wheat, *see* farm products
Wichita, Kansas, 125; *m* 59
Wisconsin, 19, 22, 45, 48, 50, 52, 86, 102, 110, 124, 126; *m* 8-9, 59, 122

climate, 45, 50
farming, 86
forests, 110
industry, 124, 126; *m* 122
land, 19, 22; *p* 2-3; *m* 8-9
minerals, 102
people, 52

Youngstown, Ohio, 14, 122; *m* 59

Acknowledgments

Grateful acknowledgment is made to the following for permission to use the illustrations found in this book:

Alabama Department Offices: Page 72
Alpha Photo Associates, Inc.: Pages 4, 10-11, 82-83; Page 95 by Zimmerman
Black Star: Page 74 by Doug Wilson
Bob Taylor: Pages 96-97
Boyne USA Resorts: Page 36
Candida: Page 20; Pages 22-23 by Bernie Donahue
Chicago Convention and Tourism Bureau: Page 58
Cyr Color Photo Agency: Page 84
DeKalb Agricultural Research, Inc.: Pages 30-31
DeWys, Inc.: Pages 54 and 55; Pages 48-49 by Fred DeWys
Ewing Galloway: Pages 98-99
Ford Motor Company: Pages 116-117
Freelance Photographers Guild: Pages 32-33, 56-57, and 119; Page 88 by James Pollock
Grant Heilman: Pages 12-13, 16-17, 85, and 106-107
Harold M. Lambert Studios, Inc.: Page 41
Homestake Mining Company: Page 103
Hormel Fine Food Products, Inc.: Pages 124-125
Industrial Development Expansion Agency: Page 25

International Harvester: Pages 92-93
John Penrod: Page 51
Kansas State Board of Agriculture: Page 90
Mackinac Bridge Authority: Pages 38-39
Michigan Department of Commerce Travel Bureau: Pages 35 and 44-45
Michigan Department of Conservation: Page 109
Mike Hanley: Pages 64-65 and 66
Missouri Tourism Commission: Pages 62-63 by Ralph W. Walker
NASA: Page 6
Photo Researchers, Inc.: Pages 46-47 by Van Bucher
Purnell Commercial Photos: Pages 42-43
Shostal Associates, Inc.: Pages 2-3, 28-29, 52-53, 76, 80-81, 100-101, 114-115, 126-127, and 128
Standard Oil of Indiana: Page 1
State of Michigan Department of Natural Resources: Pages 110-111 by Alan H. Boelter
Taurus: Pages 60-61
Texas Highway Department: Pages 26 and 113
The Art Institute of Chicago: Page 79
United States Steel: Page 123
Wide World Photos: Page 77 (both)

Grateful acknowledgment is made to Scott, Foresman and Company for the pronunciation system used in this book, which is taken from the Thorndike-Barnhart Dictionary Series. Grateful acknowledgment is made to the following for permission to use cartographic data in this book: Base maps courtesy of the Nystrom Raised Relief Map Company, Chicago 60618: Pages 14 and 15; Rand McNally & Company: Pages 8 and 9; United States Department of Commerce, Bureau of the Census: Pages 50, 89, and 94.

THE WEST

The Golden Gate Bridge across San Francisco Bay, in California. This bay is an arm of the Pacific Ocean.

† Use these questions to start students thinking about the land and climate of the West.

Part 1

Land and Climate

In the western part of the United States is a huge area of land known as the West. It covers almost one third of our country.

If you were to travel through the West, you would see many interesting sights. You would find snowy mountains and beautiful green valleys. You would find deserts and thick forests, rolling plains and steep-sided canyons. You would also see the blue water of the Pacific Ocean.

The chapters in Part 1 tell more about the land and climate of the West. As you read, try to find answers to the following questions:

†
- How many states are there in the West? What are their names?
- What are the four main land regions of the West? What is the land in each of these regions like?
- How does the climate differ from one part of the West to another? What causes these differences in climate?
- How do land features and climate affect the way people live in different parts of the West?

Along the Pacific coast of California, near the town of Carmel. The part of our country that we call the West extends all the way from Canada on the north to Mexico on the south. To the west, it is bordered by the huge Pacific Ocean.

Use Fideler Discovery Cards 10-36, or Fideler Discovery Sheets, Volume 1, pages 5-16 for additional activities.

The city of San Diego, California, as seen from an airplane. When you fly several miles above the earth's surface in an airplane, you can sometimes see places as far as 100 miles (161 km.) away. But even at this height, you can see only a very small part of the earth. Why is this so?

1 A Global View

Our earth from an airplane

Have you ever taken a trip in an airplane? If you have, you will remember the excitement you felt as the plane left the airport runway and began climbing high into the air. Before long, you were flying miles above the earth's surface. Below you were cities, farms, and forests. From your window, you looked out over a wide area. If it was a clear day, you were able to see as far as 100 miles (161 km.)† away. But the earth is so large that even at this height you could see only a small part of its surface.

Our earth from space

Until a few years ago, no one had ever been able to see more than a small part of the earth at one time. Then, in the late 1950's, the United States and the Soviet Union* began to send different kinds of spacecraft far away from the earth. Some of these spacecraft have carried persons called astronauts. Others have carried cameras or scientific equipment. So far, most of the spacecraft that have been launched have traveled around the earth. But some have journeyed to the moon or to other planets,* such as Mars and Venus.

*See Glossary
† km. means kilometer

Eastern Hemisphere

Western Hemisphere

From a spacecraft many thousands of miles out in space, it is possible to get a view of our earth as a whole.

The picture on page 6 shows a view of the earth from far out in space. This picture was taken from a United States spacecraft known as the ATS III. When the picture was taken, the spacecraft was more than 22,000 miles (35,000 km.)† away from the earth.

Continents and oceans

As you study the picture on page 6, you will notice that some of the earth's surface is hidden by clouds. In some

Our earth. The surface of our earth is covered partly with land and partly with water. The largest bodies of water are called oceans, and the largest masses of land are known as continents. Five of the earth's six continents are shown on the maps above. The continent of Antarctica is located around the South Pole, so it does not show on either of these maps.

Refer to the maps on this page. What hemisphere do we live in? What continent do we live on?

The earth from space. This photograph of the earth was taken from a United States spacecraft.

places, however, you can see land. The largest masses of land are called continents. In other places, you can see water. The largest bodies of water are oceans. They make up about three fourths of the earth's surface.

The Eastern Hemisphere

If you look at the top map on page 5, you can see the continents of Africa, Eurasia, and Australia. The western part of the great continent of Eurasia is called Europe, while the eastern part is known as Asia. Many people consider Europe and Asia to be two separate continents. The map shows that the continent of Africa lies to the south of Europe. A small part of Australia can be seen to the east of the Indian Ocean.

Refer to the picture above. What discoveries can you make about the earth from this picture?

† Are Hawaii and Alaska part of the conterminous United States? (Students may need to look up the word "conterminous" in the Glossary.)

The Western Hemisphere

The other side of the earth is known as the Western Hemisphere. The bottom map on page 5 shows that the continents of North America and South America are located in the Western Hemisphere.

Now look at the picture of the earth on page 6. With the help of the globe in your classroom, find South America in the picture. At the top left of the picture, you can also see part of North America. Much of this continent is hidden under a layer of clouds.

The United States

The map below presents a closer view of North America. Most of our own country, the United States, is on this continent. Our nearest neighbors in North America are the countries of Canada and Mexico.

Our country is made up of fifty states. Two of these, Alaska and Hawaii, are separated from all the others. Alaska lies to the northwest of Canada, on the North American continent. Hawaii is a group of islands in the Pacific Ocean. The part of our country that is made up of the other forty-eight states is called the conterminous* United States. (See map below.) †

The West

The map at the top of page 10 shows that the West is a group of eleven states in the western part of our country. The West is very large in area, covering

The United States

This map shows the location of the fifty states that make up our country. Two of these, Alaska and Hawaii, are separated from the others. Alaska is in the far northern part of North America. Hawaii is an island state in the Pacific Ocean. The other forty-eight states form the part of our country known as the conterminous* United States.

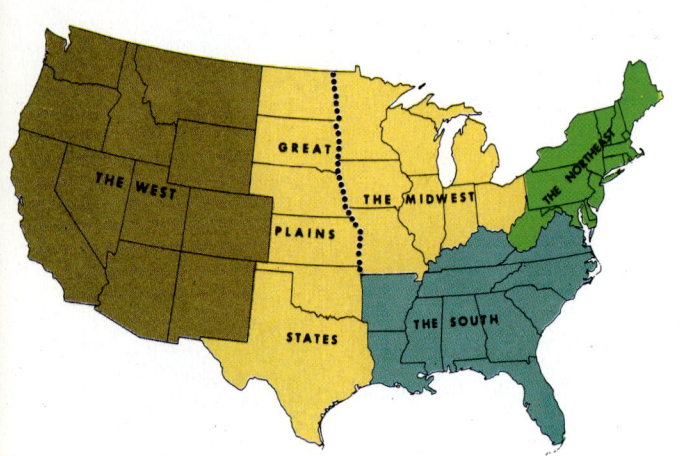

Main groups of states. The states in the conterminous United States may be divided into groups. The map above shows one way in which these states may be grouped.

almost one third of the United States. It extends all the way from Canada on the north to Mexico on the south. To the west, it is bordered by the huge Pacific Ocean.

A changing region

More than one hundred years ago, a newspaper editor in New York City wrote, "Go West, young man, go West." At that time, the part of the United States known as the West was still largely a wilderness. Almost the only people who lived in much of the West were small groups of Indians.

During the years that followed, many Americans did "go West." In some places, they found barren deserts and rugged mountains. But in other places, they found fertile lowlands with a pleasant climate. There were also rich deposits of minerals and valuable forests. Sparkling rivers flowed down from high mountain peaks. These provided water for dry farmlands. Many of the newcomers liked the West so well that they decided to stay there. Today, more than 38 million people make their homes in the West.

In the following chapters, you will discover more facts about the land, the climate, and the natural resources of the West. You will also find out why so many people have chosen to make their homes in this important part of our country.

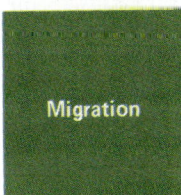

Migration

Albuquerque, New Mexico, is one of many growing cities in the West. During the last one hundred years, large numbers of people have moved to the West from other parts of the United States and from other countries. The movement of people from one country or region into another is called migration. What do you think are some reasons for the migration of people to the West? Do research in this book to find facts that will help you answer this question.

† **Thinking Together**
Imagine that you and some other members of your class are astronauts taking a trip in a spacecraft. Discuss these questions.
1. What does the earth look like from space? Can you see the land and water areas very clearly? Why? Why not?
2. What other things can you see from your spacecraft?
3. Do you think the earth is a good home for human beings? Do you think there is life anywhere except on earth? Give reasons for your answers.

† Use these questions in a class discussion about the earth.

The West 11

A Problem To Solve

How do land features in the West affect the people who live in this part of our country? To solve this problem, make hypotheses* that explain how land features in the West affect:

a. transportation
b. farming
c. where the people live

The Index will help you locate information to use in solving this problem.

See Skills Manual, "Thinking and Solving Problems"

*See Glossary

Refer to the picture above. Perhaps some of your students have visited a place like this in the West. Have them tell about their experiences.

2 Land

Imagine that you have just received a letter from a cousin who lives in another country. Your cousin has seen American movies that took place in the West. She wants to know more about this part of the United States. How would you answer your cousin's letter?

You might begin by telling your cousin that the West is a group of eleven states in the western part of our country. Then you might tell her that there are three important facts she should know about the West. Some of the maps in this book will help you understand these facts and explain them to your cousin.

A land of wide open spaces

The map on page 46 shows how many people live in different parts of the United States. Each dot on the map stands for ten thousand people. In a few places along the Pacific Ocean, there are thick clumps of dots. But in most parts of the West, there are very few dots. This map shows us that few people live in much of the West. In this chapter, you will discover some of the reasons why most of the West's people are crowded into a few small areas.

A dry land

By looking at the map on page 27, we can see how much rain falls in different parts of our country. Notice that only a small part of the West receives more than 20 inches (51 cm.)† of rainfall each year. Most farm crops need at least this amount of rainfall in

† cm. means centimeter

Dry land in Arizona. The West has large areas in which few people live. One reason why much of the West has so few people is the lack of rainfall here. What are some other reasons?

The West 13

† Refer to these pictures on pages 18 and 19. Have students locate these plateaus on the map on page 24.

order to grow well. We can tell from the map, then, that most of the West is very dry.

Now we know one reason why so much of the West is thinly populated. People need water to live. They need water for drinking, bathing, and many other uses. The lack of rainfall helps to explain why few people live in most parts of the West.

A land of mountains and high plateaus

The land in the West is higher and more rugged than the land in other parts of the United States. Look at the map on pages 8 and 9. This map shows how high the land in our country rises above the level of the sea. Notice that much of the land in the West is more than 5,000 feet (1,524 m.)† above sea level. In some places, high mountains tower above deep valleys. Between the groups of mountains are broad areas of high ground called plateaus. The pictures on pages 18 and 19 show us views of two different plateaus—the Columbia Plateau and the Colorado Plateau.

Four main regions

The West may be divided into four main parts, or regions. (See map on page 24.) The easternmost part of the West is made up of broad plains, like the one shown in the picture at right. Rising west of the plains are the Rocky Mountains. Still farther west is a huge land region that is made up largely of plateaus. It is called the Plateau Country. Between this region and the Pacific Ocean are long mountain chains separated by valleys.

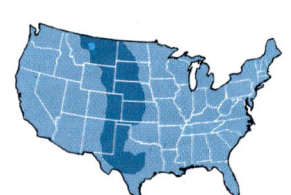

The Great Plains

The region known as the Great Plains forms a wide band extending from Canada in the north to Mexico in the south. The land in the Great Plains slopes gently upward from east to west. At the western edge of this region, some places are more than 1 mile (1.6 km.)† above sea level.

† m. means meter
† km. means kilometer

Wheat fields on the Great Plains in Colorado. In the distance are the Rocky Mountains. What do you think the machines in this picture are doing? Why do you suppose there are strips of dark earth between the lighter-colored fields of wheat? Chapter 8 will help you answer these questions.

Mesas and buttes

Most of the land in the Great Plains appears to be as level as the surface of the ocean. In some places, however, there are flat-topped hills called mesas. "Mesa" is the Spanish word for table. In other places, steep hills rise like skyscrapers above the plains. These hills are called buttes.* Many rivers that flow across the plains have carved deep valleys in the level surface of the land.

Grasslands and wheat fields

If we were to travel across the Great Plains in a car, the land would seem almost empty to us. We would see few cities or large towns. Sometimes we could look for miles in every direction

Refer to the picture above. What can you discover about wheat farming on the Great Plains? (Vast fields, mechanized farming, little manual labor, large crops.)

A cowhand roping a calf on a ranch in eastern Montana. A visitor to the Great Plains section would see many huge wheat farms and cattle ranches. What facts about the Great Plains help explain why this is so? Information in this chapter and Chapter 8 will help you answer this question.

without seeing a single farmhouse. We would notice that most of the land is covered with grass. Trees grow mainly along the banks of streams. In many places, we would see large fields of golden wheat or huge herds of grazing cattle.

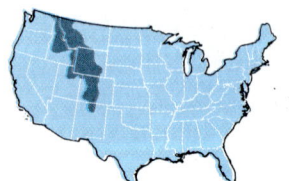

The Rocky Mountains

The Rocky Mountains rise to the west of the Great Plains. (See map on page 24.) These mountains are high and rugged. In the United States, they extend all the way from the Canadian border south into the state of New Mexico. Sparkling white snow covers the highest peaks all year long. Farther down on the mountainsides are grassy meadows. Here herds of sheep or cattle graze during the summer. On the lower slopes of the mountains there are large forests of pines and other evergreen trees.

Few people live in the Rocky Mountains. The mountain slopes are too steep and too cold for farming. It is hard to build roads and railroads through this rugged region.

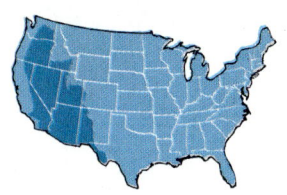

The Plateau Country

The Plateau Country is a large region that is bordered by mountains on the east, north, and west. High plateaus cover much of this region, but there are mountains and valleys in some places. This is the driest region of the West. There are few cities or large towns in the Plateau Country.

The Grand Teton Mountains of Wyoming are part of the Rocky Mountains region. Some of the rugged peaks in this region are so high that they are covered with snow all year long. Few people live in the Rocky Mountains region of the West. What do you think are the reasons for this?

The Columbia Plateau

At the northern end of the Plateau Country is the Columbia Plateau. It is named for a large river that flows through the area. Many thousands of years ago, hot, melted rock called lava poured from openings in the earth and formed the Columbia Plateau. As the lava cooled, it hardened. Little by little, wind and water wore away some of the rock to form a dark soil that is very good

Harvesting wheat on the Columbia Plateau. This picture was named for the great Columbia River. Compare the map on page 24 with the map on pages 8 and 9. What other major river also flows through this plateau?

Using Natural Resources

See Great Ideas

Fertile soil is one of the natural resources found in parts of the West. For example, the soil found on the Columbia Plateau is especially good for growing crops. Do research to discover how this soil was formed, and why it is so fertile.

Use Fideler Discovery Card 83 as an additional activity.

The Grand Canyon is in the Colorado Plateau. Millions of years ago, the land in this area was almost flat. As time passed, the Colorado River cut deeper and deeper into the earth's surface, forming the Grand Canyon. Today, this canyon is more than a mile deep in some places.

for growing crops. If we visited the northern part of the Columbia Plateau today, we would see rolling hills covered with wheat fields. In other parts of the plateau, we would see cattle grazing on grassy plains.

The Colorado Plateau

In the southeastern part of the Plateau Country is the Colorado Plateau. It is made up of many plateaus that lie several thousand feet above sea level. Here much of the land is almost flat. In some places, however, fast-flowing rivers such as the Colorado have cut deep, straight-sided valleys called canyons. One of these, the Grand Canyon, is more than a mile (1.6 km.) deep in some places. On the Colorado Plateau, there are masses of brightly colored

Refer to the picture above. Discuss why this has become one of the top tourist attractions of North America.

Joshua trees and yucca in southern Nevada. This area is part of the Basin and Range Country. Hundreds of short mountain ranges and wide valleys make up this region of the West.

rock that have been carved into strange shapes by wind and rivers. Pine forests cover the highest parts of the plateau. In other places there are wide stretches of grassland. Few roads or railroads cross this plateau. It is hard to build bridges across the deep canyons.

The Basin and Range Country

To the west and south of the Colorado Plateau there are hundreds of short mountain ranges. A range is a row of connected mountains. Between these ranges are wide basins.*

This whole area is called the Basin and Range Country. Here much of the land is so dry that few plants will grow on it. In some places the ground is dotted with sagebrush, or with cactus and other plants that can live without much water. From an airplane, the Basin and Range Country looks dusty-gray or tan. Only where water is available for irrigation* are there green farmlands. The deserts of southern California are part of the Basin and Range Country.

The northern part of the Basin and Range Country is called the Great Basin. Mountain streams that flow into the Great Basin have no way to escape to the sea. Their water collects in low spots and forms lakes. The hot sun dries up some of the water in these lakes.

the West. The map on page 24 shows us that this region contains two long mountain chains extending from north to south. The two mountain chains are separated by long valleys.

The chain of mountains to the east † has two parts. In the north is the Cascade Range. In the south is the Sierra Nevada. The peaks of these mountains are very high and steep sided.

The Cascade Range

The Cascade Range extends through Washington and Oregon into northern California. Several high, cone-shaped peaks tower above the other mountains in this area. These were formed many thousands of years ago by lava pouring out from openings in the earth called volcanoes.* Today the highest peaks of the Cascade Range are blanketed with glistening snow and ice the year around. In many places, the lower mountain slopes are covered with thick forests. There are few farms or towns in this rugged mountain area. The only low passageway through the Cascade Range is the valley of the Columbia River.

The Sierra Nevada

The Sierra Nevada gets its name from two Spanish words meaning "snowy range." This mountain range is more than 400 miles (644 km.) long. It was formed millions of years ago, when movements deep in the earth caused a huge block of stone to tilt upward into the sky. Only a few railroads and main highways cross the high, rugged Sierra Nevada. In the southern part of this range is Mount Whitney, the highest

When this happens, salt and other minerals are left behind. Therefore, some lakes in the Great Basin are very salty. The largest is Great Salt Lake. It is so salty that fish cannot live in it. Sometimes a lake dries up entirely, leaving a large patch of glistening white salt.

Pacific Mountains and Valleys

Between the Plateau Country and the Pacific Ocean is another land region of

† Refer to the map on page 24. Have students locate the Cascade Range and the Sierra Nevada on the map.

Refer to the picture and caption below. What do you think would have happened here if this had not been made a national park?

peak in the conterminous* United States. It rises 14,495 feet (4,418 m.) above the level of the sea.

The Central Valley

To the west of the high Sierra Nevada and the Cascade Range are two long valleys. One of these is the Central Valley of California, a broad lowland surrounded by mountains. This valley is about 50 miles (80 km.) wide and 450 miles (724 km.) long. In the Central Valley, the land is almost flat and the soil is fertile. This is one of the most important farming areas in the United States. Orchards, pastures, and fields of crops cover much of the land here.

Two important rivers flow through the Central Valley. One of these is the Sacramento River, which flows through the northern part of the valley. The other is the San Joaquin River, which flows through the southern part. (See the map on page 94.) These

Yosemite National Park is in a rugged mountain range called the Sierra Nevada. This range lies almost entirely in California. It is more than 400 miles (644 km.) long. In the southern part of the Sierra Nevada is Mount Whitney. It is one of the highest peaks in the United States.

two rivers join together near San Francisco Bay, and their waters flow into the bay.

The Puget-Willamette Lowland

The other valley is located in Washington and northern Oregon. It is called the Puget-Willamette Lowland. In the northern part of this valley is an inlet of the Pacific Ocean called Puget Sound. The Willamette River flows through the southern part of the valley. Here the soil is fertile, and much of the land is level enough for farming. If we were to fly over this valley in an airplane, we would see below us a patchwork of farms, meadows, and forests. We would also notice many towns and cities.

Mountains along the coast

A long chain of mountains extends from north to south along the Pacific coast of our country. These mountains

The Central Valley of California (right) lies to the west of the Sierra Nevada. This broad lowland is one of the most important farming areas in the United States. Why is this so? This chapter and Chapter 8 have information that will help you answer this question.

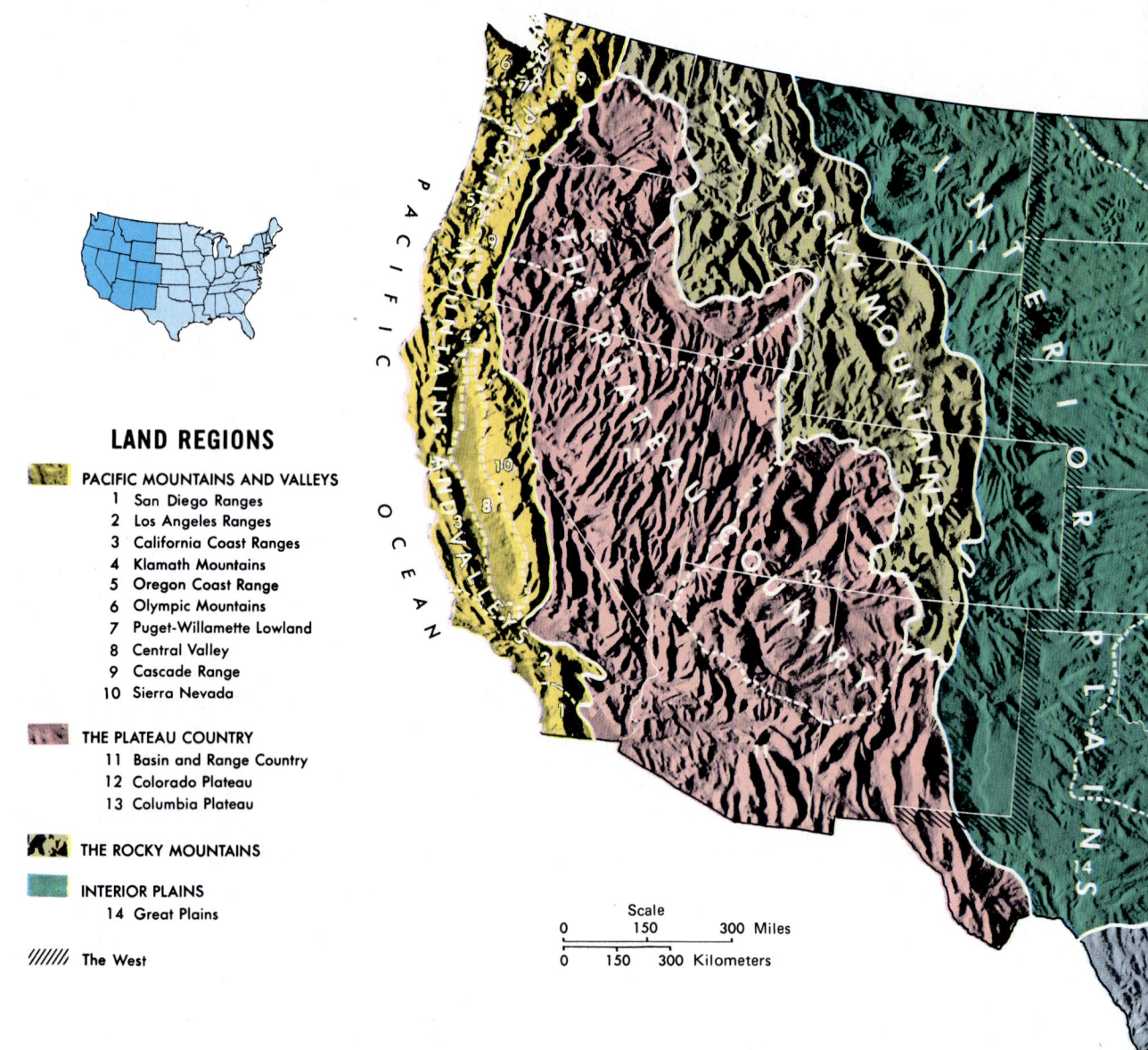

LAND REGIONS

PACIFIC MOUNTAINS AND VALLEYS
1. San Diego Ranges
2. Los Angeles Ranges
3. California Coast Ranges
4. Klamath Mountains
5. Oregon Coast Range
6. Olympic Mountains
7. Puget-Willamette Lowland
8. Central Valley
9. Cascade Range
10. Sierra Nevada

THE PLATEAU COUNTRY
11. Basin and Range Country
12. Colorado Plateau
13. Columbia Plateau

THE ROCKY MOUNTAINS

INTERIOR PLAINS
14. Great Plains

The West

are much lower than the Sierra Nevada or the Cascade Range. In some places, however, they are very steep sided. Rocky cliffs rise above the ocean in many places.

The long mountain chain along the coast is made up of several groups of mountains. (See map above.) In these mountains, much of the land is too steep and the soil is too poor for farming. Dense forests of firs, spruces, and other evergreen trees cover the mountains along the coast in Washington, Oregon, and northern California. Farther south, the forests give way to grasses and low, bushy plants.

Between the mountain ranges in southern California are several lowland areas. Although they are not very large, they are densely populated. In one lowland is Los Angeles, the largest city in the West.

† Assign these activities to help students develop social studies skills. Refer your students to the Skills Manual in this book.

† **Making Discoveries**

In this book and in other books look for information about one of the subjects below. Then write a short report about it. Use the questions given under each subject as a guide. Suggestions in the Skills Manual will help you find information and write a good report.

A. The Rocky Mountains
   1. How were the Rocky Mountains formed?
   2. About how old are the Rockies?
   3. What kinds of plants and animals are found in these mountains?
   4. How have the Rockies affected our country's history?
   5. What is the Continental Divide? (You may wish to draw a map showing the Continental Divide.)

B. The Grand Canyon
   1. How was the Grand Canyon formed?
   2. What kinds of plants and animals are found in the Grand Canyon?

Along the coast of California. Mountain ranges extend from north to south along our country's Pacific coast. These mountains are much lower than the Sierra Nevada or the Cascade Range.

Monument Valley, in Arizona. Much of the land in the West is too dry for growing crops. The land in these areas is used for grazing livestock such as cattle, sheep, and goats.

3 Climate

A visit to the dry lands of the West

It is a July afternoon, and we are riding in a car through the northern part of Nevada. (See map on page 8.) The land here is dry. Much of it is covered with sagebrush* or with clumps of grass that have turned yellow under the hot summer sun. The only trees we see are growing along the banks of streams.

By the next afternoon, we have reached southern Nevada. The sky is bright blue, and the sun is very hot. Our lips feel dry, and we are thirsty. The land here is even drier than the land we rode through before. We do not see any grass or sagebrush. Instead, we see cactus and other strange-looking desert plants. We drive many miles without seeing a river or a lake.

At last we come to a tiny town in the desert. Here we can buy gasoline and get water to drink. A thermometer in the gas station shows that the temperature is 110° F. (43° C.).† We are glad when evening comes. As we watch a beautiful red-and-gold sunset over the desert, we notice that the air is growing cooler.

†F. means Fahrenheit scale
C. means Celsius scale
*See Glossary

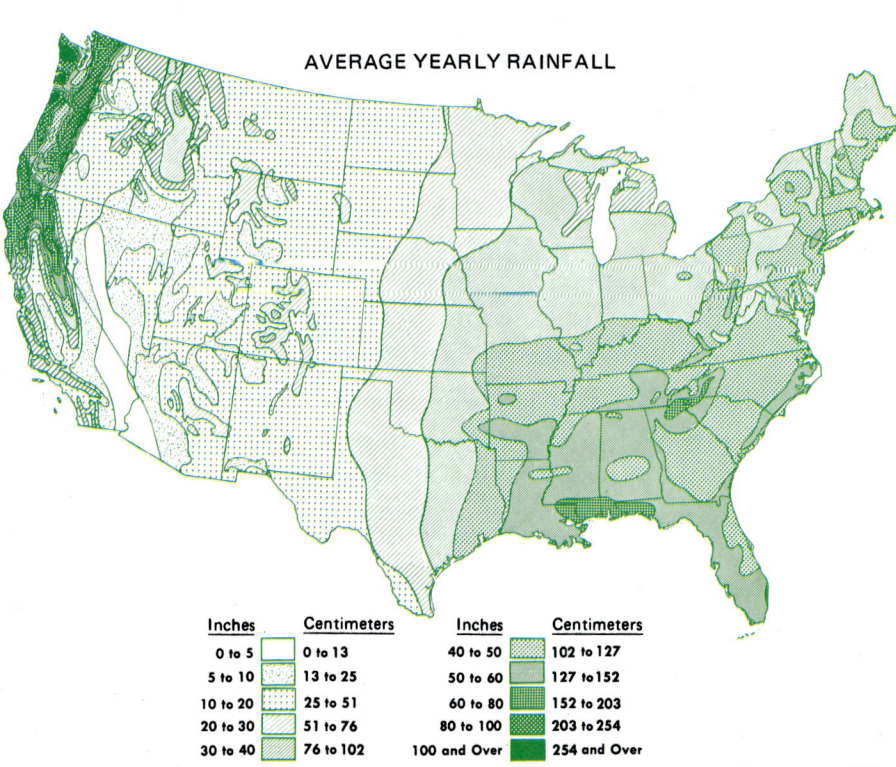

Areas of little rainfall

If we could travel all over the West, we would find many places that are like the ones we have just visited. Most parts of the West are very dry. The map on page 27 shows how much rain usually falls each year in different parts of the United States. Notice that most parts of the West receive less than 20 inches (51 cm.)† of rainfall a year. This is not enough rainfall for most trees to grow. Much of the land in these areas is covered with grass or sagebrush. These plants do not need as much water to grow as trees do.

Because the West is so dry, much of the land here is used for raising cattle, sheep, and goats. These animals can feed on the grass that grows in dry places. Most kinds of farm crops do not grow well where rainfall is less than 20 inches (51 cm.) a year. Farmers who want to grow crops in these dry lands must bring water from other places to moisten the soil. This is called irrigation. (See Chapter 9.)

Some parts of the West are so dry that they are called deserts. Here, there is too little rainfall for grass, or even sagebrush, to grow. The land is dotted with cactus, yucca,* and other desert plants.

In the desert lands of the West, weeks, or months often pass without a drop of rain. Then there will be a sudden shower that lasts only a few minutes. After the shower, bright desert flowers burst into bloom. For a short time, they make the barren desert seem like a garden.

Areas of heavy rainfall

Not all of the West is dry. In fact, one small area in the state of Washing-

ton gets more rain than any other place in the conterminous* United States. We can learn more about the wet lands of the West by driving through the mountains of the Cascade Range in Washington.

A light, gentle rain is falling as we drive along a twisting road through the

† cm. means centimeter

Dense forests grow in the coastal mountains of California, where the rainfall is heavy. What are some of the facts that help to explain why the rainiest parts of the West are in the mountains?

mountains. On each side of the road are thick forests of firs, spruces, and other evergreen trees. Sometimes we catch a glimpse of bright-green fields and pastures in a valley far below. Because everything looks so fresh and green, we know that much rain falls in this area. Farmers in the valley do not usually have to irrigate their fields, because there is enough rain for most crops to grow.

Why rainfall is heavy in some areas

Rainfall is heaviest in parts of the West where there are mountains. All year long, moist winds from the Pacific

The West 29

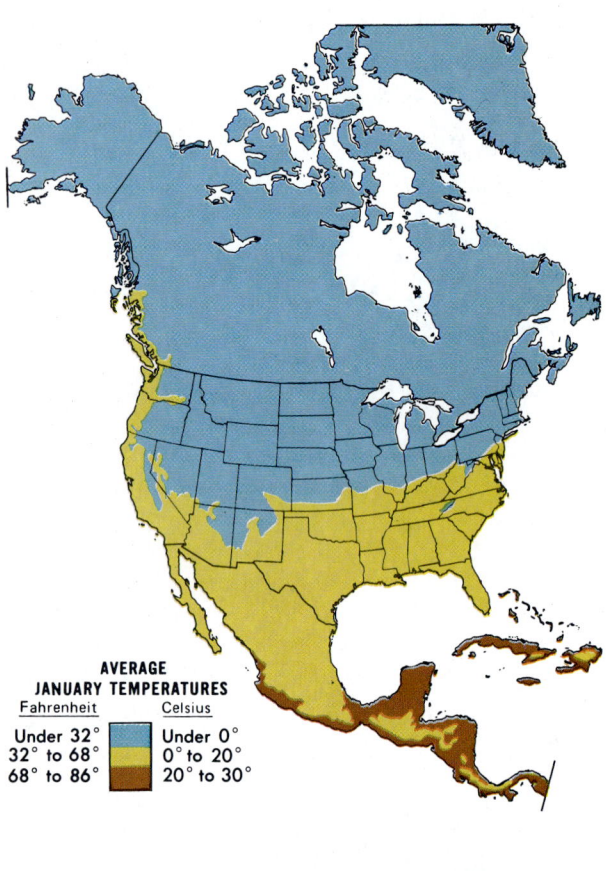

AVERAGE JANUARY TEMPERATURES
Fahrenheit / Celsius
Under 32° / Under 0°
32° to 68° / 0° to 20°
68° to 86° / 20° to 30°

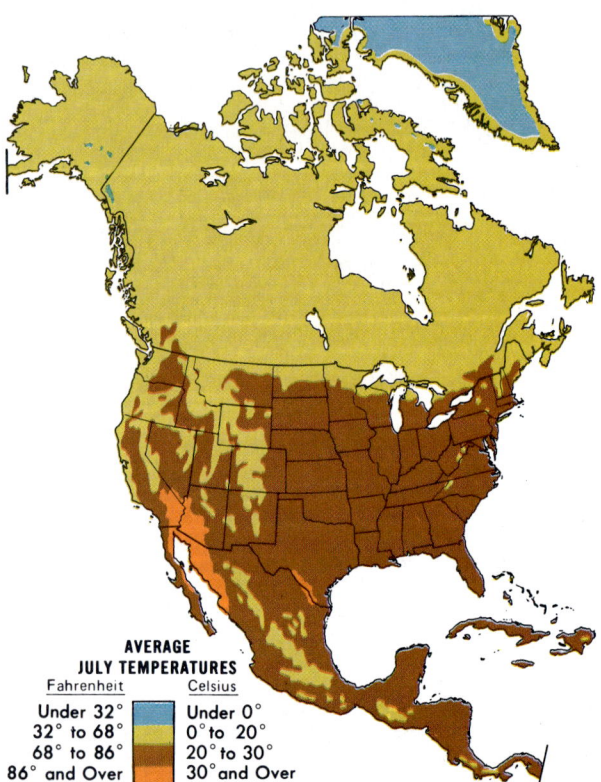

AVERAGE JULY TEMPERATURES
Fahrenheit / Celsius
Under 32° / Under 0°
32° to 68° / 0° to 20°
68° to 86° / 20° to 30°
86° and Over / 30° and Over

Ocean blow toward the western coast of the United States. These winds contain much water that has evaporated* from the ocean. As the moist winds reach the mountains, they are forced to rise. The higher they rise above the level of the sea, the cooler they become. Cool air cannot hold as much moisture as warmer air, so part of the moisture falls to earth in the form of rain or snow. For this reason, rainfall is heavy on the mountains along the Pacific coast and on the western slopes of the Sierra Nevada and the Cascade Range. It is very heavy in the western parts of Washington and Oregon. Here, the yearly rainfall may be more than 100 inches (254 cm.).

By the time the winds blowing from the west have crossed the mountains, they have lost much of their moisture. As they move down the eastern slopes of the mountains, the winds become warmer. Instead of giving off moisture, they take up moisture from the land. This is one reason why the land to the east of the mountains is so dry. We say that it lies in the "rain shadow" of the mountains.

The winds continue to blow eastward until they reach the Rocky Mountains. Again they are forced to rise and give off some of their moisture. But this time the winds do not contain as much moisture as they did when they blew in from the ocean. For this reason, the Rocky Mountains do not receive as much rainfall as the mountains that lie farther to the west.

During the winter, most of the moisture in the air falls on the mountains in the form of snow. In the high Sierra Nevada and in the Cascade Range, the snow is often very deep. The railroads

Refer to the maps and map keys above. Have students compare average January temperatures in Nevada with average July temperatures there. (Use map on pages 8-9 to locate Nevada.)

Refer to the picture below. Have you ever hiked through mountains like this? Describe your experiences.

that cross these mountains must use giant snowplows to clear the tracks so that the trains can get through. In the spring, the melting snow helps to fill the rivers of the West with fresh water.

Differences in temperature

In the West, there are great differences in temperature from one place to another. You can see this if you study the two maps on the opposite page. These maps show average temperatures

Hikers near Mount Rainier, in Washington's Cascade Range. Mount Rainier is one of the highest peaks in the West. Summer weather is cooler in the mountains than it is in the lowlands. Why is this so?

Winter in Montana. Winters in the northern parts of the Great Plains and the Plateau Country are generally very cold, while summers are often quite hot. What facts help to explain why this is so?

in North America during the months of January and July.

On the January temperature map, find the part of the West where the average temperatures are below $32°$ F. ($0°$ C.). You can tell that winters are cold in this area, because $32°$ F. is the temperature at which water freezes. In the rest of the West, the average temperatures during the month of January are between $32°$ and $68°$ F. ($0°$ and $20°$ C.). This is neither very hot nor

Refer to the picture above. Can you discover changes in cattle ranching from the days of the early settlers in the West? Explain.

either warm or hot during the summer. In other parts of the West, summers are mild. You will find out some of the reasons for these differences as you study about the climate in different parts of the West.

Climate of the plains and plateaus

In the northern parts of the Great Plains and the Plateau Country, winters are cold and summers are very warm. For example, in eastern Montana the temperature sometimes drops to -30° F. (-34° C.) on winter nights. But on a summer afternoon the temperature here may rise to more than 100° F. (38° C.).

Why are winters so cold and summers so warm in these parts of the West? First, these areas are shut off from the Pacific Ocean by high mountains. Also, they are far from any other large body of water. So they are not cooled in summer or warmed in winter by mild ocean breezes. †

Farther south in the Great Plains and the Plateau Country, winters are milder and summers are warmer than they are in the north. Usually the southern part of our country has higher temperatures than the northern part. The reasons for this are explained in "The Seasons of the Year," on pages 34 and 35.

Climate of the high mountains

Winters are cold in the Rocky Mountains, the Sierra Nevada, and other high mountains of the West. For several months each year, the ground is buried under a deep blanket of snow. Some peaks are covered with snow the year around.

During the summer, the weather in the mountains is seldom very warm.

very cold, so we can say that winters are mild in this part of the West.

Now look at the July temperature map. You can see that in some parts of the West, the average temperatures are above 68° F. Here the weather is

† Refer to the map on page 24. What mountains shut these areas off from the Pacific Ocean?

THE SEASONS

The year is divided into four natural periods, or seasons. We call them summer, autumn, winter, and spring. Each season is marked by changes in the length of day and night and by changes in temperature.

The seasons are caused by the tilt of the earth's axis and the revolution of the earth around the sun. It takes one year for the earth to revolve around the sun. On this trip, the earth remains tilted at the same angle to the path along which it travels. The chart below shows how this causes the Northern Hemisphere to be tilted toward the sun on June 21 and away from the sun on December 22. On March 21 and September 22, the Northern Hemisphere is tilted neither toward the sun nor away from it.

The chart on the left shows that on June 21 the sun shines directly on the Tropic of Cancer.* This is the northernmost point ever reached by the sun's direct rays. In the Northern Hemisphere, June 21 is the first day of summer and the longest day of the year.

The chart on the right shows that on December 22 the sun shines directly on the Tropic of Capricorn.* This is the southernmost point ever reached by the sun's direct

SUMMER IN THE NORTHERN HEMISPHERE

The chart above shows how the earth is lighted by the sun at noon on June 21, the first day of summer in the Northern Hemisphere.

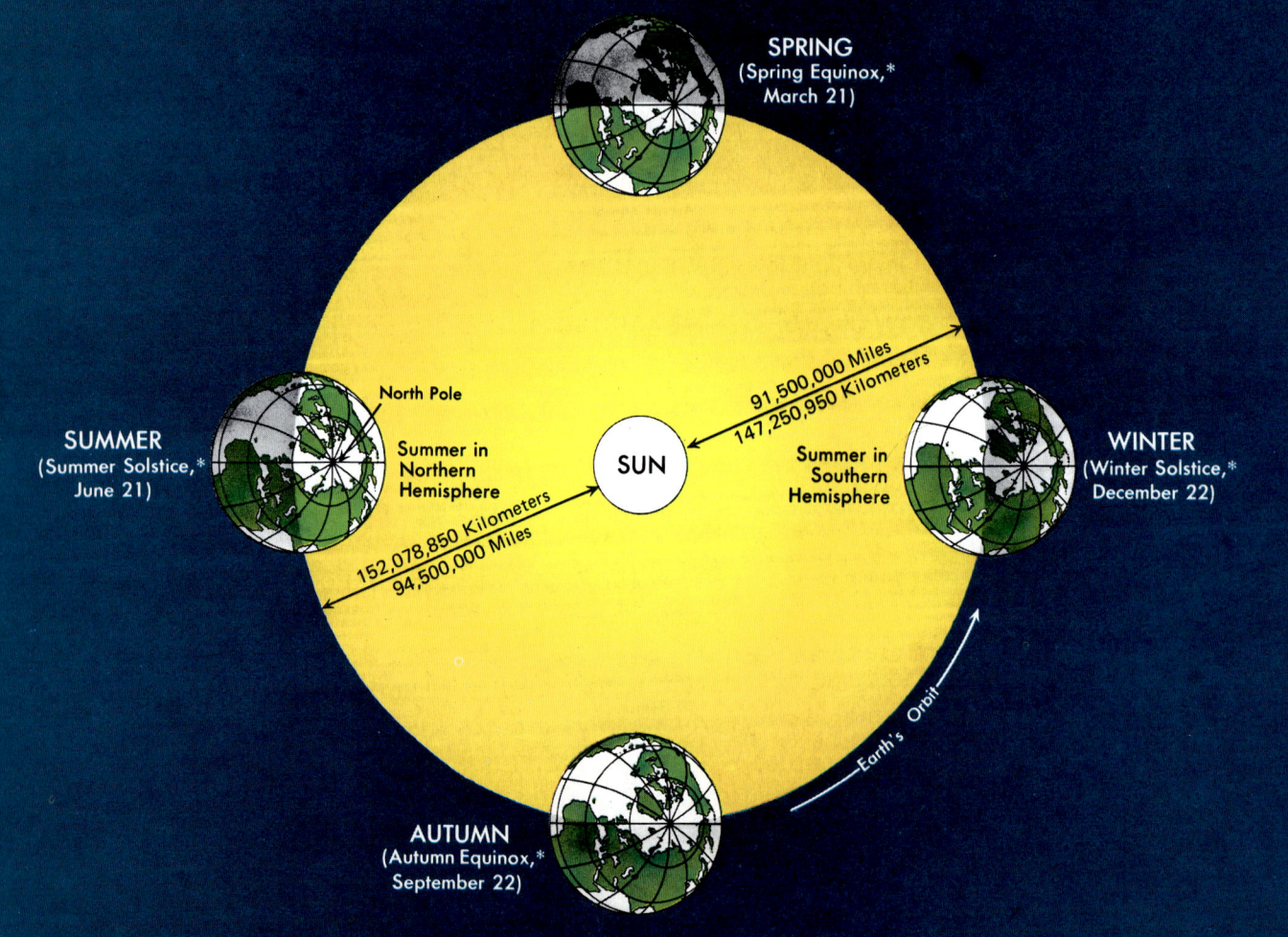

OF THE YEAR

rays. In the Northern Hemisphere, December 22 is the first day of winter and the shortest day of the year.

When one hemisphere is tilted toward the sun, the other is tilted away from the sun. For this reason, the seasons in the Southern Hemisphere are just the opposite of those in the Northern Hemisphere. Summer in the Southern Hemisphere begins on December 22, and winter begins on June 21.

Temperatures are affected by the slant of the sun's rays as they strike the surface of the earth. Study the chart below, and the picture of San Diego, California, to help you understand why this is true.

Near the equator, the sun is almost directly overhead throughout the year. For this reason, the weather near the equator is always hot, except in the mountains. In areas farther away from the equator, the sun's rays are more slanted. Therefore, the weather is usually cooler.

The southern part of the United States is nearer the equator than the northern part. This helps to explain why the weather is generally warmer in the southern part of our country than it is in the northern part.

*See Glossary

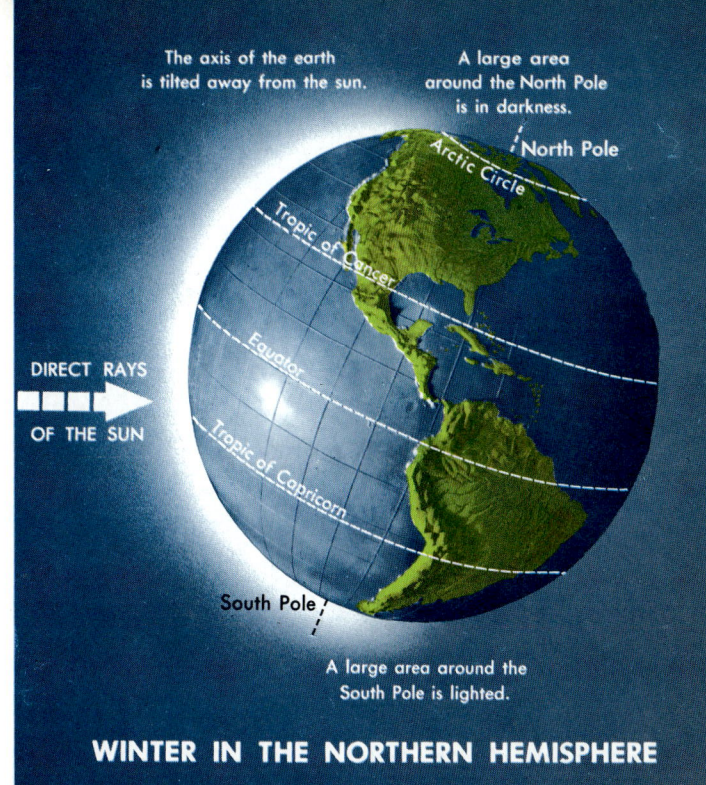

WINTER IN THE NORTHERN HEMISPHERE

The chart above shows how the earth is lighted by the sun at noon on December 22, the first day of winter in the Northern Hemisphere.

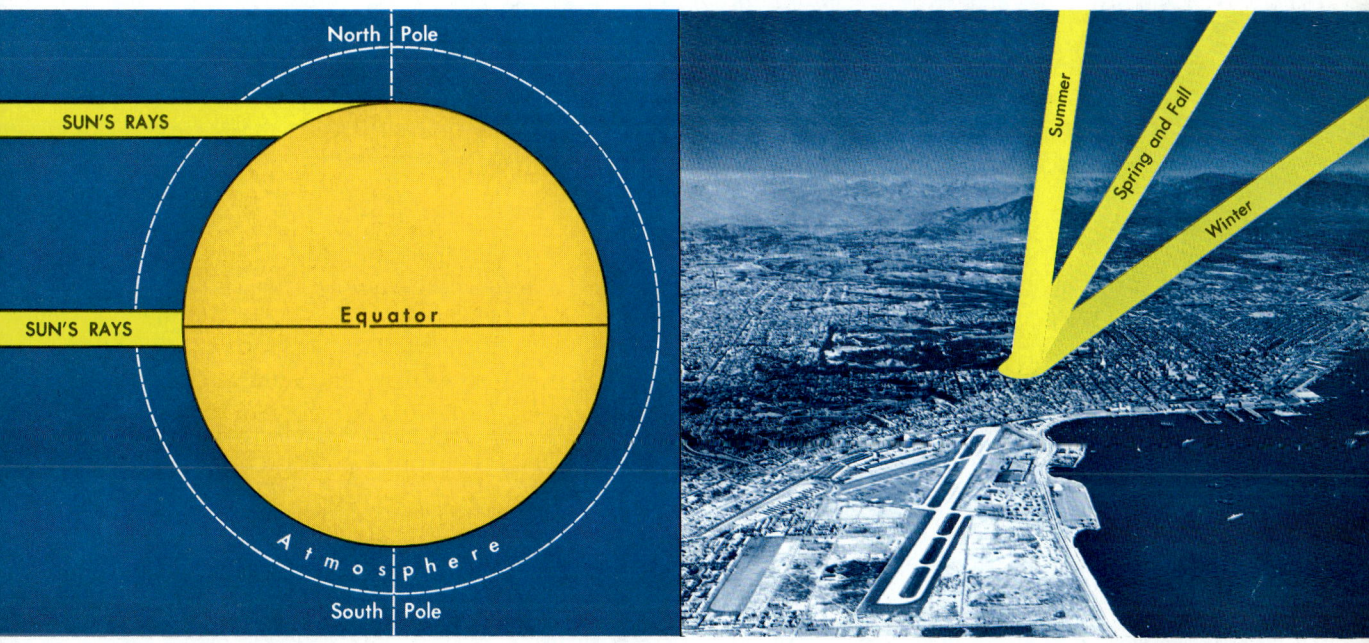

The chart above shows that when the sun's rays strike the earth at a slant, they must travel through more atmosphere, or air, than when they strike it directly. This affects temperatures because the air soaks up heat from the sun's rays. The more air the rays must pass through, the less heat they hold to warm the earth. This is one reason why temperatures are higher if the sun is directly overhead than they are if the sun is low in the sky.

This picture also helps to explain how changes in temperature are caused by the different angles at which the sun's rays strike the earth. During the summer, the noon sun is high in the sky. The rays of the sun are concentrated into small areas. For this reason, they give large amounts of heat. During the winter, the noon sun is lower in the sky. The slanting rays of the sun are spread over much wider areas, so they give less heat.

Refer to the picture and caption on these pages. Use the questions in a class discussion about meeting physical needs.

Many people come to the mountains in the summertime to enjoy the cool, refreshing air.

The mountains of the West are usually cooler than nearby lowlands because they are so much higher above the level of the sea. The higher you go above sea level, the cooler the air becomes.

As you may have learned in your science class, the earth gives off heat that it has received from the sun. Near sea level, much of this heat is held by tiny bits of dust and moisture in the air. High above sea level, the air is much cleaner and drier. It cannot hold as much heat. For this reason, the temperature is usually cooler at high altitudes* than it is at low altitudes.

In the high mountains, the growing season is less than four months long. (See map on page 38.) The growing season is the time when crops can be grown outdoors without danger of being killed by frost. Farmers cannot grow crops when the temperature is below freezing. They must plant their crops after the last heavy frost in the spring, and harvest them before the first heavy frost in the fall. Because the growing season is so short in the mountains, farmers must grow crops that do not take a long time to ripen. Among these crops are potatoes and barley.

Climate in the southern part of the West

Winters are mild all the way across the southern part of the West except in the high mountains. (See the top map on page 30.) In southern California, Arizona, and New Mexico, winter days are often warm and sunny. Snow seldom falls in these areas.

The people who live in the southernmost part of the West are able to work and play outdoors all year long. They enjoy the mild

See Needs of People

In the high mountains of the West, winters are long and cold. For several months each year, the ground is buried under a deep blanket of snow. In fact, some of the highest peaks are covered with snow even in summer. As a class, discuss the following questions. Information in this book and other books will help you prepare for your discussion.
1. Do you think the people in this picture have the same physical needs that you do? Do they need food? Clothing? Exercise?
2. In what ways does the climate of the West's high mountains affect the ways in which people meet their physical needs in the winter? In the summer?
3. At what time of the year would you most like to visit the high mountains of the West? Why do you feel this way?

The West 37

† Could crops like cotton be grown in the high mountains? What are some crops that could be grown?

winters. When they go outside, they do not have to wear heavy clothing. Many bright flowers bloom even during the winter. Thousands of people from the northern part of our country come here for winter vacations.

During the summer, the weather in the southern part of the West is usually warm or hot. There are many summer days when the temperature in the deserts rises above 100° F. (38° C.).

† In some places in the southern part of the West, the growing season lasts more than eight months. (See map below.) Here, farmers can grow cotton and other crops that ripen slowly.

Crops can be grown all year long in some parts of southern California and southern Arizona. In these areas, there is seldom a frost. Farmers can grow such warm-weather crops as oranges and lemons. They can also grow vegetables outdoors during the wintertime. Some of these vegetables are sold to people in colder parts of our country.

Climate along the Pacific coast

In most places along the Pacific coast of the West, the weather is mild the year around. (See maps on page 30.) Snow usually falls only on the mountains. The growing season is longer here than in places farther inland.

This part of the West has mild weather all year long because it lies near the Pacific Ocean. Like all large bodies of water, the ocean is warmer than the land in winter and cooler than the land in summer. All year, winds that blow eastward from the ocean bring mild weather to the lands along the coast.

The growing season is the period of time during which crops can be grown outdoors without danger of being killed by frost. In the West, there are great differences in the length of the growing season.

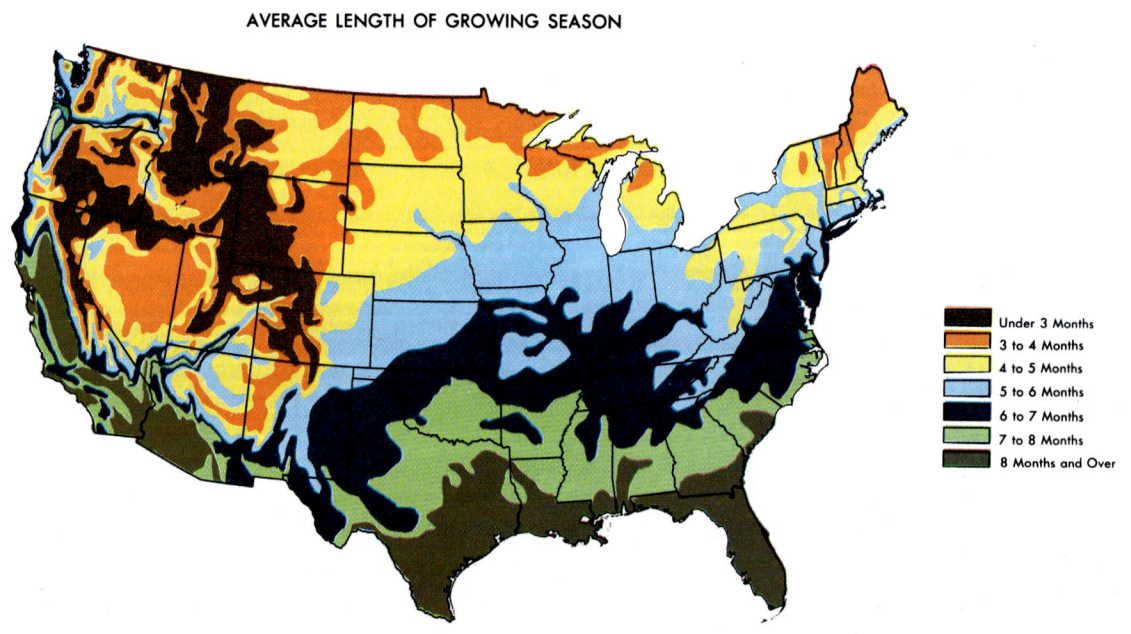

AVERAGE LENGTH OF GROWING SEASON

Under 3 Months
3 to 4 Months
4 to 5 Months
5 to 6 Months
6 to 7 Months
7 to 8 Months
8 Months and Over

Refer to the map and key above. Why do you think the length of the growing season varies so greatly from area to area in the West?

Freedom
See Great Ideas

Surfers riding a wave in the Pacific Ocean, along the coast of southern California. The climate here is mild enough for people to enjoy summer sports for many months of the year. Do you think these surfers have a feeling of freedom? What makes you think this? Have there been times in your own life when you felt completely free? When were those times? Do any persons ever have the freedom to do just as they please, or are there always limits on freedom? Think carefully about this question before giving your answer.

† **Problems To Solve**
1. Winter weather varies from place to place in the West. Winters are cold in some areas and mild in others. Why is this so? In making hypotheses* to solve this problem you will need to consider how temperatures in different parts of the West are affected by the following:
   a. distance from the equator
   b. height above sea level
   c. distance from large bodies of water

2. How does the climate in different parts of the West affect farming? To solve this problem, you will need to consider facts about each of the following:
   a. the length of the growing season in different parts of the West
   b. the amount of rainfall in these areas
   c. the kinds of crops that are grown
   d. the kinds of livestock that are raised
   Chapter 8 contains information that will be helpful in solving this problem.
   See Skills Manual, "Thinking and Solving Problems"

† Have students solve these problems.
Use Fideler Discovery Cards 26 or 29, or Fideler Discovery Sheets, Volume 1, pages 13-16 for additional activities about climate.

† Use these questions to start students thinking about the people of the West.

Part 2
People

Many different groups of people make their homes in the West. As you do research about the people of the West, you will discover why so many different groups live in this part of our country. You may also wish to find answers to the following questions.

†
- Why have so many people come to the West to live during the last one hundred years?
- Why does much of the West have few people? Why do some areas have many people?
- What are some of the largest cities in the West? Why did these cities grow up where they did?
- How are the communities in our country governed?
- What makes a successful community? Why are some communities in our country unsuccessful?
- What important artists have lived and worked in the West?

The chapters in Part 2 will help you answer these questions. Use maps, charts, and pictures, as well as text, to get the information you need.

Use Fideler Discovery Cards 57-82, or Fideler Discovery Sheets, Volume 1, pages 25-36 for additional activities.

A computer center in California. Do you think the people in this picture have the same needs as you do? Do you think they meet their needs in the same way? Explain your answers.

4 People

A growing region

In the 1840's, pioneers began moving to the West over the Oregon Trail.* Ever since then, large numbers of people have been moving to the West. Some of these people have come from other countries. But most of them have come from different parts of the United States.

Today, the population of the West is still growing rapidly. More than 38 million people now make their homes in the West. Even though so many people live in the West, this region is still not crowded. The West makes up almost one third of the area of the United States. But only about one sixth of our country's people live here.

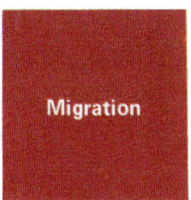
Migration

People in San Francisco, California. For more than one hundred years, large numbers of people have been moving to the West. This movement of people out of one region or country into another is known as migration. Do research in this chapter. Then answer the following questions about migration and population density in the West.

1. In what parts of the West do large numbers of people live?
2. What are some of the reasons why people may have settled in these parts of the West?
3. What part of the West would you most like to live in? Give reasons for your answer.

The West 43

Much of the West has few people

In much of the West there are few people. (See map on page 46.) In some places, a traveler can drive for many miles across lonely plains without seeing another person.

Several facts help to explain why so much of the West has so few people. As Chapter 2 explained, water is scarce in many places. People cannot live without a steady supply of fresh water. Also, farmers need water in order to grow crops.

There are some other reasons why much of the West has few people. Many areas of the West do not have railroads or paved highways. Mountains and canyons* make it hard to build them. Also, in much of the West there is very little industry to provide jobs. (See Chapter 10.)

Many people live in California

More people live in the state of California than in the other ten states of the West together.

California is now the home of about 22 million people. It has a larger population than any other state in the United States. Many Californians live in the southern part of the state. Here are the great cities of Los Angeles and San Diego. (See map on page 8.) Many people also live farther north, in an area around San Francisco Bay. The cities of San Francisco and Oakland are located here. There are also large numbers of people in the Central Valley.

Why many people live in California

There are several reasons why California has so many people. In many parts of the state, the weather is mild most of the time. Many people who used to live in places where winter is cold have moved to California. Here they enjoy pleasant weather during most of the year. People also move to California because there are many interesting places to visit. There are sandy beaches and high mountains. There are dense forests and sparkling lakes. California also has five national parks.

Many of the people in California came here to find work. In the 1940's, many huge factories were built in this state. These factories make airplanes, automobiles, clothing, and many other kinds of goods. Today, millions of people work in these factories and in other businesses.

As more people moved to California, still more jobs were created. The families that arrived each year needed homes. In order to meet this need, new houses and apartment buildings were built. This provided many jobs for builders. The newcomers also needed food, furniture, and other goods. New factories were built to make these goods. Also, new stores and shopping centers were opened. As a result, more workers were needed in factories, stores, and offices. As California's population continued to grow, more people were also needed to provide different kinds of services. These people included doctors, teachers, and police officers.

People in other parts of the West

Outside of California, there are only a few areas in the West where large numbers of people live. One of these is the Puget-Willamette Lowland in Washington and Oregon. Many cities, towns, and farms are located in this lowland. The two largest cities—Seattle,

Portland, Oregon, and **Seattle, Washington,** are in the Puget-Willamette Lowland. This is one of the few parts of the West where large numbers of people live. As you can see by the map on page 46, most of the West's densely populated areas are in California.

Have students compare the map below with the map on page 61. How important is good transportation to people who live in large cities? Explain.

Washington, and Portland, Oregon—are busy seaports. Factories and offices in these cities provide jobs for many thousands of people.

Most of the other people in the West live in or near a few large cities. (Compare the map below with the map on page 61.) These cities are located along main transportation routes. They are served by good highways, railroads, and airlines. Farmers and ranchers come from many miles away to buy the goods they need. Many people in these cities work in stores and offices. Others have factory jobs. Thousands of retired workers and other people have moved to Arizona and New Mexico. They like the warm, sunny climate there.

Many groups of people

Through the years, people have come to the West from many parts of the world. Today, people of many different races and national* origins make their homes in this part of the United States.

People of European descent

More than three fourths of the people in the West are descended from people who came to North America from Europe. Our country was settled mainly by people from the British Isles. These people brought the English language and many customs to the colonies.* It is not surprising that many people in the West are of English, Scotch, or Irish descent.

There are also many people in the West whose ancestors* came from other parts of Europe. For example, many of the people in Colorado, Washington, and Oregon are of German descent.

Mexican-Americans

More than two million Mexican-Americans live in the West. About four fifths of these people were born in the

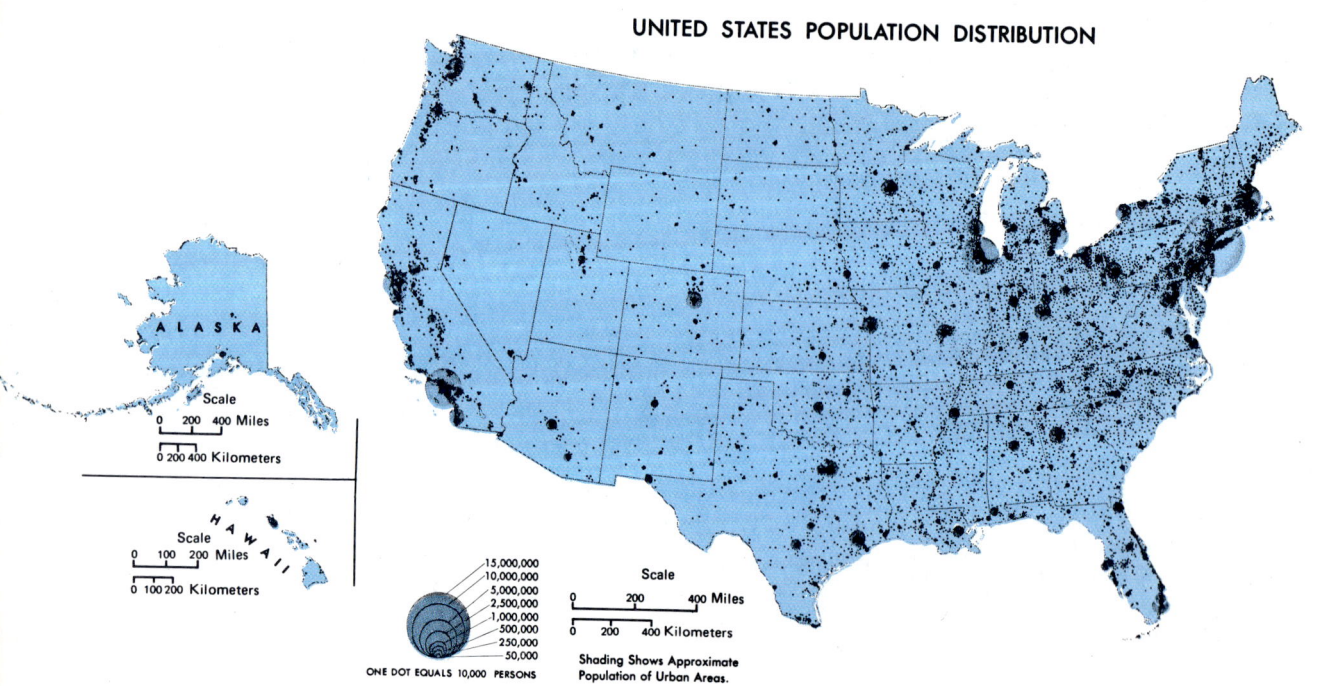

UNITED STATES POPULATION DISTRIBUTION

Language

See Great Ideas

Mexican-Americans in San Francisco. More than two million Mexican-Americans make their homes in the West. In the past, many of these people were thought of as "outsiders." This was partly because they spoke Spanish instead of English. Today, more and more Mexican-Americans are using the English language. Do you think it is important for people in our country to speak English? Why do you think this? Do you think it would be a good thing to speak both Spanish and English? Explain.

United States. The others have come here from Mexico. Some Mexican-Americans earn their living as farmers. Most of them live and work in or near Los Angeles and other large cities.

People from Mexico were coming to the West even before the Pilgrims came to America. Some of the early Mexican settlements were in areas that are now part of New Mexico or California.

Until recent years, people of Mexican descent* were often thought of as "outsiders." They spoke Spanish instead of English, and many of them dropped out of school at an early age.

Today, more Mexican-Americans are getting the education they need to hold well-paying jobs. Some are doctors, lawyers, or teachers. Others work in stores, factories, or government offices. Many of these people live in comfortable, modern homes. They enjoy the same conveniences as most other Americans.

Refer to the picture and caption above. Use the caption questions in a class discussion about language.

The West 47

Fishermen in the West. Nearly two million people of African descent make their homes in the West. Many of them live in Los Angeles, San Francisco, and the other large cities of California.

Many Mexican-Americans are also taking an active role in government. During the 1960's, thousands of Mexican-Americans registered to vote for the first time. A number of political groups have been formed by Mexican-Americans. These groups support candidates who have promised to help Mexican-Americans meet their needs and solve their problems.

People of African descent

Nearly two million people of African descent live in the West. They live mainly in the large cities of California. Many of them have moved to the West from other parts of our country.

For many years, black Americans did not enjoy the same freedoms as most other citizens. For example, some business people refused to hire black workers. Some apartment owners refused to rent to black families.

Today, laws have been passed to prevent discrimination.* Under these laws, black people have an equal opportunity with all other citizens to get good jobs. There are also laws that forbid discrimination in housing. Black people enjoy other rights and freedoms as well. As a result, more black people now have good jobs in business and industry. Some of them work in medicine, education, and other fields. Others are

† Do you think our government was right in doing this? (Discuss overall anger and mood of the country at this time.)

lawyers or government leaders. More black Americans now have the opportunities they need in order to live happy and successful lives.

People of Asian descent

Many people in the West are of Asian descent. Almost all of them are Japanese, Chinese, or Filipino. Thousands of these people live in the West's large cities. For example, there is a section called "Chinatown" in San Francisco. Large numbers of people of Chinese descent live and work in this section.

Like Mexican-Americans and blacks, people of Asian descent have often been denied rights and freedoms that other Americans enjoy. For example, during World War II,* many loyal Americans suffered from discrimination. This was because their ancestors came from Japan. When Japan became our enemy, it was feared that these people might be disloyal to our country. Because of this fear, our government moved more than 100,000 of these Japanese-Americans away from their homes on the Pacific coast. They were kept in camps that were located far inland. They were not permitted to return to their homes until the war was nearly over. †

Today, the people of Asian descent in the West enjoy the same rights and

People of Japanese descent at a festival in Seattle. Thousands of people who live in the West's large cities are of Asian descent. Many of them are Japanese. Others are Chinese or Filipino.

† How would you feel if you and your family were taken from your home and moved onto a reservation against your will? Explain your answer.

freedoms that other Americans do. They vote and hold government offices. They have an opportunity to get a good education. They also have many opportunities to hold well-paying jobs. Some are doctors or teachers. Others have their own businesses. Still others work in stores or factories.

Native Americans

Nearly 400,000 Indians, or Native Americans, live in the West. About half of these people make their homes in California and Arizona. Other states in the West with large populations of Native Americans are New Mexico and Washington.

Like the other minority* peoples in our country, Native Americans have suffered from discrimination. During the last half of the 1800's, most of the Indian tribes in the West were forced to move onto reservations.* †

Life was not easy for the people who lived on Indian reservations. In many cases, the only way to make a living was by farming. But much of the land on the reservations was not good for

A Navaho Indian woman. Nearly 400,000 Indians, or Native Americans, make their homes in the West.

See Great Ideas

The picture above shows a classroom on an Indian reservation in New Mexico. Do you think going to school is a good way of getting an education? Why do you think this? The picture on the opposite page shows a Navaho Indian woman weaving. How do you suppose she learned this skill? Do you think learning in this way can also be called education? What are some of the skills you have learned? How did you learn them?

growing crops. Also, many Indians had little interest in farming.

To add to their problems, the Indians on reservations were not allowed to govern themselves. The United States government treated them like children who had to be kept out of trouble. It gave the Indians few chances to decide things for themselves.

In recent years, the federal government has done a number of things to help the Indians on reservations. Many groups of Indians now make some of their own laws. They can also set up courts to judge Indians accused of crimes that are not very serious. The federal government has also helped to create new job opportunities for Indians. A number of factories have been built on or near the reservations. With the help of money loaned by the government, many groups of Indians have started businesses.

Work as a Social* Scientist

The picture on pages 42-43 shows people in a large city in the West. Think and work with this picture as a social scientist does. Study the picture and record your findings.

1. Where do you think this picture was taken? Why do you think this?
2. Do you think the people in this picture are similar to the people where you live? Explain your answer.
3. What does this picture tell you about ways in which the people of this city meet their needs? (See "Needs of People" at the back of this book.)
4. What does this picture tell you about ways in which people earn their living in this city?

† Have students look up the term "social scientist" in the Glossary. Assign "Work as a Social Scientist."

† Use this problem to start students thinking about cities of the West.

5 Cities

A Problem To Solve

The West is a very rapidly growing region. It has a population of more than 38 million. Yet many parts of the West are very thinly populated. For example, Wyoming is the ninth largest state in our country. It has an area as large as the states of New York and Pennsylvania together. Even so, Wyoming has a smaller population than any other state.

Almost half of the people of the West live in or near a few large cities such as Los Angeles, San Francisco, Seattle, and Denver. Why is this so? In forming hypotheses* to solve this problem, think about how the population distribution of the West is affected by the following:
1. climate
2. transportation routes
3. ways of earning a living in the West

See Skills Manual, "Thinking and Solving Problems"
*See Glossary

Rules and Government

See Great Ideas

Los Angeles is the largest city in the West and the third largest in our country. More than two and a half million people live here. Do you think so many people could live together in one city if they didn't follow certain rules? Why? Why not? What are some of the rules people must follow to live and work together successfully in large cities? Are rules also needed by people who live in small towns? Explain your answer.

† Have students look up the word "metropolitan" in the Glossary. Discuss the difference between a city and a metropolitan area.

About five out of every six people in the West live in cities or large towns. Most of the large cities here are on or near the Pacific coast. In two western states, Montana and Wyoming, there are no cities with more than 100,000 people.

† In recent years, metropolitan* areas in the West have been growing rapidly in population. (See chart at right.) Today, some metropolitan areas have more than twice as many people as they did twenty years ago.

SIX METROPOLITAN AREAS

Metropolitan Area	Population of Entire Area	Population of Central City (or Cities)
Los Angeles-Long Beach	7,004,400	2,737,000 343,000
San Francisco-Oakland	3,158,900	660,000 338,000
Anaheim-Santa Ana-Garden Grove	1,755,600	202,000 181,000 120,000
San Diego	1,623,400	805,000
Denver-Boulder	1,442,500	502,000 84,400
Seattle-Everett	1,421,700	505,000 52,800

The six largest metropolitan* areas in the West are listed above. Their populations are given in the middle column. For each of these areas, the population of the central city or cities is also given.

*See Glossary

Los Angeles

The largest city in the West is Los Angeles, California. Except for New York and Chicago, Los Angeles is larger than any other city in the United States. It spreads across a lowland in the southern part of California. To the north and east of Los Angeles are ranges of rugged mountains. The Pacific Ocean lies to the west and south.

Los Angeles and its neighboring cities have grown so close together that it is difficult to tell where one ends and another begins. Altogether, there are more than seventy-five cities in the huge metropolitan area that includes Los Angeles. The largest of these cities, except for Los Angeles, is Long Beach. South and east of Los Angeles are other metropolitan areas.

If you were to fly over the Los Angeles-Long Beach metropolitan area, you would see large groups of one-story houses. You would see schools and shopping centers. Most of the buildings you would see are low. However, in some places, there are groups of tall office buildings and hotels. Many freeways* pass through Los Angeles and its neighboring cities. They make it easier for people to travel from one place to another in this huge metropolitan area.

Industry

There are thousands of factories in and near Los Angeles. Some of them make airplanes or electronic* equipment. Other factories assemble automobiles or make tires and other automobile parts. Many factories in the Los Angeles area process* oranges, vegetables, and other crops. These crops are raised on the rich farmlands of southern California. Los Angeles is a leading producer of sports clothing, dresses, and furniture. The television and motion picture industries are also important here.

A leading seaport

Los Angeles is the most important seaport in the West. This city has one of the world's largest artificial harbors. To form this harbor, a breakwater*

The West 53

had to be built. Then channels were dug into the land. Along the channels, piers were built where ships could dock. Each year millions of tons of goods are loaded and unloaded at the port of Los Angeles.

History

Less than 150 years ago, Los Angeles was a little Mexican town. After California became a part of the United States, more people came to the Los Angeles area. They found a pleasant, sunny climate and fertile soil. There was plenty of space for homes and factories. Also, a valuable resource—oil—was found under the ground. All these things brought more people. As railroads and highways were built, people came to Los Angeles from many parts of the United States. The city grew rapidly. Today the Los Angeles metropolitan area is still growing.

San Francisco

The map on page 8 shows a large inlet of the Pacific Ocean that goes through the coastal mountains of California. This is San Francisco Bay. It looks somewhat like a lake. This is because it is almost separated from the ocean by two arms of land. The southern arm is called the San Francisco Peninsula. At the end of this peninsula* is San Francisco.

Around San Francisco Bay are many other cities and towns. The largest is Oakland. Together, San Francisco and its neighbors make up a metropolitan area of more than three million people.

To the north of the city of San Francisco is a narrow water passage called the Golden Gate. It connects the ocean with San Francisco Bay. Two great

List reasons why people settled in the Los Angeles area. Why do people continue to locate in this area?

The great city of San Francisco is bordered on the west by the Pacific Ocean and on the east by San Francisco Bay. How has San Francisco's location affected its growth?

Refer to the picture and caption above. What can you discover about San Francisco from this picture? List your discoveries.

† What other important historical event took place in our country in 1776?

bridges connect San Francisco with neighboring cities and towns. One is the Golden Gate Bridge, which runs north and south across the Golden Gate. It is one of the longest suspension* bridges in the world. The San Francisco-Oakland Bay Bridge joins San Francisco with the city of Oakland. It goes across San Francisco Bay.

A fine natural harbor

The location of San Francisco has helped to make it an important seaport. San Francisco Bay is one of the world's best natural harbors. Together with the Golden Gate, it forms the only natural passageway through the mountains along the coast of California. From San Francisco, goods can easily be shipped to inland cities or to ports in other countries. Four main railroads carry goods to and from San Francisco. Ships from many different parts of the world dock at piers along the waterfront.

Industry

Many factories have been built in the San Francisco metropolitan area. Most of them are outside the city of San Francisco. In neighboring towns and cities there is more room for growth. Among the products made in the San Francisco area are automobiles, chemicals,* paper, clothing, and frozen foods. There are large shipyards on San Francisco Bay.

History

† San Francisco began as a small Spanish fort and mission in 1776. About seventy years later, gold was discovered in California. Thousands of people came to San Francisco on their way to the goldfields. The city grew rapidly. In 1906, an earthquake started a fire that destroyed most of San Francisco. After the fire, the people worked together to rebuild their city. They made it more beautiful than it had been before. Today, San Francisco is considered one of the most beautiful cities in the United States.

Much of San Francisco is very hilly. Small streetcars called cable cars go up and down the hilly streets. They are pulled by long cables set in slots in the streets. San Francisco is also famous for a section called Chinatown. Here there are many shops and restaurants. Thousands of people of Chinese descent live and work in this part of San Francisco.

56 The West

† Why do you think one of the United States Navy's largest bases is located at San Diego? Explain.

San Diego

The city of San Diego, California, is on the Pacific coast. It is near the border between the United States and Mexico. The city lies on a lowland along San Diego Bay. It stretches inland toward the peaks of the San Diego Ranges.

An important seaport

San Diego Bay is long and narrow. It is protected from the ocean by two long peninsulas. These form an excellent harbor for oceangoing ships. This fine harbor has helped to make San Diego an important seaport. Ships from many different countries load and unload their goods here. Also, one of the United States Navy's largest bases is at San Diego. Many people in San Diego serve in the navy or work at the naval base.

San Diego is also an important fishing port. Large catches of tuna, anchovies,* and other fish are brought to San Diego. Some of these fish are canned in plants in the city.

Industry

There are many other kinds of industry in San Diego. Large factories here make airplanes and airplane parts. Other factories make electronic equipment, plastics, and boat motors. At the edge of San Diego Bay are great salt flats where ocean water is evaporated* by the sun, leaving salt. The salt is gathered by bulldozers and power shovels

San Diego lies on the Pacific coast of southern California. It is a major seaport and an important manufacturing city. Why do many retired people and tourists come to San Diego?

Seattle is Washington's largest city and most important seaport. It is located on hilly land along the shores of Puget Sound. What important industry provides jobs for many people in Seattle?

and taken to factories where it is prepared for sale.

In San Diego, the weather is mild and sunny the year around. The pleasant climate is why many retired people have chosen to make their homes in this area. Each year, large numbers of tourists come to San Diego. Here, they enjoy warm weather, beautiful scenery, and many outdoor sports.

Seattle

The largest city in the northwestern part of our country is Seattle, Washington. Seattle is on hilly land along the shores of Puget Sound, a long arm of the Pacific Ocean. East of the city is Lake Washington.

Seattle began in the 1850's as a small lumbering town. Logs were brought here from nearby forests to be sawed into lumber. The lumber was shipped to other cities along the Pacific coast. During the 1880's and 1890's, railroads were built connecting Seattle with cities in the eastern part of our country. A few years later, gold was discovered in northern Canada and Alaska. Thousands of gold-seekers stopped in Seattle to buy their supplies. The city began to grow rapidly. †

A major seaport

Seattle is one of the leading seaports along the Pacific coast. Many ships from around the world dock in Seattle's fine harbor along Puget Sound. Ships also travel between Puget Sound and Lake Washington through a canal and locks.* From Seattle, fishing boats

† Are there similarities between the early days of Seattle and the early days of San Francisco? Explain.

journey out to sea to find halibut and other fish.

Industry

Manufacturing is also important in the Seattle area. The leading industry is the manufacture of aircraft. Many of the jet passenger planes that streak across our skies were made in plants near Seattle. Shipyards along Puget Sound build fishing boats, navy ships, barges, and pleasure boats. Some factories in the Seattle area process farm crops, timber, and minerals produced in the state. For example, there are flour and grain mills, sawmills, plywood* factories, and plants that can or freeze salmon. Hydroelectric* plants located on mountain streams near Seattle provide large amounts of electric power for industry.

Each year, Seattle attracts thousands of tourists. People come to Seattle in the summer for sports such as fishing and boating. In winter there is skiing on nearby mountains.

Denver

The capital and largest city of Colorado is Denver. Denver is located along the South Platte River, near the western edge of the Great Plains. To the west of the city rise the snowcapped peaks of the Rocky Mountains. Denver is sometimes called the "Mile High City." This is because a marker on the steps of the capitol building is exactly one mile above sea level.

History

Denver was founded by settlers who came to Colorado during a gold rush in the late 1850's. The storekeepers in Denver grew rich selling supplies to miners. The miners were seeking gold, silver, and other metals in the Rocky Mountains. After railroads were built to Denver, it became an important shipping point for farm products. In recent years, many new industries have been built in or near Denver. The population has grown rapidly.

A trading city

Denver is an important trading city for many people who live on the Great Plains or in the Rocky Mountains. A number of large manufacturing firms, banks, and insurance companies have offices here. Many ranchers bring their cattle and sheep to Denver's huge stockyards to be sold. People come from many miles away to shop in Denver's fine stores.

† Refer students to the population chart on page 53. Have them compare the populations of Los Angeles, San Diego, and Seattle to the population of Denver.

Government offices

Many United States government agencies have offices in Denver. In fact, there are more government offices in Denver than in any other city except Washington, D.C. The United States Mint in Denver makes millions of our country's coins each year.

Industry

Denver is also an important manufacturing city. Some factories here use Colorado's farm products and minerals as raw materials. For example, there are sugar refineries, meat-packing plants, and oil refineries in the Denver area. Other products manufactured here include missiles, aircraft parts, mining machinery, and luggage.

Phoenix

One of the fastest-growing cities in the United States is Phoenix. It is the capital and largest city of Arizona. In 1950, only about 107,000 people lived in Phoenix. Today, the city has a population of 709,000. More than one million people make their homes in the Phoenix metropolitan area.

Trade and industry

Phoenix is located along the Salt River, in a rich farming area. Irrigated farms in the Salt River Valley produce such crops as cotton, citrus fruits, vegetables, grain, and alfalfa. Most of these farm products are brought to Phoenix to be processed or shipped to other parts of the country. There are fruit

Phoenix is the capital and largest city in Arizona. It is located along the Salt River, in the middle of a rich farming area. What are some important industries found in the Phoenix area?

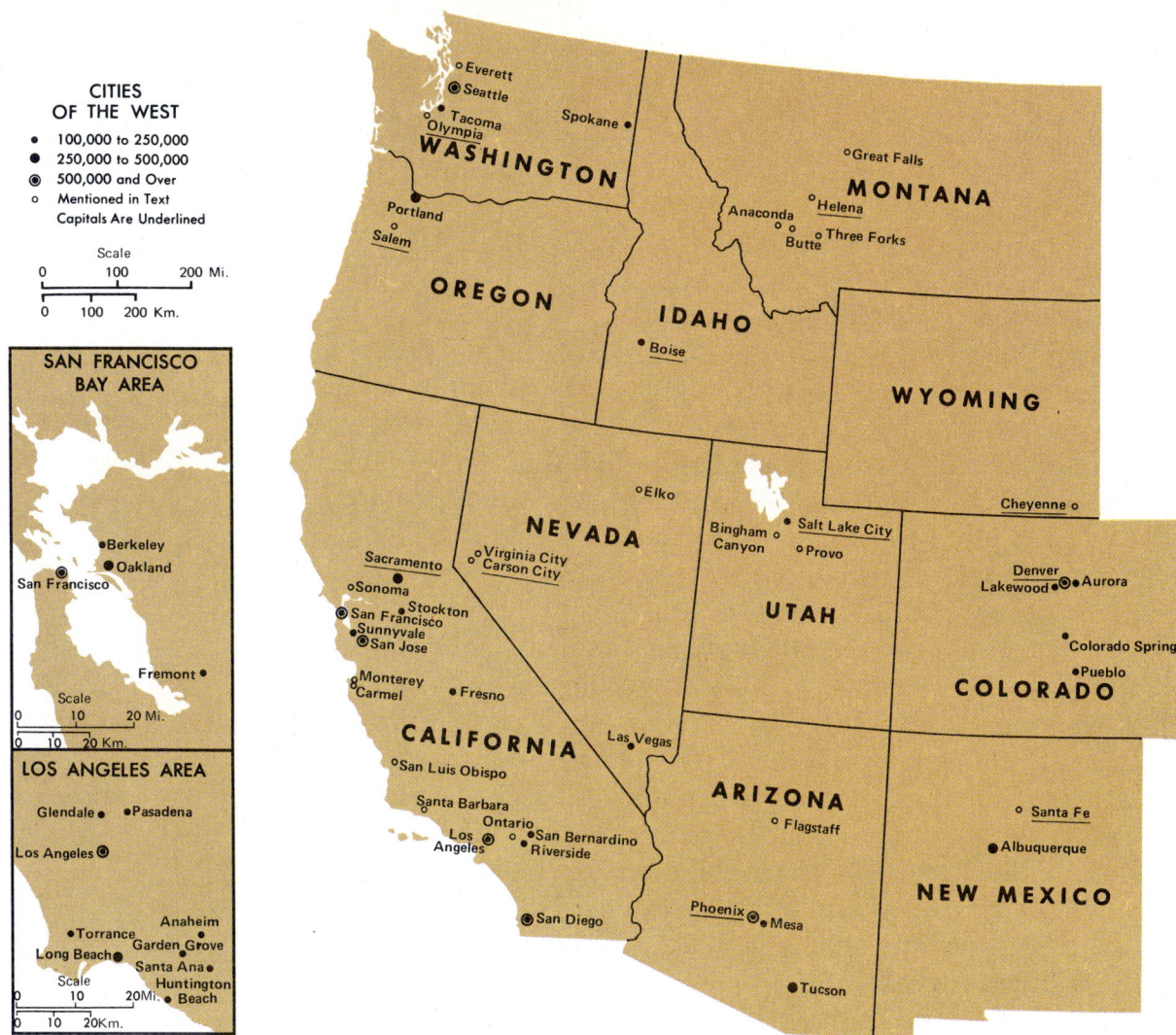

and vegetable canneries, cotton gins, grain mills, and meat-packing plants in the Phoenix area.

Phoenix has other industries as well. Factories here make aircraft parts out of aluminum. There are also factories that make electronic equipment.

Many people like to visit Phoenix. They enjoy the warm winter climate and the beautiful desert scenery nearby. There are many fine hotels, motels, and resorts in the Phoenix area. A number of people here earn their living by serving the needs of tourists.

† **Exploring Cities**
1. Do research to discover how one of the cities described in this chapter began and how it has developed. Answer the following questions in a short report.
   a. Who were the first settlers?
   b. Why did they settle here?
   c. How has the city grown in size from the time it was founded until now?

2. Describe a visit to one of the cities discussed in this chapter. Present a short report to your class. Include the following in your report:
   a. how you traveled to the city
   b. the most interesting things you saw there
   c. your opinion of what the city's most serious problems might be

† Have each student do one of these activities.

The West 61

6 Citizenship and Government

Government in Our Communities

A nation of strong communities

The United States is a nation of communities. As the map on pages 8-9 shows, our country stretches nearly 3,000 miles (4,827 km.)† from Maine to California. It also includes the far north state of Alaska and the island state of Hawaii. In this huge country, there are thousands of communities. Some are very large. For example, the cities of New York, Chicago, and Los Angeles have millions of people. Others are very small. Only a few families make their homes there.

Most of the communities in our country are good places in which to live. People in these communities are usually able to meet their basic needs. (See "Needs of People" in the Table of Contents.) For instance, most people have jobs that make it possible for them to earn a good living. Also, most people have a chance to get a good education. In these communities, most of the buildings and streets are clean and well kept. People are usually friendly and polite to one another. They enjoy working together and playing together. Most people have a feeling of pride in their community.

† In strong communities like these, most of the people share certain ideas, or beliefs. Seven of these beliefs are described on page 64. Study these beliefs carefully. Do you agree with all of them? Do you think these beliefs are important in building a strong community? Explain your answers.

Government by the people

All of the communities in our nation are alike in certain ways. For example, they all need rules, or laws, for people to live by. Of course, there must be someone to make the laws and to see that they are carried out. This means that all communities need some kind of government.

In the United States, the citizens of each community have a share in the government. They choose the people who make the laws. They also choose some of the people who carry out the laws.

In most of our communities, the government is divided into three branches. One branch makes the laws. Another carries them out. The third branch explains, or <u>interprets</u>, the laws.

† km. means kilometer

† Refer to page 64. Have students read the "Seven Important Beliefs," and then answer these questions.

Members of the Seattle City Council at work. What does the city council do? How are its members chosen? Do all communities have a group of men and women like this one? Explain.

Making the Laws

To see how the laws of a community are made, let's visit a large city in the West. We will go to Seattle, Washington. (See map on page 61.)

The city council

When we arrive in Seattle, we go to a large building in the downtown area where the Seattle City Council has its meetings. The city council makes the laws for Seattle. It also decides how the money collected in city taxes should be spent. There are nine members of the city council. They are elected by the voters of Seattle for terms of four years each.

Right now, the members of the city council are talking about a law that one of them has introduced. This law would forbid people to smoke in restaurants and other public places. A number of citizens have come to the meeting to say how they feel about the law. Some are in favor of it. Others are against it. The council members will listen to all points of view and then make their decision.

Other communities in our country also have groups of people who are elected to make the laws. These lawmaking bodies have different names, such as "city commission" or "board of aldermen." They differ from one another in a number of ways. For instance, some of them have more members than the Seattle City Council. Others have fewer members. In some communities, the lawmakers serve for less than four years at a time.

The West 63

SEVEN IMPORTANT BELIEFS THAT BUILD STRONG COMMUNITIES

1. **Every person is important.**

   Most Americans believe that every person is important. It does not matter if you are young or old, a man or a woman. You are just as important as every other person. You are important whether your skin is black, white, or some other color. You are important no matter what religion you follow or what country your grandparents came from.

2. **People have the right to govern themselves.**

   Americans believe the citizens of a country have the right to govern themselves. We think every person should be able to have some part in running our government.

3. **Decisions should be made by majority* vote.**

   In the United States, all citizens have a chance to help choose the people who run the government. They do this by voting in elections. The candidate* with the most votes is elected. This is known as majority vote. Most Americans believe the fairest way for people to govern themselves is by majority vote.

4. **All citizens should have a chance to get a good education.**

   Education is very important in a democracy. To have good government, citizens must be able to vote wisely for the people who make and carry out the laws. Most Americans believe that all young people should have a chance for a good education.

5. **Laws should be the same for all citizens.**

   Most Americans believe all citizens should be treated the same by their government. Everyone should be required to obey the same laws. People should never gain or lose any rights because of such things as the color of their skin, or how much money they have.

6. **All people have certain rights that no one can take away from them.**

   Most Americans believe that every person has a number of important rights and freedoms. Among these are freedom of speech and freedom of religion. Also every person has the right to a fair trial in a court of law. We believe that these rights cannot be taken away from any person, even by a majority vote. In a democracy, the government is expected to protect the rights of all citizens.

7. **Citizens have responsibilities as well as rights.**

   For a democracy to work, all citizens must be willing to do their part. In other words, citizens have responsibilities as well as rights. Among these responsibilities are obeying the laws of the community, taking part in the government, and doing useful work.

*See Glossary

Carrying Out the Laws

To see how the laws of a community are carried out, we will visit another large city in the West. This time we will go to Los Angeles, California.

† **The mayor**

We arrive by plane at the Los Angeles' airport and take a taxi to the City Hall. This is a tall building in the heart of the city. The mayor of Los Angeles has his office here.

We go to the mayor's office, where we meet one of his aides. This young woman tells us that the people of Los Angeles elect a mayor every four years. The mayor is in charge of carrying out the laws the city council has made. He chooses the members of about forty different commissions. Each commission has a certain job to do in the city government. For example, one commission runs the police force. Another is in charge of the city's harbor.

† Do we have a mayor? What is our mayor's name?

Refer to the picture and caption below. Use the questions in a class discussion about freedom.

In Los Angeles, the mayor has a great deal of power. But this is not true in all communities. Sometimes the mayor's only duties are to lead city council meetings and to take part in public ceremonies, such as parades. In some cities, the mayor is a member of the city council.

Many communities have a city manager instead of a mayor to run the government. The city manager is not elected by the voters. Instead, he or she is chosen by the city council.

Workers for the community

The mayor's aide tells us that about forty thousand people work for the city government of Los Angeles. These people do many different jobs. Some are police officers or fire fighters. Others are street cleaners or garbage collectors. Still others take care of the city's parks and playgrounds. There are workers who inspect houses and apartments to make sure they are safe to live in. Other people run the city's water system.

Freedom

See Great Ideas

The picture below shows Mayor Thomas Bradley of Los Angeles. During the last fifteen years, black persons have become mayors of several large American cities. In earlier times, black Americans were seldom chosen for important government jobs. What do you think were the reasons for this? Why do you suppose there has been such a change during recent years? Do you think that black Americans today have more freedom than they did in the past? Explain.

We ask the mayor's aide where the city gets the money to pay all these people. She says the money comes from taxes that people pay to the city government.

Other communities have the same kinds of government workers that Los Angeles does. But in smaller communities, fewer workers are needed.

The city's schools

Like other communities, Los Angeles has a system of public schools. There are more than 600 schools in the Los Angeles school district. About 580,000 students attend these schools.

The public schools are run by a group of men and women called the Board of Education. This board is made up of seven members, who are elected to four-year terms. The Board of Education chooses a person called a superintendent to be in charge of running the schools. Most other communities in our country also have a board of education and a superintendent of schools.

In the United States, public high schools and grade schools are free to all students. The money to run these schools comes mostly from taxes that people pay to their school districts. Some money also comes from the state and federal* governments.

Interpreting the Laws

There are law courts in most of our larger cities and towns. These courts try* people who are accused of breaking the law. They deal with crimes such as driving too fast and littering the streets. People who are arrested for more serious crimes, such as robbery, are usually tried in other courts.

Citizenship in a Strong Community

Opportunities for citizens

As you have seen, the United States is a nation of strong communities. The people in these communities have many opportunities to live a happy, satisfying life.

In a strong community, most people have steady jobs. They can do useful work and earn a good living for themselves and their families. Most people also have a chance to get a good education. This helps them to develop their talents and to accomplish goals that are important to them.

In a strong community, life is usually safe and pleasant. People can go about their business without fear of being attacked or robbed. Most of the homes are neat and well kept. The streets are clean and free of rubbish. There are parks and playgrounds where people can spend their leisure time.

In a strong community, people are friendly and helpful to one another. They have a feeling that they can trust one another. People are willing to work together on projects that will make their community a better place to live.

What makes a strong community?

A successful community does not just "happen." Every citizen must do his or her part to make the community strong. As you know, most people in a strong community follow the seven beliefs shown on page 64. For example, they believe that every person is important. They believe that all people should have the same rights and freedoms. In addition, they believe that

*See Glossary

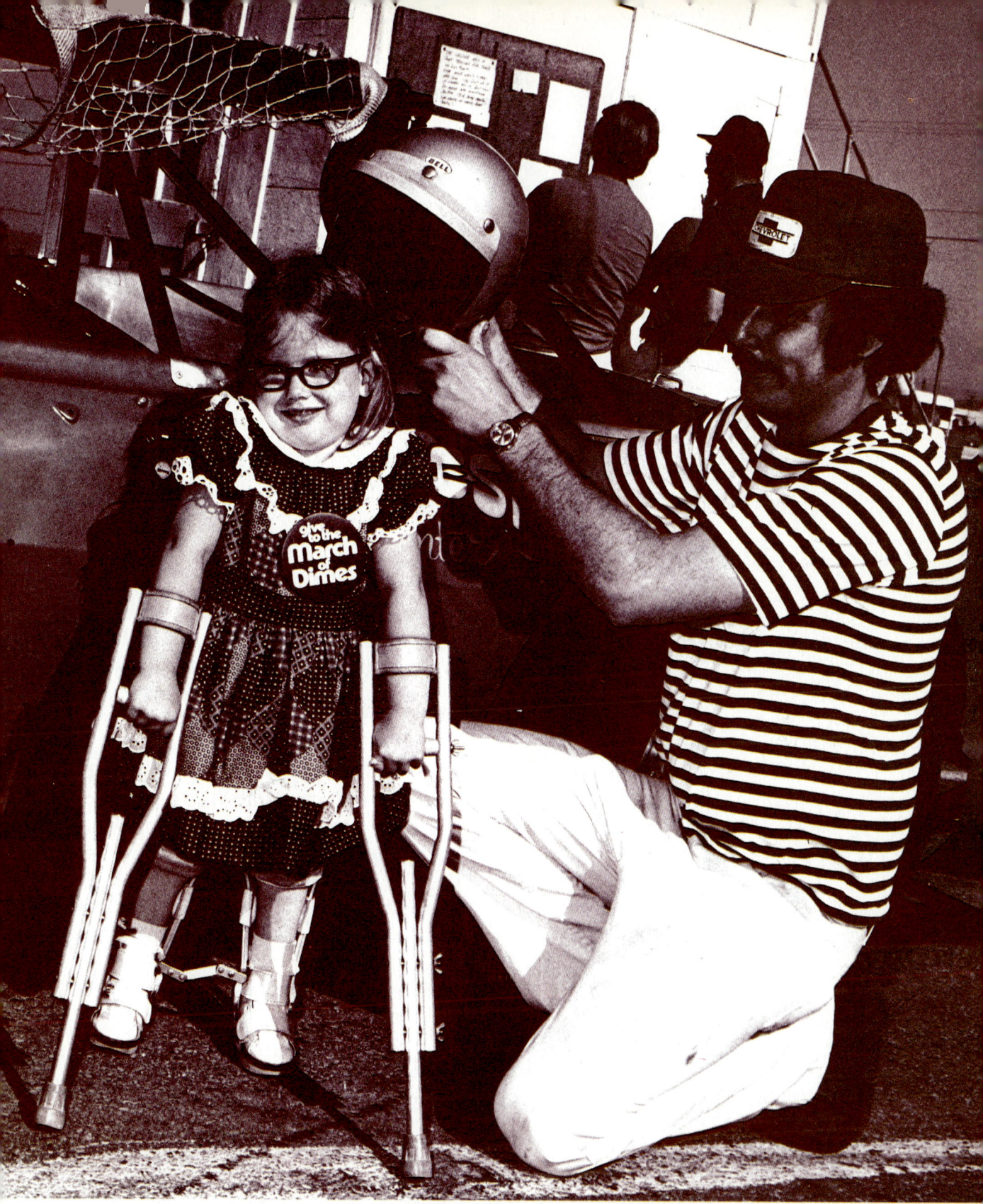

An organization called the March of Dimes provides money to help crippled children. This picture shows a race-car driver who is helping to raise money for this organization. Good citizens are willing to help out on community projects. What are some other responsibilities of a citizen?

Refer to the picture and caption above. Have students discuss responsibilities of citizens.

RESPONSIBILITIES OF CITIZENS IN A STRONG COMMUNITY

Obeying the laws

Good citizens obey the laws of their community, state, and country. Even if they think a law is unfair, they will not disobey it. Instead, they will work in a peaceful way to get the law changed.

Treating other people with respect

Good citizens treat other people the same way they would like to be treated. They try to be friendly and polite to everyone. This is because they truly believe that every person is important.

Getting a good education

In the United States, most people have an opportunity for an education. Young people are responsible for making good use of this opportunity. By learning as much as they can, they are preparing to become useful citizens when they grow up.

Doing useful work

Most Americans feel they are responsible for doing useful work. When they become adults they do not expect other people to take care of them. Instead, they expect to work hard and do their job well.

Taking part in the government

In the United States, it is important for every citizen to take part in the government. People who are over eighteen can do this by voting in all elections. Also they can work for candidates* they think would do a good job. Young people have a responsibility to learn as much as they can about their government. This will help prepare them to make wise decisions when they are older.

Cooperating with other people

Many jobs in a community cannot be done well by persons working alone. Instead, there must be cooperation among many people. Citizens of a community have a responsibility to work together. In this way, they can make their community a better place to live.

all citizens should take part in the government.

In a strong community, most people realize that they have responsibilities* as well as rights. Some of these responsibilities are shown at left. Study the list carefully. Do you agree that all citizens of a community have these responsibilities? Why? Why not? Can you think of any other responsibilities that citizens of a community have? If so, what are they?

Community Problems

Today, communities in the United States face a number of important problems. Some of these problems keep large numbers of people from meeting their basic needs. They are known as social problems. Seven of the most important social problems are shown on page 70. Let us examine one of these problems more closely.

Unsuccessful Communities

In our country, there are some communities that are not as successful as others. Many of the people who make their homes there find it hard to meet their basic needs. We will visit one of these communities to see what it is like.

A visit to an unsuccessful community

We are taking a taxi ride through a large city in the United States. Our taxicab turns down a narrow street lined with tall apartment buildings. All of the buildings on this street are run-down and shabby. Paint is peeling from the walls. Many buildings appear to be empty. Their windows are broken, and the doors are hanging loose from the hinges. Some of the buildings are

† Do you think these are all important responsibilities? Can you name others?

† **Instead of moving away, what can people do to make their communities more livable?**

streaked with black soot. It looks as though the insides of these buildings have been destroyed by fire.

We notice that the street and the sidewalks are littered with bottles and other rubbish. Someone has written all over the sidewalks and the buildings with paint. In a nearby alley, large rats are scurrying between overflowing garbage cans.

Our cab driver tells us that there is a great deal of crime in this part of the city. A person walking down the street is in danger of being robbed or beaten.

We ask the cab driver why so many buildings on this street are empty. He † says that most of the people who once lived here have moved away. Many left because they could not find any good jobs. Some left because they felt their children were not getting a good education. Other people left because they wanted to find better housing. Still others left because they were tired of living where there was so much crime. They wanted to move to a community where life was safer and more pleasant.

A street in a large American city. The insides of some of these apartment buildings have been destroyed by fire. Do you think this picture shows a successful community? Explain your answer. Why are some communities unsuccessful? What can be done to help build stronger communities?

SEVEN SOCIAL PROBLEMS

In our country, a number of serious problems prevent people from meeting their needs. These are called social problems. The government and the people of our country have been working hard to solve these problems. As we make progress toward this goal, more Americans will have happier and more successful lives. Our country's social problems include:

1. **The need for more jobs.** At the present time, about six out of every hundred workers in the United States are unable to find jobs.
2. **The high cost of living.** In recent years, the high cost of goods and services has kept many people from meeting their needs. This continuing rise in prices is called inflation.
3. **The need for better education.** Many people in our country are not getting a good education. They are not gaining the knowledge they need for good citizenship.
4. **Illness and handicaps.** Americans are among the healthiest people in the world. However, millions of people in our country suffer from serious illnesses and handicaps.
5. **Lack of freedom for certain groups.** In the past, some groups of people in our country did not have the same freedoms as other people. Today, our laws give every person the right to fair treatment and equal opportunity. Even so, some Americans still do not have all the rights and freedoms promised by our laws.
6. **Crime.** Over the years, there has been a great increase in the number of major crimes in our country. In many areas, people live in fear for their lives.
7. **Unsuccessful communities.** In many parts of the United States there are unsuccessful communities. Many of the people in these communities are not doing useful work. They are not getting the education they need to get jobs or to be good citizens. The crime rate in these communities is very high.

Why some communities are not successful

If we could travel through the United States, we would find other communities like the one we have just visited. There are many reasons why these communities are not successful. Let us explore just two of the reasons.

Communities are sometimes unsuccessful because the people there have been treated unfairly by other Americans. Often the people who live in these communities are members of minority* groups. Some are blacks or Indians. Others are Latinos* or people of Asian descent.

In the past, members of minority groups were often the victims of discrimination.* Many companies would not hire them. Or they would only give them jobs that took little skill and did not pay very much money. Often these people could not get good housing, because other Americans would not sell houses or rent apartments to them.

Sometimes members of minority groups were not given a chance to get a good education. They were not allowed to go to the same schools as other children. Often the schools they did attend were not as good as those for other children. As a result, they often grew up without the knowledge or skills they needed to earn a good living.

Today there is much less discrimination against minority groups than there used to be. But even today the members of these groups often lack many of the opportunities that other Americans have. They were treated unfairly for so long that they have not yet

† Why do you think there is less discrimination against minority groups today? Explain your answer.

† Do you agree that people should not depend on the government to solve all their problems? Discuss ways in which private business and individuals can help.

"caught up" with the rest of our citizens.

What do you think about people who discriminate against other persons? Are these people living up to the seven beliefs that build strong communities? Are they meeting their responsibilities as citizens? Give reasons for your answers.

There is another important reason why communities are unsuccessful. Some of the people who live there do not meet their responsibilities. For example, some people are not willing to do any kind of useful work. Instead, they expect other people to support them. They do not try to get a good education so that they can become useful citizens. Some of them drop out of school as soon as they are old enough to do so.

In some communities, there are people who break the laws whenever they feel like it. They may rob other people or hurt them in some way. They may break windows or start fires just for fun. These people are not treating others as they would like to be treated themselves.

Usually there are only a small number of people in a community who act in this way. But even a few of these people can cause great harm to a community. They make it hard for all the other citizens to meet their needs.

Building stronger communities

Today, many Americans are trying to solve the problem of unsuccessful communities. For instance, our federal and state governments have passed laws against discrimination. Many companies have started programs to hire members of minority groups and train them for well-paying jobs. In many communities, there are special classes for people who have not finished high school. Here, people can gain the knowledge and skills they need to earn a good living.

The federal government has spent large amounts of money to improve our nation's cities. Some of this money is being used to find jobs for people who are out of work. Some is being used to get rid of slums.* Cities are tearing down entire blocks of run-down apartment buildings and stores. In their place, they are putting up rows of modern apartment buildings where people can live without paying high rents.

All of these things can help to build stronger communities. But something more is needed also. Today, most people realize that they cannot depend on the government or on other people to solve all their problems. They must be willing to help themselves. By working together and having faith in their own abilities, they can build a better way of life. For an example of this, let us see what happened in a section of Los Angeles known as Watts.

The story of Watts

In the past, the people of Watts faced serious problems. Many of these people had been the victims of discrimination. They had settled in Watts because they could not buy houses or rent apartments in other parts of the city. In Watts there were few stores or factories that hired large numbers of workers. Most people in Watts had to go to other parts of Los Angeles to find work. But bus service between Watts and other sections was poor. Also, many families in Watts did not own

The West 71

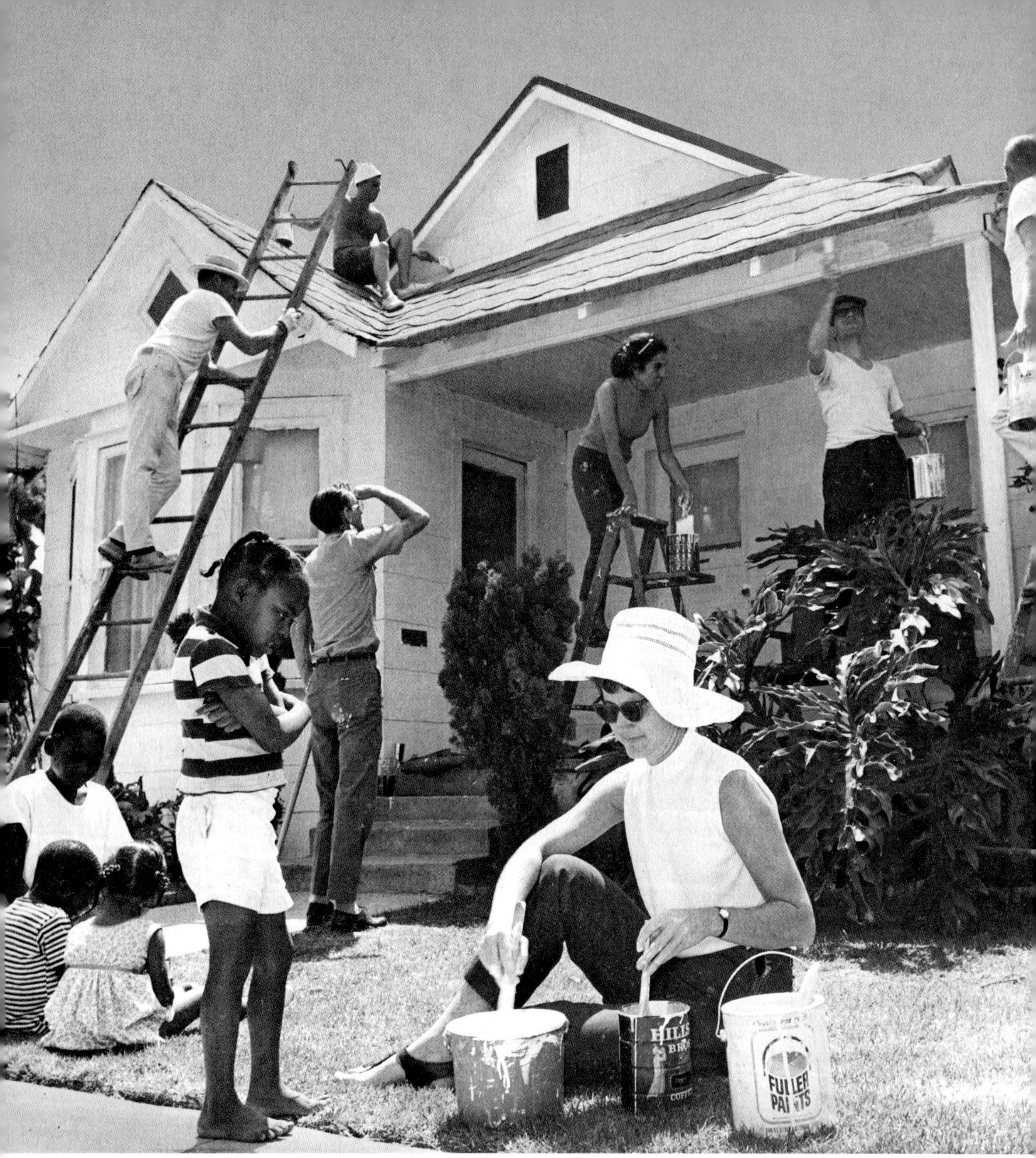

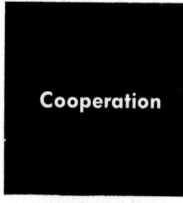

Cooperation

In the city of Los Angeles is a section known as Watts. A riot caused great damage to Watts in 1965. After the riot, the people of Watts began working together to build a stronger community. The picture above shows some citizens of Watts helping their community by painting a house. Do you think it is important for the people of Watts to work together? Why? Why not? Is it important for the members of any community to work together? Explain.

See Great Ideas

Refer to the picture and caption above. Use the questions in a class discussion about cooperation.

cars. Partly for this reason, a large number of people in Watts did not have steady jobs.

There were other problems also. Many of the houses in Watts were old and run-down. There was a great deal of crime in the area. Many people in Watts felt there was little they could do about these problems. As a result, they had given up trying.

In the summer of 1965, a riot broke out in Watts. Mobs of angry people fought with the police. They destroyed cars, broke store windows, and set fire to buildings. Thirty-four people were killed in this riot, and hundreds of others were injured.

After the riot, people in Watts began taking steps to build a stronger community. A number of citizen's groups were started for this purpose. Thousands of young people went to work repairing houses, cleaning up streets, and planting gardens. Special classes were started for people who lacked a high-school education. Jobs were found for thousands of people who had been out of work.

Today the people of Watts still lack some of the opportunities that people in other parts of Los Angeles have. But they are making steady progress toward a better way of life. The changes that have taken place in Watts show what can be done when people work together to solve their problems.

Your opportunity as a citizen

You are a citizen of a community. This is true even though you are not old enough to vote. As a citizen, you have a chance to help build a stronger community. You can do this by:

. . . obeying the laws.

. . . treating other people as you would like to be treated.

. . . doing useful work at home.

. . . trying to get a good education.

. . . learning as much as you can about your community, so you will be able to vote wisely when you are older.

If you do all of these things, you will be meeting your responsibilities as a citizen. You will also be helping to make your community a better place in which to live.

Find Out How Your Government Works

This chapter has provided certain facts about the way communities are governed. Now you may want to find out how the government of your own community works. Do research to answer the following questions.

1. Who makes the laws for your community? How are these people chosen?
2. Who is in charge of carrying out the laws for your community? How is this person or persons chosen?
3. About how many people work for your community's government? What kinds of jobs do they do?
4. What courts do you have in your community? What kinds of cases do they deal with? How do the judges in these courts get their jobs? How long do they serve?
5. Where does your community get the money it needs to run the government? Who decides how this money will be spent?

There are several ways of getting this information. Some communities put out booklets that explain how the government works. Perhaps you could get one of these booklets. Or you might plan a field trip to the offices of your community government. You might also invite someone who knows about the government of your community to speak to the class.

7 The Arts

Painters

One of the first western painters was George Catlin. His paintings and books about Indians give us valuable information about their lives and customs. *The White Cloud, Head Chief of the Iowas* is one of his most famous paintings.

Perhaps the greatest western painter was Frederic Remington. He painted or drew nearly 2,800 pictures of the West. Soldiers, Indians, and cowboys are shown in many of Remington's paintings. Some of his best-known works are *Flight of Geronimo*, *A Dash for Timber*, and *Dismounted, the Fourth Troopers Moving*.

Another important artist of the West was Charles M. Russell. Russell traveled through the West looking for adventure and freedom. He painted pictures and made sculptures.* One of his sculptures is called *Where the Best of Riders Quit*. It shows a rider being thrown from a bucking horse.

Artists Albert Bierstadt and Thomas Moran painted pictures of the West during the 1800's. Bierstadt traveled through the Rocky Mountains and northern California. Many of his paintings show the beauty of the western mountains. Among his paintings are *The Rocky Mountains* and *In the Yosemite Valley*. Moran is perhaps best known for his *Grand Canyon of the Yellowstone River*.

Georgia O'Keeffe and Mark Tobey are recent painters who have lived and worked in the West. O'Keeffe has painted many desert scenes. She has also painted pictures of such things as bones and flowers in new and different ways. One of her best-known paintings is called *Cow's Skull with Calico Roses*. During the 1920's, Tobey painted true-to-life pictures of loggers

*See Glossary

Use Fideler Discovery Cards 75-82, and Fideler Discovery Sheets, Volume 1, pages 33-36 for activities about the arts.

A painting by Frederic Remington called *Dismounted, the Fourth Troopers Moving*. Remington's true-to-life paintings and sculptures provide valuable information about life in the early West.

and sailors. His later pictures, such as *Written Over the Plains*, were painted in a more abstract* style.

Writers

During the 1800's, many poets, novelists,* and short-story writers wrote about the lives of pioneer families in the West. They also wrote about miners and cowboys. The poet Joaquin Miller lived with the Indians in California. He also lived in mining camps in the West. His most famous work is *Songs of the Sierras*.

Two important writers during the late 1800's and early 1900's were Bret Harte and Jack London. Harte was known for his poems and stories about California. Two of his best-known short stories are "The Luck of Roaring

Refer to the painting on these pages. What can you learn about the early West from this painting?

Camp" and "The Outcasts of Poker Flat."

London wrote many novels and stories. His best-known novel is *The Call of the Wild.* This book tells about the adventures of a dog that was taken from California to northern Canada.

More recent writers include John Steinbeck, William Saroyan, and Phyllis McGinley. One of Steinbeck's best-known novels is *The Grapes of Wrath.* It tells about the hardships of a family that moved from Oklahoma to California. Other well-known works by Steinbeck are *Of Mice and Men, East of Eden,* and *The Red Pony.* Among Saroyan's best-known works are his novel *The Human Comedy,* and a play called *The Time of Your Life.* McGinley wrote humorous poems about everyday life. In 1961, she won the Pulitzer* prize for poetry.

Music

Western composers* have given us many famous songs. These include "The Lone Prairie," "Streets of Laredo," and "The Chisholm Trail." Early cowboys sang these songs to help quiet their cattle and to fill the lonely hours.

Composers have also given us serious music about the West. These include

These pictures show two of the West's best-known artists. Georgia O'Keeffe (left) has painted many pictures of Western scenes. John Steinbeck (right) has written stories and novels about the people of the West. Who are some of the other painters and writers who have lived and worked in the West? What are some ways in which arts such as painting and writing can help us understand the history of a region?

Antonia Brico conducting the Los Angeles Philharmonic Orchestra in a rehearsal. Brico, who lives in Denver, Colorado, is well known as an orchestra conductor. Many people in the West enjoy listening to the fine symphony orchestras in this part of our country.

Ferde Grofé's *Grand Canyon Suite* and Hershey Kay's ballet *Western Symphony*. Aaron Copland's ballets *Billy the Kid* and *Rodeo* are other musical works about the West.

Many people also enjoy listening to the fine symphony orchestras in the West. One of our country's greatest orchestra conductors is Zubin Mehta. He conducts the Los Angeles Philharmonic Orchestra. Other well-known conductors include Edo de Waart and Antonia Brico.

Gain an Understanding

In order to gain a greater understanding of western painting, literature, or music, do one of the following:

1. Borrow a library book that shows paintings by an artist mentioned in this chapter. Choose the painting you like best. Explain to your class why you like it.
2. Read a novel by Jack London, such as *The Call of the Wild* or *White Fang*.
3. Play a recording of the *Grand Canyon Suite*. As you listen to the music, write a few sentences describing how it makes you feel.

† Have each student carry out one of these activities. Use Fideler Discovery Card 80, and Fideler Discovery Sheets, Volume 1, page 35 for additional activities.

Part 3

Earning a Living

† Use these questions to start students thinking about how people in the West earn their living.

Industry provides many jobs for people in the West. Some people work in factories where airplanes are built. Others work in plants where food is frozen or canned. In what other ways do you think people in the West earn their living? As you do research in Part 3, you may wish to discover answers to the following questions:

- What natural* resources would you † find in the West? In what ways do people in the West use these resources?
- What is dry farming? What is the most important crop grown by dry farming in the West? What other crops are raised here?
- What are the West's leading industrial cities? What are some of the products made in these cities?

*See Glossary

Pouring hot, melted copper at a smelter* in Arizona. More copper is produced in Arizona than in any other state in our country.

The West 79

8 Farming

† **A Problem To Solve**
<u>Farmers in different parts of the West raise different kinds of crops and livestock. Why is this true?</u> In making hypotheses* to solve this problem, you need to know what crops and livestock are raised in different parts of the West. Then you need to think about how raising these crops and livestock is affected by:
1. the amount of water available
2. the length of the growing season
3. the kind of land available

Chapters 2, 3, and 9 also contain information that will be helpful in solving this problem.

See Skills Manual, "Thinking and Solving Problems"

Imagine that it is more than one hundred years ago, and we are pioneers. We are making a trip across the West in a covered wagon. We plan to stop and make our home wherever we can find land that is good for farming. When we find just the right land, we will plow the soil and begin to raise crops.

The land we choose for our farm must not be too hilly or too rocky. Where hills are steep, it is hard to plant crops and to take care of them. Crops do not grow well on rocky ground.

In order to grow good crops, our farm must have fertile soil. It must also have plenty of water and sunshine. We say that soil is fertile if plants can grow well in it. If our land is in an area where rainfall is light, we must be able to get water from other places to moisten, or irrigate,* our fields. Some crops need many hours of sunshine each day and a long growing* season.

Land for raising livestock

The pioneers who came to the West many years ago found only a small amount of land that was good for growing crops. Nearly two thirds of the land is too rugged. Also, most of the West does not have enough water. In some places, the soil is not fertile. It may contain minerals that are harmful to plants. In the high mountains, the growing season is too short for most kinds of crops.

Today, just as in pioneer days, much of the land in the West is used only for raising cattle, sheep, and other livestock. These animals feed on grass,

*See Glossary

† Use "A Problem To Solve" to introduce the unit on farming.

Harvesting lettuce in California. Farming is very important to the states of the West. Why is this so? Which western state earns the most money from farm products?

which will grow where the land is too dry or too steep for crops to be grown.

Land for growing crops

A few parts of the West are very good for growing crops. These areas have fertile soil, plenty of water, and land that is fairly level. The lowlands in the southern part of the West have a warm, sunny climate and a long growing season. (Compare maps on pages 8 and 38.) Here farmers can raise many kinds of crops that cannot be grown in the northern part of our country.

Although these rich farmlands cover only a small area, the West is an important farming region. It produces more than half of the fruits and nuts and about half of the vegetables grown in the United States. Sugar beets, wheat, and cotton are other important farm products of the West. Almost two thirds of our sugar beets and more than one fourth of our wheat are grown in

Refer to the picture on these pages. What can you discover about lettuce farming in the West? (Many workers needed, stoop picking, tedious work.)

the West. Nearly one third of our cotton comes from this region. Some of the West's farm products are used by the people here. The rest are sold to people in other states and countries.

The most important farming state in the West is California. In fact, this state leads our entire country in the value of farm products. California produces more than two hundred different kinds of crops. In this chapter, we will learn about farming in California and in other parts of the West.

How important is farming to the West?

The jobs of many people in the West depend upon farming. Farmers grow crops or raise animals to sell. Other people work in factories where farm products are processed.* Still others sell farm products to stores or directly to the people who use these products. To learn more about farming in the West, let's visit an irrigated farm in the valley of the Salt River in Arizona. (See map on page 94.)

Farming on Irrigated Land

The weather is hot and sunny as we drive through the Salt River Valley. Here the land is very flat. We see green fields of cotton plants on both sides of the road. Between the fields are ditches filled with water. Some of the water from the ditches is flowing between the rows of plants. Nearby, a large stream of water from an electric pump is pouring into a ditch. This pump lifts the water from the bottom of a deep well.

We stop to watch a tractor dragging a huge scraping machine across a field. This machine is used to make the field

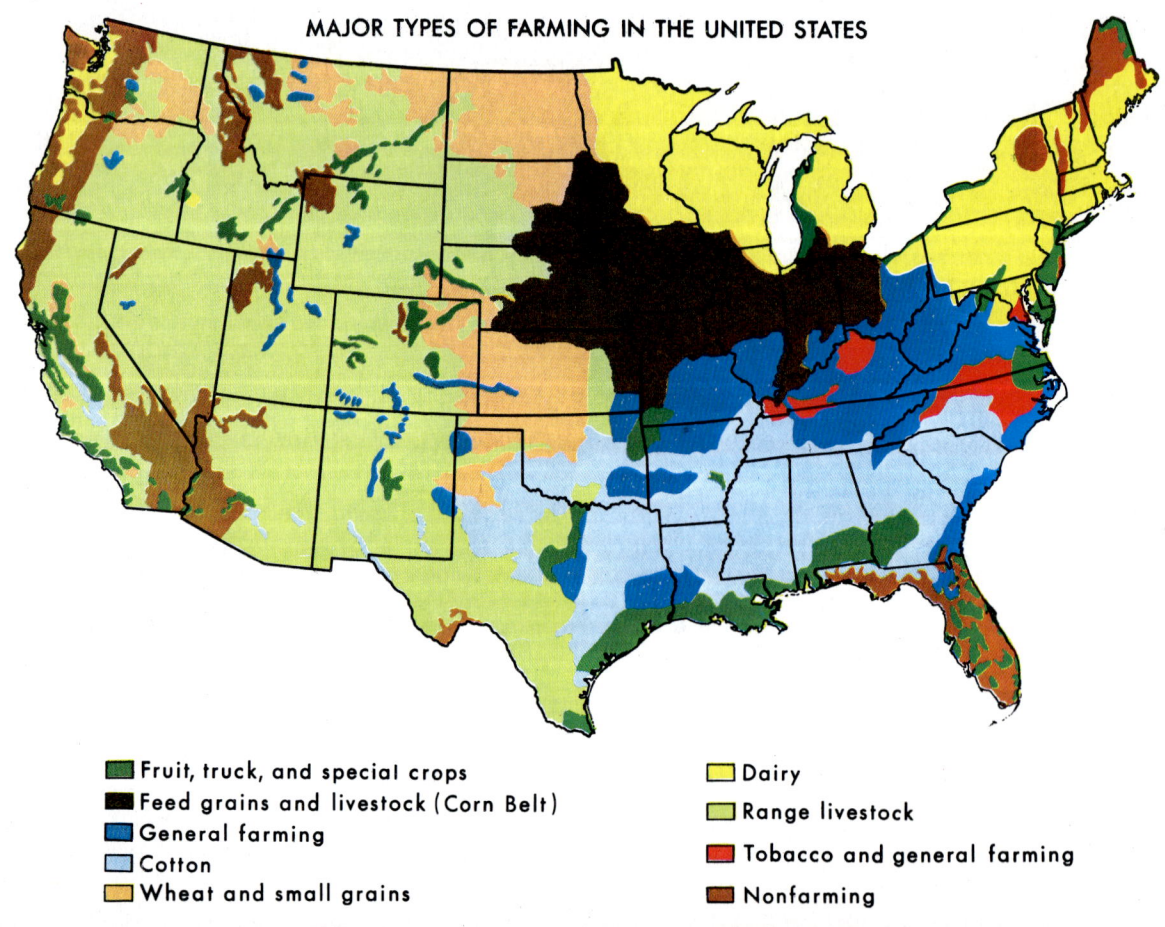

MAJOR TYPES OF FARMING IN THE UNITED STATES

- Fruit, truck, and special crops
- Feed grains and livestock (Corn Belt)
- General farming
- Cotton
- Wheat and small grains
- Dairy
- Range livestock
- Tobacco and general farming
- Nonfarming

† Refer to the map on page 94. Have students point out the location of irrigated areas.

level. Then water from the irrigation ditches can flow across it evenly.

The farmer stops his tractor and comes over to talk with us. He says that his farm is not very large—it covers only 40 acres (16 ha.).† "I like irrigation farming," he says. "I never have to worry about rainfall. When my crops need water, I pump it from under the ground. In this warm, sunny climate, I can grow crops nearly all year long."

Irrigation farming is hard work, however. First the farmer must level the land. Then he must drill a well, put in a pump, and dig irrigation ditches. Farmers who get water from reservoirs* instead of pumping it from the ground must pay for the water they receive.

Irrigated land in the West costs more money than the best farmland in other parts of the United States. This helps to explain why many irrigated farms are small. To earn a good living on these small but costly plots of land, farmers must grow crops that sell for high prices. Among the crops that are most often grown on irrigated land in the West are cotton, fruits, vegetables, and sugar beets.

Crop rotation

Like most other farmers, irrigation farmers cannot grow the same crop on the same land year after year. If they did, the soil would soon become less fertile. To keep the soil fertile, farmers must rotate their crops. In other words, they must plant different crops on the same land in different years. Many farmers rotate their other crops with a hay crop called alfalfa.* The tops of the alfalfa plant are used as feed for cattle. If the alfalfa roots and stalks are plowed into the ground, they help to put back some of the food materials that other plants take out of the soil. Alfalfa is grown on irrigated land in nearly all parts of the West.

Most crops grown on irrigated land must be planted, hoed, weeded, and harvested. In the past, these hard jobs were done mostly by people who moved from one farm to another to help with the crops. These people are called migrant workers. Today, there are still many migrant workers in the West. However, many farmers with irrigated land now use large, costly machines to do most of their planting, weeding, and harvesting.

Farmers with irrigated land sell their crops to people in many parts of the United States. Some of these products, such as fresh fruits and vegetables, must be used quickly. Otherwise, they will spoil. Such farm products are sent to other parts of the country in refrigerated cars on fast trains, or on large cargo planes.

There are irrigated farmlands in every state of the West. The map on page 94 shows us where the irrigated areas are located. These areas are often called oases. †

The Central Valley

The largest oasis in the West lies in the Central Valley of California. Here the land is almost flat, and the soil is fertile. Most of the Central Valley receives very little rainfall in the summer. The fields there must be irrigated with water from reservoirs or wells.

One of the leading crops in the Central Valley is cotton. The long, hot summers here are good for raising this crop. When the cotton is ripe, the fluffy bolls* are picked by huge machines.

† ha. means hectare

Refer to the picture and caption below. Then, refer to the picture on page 81. Can you discover the difference in the way lettuce and cotton are harvested today?

There are seeds in the cotton that must be taken out. This is done by a machine called a cotton gin.

When the seeds have been removed, the cotton is pressed into big bundles called bales. Some of these are sent to factories in the eastern part of the United States. There the cotton is spun into thread. This thread is used in weaving cloth. Some of the cotton produced in California is sent to other countries.

The Central Valley is one of the leading producers of fruits and nuts in the United States. Many grapes are grown in the Central Valley. Almost half of these grapes are dried in the sun to make raisins. Some of the grapes are made into wine. Others are sold fresh in grocery stores and fruit markets. The Central Valley has many orchards where peaches, pears, plums, figs, or olives are grown. Orange and lemon groves are located in sheltered places. The leading nut crops in the Central Valley are almonds and walnuts.

Many other crops are grown in the Central Valley. This area produces

Harvesting cotton in Arizona. Large amounts of cotton are grown on irrigated land in parts of the West where there is a long growing season. Name two important cotton-growing areas in the West.

more than twenty-five kinds of vegetables. Among the most important kinds are potatoes, tomatoes, and asparagus. Some farmers grow barley, oats, rice, or other grains.

Orange groves in southern California

Neat rows of dark-green orange trees cover much farmland near the cities of Los Angeles and Santa Barbara in southern California. (See map on page 61.) Here the climate is mild or warm the year round. California produces more oranges than any other state except Florida.

The Imperial Valley

Another important area of irrigated farmland is the Imperial Valley of southern California. This valley is in a desert near the Mexican border. Water for the farms here is brought by canals from the Colorado River. In the Imperial Valley, winter days are warm and sunny. Vegetables grown during the winter are sold to people who live in the cold parts of our country.

Other oases in the West

In the oases of Washington and Oregon, there are many fruit orchards. The climate here is just right for growing large, bright-red apples. Washington produces more apples than any other state in the United States. Other fruits grown here include pears, peaches, and cherries.

Sugar beets are grown in oases in Colorado, Idaho, and other western states. They sell for a high price, and they do not need a long growing season. The roots of the plants are used to make sugar. The stems are fed to cattle and other livestock.

Potatoes are grown throughout the northern part of the West. Like sugar beets, they can be raised where the growing season is short. They are especially important in the oases along the Snake River in Idaho. (See map on page 94.) Idaho produces more potatoes than any other state.

Many other kinds of vegetables are also grown in oases in the West. Among these vegetables are peas, beans, lettuce, carrots, and onions.

In the oases of Arizona and New Mexico, many farmers grow crops that need a long growing season. The most important is cotton. Grapefruit, dates,

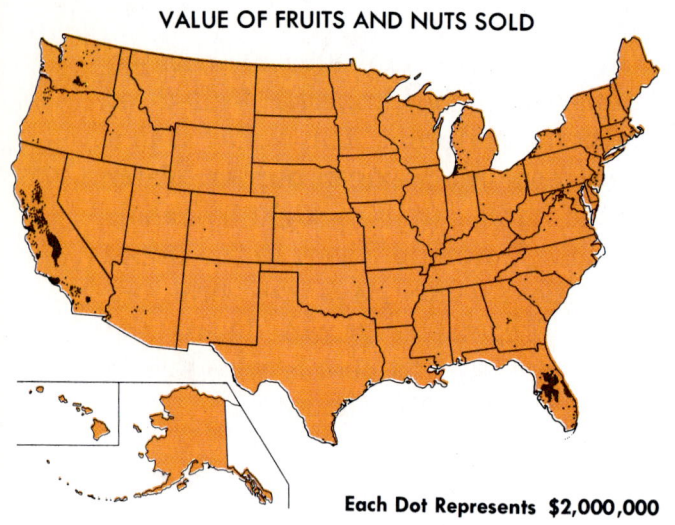

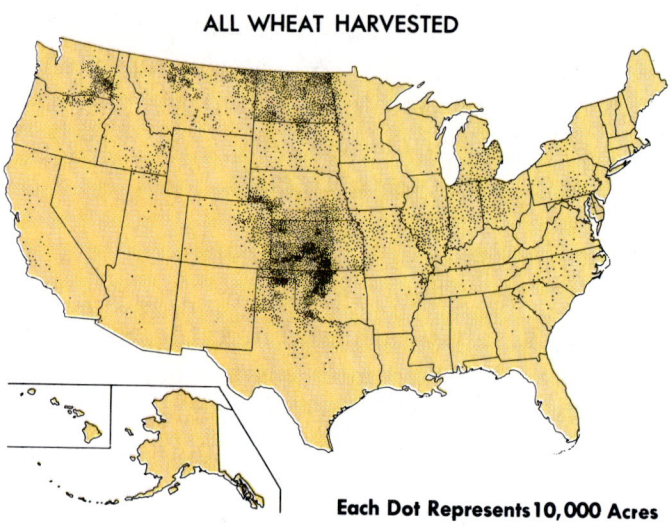

oranges, and other fruits that need a warm climate are grown in Arizona.

Dry Farming

Now we are visiting a wheat farm on the Great Plains in central Montana. (Compare maps on pages 8 and 24.) It is an afternoon in late summer. We are watching a huge machine move slowly across a field of ripe, golden wheat. This machine is a combine, which cuts, threshes,* and cleans the grain. With a combine, one person working alone can harvest many acres of wheat. Driving a combine is a hot, dusty job. The farmer is glad to have a chance to stop and talk with us.

Between the golden wheat fields we notice wide patches of brown earth on which no crops are being grown. We ask the farmer why the land is not being used. The farmer says that he plants wheat on only part of his land at one time. He leaves the rest of the land unplanted, or fallow.* "It's because the climate here is so dry," he explains. "We seldom get more than 15 inches (38 cm.)† of rainfall a year. To grow

† cm. means centimeter

† How do you think the invention of machines, like the combine, has changed farming? Explain.

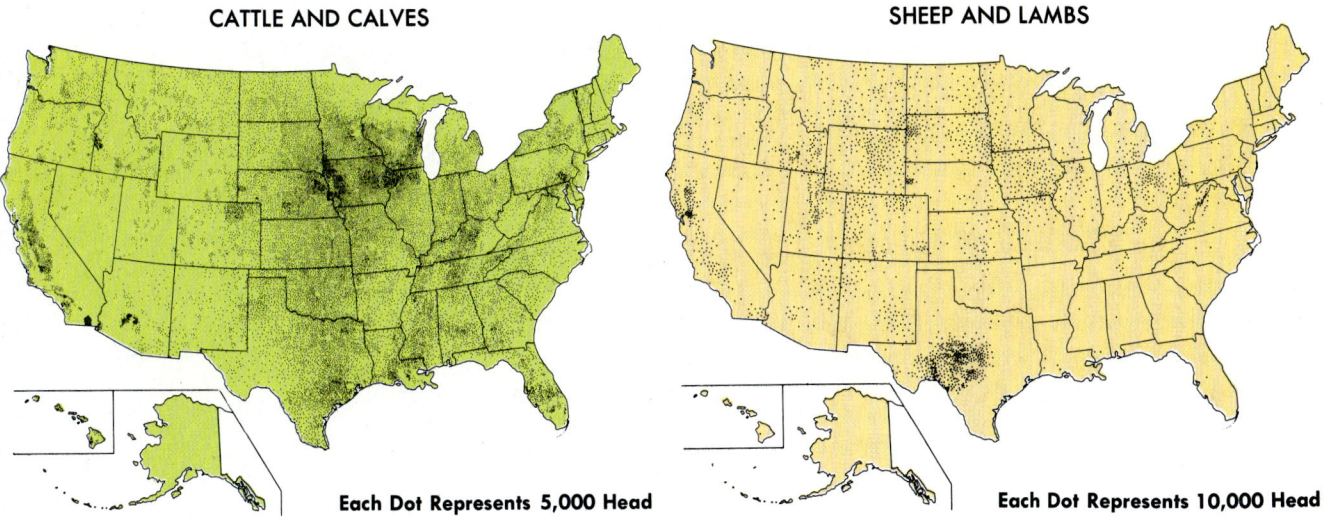

good crops, we must use rainfall from two years instead of one."

Rain that falls on fallow land is stored in the soil. Later, when crops are grown on this land, they can use the stored moisture. They will not need so much rainfall. The fallow fields must be cultivated* several times each summer to keep weeds from growing. Weeds would use some of the precious moisture in the soil.

When land is left fallow, strong winds may blow away much soil. To prevent wind erosion,* some farmers plant their wheat in strips between the fallow fields. This is called "strip-cropping." The wheat stalks slow down the wind so that it does not strike the bare soil with its full force.

The farmer tells us that his farm covers 2,000 acres (809 ha.). He needs such a large farm because he can use only about half of it each year. Because the climate is so dry, he does not get a large harvest of wheat from each acre. Therefore, he must plant many acres of wheat to pay for the combines and other expensive machines that he uses.

The farmer says he bought all this land at a much lower price than he would have had to pay for irrigated farmland.

We ask the farmer where he lives, because we can see no farmhouse. "I live in a town 10 miles (16 km.)† from here," he says. "I'm what they call a 'sidewalk farmer.' I have to be here on the farm for only a few weeks each year. During those weeks I plant and harvest my wheat. Our family would be lonely, living way out here."

The farmer tells us that the kind of farming he does is called "dry farming." This means farming without irrigation, in areas of light rainfall. Dry farming is carried on in every state in the West. However, some parts of the West are too dry even for this kind of farming.

Wheat is the most important crop grown by dry farming in the West. The top right-hand map on the opposite page shows us where the main wheat-farming areas are located. Huge amounts of wheat are raised on the Great Plains of Montana and eastern Colorado. In Montana, farmers plant their wheat in the spring. They harvest

† km. means kilometer

The West 87

it late in summer. This is called spring wheat. In eastern Colorado, winters are not so cold as they are in Montana. Farmers plant their wheat in the fall and harvest it early in the summer. This is called winter wheat.

Large amounts of wheat are also grown on the fertile Columbia Plateau in eastern Washington. Here farmers plant both winter wheat and spring wheat.

† Food that is made from the West's wheat is eaten by people throughout the United States and in other countries. When the wheat is harvested, it is taken to the nearest town. There it is stored in tall buildings called grain elevators. Later it is loaded into railroad cars and taken to flour mills in the cities.

Wheat is not the only crop grown by dry farming. Barley is an important crop in some of the dry areas of California, Montana, and other states of the West. Peas, rye, and alfalfa are also grown by dry-farming methods.

Grazing

We have learned that much of the land in the West is used for raising cattle and sheep. These animals feed on grass that grows where the land is too dry or too steep for raising crops. Feeding on grass is called grazing. More than half of all the grazing lands in the United States are in the West.

To learn more about grazing in the West, let's visit a cattle ranch in Wyoming. It is late September, which is roundup time at the ranch. All summer long, the cattle have been grazing on green pastures high in the mountains. Now the cowhands are bringing them back to a corral at the ranch headquarters. A corral is a pen where animals are kept.

The cattle that are a year old are called yearlings. They are being separated from the other animals. The yearlings have been sold to a corn farmer in the Midwest. They will be taken to a nearby town and loaded into railroad cars for their journey to the Midwest.

We ask the rancher why he sells his cattle to a midwestern corn farmer. The rancher says that the cattle he raises are very lean. This is because they feed

† What kinds of food do you eat that are made from wheat?

Using Natural Resources

See Great Ideas

The farmer shown in the picture above raises barley by using dry-farming methods. These methods make it possible to grow crops in areas that receive only 10 to 20 inches (25 to 51 cm.) of rainfall a year. Dry-farming methods provide a good example of the careful use of natural resources. Besides water, what other important resource must farmers try to save? How is this resource sometimes lost? Do you think it can ever be replaced? Why? Why not?

Refer to the picture and caption above. Have students answer the questions about natural resources.

mainly on grass. The corn farmer in the Midwest is glad to buy these lean yearlings in the fall, after he has harvested his crops. He will feed the yearlings some of his corn to fatten them. Then he will sell them for meat.

The rancher also tells us what happens to the cattle that are not sold at roundup time. These animals will be taken to nearby pastures. There they will graze until January. Then the rancher will bring them to sheds at the ranch headquarters. The cattle must be protected from the bitterly cold winter weather in this area.

During the rest of the winter, the rancher must supply his cattle with food. He has worked all summer growing alfalfa. Now he will have enough hay to feed the animals. He grows the alfalfa on a small plot of irrigated land along the banks of a stream that runs through the ranch.

Until recently, ranchers in Wyoming sent most of their cattle to farms in the Midwest to be fattened. Now, many ranchers sell large numbers of cattle to farmers who own irrigated farms in the West. The irrigation farmers fatten the cattle on farm products such as sugar beet pulp and pea vines. Many cattle are being fattened on irrigated lands in California in order to help feed the large number of people there.

In the southern part of the West, winters are warmer. Cattle can graze all year round on the same land. But the climate is so dry that cattle sometimes cannot find enough grass to eat or water to drink.

Cattle on a western ranch. Much of the land in the West is used for raising cattle and other animals. Cattle and calves are the West's leading farm product. Why do so many western farmers raise cattle?

† Refer to map on page 27. Have students point out the areas that receive at least 20 inches of rain annually.

Many ranchers in the West raise sheep instead of cattle. Sheep do not need so much water or such rich grass as cattle do. Sheep can graze in very dry areas and in mountain pastures that are too rugged for cattle. Some ranchers take their sheep to the mountains during the summer to graze on grass that grows on the mountain slopes. During the winter, the sheep graze on plateaus or in sheltered mountain valleys.

Farming Where Rain Is Plentiful

† To grow most crops without using irrigation or dry-farming methods, farmers need at least 20 inches (51 cm.) of rainfall a year. The map on page 27 shows that only a small part of the West receives this much rainfall. Most of the farmlands in the West that get more than 20 inches (51 cm.) of rain a year are located in the Puget-Willamette Lowland of Washington and Oregon.

In the Puget-Willamette Lowland, there are many dairy farms. The mild, rainy climate of this area is good for growing grass needed by dairy cows. Some of the milk from these cows is sold to people in nearby cities and towns. However, much of it is made into butter or cheese and sent to other parts of the West.

Many different kinds of crops are grown in the Puget-Willamette Lowland. Some farmers raise wheat or barley. Others grow such vegetables as beans and cabbages. There are many orchards where cherries, pears, and other kinds of fruit are grown. Berry farming is also important here. Some farmers raise flower bulbs, such as tulips, daffodils, and iris to sell to people for their gardens.

A sheep ranch in Montana. Many ranchers in the West raise sheep instead of cattle. What facts explain why this is so?

Investigate an Interesting Topic ††
Wheat is an important farm product of the West. Do research about wheat. Then write a report about it to share with your class. You may wish to use the questions below as a guide.
1. What are the parts of the wheat plant and the wheat kernel? (You may want to draw a diagram.)
2. How is wheat planted?
3. How is wheat harvested?
4. What is the difference between winter wheat and spring wheat?
5. What are some of the uses of wheat?

See "Learning Social Studies Skills" in the Skills Manual for help in finding information and in preparing your report.

†† Have students do this activity.
Use Fideler Discovery Card 100, or Fideler Discovery Sheets, Volume 1, pages 43 or 44 for additional activities.

Grand Coulee Dam on the Columbia River in Washington. The lake behind this dam supplies water to nearby areas that receive little rain. What are some ways in which people use water?

9 Natural Resources and Energy

A Problem To Solve

Why are natural resources important to the people of the West? In making hypotheses* to solve this problem, you will need to think about how the natural resources of the West have affected the following:

a. the location of towns and cities here
b. the growth of industry
c. the ways in which some of the people here earn their living

Information in Chapters 5, 8 and 10 will help you solve this problem.

See Skills Manual, "Thinking and Solving Problems"
*See Glossary

Natural resources are gifts of nature that people use to meet their needs. The part of our country we call the West is rich in natural resources. In some places, the soil is fertile and there is plenty of warm sunshine. Farmers use these natural resources in growing their crops. Rainfall is light in many parts of the West. But there are rivers and lakes that help to supply the water people need. Under the surface of the earth are large deposits of copper, oil, and other useful minerals. In some parts of the West, there are valuable forests. Also, the waters of the Pacific Ocean are rich in fish.

Water Resources

Water is one of our most important resources. People drink water. They use it to wash dishes, clothing, and other things. Factories use water in making many products. Farmers use water to raise crops and animals. Water is also used to produce electricity for homes and factories. Boats travel on waterways such as rivers and lakes. These bodies of water are also used for swimming and other sports.

Not enough water in the right places

The water that we use comes to the earth in the form of rain or snow. As you discovered in Chapter 3, rainfall is very light in most parts of the West. It is heavier in the mountains. But in these rugged areas there are few people to use the water. We can say that the West does not have enough water in the right places.

If people are to live and work in the dry parts of the West, they must get water from places where there is more rainfall. One way to do this is by building dams. To learn how dams can help supply water to dry areas, let's take a trip to the state of Washington. †

A visit to Grand Coulee Dam

We are camping on a hill high above the Columbia River. When we look at the bare, brown land around us, we can tell that this area receives little rain. In the distance we see what appears to be a huge wall that stretches across the river. This is Grand Coulee Dam.

We drive down to the dam for a closer look. There we meet a guide who explains why Grand Coulee Dam was built. She says it is like a wall that holds back the

† How do you think people in these areas obtained water before large dams were constructed? Explain your answer.

water of the Columbia River. Behind the dam, the water has formed a huge lake, or reservoir.*

Irrigation.* Some of the water in the lake is used for farming. This part of Washington is so dry that farmers must irrigate their land to grow most crops. Water for irrigation is pumped from this lake into another reservoir nearby. From there it flows through canals, ditches, and large pipes to the farms where it is needed.

Flood Control. In the past, the Columbia River sometimes rose so high that it flooded the land. Floods destroyed houses and crops. Today the dam helps to prevent floods. When the river is high, some of the water is stored in the lake behind the dam so that it will not flood the land. When the river is low, some water from the lake is allowed to flow through pipes in the dam to the river far below.

Waterpower. The dam has another important use. Water from the lake is allowed to flow through the large pipes inside the dam. The rushing water turns huge engines called turbines. These are located in two buildings called powerhouses, at the foot of the dam. The turbines run machines that produce electricity. Wires carry the electricity to many homes and factories in Washington, Oregon, and Idaho.

Water Resources

This map shows some of the most important rivers and dams in the West. It also shows areas of irrigated land.

† 1. What are three different purposes for which dams have been built in the West?
2. Compare this map with the map on page 46. What relationship do you see between the location of irrigated lands and population distribution in the West? Why do you think this relationship exists?

† Use these questions in a discussion about water resources in the West.

Irrigating a farm field in Colorado. Irrigation is an example of the wise use of water. Do you think there will always be enough water to meet people's needs? Why do you think this?

Sports. Our guide tells us that Grand Coulee Dam helps the people of this area in still another way. The lake behind the dam can be used for swimming, fishing, and other sports.

Many dams in the West

There are many other dams besides Grand Coulee in the West. Some are built of concrete.* Others are made of many layers of earth packed tightly together. The map on page 94 shows the most important of these dams.

Like Grand Coulee, these dams are useful in different ways. Many are used to store water for irrigation. Some are used mostly to prevent floods or to provide waterpower for making electricity. Still others are used to store the water needed by people who live in cities.

Pumping water from wells

Not all of the water used in the West comes from rivers and lakes. There is more water under the ground than there is in all the rivers and lakes of the West. Most of this water comes from rain and snow that fall on the mountains.

Some of the water on the mountain slopes soaks into the ground. It goes down into layers of rock beneath the soil. Because these layers are full of

† Does anyone know where the water used in our area comes from? Explain.

The West 95

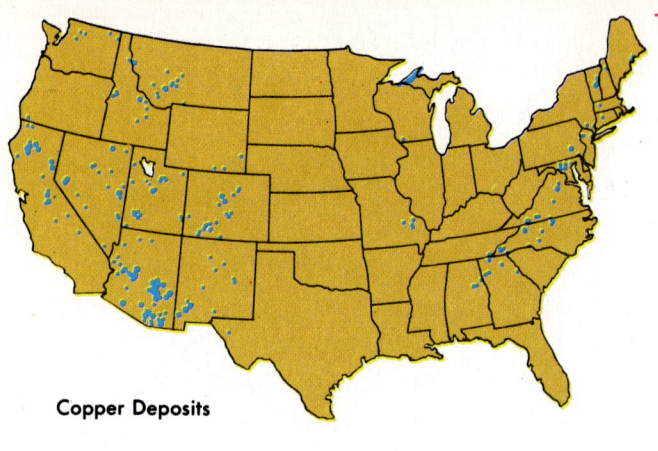

Copper Deposits

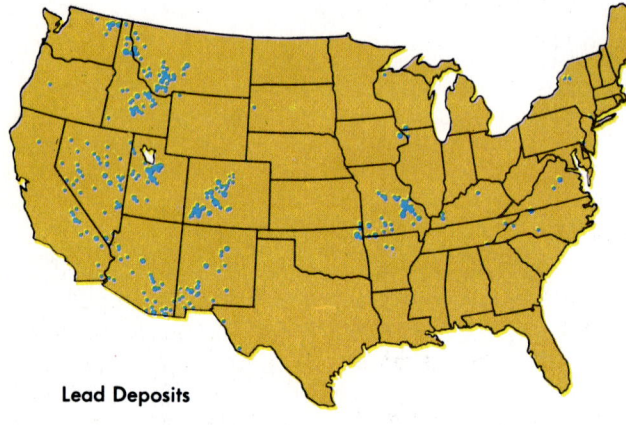

Lead Deposits

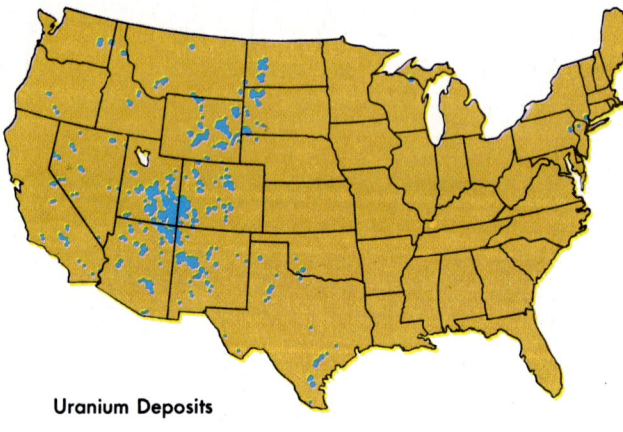

Uranium Deposits

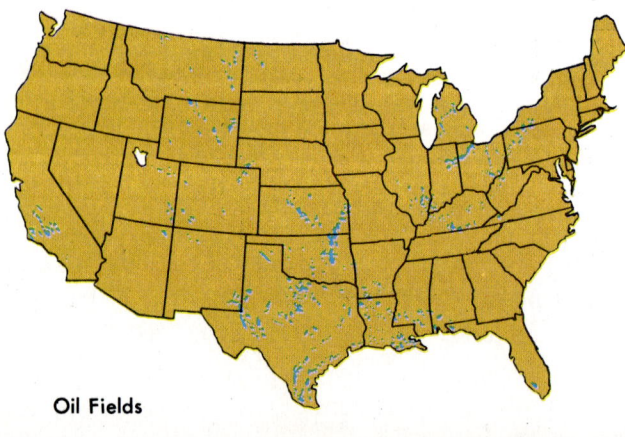

Oil Fields

† Refer to the Water Resources map on page 94. Have students point out areas on the map that are far from rivers or lakes.

tiny holes and cracks, they can hold large amounts of water, just as a sponge does. The water that remains in the soil and rock is called groundwater. Layers of rock and soil that contain groundwater often extend from mountains into nearby valleys.

When people want to get water from beneath the ground, they drill wells. Then they use pumps to bring the water to the surface. In parts of Arizona and in the Central Valley of California, farmers use large amounts of groundwater to irrigate their fields.

Why much land is not irrigated

Irrigation has helped many western farmers to grow crops in dry places. But irrigated lands cover only a very small part of the West.

It will probably never be possible to irrigate all the dry lands of the West. The main reason is that there is not enough water. The West is already using most of the water that it receives every year from rain and snow.

Many places in the West are far from † rivers or lakes that could supply water for irrigation. Water would have to be brought long distances through aqueducts.* Farmers would have to pay so much for this water that they would not be able to make a profit from growing crops.

Even where there is plenty of water, it cannot always be used for irrigation. Some water contains salt or other minerals* that are harmful to crops. Often the water cannot be used because it is full of waste materials from homes and factories. Today our government is working to clean up the water in rivers and lakes.

96

† Have students make a list of ten things they use that need energy to make them work.

Mineral Resources

Perhaps you have seen a movie or a television show about prospectors in the West. A prospector is a person who goes from place to place hunting for gold, silver, or other minerals.

There were many prospectors in the West during the 1800's. Rich deposits of gold and silver were found in California, Nevada, and other western states. Many cities and towns in the West were started by people who were looking for these valuable minerals.

Minerals are still important to people of the West. Some people work in mines or oil fields where minerals are taken from the ground. Others work in factories where these minerals are made into hundreds of products.

Energy Fuels

Three of the most valuable minerals found in the West are oil, natural gas, and coal. These are known as energy fuels, because they can be burned to
† produce energy. We need energy to give us heat and light. We also need energy to run all the machines we use in our everyday lives. (See "Meeting Our Need for Energy" at right.)

Oil

Oil, or petroleum, is a dark-colored liquid that is found in layers of rock deep in the earth. To learn how people get oil, imagine that we are driving along the Pacific coast near Long Beach, California. (See map on page 8.) From our car, we can see a group of tall steel towers. These are oil derricks. They support the long pipes and other equipment needed in drilling for oil.

Discuss some of the reasons we may be running out of oil.

Meeting Our Need for Energy

In the United States today, people get energy from a number of different sources. The chart below shows the main sources of energy in our country.

Notice that about ninety-three percent of all the energy we use comes from oil, natural gas, and coal. These energy fuels are found in deposits under the earth. They were all formed from the remains of plants and animals that lived on the earth millions of years ago.

Today the United States does not have enough oil and natural gas. New deposits of these fuels are becoming harder to find. Some experts believe we will run out of oil and natural gas by about the year 2000.

We still have enough coal under the ground to meet all our energy needs for several hundred years. But coal cannot be used as a fuel to run cars and airplanes. Also, the burning of coal causes serious air pollution. Scientists are looking for ways to change coal into liquid or a gas. They want to develop a new kind of fuel that will be cleaner and more useful than coal.

Today people are trying to make use of new sources of energy. One of these is solar energy—the energy that comes to the earth in the form of sunlight. Another is nuclear* energy. However, many problems must be solved before these new sources of energy can take the place of oil and natural gas.

*See Glossary

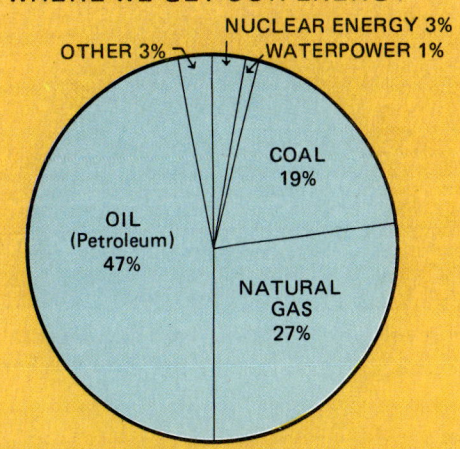

Drilling for oil. The most valuable mineral product of the West is oil. Which is the most important oil-producing state in the West? Where are some of the other oil fields in the West located?

After a well has been drilled, the derrick is taken down. It is later used at a different place. Near the derricks are several oil pumps. Long arms on the pumps rock slowly up and down as the oil is brought from the earth. The oil is sent through large pipes to factories called refineries. There it is used to make gasoline and other products.

The oil field that we see here is only one of many oil-producing areas in California. This state produces more oil than any other state in the West. Most of California's oil fields are located along the Pacific coast in the southern part of the state, or in the Central Valley.

If we could travel through other states of the West, we would see many other oil fields. Some of the largest are in the state of Wyoming. Others are in eastern Montana, northern Colorado, and southeastern New Mexico.

Oil shale

In Colorado, Utah, and Wyoming, there are huge deposits of rock called oil shale. A form of oil can be obtained from this rock by heating it. In the past, very little oil shale was mined. The reason was that it cost much more to produce oil in this way than it did to pump oil from the ground.

Today, our country is beginning to run out of oil that can be pumped from the ground cheaply. (See "Meeting Our Need for Energy" on page 97.) Also, scientists are finding less costly ways of getting oil from oil shale. In the future, it may be possible to obtain large amounts of oil from the deposits of oil shale in the West.

Natural gas

Many people in the West use natural gas for heating, cooking, and other purposes. Natural gas is found wherever there is oil. Sometimes it is also found in places under the ground where there is no oil. New Mexico and California produce more natural gas than any other states in the West. Large pipes carry the natural gas to cities and towns where it is needed.

Coal

There are vast deposits of coal in the West, especially in the states of Wyoming, Utah, Colorado, and Montana. Until a few years ago, people did not bother to mine very much coal in the West. Most of this coal was thought to be of poor quality. Also, it was far from large cities where it could be used. Sending the coal for long distances by train was expensive.

† Do you think we might use more coal in the future than we have in the past? Why? Why not?

Today, all this is changing. Coal is becoming more important as a source of energy. Some of the coal in the West is now known to be of high quality. Also, people are finding cheaper ways of moving the coal to places where it is needed. Several new coal mines have been opened in the West, and others will be opened in the future.

Most of the coal mined in the West today is used as a fuel in electric power plants. Some coal is made into a fuel called coke,* which is used in making iron and steel.

Metals

It is hard to imagine what our lives would be like without metals such as iron and copper. Metals are used in making cars, stoves, television sets, and hundreds of other products.

The West is an important producer of metals. For example, it produces more than nine tenths of all the copper and silver mined in the United States. It also supplies about two thirds of the gold and more than one fourth of the zinc mined in our country.

The map on page 24 helps explain why the West is so rich in metals. Most of this area is made up of mountains or high plateaus. Metal ores* are likely to be found in places where there are mountains.

Millions of years ago, rocks containing metal ores were buried deep under the ground. Then movements within the earth pushed masses of rock upward to form mountains. Over many thousands of years, water and ice wore away some of the rock on the mountainsides. Layers of rock that contained metal ores were uncovered in places where people could find them.

Copper

One of the most useful metals found in the West is copper. Electricity passes through this metal easily. For this reason, copper wires are used to carry electricity into homes and factories. Telephones and other appliances contain many copper wires. Because copper does not rust, it is used to make pipes that carry water. Copper is also used in making pennies and other coins.

To learn about copper mining in the West, let's visit the city of Butte, Montana. (See map on page 8.) The hill on which this city was built has been called "the richest hill on earth" because it contains so much valuable ore.

On the edge of Butte, we see a huge pit in the earth like the one shown on the opposite page. The sides of this pit have been dug out to form terraces that look like stairsteps. On some of the terraces we can see giant electric shovels scooping up loads of rock. The rock is being dumped into trucks that will carry it out of the mine.

A miner tells us that the rock will be taken to a factory nearby. There, large machines crush the rock into tiny bits. Some of these are bits of copper ore. The rest are waste materials. The ore is taken in railroad cars to a plant called a smelter. This plant is in the town of Anaconda, twenty-five miles away. In the smelter, the ore is heated in large furnaces. This separates the copper from other materials in the ore.

The copper produced at the smelter is not pure enough for some purposes. It contains small amounts of gold and other metals. Some of the copper is sent to a plant called a refinery, where most of these other metals are removed.

Refer to the map on page 8. Have students locate Butte, Montana. In what mountain range are the Butte copper mines located?

The pure copper is then sent to mills where it is made into sheets, tubes, and wires. Now it is ready to be used by other factories in making many different products.

In the West, there are many other open-pit copper mines like the one we have just visited. Some of the largest are in Arizona, Utah, and Nevada. Arizona produces more copper than any other state in our country.

Lead and zinc

Two other important metals found in the West are lead and zinc. Lead is used to make paint, car batteries, and many other products. Zinc is mixed with copper to make brass. Because zinc does not rust, it is also used as a coating for iron products such as pails. Idaho produces more lead than any other state in the West. Colorado leads the West in zinc mining.

Gold and silver

In the West today, there are very few gold miners like the prospectors of one hundred years ago. Today, nearly all of the gold and silver is mined by large companies.

An open-pit copper mine in Arizona. Copper ore is dug from open-pit mines in several states of the West. Arizona ranks first in our country in the production of this useful mineral.

Gold and silver are often found in the same ores that contain copper. Since Utah, Arizona, and Montana have large copper mines, it is not surprising that they also produce much gold and silver. Gold is also taken from a large open-pit mine near Elko, Nevada. (See map on page 61.) This is the second richest gold mine in North America.

There are large silver mines in the mountains of northern Idaho. This state produces more silver than any other state in our country.

Iron and other metals

Many other metal ores are found in the West today. One of the most important is iron ore. This ore is needed to make iron and steel. Large amounts of iron ore are mined in California, Utah, and Wyoming. Ore from these mines is sent to steel mills in California, Utah, and other states.

The West produces large amounts of uranium. This metal is used in producing nuclear* energy. There are many small uranium mines in the "Four Corners" area, where the states of Utah, Colorado, Arizona, and New Mexico come together. New Mexico is our country's leading producer of uranium.

Three other important metals found in the West are molybdenum, vanadium, and manganese. These metals are used with iron ore to make certain kinds of steel that are very hard and strong. Colorado produces over one half of the molybdenum in the United States. It is also a leading producer of vanadium. Manganese ore is mined in the states of Montana and New Mexico.

Other Minerals

The West has large deposits of other minerals besides energy fuels and metal ores. There are deposits of sand, gravel, and stone in every state of the West. Each year, people use millions of tons of these materials to build highways and buildings. Large amounts of limestone are used in making cement. California produces more cement than any other state except Texas.

Several kinds of valuable minerals are found in the Great Basin. (See page 20.) Among these minerals are salt, potash,* and borates.* Potash is also taken from underground mines in southeastern New Mexico. These are the largest deposits of potash in the United States.

Using Natural Resources

See Great Ideas

A **gravel plant in California.** Many different kinds of minerals are found in the West. Why do you think minerals are called "natural" resources? What are some other kinds of natural resources? With other members of your class, discuss ways in which people use and misuse natural resources. Some of the information you will need for your discussion may be found in this chapter. Suggestions in the Skills Manual at the back of the book will help you locate other information and hold a successful discussion.

Forest Resources

In a western forest

We are watching the sun rise over a beautiful mountain lake in Idaho. Birds are singing above us in the tall pine trees. Near the shore of the lake, we can see a mound of twigs and branches that was built by a family of beavers. Suddenly we see a mother deer and a spotted fawn as they dart through the forest.

As we are cooking breakfast over our campfire, a smiling woman in a green uniform comes up to talk with us. She is a forest ranger. Her job is to take care of the forest.

Where the West's forests are located

† The ranger tells us that we would see many forests like this one if we traveled through the West. Almost one third of the West is covered with forests. Although much of the West is too dry for trees to grow, there are large forests in the mountains. There the rainfall is heavier.

The largest forests in the West are in the Cascade Range and in the coastal mountains of Washington, Oregon, and northern California. Trees grow very well in the mild, wet climate of this area. Most of the trees are large evergreens, such as spruce, hemlock, cedar, and Douglas fir. Along the coast of northern California and southern

† Have you ever visited thick forests like this in the West or elsewhere? Have some students describe their experiences.

Cutting timber in a western forest. Forests cover almost one third of the West. Where are the largest forests located? Why are forests important to the people of the West?

† Use Fideler Discovery Card 91 (Discover products made from forest resources).

Oregon are forests of coast redwoods. These are among the tallest trees in the world.

Dense forests also grow on the western slopes of the Sierra Nevada in California. Here most of the trees are also evergreens, mostly pines and firs. In some places, there are groves of giant sequoias. These huge trees have larger trunks than the coast redwoods but are not so tall.

Because the Rocky Mountains receive less rainfall than the mountains farther west, the forests in the Rockies are not so dense. Among the main kinds of trees that grow here are pines, firs, and spruces.

Why forests are important

The wood that comes from forests † in the West is used in many different ways. Some of it is sawed into lumber. It is used for building houses, making furniture, and for other purposes. Some of the wood is made into pulp.* Paper and other products are made from this material. Many people in the West have jobs in factories that make wood products.

Forests are also important for other reasons. For example, they help to store the water that falls on the mountains in the form of rain or snow. Under the trees, the winter snow melts slowly. Some of the water sinks into the soft forest soil and trickles down the mountains beneath the ground.

If there were no forests on the mountain slopes, the sun would melt the winter snow quickly. The water would have little chance to sink into the soil. It would pour into the rivers, causing many of them to rise and flood the

The West 105

Loading logs in a western forest. Today, loggers are using our forests more wisely than they did in the past. What are some of the ways in which lumber companies are helping to conserve our forests?

land nearby. Most of the water would flow away so quickly it could not be used by the people of the West.

Trees also hold the soil. They keep it from being washed away, into rivers and streams. Without the forests, many reservoirs in the West would fill up with soil. Then these reservoirs could no longer be used to store water for irrigation.

National forests

Because forests are so valuable to everyone, they must be protected carefully. Many forests are owned by the national government. These are called national forests. (See map on page 107.) There are about one hundred national forests in the states of the West.

The national forests are used in many different ways. During the summer,

ranch owners let their sheep and cattle graze on grassy meadows among the forests. They pay the government for the use of this land. Many kinds of wild animals make their homes in the forests. Here they can find food and shelter. The national forests are also used for recreation. Each year, millions of people camp, hunt and fish, or enjoy winter sports in these forests.

Some of the trees in the national forests are cut for lumber and other purposes. Each year, the rangers decide which trees are ready for cutting. Private companies pay the government for the right to cut these trees and use the wood. The rangers make sure that new trees will grow up to replace the ones that have been cut down.

Other forests

Not all the forests in the West are owned by the national government. Some are owned by states or cities. Many forests are owned by private companies. These companies cut down some of the trees to use in making lumber, paper, and other products.

Lumbering is an important industry in the West. The chart below shows us the five states of the West that produce the most lumber. More than half of all the lumber produced in our country comes from these five states.

NATIONAL FORESTS IN THE WEST

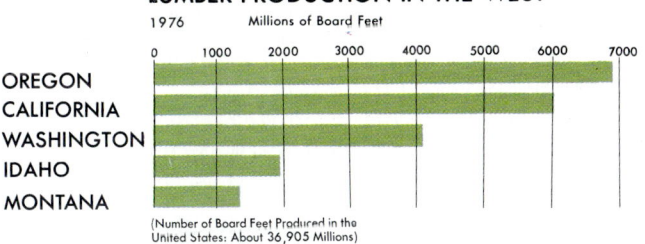

The chart above shows lumber production in the five main lumbering states of the West. More than half of all the lumber produced in our country comes from these five states.

The West 107

Fish Resources

Along the Pacific coast of the United States, fishing is an important industry. Many kinds of fish live in the waters of the Pacific Ocean. Each year millions of pounds of fish are brought to shore by fishers in California, Oregon, and Washington.

California is the most important fishing state in our country except for Alaska. About two thirds of all the fish that are caught by people in the West are brought to ports in California. To learn more about this state's fishing industry, let's visit Terminal Island in the harbor of Los Angeles.

A visit to a tuna fleet

We are standing on a long platform, called a pier. It extends into the harbor. Here the air smells of fish, salt water, and fuel oil. In the harbor, we can see the tall masts of many fishing boats. Some of these boats are large enough to hold a crew of fifteen persons.

A fisher standing on the pier tells us that the larger boats are used for tuna fishing. They have to be large and sturdy because they go far out to sea. These fishing trips may take several weeks. Sometimes the tuna fishers go all the way to South America looking for fish to catch.

We learn that the tuna swim around in the ocean in large groups called schools. When workers on a fishing boat find a school of tuna, they drop a huge net into the water. The fish are trapped by closing the net with a rope, in the same way a purse is closed with a drawstring. A powerful engine is used to pull in the net. The fish are then loaded into the boat.

Not all of California's tuna are caught with nets. On some boats, the fishers use bamboo poles. Each pole has a line and a hook hanging from the end. When a tuna is hooked, the fisher raises the pole quickly and flips the fish into the boat.

As soon as the fish are caught, they are chilled in icy salt water. Then they are put in large refrigerators so they will stay fresh. When the boat returns to port, the fish are taken to nearby factories called

In the picture above, tuna fish are being caught with poles and lines. Not all of the tuna brought to fishing ports in the West are caught in this way. Many are taken with nets. As the chart below shows, California is the West's leading fishing state. The only state in our country that earns more money from fishing is Alaska.

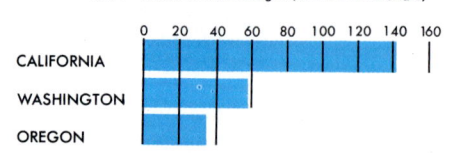

LEADING FISHING STATES IN THE WEST
1974 Value of Fish Caught (Millions of Dollars)

(Total Value of Fish Caught in the United States: $932,464,000)

Refer to the picture on these pages. What can you discover about tuna fishing? List your discoveries.

canneries. There they are cut in pieces, packed in cans, and cooked. The cans of tuna are sold in food stores all over the United States.

Los Angeles is not the only city in California with a tuna fleet. Many fishing boats dock at San Diego and other cities along the Pacific coast.

A visit to a "fish ladder"

† Now we are driving eastward from Portland, Oregon, along the south bank of the Columbia River. (See map on page 8.) On both sides of the river are steep, wooded mountains. Ahead of us we see a large dam that has been built across the river. This is Bonneville Dam.

We notice what seem to be large stairsteps. They lead up around the end of the dam and into the lake beyond. But as we come closer, we see that this "stairway" is really a series of pools. They are like the ones in the picture on page 110. Each pool is one foot higher than the one below it. Water flows down from one pool to the next in a series of waterfalls.

Suddenly we see a large fish jump out of one pool into the pool above it. Then the fish leaps into the next pool, and then the next, until it reaches the lake behind the dam. This fish is a salmon. It has just climbed a fish ladder.

A guide at the dam tells us why the fish ladder was built. She says that the

† Have students locate the Columbia River on the map on page 8.

Refer to the picture and caption below. Use the questions in a class discussion about rules and government.

Rules and Government

See Great Ideas

A "fish ladder" at Bonneville Dam on the Columbia River. The federal* government built this fish ladder to help salmon get past the dam. How did building the fish ladder help protect the supply of salmon in the West? In what other ways are the fish in our country's lakes and rivers protected? Do you think private groups and individual citizens need to help in the conservation* of our fish supply? Give reasons for your answer.

salmon here are hatched in streams that may be more than 200 miles (322 km.)† from the sea. While they are young, they swim all the way to the ocean. There they live for two to six years. When the salmon are full grown, they return to the streams to lay their eggs.

On their long journey up the rivers, the salmon often leap high over rocks and waterfalls. But they cannot leap over dams. Fish ladders are built so the salmon can get past the dams to lay their eggs. Otherwise, there would soon be no more salmon.

In Washington, Oregon, and northern California, salmon fishing is a very important industry. Thousands of people earn their living by catching salmon or working in salmon canneries.

Unlike tuna fishers, people who catch salmon do not make long trips out to sea. Some of them sail along the coast in small boats. They catch the salmon as the fish are returning to the rivers to lay their eggs. Others spread nets across the rivers to catch the fish.

Most of the salmon are taken to canneries near the river mouths. Nearly all the work in the canneries is done by machines. First the heads, fins, and tails of the salmon are cut off. Then the fish are cleaned, cut into pieces, and sealed in cans. The salmon are cooked in the cans, then shipped to all parts of our country. Not all the salmon are canned. Some are smoked or frozen. Others are sold fresh in fish markets.

Other kinds of fish.

Off the coasts of Washington and Oregon, people also catch large numbers of halibut. Some of these fish weigh several hundred pounds. Most of the halibut are sold fresh or are frozen. They are shipped to other parts of the country on fast trains with refrigerated cars.

Mackerel is one of the leading kinds of fish caught in the ocean near the coast of southern California. Fishers catch the mackerel in large nets. Some of the mackerel are canned, and some are sold fresh in fish markets.

From the ocean, people in the West get many other kinds of seafood. Among these are sea herring, sole, and sea bass. Shellfish such as crabs, shrimp, and clams are also caught. People who live near the Pacific coast can buy fresh seafood at markets.

† km. means kilometer

† **Practice Using Your Map Skills**
With the help of the map on page 8 and the maps and charts in this chapter, answer these questions.
1. Which state in the West has the most irrigated farmland?
2. Which state has the most copper?
3. Which is the leading fishing state in the West?

†† **Use Your Creativity**
Choose one of the following projects. You will find some of the information you need in this chapter. "Learning Social Studies Skills" in the Skills Manual will help you locate more information.
1. Write a report about a dam in the West that provides water both for irrigation and for making hydroelectricity. For example, you might write about Shasta Dam or Hoover Dam. You may wish to illustrate your report with diagrams or pictures.
2. Write a story about the life of a salmon. Tell where the salmon was hatched and where it spent most of its life. Also tell how it made its way upstream as a full-grown fish.

† Have each student write the answers to these questions.
†† Have students select one of these projects to research and write about.

A paper mill in Washington. Wood is the raw material used for making paper in this large factory.

10 Industry

A Visit to a Paper Mill

We are flying in a small plane over the western part of the state of Washington. On our left, we can see green forests and high mountains. On our right is a large body of water. This is Juan de Fuca Strait. It connects Puget Sound with the Pacific Ocean.

Along the shore of the strait, we see a large factory with tall smokestacks. Our pilot tells us that this is a paper mill. After our plane lands, we visit the mill to see how paper is made.

Wood for the paper mill

Our guide at the paper mill tells us that wood is the raw material used for making paper here. Each year, thousands of trees in the forests we saw from the airplane are cut down. The logs are sent to sawmills where they are made into lumber. When this is done, many tons of wood scrap are left over. This material used to be burned and wasted. Now it is used in making paper.

Large trucks and barges bring wood chips and sawdust from the sawmills to this paper mill.

Machines for making paper

Now our guide shows us what happens to the wood chips and sawdust after they arrive at the mill. We see the chips and sawdust being put into huge grinding machines.

Water is added to the ground-up material. This mixture is called pulp. The pulp now goes to the papermaking machines. There are three of these huge machines in this mill. The pulp is poured onto a screen that moves at a speed of thirteen to twenty miles an hour. (See the picture below.) As the screen moves along, much of the water is drained away. The wood fibers* in the pulp join together to form paper. Then the paper passes between heavy rollers. These rollers squeeze out the rest of the water and give the paper a smooth surface.

As the paper comes out of the machine, it is wound into huge rolls. Some of these rolls weigh more than eight tons. Next, the wide rolls are cut into narrower rolls. Now the paper is ready to be sent to customers.

*See Glossary

Part of a papermaking machine. To make paper, wood pulp is poured onto the moving screen shown below. As the screen moves along, most of the water is drained away. The wood fibers in the pulp join together to form paper.

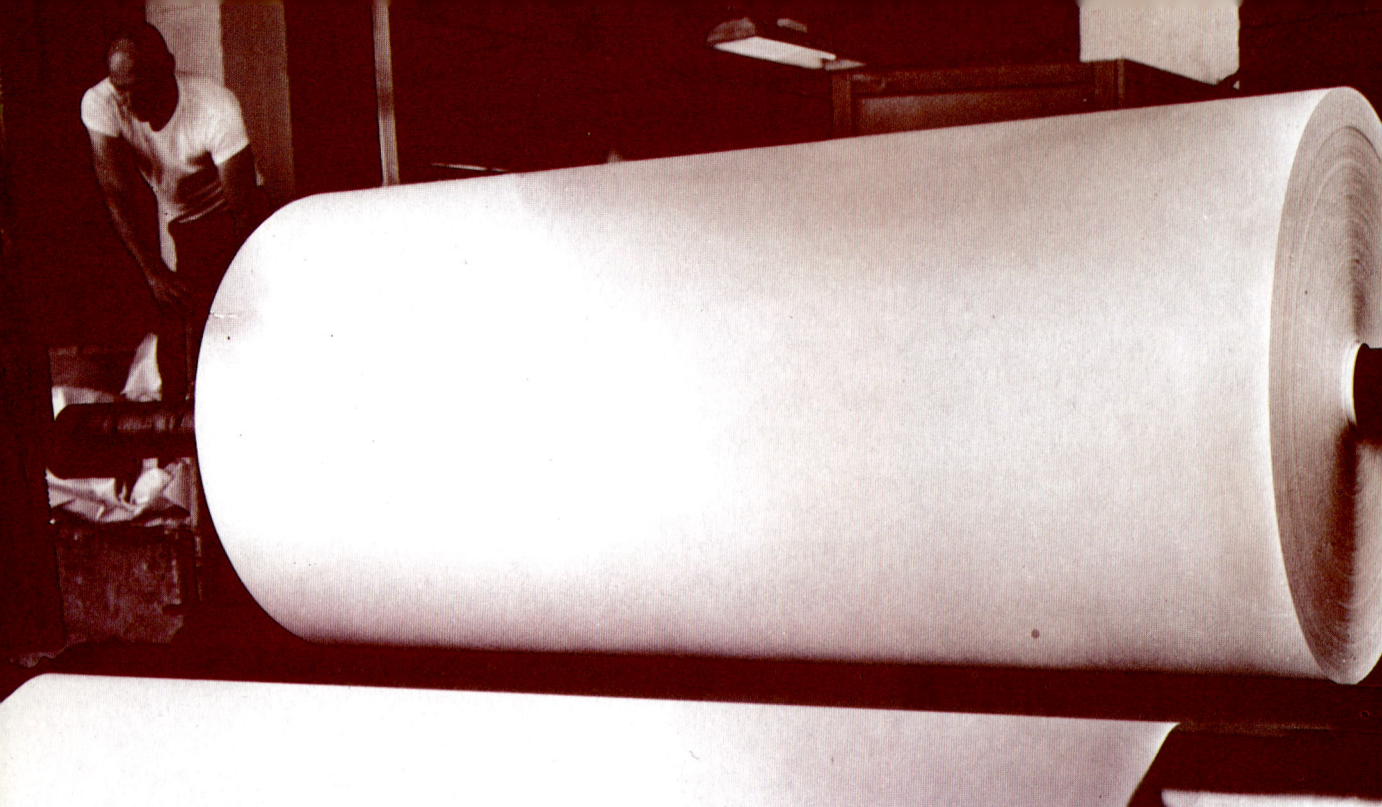

A roll of paper. The wet paper that comes from the screen (see picture on page 113) passes between heavy rollers. These rollers squeeze out the rest of the water and give the paper a smooth surface. As the paper comes out of the papermaking machine, it is wound into huge rolls.

Power for the paper mill

A large amount of electric power is needed to run the machines in this paper mill. The mill gets some of its power from a river that flows from the mountains nearby. Two power plants have been built on this river by the company that owns the paper mill. The mill also uses electric power produced at Bonneville Dam on the Columbia River.

Water for the paper mill

The nearby river supplies the paper mill with the water it needs. We learn that it takes 15,000 gallons of water to make one ton of paper. However, the mill is able to use much of this water over and over. The mill makes sure that the water is clean again before it is emptied into Juan de Fuca Strait. The plentiful supply of water here is one reason why the paper mill is located in this area.

Many workers are needed

Almost 350 people work at this mill. † Some of them run the machines. Others are managers. They direct the other workers and see that everything runs smoothly. Most of the workers live in a town near the paper mill.

Owned by a large company

Our guide tells us that the paper mill is owned by a company that has offices in many parts of the United States. This company was started a long time ago by business people who provided the money to buy machines and to pay workers. Later, many other people paid money for shares of stock* in the company. Their money helped the company to grow. Today, more than thirty

† Discuss why paper could not be made in large quantities without many workers, machines, and electricity.

† Have students solve this problem.

thousand people own stock in this company.

How the paper is used

Most of the paper made at this mill is called newsprint. It is the kind of paper used for newspapers. More than three hundred newspaper plants in the West buy paper from the company that owns this mill. Paper from this mill is also used for telephone books and catalogs. Some of the paper made here is loaded onto ships. They will carry it to cities and towns along the Pacific coast. The rest of the paper is carried from the mill on trains or in trucks.

Main Industrial Areas

The paper mill we just visited is only one of many thousands of factories in the West. Some of these factories, like the paper mill, make products from wood. Other factories refine petroleum* or produce metals from ores.* (See pages 97-102 of Chapter 9.) Still other factories in the West process* farm products such as fruits, vegetables, and meat. There are also factories that make airplanes, clothing, and many other products.

Industry is growing

Industry is growing in the West. Each year, new factories are built here. However, most of the factories in the West are in or near a few large cities, such as Los Angeles or San Francisco. (See the map below.) In many parts of the West, there is very little industry.

On our visit to the paper mill, we learned that a factory needs many things. Money is needed to start a factory and keep it operating. A factory

MAIN INDUSTRIAL AREAS OF THE WEST

A Problem To Solve †
This chapter has information about the main industrial areas of the West. <u>Why has industry developed in these areas?</u> In making your hypotheses* to solve this problem, you will need to think about how industry here has been affected by each of the following:
a. the supply of workers
b. the markets for manufactured goods
c. the supply of raw materials
d. nearness to transportation routes
Chapter 9 has information that will help you solve this problem.
See Skills Manual, "Thinking and Solving Problems"

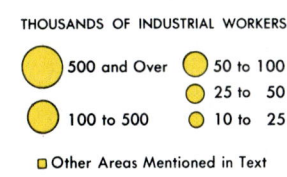

The West 115

must have raw materials. It must have machines to change the raw materials into manufactured goods. Power is needed to run the machines. A factory also needs skilled workers. Railroads and other kinds of transportation are needed to bring raw materials to factories. They are also needed to carry manufactured goods to customers. Most of these things can be found in the large industrial areas of the West.

Chapter 9 of this book tells about some of the raw materials produced in the West. Many different food products come from the farms and ranches here. In some parts of the West, there are large forests that supply factories with wood. The Pacific Ocean provides many kinds of fish. Factories get copper, lead, zinc, and other valuable minerals from the mines in the West.

The large industrial areas of the West are also well supplied with the electric power needed by factories. Power plants have been built on many rivers in the West. (See pages 94-95.) These plants use waterpower to produce large amounts of hydroelectricity.* In some parts of the West, oil and natural gas are found. These can also be used to produce electric power.

The number of people in the West is growing rapidly. Since 1950, the population of this region has increased from less than 20 million to more than 38 million. Many Americans are moving to the large cities of the West every year. Some of them are coming to these areas to get jobs in factories. For this reason, factories in or near large cities have plenty of workers. The people that arrive need such things as food,

Refer to the pictures and caption. Use the questions in the caption in a class discussion about division of labor.

clothing, houses, and cars. They buy many of the goods made in the factories of the West.

The large industrial areas of the West have good transportation systems to serve their industries. There are many fine highways in this part of our country. New ones are being built every year. Railroads and airlines connect the cities of the West with each other and with other parts of our country. From seaports on the Pacific coast, ships carry goods to all parts of the world.

Southern California

The map on page 115 shows that there are several large industrial areas near the Pacific coast in southern California. The great city of Los Angeles is located here. There are also many other cities, such as San Diego, Long Beach, Anaheim, and San Bernardino. More than one million people work in the factories of southern California. The value of the goods made in these factories is about half the value of all goods made in the West.

There are several reasons why so many industries have come to southern California. The aircraft and motion-picture industries came here because of the

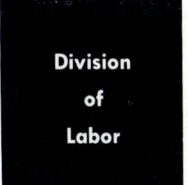

Division of Labor

See Great Ideas

What do you think would happen if the television stars in the picture at right traded jobs with the steelmakers in the picture above? Would the TV stars be very good at making steel? Would the steelmakers be able to present a good TV show? In most communities, all the work that must be done is divided into many different jobs that call for different kinds of skills. This is known as division of labor. How does division of labor help people meet their needs?

mild, sunny climate. Ranches in southern California furnish farm products for canneries and frozen-food plants. Southern California has large amounts of oil and natural gas. These are used to provide electric power for factories. As well as good land and air transportation, southern California has two large seaports. Ships from all over the world dock in the fine harbors at Los Angeles and San Diego. Some industries have come to southern California because of the large number of skilled workers. Also, products made in southern California are sold to the millions of people who live in this part of the West.

More than one third of all the factories in the West are in the Los Angeles-Long Beach industrial area. (See map on page 115.) They manufacture many different products. This area is one of the nation's leading producers of airplanes. It also has factories in which automobiles are put together. Television and motion-picture films made in the Los Angeles-Long Beach area are shown throughout the United States. Many factories in this area can or freeze fruits, vegetables, and seafood. There are also large oil refineries.* Other factories make machinery and electronic* products. The Los Angeles-Long Beach area is one of our country's leading producers of sports clothing.

Near Los Angeles are many smaller cities that make a wide variety of goods. For example, factories in Anaheim, Santa Ana, and Ontario make electronic equipment for the aircraft and space industries. Airplane engines and paint are made in Riverside. In several cities, there are plants that pro-

cess fruits and vegetables from nearby farms. The Kaiser Steel plant near San Bernardino is one of the largest steel plants in the West.

Another leading industrial city of southern California is San Diego. Many people here work in large factories that make airplanes and airplane parts. Other people work in plants that make missiles* or electronic equipment. Fishing boats, tugs, and other kinds of

Why are there so many kinds of industries in the Los Angeles-Long Beach area? Discuss the students' answers.

Workers in an airplane factory. The manufacture of airplanes is an important industry in the West.

boats are built at shipyards in San Diego. One of the nation's most important naval bases is located here. San Diego also has large canneries that process tuna and other seafood.

The San Francisco Bay area

Another part of California with many industries is the San Francisco Bay area. Among the cities here are San Francisco, Oakland, Berkeley, and San Jose. In recent years, the population of this area has been growing rapidly. There are many people to work in the factories and to buy some of the goods that are manufactured here. Factories near San Francisco Bay are served by one of the finest harbors in the world.

Thousands of factories are located in the San Francisco-Oakland industrial area. Many of these factories process

The West

fruits and vegetables grown in the Central Valley and other fertile valleys nearby. Several oil refineries and chemical* plants use oil from the Central Valley. Some factories in the San Francisco-Oakland area make tin cans, hardware, and other metal products. There are large shipyards on San Francisco Bay. Automobiles are made at several plants in the area. Other factories manufacture clothing and paper.

Several miles south of San Francisco Bay is the important manufacturing city of San Jose. One of the oldest industries in San Jose is food processing. Plums, apricots, and other kinds of fruit grown in the fertile Santa Clara Valley are brought to San Jose to be canned or frozen. There are more than sixty canneries and frozen-food plants in the San Jose area. Other factories package dried fruit.

In recent years, many new industries have come to San Jose. They have been attracted by the pleasant climate, the fine roads and railroads, and the large number of workers here. In the San Jose industrial area are an automobile plant and a missile factory. Other factories in the area make such items as electric motors, matches, carpets, and chemical sprays.

The Puget-Willamette Lowland

Outside of California, the part of the West that has the most industry is the Puget-Willamette Lowland. (Compare maps on pages 24 and 115.) Among the important manufacturing cities here are Seattle, Everett, and Tacoma in Washington, and Portland in Oregon.

Seattle and its neighboring cities, Everett and Tacoma, are all located along an arm of the Pacific Ocean known as Puget Sound. Here are deep harbors where ships can come to load and unload goods. The cities along Puget Sound are also served by fine highways and railroads. Nearby are large forests that provide wood for many different industries. Hydroelectricity is supplied by power plants that have been built on rivers in the Cascade Range.

Many factories in and near Seattle make transportation equipment. There are huge airplane plants here. Other plants make railroad cars or truck bodies. On Puget Sound, there are large shipyards.

If we were to visit the Puget Sound area, we would see many other factories. Plants that make aluminum are located here mainly because of the large supply of hydroelectric power. Large amounts of electricity are needed to produce aluminum. In Seattle there are factories in which fish are canned or frozen. Everett and Tacoma have factories that make lumber, paper, and other wood products. Wheat grown in eastern Washington is ground into flour in Seattle.

Portland, Oregon, is near the place where the Willamette River flows into the Columbia River. Ocean ships can sail up the Columbia and Willamette rivers and dock at this city. The rich farmlands of the Willamette Valley and the large forests in the mountains nearby provide raw materials for factories in the Portland area. Power plants on the Columbia and other rivers produce hydroelectricity.

Factories in Portland make many different products. Sawmills, paper

Exchange

See Great Ideas

A shipyard in Seattle. Shipbuilding is an important industry in Seattle. Some of the ships built here carry goods from our country to other parts of the world. They also bring goods back to the United States from other countries. Why do you suppose people in communities far away from each other would want to exchange goods? Do some communities have different natural resources than others? Do people in some communities have skills that are different from those of people in other communities? Explain.

mills, furniture factories, and other plants use wood from Oregon's forests. There are also plants that process fruits, vegetables, or dairy products. Some factories make bathing suits, sweaters, or other kinds of clothing. Machinery and chemicals are other important products of the Portland area.

Other industrial areas of the West

One of the largest industrial areas in the West that is not near the Pacific coast is Denver, Colorado. Denver is located in the Great Plains, a few miles east of the Rocky Mountains. It is a great transportation center. Fine highways, railroads, and airlines connect Denver with cities in other parts of our country. Food processing is the most important industry here. Many factories in the Denver area get their raw materials from farms and ranches nearby. Among these factories are meat-packing plants and sugar refineries. Electronic equipment and parts for airplanes and missiles are made here. Other factories in the Denver area make such products as mining machinery and rubber goods.

Several other cities in the West also have much industry. Many factories have been built in Phoenix and Tucson,

Working on a jet engine in Seattle, Washington. Seattle is the leading industrial city in the northwestern part of our country. Do research in this chapter and Chapter 5 to find out why Seattle is an important industrial city. What are some of the products that are made here?

The control panel in a steel plant. There are thousands of factories in the West. Most of these factories are in or near a few large cities. In much of the West, there is very little industry.

Arizona. Some of these factories make electrical equipment, chemicals, and parts for airplanes. Albuquerque, New Mexico, has meat-packing plants and lumber mills. Near Salt Lake City, Utah, there are refineries that make metals from ores that are mined nearby. Large iron and steel plants are located near Provo, Utah, and at Pueblo, Colorado. Making aluminum is important at Spokane, Washington. Aluminum plants here get the electricity they need from power plants at dams on the Columbia and other rivers.

Make Discoveries About Airplanes

Airplanes are made in several factories in the West. Do research about airplanes in other sources. Record your findings in a written report. Your report may include information about one or more of the following:

1. history and development of the airplane
2. the different kinds of airplanes
3. the parts of an airplane
4. how an airplane flies
5. how airplanes are built

"Learning Social Studies Skills" in the Skills Manual will help you find the information you need.

† Have students do research and prepare written reports.

Farming near Anchorage. Farms in Alaska produce less than one tenth of the food needed by the people here. Large amounts of food must be shipped in from other parts of the United States.

Alaska and Hawaii

Two of our states are separated from the other forty-eight. These are Alaska and Hawaii. Alaska is the largest state in our country. It is in the far northwestern part of North America. Hawaii is an island state in the Pacific Ocean. It lies about 2,400 miles (3,862 km.)† west of California.

Alaska

Land and climate

† Alaska may be divided into three regions. (See map on opposite page.) The largest is the Central Plateau. This is a region of low mountains and broad valleys. It covers over half of Alaska. Summer days in the Central Plateau are often hot. Winters here are bitterly cold.

North of the Central Plateau the land slopes gradually downward to a coastal plain along the Arctic Ocean. This region is the Arctic Slope. Much of this area is covered with ice and snow for eight or nine months each year. Summers are short and cool.

† km. means kilometer

† Refer to the map on the opposite page. Have students locate Alaska's three regions.

† Have students look up "Eskimo" and "Aleut" in the Glossary.

South of Alaska's Central Plateau is the Pacific Mountains region. This region includes several high, rugged mountain ranges. In one of these is Mount McKinley. (See map below.) It is the highest mountain in North America. Between the mountain ranges and along the coast are several lowland areas. One of these is known as the Panhandle. It extends about 500 miles (805 km.) southeastward from the main part of Alaska. The Pacific Mountains region has milder winters than the rest of Alaska. Summers here are cool and rainy.

Alaska's people

Alaska is our largest state, but it has a very small population. Only about 407,000 people live here. About four fifths of the people are white. Most of the rest are Eskimos,* Aleuts,* and Indians.

Anchorage is Alaska's largest city. It is on Cook Inlet, an arm of the Pacific Ocean. About 161,000 people live in or near Anchorage. Alaska's other cities are very small. Fairbanks, on the Central Plateau, is the home of the University of Alaska. The port city of Juneau is Alaska's capital. A new capital city

*See Glossary

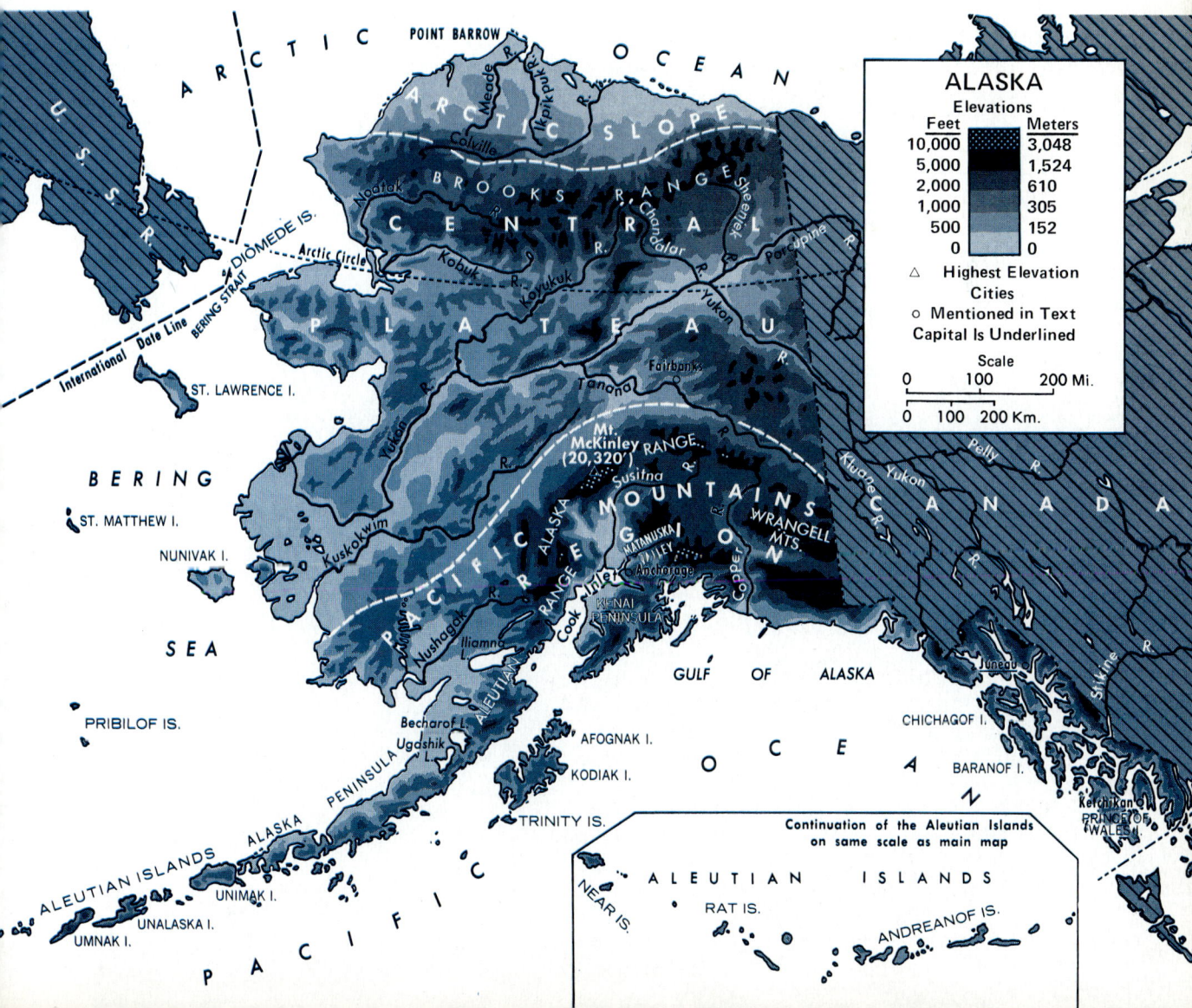

† Do you think the discovery of large oil reserves in Alaska will help our country? Discuss problems it can cause.

is being planned, however. It will be built about 35 miles (56 km.) north of Anchorage.

Many of Alaska's workers have government jobs. Others earn their living by working in hotels and other businesses that serve tourists. Some Alaskans earn their living by fishing.

Natural resources

Alaska's most valuable mineral resource is oil. There are huge deposits of oil on the Arctic Slope. Also there are large deposits of natural gas. Millions of tons of sand and gravel are mined in Alaska every year.

Alaska leads our country in the value of its fish catch. Many salmon and halibut are caught off the coast in the Pacific Ocean. Shellfish, such as crabs and shrimp, are also caught here.

Forests are another valuable resource in Alaska. Dense forests of hemlocks, spruces, and other evergreen trees cover much of the Panhandle. More than three fourths of the trees cut from Alaska's forests are made into wood pulp.* Others are cut into lumber.

Facts About Alaska		
	Number or Value	Rank
Area (square miles)	586,400	1
(square kilometers)	1,518,717	
Population	407,000	49
Capital — Juneau		
Admission Date: January 3, 1959		49
Colleges and Universities	3	44
Farm Products	$ 9,342,000	50
Dairy products	2,725,000	50
Greenhouse and nursery	2,000,000	45
Hay	1,794,000	46
Vegetables	1,064,000	50
Fish	$145,220,000	1
Timber Harvested (cubic feet)	118,995,000	23
Minerals	$448,437,000	23
Petroleum	347,408,000	9
Sand and gravel	52,788,000	6
Natural gas	21,919,000	16
Manufactures*	$179,700,000	49
Food and kindred products	57,000,000	47
Lumber and wood products	34,700,000	38
Printing and publishing	9,600,000	50

† **Building an Alaskan oil pipeline.** Alaska has huge deposits of oil on its Arctic Slope. The pipeline shown below was built to carry oil from these deposits to a seaport on the southern coast of the state. From there, the oil is shipped to refineries in other parts of the United States.

Students at the University of Hawaii. The citizens of Hawaii are descended from people who came from many different lands. Who were the first people to live in Hawaii? Where did they come from?

Hawaii

Land and climate

Hawaii lies in the middle of the Pacific Ocean. It is made up of a long chain of islands. (See map on page 8.) These islands are the tops of a great mountain range that rises from the floor of the ocean. Volcanoes* formed this range millions of years ago.

If we were to fly over the Hawaiian Islands, we would see that parts of the main islands are high and mountainous. Between the mountains, we see many deep canyons. In some places, there are broad plateaus where cattle are grazing. Fields of sugarcane and pineapples are growing in the wide, rich valleys. On some of the islands, beautiful sandy beaches stretch along the coastline.

Hawaii is famous for its delightful climate. The weather here is pleasantly warm all year round. In most places, the temperature usually does not rise above 85° F. (29° C.)† or fall below 60° F. (16° C.). The only parts of Hawaii that ever have cold weather are the high mountains.

† F. means Fahrenheit scale
C. means Celsius scale

Perhaps some of your students have visited Hawaii. Have them tell about their experiences.

A worker in a sugarcane field. The soil and climate of Hawaii are good for growing sugarcane, pineapples, coffee, and other valuable crops.

Facts About Hawaii		
	Number or Value	Rank
Area (square miles)	6,424	47
(square kilometers)	16,638	
Population	895,000	40
Capital — Honolulu		
Admission Date: August 21, 1959		50
Colleges and Universities	13	37
Farm Products	$323,257,000	41
Sugarcane	161,400,000	2
Fruits and nuts	70,793,000	7
Dairy products	21,943,000	45
Cattle and calves	18,511,000	42
Fish	$ 6,028,000	20
Timber Harvested (cubic feet)	605,000	49
Minerals	$ 42,042,000	44
Stone	21,370,000	32
Cement	17,111,000	15
Sand and gravel	2,379,000	50
Manufactures*	$412,300,000	44
Food and kindred products	206,700,000	35
Printing and publishing	53,100,000	39
Apparel and other textile products	31,000,000	36
Stone, glass, and clay products	29,400,000	42

People

The citizens of Hawaii are descended from people who came here from many different lands. The first people to live in Hawaii were Polynesians. They came here from other islands in the Pacific Ocean hundreds of years ago. Later, during the 1800's, large numbers of people began coming to Hawaii from the United States. They also came from various European countries. Others came from Japan, China, the Philippines, and other countries in Asia.

About four fifths of the people in Hawaii live on the island of Oahu. (See map on page 8.) On this island is Honolulu, the largest city in Hawaii. About 362,000 people live here. It is Hawaii's main seaport and trading city. Among the main industries in Honolulu are pineapple canning, sugar refining, and the manufacture of clothing.

Almost one fourth of all workers in Hawaii have jobs with the government. Many others earn their living by working for businesses that serve tourists. Others earn their living by growing or processing farm crops.

Natural resources

Hawaii's most important natural resources are its rich soil, its warm climate, and its beautiful scenery. The soil and climate of Hawaii are good for growing sugarcane, pineapples, coffee, and other valuable crops. Hawaii also has sandy beaches, steep mountains, and beautiful waterfalls. Many tourists come to Hawaii every year to enjoy the scenery and the climate.

The Pacific Ocean around Hawaii is a source of valuable seafood. Each year fishers bring millions of pounds of tuna and other fish to Hawaiian ports.

† Refer to the map on pages 8-9. Have students locate the island of Oahu, where most of Hawaii's people live.

Index

Explanation of abbreviations used in this Index:

p — picture *m* — map

Alaska, 124-126; *p* 124, 126; *m* 8, 125; *chart* 126
Albuquerque, New Mexico, 123; *p* 10-11; *m* 8, 61
Anchorage, Alaska, 125; *m* 125
Arizona, *p* 12-13, 78-79; *m* 8, 61, 115
   cities, *p* 60; *m* 61
   climate, 37; *p* 26-27
   farming, 82-83, 85-86; *p* 84-85
   industry, 122-123; *m* 115
   minerals, 101; *p* 101
   natural resources, 96
   people, 46, 50
arts, 74-77; *p* 74-77
   music, 76-77; *p* 77
   painters, 74-75; *p* 74-76
   writers, 75-76; *p* 76

Basin and Range Country, 20-21; *p* 20-21; *m* 24
Berkeley, California, 119; *m* 61
Bierstadt, Albert, 74
Bonneville Dam, 109-111; *p* 110; *m* 94
Bradley, Thomas, *p* 65
Brico, Antonia, 77; *p* 77
Butte, Montana, 100-101; *m* 61

California, *p* 1-5, 22-25, 28-29, 40-43, 47, 72; *m* 8, 61, 115; *chart* 107
   cities, 53-58; *p* 52, 54-57; *m* 61
   climate, 37
   farming, 82, 83-85, 88; *p* 80-81
   fishing, 108-109, 111; *chart* 108
   forests, 104; *m* 107
   growing season, 38
   industry, 117-120; *m* 115
   minerals, 97, 99; *p* 102-103
   natural resources, 96
   people, 44, 47, 48, 49, 50
Cascade Range, 21, 28-29, 30-31, 104; *p* 31; *m* 24
Catlin, George, 74
cattle, *see* farm products
Central Valley, 22-23, 44, 83-85, 96, 120; *m* 24
Chinese, *see* people, of Asian descent
cities, 52-61; *p* 12-13, 45, 52, 54-60; *m* 61
   history of, 54, 56, 58, 59
   industry, 53, 56, 57, 59, 60-61
   people, 44
   population, 53, 54, 60; *chart* 53
   See also names of cities
citizenship, 66-68, 73; *p* 67
citizenship and government, 62-73; *p* 62-63, 65, 67, 69, 72
climate, 26-39, 58, 83, 85, 87, 90, 118, 120, 124, 125, 127, 128; *p* 12-13, 26-29, 31-33, 36-37, 39; *m* 27, 30, 34-35, 38; *charts* 34-35
   in the dry lands, 27-28
   of the mountains, 33, 37
   along the Pacific coast, 38
   of the plains and plateaus, 33
   in the southern part of the West, 37-38
   in the wet lands, 28-31
   rainfall, 13-14, 17, 83, 86-87, 91; *p* 12-13; *m* 27
   seasons of the year, 34-35; *charts* 34-35
   summer, 33, 37, 38; *p* 31, 39
   temperature, 27, 31-33, 35, 37, 38; *m* 30
   winter, 32-33, 35, 37-38; *p* 32-33, 36-37
coal, *see* minerals
Colorado, *p* 14-15, 94-95; *m* 8, 61, 115
   farming, 85, 87, 88
   minerals, 101, 102
   people, 46
Colorado Plateau, 19-20; *p* 18-19; *m* 24
Colorado River, 85; *m* 94
Columbia Plateau, 18-19, 88; *p* 18; *m* 24
Columbia River, 21, 93-94, 109-111, 114, 120; *p* 92-93, 110; *m* 94
communities, 62-66, 68-73; *p* 69, 72
community problems, 68-73
continents, 5-6, 7; *p* 6; *m* 5
cooperation, *see* great ideas
Copland, Aaron, 77
copper, *see* minerals
cotton, *see* farm products
crime, *see* social problems

dams, 93-95; *p* 92-93; *m* 94
Denver, Colorado, 59-60, 122; *m* 61; *chart* 53
deserts, 28
deWaart, Edo, 77
discrimination, 48, 49, 50, 70. *See also* social problems
division of labor, *see* great ideas

earth, 4-7; *p* 6; *m* 5
Eastern Hemisphere (hem′ə sfir), 6; *m* 5
education, 66, 70, 71, 73. *See also* great ideas
electric power, 100, 114, 116, 118, 120
Elko, Nevada, 102; *m* 61
energy fuels, 97-100; *p* 98-99; *m* 96; *chart* 97
Eskimos, *see* people
Everett, Washington, 120; *m* 61; *chart* 53
exchange, *see* great ideas

Fairbanks, Alaska, 125; *m* 125
farming, 37, 80-91; *p* 14-16, 18, 23, 80-81, 84-85, 88-91, 124; *m* 82, 86, 87
farming methods,
   crop rotation, 83
   dry farming, 86-88; *p* 88-89
   irrigation, 82-83
   strip-cropping, 87
farmland, 28, 29; *p* 94-95
farm products,
   alfalfa, 60, 83, 88, 90
   barley, 37, 85, 88, 91; *p* 88-89
   cattle, 16, 19, 28, 80, 88, 91, 127; *p* 16, 90; *m* 87
   corn, *m* 82
   cotton, 38, 60, 81, 82, 83-84, 85; *p* 84-85; *m* 82
   dairy products, 91; *m* 82
   flowers, 91
   fruit, 38, 53, 60-61, 81, 83, 84, 85, 86, 91, 127, 128; *m* 82, 86
   nuts, 81, 84; *m* 86
   sheep, 28, 80, 88, 91; *p* 91; *m* 87
   sugar beets, 81, 83, 85, 90; *m* 86

PRONUNCIATION KEY: hat, āge, cāre, fär; let, ēqual, tėrm; it, īce; hot, ōpen, ôrder; oil, out; cup, put, rüle, ūse; child; long; thin; ᴛнen; zh, measure; ə represents a in about, e in taken, i in pencil, o in lemon, u in circus.

sugarcane, 127, 128; *p* 128
vegetables, 38, 53, 60-61, 81, 83, 85, 88, 91; *p* 80-81; *m* 86
wheat, 16, 19, 81-82, 86-88, 91; *p* 14-15, 18; *m* 82, 86
fish, 108-111, 126, 128; *p* 108-110; *chart* 108
fishing, 57, 59, 126
forest products, 105, 120, 122
forests, 16, 24, 29, 104-107; *p* 104-107; *m* 107; *chart* 107
freedom, *see* great ideas
fruit, *see* farm products

global view, 4-11; *p* 4-6, 10-11; *m* 5, 7-10
Golden Gate Bridge, 56; *p* 1
government, 62-66; *p* 62-63, 65
   carrying out the laws, 64-66
   city council, 63, 65; *p* 62-63
   interpreting the laws, 66
   making the laws, 63
   mayor, 64-66; *p* 65
   See also great ideas, rules and government
Grand Canyon, *p* 18-19
Grand Coulee Dam, 93-95; *p* 92-93; *m* 94
Grand Teton Mountains, *p* 16-17
Great Basin, 20-21
great ideas,
   cooperation, *p* 72
   division of labor, *p* 116-117
   education, 61, 66, 68, 71, 73; *p* 51
   exchange, *p* 121
   freedom, 48, 50; *p* 39, 65
   language, 47; *p* 47
   rules and government, 48, 51; *p* 52, 110
   using natural resources, 92-111; *p* 18, 88-89, 102-103
Great Plains, 14-16, 33, 86-88; *p* 14-15; *m* 14, 24
Great Salt Lake, 21; *m* 8
Grofé, Ferde, 77
growing season, 37, 38, 85; *m* 38

Harte, Bret, 75-76
Hawaii, 127-128; *p* 127, 128; *m* 8; *chart* 128
Honolulu, Hawaii, 128; *m* 8
hydroelectricity, 59, 116, 120

Idaho, *m* 8, 61, 115; *chart* 107
   farming, 85
   forests, *m* 107
   minerals, 101
Imperial Valley, California, 85
Indians, *see* people
industry, 112-123; *p* 78-79, 112-114, 116-119, 121-123; *m* 115

aircraft, 115, 117-118, 122, 123; *p* 118-119, 122
automobile, 118, 120
chemical, 56, 120, 122, 123
clothing, 53, 115, 122, 128
electronic equipment, 53, 57, 61, 118, 122
food processing, 53, 56, 59, 60-61, 118, 119, 120, 122, 123, 128
iron and steel, 118, 123; *p* 116-117, 123
lumbering, 107, 122; *chart* 107
metal, 120, 123
motion picture, 53, 117-118
oil refining, 60
papermaking, 56, 112-115; *p* 112-114
plastics, 57
shipbuilding, 118-119; *p* 121
television, 53, 118; *p* 117
tourist, 126, 128
transportation equipment, 53, 56, 57, 59, 60, 61, 120
iron ore, *see* minerals
irrigation, 20, 28, 83. *See also* water

Japanese, *see* people, of Asian descent
Juneau, Alaska, 125; *m* 125

Kay, Hershey, 77

land, 2, 12-25; *p* 2-3, 12-23, 25
   farming, 80-81, 82-83, 85, 86, 87, 88, 90
land regions of the West, *m* 14, 16, 17, 21, 24
   Pacific Mountains and Valleys, 21-24; *p* 22-23, 25, 31; *m* 21, 24
   Plateau Country, 17-21, 33; *m* 17, 24
   Rocky Mountains, 16, 30, 33, 59; *p* 14-15, 16-17; *m* 16, 24
language, *see* great ideas
London, Jack, 75, 76
Long Beach, California, 53; *m* 61; *chart* 53
Los Angeles, California, 24, 44, 53-54, 64-65, 73, 118; *p* 52; *m* 61; *chart* 53
   government, 64-65
   Watts section, 71-73; *p* 72

McGinley, Phyllis, 76
Mehta, Zubin, 77
metals, 100-102; *p* 101
   brass, 101

copper, 100-101
gold and silver, 101-102
lead and zinc, 101
See also minerals
metropolitan areas, 53, 54; *chart* 53
Mexican-Americans, *see* people
migrant workers, 83
migration, *p* 10-11, 42-43
Miller, Joaquin, 75
minerals, 59, 60, 97-103; *p* 98-99, 101-103; *m* 96; *chart* 97
   borates, 102
   coal, 99-100; *chart* 97
   copper, 100-101, 102, 116; *p* 101
   energy fuels, 97, 99-100; *p* 98-99; *m* 96; *chart* 97
   gold, 56, 97, 100, 101-102
   iron ore, 102
   lead, 101, 116
   limestone, 102
   manganese, 102
   molybdenum, 102
   natural gas, 99, 118, 126; *chart* 97
   oil, 97, 99, 118, 126; *p* 98-99, 126; *m* 96; *chart* 97
   potash, 102
   salt, 57-58, 102
   sand and gravel, 102, 126; *p* 102-103
   silver, 97, 100, 101-102
   stone, 102
   uranium, 102
   vanadium, 102
   zinc, 100, 101, 116
minority groups, 70
Montana, *p* 16; *m* 8, 61, 115; *chart* 107
   climate, 33; *p* 32-33
   farming, 86-88; *p* 91
   forests, *m* 107
   minerals, 100-101, 102
Monument Valley, *p* 26-27
Moran, Thomas, 74
Mount McKinley, 125; *m* 125
Mount Rainier, *p* 31
Mount Whitney, 21-22; *m* 8
music, *see* arts

Native Americans, *see* people, Indians
natural gas, *see* minerals
natural resources and energy, 92-111; *p* 92-95, 98-99, 101-110; *m* 96, 107; *charts* 97, 107, 108
Nevada, *p* 20-21; *m* 8, 61, 115
   climate, 27
   minerals, 97, 101, 102

New Mexico, *p* 10-11; *m* 8, 61, 115
  climate, 37
  energy fuels, 99
  farming, 85
  minerals, 102
  people, 46, 47, 50
North America, 7; *m* 5, 7
nuclear energy, 97, 102; *chart* 97

Oakland, California, 54, 119-120; *m* 61; *chart* 53
oceans, 5-6; *p* 6; *m* 5
oil, *see* minerals
O'Keeffe, Georgia, 74; *p* 76
Oregon, *p* 45; *m* 8, 61, 115; *chart* 107
  climate, 30
  farming, 85, 91
  fishing, 109-111; *chart* 108
  forests, 104; *m* 107
  people, 44, 46
Oregon Trail, 43

Pacific Mountains and Valleys, *see* land regions of the West
painters, *see* arts
people, 40-51, 62, 71, 73, 125, 126, 128; *p* 40-43, 47-51, 72
  Aleuts, 125
  of Asian descent, 49-50, 56, 70, 128; *p* 49
  blacks, 48-49, 70; *p* 48, 65
  of European descent, 46, 128
  Eskimos, 125
  Indians, 50-51, 70, 125; *p* 50, 51
  Latinos, 70
  Mexican-Americans, 46-48; *p* 47
  Polynesians, 128
petroleum, *see* minerals, oil
Phoenix, Arizona, 60-61, 122-123; *p* 60; *m* 61
Plateau Country, *see* land regions of the West
population, 10, 13, 14, 24, 43, 44, 46, 50, 53, 54, 116, 125; *m* 46; *chart* 53
Portland, Oregon, 46, 120, 122; *p* 45; *m* 61

ports, 53-54, 56, 57, 58-59, 108, 117, 118, 125, 128
Provo, Utah, 123; *m* 61
Pueblo, Colorado, 123; *m* 61
Puget (pū′jit) Sound, 23, 58, 112, 120
Puget-Willamette (pū′jit wə lam′-ət) Lowland, 23, 44-46, 91, 120-122; *p* 45; *m* 24

recreation, 58, 59
redwood trees, 105
Remington, Frederic, 74; *p* 74-75
reservations, 50, 51; *p* 51
reservoirs, 83
responsibilities of citizens, 68
rivers, 19, 20; *m* 94
Rocky Mountains, *see* land regions of the West
rules and government, *see* great ideas
Russell, Charles M., 74

Sacramento River, 22; *m* 94
Salt Lake City, Utah, 123; *m* 61
Salt River, 60; *m* 94
Salt River Valley, 60, 82-83
San Diego, California, 35, 44, 57-58, 118-119; *p* 4-5, 35, 56-57; *m* 61; *chart* 53
San Diego Bay, 57
San Francisco, California, 44, 54-56, 119-120; *p* 42-43, 47, 54-55; *m* 61; *chart* 53
San Francisco Bay, 23, 44, 54-56; *p* 1, 54-55; *m* 8
San Francisco Bay Area, 119-120
San Francisco-Oakland Bay Bridge, 56
San Joaquin River, 22-23; *m* 94
San Jose, California, 119; *m* 61
Saroyan, William, 76
schools, *see* education
Seattle, Washington, 44, 46, 58-59, 63, 120; *p* 58-59, 62-63, 121, 122; *m* 61; *chart* 53
sheep, *see* farm products
Sierra Nevada, (sē er′ ə nə vad′ə), 21-22, 30-31, 33, 105; *p* 22-23; *m* 24

social problems, 68-73
  crime, 69, 70
  discrimination, 70, 71
  education, 71, 73
solar energy, 97
spacecraft, 4-5
Spokane, Washington, 123; *m* 61
Steinbeck, John, 76; *p* 76
sugar beets, *see* farm products

Tacoma, Washington, 120; *m* 61
temperature, *see* climate
Terminal Island, California, 108
Tobey, Mark, 74-75
transportation, 46
Tucson, Arizona, 122-123

United States, 7, 10; *m* 7-10
Utah, *m* 8, 61

vegetables, *see* farm products
volcanoes, 21, 127

Washington, 93-95; *p* 31, 62-63, 92-93, 112-113, 121, 122; *m* 8, 61, 115; *chart* 107
  climate, 28, 30
  farming, 85, 88, 91
  fishing, 111; *chart* 108
  forests, 104; *m* 107
  people, 44, 46, 50
water, 5-6, 20-21, 93-96
  flood control, 94
  irrigation, 94-96; *p* 94-95; *m* 94
  uses of, 93-96; *m* 94
waterpower, 94, 116; *chart* 97
Watts section, *see* Los Angeles, California
Western Hemisphere (hem′ ə sfir), 7; *m* 5
wheat, *see* farm products
Willamette River, 23, 120; *m* 94
wind erosion, 87
World War II, 49
writers, *see* arts
Wyoming, *p* 16-17; *m* 8, 61, 115
  farming, 88, 90

Yosemite National Park, *p* 22-23

zinc, *see* minerals

PRONUNCIATION KEY: hat, āge, cãre, fär; let, ēqual, tėrm; it, īce; hot, ōpen, ôrder; oil, out; cup, pủt, rüle, ūse; child; long; thin; ᴛнen; zh, measure; ə represents a in about, e in taken, i in pencil, o in lemon, u in circus.

Acknowledgments

Grateful acknowledgment is made to the following for permission to use the illustrations found in this book:

A. Devaney, Inc.: Page 39
Alaska Pictorial Service: Page 124 by Steve and Delores McCutcheon
Alpha Photo Associates, Inc.: Pages 42-43 by Mac Fadyen
Annan Photo Features: Page 91
Boeing: Pages 118-119 and 122
Buddy Mays: Pages 10-11 and 51
Camera Hawaii: Page 127
Camerique Stock Photos: Page 50
City of Los Angeles, Office of the Mayor: Page 65
City of Phoenix, Office of the Mayor: Page 60
City of San Diego: Pages 4-5
Clyde Sunderland: Page 52
Crown Zellerbach Corporation: Pages 112-113, 113, and 114
De Wys, Inc.: Pages 2-3 and 47
Doug Wilson: Pages 31, 48, and 49
Dudley, Hardin, and Yang, Inc.: Pages 58-59
Freelance Photographers Guild: Pages 16-17, 22-23, 40-41, and 54-55; pages 80-81 and 90 by Willinger; pages 92-93 by Gene Ahrens; pages 106-107 by Spring
Grant Heilman: Pages 14-15, 56-57, 94-95, and 110
H. Armstrong Roberts: Pages 102-103
Jon Brenneis: Page 121
Josef Muench: Pages 26-27 and 36-37
Kaiser Steel Corporation: Pages 116-117
Los Angeles Philharmonic: Page 77
Markow Photography: Pages 18-19
Montana Chamber of Commerce: Page 16 by Browning
NASA: Page 6
NBC Studios, Burbank California: Page 117, singer Mac Davis
Oregon State Highway: Page 45
Photo Researchers, Inc.: Pages 32-33 by Joe Munroe; pages 98-99 by Jack Fields
Ray Atkeson: Page 18
San Diego March of Dimes: Page 67
San Francisco Convention & Visitors Bureau: Page 1
Shostal Associates, Inc.: Pages 23, 25, 28-29, 104-105, 123, and 128; pages 12-13, 78-79, and 84-85 by Manley
Sohio: Page 126
Sterling and Francine Clark Art Institute: Pages 74-75
The Bettmann Archive: Page 76 (right)
Tom Myers: Pages 88-89
Tuna Research Foundation: Pages 108-109
Van Cleve Photography: Pages 20-21 by David Muench
West Stock, Inc.: Pages 62-63 by Steve Meltzer
Western Ways: Page 101 by Charles W. Herbert
Wide World Photos: Pages 69, 72, and 76 (left)

Grateful acknowledgment is made to Scott, Foresman and Company for the pronunciation system used in this book, which is taken from the Thorndike-Barnhart Dictionary Series.

Grateful acknowledgment is made to the following for permission to use cartographic data in this book: Creative Arts: Pages 34 and 35; Base maps courtesy of the Nystrom Raised Relief Map Company, Chicago 60618: Page 24; Panoramic Studios: Page 5; Rand McNally & Company: Pages 8 and 9; United States Department of Commerce, Bureau of the Census: Pages 46, 86, and 87.

PICTORIAL STORY OF OUR COUNTRY

Mount Rushmore, in South Dakota, honors four of our presidents.

Discuss this picture and the question in the caption.

Our Country

Our country, the United States of America, was established just over two hundred years ago. At that time, the United States was small and weak. It was the home of less than three million people. Most of these people lived on farms or in small villages near the Atlantic coast of North America.

Today the United States is one of the largest and richest countries on earth. It stretches almost three thousand miles, from the Atlantic Ocean to the Pacific. (See the map on pages 60-61.) It also includes the far northern state of Alaska and the island state of Hawaii. Within this huge country are many large, modern cities.

Nearly 220 million people live in the United States today. Each year they produce billions of dollars' worth of goods and services. As a result, Americans live more comfortably than people in most parts of the world. Also, they enjoy a great deal of freedom to live as they please and to take part in their own government.

In the following pages, you will discover how the United States grew from a small, weak country into the powerful nation that it is today. As you read, look for certain ideas or ways of living that have helped to build our nation.

In 1976, the United States was two hundred years old. The picture at the right shows people marching in a parade to celebrate our nation's birthday. Their clothes are like the ones that people wore at the time our country was started. Two hundred years ago, the United States was small and weak. Today it is one of the largest and richest countries in the world. Are there certain ideas that helped the United States to grow? If so, what are they? This book will help you answer these questions.

An Iroquois* Indian village in what is now the state of New York. Many different groups of Indians lived in North America long ago. They used a number of things they found in the world around them to help them meet their needs. These gifts of nature are called "natural resources." What natural resources are being used by the people in the picture? Look in this book and other books to discover facts that will help you answer this question.

Using Natural Resources

See Great Ideas

1 People Build Communities in America

■ Who were the first Americans?

People have been living in what is now the United States for many thousands of years. The first Americans were people with brown skin, dark eyes, and straight, black hair. They were divided into many different groups, or tribes. Most tribes called themselves by names that meant simply "the men" or "the people." Today these early people

*See Glossary

4 History

of America are usually known as Indians, or as Native Americans.

The Indians may have come to North America from Asia. No one knows for certain how the Indians first came to North America. But many scientists believe that these people came from the continent* of Asia. There are two main reasons why they think this. First, many Indians look somewhat like the people of Asia. Second, Asia and North America are very close together in the far north. They are separated only by a narrow strip of water called the Bering Strait. (Compare map at right with map of Alaska on page 60.) Long ago, the oceans of the world were not as deep as they are today. A bridge of land may have connected Asia and North America. It would have been possible to travel from one continent to another across this land bridge.

† Scientists believe that people began coming to North America at least 25,000 years ago, and possibly more than 100,000 years ago. These people may have been hunting wild animals for food. Or they may have been trying to get away from enemies. As time passed, the Indians settled in many parts of North and South America. (See map at right.)

† These scientists are called anthropologists.

The Indian tribes of North America were not all alike. They spoke hundreds of different languages, and they had very different ways of life. For example, some tribes got most of their food by hunting animals such as deer and buffalo. Other tribes grew crops such as corn and squash for food. Still others lived mostly on fruit, seeds, and roots they gathered from wild plants.

The Indians are believed to have come from Asia across the Bering Strait. They settled in many parts of North and South America.

ROUTES OF INDIAN SETTLERS

Point out the map above. Refer students to the scale. Have them trace one or more of the Indians' longest migration routes as shown on the map. Have them measure the route (or routes) and give the distance.

History 5

A European trading ship in the 1500's. People in Europe were eager to trade with countries in eastern Asia. Why? How did the desire for trade cause Europeans to find out about America?

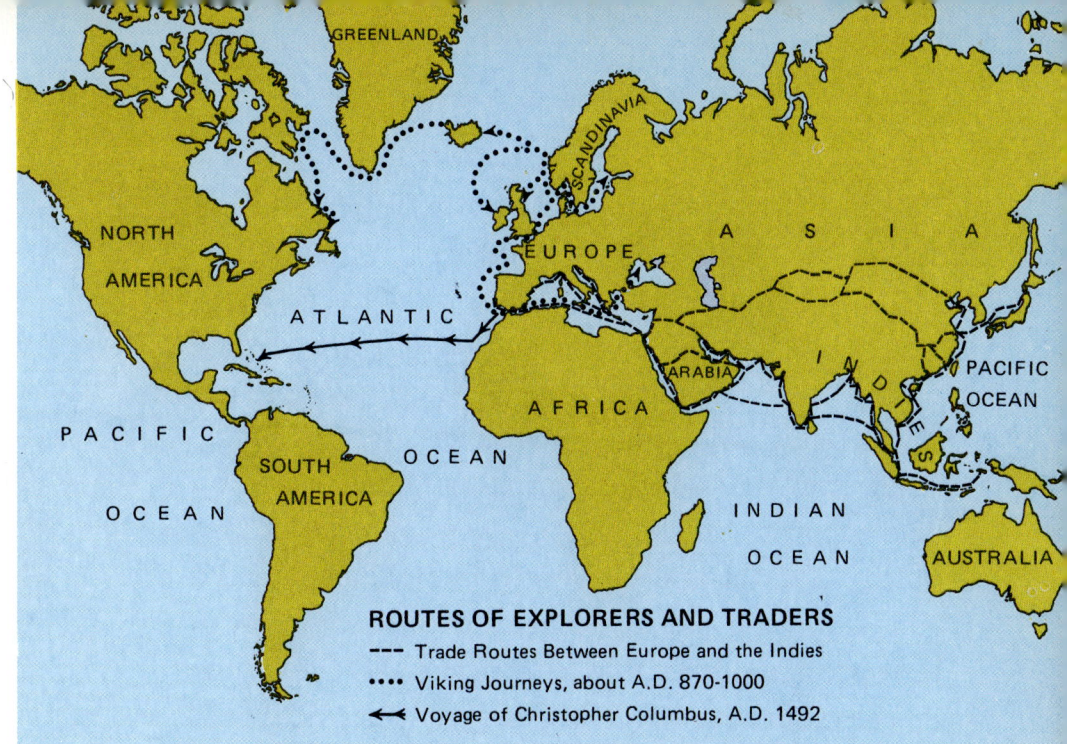

ROUTES OF EXPLORERS AND TRADERS
- - - Trade Routes Between Europe and the Indies
•••• Viking Journeys, about A.D. 870-1000
⟵ Voyage of Christopher Columbus, A.D. 1492

■ How did Europeans learn about America?

Sailors from Europe began making journeys to faraway lands. Far to the east of America, across the broad Atlantic Ocean, lay the continent of Europe. For thousands of years, people had lived in Europe without knowing anything about the lands on the other side of the ocean. Sailing ships in those days were small and not very safe. Also, sailors did not have any way to find out where they were if they sailed out of sight of land. Many people believed that the ocean was the home of terrible monsters. It is not surprising that only the most daring sailors were willing to sail very far out into the ocean.

Now and then, a ship from Europe may have reached America. For example, it seems certain that bold Viking* sailors landed on the Atlantic coast of North America about one thousand years ago. (See map above.) But news spread slowly in those days, and most Europeans never learned about such journeys.

During the early 1400's, people in Europe began to take more interest in visiting other parts of the world. Better ships

Point out the map above and refer students to the legend. Have them trace routes of the explorers. Ask: Which direction did the explorers travel in order to reach North America? Which direction did they come from?

† Columbus' ships were the Niña, the Pinta, and the Santa María.

and new kinds of tools to help sailors find their way had been developed. As a result, people were able to make longer ocean journeys.

At that time, people in Europe were eager to carry on trade with the lands in eastern Asia known as the Indies. In these lands, it was possible to get spices, silk, and other valuable goods. For years, Asian traders had been bringing these goods by land to ports on the eastern shore of the Mediterranean Sea.* Here, traders from Italy loaded the goods on their ships and carried them to cities in Europe. The prices that Europeans had to pay for these goods were much higher than the prices that the Asian traders had paid for them. Many Europeans wanted to find an ocean route to the Indies so they could buy goods directly from traders there. Then they would no longer have to pay high prices to Italian traders.

Columbus sailed westward and reached America. Some people hoped to find an ocean route to the Indies by sailing east from the southern tip of Africa. But one man had a different plan. He was an Italian sailor named Christopher Columbus. At that time, many Europeans were already saying that the earth was round. Columbus agreed with them. He was sure he could reach Asia by sailing westward across the Atlantic Ocean.

Queen Isabella of Spain agreed to give Columbus the money and ships that he needed for his journey. † In August of 1492, Columbus and his crew left Spain in three tiny ships. They sailed for many weeks until they reached a small island off the coast of North America. Columbus thought he had reached the Indies, so he called the people

he found there "Indians." After visiting other islands, he returned to Spain with the news of his exciting discovery.

Before long, other explorers from European countries were sailing westward to see the lands Columbus had found. They soon realized that Columbus had not reached Asia after all. Instead, he had reached a completely new part of the world.

Many people came from Europe to America. In the years that followed the voyage of Columbus, people from several European countries came to America. Some of them were searching for a water route through America to Asia. Others were hoping to find gold and silver or other kinds of treasure. Still others wanted to bring their religion, Christianity, to the Indians.

A Spanish explorer named Francisco Coronado was one of the first Europeans to visit the southwestern part of the United States. He led an army through this area in 1540. Why did Coronado come? What were some of the other reasons why people from Europe came to America?

† Some of these rich cities were parts of the ancient Aztec and Inca civilizations.

■ What part did the Spanish play in settling America?

The Spanish built missions and forts in what is now the United States. The first Europeans to settle in America at this time came from Spain. Spanish explorers found rich Indian cities in Mexico and South America. They fought the Indians and took over their lands. In this way, they won a great fortune in gold and silver for Spain.

Hoping to find more riches, other Spaniards journeyed far into North America. They found little gold and silver there. But their journeys made it possible for Spain to claim a large area in what is now the United States.

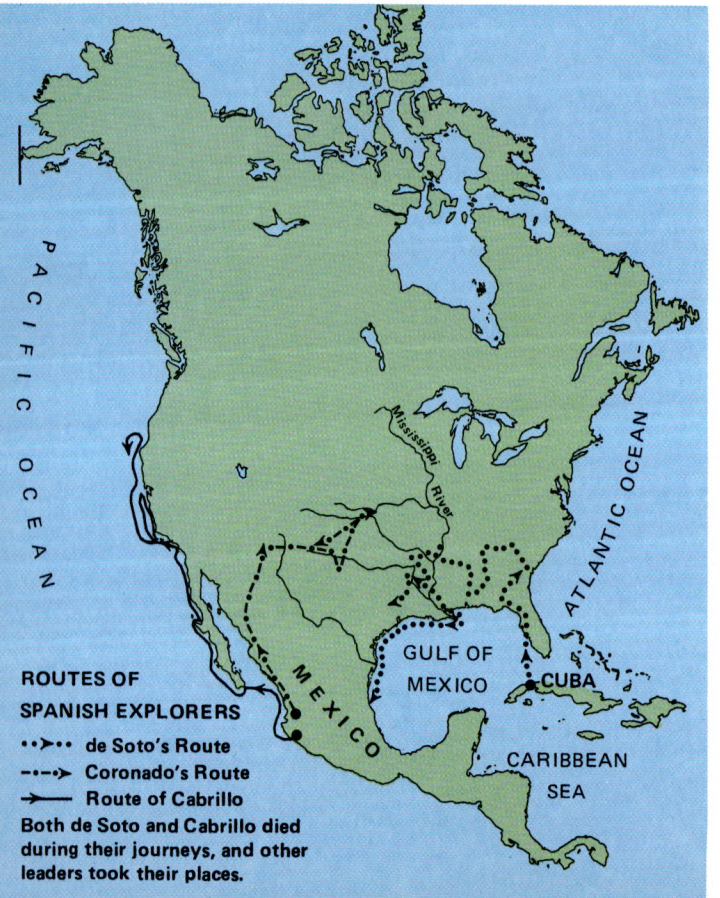

ROUTES OF SPANISH EXPLORERS
··▷·· de Soto's Route
---▷ Coronado's Route
→ Route of Cabrillo
Both de Soto and Cabrillo died during their journeys, and other leaders took their places.

The map at the left shows the routes of three Spaniards who visited different parts of North America in the 1500's. In 1539, Hernando de Soto started on a journey through what is now the southeastern part of our country. He was the first European to see the Mississippi River. In 1540, Francisco Coronado started out from Mexico to look for rich cities that were said to lie farther north. He journeyed for hundreds of miles over deserts and mountains, but he never found the cities he was seeking. Juan Cabrillo was the first European to visit California. He sailed along the Pacific coast in 1542.

The mission of San Xavier is near Tucson, Arizona. (See map on pages 60-61.) It was built by Spanish missionaries in the 1700's. What is a missionary? If you do not know, look in the Glossary at the back of this book. The missionaries spent much time learning to speak the languages spoken by the Indians. Why was it important for them to do this? If people do not speak the same language, how can they tell their ideas to one another?

† As time passed, Spanish settlers began coming here to live. They built missions where the Indians could come to learn about Christianity. (See the picture above.) They also built forts to protect their settlements from being attacked by enemy Indians or by soldiers from other European countries. The first Spanish settlements were established in Florida during the 1500's. Later, other Spanish settlements were started in Texas, New Mexico, Arizona, and California.

† Point out that a number of the early missions (like the one pictured above) can still be seen today. Perhaps some of your students have visited old missions like this. Have them tell about their experiences.

Father Jacques Marquette was a French missionary. He and a fur trader named Louis Joliet went much of the way down the Mississippi River in 1673. They were searching for a water route that would lead to Asia. Do you think they found it? Give reasons for your answer.

■ Which lands were settled by the French, Dutch, and Swedish?

France claimed a huge amount of land in North America. People from France also visited North America during the 1500's and 1600's. Some sailed along the Atlantic coast. Others traveled up the St. Lawrence River in what is now Canada. (See the map on pages 60-61.) Later, other French explorers made journeys through the Great Lakes* and along the Mississippi River. They claimed a huge amount of land for France. The left-hand map on page 21 shows the French territory in North America.

During the 1600's and 1700's, people from France came to North America to live. Some were traders who bought valuable furs from the Indians in exchange for goods such as cloth, knives, and beads. These furs were sent to Europe, where they could be sold for high prices. Other French people who came to America were soldiers, missionaries, fishers, or farmers.

Have a student read the caption to the above picture aloud. Have someone answer the question. Call attention to the left-hand map on page 21 showing French territory in North America.

New Amsterdam was a Dutch settlement along the Hudson River. It later became New York City. What does the picture tell you about New Amsterdam?

The Dutch and Swedish settled near the Atlantic coast. Other European countries also started settlements in North America during the 1600's. Two of these countries were Holland and Sweden. There were Dutch* settlements along the Hudson River in what is now New York State. (See map at right.) The Swedish settled along the Delaware River. But these settlements were small and weak. By 1700, all of them had been taken over by the country of England.

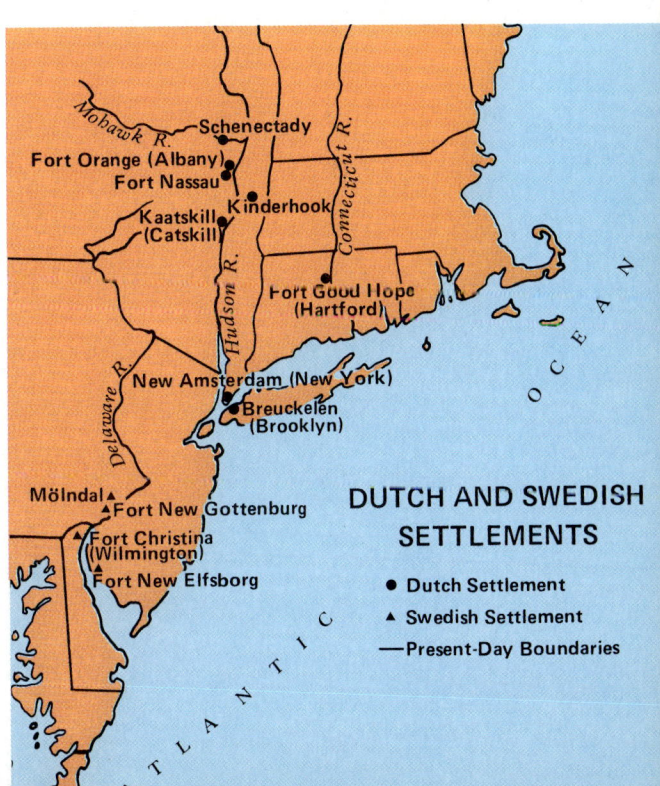

Compare John Cabot's landing on North America to Neil Armstrong's landing on the moon.

■ Why did the English decide to start settlements in America?

The English were slow to settle the lands they claimed. The first explorer from England to visit America was John Cabot. In 1497 he and his men sailed westward across the Atlantic Ocean in search of a water route to the Indies. When they reached the coast of Canada, they claimed the land for the English king.

For many years, the English did not try to settle the lands that Cabot had visited. But as time went on, English leaders became more interested in starting colonies* in America.

† Have your students imagine that they are some of the first settlers in Jamestown. Have them write letters describing their life in the colony.

From these colonies, the English could buy goods that they could not produce in large enough amounts in England. Among these goods were logs and animal furs. In return, traders in England could sell large amounts of cloth, hardware, and other English goods to the American settlers. At that time, England, France, Holland, and Spain were all rivals of one another. The English decided that if they started colonies along the Atlantic coast, the other European countries would be less likely to claim this land for themselves.

An English settlement was started in Virginia. In † 1607, a group of English traders sent about one hundred people to what is now Virginia. There the colonists started a settlement called Jamestown. This was the first successful English settlement in America. At first, life was very hard for the settlers. Many of them died of hunger or sickness. Others were killed by the Indians, who were angry because the settlers often treated them badly. In spite of these troubles, Jamestown kept going. During the years that followed, people from England started many other settlements along the Atlantic coast of North America.

People came to America in search of freedom and a better way of life. Why were so many English people willing to leave their homes and make the long,

Loyalty

See Great Ideas

John Cabot landed on the Atlantic coast of Canada in 1497. Do you think sailors like Cabot could have made successful journeys without the help of loyal followers? Explain your answer. What might have happened if these followers had not been loyal?

15

† Ask: Do you think Americans could be put in prison today for not attending a certain church? Why? Why not? (Religious freedom is guaranteed in the Bill of Rights.)

dangerous journey to America? For one thing, people who lived in England at that time did not have very much freedom. All English men and women were expected to belong to the Church of England, which was headed by the king. People who belonged to other churches could be put into prison. This was why the Pilgrims* and certain other groups of people decided to move to America. In that faraway land, they would be free to worship as they pleased.

During the 1600's, it was hard to make a good living in England. Most of the farmland was owned by a small number of wealthy families. In earlier times, many English people had been farmers who rented land from these rich landowners. But as time passed, the landowners found they could make more money by

Using Tools

See Great Ideas

Jamestown, Virginia, was the first long-lasting English settlement in America. The picture below shows the settlers building a fort along the banks of the James River. What tools are the people in this picture using? Can you think of some other tools that the settlers might have needed in order to build their fort? Would it have been possible for the European settlers to make homes in the wilderness without using tools? Explain your answer.

raising sheep for wool. They began using their fields as pastures for sheep. Many farmers could not find any land to rent, and it was not easy to get other jobs.

In America, there were large areas of fertile land that had not yet been settled. Farmers could get all the land they wanted free, or at a very low cost. All kinds of workers were needed in America, so anyone who was willing to work hard could be fairly sure of getting a good job. The hope of a better life brought many settlers to America.

■ What was life in the British colonies like?

The colonies grew in population. As the years passed, more and more people made their homes in England's colonies. Settlers came not only from England but also from Ireland, Germany, France, and other European countries. In the meantime, England had joined with the neighboring country of Scotland to form the kingdom of Great Britain.

By 1750 there were thirteen British colonies in North America. (See the map above.) Together these colonies had a population of more than one million. Most of the colonists lived on the Atlantic coast or along

Thirteen British colonies grew up along the Atlantic coast of North America. Which four colonies made up the area known as New England? What were the four Middle Colonies? What were the five Southern Colonies?

rivers that flowed into the ocean. The rest of what is now the United States was mostly a wilderness.

How people in the British colonies made their living. About nine out of every ten colonists in America earned their living by farming. However, there were fewer farmers in New England than in the other colonies. Much of the land in New England was hilly, and the soil was thin and stony. But there were valuable forests in New England, and the

Exchange

See Great Ideas

A street in Philadelphia, the largest city in the British colonies. Philadelphia grew up along the Delaware River. Ships could sail up the river from the Atlantic Ocean to load and unload their goods. As time passed, Philadelphia became an important center for trade. Another word for trade is "exchange." How do you think exchange helped the thirteen colonies to grow?

Atlantic Ocean was rich in fish. Along the coast were many bays where ships could be safe from storms. Boston and other busy cities grew up here. Many people in New England earned their living from the sea. Some of them built ships. Others were sailors, fishers, or traders.

In the Middle Colonies, there were larger areas of level land with rich soil. Farmers here produced large amounts of wheat, beef, and other goods. They sold these goods to people in all of the colonies and also Great Britain. The Middle Colonies were rich in iron ore,* wood, and other resources. Cities like New York and Philadelphia grew up along the Atlantic coast, where there were good harbors for ships.

In the Southern Colonies, the land and climate* were good for farming. Summers were long and hot. There was plenty of rainfall, and the soil in many places was rich. Some of the colonists started large farms called plantations. There they grew crops such as tobacco and indigo.* These crops could be shipped to Europe and sold there for high prices. Much of the work on the plantations was done by black people who had been brought from Africa as slaves.

In colonial days, slavery was carried on in many parts of the world. To get slaves, traders from England and other European countries sailed along the coast of Africa. They gave cloth and other valuable goods to African rulers in exchange for prisoners who had been captured in war. The prisoners were loaded into ships and taken to America. Many died of hunger or sickness along the way. Those who lived were sold to the American settlers. By the late 1700's, about one fifth of all the people in the British colonies were black men and women from Africa.

Call attention to the picture on these pages. What can you discover about life in early Philadelphia from this picture?

Discover Our Country's Story

1. Why did the first people who lived in America become known as Indians?
2. Why did people in Europe want to find an all-water route to Asia?
3. How did Christopher Columbus hope to reach Asia? Was he successful? Explain your answer.
4. What parts of the United States were settled by people from Spain?
5. What happened to the Dutch and Swedish settlements in America?
6. Why was Jamestown important in American history?
7. Why did the Pilgrims decide to come to America?
8. Why were there fewer farmers in New England than in the other colonies?
9. Why were the Southern Colonies so well suited to farming?
10. In colonial days, most people did not think it was wrong to own slaves. Why do you suppose they felt this way?

You may wish to use these questions for class discussion.

† George Washington helped to fight the French during this war as an aide to the British commander, General Braddock.

2 The American Communities Form a Nation

■ How did Britain win control of France's lands in North America?

France and Great Britain went to war. At the same time the British colonies were growing larger, France and Great Britain began to quarrel. Both countries claimed an area that lay mostly between the Appalachian Mountains and the Mississippi River. (Compare the left-hand map on page 21 with the map on pages 60-61.) † This helped to bring about the French and Indian War,* which began in 1754.

At first, the French seemed to be winning the war. They had good army leaders, and they were helped by several Indian tribes. But there were about twenty times as many people in the British colonies as in the French colonies. Also, Britain had a stronger navy than France. As a result, the British could send more troops and supplies to America.

After years of fighting, the British defeated the French. A treaty* of peace was signed in 1763. Under this treaty, France lost its huge empire in North America. (See right-hand map on page 21.) Britain now ruled over nearly all the land in the eastern part of the continent.

■ Why were the American colonists unhappy under British rule?

A quarrel arose between Great Britain and the colonies. After the French and Indian War, the American colonists began to grow more and more unhappy under British rule. One reason for this was that the colonists were not free to carry on business as they pleased. For example, Britain would not allow the colonists to sell goods directly to foreign countries such as France and Holland. These goods had to be sent to England first. Also, goods that were shipped into and out of the colonies had to be carried in British ships. Some kinds of goods that were made in America could not be sold anywhere except in the colony where they were made. The purpose of all these laws was to help traders and shipowners in Great Britain.

Most people in the colonies strongly disliked the British trade laws. They believed these laws hurt their business and caused them to pay higher prices for goods they bought

*See Glossary

20 History

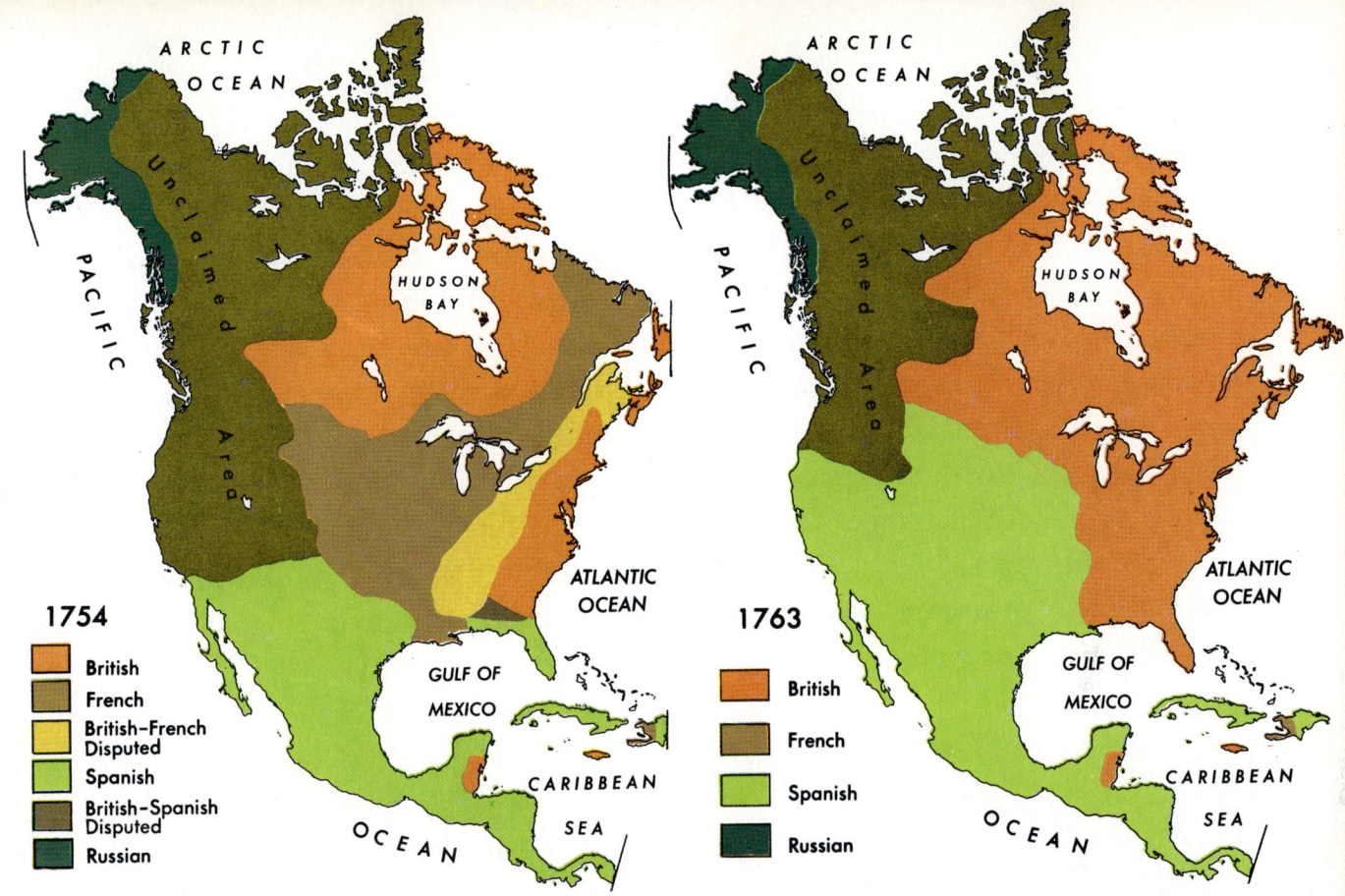

Before and after the French and Indian War. These maps show the lands in North America that belonged to different countries of Europe. The French and Indian War started in 1754. At that time, Great Britain and France both claimed huge amounts of land in North America. At the end of the war, in 1763, France had to give up nearly all of its great empire.

from Britain and other lands. Many colonists broke the laws by trading secretly with foreign countries.

In order to make sure that the trade laws were obeyed, British officers were sent to the colonies to hunt for people who were breaking these laws. The officers were given papers called writs of assistance, which allowed them to search any home or business place in the colonies. The colonists felt that the writs of assistance took away some of their rights as British citizens.

Many colonists had expected that they would be allowed to settle west of the Appalachian Mountains after the French were defeated. But the British were afraid that this would cause trouble with the Indians who lived there. In 1763 the British government sent out an order telling the settlers not to move into the lands west of the Appalachian Mountains.

The colonists became even more unhappy when the British Parliament* passed laws that made them pay certain taxes to Britain. The colonists were not allowed to choose any people to represent them in Parliament, so they felt Parliament had no right to tax them. In the past, the lawmaking body of each colony had decided what taxes people would have to pay. It seemed to the colonists that the British leaders were trying to take away their right to govern themselves.

Americans protested against the British laws. The colonists showed their anger toward Britain in several ways. In some communities, British officers were attacked by groups of citizens. Sometimes British goods were destroyed. For example, colonists who were dressed as Indians dumped a load of tea into the harbor of Boston. This was known as the Boston Tea Party. Many colonists refused to buy any more goods from Great Britain until the laws were changed.

† Have someone look up "First Continental Congress" in the Glossary and read the definition aloud.

■ How did the colonists gain their independence?

The Revolutionary War began. As time went on, it became clear that the British government was not going to change its ways. Many Americans began to think that stronger measures were needed. In 1774, a number of colonial leaders met in Philadelphia to talk about their troubles with Britain. This meeting † was known as the First Continental Congress.* In each colony, groups of citizens began to gather weapons and meet for army drill. In Massachusetts these people were called minutemen, because they could be ready for battle only a few minutes after receiving a warning.

In April of 1775, the British general in Massachusetts sent a group of soldiers from Boston to the nearby villages of Lexington and Concord. The soldiers were ordered to get the weapons and gunpowder that had been stored there by the colonists. Fighting broke out between the British soldiers and a group of minutemen. This was the start of the Revolutionary War.

News of the fighting soon spread from Massachusetts to the other colonies. A short time later, the Second Continental Congress met in Philadelphia. For several years, this Congress led the thirteen colonies in their fight against Britain.

See Great Ideas

The picture at the left shows an American lawyer named James Otis speaking in a courtroom against the writs of assistance. (See page 21.) Do you think that the American colonists were used to having very much freedom? Explain. What part do you think the idea of freedom played in the colonists' fight against British rule?

The picture above shows the Second Continental Congress meeting in Philadelphia on July 4, 1776. The Declaration of Independence is being presented to the Congress for its approval.

Colonial leaders signed the Declaration of Independence. When the war began, most of the American colonists still felt a strong loyalty toward Great Britain. But as the fighting went on, many people came to feel that the colonies should break away from Britain and form an independent nation. If the colonies were no longer under British rule, they could govern themselves as they pleased. They could build up new industries and trade freely with all countries. People could settle anywhere without having to ask the British government.

By the summer of 1776, most members of the Second Continental

Why did most people in the Congress believe that the American colonies should break away from Britain? Why did they feel it was important to have a written Declaration of Independence?

Congress were in favor of independence. Thomas Jefferson and several others were asked to prepare a statement that would explain why the colonists wanted to be free of British rule. This statement became known as the Declaration of Independence. It was approved by the Second Continental Congress on July 4, 1776. Today, we think of July 4 as the "birthday" of our country.

Americans finally won their fight for freedom. Even after the Declaration of Independence was signed, the colonists were not yet free of British rule. The Revolutionary War went on for seven more years. At times, it seemed certain that the

Americans would be defeated. They were fighting a rich and powerful nation. The American soldiers did not have much training. Also, they lacked proper food, clothing, and weapons. Many people in America were not in favor of independence. These people helped the British in a number of ways.

In spite of these troubles, the colonists refused to give up. The American soldiers were fighting to win freedom and to protect their homes, so they showed great loyalty and bravery. The American general, George Washington, was a wise and strong leader. Also, the colonists received much valuable aid from Britain's enemy, France. The French government gave money, weapons, and soldiers to help the Americans.

At Yorktown, Virginia, in 1781, a British army gave itself up to American and French troops led by George Washington. What problems did the American colonists face during the Revolutionary War? Why were they able to overcome these problems and win their freedom from British rule?

† Have someone look up "constitution" in the Glossary and read the definition aloud.

In 1781, a British army gave itself up to General Washington at the village of Yorktown, Virginia. Now the British government knew that it had lost the war. A treaty of peace was signed in 1783. In this treaty, Britain agreed that the United States was a fully independent country. The new nation stretched from the Atlantic Ocean to the Mississippi River, and from Canada to Florida. (See the map on page 34.)

■ What kind of government was established in the new nation?

The United States did not have a strong national government. When the war ended, the American people faced an important problem. The thirteen states that had won their independence were not really united. Most people had a greater feeling of loyalty to the state in which they lived than they did to the nation.

The national government of the United States was very weak. It could pass laws, but it had no way of making sure that these laws were carried out. Also, it did not have the power to raise the money it needed to carry on its work. Many people were afraid that there would soon be thirteen small, weak countries instead of one large, strong nation.

A new plan of government was written. In 1787, leaders from the different states held a meeting in Philadelphia. They wanted to talk about ways of making the national government stronger. These people decided to write a new plan of government, or constitution,* for the United States.

For almost four months, the American leaders argued about the kind of government that the United States should have. There were many different ideas. Sometimes it seemed that the meeting would never reach

History 27

Cooperation

See Great Ideas

The picture at the right shows a crowd of people watching George Washington become the first president of the United States. This happened in New York City in 1789. Do you think cooperation was needed in order to set up a new government for the United States? Could this government have been successful if people had not been willing to work together? Explain.

its goal. But the people at the meeting knew that if they did not cooperate, the United States might fall apart. They agreed to settle their differences.

At last, the leaders in Philadelphia were done with their work. On September 17, 1787, most of them signed their names to the new Constitution of the United States.

The Constitution set up a federal* form of government. Under this plan, the national government would be much stronger than it had been before. For example, it would be able to carry out national laws and settle arguments between states. It would also be able to collect taxes to carry on its work. But the states would still have power to deal with many other kinds of matters.

The national government would be divided into three branches. One branch, Congress, would make the laws. Another branch—headed by the president—would see that the laws were carried out. The third branch would be made up of the Supreme Court* and other national courts.

The Constitution was approved. Before the new plan of government could become law, it had to be accepted by at least nine states. Many people did not want the Constitution. They thought it gave too much power to the national government. Others were in favor of the Constitution, because they thought a strong national government would be able to take care of some of the country's problems.

By the summer of 1788, nine states had approved the Constitution. Now the new government could begin work.

Have students study the picture on these pages. Ask: How do you think the American colonists felt when they gained their freedom? What does this picture tell you about the inauguration of our first president? Explain.

Elections were held to choose a president, a vice-president, and members of Congress. George Washington was elected president. He chose a group of people to help him run the government. This group became known as the Cabinet. Plans were made to build a capital city called Washington in an area along the Potomac River known as the District of Columbia. (Find Washington, D.C., on the map on pages 60-61.)

Discover Our Country's Story
1. Why were the British able to win the French and Indian War?
2. Why did the colonists feel that the British Parliament had no right to tax them?
3. How did the Revolutionary War begin?
4. What caused the British government to decide that it had lost the war in America?
5. Why was a constitution needed for the United States? Is the United States Constitution still being used today? How can you find out?
6. Why were some people against the new Constitution? Why were other people in favor of it? Which side won?

Use the questions on this page for class discussion.

3 The Nation Grows

■ Why did many Americans move west of the Appalachian Mountains?

Pioneers built homes in the wilderness. After the United States became a nation, thousands of settlers moved from the Atlantic coast to the lands west of the Appalachian Mountains. (See map on pages 60-61.) Here they could buy good farmland at a very low cost. Some of the settlers followed trails that led through passes in the mountains. Others went by boat down the Ohio River.

The settlers who built new homes west of the mountains faced many hardships and dangers. Often, thick forests had to be cleared away be-

† Discuss a major reason many people settled west of the Appalachian Mountains. (Good farmland could be bought inexpensively.)

Rules and Government

See Great Ideas

This picture shows Daniel Boone leading settlers through a pass in the Appalachian Mountains. During the late 1700's, many American families moved west of the mountains to make new homes. Do you think these settlers needed to follow certain rules in order to get along with one another? Do you think they needed some form of government? Explain your answer.

fore the land could be used for farming. The pioneer families had to raise their own food and build their own cabins. They also had to make most of their own furniture and clothing. Sometimes they were attacked by Indians who did not want strangers moving into their hunting grounds. Many settlers died of diseases such as smallpox* and cholera.*

In spite of these troubles, more and more people came to the lands west of the Appalachian Mountains. Towns and cities began to grow up here. As the territories between the Appalachians and the Mississippi River grew in population, they were allowed to enter the Union* as states.

■ How did life in America change during the early 1800's?

Factories were built to make goods needed by Americans. At the time the United States became a nation, most of the goods people used in their homes were made by hand. But a great change was taking place in England. Machines † were being made that could do spinning, weaving, and other jobs that people had always done by hand. These machines were too large to be put in people's homes. Instead, large buildings called factories were built. Then workers were hired to come to the factories and run the machines.

Near the end of the 1700's, people in America learned how to make some of the new machines. They built a number of textile* mills, where cotton was spun into thread. These were the first real factories in the United States.

New England was very well suited to manufacturing. In this part of the country, there were wealthy business people

*See Glossary

† This was the beginning of the Industrial Revolution.

Have your students study the picture on these pages. Ask: What do you think it would be like to ride on a train like this? Do you think it would be comfortable? Explain.

who had money to spend for building factories. Since there was little good farmland in New England, many people were looking for other ways to earn a living. They could be hired to work in factories. Also, New England had a number of rivers and streams that could supply waterpower to run the new machinery.

By the early 1800's, there were many factories in New England. They made clothing, guns, tools, and many other things needed by America's growing population.

Better means of transportation were developed. When the United States was started, it was hard to go from one part of the country to another. Nearly all the roads were narrow, bumpy, and often muddy. People journeyed over these roads on horseback, or in wagons or stagecoaches. Often it was easier to go by boat, but water transportation was very slow. Because it cost so much to ship goods from place to place, there was little trade between different parts of the country.

A railroad train in New Jersey during the 1830's. How is this train different from the ones that are used today? What other kinds of transportation do you see in this picture?

† Point out that steam engines were used on railroads in many parts of our country until 1960. They are still widely used today in many underdeveloped countries.

During the early 1800's, great improvements were made in transportation. New roads with hard surfaces were built in many places. Canals were dug to connect waterways such as rivers and lakes. The most important was the Erie Canal in New York State. By using the Erie Canal, people could go by water from the Atlantic coast to the Great Lakes. Large amounts of goods were also carried over this route.

At the same time, people were starting to use a new form of power to run machinery. This was steam power. The first successful steam* engine had been made in the 1760's. Before long, steam engines were being used to run boats and trains. By the middle 1800's, there were hundreds of steamboats on our country's rivers and on the Great Lakes. Railroad lines were being built to connect all the important cities in the United States.

Our country grew rapidly in population. In the early 1800's, the number of people who lived in the United

In the 1800's, trains and steamboats became important means of transportation in the United States. How do you suppose this affected trade between different parts of our country?

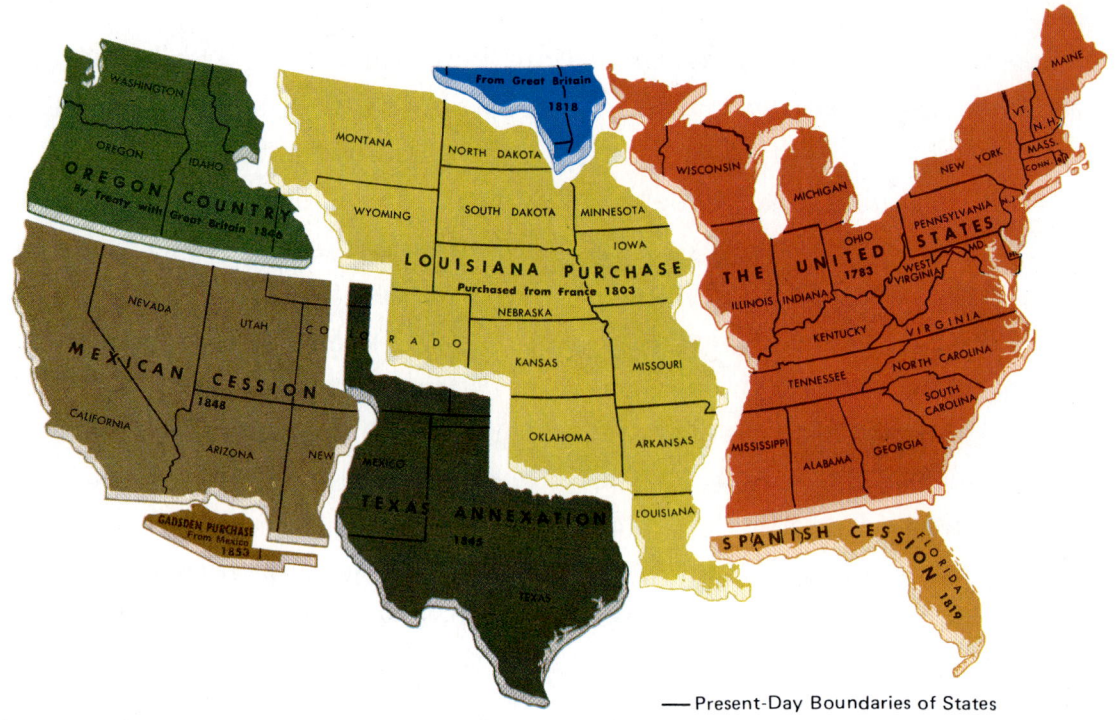

— Present-Day Boundaries of States

How our country grew. The red area on this map shows the size of the United States at the time that our country won its freedom from Great Britain. Later, other pieces of land were added to our country. For example, the United States gained Florida from Spain in 1819.

States grew larger than ever before. More than two million people came here from Ireland, Germany, and other places in Europe. Most of these people were seeking greater freedom or a better way of life. Many of them settled in cities along the Atlantic coast. Others went westward to build new homes on the frontier.

■ How did the United States gain land west of the Mississippi?

The United States bought Louisiana. To the west of the Mississippi River lay a huge piece of land called Louisiana. In 1803, the United States bought this land from France. (See map above.) President Thomas Jefferson sent a group of explorers led by Meriwether Lewis and William Clark to learn more about this new part of our country. Lewis and Clark journeyed all the way across the Louisiana Territory. (See map on page 36.) Then they went westward through the mountains to the Pacific Ocean. They brought back many useful facts about the places they had visited. During the years that followed, thousands of settlers moved

Have students study the map above. Have someone give the date each piece of land was added to our country. What two pieces of land are not shown on the map? (Alaska and Hawaii.)

into the Louisiana Territory to make their homes.

Texas became part of the Union. In 1821, the people of Mexico won their freedom from Spain. At that time, Mexico took over all the Spanish lands in the western part of North America. (Compare the map below with the maps on page 21.) There were Mexican settlements in Texas, California, and other places. However, these settlements were mostly small and far apart.

During the 1820's, settlers from the United States began moving into Texas. The government of Mexico had told them they could settle there. But as time passed, a quarrel arose between the American settlers and the Mexican government. Even though the settlers had promised to be loyal to Mexico, they still thought of themselves as Americans. In 1835, the settlers revolted. About a year later, they were able to break away from Mexican rule.

The settlers had won their independence from Mexico, but they did not want Texas to remain a separate country. They hoped it would become part of the United States. In 1845, our government annexed* Texas. This made people in Mexico angry. They believed the United States had been trying all along to take over this area.

The United States gained California and other lands from Mexico. About the same time, American settlers were also moving into California. Like the Texans, these people did not wish to live under Mexican rule. They wanted the United States to take over California too.

In 1846, a war broke out between Mexico and the United States. After about a year of fighting, the United States won this war. Mexico then had to sell California and other lands

THE UNITED STATES AND MEXICO IN 1821

---Present-Day Boundary Between the United States and Mexico

Refer to the map on this page. Have students compare this map and the map on pages 60-61 to identify the states that the United States annexed from Mexico after 1821.

Have your students look at the map below. Using the map on pages 60-61, have them discover what present-day states Lewis and Clark traveled through to reach their final destination.

in the Southwest to the United States. (See map on page 34.)

Britain and the United States divided the Oregon Country. Along the Pacific coast was a large piece of land known as the Oregon Country. Both the United States and Great Britain wanted to own it. For a time, it seemed likely that the two countries would go to war over the Oregon Country. But in 1846 they settled their differences by signing a treaty. Under this agreement, the United States got nearly all of the Oregon Country south of a line that stretched from the Rocky Mountains to the Pacific Ocean. Britain took the land north of this line.

■ Why did many people come to the western part of our country?

Pioneers in covered wagons traveled across the West. Years before the United States gained part of the Oregon Country, Americans were coming to this area. In the Oregon Country, there were pleasant valleys where the soil and climate were very good for farming. Many Americans wanted to move to the Oregon Country because they thought they could make a better living there.

Most of the settlers went westward over a route known as the Oregon Trail. (See map on this page.) They carried their belongings in covered wagons that were pulled by oxen or horses. The journey along the two-thousand-mile trail took about six months. It was very hard and dangerous. The settlers had to cross high mountains, wide rivers, and empty deserts. Many people died of sickness or were killed in fights with Indians. But settlers kept on coming.

The search for gold and silver brought many settlers. In 1848, a discovery was made that brought thousands of people to California. An American settler found tiny bits

ROUTES TO THE WEST

····· Westbound Route of Lewis and Clark, 1804-1805
—— Oregon Trail
······ First Railroad Across the West
—— Present-Day Boundaries of States

Pioneers going to the Oregon Country. These people have removed the wheels from their covered wagon and put it on a raft to float down a river. During the 1800's, many people moved to the West to make use of the natural resources there. What were some of these resources?

of gold in a mountain stream near Sacramento. (See map at left.) News of this exciting discovery soon spread to the eastern part of the United States. Before long, thousands of settlers were going to California by ship or by covered wagon in order to hunt for gold. This was known as the "gold rush." The number of people in California grew rapidly. Only two years later, California became a state in the Union.

In the years that followed, large deposits of gold and silver were found in Nevada, Colorado, and other parts of the West. Each discovery brought many miners. Large towns grew up quickly wherever gold and silver were found. Most of these "boomtowns" lasted only a few years, until the gold and silver

Call attention to the picture above. What can you discover about pioneer life from this picture?

† You may add that the two railroads were joined near Great Salt Lake with a spike made of gold.

ran out. But a few mining towns—such as Denver, Colorado—grew into important cities.

Railroads brought many people to the West. For years, people had dreamed of a railroad that would connect the eastern part of the United States with the Pacific coast. In the 1860's, two companies began this difficult task. Workers for one company began laying track westward from Omaha, Nebraska. (See map on page 36.) The other company's workers started east from Sacramento, California. The two railroad lines finally met near Great Salt Lake in Utah in 1869. †

As time passed, other railroads were built across the West. Now settlers could travel westward by train instead of making the long, dangerous journey by covered wagon. Soon, people were moving west in growing numbers.

An Indian camp on the Great Plains. Why were the Indians unhappy to see white settlers coming to the West? What changes took place in the Indians' way of life after the settlers came?

† Discuss what might have happened if the Indian tribes had cooperated with one another.

The Indians lost their land and their way of life. Many different tribes of Indians lived in the West at the time that white people began coming here. The Indians did not like to have white people settle on their land. Often they had good reasons for being unhappy. For example, in the early 1800's huge herds of buffalo roamed the Great Plains.* The Indians of the plains hunted buffalo to get meat, hides, and other things they needed. But as the years passed, most of the buffalo were killed by white hunters. Then the Indians could no longer find enough buffalo to meet their needs.

In the last half of the 1800's, a number of battles took place between the Indians and United States soldiers. The Indians fought bravely. But they were much fewer in number than the white people, and some of the tribes were not willing to cooperate with each other. Also, the whites had better weapons. At last, the Indians gave up. They had to sell most of their land to the whites and move to places called reservations.*

Farmers came to the Great Plains to make their homes. After railroads were built across the Great Plains, many farmers began to settle in this part of the country. They came because they could get good farmland free or at a very low price. In return for building railroad lines, some companies had been given large amounts of land by the government. They were willing to sell this land cheaply to settlers. Also, the government gave land to people who were willing to farm it for five years.

Life was not easy for the families who settled on the Great Plains. Summers were hot and winters were freezing cold. In most places, the land was covered with thick grass that made it hard to plow the soil. Strong winds or hail sometimes destroyed whole fields of crops. Weeks or months might pass without any rain. Often farmers had to dig deep wells in order to get water. They had to put fences of barbed wire around their fields to keep wandering herds of cattle from eating their crops.

Pioneer farmers on the Great Plains. These people are plowing land so they can plant crops. Why was life very hard for many of the families who settled on the Great Plains?

Some settlers became so unhappy with their hard life that they moved back east. But others refused to give up. Through hard work and courage, they changed the Great Plains into an important farming area.

Discover Our Country's Story

1. What were some problems faced by the settlers who moved west of the Appalachian Mountains?
2. Why was New England a good place for building factories?
3. Why was there little trade at first between different parts of our country?
4. Why was Lewis and Clark's journey important to the United States?
5. Why were the people of Mexico angry when Texas became part of the United States?
6. Why did large numbers of people begin coming to California in 1848?
7. What were "boomtowns"? What happened to most of these towns?
8. How was the building of railroads important to the history of the West?
9. Why did the Indians lose most of the battles they fought against United States soldiers?
10. Why did many farmers come to the Great Plains during the last half of the 1800's?

You may wish to use these questions for class discussion.

† You may wish to assign students to do research about Abraham Lincoln from books in your school library. You may have several students work together to prepare a special class report about Lincoln.

4 The Union Is Saved

■ How did the United States become a divided country?

The North and the South had different ways of life. In the early 1800's, there were important differences between the northern and southern parts of our country. Hundreds of factories had been built in the North. Many people there lived in cities or large towns. In the South, there were few cities and only a small number of factories. Most people made their living by farming. In some places, there were plantations. On these large farms, cotton was usually the main crop. The owners sold large amounts of cotton to factories in the North and in Europe.

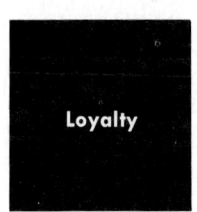

Loyalty

See Great Ideas

† Abraham Lincoln was president of the United States at the time that a war broke out between the northern and southern parts of our country. This great struggle became known as the Civil War. Why is Abraham Lincoln remembered today as one of our greatest presidents? How did Lincoln show his loyalty to his country? How did he show his loyalty to certain ideas, such as the idea of freedom for all people? You will need to read more about Lincoln in other books to find the answers to these questions.

† Why did people in the North pass laws making slavery illegal?

Large numbers of slaves worked on plantations in the South. Much of the work on southern farms was done by black people. On page 18, you read how blacks were brought from Africa in colonial days as slaves. These people did not have the freedom to live where they wished or to work at jobs of their own choosing. They had to work all their lives for the white plantation owners.

In colonial days, slavery had been allowed in the North also. But it had never been very profitable there, because farms were much smaller. Also, many people in the North believed that slavery was wrong. By 1800, most states in the North had passed laws saying that people could not own slaves.

Americans disagreed about slavery and other matters. Some people in the North believed that slavery should be ended everywhere in the United States. These people made speeches and wrote books attacking

A slave market in Virginia before the Civil War. White people in the South often said that black people did not mind being slaves. Do you think they were right? Why? Why not? Do you think that human beings everywhere have a deep desire for freedom? Explain.

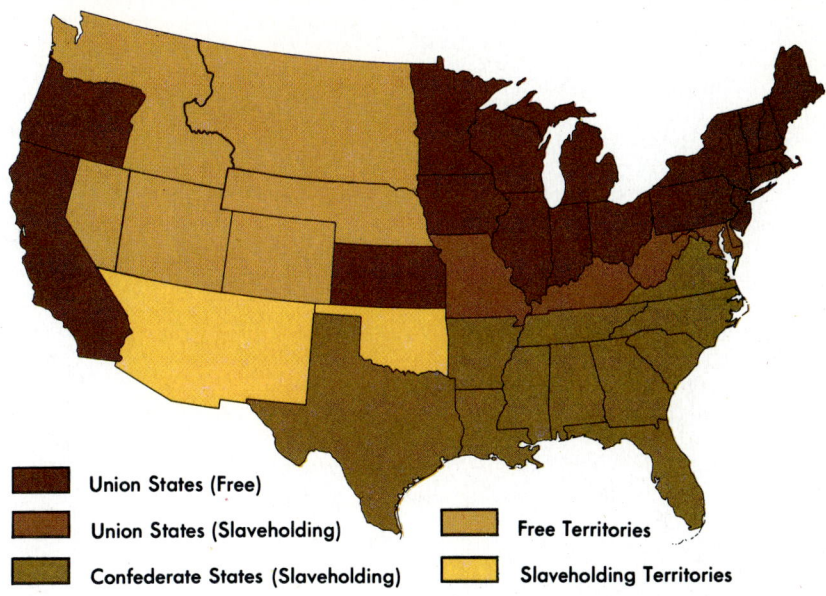

A Divided Country

The map at the right shows the United States at the time of the Civil War. Slavery was allowed in all the Confederate states. It was not allowed in most states of the Union. These were known as free states. A few states, such as Missouri and Kentucky, allowed slavery but remained loyal to the Union. The western part of Virginia stayed with the Union when the rest of the state joined the Confederacy. It later became the state of West Virginia.

- Union States (Free)
- Union States (Slaveholding)
- Confederate States (Slaveholding)
- Free Territories
- Slaveholding Territories

slavery. Sometimes they helped black people in the South to escape from their masters. As time passed, more people in the North began to agree with their views.

This movement to do away with slavery made most white people in the South very angry. They were afraid they would not be able to keep up their way of life if they did not have slaves to work for them.

People in the North and the South also disagreed about other matters. One of these was the question of states' rights. Most leaders in the North believed that laws made by the federal government should always be obeyed by the states. On the other hand, many southern leaders believed that states did not have to obey federal laws if they thought these laws were unfair. Some even said that states had the right to leave the Union.

■ How did the Civil War affect our country?

The quarrel between the North and the South led to war. In 1860, Abraham Lincoln became president of the United States. This alarmed many white people in the South, because they thought Lincoln would try to end slavery. Before long, eleven states in the South broke away

Have your students study the map and legend above. Was our state a free state or a slaveholding state (or territory) at the time of the Civil War?

The Battle of Mobile Bay was an important navy battle in the Civil War. It took place in 1864 near Mobile, Alabama. (See map on pages 60-61.) Who won the Battle of Mobile Bay? Why was this battle so important? Look in other books to find answers to these questions.

You may wish to discuss the Emancipation Proclamation.

from the Union. They formed a new nation known as the Confederate States of America, or the Confederacy.

In April, 1861, a war broke out between the North and the South. This became known as the Civil War.* It lasted four years and took the lives of more than half a million Americans.

The war ended in victory for the North. For a time, the South appeared to be winning the war. But the North was stronger in several ways. It had more than twice as many people as the South, and much more wealth. There were more factories in the North to make weapons and other things the soldiers needed. In addition, the North had better railroads. The North was aided by thousands of black soldiers who fought for the Union. Also, President Lincoln was a very † wise and strong leader.

These advantages helped the North to win the war. In the spring of 1865, the Confederate armies surrendered to the armies of the Union.

Two important results of the Civil War. The victory of the North caused two important things to happen. First, the eleven Confederate states were brought back into the Union. Second, slavery was ended in all parts of the United States.

*See Glossary

Discover Our Country's Story
1. What were some important differences between the North and the South during the early 1800's?
2. Why did slavery come to an end in the North?
3. How did people in the North and the South disagree on the question of states' rights?
4. Why were many white people in the South alarmed when Abraham Lincoln became president?
5. Why was the North able to win the Civil War?

† Make the students aware the South also had some strong leaders. Discuss some of them.

† Ask: Do you think railroads played an important part in the growth of industry and trade? Explain your answer.

5 Our Country Becomes a World Leader

■ How did the United States become a great manufacturing nation?

The Civil War helped industry to grow. During the Civil War, industry grew rapidly in the United States. The American soldiers needed large amounts of such things as clothing, food, and weapons. To help meet these needs, new factories were started. And many older factories made more goods than ever before.

† After the war, industry grew even faster. There were now more people in the United States, so there were more customers for the goods that factories made. Also, the new railroads made it possible to ship goods quickly and cheaply from one place to another. Because of this, factories could sell their goods to people in all parts of the country.

Inventors discovered new ways of making goods. Another reason why industry grew so rapidly was that people found new ways to make use of our country's rich natural resources. For example, there were large deposits of coal and iron ore in the United States. Coal and iron ore could be used in making steel. Although steel was a very useful metal, it had always been slow and costly to produce. But in the 1850's,

Using Natural Resources
See Great Ideas

The picture at right shows a group of ironworkers in New York State. During the last half of the 1800's, Americans discovered new ways of using certain natural resources to meet their needs. What were some of these resources? How did the new discoveries affect the growth of industry in the United States?

people found a way to make large amounts of steel rapidly and cheaply. Soon many steel plants were built in the United States. The steel was used by other factories in making many different kinds of goods.

People were also discovering new ways of using natural resources to produce heat, light, and power. One of these resources was a dark, oily liquid that came out of the ground in certain places. This was called petroleum. For a long time, people thought petroleum was worthless. But then they found that it could be made into kerosene* and other valuable products. Kerosene became widely used as a fuel in lamps and stoves.

People in America were also learning about a new form of power called electricity. In 1879, Thomas Edison made the first successful electric light. Edison and other inventors also developed machines that could make large amounts of electricity.

*See Glossary

Photograph courtesy of the Ford Archives

Using Tools

See Great Ideas

The picture above shows Henry Ford and his wife, Clara Bryant Ford, in a workshop behind their home in Detroit, Michigan. The year was 1896, and Henry Ford was just finishing work on his first automobile. Ford was not the first person ever to build an automobile, but he was the first to make cars that were cheap enough for most people to buy. Can you explain how he did this?

Soon electricity was being used to run many kinds of machinery.

About the same time, people were discovering new ways of sending messages from place to place. Alexander Graham Bell invented the first telephone in 1876. Radio was another new form of communication.* It was developed in the early 1900's.

† How do you think the development of new farm machines helped to change the lives of farmers?

Because of new inventions, transportation was also improved. The first automobiles were built in the late 1800's by people in Europe and the United States. In 1903, two brothers from Ohio named Wilbur and Orville Wright built the first successful airplane.

Factory owners discovered better ways of making goods. As the years passed, factory owners in the United States found new and better ways of making goods. One of the most important of these was the assembly-line method. It was developed mostly by an auto maker named Henry Ford. The frame of an automobile was put on a large belt that moved slowly past a line of workers. Each worker added a different part to the frame until the car was finished.

The assembly-line method made it possible to build large numbers of cars at a price most people could pay. It worked so well that factories began to use it in making many different kinds of goods.

All of these new discoveries helped industry to grow rapidly in the United States. By the early 1900's, our country was producing more factory goods than any other country.

■ How did great cities grow up in the United States?

People moved from farms to cities. Before the Civil War, only one out of every five Americans lived in a city or large town. But in the years that followed, great changes took place in
† people's way of living. Farmers began to use new machines and better ways of farming. These made it possible for one farmer to raise enough food for many people. At the same time, more workers than ever before were needed in factories, stores, and offices. Thousands of people moved from farms to cities to get jobs. As more and more newcomers arrived, the cities grew rapidly. For example, Chicago was more than twenty times as large in 1910 as it was in 1860. By 1910 nearly half of all Americans lived in cities or large towns.

Immigrants* came from many lands. Many of the people who settled in the growing cities were immigrants from other lands. Between 1865 and 1915, more than twenty-six million people came to the United States to live. Most of them were from European countries such as Germany, Italy, Sweden, and Poland. Some also came from Mexico, Canada, and other countries in North and South America. A much smaller

*See Glossary

History 49

Division of Labor

See Great Ideas

The picture above shows a famous street called the Bowery in New York City during the 1890's. In the years that followed the Civil War, American cities grew rapidly. What were some of the reasons for this? Was there *more* division of labor in the cities than in the country? Or was there *less*? How do you think this affected the number of people who wanted to move from the farms to the cities? Look for "Great Ideas" on the Contents page to find information that will help answer these questions.

number of people came from China, Japan, and other countries in Asia.

Most of these people came to America because they had heard it was a "land of opportunity." In the lands where they were born, they had found it hard to earn a good living. They hoped it would be easier to find good jobs in America. Some people came to America because they wanted more freedom than they could have in their own countries.

Life was not easy for most of the immigrants at first. These people were often very poor. Because most of them did not have any special training, they could not get good jobs. Many could not speak English when they arrived. Often they found it hard to give up their old ways of

Refer to the picture on these pages. Ask: What can you discover from this picture about life in New York City in the 1890's? Make a list of your discoveries.

doing things and learn a new way of life. Some of them were treated unkindly by other people in America. This was partly because they seemed strange and "different." Also, many Americans were afraid the newcomers would take their jobs away from them by working for less money.

As time passed, life became easier for most of the immigrants. The children and many of the older people went to school. There they learned the English language and American ways. As they gained more education, they were able to get better jobs. Many of our country's leaders during the last one hundred years have been immigrants or sons and daughters of immigrants. †

■ How did the United States become involved in world problems?

Americans began to take more interest in other countries. During the 1700's and 1800's, most Americans paid little attention to what was happening in other parts of the world. Wide oceans separated America from Europe, Asia, and Africa. Transportation and communication were still quite slow. Americans were interested mostly in developing the resources of their own huge country.

As time passed, an important change began to take place. The United States was now becoming one of the richest and strongest countries in the world. It was carrying on more and more trade with other nations. Many Americans felt the United States should play a more important part in the world.

A chance to do this came in 1898, when the United States went to war against Spain. At that time, Spain ruled the island of Cuba in the West Indies. American soldiers were sent to Cuba to help the people of that island win their independence from Spain. After a few months of fighting, the Americans defeated the Spanish. Spain had to

† Some of your students may have parents or grandparents that came from other countries. You may have several students tell the class about their families.

† Have someone look up "Nazi" in the Glossary and read the definition aloud.

give Cuba its freedom. The United States became owner of two Spanish possessions. These were the island of Puerto Rico, in the West Indies, and the Philippine Islands, off the coast of Asia. About the same time, the United States took over the Hawaiian Islands.

The United States entered a war in Europe. In 1914, a terrible war broke out between two groups of countries in Europe. On one side were the Central Powers, which included Germany and Austria-Hungary. On the other side were Britain, France, Russia, and several other countries. They were called the Allies. The great struggle between the Allies and the Central Powers became known as World War I.

At first, the United States tried to stay out of the war in Europe. But German submarines began to attack Allied ships in the Atlantic Ocean. A number of Americans on these ships were killed. The Germans also did other things that made the American people angry. In 1917 the United States joined the war on the side of the Allies. American soldiers were sent to Europe to fight. In the fall of 1918, the Central Powers finally gave up.

Another war took the lives of many Americans. For a few years, there was peace in most parts of the world. But in 1933 † a group of people called the Nazis* took over the government in Germany. Their leader, Adolf Hitler, wanted to conquer other countries and make Germany the most powerful nation in Europe. The leaders of Italy and Japan also decided to go to war to gain more lands. Together, these three countries became known as the Axis. They were opposed by Britain, France, the Soviet Union, and other countries. In 1939, Germany attacked the neighboring country of Poland. This was the start of World War II.

Again, people in the United States hoped to stay out of war. But in 1941, Japanese airplanes made a surprise attack on a large group of American warships docked at Pearl Harbor in

the Hawaiian Islands. This attack brought our country into the war against the Axis. Millions of Americans were sent to fight in many parts of the world.

By working together, the United States and its allies were able to defeat the Axis. First Italy and then Germany surrendered to the Allied armies. In the meantime, scientists who were working for the United States government built a powerful new weapon called the atomic bomb. In August, 1945, atomic bombs destroyed two Japanese cities. Partly because of this, Japan gave up the war a short time later.

The United Nations was formed to work for world peace. By the end of World War II, many people had come to believe that there must never again be a world war. Atomic bombs and other weapons had become too powerful. If these new weapons were ever used in another war, they might destroy all life on earth.

An American battleship on fire after the Japanese attack at Pearl Harbor in 1941. Where is Pearl Harbor? Why was the attack at Pearl Harbor so important in American history?

Cooperation

See Great Ideas

The picture above shows people from different countries at a meeting of the United Nations in New York City. What is the United Nations? Why was the United Nations formed? Do you think it is important for countries to cooperate with one another in order to solve their problems? Give facts to explain your answer. What sometimes happens when countries do not cooperate?

In 1945, most countries of the world joined together in forming a new organization to work for world peace. This was the United Nations. Today about 150 countries are members of the United Nations, which meets in New York City. The United Nations tries to settle disagreements that might lead to war. It also tries to help the poorer countries of the world provide a better way of life for their people.

Communism spread to many parts of the world. After World War II ended, the United States was faced with a new problem. For almost thirty years, the Soviet Union had been ruled by a group of people who were known as Communists.* The Communists believed that industry,

Refer to the picture above. Have students read the caption. Use the questions for a class discussion.

trade, and most other activities in a country should be run by the government. They wanted people all over the world to follow the Communist way of life.

For a time, it seemed to many Americans that the Communists might reach their goal. Communist governments came to power in several countries of eastern Europe, such as Poland and Hungary. In 1949 the huge country of China also fell under Communist rule.

Most people in the United States were strongly against communism. They were afraid it could take away their freedom. The United States made agreements with a number of friendly countries in Europe and Asia. These countries promised to help each other in case of a Communist attack.

The struggle between the Communist countries and the non-Communist countries became known as the Cold War. Both sides made their armies larger. They also developed new weapons and war equipment, such as hydrogen* bombs and guided* missiles. Sometimes real fighting broke out between the two sides. For example, there was a war between Communist and non-Communist forces in the small Asian country of Korea. This war lasted from 1950 to 1953. Another war took place in the Asian country of Vietnam from 1957 to 1975. About half a million American soldiers were killed or wounded in these two wars.

In the last few years, the Communist and non-Communist countries have grown a little more friendly toward one another. Some people believe that the Cold War is mostly over. Other people think that the Cold War will last as long as the Communist and non-Communist countries have such different ways of life.

Discover Our Country's Story

1. How did the Civil War help American industry to grow? Why did industry keep on growing after the war was over?
2. What important changes took place in transportation and communication during the late 1800's and early 1900's?
3. Why did many people from Europe come to America after 1865?
4. Why did many immigrants have a hard time when they first came to America?
5. Why did most Americans take little interest in other countries during the 1700's and 1800's?
6. What were some things that happened because of the Spanish-American War?
7. Why did the United States take part in World War I? Why did it take part in World War II?
8. What was the Cold War, and how did it come about?

You may wish to use the questions on this page for class discussion or evaluation.

6 Years of Amazing Change

A giant rocket takes off from the earth for a flight into space. Do you think space flights will be important to Americans in years to come? Explain.

■ How have science and industry changed American life?

In the last thirty years, great changes have taken place in our country. Today our way of life is very different from what it was in the past.

Changes brought about by science. Some of these changes have been brought about by science. For example, scientists have learned how to use the energy* stored in atoms.* This energy can be used to make powerful weapons. It can be used to produce electricity. Also, rockets have been built to carry people far from the earth. American astronauts* have already landed on the moon. Someday they may be able to make even longer trips in space. †

Changes caused by industry. Important changes have also been taking place in industry. Many new machines have been invented. Some of these machines do not need people to guide them. They can run by themselves. The use of

*See Glossary

† Point out that sending astronauts into space requires the cooperation of thousands of people.

Is all change progress? Discuss how progress in one area of our life may create problems in another area. (Pollution is an example.)

machines like these is called automation. Other new machines can do the hardest math problems in a few seconds. These machines are called computers.

The new machines have helped industry to grow. By using them, workers can produce more goods than ever before. (See the charts below.) This is why most Americans have a comfortable way of life. They can afford to buy many kinds of goods. For example, most American families own cars and television sets. This is not true in many other countries. There, only a few rich families can buy such things.

Pollution is a serious problem. The growth of our industry has brought many good things to people in the United States. But it has also led to some major problems. One of these is pollution.*

Air pollution is caused in several ways. People burn fuels such as coal and oil to heat their buildings. They also burn these fuels to produce electricity. Sometimes rubbish is burned to get rid of it. The smoke from all these fires goes into the air. There

Great changes have taken place in our country in the last thirty years. Some of these changes are shown on the charts below. The chart at left shows the number of people in the United States. Our population has grown from about 152 million in 1950 to almost 220 million today. The middle chart shows the value of all goods and services produced in our country. As you can see, production has grown very rapidly since 1950. The chart at right shows the average family income in the United States. The average family income grew from about $3,300 in 1950 to about $13,700 in 1975. It is still growing rapidly today.

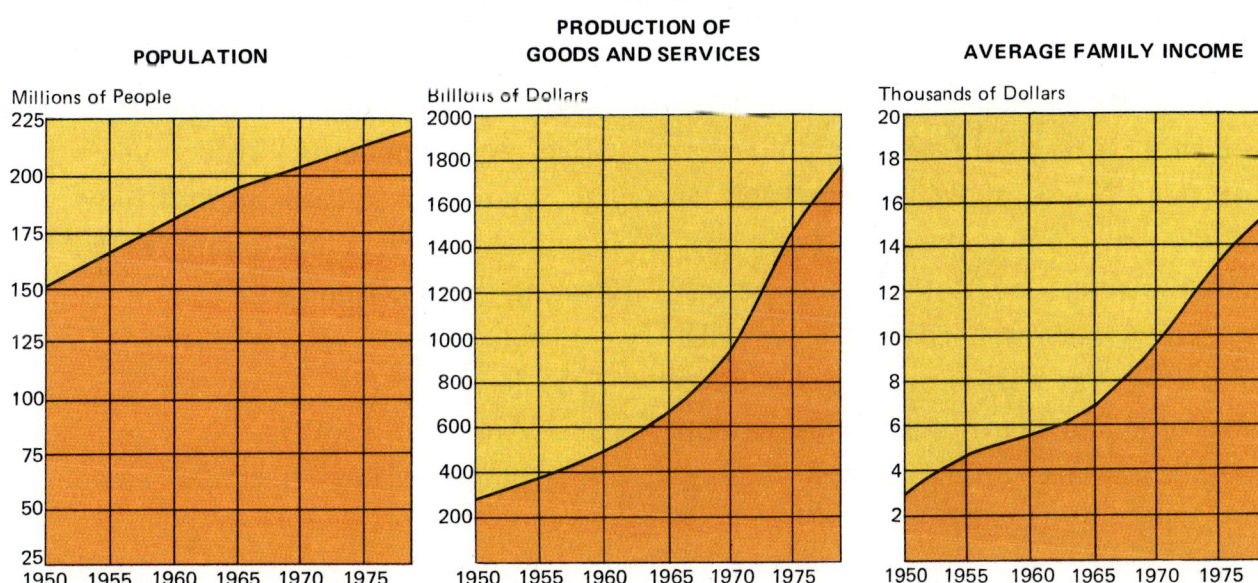

Our Changing Nation

† Point out that the United States imports nearly half the oil we use.

it mixes with fumes from cars, trucks, buses, and airplanes.

Water can become polluted also. This happens when cities and factories dump their waste materials into rivers and lakes.

Today many Americans are worried about pollution. Scientists have found that people can become very sick from breathing polluted air. Polluted water is not safe for drinking, bathing, and other uses. Our country's leaders are seeking ways to stop pollution. They want to make our air and water clean again.

The need to use resources carefully. The growth of industry has led to another problem. Each year, American factories use huge amounts of natural resources. Today some of these resources are starting to run out. For example, we no longer produce enough oil, or petroleum,* to meet our needs. So we must buy large amounts of oil from other countries. If these countries ever stopped selling us oil, we would be in serious trouble. †

In the future, we will have to use our resources more carefully to keep from running out. We must also find new ways of getting the things we need. For instance, sunlight is a source of energy that will never be used up. Some people are now using sunlight to heat their houses. Someday it may also be possible to use sunlight in producing electric power.

■ How has the concern for human needs changed American life?

Basic needs of people. All people on earth are alike in certain ways. They all have needs they must meet in order to live happy, useful lives. These are called basic human needs. (See "Needs of People" in Table of Contents.) For example, every person needs food, clothing, and shelter. Every person needs goals to work for. Every person needs a chance to think and learn. And every person needs some kind of faith. Today, Americans are trying to make sure that all our citizens have a chance to meet their basic human needs.

Some people did not have equal rights and freedoms. Thirty years ago, many Americans did not have an equal chance to meet their needs. Among these people were:

. . . blacks
. . . Jews*
. . . American Indians
. . . people whose ancestors* came

from certain countries, such as Mexico, Puerto Rico, China, and Japan.

These people lacked a number of the rights and freedoms that other Americans enjoyed. For example, in some places black children could not go to the same schools as white children. Some hotels and resorts would not admit Jews as guests. Mexican-Americans were sometimes

Freedom

See Great Ideas

The picture above shows a civil rights march in Boston, Massachusetts, during the 1960's. What do we mean by "civil rights"? Why did some Americans feel they needed to hold marches for civil rights? Did the civil rights movement succeed in reaching its goals? Give facts to back up your answer. Are there still any people in our country today who do not enjoy the same rights and freedoms as other Americans? If so, who are they?

Refer to the picture above. Use the questions for discussion.

† Dr. Martin Luther King, Jr., was a well-known leader of the civil rights movement. In 1964, he received the Nobel Peace Prize for his great freedom work.

refused jobs that other Americans could get easily. Some people would not sell houses or rent apartments to Indian families.

Women, too, were often treated unfairly in our country. For example, some companies would not hire women for certain jobs. If they did hire women, they would often pay them less money than men. This was true even if the women did exactly the same kind of work.

People work for equal rights and freedoms. During the 1950's, an important change took place. Some of the people who had been treated unfairly began to demand equal rights. They held marches and public meetings to call attention to what they wanted. Soon they were joined by other Americans who supported their fight for freedom. This became known as the civil* rights movement.

As time passed, the civil rights movement began to reach its goals. Our federal and state governments passed laws to protect the rights of minority* groups. Today it is against the law to treat a person unfairly just because that person belongs to a certain group. Women and minority groups now enjoy more rights than ever before in our history.

Today some people cannot meet their needs. Even today, however, many Americans find it hard to meet their needs. For example, millions of people cannot find steady jobs. Sometimes this is because they are too old, or their health is poor. They may not have the education or the skills needed to get a well-paying job. Sometimes there are simply not enough jobs for all the people who need them.

Usually, people who lack steady jobs do not have much money. They cannot afford to buy the proper kinds of food, clothing, and shelter. Many of them live in run-down areas called slums. When they become ill, they cannot afford medical care. Sometimes their illnesses keep them from holding full-time jobs.

Business and government are helping. Many things are being done to help Americans who have trouble meeting their needs. For instance, our government runs training programs for workers without jobs. Here, people learn skills they can use in industry. Business companies also carry on programs of this kind. Many cities have built apartment buildings where people can live without paying very much money. Our government provides money for people who are too old or too ill to hold steady jobs.

Government programs have helped many Americans to meet their needs. But these programs often cost a lot of money. Also, many people are needed to carry them out. Today, more than sixteen million Americans work for the government. Our national government spends more than thirteen times as much money each year as it did in 1948. Most of this money comes from taxes that our citizens must pay to the government.

Doing our part as citizens. In the years to come, many more exciting

Rules and Government
See Great Ideas

The picture below shows a woman scientist at work. In the past, women could work only at certain kinds of jobs. Today, all kinds of jobs are open to women. How did laws help to bring about this change? Sometimes people think that laws take away part of their freedom. But can laws also protect a person's freedom? If so, how?

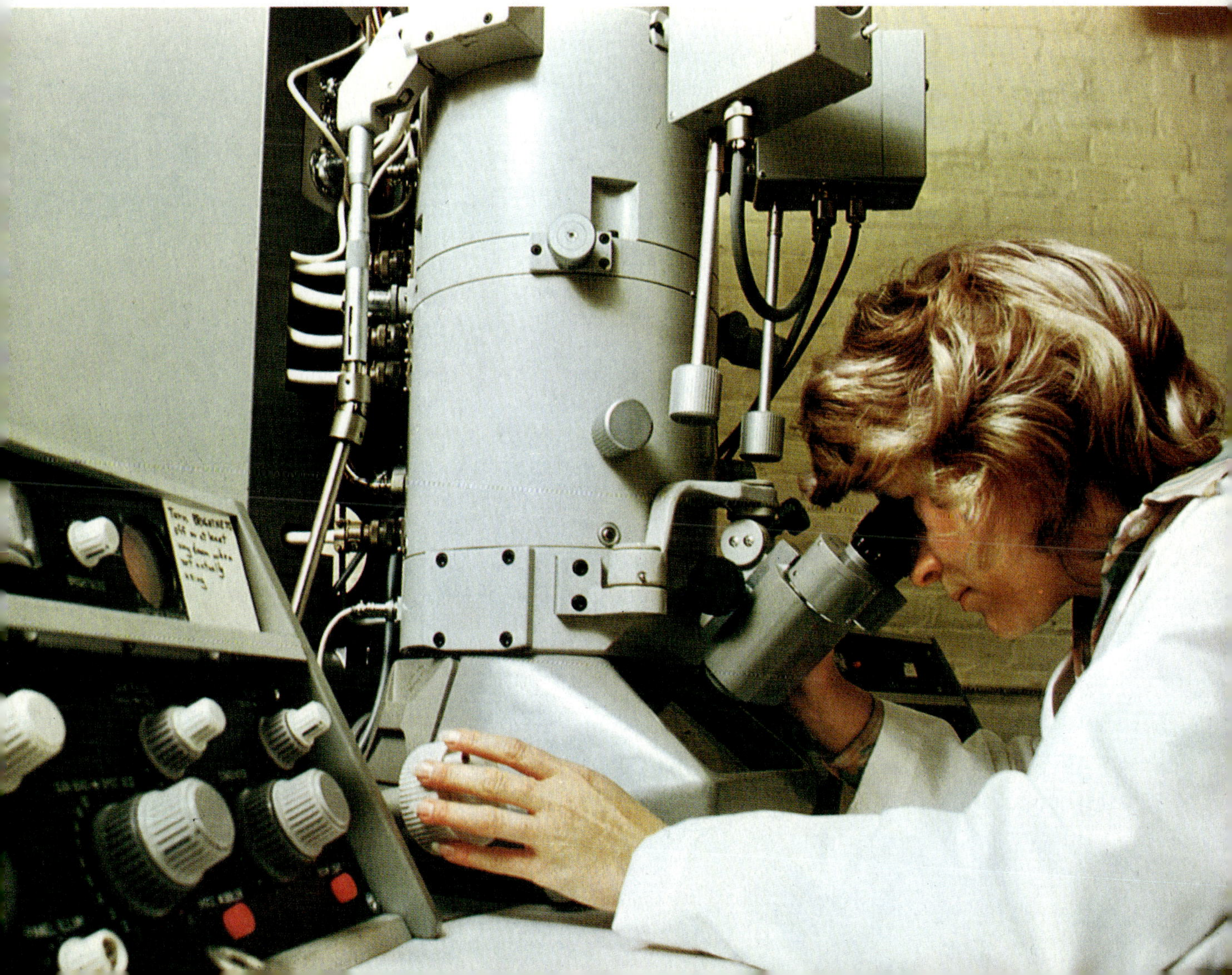

Education
See Great Ideas

Working on a classroom project. In our country today, most young people have a chance to get a good education. Nearly all children attend grade school and high school. Many students also go on to college. Do you think education is one of the great ideas that have built our nation? What would happen if most of our citizens did not have a good education? Would our government be able to do its job well? Give reasons for your answers.

changes will take place in our country. Will these changes be good or bad? The answer is largely up to us. We must all do our part as citizens. We must continue to live by the great ideas that built our nation—ideas such as freedom, loyalty, and cooperation. In this way, we can make our country even better and stronger than it is today.

Discover Our Country's Story
1. What important changes have taken place in the United States during the last thirty years? How have these changes affected your family?
2. Why is pollution a serious problem today? What are some examples of pollution in your own community?
3. What is being done today to help people who have trouble meeting their needs?
4. In what ways do you think the United States will change in the years ahead?

You may wish to use the questions on this page for class discussion.

Index

Explanation of abbreviations used in this Index: *p* — picture   *m* — map

Allies, 52
animals, 5, 17, 39
Asia, 5, 8, 9
assembly-line method, 49
astronauts, 56
atomic bomb, 53
automation, 57
automobiles, 49; *p* 48

Battle of Mobile Bay, *p* 44-45
Bell, Alexander Graham, 48
Bering Strait, 5; *m* 5
birthday of our country, 25; *p* 2-3
blacks, *see* people
Boone, Daniel, *p* 30-31
Boston, Massachusetts, 18; *p* 59
Boston Tea Party, 22
Britain, *see* Great Britain

Cabinet, 29
Cabot, John, 14; *p* 14-15
Cabrillo (kä brēl´ yō), Juan, *m* 10
California, 11, 35
Chicago, Illinois, 49
China, 55
cities, 49. See also names of cities
civil rights, 62; *p* 59
Civil War, 43-45, 46; *p* 44-45; *m* 43
coal, *see* minerals
Cold War, 55
colonies,
   British, 17-18, 20; *m* 17
   English, 14-15, 17
   French, 20
   Middle Colonies, 18; *m* 17
   New England, 17-18; *m* 17
   Southern Colonies, 18; *m* 17
Columbus, Christopher, 8-9; *m* 7
communism, 54-55
communities, early, 4-18
computers, 57
Confederate States of America, 45; *m* 43
Congress, 28, 29
Constitution, (kon´ stə tü´ shən) of the United States, 27-28
Continental Congress, First, 23
Continental Congress, Second, 23, 24-25; *p* 24-25
Coronado, Francisco, *p* 8-9; *m* 10
covered wagon, *p* 37
Cuba, 51-52

de Soto, Hernando, *m* 10
Declaration of Independence, 24, 25; *p* 24-25
divided country, 41; *m* 43

earning a living, 17, 41, 50, 51
Edison, Thomas, 47
electricity, 47-48, 56, 58
energy, 56, 58
Erie Canal, 33
Europeans, *see* people
explorers, 8-10, 12, 14; *p* 8-9, 12-13; *m* 7, 10

factories, 31, 32, 41, 45
farmers, 16, 17, 18, 39; *p* 40
farm products, 5, 18, 41
Ford, Henry, 49; *p* 48
forts, 10, 11
France, 26, 52
freedom, *see* great ideas
French and Indian War, 20; *m* 21

Germany, 52
gold, *see* minerals
goods and services, *chart* 57
government,
   British, 23
   national, 27-28
   spending, 62, 63
Great Britain, 17, 18, 24
great ideas,
   cooperation, *p* 28-29, 54
   division of labor, *p* 50-51
   education, *p* 64
   exchange, *p* 18-19
   freedom, 2, 16, 55, 58, 59; *p* 22-23, 59
   language, *p* 10-11
   loyalty, *p* 14-15, 41
   rules and government, 43; *p* 30-31, 63
   using natural resources, 4, 46, 58; *p* 4, 37, 46-47
   using tools, 8; *p* 16, 48
Great Lakes, 12, 33
Great Plains, 39-40; *p* 40
guided missiles, 55

Hawaiian Islands, 52, 53
Hitler, Adolf, 52
hydrogen bombs, 55

immigrants, 49-51
income, family, *chart* 57
Indians, *see* people
Indies, 8, 14; *m* 7
industry, 46-47, 56, 57, 58; *p* 46-47; *chart* 57
inventions, 48-49, 56
iron ore, *see* minerals

Jamestown, Virginia, 15; *p* 16
Japan, 52, 53
Jefferson, Thomas, 25, 34
Joliet, Louis, *p* 12-13

Korean War, 55

laws, 22, 62
Lewis and Clark, 34; *m* 36
Lincoln, Abraham, 43, 45; *p* 41
Louisiana Purchase, 34-35; *m* 34

machines, 31, 56-57
manufacturing, 31-32
Marquette, Father Jacques, *p* 12-13
Mexico, 35
minerals,
   coal, 46
   gold, 9, 10, 37-38
   iron ore, 18, 46
   petroleum, 47, 58
   silver, 9, 10, 36-37
minority groups, 62
minutemen, 23
missionaries, 12; *p* 12-13
missions, 10, 11; *p* 10-11
Mississippi River, 12, 20; *p* 12-13; *m* 10
Mount Rushmore, *p* 1

Native Americans, *see* people, Indians
New Amsterdam, *p* 13
New England, 17-18
New York City, 18; *p* 13, 28-29, 50-51

oil, *see* minerals, petroleum
Oregon Country, 36; *m* 34
Oregon Trail, 36; *m* 36

Parliament, 21-22
Pearl Harbor, 52-53; *p* 52-53
people,
   basic needs, 58
   blacks, 18, 42, 43, 58, 59; *p* 42-43
   Europeans, 7-17; *p* 6-9, 12-16
   first Americans, 4-5
   French, 12
   Indians, 4-5, 9, 10, 11, 12, 20, 21, 31, 39, 58, 62; *p* 4, 38-39; *m* 5
   Jews, 58, 59
   Mexican-Americans, 59
   Spanish, 10-11; *p* 8-9; *m* 10

PRONUNCIATION KEY: hat, āge, cāre, fär; let, ēqual, tėrm; it, īce; hot, ōpen, ôrder; oil, out; cup, pu̇t, rüle, ūse; child; long; thin; ᴛʜen; zh, measure; ə represents a in about, e in taken, i in pencil, o in lemon, u in circus.

History 65

petroleum, *see* minerals
Philadelphia, Pennsylvania, 18, 23, 27, 28; *p* 18-19
Pilgrims, 16
pioneers, *see* settlers
plantations, 18
pollution, 57-58
population, 2, 17, 33-34; *chart* 57

radio, 48
railroads, *see* transportation
Revolutionary War, 23-27; *p* 26-27
rockets, 56; *p* 56
Russia, *see* Soviet Union

schools, *p* 64
science, 56; *p* 63
settlements, 11, 13, 15, 35; *p* 13, 16, 18-19; *m* 13
settlers, 5, 11, 17, 21, 30-40; *p* 30-31, 37; *m* 5

silver, *see* minerals
slavery, 18, 42-43; *m* 43
slaves, *p* 42-43
slums, 62
Soviet Union, 52, 54
space flight, 56; *p* 56
Spanish-American War, 51
states' rights, 43
steam engine, 33
steam power, 33
steel, 46-47
Supreme Court, 28

taxes, 21, 63
telephone, 48
Texas, 11, 35; *m* 34
textile mills, 31
trade, 20-21, 32, 51; *p* 6-7
traders, 8, 12, 15, 18; *m* 7
transportation, 32-33; *p* 32-33
treaties, 20, 27

unemployment, 62
Union, the, 45; *m* 43
United Nations, 53-54; *p* 54
United States, *m* 60-61
  growth of, *m* 34
  possessions, 52
using natural resources, *see* great ideas

Vietnam War, 55
Vikings, 7; *m* 7

Washington, D.C., 29
Washington, George, 26, 27, 29; *p* 26-27, 28-29
West Indies, 51, 52
women, 62; *p* 63
World War I, 52
World War II, 52-53; *p* 52-53
Wright brothers, 49

Yorktown, Virginia, 27; *p* 26-27

Acknowledgments

Grateful acknowledgment is made to the following for permission to use the illustrations found in this book:

American Heritage: Pages 8-9, painting by Frederic Remington
Anheuser-Busch, Inc.: Pages 12-13, courtesy of August A. Busch, Jr.
Cincinnati Art Museum: Pages 38-39, bequest of Mrs. W. D. Julian
Confederation Life Collection: Pages 14-15
Ford Archives: Page 48, painting by Norman Rockwell
Francis G. Mayer, Art Color Slides, New York City: Pages 42-43, painting by Eyre Crowe
Grant Heilman: Pages 10-11 by Alan Pitcairn
H. Armstrong Roberts: Pages 1, 2-3, 52-53, and 63
Herb Orth, LIFE Magazine, © Time Inc.: Pages 22-23
Ken Heyman: Page 64
Kennedy Galleries, New York: Pages 32-33
Metropolitan Museum of Art: Pages 46-47, painting by John Ferguson Weir, gift of Lyman G. Bloomingdale, 1901
Museum of the City of New York: Pages 50-51
NASA: Page 56
New York Public Library: Page 13; pages 18-19, engraving by William Birch and Son
Phillip Gendreau: Page 41
The Fideler Company: Pages 4, 6-7, 28-29, 30-31, and 40
Thomas Williams: Page 16
United Nations: Page 54
United States Department of Commerce, Bureau of Public Roads: Page 37
Van Cleve Photography: Page 59 by David Kelley
Wadsworth Atheneum, Hartford, Conn.: Pages 44-45
Yale University Art Gallery: Pages 24-25 and 26-27, paintings by John Trumbull

Grateful acknowledgment is made to Scott, Foresman and Company for the pronunciation system used in this book, which is taken from the Thorndike-Barnhart Dictionary Series. Grateful acknowledgment is made to Rand McNally & Company for cartographic data on pages 60-61 and for permission to use the globes in this book.

SKILLS MANUAL

CONTENTS

Thinking 1
Solving Problems 2
Learning Social Studies Skills 3
    How To Find Information
        You Need 4
    Evaluating Information 5
    Making Reports 7
    Holding a Group Discussion 9
    Working With Others 9
    Building Your Vocabulary 10
Learning Map Skills 10

Thinking

One of the main reasons you are attending school is to learn how to think clearly. Your social studies class is one of the best places in which to grow in the use of your thinking skills. Here you will learn more about using the thinking skills that will help you understand yourself, your country, and your world.

There are seven different kinds of thinking skills. As you use all seven, you will become more successful in school and in life. You will be able to understand yourself and your world much better. You will be a happier and more useful citizen as well.

Seven kinds of thinking

1. **Remembering** is the simplest kind of thinking. Everything you can remember is called your store of knowledge.

   Example: Remembering facts, such as the names of state capitals.

2. **Translation** is changing information from one form into another.

   Example: Reading a map and putting into words the information you find there.

3. **Interpretation** is discovering how things relate to each other, or how things are connected.

   Example: Comparing two pictures to decide in what ways they are alike or in what ways they are different.

4. **Application** is using your knowledge and skills to solve a new problem.

   Example: Using social studies skills to prepare a written report.

5. **Analysis** is the kind of thinking you use when you try to find out how something is organized, or put together. When you

use this kind of thinking, you separate complicated information into its basic parts. Then you can see how they were put together and how they are related to each other.

Example: Separating main ideas from supporting facts.

6. **Synthesis** is putting ideas together in a form that not only has meaning but is also new and original.

Examples: Painting a picture; or writing something original, which might be a paragraph or an entire poem, story, or play.

7. **Evaluation** is the highest level of thinking. It is judging whether or not something meets a given standard.

Example: Deciding which of several different sources of information is the most reliable; or judging the success of a class discussion.

Solving Problems

The social studies will be more worthwhile to you if you learn to think and work as a scientist does. Scientists use a special way of studying called the problem-solving method. During the 1900's, the use of this method has helped people gain much scientific knowledge. In fact, we have gained more scientific knowledge during the 1900's than people had discovered earlier throughout the history of human beings on this planet.

The problem-solving method is more interesting than simply reading a textbook and memorizing answers for a test. By using this method, you can make your own discoveries. Using the problem-solving method will also help you learn how to think clearly. It will involve you in using all of the seven different kinds of thinking skills. To use this method in learning about our country, you will need to follow these steps.

1. **Choose an important, interesting problem** that you would like to solve. (A sample problem to solve is given on the opposite page.) Write the problem down so that you will have clearly in mind what it is you want to find out. If there are small problems that need to be solved in order to solve your big problem, list them, too.

2. **Think about all possible solutions** to your problem. List the ones that seem most likely to be true. These possible solutions are called "educated guesses," or hypotheses. You will try to solve your problem by finding facts to support or to disprove your hypotheses.

Sometimes you may wish to do some general background reading before you make your hypotheses. For example, if you were going to solve the sample problem on the opposite page, you might want first to read about the land features of the Northeast. Then, make your hypotheses based on what you have discovered.

3. **Test your hypotheses** by doing research. This book provides you with four major sources of information. These are the pictures, the text, the maps, and the Glossary. To find the information you need, you may use the Table of Contents and the Index. The suggestions on pages 4-7 will help you find and evaluate other sources of information.

As you do research, make notes of all the information that will either support your hypotheses or disprove them. You may discover that information from one source does not agree with information from another. If this should happen, check still further. Try to decide which facts are correct.

4. Summarize what you have learned. Your summary should be a short statement of the main points you have discovered. Have you been able to support one or more of your hypotheses with facts? Have you been able to prove that one or more of your hypotheses is not correct? What new facts have you learned? Do you need to do more research?

You may want to write a report about the problem. To help other people share the ideas you have come to understand, you may decide to include maps, pictures, or your own drawings with your report. You will find helpful suggestions for writing a good report on pages 7 and 8.

A sample problem to solve

As you study our country, you may wish to try to solve problems about our country as a whole. Or, you may wish to study one major region. The following sample problem to solve is about the Northeast as a region.

Mountains and rolling hills make up much of the Northeast. Very little of this part of our country is low and level. <u>How do the land features of the Northeast affect the lives of the people?</u> In forming hypotheses to solve this problem, you will need to think about how the land features of the Northeast affect the following:

a. where the cities grew up
b. industry
c. farming

The suggestions on the next two pages will help you find the information you need for solving this problem.

Learning Social Studies Skills

What is a skill?

A skill is something that you have learned to do well. To learn some skills, such as swimming or playing baseball, you must train the muscles of your arms and legs. To learn others, such as typing, you must train your fingers. Still other skills call for you to train your mind. For instance, reading with understanding is a skill that calls for much mental training. The skills that you use in the social studies are largely mental skills.

Why are skills important?

Mastering different skills will help you to have a happier and more satisfying life. You will be healthier and enjoy your free time more if you develop skills needed to take part in different sports. By developing art and music skills, you will be able to share your feelings more fully. It is even more important for you to develop your mental skills. These skills are the tools that you will use in getting and using the knowledge you need to live successfully in today's world.

Developing a skill

If you were to ask fine athletes or musicians how they gained their skills, they would probably say, "Through practice."

To develop mental skills, you must practice also. Remember, however, that a person cannot become a good ballplayer if he or she keeps throwing the ball in the wrong way. A person cannot become a fine musician by practicing the wrong notes. The same thing is true of mental skills. To master them, you must practice them correctly.

The following pages have suggestions about how to perform correctly several important skills needed in the social studies. For example, to succeed in the social studies you must know how to find the information you need. You need to know how to prepare reports and how to work with others on group projects. Study these skills carefully, and use them.

How To Find Information You Need

Each day of your life you seek information. Sometimes you want to know certain facts just because you are curious. Most of the time, however, you want information for some certain reason. If you enjoy baseball, for instance, you may want to know how to figure batting averages. If you collect stamps, you need to know how to find out what countries they come from. As a student in today's world, you need information for many reasons. As an adult, you will need even more knowledge in order to live successfully in tomorrow's world.

You may wonder how you can possibly learn all the facts you are going to need during your lifetime. The answer is that you can't. Therefore, knowing how to find information when you need it is very important to you. Following are suggestions for finding good sources of information and for using these sources to find the facts that you need.

Written Sources of Information

Books

You may be able to find the information you need in books that you have at home or in your classroom. To see if a textbook or other nonfiction* book has the information you need, look at the table of contents and the index.

Sometimes, you will need to go to your school or neighborhood library to find books that have the information you want. To make the best use of a library, you should learn to use the card catalog. This is a file that contains information about the books in the library. Each nonfiction book has at least three cards, filed in alphabetical order. One is for the title, one is for the author, and one is for the subject of the book. Each card gives the book's special number. This number will help you to find the book. All the nonfiction books in the library are arranged on the shelves in numerical order. If you cannot find a book that you want, the librarian will help you.

Reference volumes

You will find much useful information in certain books known as reference volumes. Among these are dictionaries, encyclopedias, atlases, and other special books. Some companies publish a book each year with facts and figures and general information about the events of the year before. Such books are generally called yearbooks, annuals, or almanacs.

Newspapers and magazines

These are important sources of up-to-date information. Sometimes you will want to look for information in papers or magazines that you do not have at home. You can almost always find the ones you want at the library.

The *Readers' Guide to Periodical Literature* is kept for use in most libraries. It will direct you to magazine articles about the subject you are interested in. This is a series of volumes that list articles by title, author, and subject. In the front of each volume is an explanation of the abbreviations used to indicate the different magazines and their dates.

Booklets, pamphlets, and bulletins

You can get many materials of this kind from local and state governments, as well as from our federal government. Chambers of commerce, travel bureaus, trade organizations, private companies, and embassies of other countries publish materials that have a wealth of information.

Many booklets and bulletins give correct information. Remember, however, that some of them were written to promote certain goods or ideas. Information from such sources should be checked carefully.

*See Glossary

Reading for Information

The following suggestions will help you to save time and work when you are looking for information in books and other written materials.

The table of contents and the index

The table of contents appears at the beginning of the book and generally is a list of the chapters in the book. By looking at this list, you can almost always tell if the book has the kind of information you need.

The index is a more detailed list of the things that are talked about in the book. It will help you find the pages on which specific facts are talked about. In most books, the index is at the back. Encyclopedias often place the index in a separate volume.

At the beginning of an index, you will generally find an explanation that makes it easier to use. For instance, the beginning of the Index for this book tells you that *p* means picture and *m* means map.

The topics, or entries, in the index are arranged in alphabetical order. To find all the information you need, you may have to look under more than one entry. For example, to find out what pages of a social studies book have information about cities, you would look up the entry for cities. You could also see if cities are listed by their own names.

Skim the written material

Before you begin reading a chapter or a page, skim it to see if it has the information you need. In this way you will not waste time reading something that is of little or no value to you. When you skim, you look mainly for topic headings, topic sentences, and key words. Imagine you are looking for the answer to the question: "What are the people in the West doing to conserve their forest resources?" In a book about the West or about the United States, you might look for a topic heading that mentions forest resources. When you find this heading, you might look for the key words, "conserving forests."

Read carefully

When you think you have found the page that has the information you are looking for, read it carefully. Does this page tell you exactly what you want to know? If not, you will need to look further.

Other Ways of Getting Information

Direct experience

What you see or live through for yourself may be a good source of information if you have watched carefully and remembered accurately. Firsthand information can often be obtained by visiting places in your community or nearby, such as museums, factories, or government offices.

Radio and television

Use the listings in your local newspaper to find programs about the subjects in which you are interested.

Movies, filmstrips, recordings, and slides

Materials on many different subjects are available. You can get them from schools, libraries, museums, and private companies.

Resource people

Sometimes, you will be able to get information by talking with a person who has special knowledge. Once in a while, you may wish to invite someone to speak to your class and answer questions.

Evaluating Information

During your lifetime, you will constantly need to evaluate what you see, hear, and read. Information is not true or worthwhile simply because it is presented on television or is written in a book, magazine, or newspaper. The following suggestions will help you in evaluating information.

Primary and secondary sources of information

A primary source of information is a firsthand record. For instance, a photograph taken of something while it is happening is a primary source. So is the report you write about a field trip you take. Original documents, such as the Constitution of the United States, are primary sources also.

A secondary source is a secondhand report. If you write a report about what someone else told you he or she saw, your report will be a secondary source of information. Another example of a secondary source is a history book.

Advanced scholars like to use primary sources whenever possible. However, these sources are often difficult to obtain. Most students in elementary and high school use secondary sources. You should always be aware that you are using secondhand information when you use a secondary source.

Who said it and when was it said?

The next step in evaluating information is to ask, "Who said it?" Was she a person with special training in the subject about which she wrote? Was he a newsman who is known for careful reporting of the facts?

Another question you should ask is "When was it said?" Changes take place rapidly in our world, and the information you are using may be out of date. For instance, suppose you are looking for information about a country. If you use an encyclopedia that is five years old, much of the information you find will not be correct.

Is it mostly fact or opinion?

The next step in evaluating information is to decide if it is based on facts or if it consists mostly of unsupported opinions. You can do this best if you know about these three kinds of statements:

1. <u>Statements of fact that can be checked.</u> For example, "Voters in the United States choose their representatives by secret ballot" is a statement of fact that can be checked by finding out how voting is carried on in different parts of our country.
2. <u>Inferences, or conclusions that are based on facts.</u> The statement "The people of the United States live in a democracy" is an inference. This inference is based on the fact that the citizens choose their representatives by secret ballot, and on other facts that can be proved. It is important to remember that inferences can be false or only partly true, even though they are based on facts.
3. <u>Value judgments, or opinions.</u> The statement "It is always wrong for a country to go to war" is a value judgment. Since a value judgment is an opinion, you need to look at it very carefully. On what facts and inferences is it based? What facts and conclusions do you think form the basis of the opinion, "It is always wrong for a country to go to war"? Do you agree or disagree with these conclusions? Trustworthy writers or reporters are careful to let their readers know which statements are their own opinions. They also try to base their opinions as much as possible on facts that can be proved.

Why was it said?

The next step in evaluating information is to find out the purpose for which it was prepared. Many books and articles are prepared in an honest effort to give you accurate information. Scientists writing about new scientific discoveries will generally try to report their findings as accurately as possible. They will be careful to distinguish between things they have actually seen and conclusions they have drawn from their observations.

Some information, however, is prepared mostly to persuade people to believe or act a certain way. Information of this kind is called propaganda.

Some propaganda is used to promote causes that are generally thought to be good. A picture that shows Smokey the Bear and the words "Only you can prevent forest fires" is an example of this kind of propaganda.

Propaganda is also used to make people support causes they would not agree with if they knew more about them. This kind of propaganda may be made up of information that is true, partly true, or false. Even when it is true, however, the information may be presented in such a way as to mislead you.

Propaganda generally appeals to people's feelings rather than to their thinking ability. For this reason, you should learn to recognize information that is propaganda. Then you can think about it calmly and clearly, and evaluate it intelligently.

Making Reports

There are many times when you need to share information or ideas with others. Sometimes you will need to do this in writing. Other times you will need to do it by speaking. One of the best ways to develop your writing and speaking skills is by making written and oral reports. The success of your report will depend on how well you have organized your material. It will also depend on your skill in presenting it. Here are some guidelines that will help you in preparing a good report.

Decide upon a goal

Have your goal clearly in mind. Are you mostly interested in sharing information? Do you want to give your own ideas on a subject? Or are you trying to persuade other people to agree with you?

Find the information you need

Be sure to use more than one source. If you are not sure how to find information about your subject, read the suggestions on pages 4 and 5.

Take good notes

To remember what you have read, you must take notes. Before you begin taking notes, however, you will need to make a list of the questions you want your report to answer. As you do research, write down the facts that answer these questions. You may find some interesting and important facts that do not answer any of your questions. If you feel that they might be useful in your report, write them down, too. Your notes should be short and in your own words except when you want to use quotations. When you use an exact quotation, be sure to put quotation marks around it.

You will be able to make the best use of your notes if you write them on file cards. Use a separate card for each statement or group of statements that answers one of your questions. To remember where your information came from, write on each card the title, author, and date of the source. When you have finished taking notes, group the cards according to the questions they answer.

Make an outline

After you have reviewed your notes, make an outline. This is a general plan that shows the order and the relationship of the ideas you want to include in your report. The first step in making an outline is to pick out the main ideas. These will be the main headings in your outline. (See sample outline below.) Next, list under each of these headings the ideas and facts that support or explain it. These related ideas are called subheadings. As you arrange your information, ask yourself the following questions.

a. Is there one main idea I must put first because everything else depends on this idea?
b. Have I arranged my facts in such a way as to show relationships among them?

c. Are there some ideas that will be clearer if they come after other ideas have been explained?
d. Have I included enough facts so that I can end my outline with a summary statement or a logical conclusion?

When you have finished your first outline, you may find that some parts of it are too short. If so, you may wish to do more research. When you feel that you have enough information, make your final outline. Remember that this outline will serve as a guide for your finished report.

Example of an outline

The author of this Skills Manual prepared the following outline before writing "Making Reports."

I. Introduction
II. Deciding upon a goal
III. Finding information
IV. Taking notes
   A. List main ideas to be researched
   B. Write on file cards facts that support or explain these ideas
   C. Group cards according to main ideas
V. Making an outline
   A. Purpose of an outline
   B. Guidelines for arranging information
   C. Sample outline of this section
VI. Preparing a written report
VII. Presenting an oral report

Special guidelines for a written report

Using your outline as a guide, write your report. The following suggestions will help you to make your report interesting and clear.

<u>Create word pictures that your readers can see in their minds.</u> Before you begin, imagine that you are going to make a movie of the subject you plan to write about. What scenes would you like to show? Next, think of the words that will bring these same pictures into your readers' minds.

<u>Group your sentences into good paragraphs.</u> It is generally best to begin a paragraph with a topic sentence that says to the reader, "This is what you will learn about in this paragraph." The other sentences in the paragraph should help to support or explain the topic sentence.

<u>A sample paragraph.</u> Below is a sample paragraph from a textbook about the northeastern part of our country. The topic sentence has been underlined. Notice how clear it is and how well the other sentences support it. Also notice how many pictures the paragraph puts in your mind.

<u>One of the most interesting sights in the Erie-Ontario Lowland is beautiful Niagara Falls.</u> These falls are located on the Niagara River, which forms part of the border between the United States and Canada. The Niagara River flows northward from Lake Erie to Lake Ontario. About halfway between these two lakes, the river plunges over a steep cliff, forming Niagara Falls. Each year, thousands of tourists come to see these famous falls. Waterpower from the falls is used to produce electricity for factories and homes in both the United States and Canada.

<u>Other guidelines.</u> There are two other things to remember in writing a good report. First, use the dictionary to find the spelling of words you are not sure about. Second, make a list of the sources of information you used. Put this list at the beginning or end of your report. This list is called a bibliography.

Special guidelines for an oral report

When you are going to give a report orally, you will also want to arrange your information in a logical order by making an outline. Prepare notes to guide you during your talk. These notes should be complete enough to help you remember all the points you want to make. You may even write out certain parts of your report that you would rather read.

When you present your report, speak directly to your audience. Pronounce your words correctly and clearly. Remember to speak slowly enough for your listeners to follow what you are saying. Use a tone of voice that will hold their interest. Stand up straight, but try not to be too stiff. Remember, the only way to improve your speaking skills is to practice them correctly.

Holding a Group Discussion

One of the important ways in which you learn is by exchanging ideas with other people. You do this often in everyday conversation. You are likely to learn more, however, when you take part in the special kind of group conversation that we call a discussion. A discussion is more orderly than a conversation. It generally has a definite, serious purpose. This purpose may be the sharing of information or the solving of a problem. In order to reach its goal, the discussion group must arrive at a conclusion or make a decision of some kind.

The guidelines below will help you to have a successful discussion.

Be prepared

Think about the subject to be discussed ahead of time. Prepare for the discussion by reading and taking notes. You may also want to make an outline of the ideas you want to share with the group.

Take part

Take part in the discussion. Express your ideas clearly and in as few words as possible. Be sure that the statements you make and the questions you ask deal with the subject being talked about.

Listen and think

Listen thoughtfully to others. Encourage all of the members of the discussion group to express their ideas. Do not make up your mind about a question or a problem until all of the facts have been given.

Be courteous

When you speak, address the whole group. Ask and answer questions politely. When you do not agree with someone, give your reasons in a friendly way.

Working With Others

In school and throughout life, you will find that there are many things that can be done better by a group than by one person working alone. Some of these projects would take too long to finish if they were done by one person. Others have different parts that can be done best by people with different talents.

Before your group begins a project, you should decide several matters. First, decide exactly what goal you are trying to reach. Second, decide what part of the project each person should do. Third, decide when the project is to be finished.

Do your part

Remember that the success of your project depends on every member of the group. Be willing to do your share of the work and to accept your share of the responsibility.

Follow the rules

Help the group decide on reasonable rules. Then follow them. When a difference of opinion cannot be settled by discussion, make a decision by majority* vote.

Share your ideas

Be willing to share your ideas with the group. When you present an idea for discussion, be prepared to see it criticized or even rejected. At the same time, have the courage to stand up for an idea or a belief that is really important to you.

Be friendly, thoughtful, helpful, cheerful

Try to express your opinions seriously and sincerely without hurting others or losing their respect. Listen politely to the ideas of others.

Learn from your mistakes

Look for ways in which you can be a better group member the next time you work with others on a project.

Building Your Vocabulary

When you do research in many different kinds of reading materials, you are likely to find several words you have never seen before. If you skip over these words, you may not fully understand what you are reading. The following suggestions will help you to discover the meanings of new words and build your vocabulary.

1. See how the word is used in the sentence. When you come to a new word, don't stop reading. Read on beyond the new word to see if you can discover any hints as to what its meaning might be. Trying to figure out the meaning of a word from the way it is used may not give you the exact definition. However, it will give you a general idea of what the word means.

2. Sound out the word. Break the word up into syllables, and try to pronounce it. When you say the word aloud, you may find that you know it after all but have simply never seen it in print.

3. Look in the dictionary. When you think you have figured out what a word means and how it is pronounced, look it up in the dictionary. First, check the pronunciation. Have you pronounced it correctly? Then, check the meaning of the word. Remember, most words have more than one meaning. Did you decide on the right definition?

4. Make a list of the new words you learn. In your own words, write a definition of each word you place on your list. Review this list from time to time.

Learning Map Skills

The earth is a sphere

Our earth is round like a ball. We call anything with this shape a sphere. The earth is, of course, a very large sphere. Its diameter* is about 8,000 miles (12,874 kilometers*). Its circumference* is about 25,000 miles (40,233 kilometers). The earth is not quite a perfect sphere. It is somewhat flat at the North and South poles.

Globes and maps

The globe in your classroom is also a sphere. It is a small-size copy of the earth. The surface of the globe shows the shapes of the areas of land on the earth. It also shows the shapes of the different bodies of water. By looking at the globe, you can see exactly where the continents,* islands, and oceans are. Globes are made with the North Pole at the top. But they are often tipped to show the way the earth is tipped. Maps are flat drawings. They may show part or all of the earth's surface.

Scale

Globes and maps give information about distance. When you use them, you need to know what distance on the earth is represented by a given distance on the globe or map. This relationship is called the scale. The scale of a globe or map may be shown in several different ways.

On most maps, the scale is shown by a small drawing. For example:

```
         0       200       400   Miles
Scale    |--------|---------|
         0       322       644   Kilometers
```

Sometimes, the scale is shown in this way:
1 inch = 400 miles (644 kilometers).

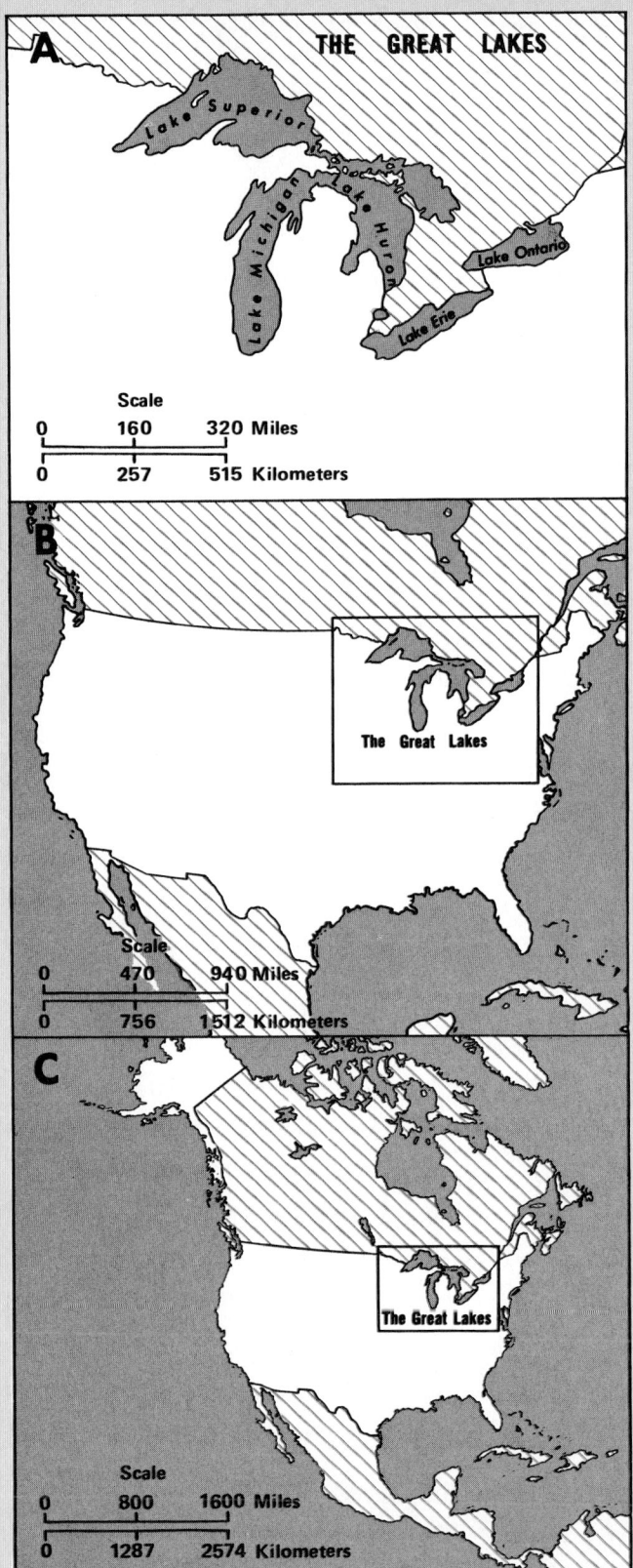

The Great Lakes area is a different size on each of the three maps above. This is because one inch on each of these maps represents a different distance on the earth.

Finding places on the earth

Map makers, travelers, and other interested people have always wanted to know just where certain places are. Over the years, a very accurate way of giving such information has been worked out. This system is used all over the world.

In order to work out a means of finding anything, you need starting points and a measuring unit. The North and South poles and the equator are the starting points for the system we use to find places on the earth. The measuring unit for our system is called the degree (°).

Parallels show latitude

When we want to find a place on the earth, we first find out how far it is north or south of the equator. This distance measured in degrees is called north or south latitude. The equator stands for zero latitude. The North Pole is located at 90 degrees north latitude. The South Pole is at 90 degrees south latitude.

All points on the earth that have the same latitude are the same distance from the equator. A line connecting such points is called a parallel. This is because it is parallel to the equator. (See globe D on the next page.)

Meridians show longitude

After we know the latitude of a place, we need to know its location in an east-west direction. This is called its longitude. The lines that show longitude are called meridians. They are drawn so as to connect the North and South poles (See globe E on the next page.) Longitude is measured from the meridian that passes through Greenwich, England. This line of zero longitude is called the prime meridian. Distance east or west of this meridian measured in degrees is called east or west longitude. The meridian of 180 degrees west longitude is the same as the one of 180 degrees east longitude. This is because 180 degrees is exactly halfway around the world.

11

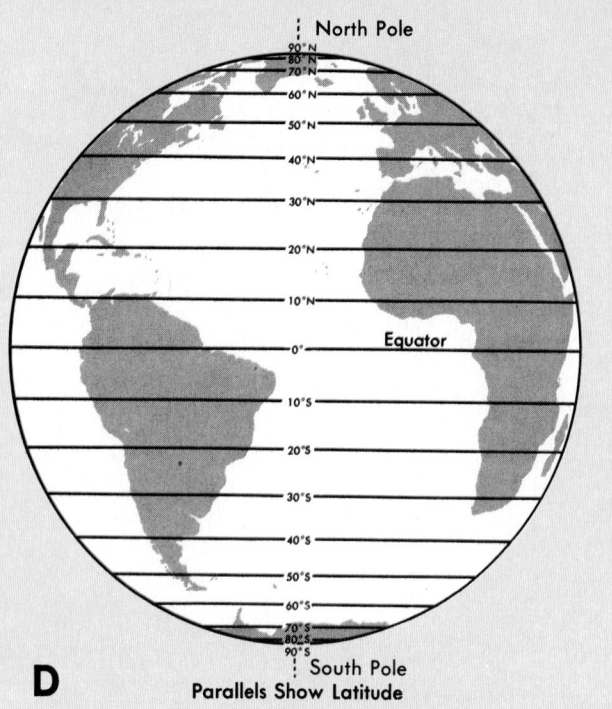

D Parallels Show Latitude

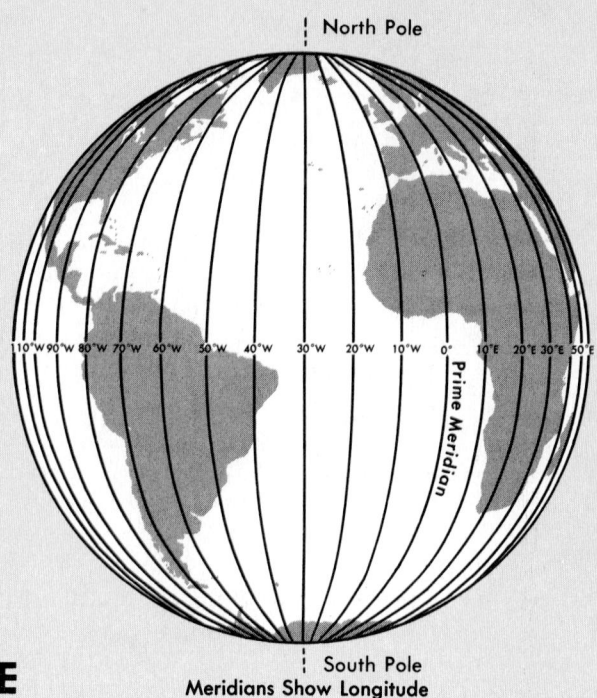

E Meridians Show Longitude

Finding places on a globe

The location of a certain place might be given to you like this: 30° N 90° W. This means that this place is located 30 degrees north of the equator, and 90 degrees west of the prime meridian. See if you can find this place on the globe in your classroom. It is helpful to remember that parallels and meridians are drawn every ten or fifteen degrees on most globes.

The round earth on a flat map

An important fact about a sphere is that you cannot flatten out its surface perfectly. To prove this, you might do the following. Cut an orange in half. Scrape away the fruit. You will not be able to press either piece of orange peel flat without crushing it. If you cut one piece in half, however, you can press these smaller pieces nearly flat. Next, cut one of these pieces of peel into three smaller pieces, shaped like those in drawing F on the opposite page. You will be able to press these pieces quite flat.

A map like the one shown in drawing F can be made by cutting the surface of a globe into twelve pieces shaped like the smallest pieces of your orange peel. Such a map would be accurate. However, an "orange-peel" map is not easy to use, because the continents and oceans are cut apart.

A flat map can never show the earth's surface as truthfully as a globe can. On globes, shape, size, distance, and direction are all accurate. A single flat map of the world cannot be drawn to show all four of these things correctly. But flat maps can be made that show some of these things accurately. The different ways of drawing maps of the world to show different things correctly are called map projections.

The Mercator projection

Drawing G, on the opposite page, shows a world map called a Mercator projection. When you compare this map with a globe, you can see that continents, islands, and oceans have almost the right shape. On this kind of map, however, North America seems larger than Africa. This is not true. On Mercator maps, lands far from the equator appear larger than they are.

Because they show true directions, Mercator maps are very useful to sailors and fliers. For instance, the city of Lisbon, Portugal, lies almost exactly east of Baltimore, Maryland. A Mercator map shows that a ship could reach Lisbon by sailing from Baltimore straight east across the Atlantic Ocean. A plane could also reach Lisbon by flying straight east from Baltimore.

The shortest route

Strangely enough, the best way to reach Lisbon from Baltimore is not by going straight east. There is a shorter route. In order to understand why this is so, you might like to do the following.

On your classroom globe, find Lisbon and Baltimore. Both cities lie just south of the 40th parallel. Take a piece of string and connect the two cities. Let the string follow the true east-west direction of the 40th parallel. Now, draw the string tight. Notice that it passes far to the north of the 40th parallel. The path of the tightened string is the shortest route between Baltimore and Lisbon. The shortest route between any two points on the earth is called the great* circle route.

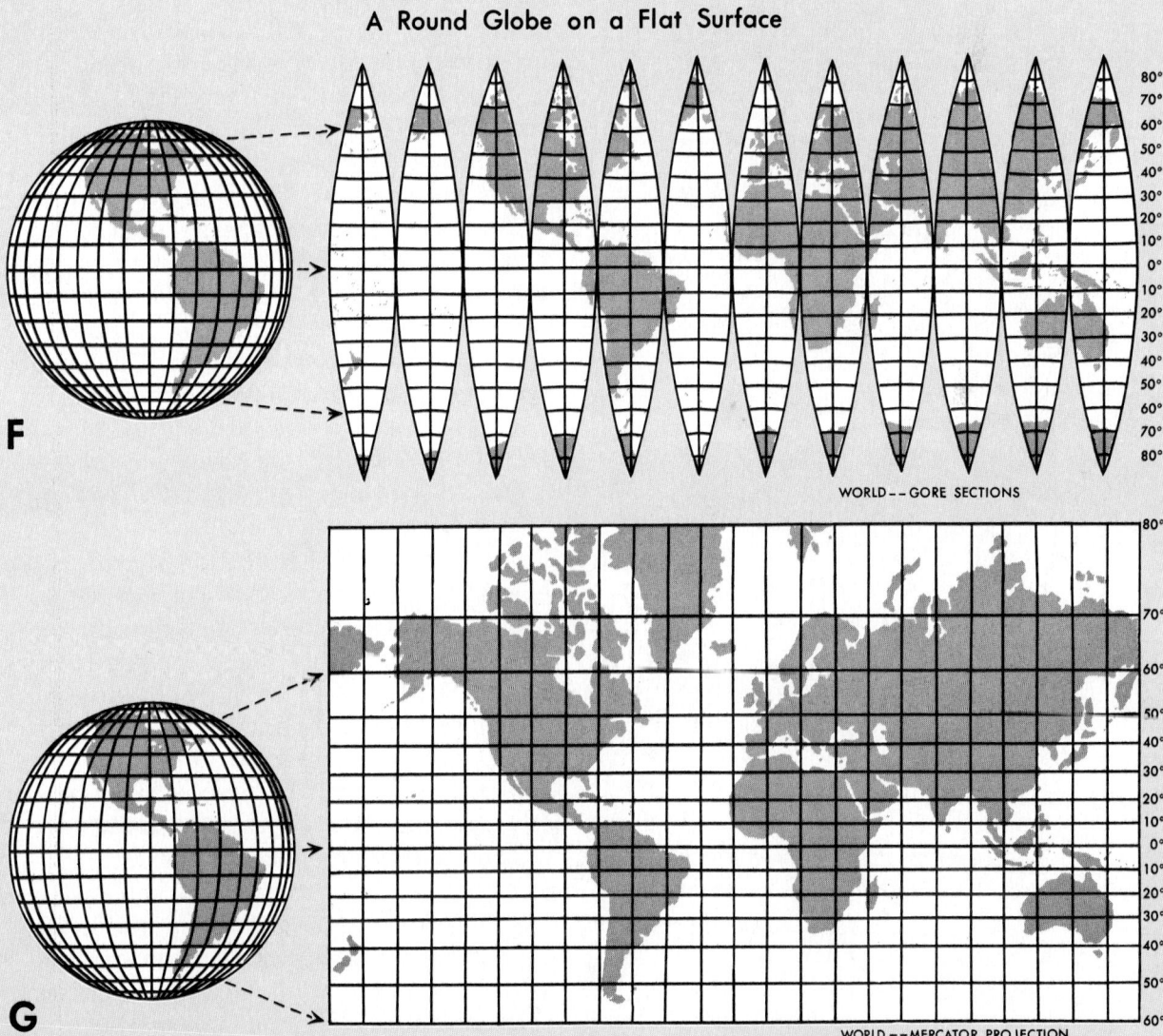

A Round Globe on a Flat Surface

F — WORLD--GORE SECTIONS

G — WORLD--MERCATOR PROJECTION

13

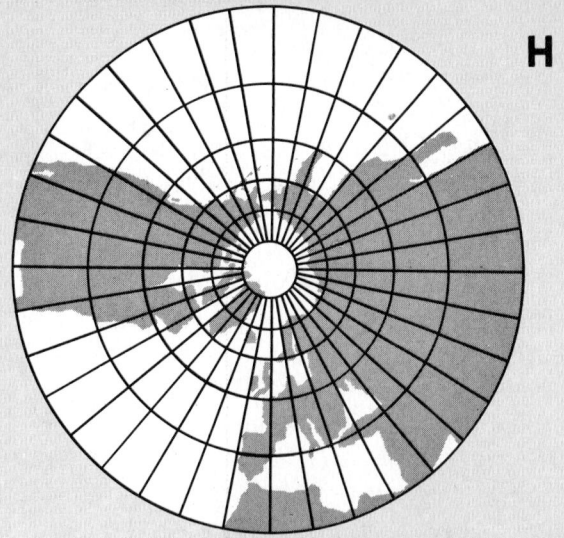

GNOMONIC PROJECTION

The gnomonic (nō mon′ ik) **projection**

Using a globe and a piece of string is not a very handy or accurate way of finding great circle routes. Instead, sailors and fliers use a special kind of map called the gnomonic projection. (See drawing H, at left.) On this kind of map, the great circle route between any two places can be found simply by drawing a straight line between them.

Special-Purpose Maps

Maps that show part of the earth

For some uses, we would rather have maps that do not show the whole surface of the earth. A map of a very small part of the earth can be drawn more accurately than a map of a large area. It can also include more details.

Drawing I, on this page, shows a photograph and a map of the same small part of the earth. The drawings on the map that show the shape and location of things on the earth are called symbols. The small drawing that shows directions is called a compass* rose.

Maps for special purposes

Maps can show the location of many different kinds of things. For instance, a map can show what minerals are found in certain places, or what crops are grown. A small chart that lists the symbols and their meanings is usually included on a map. This is called the key.

Symbols on some geography maps stand for the amounts of things in different places. For instance, map J, at left, gives information about the number of people in the southwestern part of the United States. The key tells the meaning of the symbols. In this case the symbols are dots and circles.

On different maps, the same symbol may stand for different things and amounts.

Each dot on map J stands for 10,000 persons. On other maps, a dot might represent 5,000 sheep or 1,000 bushels of wheat.

There are other ways of giving information about quantity. Different designs or patterns may be used on a rainfall map to show the areas that receive different amounts of rain each year.

Relief Maps
The roughness of the earth's surface

From a plane, you can see that the earth's surface is rough. You can see mountains and valleys, hills and plains. For some uses, globes and maps that show these things are needed. They are called relief globes and maps.

Since globes are three-dimensional* copies of the earth, you may wonder why most globes do not show the roughness of the earth's surface. The reason for this is that the highest mountain on the earth is not very large when it is compared with the earth's diameter. Even a very large globe would be smooth nearly everywhere.

In order to make a relief globe or map, you must use a different scale for the height of the land. You might start with a large flat map. One inch on your flat map may stand for a distance of 100 miles (161 kilometers) on the earth. Now you are going to make a small copy of a mountain on your map. On the earth, this mountain is two miles (3.2 kilometers) high. If you let one inch stand for this height on the earth, your mountain should rise one inch above the flat surface of your map. Other mountains and hills should be copied on this same scale.

By photographing relief globes and maps, flat maps can be made that show the earth much as it looks from an airplane. Map K, at right above, is a photograph of a relief map. Map L is a photograph of a relief globe.

Topographic maps

Another kind of map that shows the roughness of the earth's surface is called a topographic, or contour, map. On this kind of map, lines are drawn to show different heights of the earth's surface. These are

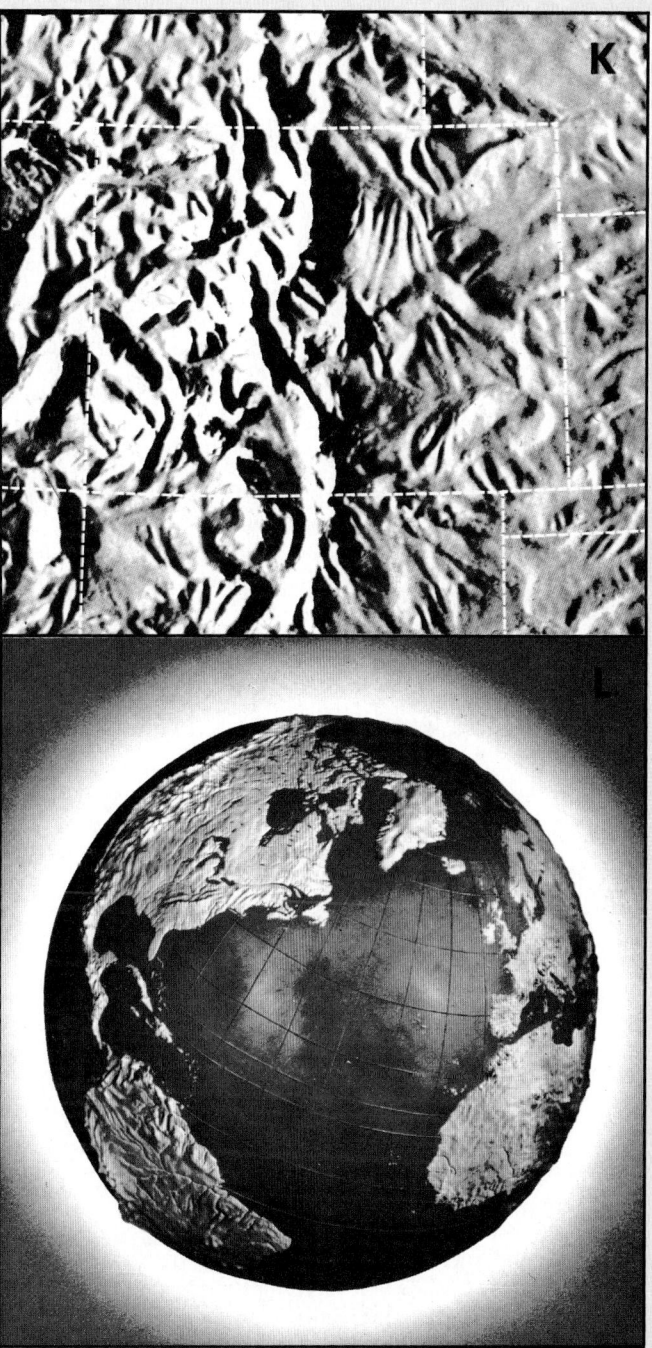

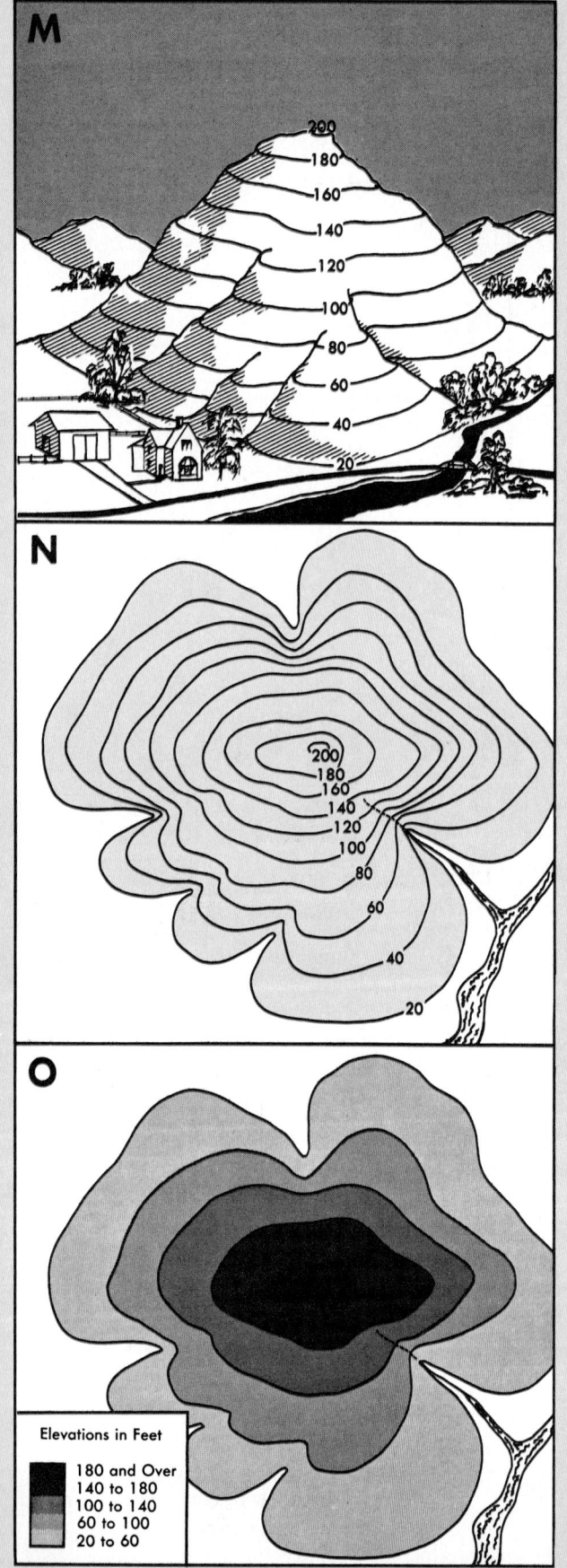

called contour lines. The maps on this page help to explain how topographic maps are made.

Map M is a drawing of a hill. Around the bottom of the hill is our first contour line. This line connects all the points at the base of the hill that are exactly twenty feet above sea level. Higher up the hill, another contour line is drawn. It connects all the points that are exactly forty feet above sea level. A line is also drawn at a height of sixty feet. Other lines are drawn every twenty feet until the top of the hill is reached. Since the hill is shaped somewhat like a cone, each contour line is shorter than the one just below it.

Map N shows how the contour lines in the drawing of the hill M can be used to make a topographic map. This map gives us a great deal of information about the hill. Since each line is labeled with the height it stands for, you can tell how high the different parts of the hill are. It is important to remember that land does not really rise in layers, as you might think when you look at a topographic map. Wherever the contour lines are far apart, you can be sure that the land slopes gently. Where they are close together, the slope is steep. With practice, you can picture the land in your mind as you look at such a map. Topographic maps are especially useful to people who design such things as roads and buildings.

On a topographic map, the spaces between the contour lines may be filled in with different shades of a color. If a different shade of brown were used for each different height of land shown in map N, there would be ten shades. It would be very hard for you to tell these different shades of brown apart. Therefore, on map O, at left, black and four shades of brown were used to show differences in height of forty feet. The key shows the height of the land represented by the different shades. On some topographic maps, different colors are used to stand for different heights.

Needs of People

All people on earth must meet certain needs in order to be healthy and happy. Scientists who study human beings tell us that these basic needs are the same for everyone. It does not matter if you are rich or poor... tall or short... fat or thin... dark-skinned or light-skinned. You have the same basic needs as everyone else.

There are three kinds of basic needs. These are: physical needs, social needs, and the need for faith.

Physical Needs

Some basic needs are so important that people will die or become seriously ill if they fail to meet them. These are called physical needs. They include the need for each of the following:
1. air
2. water
3. food
4. protection from heat and cold
5. sleep and rest
6. exercise

Although all people share these needs, they do not all meet them in the same way. How do you meet your physical needs?

Social Needs

People also have social needs. They must meet these needs in order to have a happy and useful life. Social needs include:

An outdoor concert in Louisville, Kentucky. All people on earth have certain basic needs. Some of these are called social needs. For example, feeling that you belong to a group is a social need. Do you think the members of this orchestra have a feeling of belonging to a group? Why do you think this? What are some other basic needs that all people share?

1. Belonging to a group. All people need to feel they belong to a group of people who respect them and whom they respect. Belonging to a family is one of the main ways people meet this need. What can the members of a family do to show that they love and respect each other? How do the members of your family help one another?

Having friends also helps people meet their need for belonging to a group. What groups of friends do you have? Why are these people your friends? Do you suppose young people in other countries enjoy doing the same kinds of things with their friends as you enjoy doing with your friends? Why? Why not?

2. Goals. To be happy, every person needs goals to work for. What goals do you have? How can working toward these goals help you have a happy life? What kinds of goals do you think other young people in our country have?

3. A chance to think and learn. All people need a chance to develop and use their abilities. They need opportunities to find out about things that make them curious. What would you like to learn? How can you learn these things? How can developing your abilities help you have a happy life?

4. A feeling of accomplishment. You share with every other person the need for a feeling of accomplishment. All people need to feel that their lives are successful in some way. What gives you a feeling of accomplishment? Can you imagine what life would be like if you never had this feeling?

The Need for Faith

In addition to physical and social needs, all people also have a need for faith. You need to believe that life is precious and that the future is something to look forward to. You may have different kinds of faith, including the following:

1. Faith in yourself. In order to feel secure, you must have faith in your own abilities. You must feel that you will be able to do some useful work in the world and that you will be generally happy. You must believe that you can work toward solving whatever problems life brings to you. How do you think you can build faith in yourself?

2. Faith in other people. You also need to feel that you can count on other people to do their part and to help you when you need help. What people do you have faith in? What do you think life would be like without this kind of faith?

3. Faith in nature's laws. Another kind of faith that helps people face the future with confidence is faith in nature's laws. The more we learn about our universe, the more certain we feel that we can depend on nature. How would you feel if you couldn't have faith in nature's laws?

4. Religious faith. Throughout history, almost all human beings have had some kind of religious faith. Religion can help people understand themselves and the world they live in. It can bring them joy, and it can give them confidence in times of trouble. Religion can also help people live together happily. For example, most religions teach people to be honest and to love and help their neighbors.

Meeting Needs in Communities

No person can meet his or her needs alone. Only by living and working with others can a person have a happy, satisfying life. For this reason, people everywhere on earth have always lived in communities.

Over the years, people have followed certain ideas or ways of living that help them to live together in communities. We call these the "great ideas." In other parts of this book, you can discover how the great ideas have helped people in the United States to meet their basic needs.

Great Ideas That Built Our Nation

People have been living in America for thousands of years. During this time, they have always met their needs in communities. No one can meet his or her needs all alone. Only by living and working with other people can a person have a happy, satisfying life.

In order to make community life successful, people have developed certain ways of living. We call these the "great ideas." Let us examine ten great ideas that have been important in our country's history.

cooperation	using tools
loyalty	division of labor
freedom	exchange
rules and government	language
using natural resources	education

What great ideas do you think are illustrated by the pictures on this page?
1. Cutting timber in a western forest.
2. The city of Los Angeles, California.
3. A factory worker in Rhode Island.

Exploring the moon. The astronaut is driving a lunar roving vehicle on the moon. At left is the lunar module that brought him to the moon from a spacecraft circling high overhead.

Cooperation

A Great Idea

Working together is called cooperation. This is one of the great ideas that helped build our nation. For example, the early settlers in America needed to cooperate. They worked together to provide the food they needed. In what other ways do you think the early settlers cooperated with one another?

How is cooperation important to communities today? What are some important jobs that require cooperation? What are some other examples of cooperation in the community where you live? Do you think our country could have sent astronauts to the moon if people had not worked together on the space program? Explain.

Loyalty
A Great Idea

People discovered long ago that in order to live together successfully in a community, they had to be loyal to each other. People were willing to do unpleasant or difficult tasks simply because they felt a strong sense of loyalty to their community. Members of families had to be loyal to each other in order to have a happy family life.

In every truly successful community on the earth today, people are usually loyal to each other. They are loyal to their community, their country, and their leaders. Do you think the astronaut shown on page 20 is loyal to our country? What are some things you can do to show that you are loyal to our country? Do you think that the leaders of a community should be loyal to the people? Why do you think this?

The people in successful communities are also loyal to their ideas and beliefs. Most people in our country, for example, are loyal to the principles of democracy, and to the ideas of freedom, justice, and equality. In addition, they are loyal to their religious faith.

Boy scouts looking at a statue of Abraham Lincoln. Lincoln was president of our country during the Civil War.* Why do you think Lincoln is honored today? Is it partly because of his loyalty to certain principles, such as the idea of freedom for all people? Explain your answer.

Do you think boy scouts need to be loyal to certain persons and ideas? Is loyalty important to organizations such as the Boy Scouts of America? Why? Why not?

*See Glossary

Freedom
A Great Idea

The idea of freedom has been important to Americans since the early days of our country's history. Many of the settlers who came to America from Europe during the 1600's and 1700's were seeking more freedom than they had in their homelands.

By the middle of the 1700's, there were thirteen British colonies along the Atlantic coast of North America. During the 1760's and early 1770's, Britain began to take away some of the freedoms the colonists had enjoyed. On July 4, 1776, representatives of the thirteen colonies approved the Declaration of Independence. In this famous document, the colonists declared

Minutemen fighting British troops at Concord, Massachusetts. Minutemen were American colonists who fought to gain freedom from British rule during the Revolutionary War. They were called minutemen because they could be ready for battle in only a few minutes. Why did the colonists want to be free from British rule? You may wish to do research to discover answers to this question.

The White House, the home of our country's president. In the United States, all citizens are free to take part in electing the president and other government leaders.

their freedom from British rule. They set up a new nation called the United States of America.

At the time our country was founded, there were many people here who did not enjoy all the same rights and freedoms as other Americans. For example, most black people lived in slavery. They were forced to work all their lives for white masters. The Civil War* finally led to the ending of slavery throughout the United States.

For a long time after the founding of our country the freedom of women was limited in certain ways. For instance, women could not vote in elections or testify as witnesses in a court of law. A married woman had no right to any property of her own. Any wages that she earned became the property of her husband.

Gradually women began to gain more rights and freedoms. One state after another passed laws giving married women the right to own property. The Nineteenth Amendment to the Constitution, which became law in 1920, guaranteed to women throughout the United States the right to vote.

Today most Americans enjoy a large amount of freedom. For example, they are free to live where they please and to work at jobs of their own choosing. They can express their ideas freely without fear of punishment. They are also free to worship God in their own way, or not to worship at all if they so desire.

Are there any people in the United States today who do not enjoy as much freedom as other Americans? Who are they? What is being done to help these people gain more freedom?

Rules and Government
A Great Idea

People in every community need to follow rules in order to live together successfully. Why is this true? What kinds of rules do people in your own community follow? How do these rules make life safer and more pleasant for everyone? What would it be like to live in a community that had no rules?

In every community, there must be a person or a group of persons to make the rules and see that they are carried out. In other words, all communities need some form of government. Who makes the rules in your local community? Who enforces the rules that these people make?

Although every successful community has some form of government, not all governments are alike. The United States is a democracy. This means that its citizens have a share in governing themselves. Do you think it is important for people to take part in their own government? Why do you think this?

A committee meeting in California. These men and women are all members of the California legislature, which makes the laws for that state. Do you think laws are necessary? Why? Why not?

Pouring melted steel into molds in a Pennsylvania steel plant. Many important products are made from steel. Do research to discover what mineral resources are used in making steel.

Using Natural Resources

A Great Idea

The picture above shows a farmer growing crops in an irrigated* field in the West. In growing crops, farmers use certain natural resources. By "natural resources" we mean any gifts of nature that people use to meet their needs. Some important natural resources are listed below. Which of these do you think farmers use?

air	water	wild animals
soil	sunshine	wild plants
	minerals	

Over the years, people in various parts of the world learned how to make greater use of the earth's resources. The world's first farmers began to use soil, sunshine, and rain to grow crops. They also began to raise animals for food. Later, people began to use different metals for making tools and weapons.

Today, we use hundreds of natural resources in meeting our needs. Stone and trees are just as important to us as they were to earlier people. We use these materials both in building and manufacturing. Farmers today use sunshine, soil, and water, just as early people did. Minerals such as coal and iron ore are among our most valuable resources. What are some natural resources that are used by people in your community?

A lumber mill in Florida. Lumber is one of the many valuable products we get from forests.

People have always depended on the earth's resources to help them in meeting their needs for food, clothing, and shelter. Early people hunted wild animals for food and for skins to make clothing. They added to the food supply by gathering the fruits, seeds, and roots of wild plants. These early people lived in caves or built shelters from tree branches, mud, or animal skins. They used wood, stones, bones, and shells to make tools and weapons. Compared to people who lived later, however, the people of early times made very little use of the natural resources in the world around them.

Using Tools
A Great Idea

A tool is anything that people use to help them do work. Some tools, such as hammers and shovels, are very simple. Other tools are large or complicated. Tools that have a number of moving parts are called machines. What kinds of tools do you have in your home? How do these tools help the members of your family to meet their needs?

The early settlers who came to our country brought with them several important kinds of tools. Among these were guns and axes. With their rifles, the settlers killed wild animals to get meat for food and skins for making clothing. They also used guns

A huge scoop used for mining phosphate* rock. This scoop is pulled across the phosphate rock deposit to gather up large amounts of the mineral. Then a giant crane lifts the filled scoop and empties it into a bin. Do you think it would be possible to produce large amounts of minerals without the use of tools such as these? Explain.

Cutting down trees in colonial days. The early settlers in America used axes to clear the land so they could grow crops. They used the logs for building cabins.

to protect themselves from unfriendly Indians. With their axes, they chopped down trees in the forests so they could use the cleared land for growing crops. Axes were also used to cut logs for building cabins.

Today people in our country use many kinds of modern machines to produce the goods they need. Many of these machines are very complicated and are run by electricity. Do you think that people who use modern machines can have more goods to enjoy than people who use only a few simple tools? Why do you think this?

A worker in a textile factory in Hawaii. In a factory, the work is divided among people who do different jobs. This is known as division of labor.

Division of Labor

A Great Idea

In every community, not all the people do exactly the same kind of work. Instead, they work at different jobs. For example, some people earn their living by farming. Others work in factories or offices. Dividing up the work of a community among people who do different jobs is known as division of labor. By using division of labor, people are able to obtain more goods and services than they could if they tried to meet all of their needs by themselves. Why do you suppose this is so?

Division of labor also makes it possible for each person to work at the job he or she can do best. For example, this textile worker (see picture above) is very skillful at his job. He also enjoys it very much. He probably would not like to do some other kind of work that did not require the skills he has learned. On the other hand, the people who produce the food, appliances, and other things he buys might not enjoy the kind of work he does.

Division of labor also helps people produce many useful things that one person working alone could not produce. Do you think it would ever be possible for one person to make and use all of the many tools needed to manufacture such things as automobiles and refrigerators?

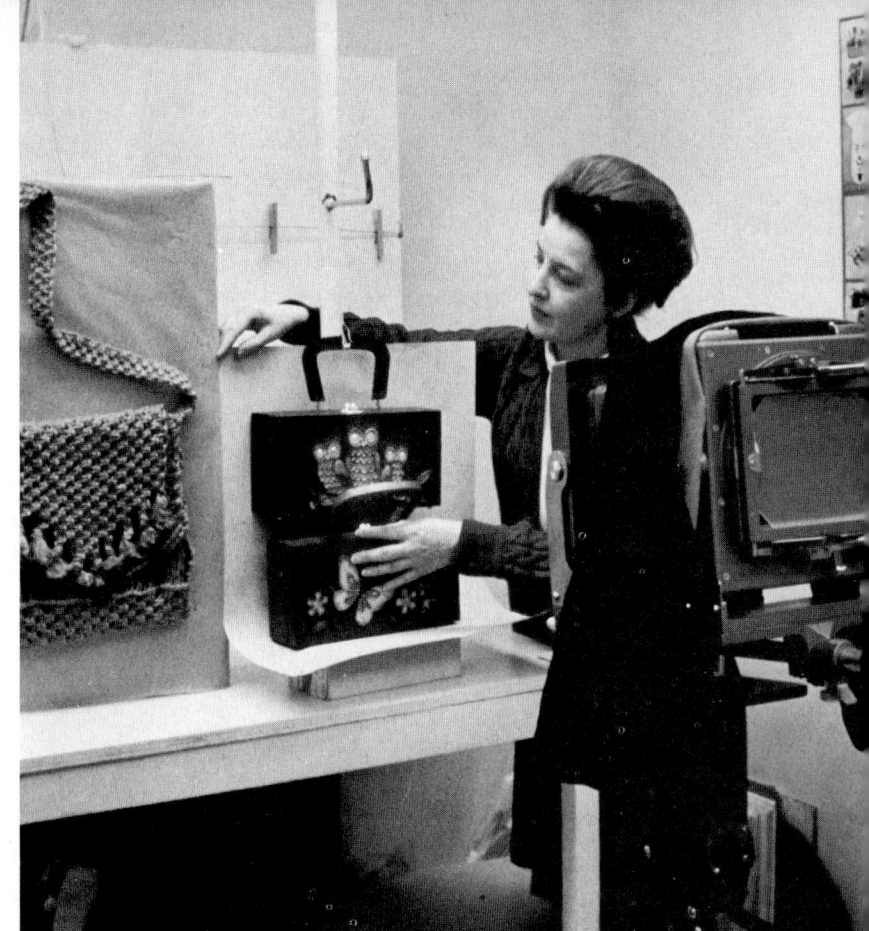

This photographer is preparing to take a picture of some handbags for a magazine advertisement.

The people shown below are members of a hospital operating team. Like the photographer, they provide a service instead of helping to make a product. Other people who perform services are teachers, lawyers, telephone operators, and police officers.

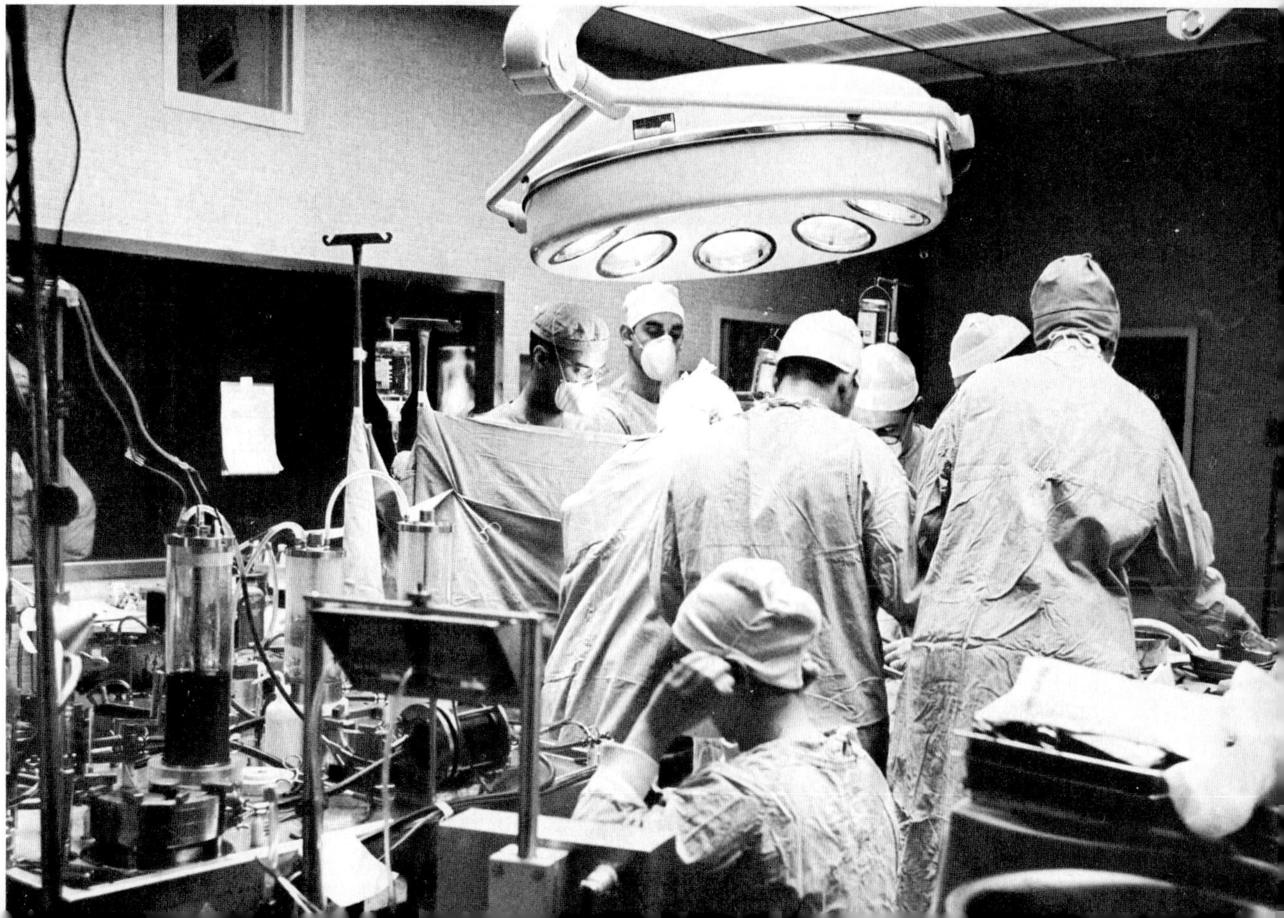

Shopping for food. What will this woman give the store in exchange for the things she needs? Do you think it would be possible for her to get these things without using the idea of exchange?

Exchange

A Great Idea

When people use division of labor, they need to exchange goods and services with each other. In this way, they can get goods and services they do not produce themselves. What would it be like to live in a community where people did not use the great idea of exchange? Explain.

In early times, people often traded goods and services directly with each other. Today most people work at jobs where they earn money. They use this money to buy the goods and services they need. Do you think money makes it easier to carry on exchange? Give reasons for your answer.

Language
A Great Idea

Throughout history, people have felt the need to communicate with each other. In order to work together, people need to share their ideas and feelings. Early people communicated in several ways. For example, they smiled, frowned, made gestures with their hands, and drew pictures. Their most important way of communicating, however, was by speaking. Scientists who have studied the beginnings of language believe that all human beings—even those who lived in earliest times—have had some form of spoken language.

Human beings did not develop written language until about five thousand years ago. Writing made it possible for people to store information so that it could be used at a later time. Writing also enabled people to communicate over long distances. Today, almost every language in the world can be written as well as spoken.

Every day, you use language to communicate with others. You talk with your family and your friends. On school days, you talk with your teachers and the other members of your class. You write notes and letters. You write out much of your schoolwork. Do you think it is important to use spoken language in such a way as to communicate clearly with other people? Why do you think this? Do you think it is important to be able to put your thoughts and feelings into writing? Explain.

People in New York City's Chinatown. What does this picture tell you about language in our country?

Education

A Great Idea

In every community, the older people pass on their ideas and skills to the younger people. This is one kind of education. Do you think it would be possible to have a successful community without education? Why? Why not?

In early times, parents taught their children most of the things they needed to know. Today, most American children get a large part of their education in school. Do you think education is important for every person? Why do you think as you do?

High school students in a science class. In most parts of the world, young people receive much of their education in school. Do you think education is important for everyone? Why? Why not?

Word List
(Glossary)

Complete Pronunciation Key

The pronunciation of the word is shown just after the word, in this way: **Iroquois** (ir′ ə kwoi). The letters and signs used are pronounced as in the words below. The mark ′ is placed after a syllable with a primary or strong accent, as in the example above. The mark ′ after a syllable shows a secondary or lighter accent, as in **electronic** (i lek′ tron′ ik).

a	hat, cap	j	jam, enjoy	u	cup, butter
ā	age, face	k	kind, seek	ù	full, put
ã	care, air	l	land, coal	ü	rule, move
ä	father, far	m	me, am	ū	use, music
b	bad, rob	n	no, in		
ch	child, much	ng	long, bring	v	very, save
d	did, red	o	hot, rock	w	will, woman
		ō	open, go	y	young, yet
e	let, best	ô	order, all	z	zero, breeze
ē	equal, see	oi	oil, voice	zh	measure, seizure
ėr	term, learn	ou	house, out		
		p	paper, cup		
f	fat, if	r	run, try	ə	represents:
g	go, bag	s	say, yes		a in about
h	he, how	sh	she, rush		e in taken
		t	tell, it		i in pencil
i	it, pin	th	thin, both		o in lemon
ī	ice, five	TH	then, smooth		u in circus

abstract. Refers to a painting or a sculpture that does not look like a person or an object. Instead, the work of art represents the artist's ideas or feelings about a subject.

Aleutian (ə lü′ shən) **Islands.** A long chain of islands that are part of Alaska. The Aleutians extend southwestward into the Pacific Ocean.

Aleuts (al′ ē üts). A group of people who live on the Aleutian Islands and in other parts of Alaska. Their language and customs are similar to those of the Eskimos. Many Aleuts earn their living by fishing, raising sheep, or hunting fur seals. See **Aleutian Islands.**

alewife. A fish of the herring family. It is found along the Atlantic coast and in the Great Lakes. Alewives are sometimes used for food. They are also made into products such as oil and fertilizer.

alfalfa. A plant with cloverlike leaves. Hay made from alfalfa is used as food for farm animals.

altitude. Height above the level of the sea. For example, a mountain that rises 10,000 feet (3,050 meters) above sea level has an altitude of 10,000 feet.

ammonia (ə mōn′ yə). A colorless gas with a sharp smell. The ammonia used for cleaning around the house is really ammonia dissolved in water. Ammonia is an important chemical used in industry. It is used in making products such as fertilizers and explosives.

ancestors. People from whom one is descended. They include your grandparents, great-grandparents, and others farther back in your family.

anchovy (an′ chō vē). A very small fish, used mainly in sauces and relishes.

annex. To make one territory part of another.

Appalachian (ap/ə lā/chən) **Plateau.** The westernmost section of the Appalachian Highlands region. See **plateau**.

aqueduct (ak/ wə dukt). A canal, tunnel, or large pipe for carrying water. An aqueduct usually carries the water from a river or a lake to the place where it is to be used.

Arab. Refers to a group of people who live mainly in northern Africa and Southwest Asia. Arabs speak the Arabic language. Most of them follow the religion of Islam. See **Islam**.

architecture. The art of designing buildings.

astronaut. A pilot or a crew member of a spacecraft.

atomic energy. Energy that is stored in atoms. See **atoms**.

atoms. Pieces of matter too small to be seen except with a special microscope. When atoms are split or combined in certain ways, great amounts of energy are released. This energy can be used for many purposes, including the production of electricity.

automation. The use of machinery that needs only a few, if any, people to run it.

bale. A large bundle of material that is squeezed together and tied with rope, wire, or straps.

basic chemicals. Common chemicals that are produced in large amounts for use in industry. Ammonia and certain strong acids are examples of basic chemicals. See **chemicals**.

basin. An area of land that is largely surrounded by higher land. Also, the total area of land that is drained by a river and its branches.

bauxite (bôk/ sīt). An ore that is the chief source of aluminum. See **ore**.

bearings. Objects such as metal balls and rollers that enable one part of a machine or a mechanical device to slide smoothly over or around another part. Ball bearings are used in roller-skate wheels, for example.

bill. A suggested law to be voted on by a legislature. See **legislature**.

bituminous (bə tü/ mə nəs) **coal.** Another name for high-grade soft coal. This is the most plentiful and important type of coal.

blackout. A period of time during which electricity is cut off from an area.

blast furnace. A furnace in which iron is made from iron ore. It is called a blast furnace because a strong blast of air is blown into the bottom of the furnace.

bluegrass. Any one of about 200 kinds of grass with bluish green stems and blue flowers. The best known is Kentucky bluegrass, a useful lawn and pasture grass.

boll (bōl). The seed pod of a plant such as cotton. The white fibers found in cotton bolls are used to make cotton cloth.

borates. A group of certain chemicals that are somewhat like salt. Several borates are found in nature as minerals. A common borate is called borax. It is used for softening water and for cleaning. See **chemicals**.

breakwater. A wall built in the water to protect a harbor or a beach from waves. Breakwaters are usually built of stone and concrete.

British Parliament. See **parliament**.

Buddhism (bùd/ iz əm). A religion founded in India about 2,500 years ago. It teaches that selfishness is the cause of all sorrow, and that brotherly love among all people is the way to happiness.

butte (būt). A flat-topped hill that rises steeply from the land around it. A butte is somewhat like a mesa, but smaller. See **mesa**.

cancer. A serious disease marked by a harmful growth or growths in the body.

Cancer, Tropic of. See **Tropic of Cancer**.

candidate. A person who seeks a job or an office, such as president. Each candidate in an election hopes to get the most votes.

canyon. A valley with high, steep sides.

capital. A city that serves as the center of government for a country or a state. In economics, "capital" refers to wealth that is used to produce more wealth. Money, factory buildings, and machines are important forms of capital.

capitol. A building in which lawmakers meet. When spelled with a capital "C," this word means the building in Washington, D.C., where the United States Congress meets. See **United States Congress**.

Capricorn, Tropic of. See **Tropic of Capricorn**.

carbon. A common substance found in nature in many different forms. A diamond is pure carbon. So is graphite, the black writing material in your pencil. Anthracite, a high-quality coal, is almost entirely carbon. Carbon is found in all living things, in many kinds of rock, and in petroleum.

cash crops. Crops that farmers raise to be sold, rather than to be used by themselves and their families.

Celsius (sel′sē əs). Refers to a scale for measuring temperature. On the Celsius scale, which is part of the metric system, 0° represents the freezing point of water and 100° represents the boiling point. To change degrees Celsius to degrees on the Fahrenheit scale, multiply by 1.8 and add 32. See **metric system** and **Fahrenheit**.

centimeter (sen′tə mē′tər). A unit in the metric system for measuring length. It is equal to about .39 inch. See **metric system**.

cession. The giving up of territory by one country to another.

chemicals. Substances that are made when two or more substances act upon one another. Examples are salt, soda, ammonia, and aspirin.

chemist. A person who studies, tests, or makes chemicals. A chemist usually works in a laboratory. See **chemicals**.

cholera. A disease caused by polluted food or water. Early settlers who traveled west often had to use whatever food or water they could find. Many became sick or died.

Christianity. A religion that is followed by more people than any other religion in the world. It is based on the teachings of Jesus Christ, who lived nearly two thousand years ago. There are three main branches of Christianity. These are the Roman Catholic Church, the Eastern Orthodox churches, and the Protestant churches.

circumference (sər kum′ fər əns). The distance around something, such as a circle or a ball.

citrus fruit. Any of several kinds of fruit. Oranges, grapefruit, lemons, and limes are some of the common citrus fruits.

civil rights. The rights and freedoms that belong to a person as a member of a community, a state, or a country. There are many different civil rights. Among them are the right to speak freely and to attend the church of one's choice. Others are the right to own property, the right to a fair trial, and the right to get a job or a place to live without discrimination. (See **discrimination**.) Sometimes the right to vote is also thought of as a civil right.

Civil War, 1861-1865. A war between the northern and southern parts of our country. The northern states were called the Union. The southern states were called the Confederacy. The Union won the Civil War.

climate. The average weather conditions of a given place over a period of many years.

coke. A fuel made by roasting coal in special ovens from which the air has been shut out.

coking coal. Coal that is good for making coke. See **coke**.

colonial. Refers to a certain period of time in the history of the United States. The colonial period began when the first European colonies were started in America. It lasted until the thirteen British colonies became the United States.

colony. A settlement outside the country that controls it. In American history, usually means any one of thirteen colonies along the Atlantic coast. These colonies were started by people from England in the 1600's and 1700's. Later, the thirteen colonies became the United States.

commercial (kə mėr′ shəl). Having to do with business or trade.

communicate. To share ideas and feelings with other people. Speaking and writing are two of the most important ways of communicating.

communication. Sharing ideas and feelings with other people. Speaking is the main way in which we communicate with people who are near enough to hear us. Writing helps us communicate with people who are not close by. Other means of communicating over a distance include such things as the telegraph, radio, and television.

Communist. Refers to certain countries in which the government controls industry, farming, trade, education, and most other activities. The word Communist also refers to political parties and to people who favor such a system of government control.

compass rose. A small drawing put on a map to show directions. Here are three examples of compass roses:

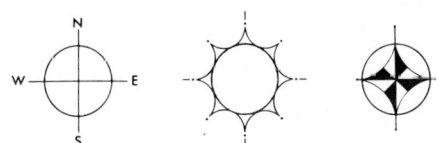

PRONUNCIATION KEY: h**a**t, **ā**ge, c**ā**re, f**ä**r; l**e**t, **ē**qual, t**ė**rm; **i**t, **ī**ce; h**o**t, **ō**pen, **ô**rder; **oi**l, **ou**t; c**u**p, p**u̇**t, r**ü**le, **ū**se; **ch**ild; lo**ng**; **th**in; **FH**en; **zh**, measure; **ə** represents **a** in about, **e** in taken, **i** in pencil, **o** in lemon, **u** in circus. For the complete key, see page 35.

complicated. Made up of a number of different parts.

composer. A person who writes music.

computer. A machine that stores information and uses this information to solve difficult problems.

concrete. A hard, strong material that is used for such things as buildings and roads. Concrete is made by mixing cement, sand, gravel, and water. This mixture becomes hard as it dries.

conservation. Saving or protecting something so it will not be wasted. For example, forests and soil need to be conserved.

conserve. To protect or keep safe.

constitution. A set of rules telling how a country or a state is supposed to be governed. When this word is written with a capital "C," it usually means the Constitution of the United States. Our Constitution was adopted in 1788. It has been in use ever since.

conterminous (kən tėr′mə nəs) **United States.** The forty-eight states of the United States that are enclosed by an unbroken boundary. The word conterminous means "having the same boundary."

continent. One of the six largest land areas on the earth. These are Eurasia, Africa, North America, South America, Australia, and Antarctica. Some people think of Eurasia as two continents—Europe and Asia.

Continental Congress. A meeting of leaders from the colonies in America that later joined together to form the United States. There were two Continental Congresses. The First Continental Congress met in 1774 to discuss the quarrel between the colonies and Great Britain. The Second Continental Congress met in 1775, soon after the Revolutionary War began. On July 4, 1776, it approved the Declaration of Independence. For several years after this, the Second Continental Congress served as the government of the United States.

conveyor belt. A moving belt, usually made of canvas, rubber, or metal, that carries things from one place to another.

cowhand. A person who takes care of cattle.

crop rotation. A way of farming in which different crops are raised on the same land in different years.

crude oil. Petroleum as it comes from the ground.

cultivate. To break up the soil around the roots of growing plants, mainly for the purpose of killing weeds. Also, to prepare and use land for growing crops.

Declaration of Independence. A public statement made by leaders of the American colonies on July 4, 1776. This statement said that the colonies were independent, or free, of Great Britain.

Delmarva Peninsula. A peninsula along the Atlantic coast of the United States. It is about 180 miles (290 kilometers) long and 70 miles (113 kilometers) across at its widest part. Most of the state of Delaware and parts of Maryland and Virginia lie on this peninsula.

democracy. A country in which people govern themselves. The people choose their leaders and make decisions by majority vote. See **majority.**

density of population. The average number of people per square mile, square kilometer, or some other unit of area, in a given place. Density of population may be found by dividing the total number of people in an area by the number of square miles or other units of the area.

depressed area. An area where many of the people are unable to find jobs.

descent. Birth or ancestry. For example, we might say that a certain person born in the United States is of French descent. This means that some or all of that person's ancestors were born in France.

diameter (dī am′ə tər). A straight line that joins opposite sides and passes through the center of something, such as a circle or a ball. Also, the length of such a straight line.

diesel (dē′ zəl) **engine.** A kind of engine often used in trucks and trains. Instead of gasoline, it burns a petroleum product called diesel oil.

discrimination. Keeping rights and freedoms from people because they belong to certain groups. Usually, people are discriminated against because they belong to minority groups. (See **minority group.**) Although women are not a minority group, they have also suffered from discrimination.

District of Columbia. A piece of land set apart as the home of the federal government of the United States. The District of Columbia lies in the eastern part of our country, between Maryland and Virginia. It is not part of any state. Washington, our national capital city, covers the entire area of the District of Columbia.

drift mine. A type of mine in which a tunnel is dug into the side of a hill.

drought (drout). A long period of dry weather.

dry farming. A way of farming used in areas where there is little water. Dry farmers in these areas raise crops that need little moisture. They leave part of their land idle, or fallow, each year. This lets the soil store up moisture.

Dutch. People from the Netherlands. (See **Netherlands**.) Also, the language spoken by these people.

Eastern Orthodox (ôr′ thə doks). Refers to one of the three main branches of Christianity. (See **Christianity**.) Most of the churches that belong to this branch are in western Asia and eastern Europe. Eastern Orthodox also refers to the members of these churches.

ecology (ē kol′ ə jē). Refers to the relationships living things (plants, animals, and human beings) have to each other and to their environment. Also, the study of these relationships. See **environment**.

electric power. Electricity.

electric power plant. A plant that uses machines called generators to produce electricity. The generators are run by other machines called turbines, which are usually powered by steam. Turbines may also be powered by the force of falling water.

electron. The smallest possible amount of electricity.

electronic (i lek′tron′ik). Refers to certain kinds of electrical devices, such as vacuum tubes and transistors. Also refers to products that use such devices. Radios, television sets, and computers are examples of electronic products.

electron microscope. A microscope is a special tool used by scientists for making very tiny things look larger. An electron microscope is different from a regular microscope in that it uses a beam of electrons instead of light to show the shape of an object. See **electron**.

energy. Power, or force, that can be used to do work. In earliest times, people used only their own muscles to do work. Since then, they have learned to use many other sources of energy. Some of these are wind, flowing water, and fuels such as coal, oil, and natural gas.

engineer. A person who plans or builds such things as machinery, bridges, and roads.

engineering. The kind of work that engineers do. See **engineer**.

environment (en vī′ rən mənt). Everything that surrounds living things and influences their growth and development. The environment of a person includes such things as air, sunlight, water, land, plants, animals, and other people.

equator (i kwā′ tər). An imaginary line around the earth, dividing it into a northern half and a southern half.

equinox (ē′ kwə noks). Either of two times of the year when the sun shines directly on the equator. They take place about March 21 and September 22. At these two times, day and night are each twelve hours long everywhere on the earth.

Erie Canal. A canal in New York State. It connected the Hudson River, near the city of Albany, with the port city of Buffalo, on Lake Erie. It was finished in 1825. In the early 1900's, the Erie Canal became part of a larger system of canals called the New York State Barge Canal.

erosion. The wearing away of the earth's surface by the forces of nature. These forces include falling rain, running water, ice, wind, and waves. Erosion may be helpful to people, as when soil is formed from rock. Or it may be harmful, as when rich soil is washed away.

Eskimos. Certain people who live in the far northern parts of North America and eastern Asia. The Eskimos in Alaska include two groups. These are the Inuit and the Yupiit. Many Eskimos earn their living by hunting and fishing. Others have jobs in factories and offices.

essay. A piece of writing that usually tells what the writer thinks about a subject.

etcher. An artist who uses acid to make a design or a picture on a metal plate. The plate is then inked and used to print copies of the design or picture.

Eurasia (yu rā′ zhə). The largest continent on the earth. It is sometimes thought of as two separate continents—Europe and Asia. See **continent**.

evaporate (i vap′ ə rāt). To change from a liquid to a gas or vapor. For example, when the water on a wet sidewalk disappears, it is said to evaporate. The water changes into a gas called water vapor, which mixes with the air.

explosives. Substances that can be exploded. For example, the gunpowder used in firecrackers is an explosive.

PRONUNCIATION KEY: hat, āge, cāre, fär; let, ēqual, tėrm; it, īce; hot, ōpen, ôrder; **oil, out;** cup, pu̇t, rüle, ūse; **child; lo**ng; **th**in; ᵺHen; **zh,** measure; ə represents **a** in about, **e** in taken, **i** in pencil, **o** in lemon, **u** in circus. For the complete key, see page 35.

export (ek spôrt′). To send goods from one country or region to another, especially for the purpose of selling them. These goods are called exports (eks′pôrts).

fallow. Farmland on which no crop is being grown is said to be fallow.

Fahrenheit (far′ ən hīt). Refers to a scale for measuring temperature in which the freezing point of water is represented by 32° and the boiling point by 212°. See **Celsius**.

federal. A system of government in which the constitution gives great powers to the central government to govern the country, yet leaves control of local affairs to the states. The national government, as separate from the governments of the states, is called the federal government.

feedlot. A place where cattle are kept while being fattened for market.

fertile. Good for producing crops.

fertilizer. A substance that farmers add to their soil. The fertilizer helps the soil produce more and better crops.

fiber. A thread or a threadlike part.

fiction. Novels, short stories, and other writings that tell about people and happenings that are not real.

Filipino (fil′ ə pē′ nō). Refers to people from the Philippines or people whose ancestors were from the Philippines. See **ancestors**.

First Continental Congress. See **Continental Congress**.

fission. The splitting or breaking apart of atoms in a way that releases large amounts of energy. See **atoms**.

fossil. The remains or traces of a plant or an animal that lived long ago. For example, an animal bone that has turned into rock is called a fossil. The fossil fuels—coal, oil, and natural gas—were formed from the remains of plants and animals that lived millions of years ago. Over the years, the forces of nature changed these remains into the fuels we take from the earth today. Sometimes you can actually see the pattern of a fern in a piece of coal.

foundry. A place where melted metal is poured into hollow forms called molds. When the metal cools, it hardens into the desired shape. Then the mold is removed.

freeway. A broad highway that is designed to carry heavy traffic at high speeds. Freeways have no traffic lights or crossroads.

French and Indian War, 1754-1763. A war in North America. In this war, Great Britain and its American colonies defeated the French. Indians fought on both sides. As a result of the war, Great Britain took over most of the land that the French had claimed in North America.

frontier (frun tir′). An area that lies between settled lands and the wilderness.

fusion. The combining of atoms in a way that releases large amounts of energy. See **atoms**.

generator. A machine used to make electricity. In electric power plants, the generators are usually run by other machines called turbines. The turbines are run by the force of steam or of falling water.

Georgian (jôr′ jən) **style.** A style of building much used in Britain and its colonies in the 1700's and early 1800's. A house built in the Georgian style was usually very impressive. It had a central doorway, often with tall columns. On each side of the doorway were the same number of windows.

gin (jin). A machine that separates cotton fibers from seeds and other materials. The fibers are pulled through holes that are too small to let the seeds and other materials through.

glacier (glā′ shər). A mass of ice that moves slowly down a slope or valley.

Great Britain. A large island that lies off the western coast of Europe. It includes three parts—England, Scotland, and Wales. Long ago, these were three countries with different rulers. Wales was joined to England during the 1500's. Then, in 1707, England and Wales were united with Scotland to form the kingdom of Great Britain. The ruler of Great Britain also ruled the British colonies in America. Later, the northern part of Ireland became part of the kingdom of Great Britain. Today, the official name for this country is "The United Kingdom of Great Britain and Northern Ireland."

great circle. Any imaginary circle around the earth that divides its surface exactly in half. The equator, for example, is a great circle. The shortest route between any two points on the earth always lies on the great circle that passes through them.

Great Lakes. Five huge lakes in the central part of North America. These are Lakes Superior, Michigan, Huron, Erie, and Ontario.

Great Lakes-St. Lawrence Waterway. A great inland waterway that includes the St. Lawrence

River, the five Great Lakes, and several smaller connecting waterways. The system of canals, dams, and locks on the St. Lawrence between Lake Ontario and the city of Montreal, Canada, is known as the St. Lawrence Seaway. See **lock.**

Great Plains. A part of our country that is made up of broad, level plains. It lies east of the Rocky Mountains and extends from Canada to Mexico.

Great Valley. A long chain of valleys in the eastern part of the United States. The Great Valley forms a large part of the Appalachian Ridges and Valleys section of the Appalachian Highlands.

gristmill. A mill for grinding grain.

groundwater. Water that soaks into the ground and collects in layers of soil and rock. This is the water that supplies wells and springs.

growing season. The period of time when crops can be grown outdoors without danger of being killed by frost.

guided missile. A kind of rocket that can be used to carry bombs to enemy countries during a war. Some guided missiles are directed by radio signals sent from the ground. Others are guided by an electronic device inside the missile. See **electronic.**

hardwood. Refers to trees that have broad leaves, rather than needles. Oaks and maples are examples of hardwood trees.

hectare (hek′ tãr). A unit in the metric system for measuring area. It is equal to about 2.47 acres. See **metric system.**

Huguenots (hū′ gə nots). The name given to the Protestants in France during the 1500's and 1600's. The Huguenots were often made to suffer by French Roman Catholics. Thousands of Huguenots were put in prison or killed. Many fled to other countries. See **Protestant** and **Roman Catholic.**

humid (hū′ mid). Refers to air that contains a large amount of moisture.

hydrochloric acid. A strong, colorless acid. It is widely used in industry for cleaning metals. It is also used in dyeing and in food processing.

hydroelectric (hī′ drō i lek′ trik). Refers to hydroelectricity. See **hydroelectricity.**

hydroelectricity (hī′ drō i lek′ tris′ ə tē). Electricity produced from waterpower.

hydrogen bomb. A very powerful bomb. In this kind of bomb, atoms are combined in a way that releases large amounts of energy. See **atoms.**

hypotheses (hī poth′ ə sēz). Possible answers or solutions to a problem. Sometimes hypotheses are called "educated guesses." A hypothesis may turn out to be wrong. But it helps us find the right answer.

illustrate. To explain or to show more clearly with diagrams, maps, or pictures.

immigrant. A person who moves into a country or region with the purpose of making a new home there.

immigration. Moving into a country or region with the purpose of making one's home there. Also, the movement of immigrants into a country or region.

import. To bring goods into a country or region from another country or region, especially for the purpose of selling them. These goods are called imports.

income. The money a person or a business makes during a given period of time. For example, a person's yearly income might include wages for a job plus profits from a business. See **profit.**

indigo (in′ də gō). A plant from which a deep-blue dye is made. Also, the name of the dye.

insurance. A means of protection that provides money in case of illness, accident, or some other event.

Intracoastal (in′ trə kōs′ təl) **Waterway.** A protected water route used by boats along the Atlantic and Gulf coasts of our country. It includes rivers, bays, and canals.

invest. To use money for the purpose of making more money.

iron ore. A rocklike mineral that contains enough iron to make it worth mining.

Iroquois (ir′ ə kwoi). A group of Indian tribes that once lived mostly in what is now lower Canada and central New York State.

irrigate. To supply dry land with water. Ditches, canals, pipelines, and sprinklers are common means used to irrigate farmlands.

irrigated truck farm. A vegetable farm to which water is supplied by such means as ditches, canals, pipelines, and sprinklers. See **truck farm.**

PRONUNCIATION KEY: hat, āge, cãre, fär; let, ēqual, tėrm; it, īce; hot, ōpen, ôrder; oil, out; cup, p u̇t, rüle, ūse; **child; lo ng; th**in; ₮Hen; **zh,** measure; ə represents **a** in about, **e** in taken, **i** in pencil, **o** in lemon, **u** in circus. For the complete key, see page 35.

irrigation. The act or practice of irrigating. See **irrigate**.

Islam (is′ ləm). One of the world's major religions. Islam was founded by an Arabian prophet named Mohammed, who was born in A.D. 570. According to this faith, there is only one God, called Allah, and Mohammed is his prophet. Followers of Islam are called Moslems, or Muslims.

Jew. A member of a group of people held together for more than three thousand years by their history and their religious faith. The history of the Jews began in southwestern Asia, probably about 1900 B.C. The Jewish faith, called Judaism, is one of the world's major religions. See **Judaism**.

Judaism (jü′ dā iz əm). One of the world's major religions. It is based on the teachings of the Old Testament, and on the Talmud, which is an interpretation of these teachings. Followers of Judaism are called Jews. The main beliefs of Judaism are that there is only one God, that God is good, and that God wants people to follow his laws. Two other major religions, Christianity and Islam, grew out of Judaism.

jury. A group of persons who serve in a court of law. The jury studies the facts and decides whether or not the person charged with a crime is guilty.

kaolin (kā′ ə lin). A fine, white clay used to make chinaware.

kerosene. An oily liquid that is usually made from petroleum. One hundred years ago, many people used kerosene as a fuel in lamps and stoves. Today, kerosene is used mainly as a fuel in jet airplanes.

Korean War, 1950-1953. A war between North Korea and South Korea, two countries in eastern Asia. The United Nations sent soldiers to help South Korea. Many of these soldiers were Americans. See **United Nations**.

kilometer (kə lom′ ə tər). A unit in the metric system for measuring length. It is equal to about .62 mile. See **metric system**.

labor union. A group of workers who have joined together to deal with their employers on such matters as higher wages and better working conditions.

Latino. A person who was born in Latin America or whose ancestors were Latin Americans. Latin America includes all of North and South America south of the United States. For example, people from Mexico, Cuba, and Puerto Rico are Latinos.

latitude. Distance north or south of the equator, measured in units called degrees.

legal. Refers to anything that is allowed by law. Also refers to anything having to do with the law or courts of law.

legislature. A group of persons who have the power to make laws for a state or a country.

Lent. A special period observed by many Christian churches before Easter. People often give up certain foods or say extra prayers during this time.

levees. High, wide walls made of earth or concrete. They are built along rivers or lakes to prevent flooding.

lignite. A low-grade coal that is about half carbon and half water. (See **carbon**.) When lignite is burned, it gives off less heat than coal that contains more carbon.

lint. The long fibers obtained from the cotton plant.

livestock. Farm animals such as cattle, hogs, sheep, horses, and chickens.

lock. A section of a canal or river that is used to raise or lower ships from one water level to another. Gates at each end permit ships to enter or leave the lock. When a ship is in the lock, the gates are closed. The water level in the lock is raised or lowered to the level of the part of the canal or river toward which the ship is going. Then the gates in front of the ship are opened, and the ship passes out of the lock.

majority (mə jôr′ ə tē). Usually, any number over half. The term "majority vote" refers to a way in which groups of people make decisions. In this system, important questions are decided and people are elected to office by the largest number of votes.

Manhattan. One of the five boroughs into which New York City is divided. The Borough of Manhattan consists mainly of an island, also called Manhattan, that lies at the mouth of the Hudson River. It also includes several very small islands nearby.

manufactures (man′ yə fak′ chərz). This word usually means goods that are produced in factories. Sometimes, fact tables show dollar figures for manufactures. These figures represent the value added to goods or raw materials by factories in a certain area. The value added is figured out in an interesting way. From the amount of money received from the sale of goods, the cost of the materials needed to make them is subtracted. The amount of money left is the value added by the factories.

Mediterranean (med′ə tə rā′nē ən) **Sea**. An inland sea about 2,330 miles (3,749 kilometers) long. It lies south of Europe, west of Asia, and north of Africa.

menhaden (men hā′ dən). A fish found along the Atlantic and Gulf coasts of the United States. Menhaden are chiefly used to make fertilizer, cattle feed, and oil.

mesa (mā′sə). A small plateau that rises steeply from the land around it. (See **plateau**.) A mesa has a flat top. Mesa is a Spanish word that means table.

mesquite (mes kēt′). A spiny, low-growing tree with long roots. It grows in the southwestern part of the United States and in other dry lands. Parts of the mesquite plant are eaten by cattle.

meter. In the metric system, the basic unit for measuring length. It is equal to 39.37 inches. See **metric system**.

metric system. A system of measurement used in many countries throughout the world, especially in science. In this system, the meter is the basic unit of length.

metropolitan (met′rə pol′ə tən) **area.** A thickly populated area that includes at least one large central city. Besides the central city, a metropolitan area usually includes several smaller towns and settled sections.

Midwest. A part of the United States. The Midwest includes the states of Illinois, Indiana, Iowa, Michigan, Minnesota, Missouri, Ohio, and Wisconsin.

mineral. Any of certain substances found in the earth. Diamonds and coal are examples of minerals.

minority (mə nôr′ə tē) **group.** A group of people who differ in race, religion, or national origin from the people who make up the largest group in a country or a region.

missile. A weapon, such as a bomb or rocket, that travels through the air without a pilot. Missiles may be guided by radio signals from the ground. They may also be guided by an electronic device within the missile. See **electronic**.

missionary. A person who is sent out by a religious group to persuade other people to follow the same religion.

mohair. The long, silky hair of the Angora goat. Also, yarn or cloth made of mohair.

mold. A hollow container in which something can be shaped. For example, liquid Jello is poured into a mold. After it has become solid, it may be turned out in the shape of the mold.

monuments. Objects or structures, such as buildings, put up to keep people or events from being forgotten.

mural. A picture, usually very large, that is painted on a wall.

national origin. Generally refers to the country where a person was born, or where one's parents or grandparents were born.

natural resources. Useful things found in nature, such as soil, water, trees, and minerals. See **mineral**.

Nazi (nät′sē). Refers to a political party in Germany called the National Socialists. This undemocratic party controlled the country from 1933 to 1945. Adolf Hitler was leader of the National Socialists and dictator of Germany. Under his leadership, Germany tried to gain control of much of the world. See **World War II**.

Netherlands. A small country in northwestern Europe. The Netherlands is often known as Holland, although this name really refers only to part of the country.

newsprint. An inexpensive, coarse paper made mostly from wood pulp. It is mainly used for newspapers.

Nobel Prize. Any one of several prizes given each year for important work in such fields as science, writing, and world peace.

nonfiction. Writing that deals with real people and events.

nonmetallic minerals. Minerals that do not provide metals. (See **mineral**.) Examples of nonmetallic minerals are sulfur and limestone.

novel. A long story, usually telling about people who did not really live and events that did not really happen.

novelist. A person who writes long stories, called novels. Usually, the people in a novel did not really live, and the events did not really take place.

nuclear (nü′ klē ər). Refers to the production or use of atomic energy. See **atomic energy**.

PRONUNCIATION KEY: hat, āge, cāre, fär; let, ēqual, tėrm; it, īce; hot, ōpen, ôrder; oil, out; cup, put, rüle, ūse; child; long; thin; ᴛHen; zh, measure; ə represents a in about, e in taken, i in pencil, o in lemon, u in circus. For the complete key, see page 35.

Old State House. A building in Boston where the government leaders of the Massachusetts Bay Colony met. Later, the Old State House served as the first capitol for the state of Massachusetts. (See **capitol**.) This building is now used as a museum.

ore. Rock or other material that contains enough metal to make it worth mining.

Oregon Trail. The main route taken by the pioneers who traveled westward in the mid-1800's to settle in what is now the state of Oregon. This trail went from Independence, Missouri, to the Willamette Valley in Oregon.

oxygen (ok′sə jən). A colorless, odorless, tasteless gas. It makes up about one fifth of the air we breathe. Combined with other substances, oxygen is found in all plants and animals. It is also found in water and in many kinds of rock.

parliament (pär′lə mənt). In some countries, a group of people who make the laws. In many ways a parliament is like the Congress of the United States. When "parliament" is spelled with a capital "P," it usually means the parliament of Great Britain.

pasteurize (pas′chə rīz). To heat a liquid such as milk to a high temperature and then cool it rapidly. This process kills harmful germs.

patchwork. Pieces of cloth of different colors and shapes, which have been sewed together. Also, anything that looks like patchwork.

patchwork quilt. A warm covering for a bed. The top is made from patches of cloth, of different colors and shapes. These have been sewed together.

peninsula (pən in′sə lə). An area of land that is almost surrounded by water. It is connected to a larger area of land.

petrochemicals (pet′rō kem′ə kəlz). Chemicals obtained from petroleum or natural gas. Petrochemicals are used in making hundreds of products, such as paint, fertilizer, and synthetic rubber. See **chemicals**.

petroleum. Also called oil. A thick oily liquid that comes from the earth. Petroleum may be dark brown or greenish black in color. Gasoline and many other useful things are made from petroleum.

phosphate rock. A kind of rock that contains chemicals needed by plants. It is ground up and used in making fertilizer. See **chemicals**.

Piedmont (pēd′mont) **Plateau.** A section of the Appalachian Highlands that extends from New York into Alabama. Most of the land in the Piedmont is gently rolling or hilly.

Pilgrims. A group of English colonists who came to America in 1620. The Pilgrims had left England because they had not been allowed to worship God as they pleased. They started a colony called Plymouth in what is now Massachusetts.

planet. The earth or any one of the other heavenly bodies that move around the sun. The nine main planets are Mercury, Venus, Earth, Mars, Jupiter, Saturn, Uranus, Neptune, and Pluto.

plateau (pla tō′). A large, generally level area of high land.

plywood. A material made by gluing together thin sheets of wood.

polio. A short form of the word poliomyelitis. This is a serious disease that causes fever and weakness of the muscles. Some people die from polio and some become lame.

pollute. To make something dirty or impure.

pollution. Making something dirty. For example, air or water may become polluted.

population. The total number of people living in any particular place. See **density of population**.

potash. See **potassium salts**.

potassium salts. A group of certain chemicals, many of which are found in nature as minerals. Most of them are commonly referred to as potash. Potassium salts are used in making fertilizer, medicine, photographic supplies, and many other products. See **chemicals**.

prairie. A large area of level or rolling land covered with grass. A prairie usually has no trees.

prejudice. An opinion that is formed without knowing all the facts. The dislike for a person just because he or she belongs to a different group is a common kind of prejudice.

process. A method or way of doing something, or the steps taken to get a thing done. Also, to treat foods or other substances in some special way to make them more useful. For example, corn is said to be processed when it is canned or made into cornflakes.

produce (prə düs′). To make or to raise. For example, factories produce manufactured goods. Farms produce crops and livestock.

profit. The money earned by a business. It is the amount of money taken in, minus the money spent in running the business.

Protestant. Refers to one of the three main branches of Christianity. Also, a member of any one of the many different Protestant groups, such as the Methodists, Baptists, or Presbyterians. See **Christianity**.

prune. To cut off dead or useless parts of a tree, bush, or other plant. Usually, a plant is pruned to give it a better shape or to aid its growth.

Puerto Rico (pwer′ tō rē′ kō). An island about 1,000 miles (1,609 kilometers) southeast of Florida. The United States has had control of Puerto Rico since 1898. Today, this island governs itself with the help of the United States.

Puget-Willamette (pū′ jit wə lam′ ət) **Lowland.** A long valley in the western part of Oregon and Washington. It is about 350 miles (563 kilometers) long and 50 miles (80 kilometers) wide.

Pulitzer (pū′ lit sər) **Prize.** Any one of several prizes given each year in the United States for good work in such fields as newspaper writing, literature, music, and cartooning. The prizes are named for Joseph Pulitzer (1847-1911), a newspaper editor and publisher. Pulitzer left a large amount of money for these prizes.

pulp. A soft, damp material usually made from wood or rags. It is used in making paper.

purify. To make pure or clean.

pyrites (pī rī′tēz). Various minerals that include sulfur combined with metals such as iron, copper, and nickel. Both copper and nickel may be produced by smelting ores that contain pyrites, but it is not practical to obtain iron in this way. (See **smelting.**) A gas formed during the smelting process is used to make sulfuric acid, which is an important industrial chemical. The gas is also used in refrigeration.

quarry (kwôr′ē). An open pit in the earth from which stone is taken for use in building.

rain shadow. An area is said to lie in a rain shadow if mountains shelter it from moist winds. When moist winds rise to go over mountains, they are cooled and lose moisture in the form of rain or snow. By the time they have crossed the mountains, they are drier. As the winds move down to the lower land on the other side of the mountains, they become warmer. This causes them to take up moisture instead of losing it. Thus the land in the rain shadow is drier than the land on the other side of the mountains.

raw materials. Substances that can be manufactured into useful products. For example, iron ore is the main raw material needed for making iron and steel. Many manufacturing plants use steel as a raw material for making machinery and other metal products.

raw sugar. A form of sugar obtained from the juice squeezed from sugarcane. It is yellowish brown in color because the sugar crystals are covered with a thin film of molasses. Raw sugar is refined to produce the white sugar sold in stores.

recession (ri sesh′ən). A time when business activity slows down and many people are put out of work.

refinery. A place where useful products are made from something found in nature. For example, petroleum is made into gasoline, kerosene, and other useful products in a refinery.

research. A careful search for facts or truth about a subject.

reservation. An area of land owned by the government and set aside for some special use. Especially, an area set aside for use by Indians.

reservoir. A lake that stores large amounts of water until it is needed. The water may be used in homes, in manufacturing, or for farming. A reservoir may be a natural lake. Or it may be a lake formed by a dam on a river.

responsibility. Duty. Something that a person ought to do because it is the right thing to do, such as obeying the law.

retail (rē′tāl). Refers to stores that sell goods directly to the people who will use the products. Grocery stores and department stores are examples of retail stores.

Revolutionary War, 1775-1783. A war between Great Britain and thirteen British colonies in America. The colonies won the war and became states in a new country. This was the United States.

rickets. A disease of children in which the bones are not straight. It is caused by a lack of sunlight or a lack of vitamin D in the diet.

Roman Catholic. Refers to a church that is one of the three main branches of Christianity. Also refers to members of this church. See **Christianity.**

rosin. A hard, brittle substance that is made, along with turpentine, from the sap of living pine trees or from dead pinewood. Rosin is used in products such as paint, varnish, and soap.

PRONUNCIATION KEY: hat, āge, cãre, fär; let, ēqual, tėrm; it, īce; hot, ōpen, ôrder; oil, out; cup, pu̇t, rüle, ūse; child; long; thin; ᴛHen; zh, measure; ə represents a in about, e in taken, i in pencil, o in lemon, u in circus. For the complete key, see page 35.

sagebrush. A low, bushy plant with grayish green leaves. Sagebrush grows in the western part of the United States. It is sometimes used for fuel. It is also used as winter feed for sheep and cattle.

Scandinavia. A large area in northern Europe that includes the countries of Norway, Sweden, and Denmark.

scientist. An expert in some branch of science. A scientist makes an orderly study of natural laws and facts about nature.

scrap. Metal that is thrown away. Steel scrap is often used to replace part of the iron ore needed to make steel. Each ton of steel scrap used saves two tons of iron ore.

sculptor. An artist who makes figures or statues, usually of marble, wood, metal, or some other hard material.

sculptures. Works of art that are three-dimensional. (See **three-dimensional.**) For example, a statue made of marble, wood, or some other hard material.

sea level. The level of the surface of the sea. All surfaces on land are measured according to their distance above or below sea level.

Second Continental Congress. See **Continental Congress.**

segregation (seg′ rə gā′ shən.) In the United States, the separation of black people from white people, either by law or by custom. Under segregation, blacks generally attend separate schools, eat in separate restaurants, and sit in separate sections of buses. In many cases, they also live in separate sections of cities.

shale. A kind of rock that was probably formed from clay.

silage (sī′lij). Chopped green cornstalks or other plants that have been stored in a silo. A silo is an airtight building, usually shaped like a cylinder. Silage is used to feed cattle or other livestock.

slag. The waste material that is produced when ore is smelted to obtain metal. See **smelt.**

slate. A dark-colored rock, usually bluish gray, that splits easily into thin layers. Slate is used to make shingles, blackboards, and other items.

slum. A crowded, run-down part of a city or town. Most of the people who live in slums are very poor.

smallpox. A serious disease from which many people once died.

smelt. To separate the metal from the other materials in ore by melting the ore in a special furnace.

smelter. A place where smelting is done. Also, a furnace in which ore is smelted. See **smelt.**

smelting. The process by which metal is obtained from ore.

social scientist. A person who is skilled in any of the social sciences. These are sciences that deal with people. They include history, geography, and economics.

solar system. Our sun and the planets and smaller heavenly bodies that revolve around it.

solstice (sol′ stis). Either of two times of the year when the direct rays of the sun are farthest from the equator. This occurs about June 21 and about December 22.

South. A region of the United States, which includes Alabama, Arkansas, Florida, Georgia, Kentucky, Louisiana, Mississippi, North Carolina, South Carolina, Tennessee, and Virginia. "South" also refers to the states that opposed the Union in the Civil War. See **Civil War.**

Soviet Union. Short name for the Union of Soviet Socialist Republics, or U.S.S.R. Also called Russia. This country is located in Eurasia. See **Eurasia.**

State Supreme Court. In most states, the highest court of law.

standard of living. The way of living in a community or a country that people think of as necessary for a happy, satisfying life. In a country with a high standard of living, many different goods and services are thought of as necessary for most of the people. In a country with a low standard of living, many of these same things are enjoyed by only a few very wealthy people.

steam engine. An engine that is run by steam. To produce the steam, water is heated by burning a fuel such as coal or oil. Steam engines are often used to run trains and ships. They are also used in power plants to produce electricity.

stock. The total capital of a corporation. (See **capital.**) The stock of a company is usually divided into small portions called shares. A person may buy one or more of these shares. He or she then owns part of the business.

strike. The stopping of work by a group of workers. The purpose of a strike is usually to force a business to pay higher wages or provide better working conditions.

strip-mining. A way of digging up minerals that are deposited in flat strips near the surface of the earth. To reach these deposits, the layers of soil and rock that lie on top of the minerals must be removed.

suburb. An outer part of a city, or a smaller community near a city.

sulfuric (sul fyu̇r′ ik) **acid**. A heavy, colorless, oily liquid. It is used in refining petroleum and in making fertilizers, chemicals, steel, and plastics.

Supreme Court. The most important court of law in the United States. It meets in the nation's capital, Washington, D.C. The Supreme Court has nine judges, who are called justices. Their job is to make sure that our country is being governed according to the rules in the Constitution. See **constitution**.

suspension bridge. A bridge hung from thick wire ropes called cables. The cables are fastened to high towers on each side of the water or gap to be bridged.

synthetic (sin thet′ ik). Refers to certain substances such as plastics and nylon, developed to replace similar natural materials.

terminus. The end of a transportation route.

textile. Cloth, or the thread used to make cloth.

three-dimensional (də men′ shə nəl). Refers to anything that has height, length, and width.

thresh. To separate the grain from the husks and stems of the plant.

tinplate. Thin sheets of steel that have been coated with tin.

tobacco. A plant that is used mainly for making products such as cigars and cigarettes. In recent years, scientists have discovered that the use of tobacco products is harmful. They have reported that smoking helps to cause cancer, heart trouble, and other serious diseases.

treaty. An agreement, usually in writing, between two or more nations.

Tropic of Cancer. An imaginary line around the earth, about 1,600 miles (2,574 kilometers) north of the equator.

Tropic of Capricorn. An imaginary line around the earth, about 1,600 miles (2,574 kilometers) south of the equator.

tropics. The part of the earth that lies between the Tropic of Cancer and the Tropic of Capricorn. The weather in the tropics is generally hot all year round. See **Tropic of Cancer** and **Tropic of Capricorn**.

truck farm. A farm on which vegetables are raised to be sold. One meaning of the word "truck" is to trade things. Formerly vegetables often were traded for other products.

try. To bring a person before a judge or jury in a court of law. The judge or jury decides whether or not the person is guilty of breaking a law.

turbine. An engine commonly run by the force of water or steam striking against blades. Turbines are used to run electric generators. See **generator**.

turpentine. An oily liquid prepared from the sap of living pine trees or from dead pinewood. It is often used for thinning paints and varnishes.

Union. The United States of America. During the Civil War, the northern states were called the Union. See **Civil War**.

United Nations. An organization of countries from all over the world. It was started in 1945 to work for world peace. About 150 countries now belong to the United Nations.

United States Congress. The lawmaking, or legislative, branch of the United States government. It is made up of the Senate and the House of Representatives.

United States Supreme Court. See **Supreme Court**.

Upper Peninsula. The northern part of the state of Michigan. It lies mainly between Lake Superior and Lake Michigan.

uranium (yu̇ rā′ nē əm). A very heavy, silver-white metal. It is important as the source of certain materials used to produce atomic energy. See **atomic energy**.

urban. Having to do with cities or large towns.

victim. A person who is harmed by something or someone.

Vikings. People who lived along the seacoast in Scandinavia about one thousand years ago. (See **Scandinavia**.) The Vikings were fine sailors and fierce warriors. They often invaded other countries in northern Europe. Some of them settled on the islands of Iceland and Greenland.

volcano. An opening in the earth's crust through which melted rock, called lava, and other materials are forced to the surface. These materials often build up to form a hill or mountain, also called a volcano.

weather. The condition of the air or atmosphere at a given time and place. A description of weather includes such things as wind, sunshine, temperature, and moisture. The average weather conditions of a particular place

---

PRONUNCIATION KEY: hat, āge, cãre, fär; let, ēqual, tėrm; it, īce; hot, ōpen, ôrder; oil, out; cup, pu̇t, rüle, ūse; child; long; thin; ᴛHen; zh, measure; ə represents a in about, e in taken, i in pencil, o in lemon, u in circus. For the complete key, see page 35.

West Indies. A large group of islands in the Atlantic Ocean. They lie between the United States and South America. The West Indies got their name because Columbus thought he had reached lands in eastern Asia called the Indies.

wholesale. Having to do with selling large amounts of goods to businesses for resale. For example, a wholesale hardware company might buy a large amount of hammers from the manufacturer. The wholesale company would then sell the hammers to hardware stores throughout our country. These hardware stores, which sell the hammers to the people who are going to use them, are called retail stores. See **retail**.

wood pulp. See **pulp**.

World War I, 1914-1918. A war that was fought in many parts of the world. On one side were the Central Powers. These were Germany, Austria-Hungary, Turkey, and Bulgaria. They were defeated by the Allies. These included Great Britain, France, Russia, Japan, the United States, and other countries.

World War II, 1939-1945. A war that was fought in many parts of the world. On one side were the Allies, which included the United States, Great Britain, the Soviet Union, France, and many other countries. On the other side were the Axis Powers, which included Germany, Italy, and Japan. The Allies defeated the Axis Powers.

X-ray. A ray that can go through substances that light cannot go through. X-rays can be used to photograph such things as broken bones inside the body.

yucca (yuk′ə). Any of several plants of the lily family that grow in warm, dry areas. Some yucca plants are short but others are as tall as trees. The leaves of the yucca are usually stiff, narrow, and pointed. Yucca flowers are white.

Acknowledgments

Grateful acknowledgment is made to the following for permission to use the illustrations found in the Thinking Aids section of this book:

A. Devaney, Inc.: Page 26
Alpha Photo Associates, Inc.: Pages 21 and 27
Camera Hawaii: Page 30
De Wys, Inc.: Page 23
Field Enterprises: Pages 22-23, painting by Frederick Coffey Yohn
Grant Heilman: Page 34
H. Armstrong Roberts: Pages 31 (lower) and 33
Kaiser Steel Corporation: Page 19 (lower left)
Louisville Chamber of Commerce: Page 17
Magnum Photos, Inc.: Page 31 (upper)

NASA: Page 20
Shostal Associates, Inc.: Page 19 (upper left and lower right)
Sirlin Studios: Pages 24-25
Texasgulf: Pages 28-29
The Fideler Company: Page 29 by Adrian Beerhorst
United States Department of Agriculture, Soil Conservation Service: Pages 26-27
United States Department of Interior, Bureau of Reclamation: Page 32

Grateful acknowledgment is made to Scott, Foresman and Company for the pronunciation system used in this book, which is taken from the Thorndike-Barnhart Dictionary Series. Grateful acknowledgment is made to the following for permission to use cartographic data in this book: Creative Arts: Bottom map on page 15; Base maps courtesy of the Nystrom Raised Relief Map Company, Chicago 60618: Top map on page 15; United States Department of Commerce, Bureau of the Census: Bottom map on page 14.